Fifty Years of
FOREIGN AFFAIRS

Fifty Years of
FOREIGN AFFAIRS

EDITED BY

HAMILTON FISH ARMSTRONG

*with James Chace, Carol Kahn,
and Jennifer Whittaker*

Published for the

COUNCIL ON FOREIGN RELATIONS

by

PRAEGER PUBLISHERS

New York · Washington · London

PRAEGER PUBLISHERS
111 Fourth Avenue, New York, N.Y. 10003, U.S.A.
5, Cromwell Place, London SW7 2JL, England

Published in the United States of America in 1972
by Praeger Publishers, Inc.

© 1972 by Council on Foreign Relations, Inc.

Library of Congress Catalog Card Number: 72–76447

The Council on Foreign Relations is a nonprofit institution devoted to the study of political, economic, and strategic problems as related to American foreign policy. It takes no stand, expressed or implied, on American policy. The authors of books published under the auspices of the Council are responsible for their statements of fact and expressions of opinion. The Council is responsible only for determining that they should be presented to the public.

For a partial list of Council publications, see page 499

Printed in the United States of America

CONTENTS

Contents

Preface

To my surprise, I have discovered that in its fifty years of life *Foreign Affairs* has published over 2,600 articles. Even an editor who watched as the face of the world changed through those fifty years marvels, when confronted with the unexpected magnitude of the figure, that there was indeed such a number of subjects demanding attention and that authors were found equipped to deal with them. We have mined this accumulation of riches and chosen thirty-one articles for republication in this anniversary volume. To make the right choice was impossible. There was an immense variety of precious materials, and there was no test that could be used for judging their present relative value.

The articles chosen cannot be called the "best" of the period. Some are reprinted because they describe a problem or situation that has a parallel today and that again (or still) weighs on our minds. Some define policy decisions that ought to be made, and often were not. Others themselves influenced the making of important decisions. One or two profiles of individuals are included because their excellence as works of art made it impossible to overlook them. Unfortunately, some valuable articles had to be omitted simply because of their length.

I hope the articles selected will not only seem right for their intrinsic value but also that they will substantiate the editorial policy laid down in a note in the first issue of *Foreign Affairs* and reprinted in each issue ever since, namely, that articles would not represent any consensus of opinions, since some writers would flatly disagree with others, but would show, rather, a broad hospitality to divergent ideas as a means of encouraging the American public to think for itself about foreign policy.

As the reader glances through the table of contents of this volume, he will be struck, I hope, by the variety of political views held by the authors, running from N. Bukharin, the leading communist theoretician, eventually purged and shot by Stalin, to Secretary of State John Foster Dulles, author of the massive retaliation policy. If so, he may be as surprised as were early readers of the review, who expected it to be stuffy, to find Harold Laski, W. E. B. DuBois, and John Dewey among its early contributors. Although the present volume does not pretend—could not pretend—to give a conspectus of the history of the past fifty years; it does provide some useful milestones along the route that was traveled. Probably the best estimate of the opening phases of Soviet foreign policy was made in an article in the first issue by Archibald Cary Coolidge of Harvard University, the leading Slavic scholar of the time and editor of *Foreign Affairs* from the start until 1928. (I was his managing editor in those years.) The article attracted the attention of Lenin himself, and the copy he marked is in my possession. Since the publication of Coolidge's contribution, some 220 articles on Soviet problems and the situation of communism in general have appeared in the pages of the review, more, I imagine, than in any other general American periodical in the period. The most influential, probably, and certainly the one most often reprinted, was "The Sources of Soviet Conduct," by George Kennan, signed "X," written twenty-five years after Coolidge's and incorporated, like his, in the present volume.

From the start, the editors of *Foreign Affairs* have enjoyed a rare independence from interference by its parent, the Council on Foreign Relations. There can be few if any examples of a similar intellectual generosity on the part of those materially responsible for maintaining a periodical toward those in charge of editing and producing it. A second element making it possible for the editors to follow a completely independent editorial course is that *Foreign Affairs* has had no connection, financial or otherwise, with any agency of the U.S. Government. In the early days, the State Department was annoyed when we printed articles critical of government policies. The view now seems to be accepted that the hostile and the appreciative have been held pretty well in balance and that the over-all advantages of helping to create public understanding of international problems more than offset the inconvenience of sharp criticism of particular policies.

In both these respects, the lot of the editors of *Foreign Affairs* has been ideal. We have made mistakes, but they have been our own mistakes, not foisted on us from any external source.

As I look back on the long roster of articles published in these fifty years and recall the pleasant tension that attended the preparation of each issue, and the enjoyment there was in even the frantic negotiations that led to the writing of this or that article. I realize that our editorial task has been much more a joy than work. May Mr. Coolidge's and my successors find this as true in the years ahead as it has been in the past half-century.

HAMILTON FISH ARMSTRONG

¶ A Requisite for the Success of Popular Diplomacy

by Elihu Root   (September, 1922)

The article which Elihu Root wrote for the first issue of Foreign Affairs *in the autumn of 1922 has become something of a classic. The thesis was a simple one: Since the people in a democracy are responsible for the control and conduct of foreign policy, they should learn the business.*

Elihu Root was, in 1922, our most eminent elder statesman. He had been Secretary of War under McKinley, Secretary of State under Theodore Roosevelt, United States Senator from 1909 to 1915, and Ambassador Extraordinary to Russia in 1917. Now seventy-seven, he wrote out of deep concern for the safety of his country, launched on waters his experience told him were more perilous than most of his fellow citizens perceived or, at any rate, were willing to admit. Two years earlier, the United States had rejected the Treaty of Versailles, the Covenant of the League of Nations and the military guarantee to France; only the previous year, it had concluded a separate peace with Germany. Domestic affairs engrossed the American mind.

In so far as problems of foreign relations impinged at all on the public consciousness, it was in the form of questions left over from the recent time of troubles. On most of them, the American public had opinions but, as events were to show, not much knowledge. Should the United States join the World Court? Leaders of both parties advocated it; a majority of Republicans opposed it; and public opinion soon forgot it. How rapidly could the moral satisfactions and dollar savings of disarmament be achieved? A rapprochement *with Japan in this connection was applauded, but a reduction in the strength of the British fleet relative to our own was vaguely thought to be an even more important American objective. And the war debts? That they should be paid was obviously a matter of simple right and wrong. Calvin Coolidge was to state this with the force of moral virtue unhampered by knowledge: "They hired the money, didn't they?" And* how *were they to be paid? If Presidents Harding, Coolidge, and Hoover understood the exchange problem involved in asking for payment in dollars and refusing to admit the imports that alone could produce them, they did not by word or act reveal it. And, if this was the attitude of our leaders, how was the public to know better?*

One way for the public to "know better" on these and other similar problems was to approach them in the attitude recommended by Elihu Root in such simple and reasonable language. After half a century, his advice is still good.

A REQUISITE FOR THE SUCCESS OF POPULAR DIPLOMACY

By Elihu Root

THE control of foreign relations by modern democracies creates a new and pressing demand for popular education in international affairs. When the difficult art of regulating the conduct of nations toward each other, in such a way as to preserve rights and avoid offense and promote peaceful intercourse, was left to the foreign offices of the world the public in each country could judge policies by results, and, in the various ways by which public opinion expresses itself, could reward or punish the success or failure of government. To perform that particular function it was not very important that the public should be familiar with the affairs out of which success or failure came. That condition, however, is passing away. In the democratic countries generally, the great body of citizens are refusing to wait until negotiations are over or policies are acted upon or even determined. They demand to know what is going on and to have an opportunity to express their opinions at all stages of diplomatic proceedings. This tendency is due partly to a desire to escape from certain well recognized evils in diplomacy as it has been practiced. It is due in part doubtless to the natural disposition of democracies to revert to the conditions which existed before the invention of representative government and thus to avoid the temporary inequalities involved in delegations of power to official representatives however selected.

The new condition has undoubtedly been accelerated by the great war and its lessons. We have learned that war is essentially a popular business. All the people in the countries concerned are enlisted in carrying it on. It cannot be carried on without their general participation. And whoever wins the war all the people of all the countries involved suffer grievous consequences. There is a general conviction that there has been something wrong about the conduct of diplomacy under which peoples have so often found themselves embarked in war without intending it and without wishing for it and there is a strong desire to stop that sort of thing. Democracies determined to control their own destinies object to being led, without their knowledge, into situations where they have no choice.

The demand for open diplomacy and contemporaneous public information, although in its application there is frequently an element of mere curiosity or news gathering business, nevertheless rests upon the substantial basis of democratic instinct for unhampered self-government. It is incident to the awakening sense of opportunity which, among the unskilled majority, has followed the exercise of universal suffrage, the spread of elementary education, and the revelation of the power of organization. The change is therefore not to be considered as temporary but as a step in the direct line of development of democratic government, which, according to the nature of democracies, will not be retraced. The new conditions and such developments as may grow from them, are the conditions under which diplomacy will be carried on hereafter. Of course, as in all practical human affairs, limitations and safeguards will be found necessary, but the substance will continue, and public opinion will be increasingly not merely the ultimate judge but an immediate and active force in negotiation.

The usefulness of this new departure is subject to one inevitable condition. That is, that the democracy which is undertaking to direct the business of diplomacy shall learn the business. The controlling democracy must acquire a knowledge of the fundamental and essential facts and principles upon which the relations of nations depend. Without such a knowledge there can be no intelligent discussion and consideration of foreign policy and diplomatic conduct. Misrepresentation will have a clear field and ignorance and error will make wild work with foreign relations. This is a point to which the sincere people who are holding meetings and issuing publications in opposition to war in general may well direct their attention if they wish to treat the cause of disease rather than the effects. Given the nature of man, war results from the spiritual condition that follows real or fancied injury or insult. It is a familiar observation that in most wars each side believes itself to be right and both pray with equal sincerity for the blessing of heaven upon their arms. Back of this there must lie a mistake. However much ambition, trade competition, or sinister personal motives of whatever kind, may have led towards the warlike situation, two great bodies of human beings, without whose consent war cannot be carried on, can never have come to two diametrically opposed genuine beliefs as to the justice of the quarrel without one side or the other, and probably both, being mistaken about their country's rights and their country's duties. Here is the real advantage of the change from the old diplomacy to the new. Irresponsible governments may fight without being in the least degree mistaken about their rights and duties. They may be quite willing to make cannon fodder of their own people in order to get more territory or more power; but two democracies will not fight unless they believe themselves to be right. They may have been brought to their belief by misrepresentation as to facts, by a misunderstanding of rules of right conduct, or through having the blank of ignorance filled by racial or national prejudice and passion to the exclusion of inquiry and thought; but they will fight not because they mean to do wrong but because they think they are doing right. When foreign affairs were ruled by autocracies or oligarchies the danger of war was in sinister purpose. When foreign affairs are ruled by democracies the danger of war will be in mistaken beliefs. The world will be the gainer by the change, for, while there is no human way to prevent a king from having a bad heart, there is a human way to prevent a people from having an erroneous opinion. That way is to furnish the whole people, as a part of their ordinary education, with correct information about their relations to other peoples, about the limitations upon their own rights, about their duties to respect the rights of others, about what has happened and is happening in international affairs, and about the effects upon national life of the things that are done or refused as between nations; so that the people themselves will have the means to test misinformation and appeals to prejudice and passion based upon error.

This is a laborious and difficult undertaking. It must be begun early and continued long, with patience and persistence, but it is the very same process as that by which all the people of the great democracies have learned within their own countries to respect law and to follow wise and salutary customs in their communities, and to consider the rights of others while they assert their own rights, and to maintain orderly self-government.

It so happens that our own people in the United States have been peculiarly without that kind of education in foreign affairs. Not only have we been very busy over the development of our own country and our own institutions, but our comparatively isolated position has prevented the foreign relations of the old world from becoming matters of immediate vital interest to the American people, and they have not been interested in the subject. Naturally enough a great part of our public men have neglected to study the subject. The great body of Americans in office would study questions of transportation and tariff and internal improvements and currency because their constituents were interested in these subjects; but there was no incentive for them to study foreign affairs because their constituents were indifferent to them. The conditions are now widely different. Our people have been taught by events to realize that with the increased intercommunication and interdependence of civilized states all our production is a part of the world's production, and all our trade is a part of the world's trade, and a large part of the influences which make for prosperity or disaster within our own country consist of forces and movements which may arise anywhere in the world beyond our direct and immediate control. I suppose that the people of the United States have learned more about international relations within the past eight years than they had learned in the preceding eighty years. They are, however, only at the beginning of the task.

The subject is extensive and difficult and a fair working knowledge of it, even of the most general kind, requires long and attentive study. Underlying it are the great differences in the modes of thought and feeling of different races of men. Thousands of years of differing usages under different conditions forming different customs and special traditions have given to each separate race its own body of preconceived ideas, its own ways of looking at life and human conduct, its own views of what is natural and proper and desirable. These prepossessions play the chief part in determining thought and action in life. Given two groups of men, each having a different inheritance of custom and tradition, and each will have a different understanding of written and spoken words, of the reasons for conduct and the meaning of conduct, and each will to a very considerable degree fail to understand the other. Neither can judge the other by itself. If the instinctive occidental reformer and the instinctive oriental fatalist are to work together they must make biological studies of each other. Add to these differences the selfish passions which have not yet been bred out of mankind and there inevitably follow in the contacts of international intercourse a multitude of situations which cannot be solved by the men of any one nation assuming that the rest of the world is going to think and feel as they themselves do and to act accordingly.

The organization of independent nations which has followed the disappearance of the Holy Roman Empire is in the main the outgrowth of that progress in civilization which leads peoples to seek the liberty of local self-government according to their own ideas. Whatever may be the form of local governments there can be no tyranny so galling as the intimate control of the local affairs of life by foreign rulers who are entirely indifferent to the local conceptions of how life ought to be conducted. National independence is an organized defense against that kind of tyranny. Probably the organization of nations is but a stage of development but it is the nearest that mankind has yet come towards securing for itself a reasonable degree of liberty with a reasonable degree of order.

It is manifest that the differences of thought and feeling and selfish desire which separate nations in general have to be dealt with in particular in the multitude of controversies which are sure to arise between them and between their respective citizens in a world of universal trade and travel and inter-communication. The process of such adjustment without war is the proper subject of diplomacy. During some centuries of that process many usages have grown up which have been found necessary or convenient for carrying on friendly intercourse, and many of these have hardened into generally accepted customs in manners or in morals which no longer require to be discussed but which every nation has a right to assume that other nations will observe. Many rules of right conduct have been accepted and universally agreed upon as law to govern the conduct of nations. In England and America these rules of international law are authoritatively declared to be a part of the municipal law of the country enforceable by the courts. In this way the nations founded upon differences have been gradually rescuing from the field of difference and controversy, and transferring to the field of common understanding and agreement, one subject after another of practical importance in the affairs of the world. The process is in the direction of that unity of thought and feeling, the absence of which hitherto has caused the failure of all schemes and efforts for the unity of mankind. The study of international relations means not only study of some particular controversy but study of this long history of the process of adjustment between differing ideas and of the prejudices and passions and hitherto irreconcilable differences which have baffled adjustment and which affect the relations and probable conduct of the nations concerned. All these are in the background of every international question and are often of vital importance to its right understanding.

The process I have described has created a community of nations. That community has grown just as communities of natural persons grow. Men cannot live in neighborhood with each other without having reciprocal rights and obligations towards each other arising from their being neighbors. The practical recognition of these rights and obligations creates the community. It is not a matter of contract. It is a matter of usage arising from the necessities of self-protection. It is not a voluntary matter. It is compelled by the situation. The neighbors generally must govern their conduct by the accepted standards or the community will break up. It is the same with nations. No nation whose citizens trade and travel; that is to say, no nation which lives in neighborhood with other nations need consider whether or not it will be a member of the community of nations. It cannot help itself. It may be a good member or a bad member, but it is a member by reason of the simple fact of neighborhood life and intercourse. The Bolshevik rulers of Russia are illustrating this. They have been trying to repudiate all the obligations resulting from their country's membership in the community of nations, and one result is that intercourse is impossible.

This great fact of the community of nations is not involved at all in any question about the "League of Nations" or any other association of nations founded upon contract. The "League of Nations" is merely a contract between the signers of the instrument by which they agree to super-add to the existing usages, customs, laws, rights, and obligations of the existing community of nations, certain other rights and obligations which shall bind the signers as matter of contract. Whether a country enters into that contract or not, its membership of the community of nations continues with all the rights and obligations incident to that membership.

A self-respecting democracy which undertakes to control the action of its government as a member of this community of nations, and wishes to respond fairly and fully, not only to the demands of its own interests, but to the moral obligations of a member of the community, is bound to try to understand this great and complicated subject so that it may act not upon prejudice and error but upon knowledge and understanding.

There is one specially important result which should follow from such a popular understanding of foreign affairs. That is, a sense of public responsibility in speech and writing, or perhaps it would be better stated as a public sense of private responsibility for words used in discussing international affairs. More fights between natural persons come from insult than from injury. Under our common law, libel was treated as a crime, not because of the injury which it did to the person libeled, but because it tended to provoke a breach of the peace. Nations are even more sensitive to insult than individuals. One of the most useful and imperative lessons learned by all civilized governments in the practice of international intercourse has been the necessity of politeness and restraint in expression. Without these, the peaceful settlement of controversy is impossible. This lesson should be learned by every free democracy which seeks to control foreign relations.

It cannot, however, be expected that every individual in a great democracy will naturally practice restraint. Political demagogues will seek popularity by public speeches full of insult to foreign countries, and yellow journals will seek to increase their circulation by appeals to prejudice against foreigners. Hitherto these have been passed over because the speakers and writers were regarded as irresponsible, but if the democracy of which the speakers and publishers are a part is to control international intercourse that irresponsibility ends, and it is the business of the democracy to see to it that practices by its members which lead directly towards war are discouraged and condemned. Offenses of this character are frequently committed in this country by political speakers and sensational newspapers and because we are a great nation the expressions used become known in the other countries concerned and cause resentment and bitter feeling. What especially concerns us is that these are very injurious offenses against our own country. Such public expressions by our own citizens bring discredit upon our country and injure its business and imperil its peace. They answer to the description of crime in the old indictments as an act "against the peace and dignity" of the State. They will practically cease whenever the

American public really condemns and resents them so that neither public office nor newspaper advertising or circulation can be obtained by them. That will come when the American public more fully understands the business of international intercourse and feels a sense of the obligations which it incurs by asserting the right to control the conduct of foreign relations.

¶ RUSSIA AFTER GENOA AND THE HAGUE
by Archibald Cary Coolidge ("K")   (September, 1922)

Although he had just become Editor of the newly established Foreign Affairs, *Archibald Cary Coolidge was persuaded only reluctantly to write an article for its first issue. He was the obvious American equipped to undertake a special task—to estimate the possibilities for greatness or destruction revealed in the first phase of the Bolshevik Revolution in Russia. After serving in the American Legation in St. Petersburg in 1890–91, where he perfected his Russian, he had visited Russia repeatedly and traveled to remote regions.*

In agreeing to write the article, Coolidge made two stipulations, one that it appear anonymously—it therefore was signed "K"—the other that it be placed last in the magazine. He did not make the conditions out of false modesty but because he did not want Foreign Affairs *to be involved in any controversial opinions he might express. The article dealt with the problems of the new Russian state just emerging into world politics, enumerating them without bias and with amazing foresight. He warned that, although Russia renounced imperialistic ambitions, this did not mean that it was indifferent to legitimate national interests, even if it was not able at the moment to assert them effectively. And, on the much debated question of recognition (finally settled by President Franklin D. Roosevelt in 1933), he pointed out that to recognize a government did not imply that we admired it; trading with Russia would not make us responsible for the practices of Lenin and Trotsky any more than the crimes of Sultan Abdul-Hamid had been deemed a bar to American commerce with Turkey.*

But turn now to Coolidge's own measured discussion of these matters and understand why Lenin himself hurriedly procured a copy of the first issue of Foreign Affairs *and marked in it what he considered Coolidge's salient points.*

RUSSIA AFTER GENOA AND THE HAGUE

By K

NOW that the smoke of the verbal battles between the Russian and the non-Russian participants in the last two international conferences has lifted, we can begin to estimate what results have been attained by the many weeks of earnest, not to say acrimonious, discussion between the representatives of assembled Europe. Few will deny that these results have been meagre compared with the hopes entertained at the outset. Some will even declare that no progress whatever towards a reconstruction of the world has come from these meetings of "best minds." Others will take a rosier view, but it is too early yet to reach many definite conclusions about questions with such intricate and far reaching ramifications. We can only distinguish certain immediate and obvious phenomena.

One of these is that there has been a clearing of the atmosphere. Europe may feel no nearer to seeing her way out of her difficulties, but she knows better where she stands and what are the circumstances with which she has to deal. This is particularly true in regard to Russia, the great mystery of the last four years. The Soviet republic has come out of its seclusion, it has shown itself willing, nay eager, to talk with other states. As yet it has been officially recognized by but few, but it has reassumed a position in the concert of the powers whether the others like it or not. Its present standing, its attitude and aims, should be clearly understood, for Russia is too large a part of the world to be ignored with impunity.

When in October last Chicherin sent out his first note proposing an international conference on Russian affairs and offering as a *quid pro quo* for assistance the recognition of Russian pre-war debts, not many people realized just what were the situation and reasoning of the Soviet Government. Their overture was generally regarded as the appeal of a hopeless bankrupt forced at last by desperate necessity to recognize the error of his ways and to beg for succor at the hands of those he had grievously injured. Even if we admit that there was justification for this opinion it was at best only a half truth. It was equally true that the ruling Communists had never felt more firmly on their feet than they did at that very moment, and not without reason.

The Russian Socialist Federated Soviet Republic was just completing the fourth year of its stormy existence, during which it had had innumerable difficulties to overcome and obstacles to surmount. Although by its own admission it could count on the active support of only a minority of the population and had had arrayed against it the vast majority of those who had formerly been the leaders in every form of public life, private enterprise or intellectual activity, although it had been undermined by the plots of reactionaries, social revolutionists, even anarchists, it had survived. It had fought against Germans, English, French, Americans, Japanese, Poles, Czechoslovaks, against Cossacks and other discontented elements within led by thousands of trained officers and armed and provisioned from without; it had seen most of its territory overrun at one time or another; and yet it had emerged triumphant. By the autumn of 1921 every assault, native or foreign, had failed. Only in the Far East under Japanese protection there was still military opposition, but even there it was diminishing. Peace had been concluded with Poland and with the Baltic states, for these were alien elements in the body politic which Communist Russia let go with little apparent regret and in full conformity with her theories. She had regained control in the Caucasus, she had concluded political treaties and was on friendly terms with Persia, Afghanistan and Turkey. It is true she still professed to fear attack in the east from Japan and in the west from Poland and Rumania supported by France, her newspapers and orators still harped on the evil designs of her capitalistic foes, but such talk was chiefly intended to stimulate the patriotism of the masses and particularly of the army. In reality, never before had Soviet Russia been so free from the menace either of foreign invasion or of serious insurrection.

This last fact was not due to any marked increase in popularity of the Communist regime. There was scant evidence of anything of the sort. But all open opposition had been beaten down. Every conspiracy had been ruthlessly suppressed. The peasantry who formed the immense majority of the population no longer manifested active discontent. What they asked for was to be let alone, and the Soviet Government had learned the wisdom of respecting this wish. The remnants of the former upper and educated classes were now thoroughly cowed by the terror they had lived through. The hundreds of thousands of irreconcilable refugees abroad were innocuous and were getting more and more

out of touch even with their like in their native land. The component parts of the loosely federated state acted together with
sufficient unity of purpose and were under the same rigorous
general control. Doubtless disorder still prevailed in outlying
districts and little heed was paid in some regions to the writ of the
central authorities, but these were but local manifestations which
could be dealt with in time. Altogether, Soviet Moscow felt it
had been victorious in both foreign and domestic affairs and it
was as far as possible from any such sentiment as contrition.

On the other hand, there were two painful truths which the
blindest adherent of Bolshevism could not deny or explain away.
First, in spite of Communist propaganda, no other country as yet
followed more than temporarily the Russian example; second,
in Russia itself the economic situation was utterly disastrous. In
the early days the hopes of the Communists had been high. The
Bolshevik triumph was to be but a step in the world wide revolution which should soon extend to all lands. For a space, especially in the year 1919, the outlook was promising. In Germany the Spartacus movement threatened the existence of the
new republic. At Budapest the red terror was installed by Bela
Kuhn, the disciple of Lenin. At Vienna the weak government
seemed likely to collapse at any moment. If this happened the
example of Hungary and Austria could not but affect Rumania
and Jugoslavia. Italy was reported to be full of seething discontent and should Italy raise the red flag France with her traditions of the Paris commune, the precursor of the Moscow one,
must surely follow. Then the turn of England would come and
sooner or later that of the United States. This was the doctrine
which Communist writers and speakers (and none others were
allowed) preached to thousands of eager believers throughout
Soviet Russia.

But the prophecies did not come true. Every one of the
supposedly tottering bourgeois governments succeeded in maintaining itself, growing stronger rather than weaker as time went
on. Worse still, the regime of Bela Kuhn was quickly overthrown
in Hungary, to the intense disappointment of Moscow. Of
course, the certainty of the ultimate triumph of Communistic
ideas everywhere was still proclaimed, but as the months followed
each other that triumph began to look discouragingly remote.
All the strenuous efforts of Bolshevist propaganda had produced
but meagre results, and the natural consequence was a feeling of

disillusionment and lassitude. The official tone might remain the same, the more ardent spirits might continue to dream and to plot, but the abler and harder headed men at the helm, sobered by stern experience in facing the difficulties of actual administration, had been brought to see that their first task was to make the best of conditions as they were. The capitalistic states of the world existed; they were in no hurry to come to an end; they could help Russia as well as harm her. As they now seemed disposed at least to leave her alone, was it not wisdom to stop wasting efforts on their conversion and to find out on what terms it was possible to live with them?

These arguments were reinforced by the appalling nature of the economic situation in which Soviet Russia found herself. Such a colossal catastrophe the world had never witnessed. Not only had factories and mines almost ceased to produce, but transportation had broken down; tools, clothes, shoes and other necessities of decent life were becoming unprocurable. Vast masses of peasantry with no stocks in reserve were raising but a fraction of the crops they formerly had and were concealing and hoarding what they did raise. Thus the threat of famine on a gigantic scale needed only a single bad harvest to make it become a terrific reality.

Of course it was explained that these evils were due to the sins of the former tsarist regime and to bourgeois exploitation, to war, to insurrection, to the intervention of foreign armies, to the blockade which had been instituted against the Russian labor republic by its capitalist foes, and to their continued machinations without and within. But granting all this, though these explanations had been repeated so often that the effect was beginning to wear off, the fact remained that the Communist promised land was becoming a hell on earth, not only to such of the hated bourgeoisie as still managed to survive, but to pretty much every one else within its borders. Something had to be done to remedy the situation, even if certain sacred principles of Communist theory went by the board.

Already by the end of the year 1920 the Soviet leaders and especially Lenin, who with his strange cynical frankness seems to take a positive delight in pointing out the errors which he and his have committed, had made up their minds that they must embark on a new policy. They had come to recognize that in a country where nine-tenths of the people were peasants it was impossible to maintain a government supported only by the factory population. It had become evident, too, that the peasants could not be won over unless they were assured not only of the practical possession of their land but of the right to dispose of its products. Experience had shown that if they were to be deprived of their surplus produce (theoretically in return for manufactured goods which the ruin of industry had rendered it impossible to supply) they would answer by raising only what food was requisite for their immediate needs. There was no escaping the conclusion that they did not appreciate the beauties of Communism and for the present at least were unteachable. Therefore, as the life of Russia depended upon them, their terms must be accepted. The system of compelling them to hand over to the state everything not needed for their own requirements and those of their families had to be given up. The government surrendered, and it was enacted that henceforth after paying a moderate tax in kind the peasant should be at liberty to sell whatever he had raised, which implied in practice a recognition of his ownership of the land.

This enactment made an irreparable breach in the system under which Soviet Russia had been administered since the winter of 1917. It meant the beginning of what was almost a new revolution, for it did not and could not stand by itself. If the peasant might own and sell, then others must be allowed to. Why should he be the only person allowed to dispose of the fruits of his labors, and if people were to sell they must also have the means to buy. The Soviet authorities had never been able really to put an end to all private trade, indeed, in the cities, they had often winked at the illicit sale of food without which there would have been much more actual starvation. They now proceeded to re-establish the right of private property and of buying and selling, the government reserving to itself only the making of regulations and also the monopoly of certain products and key industries, including export. This is the famous "new economic policy" or "strategic retreat," which was elaborated by a long series of decrees in 1921 and the first part of 1922.

Under this policy Russia has reverted to something like her former life. The markets and the business streets of Moscow are once more crowded; many shops have been opened though there is but little variety in the goods, largely second-hand, which they have to offer; tickets for railways, tramways and theatres again

have to be paid for. All this is obviously in violation of the
principles on which the Soviet republic was proclaimed and
which it long tried to enforce, and the process has been watched
with disapproval and alarm by the more uncompromising left
wing of the Communist party, who have asked where it was to
end. But the necessity of a change was so clear that it has been
put through without open opposition.

But the "new economic policy" did not relate to internal affairs
alone, for the need of assistance from abroad has likewise been
urgent. It is true that the Soviet Government and its partisans
declared that Russia, the land of boundless natural resources,
was capable of recovering her prosperity unaided, yet even they
did not profess that in that case her recovery could be other
than a slow and painful one. If she wished to get quickly on her
feet, to provide a new plant in place of what had been destroyed,
to make a vast number of indispensable repairs and to procure
necessary articles of many kinds, in order to set her industries
going again on their former scale, not to speak of the tapping of
new sources of wealth, she could do so only with the aid of a great
amount of capital and that capital she could not furnish herself;
she must turn to foreigners, however much she might condemn
their principles. Foreign capital could be obtained only from
loans or in return for concessions, foreign goods could come in
only by trade and nothing of the sort could be hoped for as
long as Soviet Russia remained an outcast among the nations.
If she must get outside assistance from abroad, the sooner she
entered into normal relations with the rest of the world the
better. The capitalist states might be unregenerate but she
could not afford to wait till they had learned the error of their
ways. She required immediate help and as a first step to this she
wanted recognition.

That this help must be paid for in some way was evident, but
the Soviet leaders believed they were in a position to bargain.
They too had heard the widespread cry that the peace and prosperity of the world could not be restored until Russia had been
once more admitted into the comity of nations and should again
contribute by her efforts and from her huge resources to the
welfare of mankind. They also know that in the capitalistic
countries there were men who hoped splendid things from a
reopening of Russian trade. No wonder, then, that the Moscow
papers asserted that "Europe needs Russia as much as Russia

needs Europe." What they did not perhaps appreciate was that there were millions of good people all over the globe who regarded Bolsheviks as little better than wild beasts.

The Soviet Government itself was naturally well aware that it would be met at the outset of any negotiations by the question whether it was prepared to recognize the tremendous claims against it. It was ready with its reply. The claims of foreign states against Russia could be divided into two categories, first, pre-war debts, and, secondly, war debts and claims for reparation for the destruction and confiscation of foreign property. As an offset to this second class of demands the Russians could bring up their own counter claims which were even more tremendous than the claims of the Allies, or at any rate could be made so if the occasion required. And these counter claims could not be waived aside as midsummer madness. They were based on quite enough international law and precedent to offer a presentable case before an impartial tribunal, could such a one be conceived of. The Allied powers without formal declaration of war with Soviet Russia had for years not only abetted and fostered countless plots against her, and furnished openly or covertly weapons, munitions, military instructors to armed forces who were trying to overthrow her government, but had also actually sent their armies into her territory. If Great Britain had once had to pay more than fifteen million dollars damages (the case had been specially studied up in Moscow) for having allowed the *Alabama* to sail from England to prey on commerce during the American Civil War, how much did the Allied and Associated Powers owe for their continual intervention in the Russian one? To be sure, the Allies had never recognized the Soviet Government and if it had been overthrown their intervention would have been counted to them by its successor as righteousness. But it had not been overthrown. It had maintained itself and its claims could not be ignored. If the South had been victorious Great Britain would not have had to pay an indemnity for the exploits of the *Alabama*. As the North was, she did. The logic of facts has to be taken into consideration.

We need not, however, suppose that the Soviet Government has expected that its claims on this score will be satisfied. Their value consists in their capacity of being used as an offset to Allied claims for compensation or war debt. This applies to the United States as well as to Great Britain and France. Some day the

Americans may have to charge off the couple of hundred millions Russia now owes them as war debt and put it down as part of the cost of their expeditions to Archangel and Vladivostok.

As to pre-war debts, although Soviet Russia demurred in theory at recognizing an obligation to repay sums which had served to strengthen the former oppressive autocracy and militarism, in practice she could hardly hope to obtain the new loans she so ardently desired if at the same time she calmly repudiated her old ones. Here was her chance to make a concession. While refusing to admit a moral liability for these debts, she would express a willingness to meet them, though just to what extent need not be specified but would depend on the bargain she could drive later.

The country which would profit the most by this concession was the one which had been the bitterest and most active enemy of the Bolshevik regime from the first, and was most cordially detested by Moscow in return, namely France. Her attitude was still one of uncompromising hostility, and crowned with victory she was now the predominant power on the European continent. But it was in France that by far the largest portion of Russian pre-war debt was held and that not by a few millionaires but by tens of thousands of small investors. In order to protect their interests France would have to put her pride in her pocket, forget past grievances and present antipathies and come down to business. If she continued aloof and hostile, she would be in danger of sacrificing what she had invested in the past, as well as the special opportunities now offered.

With England the situation was even simpler. English conservatives might dislike Bolshevism—and England had done much to aid the enemies of the Soviets, especially in the warfare of Denikin—but the English are a practical people who accept the decision of facts. The Soviet Government was now firmly established. As England lives by her exports, her millions of unemployed were a sufficient reason for her to make every effort to open up new markets and to re-establish old ones. Why should she not come to terms with Russia, especially as her holdings of pre-war debts were much less serious than those of France? Lloyd George had intermittently given encouragement to the idea. As early as March 16, 1921, an agreement had been concluded which not only permitted Anglo-Russian trade, but sanctioned the residence of a Russian commercial agent in London.

So far this had not led to any particular results, but the ice was broken.

The attitude of the United States presented a peculiar problem. As the richest, most successful bourgeois capitalistic state of the day, the United States embodies the most advanced type of the form of society which Communists regard it as their chief object in life to destroy, but as it has the largest amount of available capital it is the country which can do the most to build up Russia and finally it is the one which has shown itself by far the most generous in relieving Russian distress. Whatever might be the differences in their social conceptions, the advantage to Moscow of cultivating friendly relations with Washington was indisputable. This ought not to be difficult. The Americans have the reputation of caring for the almighty dollar and here was Moscow willing to offer them special opportunities to obtain a great number of dollars by the exploitation of untapped Russian resources. Yet, strange to say, America, which had no particular quarrel with Russia, which had not been injured by the breaking of an alliance with her as had England and France, which had no conflicting ambitions and several common interests and which was showing herself such a friend in need to starving Russians, nevertheless remained coldly aloof, haughtily refusing to recognize the Soviet Government or to have any dealings with it except in dispensing charity. To be sure, President Wilson in a direct communication had urged it not to make peace with Germany and this might be regarded as a recognition of sorts, but his appeal had fallen on deaf ears, and there had been no further official intervention. Later the Bullitt mission had aroused Soviet hopes but it had led to nothing but controversy. Since then not only had the Wilson administration refused recognition but the Harding one, by Mr. Hughes' declaration of March 25, 1921, had taken an equally uncompromising stand, nay, it had gone further, for it had invited other powers to a conference in Washington to discuss questions of the Pacific and of the Far East without the participation of Russia, in flagrant disregard of the fact that she was one of those most interested in just such questions. Chicherin had protested in July and again in November in vigorous but dignified language and had declared that any decisions reached would be for her null and void. The statement that the United States would act as the "moral trustee" for Russia seemed like adding insult to injury, and it was freely asserted in Moscow that

America at the Washington conference would try to buy concessions from the Japanese in other places by giving them a free hand in Siberia. Instead she showed she took her trusteeship seriously and did what she could to get them out of there.

Some would say that a bond was created between Soviet Russia and the United States by their similar attitude towards the League of Nations. The reasons influencing the two might not be quite the same, but the tone in regard to it of, for instance, the Boston *Transcript* differed little from that of the *Pravda*. If a common dislike draws nations together, abstention of the United States and Russia from the League should help to bring them closer to each other and to Germany.

When in the summer of 1921 in answer to the appeal of Maxim Gorki the American Relief Administration, whose president is the Secretary of Commerce, consented to enter Russia, it was hard for the Communists to believe that these bourgeois dispensers of charity were without secret political aims, and when this became self-evident it was harder still for them to understand why if the American people were willing to feed the hungry they should not be willing to do lasting good in a form that would be advantageous to themselves also by accepting the hand that was proffered them, entering into cordial relations, and taking part in the work of Russian economic regeneration. It was work, too, such as ought to appeal irresistibly to the daring imagination so characteristic of Americans, for it was not a matter of slowly building up a trade or of petty concessions but of immediate enterprises on the grandest scale with the promise of marvelous results. Why then did they hold back? Verily these Americans were strange people.

In the above reasoning there were two flaws which the rulers of the Soviet state did not, indeed could not be expected to, appreciate in their full seriousness. To begin with, in all the states with which they now wished to deal public opinion, or a large part of it, looked on them with unaffected moral reprobation, not to say actual loathing. To recognize the regime they had established was to condone crime. The tales of atrocities they had committed had shocked the civilized world; their denials and counter-charges had found little credence. Their machinations and their propaganda had spread alarm everywhere and their wild rantings as well as those of their controlled newspapers about the wickedness of the bourgeoisie and the necessity of wading through blood to a world revolution were not calculated to win them friends in countries where the bourgeoisie and capitalists were influential, not to say dominant. Secondly, even granting that a good many people were inclined to overlook the misdeeds credited to the Bolsheviks, the question still remained, were they to be trusted? What guarantee could they offer that they would keep their word? Was it not more than likely that after they had lured foreign capital by fair promises they would so hamper its operation that it could make no profit, and when they were ready they would end by confiscating it as they had done before? Was there anything in their character or record which entitled them to be trusted? The Russian answer to this, that decrees, laws, nay whole codes were being promulgated with bewildering activity, guaranteeing all sorts of rights to foreigners as well as to natives, was not wholly convincing. The Soviet Government in its administrative routine may vie with any other in its wilderness of red tape, but it can turn out as many laws as it wants with incomparable speed. By the same token it can repeal them with equal facility. A realization of this may even have lurked in the minds of the creators of the "new economic policy."

This policy having once been decided upon for foreign as well as for domestic affairs, the next question was that of procedure. The Soviet Government, however desirous of recognition and of financial help, and however prepared to make concessions in return, did not propose to appear as a suppliant, or to give up more than it had to. It trusted to its own wits and in Chicherin it possessed a spokesman who had already proved that he could hold his own in dialectics against any opponent he encountered. He opened his campaign with his note of October 29, 1921, in which while asserting that Soviet Russia was not legally or morally bound by the debts of the former regime, nevertheless in view of her need of immediate assistance he stated she would consent to see what she could do towards meeting foreign claims. He therefore proposed that an international congress should be called which should recognize her government and devise the means necessary to bring about her economic rehabilitation.

This overture met with a chilling reception. Such replies as were received were unfavorable. But Moscow went on its way and though within its borders famine and distress became ever more grievous, its international position continued to improve. German and Norwegian trade delegations arrived in Moscow, the

frontier with Esthonia was finally settled and a treaty was signed
with Austria. The meeting of the Ninth Soviet Congress showed
that there was at least no open dissension in the ranks of the
faithful. Trotski's speech which was largely devoted to foreign
affairs breathed confidence, and though sharp in its denunciations
of the actions of certain other powers, it was not at bottom
bellicose. And soon the much desired happened. On January
6, 1922, the meeting of premiers at Cannes invited Soviet Russia
to attend a general European Conference at Genoa.

There was no hesitation shown about accepting and few
attempts to conceal the satisfaction at what the newspapers
called "our victory." A strong delegation was chosen, including
in theory Lenin himself, though there can have been little serious
intention of having him risk his health, not to say his life, merely
to satisfy idle curiosity abroad. Chicherin was competent to
conduct the Russian case, which had been carefully prepared
long before. Meanwhile the making of reassuring laws continued.
On February 6th the famous "Cheka," or Extraordinary Commission, whose ruthless exploits had rendered it a name of terror
to millions, was formally abolished.

As a preliminary move, the Russian delegates to Genoa on their
way through Riga signed an agreement with Poland, Esthonia
and Latvia confirming existing treaties and promising to facilitate
trade and communications between the two parties. The representatives of the other three states also officially expressed the
opinion that a general recognition of the Soviet Government
would be helpful to the reconstruction of Europe. In Berlin the
Russian delegates carried on negotiations which were soon to
have important results. All told, they were proceeding to a meeting at which they might gain a good deal and stood to lose but
little, for if they could not obtain collective assistance they were
confident that profiting by mutual jealousies they could make
some satisfactory bargains with individual powers.

They had, however, met with one severe disappointment before
they started. On March 8 Secretary Hughes definitely declined
the invitation to the United States to take part in the Conference.
This deprived it of half its value for Moscow. What Russia
wanted was recognition and above all money. Without American
recognition that of Europe was of less consequence, for only the
United States was rich enough to lend on a large scale. We may
well surmise, therefore, that the absence of American repre-

sentatives seriously affected the conduct of the Russians both at Genoa and The Hague.   They now felt they had less to gain by making concessions and accordingly less reason for making them. Even Lenin's defiant speech to the Congress of Metal Workers at Moscow on March 6th may have been so influenced, for by that time the American refusal could be foreseen.   He declared that if need be Russia would say, "All attempts to impose upon us terms as if we were vanquished are outright nonsense to which it is not worth while to reply.   We are entering into relations as merchants and we know what you owe us and we owe you, and what legitimate and even exorbitant profit you may extort from us.   We have a great number of proposals, the number of agreements grows and will grow, whatever the relations between the three or four victorious powers; a postponement of this conference will be a loss for yourselves, because by postponing it you will prove to your own people that you do not know what you want and that you are suffering from disease of the will."   Turning to internal politics he told his enemies, "You challenged us to a desperate fight in 1917, and in reply we took recourse to terror, and again to terror—and will use it still again if you try it again," and as for 'the new economic policy' "we can say now that this retreat as far as concessions made to the capitalists are concerned is now ended."

In Europe, on the other hand, even it would seem in government circles, there existed a widespread belief that the economic situation in Russia was such that however much her representatives might bluff and bluster at the outset, in the end they would have to submit to almost anything.   It would therefore be possible, as well as desirable, to impose not only stringent terms for the repayment of old debts, but elaborate and humiliating conditions for future benefits.

We need not enter here into the story of the Genoa conference. Both sides began by putting forward their demands in extreme form—the principal Allies in the report of the preliminary conference held in London, the Russians in a memorandum they drew up in reply stating counter claims which appeared to the Allied powers utterly extravagant, not to say impertinent.   In the weeks of wrangling that followed both sides made concessions but they never were near real agreement.   From the first the Russians made it plain that they meant to be treated as equals, not as culprits or supplicants.   They took the tone that they came to offer as well as to ask and in debate they did not shrink from irritating their opponents by sharp rejoinders. Yet although their demands made Europe gasp they were quite ready to bargain, indeed it sometimes seemed that there was no principle they would not sacrifice if only they could make sure of a large loan. It is not surprising that the conference ended as it did; it could hardly have done otherwise.

But if, owing to the absence of the Americans, the Russians at Genoa had not expected real financial help, they had no cause to be disappointed with the outcome of the conference. For one thing, they had found what they had long desired, a platform from which they could speak with a certainty of being listened to. They did not particularly care if they were disapproved of and stirred up anger. They had not come for sympathy but to assert themselves, and to obtain practical if not formal recognition. This they had achieved. The recognition they had won might not be friendly but it was real. To pretend not to recognize a government after arguing and trying to reach an agreement with it for long weeks, with the whole world following every move in the game, was almost ludicrous. The Soviet republic had indeed won the *de facto* recognition of Europe. It could afford to wait a while for the *de jure*, especially as thanks to American assistance the horrors of the famine were being combatted with some measure of success.

At the same time, the Russian delegates had not forgotten the other string to their bow, the opportunity for conversations with separate powers. The situation was promising. France and of late even Italy, ordinarily the faithful henchman of England, had shown themselves willing, although still theoretically at war with the Ottoman Empire, to make pacts with the Turks at Angora behind the back of their British ally. The desire of the Italians for a commercial treaty with Russia was well known and negotiations were already well under way. There was nothing to hinder the Soviet delegates at Genoa or afterwards at The Hague from dealing secretly with single states as well as openly with a number. This they proceeded to do.

On April 15th the Genoa Conference and the world were astonished by the news that Germany and Russia had just signed a formal treaty at Rapallo a few miles away. In its terms it was sound and statesmanlike. The two countries entered once more into normal relations, granting each other equal rights and privileges. By a particularly sensible provision all the claims each might have against the other were swept away, thus disposing of a vast mass of complicated and contentious matter, which could be handled in no other fashion without endless difficulties and possibilities of trouble. The Treaty of Versailles had recognized the right of Russia to German reparation payments. But now bygones were to be bygones. The two mighty former empires had fallen and their old quarrels were but memories. The two new and struggling republics needed the help which each could give the other.

Later history will show some day whether in the long run Russia or Germany will have profited the more by the treaty of Rapallo. At the time it was signed there is no doubt as to which gained by it. However ultimately advantageous it might be to Germany, she ran just then all the risks and paid all the penalties. She doubtless had a theoretical right to conclude the agreement, which was not unlike the one made by Poland, Esthonia and Latvia with Russia a few weeks before, but she chose the worst moment to do it. She prejudiced her case by an appearance of double-dealing, and she heightened the alarm of France, which it was her interest to allay, as well as weakened the hands of Lloyd George, on whom she depended and who was trying to do what he could for her. As a punishment for putting this spoke in the Allied wheel she had to accept the humiliation of being excluded from all further meetings in which Russian affairs were debated.

But Russia received no punishment. If she had worried England and France, why so much the better. It would make them more amenable to reason by showing them she could turn elsewhere. At the dramatic moment she had won an advantage which not only strengthened her immediate position but laid the foundation for greater things in the future.

Towards the close of the conference the news of the Shell oil concession created another sensation, though of a milder sort. The relations between the Shell Company and the British Government were enough to make the transaction interesting. Presently, too, the conference woke up to the fact that the intention of the Russians to redivide their oil districts in such a manner as to exploit them in large concessions to the best advantage, though economically wise, conflicted hopelessly with the return of oil properties to their former foreign owners. All that the Russians were willing to do was to offer not compensation but a certain priority in new concessions. At the last, when the conference ended without agreement, they took back all offers of any kind they had made and rested on their original positions.

When the time came for fresh attempts at accord at The Hague, the prospect was discouraging from the start. The United States had again refused to take part and the tone of the Russian delegates was not conciliatory, nor did the fact that they were long held aloof by the non-Russians and invited only to meet sub-commissions improve their disposition. On the other hand they seemed ready to go on talking indefinitely, it was suspected with ulterior motives, and there was again the feeling that they might be willing to sacrifice many principles if only offered money enough. They boldly asked for a huge amount. But the uselessness of further discussion soon became so increasingly evident that the conference broke up, this time with complete acknowledgment of failure, as it made no suggestion of further meetings.

To the self denying ordinance of the non-Russians, adhered to by the United States, that they would frown upon any acquisition by their nationals of Russian concessions which included property that had once belonged to other foreigners, the Soviet Government replied soon after by granting an oil concession to Germans, Germany not having been invited to The Hague. Although this concession did not include any former foreign property the retort was unmistakable.

On June 5th a treaty was signed between Russia and Czechoslovakia. Some of the provisions are significant. Questions of indemnity or return of property are postponed. Also, although it is stated that the treaty is not meant to anticipate the recognition *de jure* of the Soviet republic, nevertheless the chiefs and two other members of the principal mission of each country in the territory of the other are to have diplomatic privileges, and local agents are to have consular ones. In other words there is recognition in all but the name.

Since the close of the Genoa Conference the attitude of Moscow has perceptibly stiffened, whether it be owing to favorable crop reports which make the Communist rulers feel more independent of outside help, as is shown in their hampering even the work of the American Relief Administration, or whether it be due to an increase of influence of the left wing of the party, thanks to the incapacitation of Lenin, or whether to some other cause. This has manifested itself in a refusal to ratify the treaty of commerce which Chicherin concluded with Italy just before his departure from there, and still more in the fresh contempt exhibited for the opinion of the outside world. The way in which the recent trial of social revolutionists has been conducted was enough to alienate the sympathies of all but the Communistic fraction of European and American socialists, and the treatment of the clergy accused of resistance to the law confiscating church property for famine relief has looked, in spite of the charitable purport of the measure itself, like odious religious persecution. On the credit side we note a proposition, with whatever intention, to discuss the reduction of armaments.

In her external relations, as in her internal conditions, Soviet Russia presents a changing picture. Predictions as to the future are hazardous. We can do little more than note a few salient facts and guess at certain tendencies.

In Europe Russia no longer borders on any state of the first rank, such as Germany and Austria, but on five smaller ones, Finland (which now separates her from Sweden and Norway), Esthonia, Latvia, Poland and Rumania. All of these are composed, wholly or in part, of territory which until recently was hers, or at least under her sovereignty. Today she has recognized their independence in accordance with the principles she professes, and she has been liberal in the drawing of frontier lines, notably in the case of Finland to whom she has made a pure gift of the district of Pechenga in the extreme north simply because it is of greater value to Finland, which thereby gains a port of access to the Arctic Ocean, than it is to Russia, which has plenty of sea coast on the Arctic, though nowhere else. Examples of such generosity between nations are rare. Nevertheless, Russia's European neighbors are much afraid of her. She is still far larger and possesses far more ultimate resources than all of them put together; she still maintains on paper a standing army of over a million men. They fear that her renunciation of the former borderlands of the empire may have been due only to the necessities of the moment and might be taken back at the first convenient opportunity. There are enough Communists in these states to furnish Moscow with pretexts for interfering if it wishes to do so. They are aware, also, that not only have most of the Russians in exile refused to accept the shrinkage of their country as permanent but that Soviet policy itself seems to be inspired by more nationalistic sentiment than it was a while ago. The example of the way Soviet governments were established with the aid of Russian soldiers in the three republics of the Caucasus is not reassuring.

On the other hand, a policy of reconquest on the part of Russia would inevitably provoke a coalition against her. Poland and Rumania are bound together by an alliance which represents a population of over forty million people and a very considerable military strength. They would have allies and they could count on much indirect assistance and perhaps active support from France. The Baltic states are far weaker and more exposed and one of them, Lithuania, from hatred of Poland leans towards Russia. In their case the danger to their independence lies not so much in their having belonged to Russia for two centuries as in the fact that they constitute her natural sea coast on the Baltic. Many wiseacres declare that it is impossible for her to do without them. One may reply that Germans have held the same views about Belgium, Holland and Denmark, and that these views are today not generally accepted. But peril is there and will continue. To meet it the Baltic republics must rely not only on their own sturdy resistance but on outside aid. Poland, for instance, can hardly leave them to their fate, even if she does not covet them for herself as she is suspected of doing. The condition of the Russian army is not of the best, especially for an offensive campaign, and the difficulties of arming, supplying and handling large masses of men would be great just now. Finally, in fairness to the Soviet Government, one must admit that in spite of rude language and non-fulfillment of some of the minor provisions of its treaties, it has shown no serious signs of deliberate intent to violate them.

With one of her neighbors Russia still has unsettled questions of such importance that under other circumstances they might easily lead to war. Profiting by the Russian revolution and the ensuing confusion, Rumania, on the ground of historical right and more or less with the consent of the inhabitants, about half of whom are Rumanians, has possessed herself of the former Russian province of Bessarabia. This annexation has never been recognized by Moscow. On the other hand, the Bolsheviks appropriated to their own use the Rumanian gold reserve which at the time of the war had been sent to Russia for greater security. Naturally Rumania claims it back. The Soviet Government probably cares no more for Bessarabia (except perhaps the

Ukrainian part of it) than it did for other lands it has ceded, but as the Rumanian gold has long been spent and would be inconvenient to return, the obvious course to follow is to keep open the dispute. If Rumania would buy Russian recognition of the *fait accompli* by abandoning the demand for her stolen gold, Moscow would hardly object, and this may be the ultimate solution, but so far Rumania has been unwilling to accept it. Neither side, however, is ready to go to war over these questions.

The threat of an attack upon Russia herself, in her hour of weakness, by her neighbors, especially Poland and Rumania aided and abetted by France, has been a favorite theme of Bolshevik oratory. We may take it that most of this has been for popular consumption, though she has had some genuine grievances to complain of, for the territory of her neighbors has been used as a base of operations for insurrections in her own. Still, if she has entertained real apprehensions, as she seems to have, this betrays more weakness than she has usually been credited with. Some Communists may even desire foreign aggression, for it would once more rally disaffected elements to the support of the government. But these small states will hardly be foolish enough to molest their gigantic neighbor, weak as she now is, if she leaves them alone. They have already got in full the boundaries they are entitled to, and even the desire of Poland and Rumania to see a really independent Ukraine which shall serve as a buffer between them and Moscow is moderated by the knowledge that such a Ukraine would be more nationalistic in character and would demand from them their Ukrainian territories with more insistance and asperity than Moscow does.

Of the great powers France is the one whose relations with Soviet Russia are the worst and not improbably may remain so for a good while to come. Some Frenchmen, to be sure, think that it will be easier to reach an agreement by separate treaty than it has been by general international convention. They may be right, but France has much to claim from Russia and comparatively little to offer these days when she no longer has moneys to lend. This puts her at a disadvantage in negotiating with an adversary as unsentimental as the Bolsheviks. But neither country at this moment is in a position to do the other great harm. England has more to offer and fewer claims to present. She is less embittered, and is also in greater need of Russian trade and of tolerable political relations, for she is more vulnerable. Moscow has enough means of action in the Mohammedan and Asiatic world to make trouble for her in several countries, notably in Afghanistan and India.

Many people regard the recent treaty of Rapallo between Germany and Russia as only a first step towards closer relations and perhaps actual alliance. Some would say it existed already. There are indeed many ways in which the two countries might help one another. German industry could furnish Russia with the chief articles of which she is in pressing need; German science and technical skill could guide the upbuilding of her industries, the reopening and the administration of her mines, the construction of great public works and likewise the training of her armies, although at least Trotski would assert they are trained already. The trouble is all these benefits have to be paid for in cash—paper roubles and other forms of Soviet credit will not do—and Russia has not the cash to pay for them. Besides, though she wishes to use the Germans and has a wholesome respect for their abilities, she does not intend to put herself into their hands for exploitation. For her part she cannot give them the thing they would value most, military security. Russian armies today could not keep the French out of Berlin. Even if they could they would not be welcome. It looks, accordingly, as if Moscow and Berlin will not become intimate; but, though they have little trust in each other, they will remain on friendly terms. They have one common bond, which has helped to keep them together in the past and may again, their deep dislike for Poland.

Although in principle the foreign policy of the Soviet republic is based on internationalism and in practice is dominated by the necessities of the moment, some of the traditions of the former empire have not been forgotten. The Russia of today declares she has renounced imperialistic ambitions but that this does not mean she is indifferent to legitimate national interests even if she is not now in a position to assert them effectively. This is true of her policy both in the Near and in the Far East. She no longer menaces Turkey, indeed she is on excellent terms with the Angora Government, but she has not lost her right to be heard in questions regarding Constantinople and the Straits which will always remain of vital importance to her southern trade. She will therefore not accept as valid any international arrangements concerning them made without her participation.

The same principle holds in regard to the Far East. Russia has given fair warning that the agreements reached at the Washington Conference do not exist as far as she is concerned. Her right to take this stand is unquestionable but she will make no complaint if the policy of Mr. Hughes results in the evacuation of Siberia and northern Sakhalin by the Japanese, a thing she earnestly desires but is too weak to bring about unaided. At any rate, she means some day to assert herself once more in this part of the world, though she may do so in the name of the Far Eastern republic which, without being a Soviet state, is none the less in her eyes a member of the Russian Federation. If the Americans, in the meanwhile, are willing to pull her chestnuts out of the fire for her so much the better. And now Japan has just manifested a willingness to enter into conference with her.

In her future dealing with China, as with Turkey, she will have the considerable advantage that she alone of the great powers has agreed under certain conditions to surrender all claim to consular jurisdiction and other capitulations of the sort which have seemed so necessary for the protection of Europeans in the past, but which are so resented by Chinese and Turks today. She has also given back her share of the famous concession of special rights along the Manchurian railway, thereby ingratiating herself with the Chinese and making the position of the Japanese in South Manchuria more awkward.

And finally as to America, the self-appointed moral trustee, the benefactor who has dispensed such charity as no people ever before bestowed on another and at the same time the stern critic who declines to recognize the government she has been cooperating with in feeding millions of its people—what is she going to do? Her position is morally strong, for in her condemnation as in her charity she has been guided by unselfish considerations. In no other country is there more genuine horror of the Bolsheviks as men of blood without ruth or faith who have wrought a havoc unparalleled in history. Are they to be helped and comforted because they have got to the end of their rope and after limitless wanton destruction have shown themselves incapable of creating or rebuilding? Their methods are still those of brutal terror under which no one but the ruling minority can feel secure. Of what value are the promises of men whose highest aim is to subvert the very basis of the society on which our civilization is founded and who believe that every means to this end is justified? Some of these men may be honest fanatics of a dangerous kind, others are mere criminals. To grasp their hand in friendship is to touch pitch and be defiled.

To this some reply denying the accusations or putting much of the blame elsewhere. Still others believe that even granting the truth of the charges it does not follow that because we disapprove of the rulers of a country we should have no dealings with the people who suffer most from their rule. The progress of mankind has come through intercourse, and if we wish to aid the unfortunate millions of Russia, the way to do so is not to leave them alone or even merely to pauperize them with charity, but to help them to get to their feet again. Free communications with the outside world would be an inestimable boon to many of them. Shall we refuse to sell sorely needed farm instruments to the Russian peasants because we dislike the Moscow Soviet? To recognize the government of a country does not imply that we admire it, it is merely to take note of an existing fact. If the crimes of Sultan Abdul Hamid were not deemed a bar to American commerce and to the necessary official relations with Turkey, why should trading with Russia make us responsible for the practices of Lenin and Trotski?

But apart from ethical considerations there are other reasons which explain the hesitation felt by many governments, and notably the American, about recognizing officially the present regime. Among these is doubt as to its duration and to what may succeed it. This is no mere question of change of personnel such as has often occurred in Latin America and elsewhere, but of something much more fundamental. Today we can see four possibilities of development in the case of Russia, any one of which would be of world-wide importance and any one of which might be precipitated by the permanent disappearance from the scene of Lenin, an event which in view of the state of his health may occur at any time, if it has not occurred already. The part which he has played has been so great and the place which he has held has been so commanding that by his departure he would leave a gap difficult to fill. A struggle for power between those next in line, of whose relative strength we know almost nothing, might lead to far-reaching results.

These four obvious possibilities are, first, a counter revolution, though not necessarily in favor of monarchy, such a one as was attempted by Kolchak, Denikin, Wrangel and others. This is still the dream of hosts of Russian exiles and of an unknown proportion of the population of Russia itself. The previous attempts to bring it about have failed and there seems no particular reason for expecting that others would succeed now.

Second, the "new economic policy" may continue to spread and may take deep root, the new codes of law may supplant the arbitrary dictatorship of the proletariat, the bourgeoisie may be able to raise its head again, and the men directing the ship of state, taught by experience, may abandon in practice many of their previous theories and methods. In other words, the Russian Republic may undergo the same sort of transformation as did the first French republic after the reign of terror. Even now a few more changes would make Soviet legislation not very different from that of the other new socialistically inclined republics.

Third, there may be a reaction to the left. If, for instance, Trotski or Zinoviev succeeds to the place of Lenin, we may witness a return to the attempt to govern on purely Communistic principles accompanied by increased activity in propaganda abroad.

Fourth, even without dissension in the Communist ranks or attack from without or within, the economic condition of Soviet Russia may become so deplorable and transportation break down to such an extent that the central government will lose its control and the country fall into anarchy, breaking up into fragments, each mindful only of its own wants. How far such a process of disruption might go and whither it would lead is beyond our ken, but of this we may be sure: it would mean confusion and misery such as would stagger the imagination.

¶ LENIN

by Victor Chernov   (March, 1924)

*His dominating mind and will and his shrewd judgment of coming events
enabled Lenin to create a small but relatively disciplined party and then, using
it as a fulcrum of power, seize the revolutionary opportunity of 1917. His interpretation of Marxism led him to a new type of state and a new type of
international revolutionary general staff, both based on the concept of a "permanent civil war." The Russian protest movement had thrown up a host
of dedicated idealists, more than a few terrorists, and many martyrs. It
was less notable for producing men of will and action. In this brief portrait,
sketched just after Lenin's death, Victor Chernov (1873–1952) drew on a long,
deep, but not personally intimate knowledge of his fellow revolutionary and
bitter political rival.*

*Chernov was expelled from the university at twenty for his leading part in
student protests against the Tsarist regime, and from then on he was a professional revolutionary. Drawing on Russian populist traditions, on Marxism, and
on an extensive knowledge of Western economics and sociology, Chernov developed and propagated an eclectic but powerful concept of peasant revolution
as Russia's future path. The Socialist Revolutionary Party, of which Chernov
was a principal founder, called for a democratic republic, political freedom, and
the free use of the land by those who till it. In 1917, he returned to Russia from
long exile to find his followers sharply divided. Some wanted to continue the
war to defend the achievements of the Revolution; others demanded immediate
peace at any price; still others, like Chernov, hoped to organize support in both
warring camps for a negotiated peace. The Socialist Revolutionary ranks were
also split on the question of whether to divide all the land immediately among
the peasants by direct action or to wait for the Constituent Assembly to act in
an orderly way.*

*The elections to the Constituent Assembly gave the Socialist Revolutionaries
and their allies a clear majority. On January 5, 1918, Chernov was elected
President of the Assembly, which, after one day's session, was dispersed by
force at Lenin's command. After continuing the underground struggle against
Bolshevik rule for several years, Chernov was forced to leave Russia again and
found refuge in the West. His one major work in English translation is* The
Great Russian Revolution *(1936), an analysis of the failure of the democratic
forces in the 1917 Revolution.*

LENIN

By *Victor Chernov*

LENIN is dead—this time dead physically, for spiritually and politically he has been dead a year at least. We have got in the habit of speaking of him as a thing of the past; and for that very reason it will not be difficult now to write of him dispassionately.

Lenin was a great man. He was not merely the greatest man in his party; he was its uncrowned king, and deservedly. He was its head, its will, I should even say he was its heart were it not that both the man and the party implied in themselves heartlessness as a duty. Lenin's intellect was energetic but cold. It was above all an ironic, sarcastic, and cynical intellect. Nothing to him was worse than sentimentality, a name he was ready to apply to all moral and ethical considerations in politics. Such things were to him trifles, hypocrisy, "parson's talk." Politics to him meant strategy, pure and simple. Victory was the only commandment to observe; the will to rule and to carry through a political program without compromise, that was the only virtue; hesitation, that was the only crime.

It has been said that war is a continuation of politics, though employing different means. Lenin would undoubtedly have reversed this dictum and said that politics is the continuation of war under another guise. The essential effect of war on a citizen's conscience is nothing but a legalization and glorification of things that in times of peace constitute crime. In war the turning of a flourishing country into a desert is a mere tactical move; robbery is a "requisition," deceit a strategem, readiness to shed the blood of one's brother military zeal; heartlessness towards one's victims is laudable self-command; pitilessness and inhumanity are one's duty. In war all means are good, and the best ones are precisely the things most condemned in normal human intercourse. And as politics is disguised war, the rules of war constitute its principles.

Lenin was often accused of not being and of not wanting to be an "honest adversary." But then the very idea of an "honest adversary" was to him an absurdity, a smug citizen's prejudice, something that might be made use of now and then jesuitically in one's own interest; but to take it seriously was silly. A defender of the proletariat is under an obligation to put aside all scruples in dealings with the foe. To deceive him intentionally, to calumniate him, to blacken his name, all this Lenin considered as normal. In fact, it would be hard to exceed the cynical brutality with which he proclaimed all this. Lenin's conscience consisted in putting himself outside the boundaries of human conscience in all dealings with his foes; and in thus rejecting all principles of honesty he remained honest with himself.

Being a Marxist, he was a believer in "class struggle." As an individual contribution to this theory he used to confess his belief that civil war was the unavoidable climax of class struggle. We may even say that to him class struggle was but the embryo of civil war. Dissent in the party, whether serious or merely trifling, he often tried to explain as an echo of class antagonisms. He would then proceed to eliminate the undesirable by cutting them off from the party, and in doing this he "honestly" resorted to the lowest means. After all, is not a non-homogeneous party an illegitimate conglomeration of antagonistic class-elements? And all antagonistic class-elements should be treated according to the precept "war is war."

His whole life was passed in schisms and factional fights within the party. From this resulted his incomparable perfection as a gladiator, as a professional fighter, in training every day of his life and constantly devising new tricks to trip up or knock out his adversary. It was this lifelong training that gave him his amazing cool-headedness, his presence of mind in any conceivable situation, his unflinching hope "to get out of it" somehow or other. By nature a man of single purpose and possessed of a powerful instinct of self-preservation, he had no difficulty in proclaiming *credo quia absurdum* and was much like that favorite Russian toy, the Van'ka-Vstan'ka boy, who has a piece of lead in his rounded bottom and bobs up again as fast as you knock him down. After every failure, no matter how shameful or humiliating, Lenin would instantly bob up and begin again from the beginning. His will was like a good steel spring which recoils the more powerfully the harder it is pressed. He was a hardy party leader of just the kind necessary to inspire and keep up the courage of his fellow fighters and to forestall panic by his personal example of unlimited self-confidence, as well as to bring them to their senses in periods of high exaltation when it would be extremely easy for them to become "a conceited party," as he used to say, resting on their laurels and overlooking the perils of the future.

This singleness of purpose was the thing that most imposed respect among his followers.   Many a time when Lenin managed to survive, thanks only to some blunder of his foes, the credit for his survival was attributed to his unflinching optimism.   Often it used to be mere blind luck—but then blind luck mostly comes to those who know how to hold out through a period of desperate ill-luck.   Most persons soon give up.   They do not care to sacrifice their strength in evidently futile attempts; they are sensible —and it is this good sense that precludes good luck.   There is some supreme common sense, on the other hand, in a man who will spend his last ounce of energy in spite of all odds,—in spite of logic, destiny and circumstance.   And with such "unreasonable common sense" nature endowed Lenin to excess.   Thanks to this tenacity he more than once salvaged his party from apparently inextricable straits, but to the masses at large such occurrences were miracles and were ascribed to his genius of foresight.   Foresight on a large scale, however, was the very thing he lacked.   He was a fencing master first of all, and a fencer needs only a little foresight and no complicated ideas.   In fact, he must not think too much; he must concentrate on every movement of his adversary and master his own reflexes with the quickness of inborn instinct, so as to counter every hostile move without a trace of delay.

Lenin's intellect was penetrating but not broad, resourceful but not creative.   A past master in estimating any political situation, he would become instantly at home with it, quickly perceive all that was new in it and exhibit great political and practical sagacity in forestalling its immediate political consequences. This perfect and immediate tactical sense formed a complete contrast to the absolutely unfounded and fantastic character of any more extensive historical prognosis he ever attempted—of any program that comprised more than today and tomorrow. The agrarian plan worked out by him in the nineties for the Social-Democratic Party, something he had been toiling over and digesting for ten years, met with complete failure, an accident which never prevented him subsequently from hastily borrowing from the Social-Revolutionaries agrarian slogans which he previously had spent much effort in combating.   His concrete plans of attack were superbly practical; but his gran-

diose program of action after victory, which was to cover a whole
historical period, went to pieces at the first touch of reality.   His
"nearer political outlook" was unexcelled; his "further political
outlook" went permanently bankrupt.

As a man who already had the truth in his pocket he attached
no value to the creative efforts of other seekers after truth.   He
had no respect for the convictions of anyone else, he had none of
the enthusiastic love of liberty which marks the independent
creative spirit.   On the contrary, he was dominated by the
purely Asiatic conception of a monopoly of press, speech, justice,
and thought by a single ruling caste, agreeing therein with the
alleged Moslem saying that if the library of Alexandria contained
the same things as the Koran it was useless, and if it contained
things contrary it was harmful.

Granting that Lenin was absolutely lacking in creative genius,
that he was merely a skilful, forcible and indefatigable expounder
of other thinkers' theories, that he was a man of such narrowness
of mind that it could almost be called limited intelligence, nevertheless he was capable of greatness and originality within those
limitations.   His power lay in the extraordinary, absolute lucid-
ity—one might almost say the transparency—of his propositions.   He followed his logic unflinchingly even to an absurd conclusion, and left nothing diffuse and unexplained unless it were
necessary to do so for tactical considerations.   Ideas were made
as concrete and simple as possible.   This was most evident in
Lenin's rhetoric.   He never was a brilliant orator, an artist of
beautiful speech.   He would often be coarse and clumsy, especially in polemics, and he repeated himself continually.   But
these repetitions were his very system and his strength.   Through
the endless re-digesting, uncouth pounding and clumsy jokes
there throbbed a live, indomitable will that would not be devi-
ated by an inch from the appointed path; it was a steady, elemental pressure whose monotony hypnotized the audience.   One
and the same thought was expressed many times in many
different shapes till finally in one way or another it penetrated
each individual brain; then, as a drop of water perforates the
rock, constant repetition was applied to implant the idea into
the very essence of the hearer's intelligence.   Few orators have
known how to achieve such admirable results by dint of repetition.   Besides, Lenin always *felt* his audience.   He never rose
too high above its level, nor did he ever omit to descend to it at

just the necessary moment, in order not to break the continuity of the hypnosis which dominated the will of his flock; and more than any one he realized that a mob is like a horse that wants to be firmly bestrode and spurred, that wants to feel the hand of a master. When needed he spoke as a ruler, he denounced and whipped his audience. "He's not an orator—he's more than an orator," someone remarked about him, and the remark was a shrewd one.

The will of Lenin was stronger than his intellect, and the latter was everlastingly the servant of the former. Thus when victory was finally won after years of clandestine toil he did not embark upon the task of embodying his ideas as would a constructive socialist who had pondered over his creative work in advance; he merely applied to the new, creative phase of his life's program the same methods which had been used in his destructive struggle for power, "On s'engage et puis on voit"—he was very fond of these words of Napoleon's.

Lenin has often been painted as a blind dogmatist, but he never was such by nature. He was not the kind to become attached for better or worse to a symmetrically finished system, he merely set his mind on succeeding in his political and revolutionary gamble, where to catch the proper moment meant everything. This is how he often became a quack, an experimenter, a gambler; this is why he was an opportunist, which is something diametrically opposed to a dogmatist.

Many critics have thought Lenin greedy for power and honors. The fact is he was organically made to rule and simply could not help imposing his will on others, not because he longed for this but because it was as natural for him to do so as it is for a large astral body to influence the planets. As for honors, he disliked them. His heart never rejoiced in pomp. Plebeian in his tastes and by his inmost nature, he remained just as simple in his habits after the October revolution as he had been before. He has often been represented, too, as a heartless, dry fanatic. This heartlessness of his was purely intellectual and therefore directed against his enemies, that is, against the enemies of his party. To his friends he was amiable, good-natured, cheerful, and polite, as a good comrade should be; so it was that the affectionate, familiar "Iliich" became his universally accepted name among his followers.

Yes, Lenin was good-natured. But good-natured does not

mean good-hearted. It has been observed that physically strong people are usually good-natured, and the good nature of Lenin was of exactly the same description as the amiability of a huge Saint Bernard dog toward surrounding pups and mongrels. So far as we can guess, real good-heartedness most probably was considered by him one of the pettiest of human weaknesses. At least it is a fact that whenever he wanted to annihilate some Socialist adversary he never omitted to bestow upon him the epithet of "a good fellow." He devoted his whole life to the interests of the working class. Did he love those working people? Apparently he did, although his love of the real, living workman was undoubtedly less intense than his hatred of the workman's oppressor. His love of the proletariat was the same despotic, exacting, and merciless love with which, centuries ago, Torquemada burned people for their salvation.

To note another trait: Lenin, after his own manner, loved those whom he valued as useful assistants. He readily forgave them mistakes, even disloyalty, though once in a while calling them sternly to task. Rancor or vengefulness were alien to him. Even his foes were not live, personal enemies but certain abstract factors to be eliminated. They could not possibly excite his human interest, being simply mathematically determined points where destructive force was to be applied. Mere passive opposition to his party at a critical moment was a sufficient reason for him to have scores and hundreds of persons shot without a moment's consideration; and with all this he was fond of playing and laughing heartily with children, kittens and dogs.

It has been said that what the style is the man is. It would be even truer to say that what the thought is the man is. If it has been given to Lenin to leave any imprint of himself upon the doctrine of class struggle it is to be found in his interpretation of the dictatorship of the proletariat, an interpretation permeated with the conception of that will which was the essence of his own personality. Socialism means the enfranchisement of labor; and the proletariat is the warp and woof of the working mass. In the proletariat itself, however, there are purer and less pure strains of proletarians. Now if a dictatorship of the proletariat over the working masses is required there must be, on the same principles, within the proletariat itself a vanguard-dictatorship over the proletarian rank and file. This must be a kind of quintessence, a true Proletarian Party. Within this Proletarian

Party there must likewise be an inner dictatorship of the sterner elements over the more yielding ones. We have thus an ascending system of dictatorships, which culminates and could not help culminating in a personal dictator. Such Lenin came to be.

His theory of concentric dictatorships,—which reminds one of the concentric circles of Dante's Inferno,—thus developed into a universally applicable theory of Socialist dictatorial guardianship over the people, that is, into the very antithesis of true Socialism as a system of economic democracy. This favorite and most intimate conception of Lenin—and the only one really his own—was a *contradictio in adjecto*. Such an inner contradiction could not help but become, ultimately, a source of disintegration inside the party he had created.

He is dead. His party is now headed by men whom for a long period of years he moulded after his own image, who found it easy to imitate him but who are finding it extremely difficult to continue his policy. That party as a whole is now beginning to experience the fate of its supreme leader: gradually it is becoming a living corpse. Lenin is no longer there to galvanize it with his surplus energy; he spent himself to the dregs—spent himself on a party which is now, in its turn, exhausted. Over his freshly made grave it may for a moment draw closer together and pronounce vows of fidelity to the revered teacher who has told it so much in the past, but who today is telling it no more, and who will tell it no more in the future. Then it will fall back into everyday life and again be subject to the law of disintegration and dissolution.

¶ WORLDS OF COLOR
by W. E. B. DuBois   (April, 1925)

Contemporaneous with the story of the evolution of the British Empire during the interwar years, and woven into it, was the demand of the colored races for political and economic justice at the hands of the white race. W. E. B. DuBois, whose "Worlds of Color" appeared in the April, 1925, Foreign Affairs, *was one of the great leaders of the movement. Born in Massachusetts in 1868, he took degrees at Fisk and Harvard universities and at the University of Berlin, taught history and economics at Atlanta and Wilberforce universities, organized the Niagara Movement, which produced the National Association for the Advancement of Colored People, and was the prime mover in the calling of the first Pan-African Congress, which met in Paris in 1919. As Editor of* Crisis *and author of many books, his voice was among the most powerful and effective in arousing the members of the black race to their opportunities and their responsibilities and in educating members of the white race to their obligations and to the danger of complacency. Many years before most, and possibly more than any other man, he helped shape the attitude of American Negroes to a militant demand for their rights (as he himself phrased it) as members of society.*

In his latter days, DuBois championed the belief that only through socialism could Negroes achieve these rights. As is natural enough for one whose task was to arouse and awaken, he used the methods of combat—broad, hard strokes, not fine distinctions. In the perspective of nearly fifty years, the configuration of the world is vastly different. The British Empire is no more—all its former African colonies have gained their independence with the exception of Rhodesia, which unilaterally declared it in 1965. And in the United States civil-rights legislation has been enacted, acknowledging many of the rights DuBois wrote of. It may nonetheless be noted that tragedies more terrible and defeats more humiliating than any forecast in 1925 have occurred—and that the final results of complacency and injustice have not yet been registered.

WORLDS OF COLOR

By W. E. B. DuBois

ONCE upon a time in my younger years and in the dawn of this century I wrote: "The problem of the Twentieth Century is the problem of the color line." It was a pert phrase which I then liked and which since I have often rehearsed to myself, asking how far was it prophecy and how far speculation? Today, in the last year of the century's first quarter, I propose to examine this matter again, and more especially in the memory of the great event of these great years, the World War. How deep were the roots of this catastrophe entwined about the color line? And of the legacy left, what of the darker race problems will the world inherit?

THE LABOR PROBLEM

Most men would agree that our present Problem of Problems is what we call Labor: the problem of allocating work and income in the tremendous and increasingly intricate world-embracing industrial machine which we have built. But, despite our study and good-will, is it not possible that our research is not directed to the right geographical spots and our good-will too often confined to that labor which we see and feel and exercise right around us rather than to the periphery of the vast circle and to the unseen and inarticulate workers within the World Shadow? And may not the continual baffling of our effort and failure of our formula be due to just such mistakes? At least it will be of interest to step within these shadows and, looking backward, view the European and white American labor problem from this external vantage ground—or, better, ground of disadvantage.

With nearly every great European empire today walks its dark colonial shadow, while over all Europe there stretches the yellow shadow of Asia that lies across the world. One might indeed rede the riddle of Europe by making its present plight a matter of colonial shadows and speculate wisely on what might not happen if Europe became suddenly shadowless—if Asia and Africa and the islands were cut permanently away. At any rate here is a field of inquiry, of likening and contrasting each land and its far off shadow.

THE SHADOW OF PORTUGAL

I was attending the Third Pan-African Congress and I walked to the Palacio dos Cortes with Magellan. It was in December, 1923, and in Lisbon. I was rather proud. You see Magalhaes (to give him the Portuguese spelling) is a mulatto—small, light-brown and his hands quick with gestures. Dr. José de Magalhaes is a busy man: a practising specialist; professor in the School of Tropical Medicine whose new buildings are rising; and above all, deputy in the Portuguese Parliament from São Thomé, Africa. Thus this Angolese African, educated in Lisbon and Paris, is one of the nine colored members of European Parliaments. Portugal has had colored ministers and now has three colored deputies and a senator. I saw two Portuguese in succession kissing one colored member on the floor of the house. Or was he but a dark native? There is so much ancient black blood in this peninsula.

Between the Portuguese and the African and near African there is naturally no "racial" antipathy—no accumulated historical hatreds, dislikes, despisings. Not that you would likely find a black man married to a Portuguese of family and wealth, but on the other hand it seemed quite natural for Portugal to make all the blacks of her African empire citizens of Portugal with the rights of the European born.

Magalhaes and another represent São Thomé. They are elected by black folk independent of party. Again and again I meet black folk from São Thomé—young students, well-dressed, well-bred, evidently sons of well-to-do if not wealthy parents, studying in Portugal, which harbors annually a hundred such black students.

São Thomé illustrates some phases of European imperialism in Africa. This industrial rule involves cheap land and labor in Africa and large manufacturing capital in Europe, with a resultant opportunity for the exercise of pressure from home investors and the press. Once in a while—not often—a feud between the capitalists and the manufacturers at home throws sudden light on Africa. For instance, in the Boer War the "cocoa press" backed by the anti-war Liberals attacked the Unionists and exposed labor conditions in South Africa. In retaliation, after the war and when the Liberals were in power, the Unionists attacked labor conditions in the Portuguese cocoa colonies.

For a long time the cocoa industry flourished on the islands of
São Thomé and Principe, on large plantations run by Portuguese and backed by English capital. Here under a system of
labor recruiting and indentures which amounted to slavery these
little islands led the world in cocoa production and here was the
basis of the great English and American cocoa industry. When
this system was attacked there immediately arose the situation
which is characteristic of modern industrial imperialism and
differentiates it from past imperialism. Modern expansion has
to use democracy at home as its central authority. This democracy is strangely curbed by industrial organization but it does
help select officials, and public opinion, once aroused, rules.
Thus with a democratic face at home modern imperialism turns
a visage of stern and unyielding autocracy toward its darker
colonies. This double-faced attitude is difficult to maintain
and puts hard strain on the national soul that tries it.

In England the attack of the Unionists on the Liberals and
the "cocoa press," proving slavery on the São Thomé plantations, led to a demand for drastic labor reform in Portuguese
Africa. Now the profits of the great Portuguese plantation
owners could not afford this nor could they understand this
sudden virtue on the part of capitalists who had known all
along how labor was "recruited." They charged "hypocrisy,"
not understanding that English capitalists had an inconvenient
democracy at home that often cracked its whip over them. The
cocoa industry was forced by public opinion to boycott Port-
guese cocoa; the great Portuguese proprietors were forced to
give place to smaller Negro and mulatto cultivators who could
afford smaller profits. At the same time the center of cocoa
raising crossed the straits and seated itself in the English colonies
of the Gold Coast and Nigeria, formerly the ancient kingdoms
of Ashanti, Yoruba, Haussaland and others. Thus in this part
of Portuguese Africa the worst aspects of slavery melted away
and colonial proprietors with smaller holdings could afford to
compete with the great planters; wherefore democracy, both
industrially and politically, took new life in black Portugal.
Intelligent black deputies appeared in the Portuguese parliaments, a hundred black students studied in the Portuguese universities and a new colonial code made black men citizens of
Portugal with full rights.

But in Portugal, alas! no adequate democratic control has

been established, nor can it be established with an illiteracy of 75 percent; so that while the colonial code is liberally worded and economic power has brought some freedom in São Thomé, unrestrained Portuguese and English capital rules in parts of Angola and in Portuguese East Africa, where no resisting public opinion in England has yet been aroused.

The African shadows of Spain and Italy are but drafts on some imperial future not yet realized, and touch home industry and democracy only through the war budget. As Spain is pouring treasure into a future Spanish Morocco, so Italy has already poured out fabulous sums in the attempt to annex north and northeast Africa, especially Abyssinia. The prince who yesterday visited Europe is the first adult successor of that black Menelik who humbled Italy to the dust at Adowa in 1896.

Insurgent Morocco and dependent Egypt, independent Abyssinia and Liberia are, as it were, shadows of Europe on Africa, unattached, and as such they curiously threaten the whole imperial program. On the one hand they arouse democratic sympathy in home lands which makes it difficult to submerge them; and again they are temptations to agitation for freedom and autonomy on the part of other black and subject populations.

THE SHADOW OF BELGIUM

There is a little black man in Belgium whose name is Mfumu Paul Panda. He is filled with a certain resentment against me and American Negroes. He writes me now and then but fairly spits his letters at me and they are always filled with some defense of Belgium in Africa or rather with some accusation against England, France and Portugal there. I do not blame Panda although I do not agree with his reasoning. Unwittingly, the summer before last, I tore his soul in two. His reason knows that I am right but his heart denies his reason. He was nephew and therefore by African custom heir of a great chief who for thirty years, back to the time of Stanley, has coöperated with white Belgium. As a child of five young Panda was brought home from the Belgian Congo by a Belgian official and given to that official's maiden sister. This sister reared the little black boy as her own, nursed him, dressed him, schooled him, and defended against the criticism of her friends his right to university training. She was his mother, his friend. He loved her and revered her. She guided and loved him. When the second

Pan-African Congress came to Brussels it found Panda leader of the small black colony there and spokesman for black Belgium. He had revisited the Congo and was full of plans for reform. And he thought of the uplift of his black compatriots in terms of reform. All this the Pan-African Congress changed. First it brought on his head a storm of unmerited abuse from the industrial press: we were enemies of Belgium; we were pensioners of the Bolshevists; we were partisans of England. Panda hotly defended us until he heard our speeches and read our resolutions.

The Pan-African Congress revealed itself to him with a new and unexplicable program. It talked of Africans as intelligent, thinking, self-directing and voting men. It envisaged an Africa for the Africans and governed by and for Africans and it arraigned white Europe, including Belgium, for nameless and deliberate wrong in Africa. Panda was perplexed and astonished; and then his white friends and white mother rushed to the defense of Belgium and blamed him for consorting with persons with ideas so dangerous and unfair to Belgium. He turned upon us black folk in complaining wrath. He felt in a sense deceived and betrayed. He considered us foolishly radical. Belgium was not perfect but was far less blood guilty than other European powers. Panda continues to send me clippings and facts to prove this.

In this last matter he is in a sense right. England and France and Germany deliberately laid their shadow across Africa. Belgium had Africa thrust upon her. Bismarck intended the Congo Free State for Germany and he cynically made vain and foolish Leopold temporary custodian; and even after Bismarck's fall Germany dreamed of an Africa which should include the Congo, half the Portuguese territory and all the French, making Germany the great and dominant African power. For this she fought the Great War.

Meantime, and slowly, Belgium became dazzled by the dream of empire. Africa is but a small part of Britain; Africa is but a half of larger France. But the Congo is eighty-two times the size of little Belgium, and at Tervurien wily Leopold laid a magic mirror—an intriguing flash of light, set like a museum in rare beauty and approached by magnificent vistas—a flash of revealing knowledge such as no other modern land possesses of its colonial possessions. The rank and file of the Belgians were

impressed. They dreamed of wealth and glory. They received
the Congo from Leopold as a royal gift—shyly, but with secret
pride. What nation of the world had so wonderful a colony!
And Belgium started to plan its development.

Meantime the same power that exploited the Congo and made
red rubber under Leopold—these same great merchants and
bankers—still ruled and guided the vast territory. Moreover
Belgium, impoverished by war and conquest, needed revenue as
never before. The only difference, then, between the new Congo
and the old was that a Belgian liberal public opinion had a right
to ask questions and must be informed. Propaganda intimating
that this criticism of Belgium was mainly international jealousy
and that the exploitation of black Belgium would eventually
lower taxes for the whites was nearly enough to leave the old
taskmasters and methods in control in spite of wide plans for
eventual education and reform.

I remember my interview with the socialist Minister for
Colonies. He hesitated to talk with me. He knew what socialism had promised the worker and what it was unable to do for
the African worker, but he told me his plans for education and
uplift. They were fine plans, but they remain plans even today
and the Belgian Congo is still a land of silence and ignorance,
with few schools, with forced industry, with all the land and
natural resources taken from the people and handed over to the
State, and the State, so far as the Congo is concerned, ruled
well-nigh absolutely by profitable industry. Thus the African
shadow of Belgium gravely and dangerously overshadows that
little land.

THE SHADOW OF FRANCE

I know two black men in France. One is Candace, black
West Indian deputy, an out-and-out defender of the nation and
more French than the French. The other is René Maran, black
Goncourt prize-man and author of "Batouala." Maran's attack
on France and on the black French deputy from Senegal has
gone into the courts and marks an era. Never before have
Negroes criticized the work of the French in Africa.

France's attitude toward black and colored folk is peculiar.
England knows Negroes chiefly as colonial "natives" or as
occasional curiosities on London streets. America knows
Negroes mainly as freedmen and servants. But for nearly two

centuries France has known educated and well-bred persons of
Negro descent; they filtered in from the French West Indies,
sons and relatives of French families and recognized as such
under the Code Napoleon, while under English law similar folk
were but nameless bastards. All the great French schools have
had black students here and there; the professions have known
many and the fine arts a few scattered over decades; but all this
was enough to make it impossible to say in France as elsewhere
that Negroes cannot be educated. That is an absurd statement
to a Frenchman. It was not that the French loved or hated
Negroes as such; they simply grew to regard them as men with
the possibilities and shortcomings of men, added to an unusual
natural personal appearance.

Then came the war and France needed black men. She recruited them by every method, by appeal, by deceit, by half-
concealed force. She threw them ruthlessly into horrible
slaughter. She made them "shock" troops. They walked from
the tall palms of Guinea and looked into the mouths of Krupp
guns without hesitation, with scarcely a tremor. France watched
them offer the blood sacrifice for their adopted motherland with
splendid *sang-froid*, often with utter abandon.

But for Black Africa Germany would have overwhelmed
France before American help was in sight. A tremendous wave
of sentiment toward black folk welled up in the French heart.
And back of this sentiment came fear for the future, not simply
fear of Germany reborn but fear of changing English interests,
fear of unstable America. What Africa did for France in military protection she could easily repeat on a vaster scale; wherefore France proposes to protect herself in future from military
aggression by using half a million or more of trained troops from
yellow, brown and black Africa. France has 40,000,000 Frenchmen and 60,000,000 Colonials. Of these Colonials, 845,000
served in France during the war, of whom 535,000 were soldiers
and 310,000 in labor contingents. Of the soldiers, 440,000 came
from north and west Africa. The peace footing of the French
army is now 660,000, to whom must be added 189,000 Colonial
troops. With three years service and seven years reserve,
France hopes in ten years time to have 400,000 trained Colonial
troops and 450,000 more ready to be trained. These Colonial
troops will serve part of their time in France.

This program brings France face to face with the problem of

democratic rule in her colonies. French industry has had wide experience in the manipulation of democracy at home but her colonial experience is negligible. Legally, of course, the colonies are part of France. Theoretically Colonials are French citizens and already the blacks of the French West Indies and the yellows and browns of North Africa are so recognized and represented in Parliament. Four towns of Senegal have similar representation; but beyond this matters hesitate.

All this, however, brings both political and economic difficulties. Diagne, black deputy from Senegal, was expelled from the Socialist Party because he had made no attempt to organize a branch of the party in his district. And the whole colonial bloc stand outside the interests of home political parties, while these parties know little of the particular demands of local colonies. As this situation develops there will come the question of the practicability of ruling a world nation with one law-making body. And if devolution of power takes place what will be the relation of self-governing colonies to the mother country?

But beyond this more or less nebulous theory looms the immediately practical problem of French industry. The French nation and French private industry have invested huge sums in African colonies, considering black Africa alone. Dakar is a modern city superimposed on a native market-place. Its public buildings, its vast harbor, its traffic are imposing. Conakry has miles of warehouses beneath its beautiful palms. No European country is so rapidly extending its African railways—one may ride from St. Louis over half way to Timbuktu and from Dakar 1,500 miles to the Gulf of Guinea.

The question is, then, is France able to make her colonies paying industrial investments and at the same time centers for such a new birth of Negro civilization and freedom as will attach to France the mass of black folk in unswerving loyalty and will to sacrifice. Such a double possibility is today by no means clear. French industry is fighting today a terrific battle in Europe for the hegemony of reborn Central Europe. The present probabilities are that the future spread of the industrial imperialism of the West will be largely under French leadership. French and Latin imperialism in industry will depend on alliance with western Asia and northern and central Africa, with the Congo rather than the Mediterranean as the southern boundary.

Suppose that this new Latin imperialism emerging from the Great War developed a new antithesis to English imperialism where blacks and browns and yellows, subdued, cajoled and governed by white men, form a laboring proletariat subject to a European white democracy which industry controls; suppose that, contrary to this, Latin Europe should evolve political control with black men and the Asiatics having a real voice in Colonial government, while both at home and in the colonies democracy in industry continued to progress; what would this cost? It would mean, of course, nothing less than the giving up of the idea of an exclusive White Man's World. It would be a revolt and a tremendous revolt against the solidarity of the West in opposition to the South and East. France moving along this line would perforce carry Italy, Portugal and Spain with it, and it is the fear of such a possible idea that explains the deep seated resentment against France on the part of England and America. It is not so much the attitude of France toward Germany that frightens white Europe, as her apparent flaunting of the white fetish. The plans of those who would build a world of white men have always assumed the ultimate acquiescence of the colored world in the face of their military power and industrial efficiency, because of the darker world's lack of unity and babel of tongues and wide cleft of religious difference. If now one part of the white world bids for dark support by gifts of at least partial manhood rights, the remainder of the white world scents treason and remains grim and unyielding in its heart. But is it certain that France is going to follow this program?

I walked through the native market at St. Louis in French Senegal—a busy, colorful scene. There was wonderful work in gold filigree and in leather, all kinds of beads and bracelets and fish and foods. Mohammedans salammed at sunset, black-veiled Moorish women glided like sombre ghosts with living eyes; mighty black men in pale burnooses strode by,—it was all curious, exotic, alluring. And yet I could not see quite the new thing that I was looking for. There was no color line particularly visible and yet there was all the raw material for it. Most of the white people were in command holding government office and getting large incomes. Most of the colored and black folk were laborers with small incomes. In the fashionable cafés you seldom saw colored folk, but you did see them now and then and no one seemed to object. There were schools, good schools, but they fell short of anything like universal education for the natives. White and colored school children ran and played together, but the great mass of children were not in school.

As I look more narrowly, what seemed to be happening was this: the white Frenchmen were exploiting black Africans in practically the same way as white Englishmen, but they had not yet erected or tried to erect caste lines. Consequently, into the ranks of the exploiters there arose continually black men and mulattoes, but these dark men were also exploiters. They had the psychology of the exploiters. They looked upon the mass of people as means of wealth. The mass therefore had no leadership. There was no one in the colony except the unrisen and undeveloped blacks who thought of the colony as developing and being developed for its own sake and for the sake of the mass of the people there. Everyone of intelligence thought that Senegal was being developed for the sake of France and inevitably they tended to measure its development by the amount of profit.

If this sort of thing goes on will not France find herself in the same profit-taking colonial industry as England? Indeed, unless she follows English methods in African colonies can she compete with England in the amount of profit made and if she does not make profit out of her colonies how long will her industrial masters submit without tremendous industrial returns? Or if these industrial returns come, what will be the plight of black French Africa? "Batouala" voices it. In the depths of the French Congo one finds the same exploitation of black folk as in the Belgian Congo or British West Africa. The only mitigation is that here and there in the Civil Service are black Frenchmen like René Maran who can speak out; but they seldom do.

For the most part, as I have said, in French Africa educated Africans are Europeans. But if education goes far and develops in Africa a change in this respect must come. For this France has a complete theoretical system of education beginning with the African village and going up to the colleges and technical schools at Goree. But at present it is, of course, only a plan and the merest skeleton of accomplishment. On the picturesque island of Goree whose ancient ramparts face modern and commercial Dakar I saw two or three hundred fine black boys of high school rank gathered in from all Senegal by competitive tests and taught thoroughly by excellent French teachers in accordance with a curriculum which, as far as it went, was equal to that of any European school; and graduates could enter the higher schools of France. A few hundred students out of a black population of nineteen millions is certainly but a start. This development will call for money and trained guidance and will interfere with industry. It is not likely that the path will be followed and followed fast unless black French leaders encourage and push France, unless they see the pitfalls of American and English race leadership and bring the black apostle to devote himself to race uplift not by the compulsion of outer hate but by the lure of inner vision.

As yet I see few signs of this. I have walked in Paris with Diagne who represents Senegal—all Senegal, white and black, —in the French parliament. But Diagne is a Frenchman who is accidentally black. I suspect Diagne rather despises his own black Wolofs. I have talked with Candace, black deputy of Guadaloupe. Candace is virulently French. He has no conception of Negro uplift, as apart from French development. One black deputy alone, Boisneuf of Martinique, has the vision. His voice rings in parliament. He made the American soldiers keep their hands off the Senegalese. He made the governor of Congo apologize and explain; he made Poincaré issue that extraordinary warning against American prejudice. Is Boisneuf an exception or a prophecy?

One looks on present France and her African shadow, then, as standing at the parting of tremendous ways; one way leads toward democracy for black as well as white—a thorny way made more difficult by the organized greed of the imperial profit-takers within and without the nation; the other road is the way of the white world, and of its contradictions and dangers English colonies may tell.

THE SHADOW OF ENGLAND

I landed in Sierra Leone last January. The great Mountain of the Lion crouched above us, its green sides trimmed with the pretty white villas of the whites, while black town sweltered below. Despite my diplomatic status I was haled before the police and in the same room where criminals were examined I was put through the sharpest grilling I ever met in a presumably civilized land. Why? I was a black American and the English fear black folk who have even tasted freedom. Everything that America has done crudely and shamelessly to suppress the Negro, England in Sierra Leone has done legally and suavely so that the Negroes themselves sometimes doubt the evidence of their own senses: segregation, disfranchisement, trial without jury, over-taxation, "Jim Crow" cars, neglect of education, economic serfdom. Yet all this can be and is technically denied. Segregation? "Oh no," says the colonial official, "anyone can live where he will—only that beautiful and cool side of the mountain with fine roads, golf and tennis and bungalows is assigned to government officials." Are there black officials? "Oh yes, and they can be assigned residences there, too." But they never have been. The Negroes vote and hold office in Freetown—I met the comely black and cultured mayor—but Freetown has almost no revenues and its powers have been gradually absorbed by the autocratic white colonial government which has five million dollars a year to spend. Any government prosecutor can abolish trial by jury in any case with the consent of the judge and all judges are white. White officials ride in special railway carriages and I am morally certain—I cannot prove it—that more is spent by the government on tennis and golf in the colony than on popular education.

These things, and powerful efforts of English industry to reap every penny of profit for England in colonial trade, leaving the black inhabitants in helpless serfdom, has aroused West Africa, and aroused it at this time because of two things—the war, and cocoa in Nigeria. The burden of war fell hard on black and British West Africa. Their troops conquered German Africa for England and France at bitter cost and helped hold back the Turk. Yet there was not a single black officer in the British army or a single real reward save citations and new and drastic taxation even on exports.

But British West Africa had certain advantages. After the decline of the slave trade and before the discovery that slavery and serfdom in Africa could be made to pay more than the removal of the laboring forces to other parts of the world, there was a disposition to give over to the natives the black colonies on the fever coast and the British Government announced the intention of gradually preparing West Africans for self-government. Missionary education and the sending of black students to England raised a small Negro intelligentsia which long struggled to place itself at the head of affairs. It had some success but lacked an economic foundation. When the new industrial imperialism swept Africa, with England in the lead, the presence of these educated black leaders was a thorn in the flesh of the new English industrialists. Their method was to crowd these leaders aside into narrower and narrower confines as we have seen in Sierra Leone. But the Negroes in the older colonies retained possession of their land and, suddenly, when the cocoa industry was transferred from Portuguese Africa, they gained in one or two colonies a new and undreamed of economic foundation. Instead of following the large plantation industry, cocoa became the product of the small individual native farm. In 1891 a native sold eighty pounds of the first cocoa raised on the Gold Coast. By 1911 this had increased to 45,000 tons and in 1916 to 72,000 tons. In Nigeria there has also been a large increase, making these colonies today the greatest cocoa producing countries in the world.

Moreover this progress showed again the new democratic problems of colonization, since it began and was fostered by a certain type of white colonial official who was interested in the black man and wanted him to develop. But this official was interested in the primitive black and not in the educated black. He feared and despised the educated West African and did not believe him capable of leading his primitive brother. He sowed seeds of dissension between the two. On the other hand, the educated West African hated the white colonial leader as a supplanter and deceiver whose ultimate aims must be selfish and wrong; and as ever, between these two, the English exploiting company worked gradually its perfect will.

Determined effort was thus made by the English, both merchants and philanthropists, to cut the natives off from any union of forces or of interests with the educated West Africans. "Protectorates" under autocratic white rule were attached to the colonies and the natives in the protectorates were threatened with loss of land, given almost no education and left to the mercy of a white colonial staff whose chief duty gradually came to be the encouragement of profitable industry for the great companies. These companies were represented in the governing councils, they influenced appointments at home and especially they spread in England a carefully prepared propaganda which represented the educated "nigger" as a bumptious, unreasoning fool in a silk hat, while the untutored and unspoiled native under white control was nature's original nobleman. Also they suggested that this "white" control must not admit too many visionaries and idealists.

This policy has not been altogether successful, for the educated Negro is appealing to English democracy and the native is beginning to seek educated black leadership. After many vicissitudes, in 1920 a Congress of West Africa was assembled on the Gold Coast, and from this a delegation was sent to London "to lay before His Majesty the King in Council through the colonial ministry certain grievances." This was an epoch-making effort and, as was natural, the Colonial Office, where imperial industry is entrenched, refused to recognize the delegation, claiming that they did not really represent black West Africa. Nevertheless, through the League of Nations Union and the public press this delegation succeeded in putting its case before the world. They described themselves as "of that particular class of peaceful citizens who, apprehensive of the culminating danger resulting from the present political unrest in West Africa—an unrest which is silently moving throughout the length and breadth of that continent—and also appreciating the fact that the present system of administration will inevitably lead to a serious deadlock between the 'Government and the Governed,' decided to set themselves to the task of ameliorating this pending disaster by putting forward constitutionally a programme, the carrying of which into operation will alleviate all pains and misgivings."

The final resolutions of the Congress said, "that in the opinion of this Conference the time has arrived for a change in the Constitution of several British West African colonies, so as to give the people an effective voice in their affairs both in the Legislative and Municipal Governments, and that the Conference pledges itself to submit proposals for such reforms."

The reasons for this demand are thus described:

"In the demand for the franchise by the people of British West Africa, it is not to be supposed that they are asking to be allowed to copy a foreign institution. On the contrary, it is important to notice that the principle of electing representatives to local councils and bodies is inherent in all the systems of British West Africa. . . . From the foregoing it is obvious that a system by which the Governor of a Crown Colony nominates whom he thinks proper to represent the people is considered by them as a great anomaly and constitutes a grievance and a disability which they now request should be remedied."

Since the war not only has West Africa thus spoken but the colored West Indies have complained. They want Home Rule and they are demanding it. They asked after the war: Why was it that no black man sat in the Imperial Conference? Why is it that one of the oldest parts of the empire lingers in political serfdom to England and industrial bondage to America? Why is there not a great British West Indian Federation, stretching from Bermuda to Honduras and Guiana, and ranking with the free dominions? The answer was clear and concise—Color.

In 1916 a new agitation for representative government began in Grenada. The fire spread to all the West Indies and in 1921 a delegation was received by the Colonial Office in London at the same time that the Second Pan-African Congress was in session.

Here were unusual appeals to English democracy—appeals that not even commercial propaganda could wholly hush. But there was a force that curiously counteracted them. Liberal England, wanting world peace and fearing French militarism, backed by the English thrift that is interested in the restored economic equilibrium, found as one of its most prominent spokesmen Jan Smuts of South Africa, and Jan Smuts stands for the suppression of the blacks.

Jan Smuts is today, in his world aspects, the greatest protagonist of the white race. He is fighting to take control of Laurenço Marques from a nation that recognizes, even though it does not realize, the equality of black folk; he is fighting to keep India from political and social equality in the empire; he is fighting to insure the continued and eternal subordination of black to white in Africa; and he is fighting for peace and good will in a white Europe which can by union present a united front to the yellow, brown and black worlds. In all this he expresses bluntly, and yet not without finesse, what a powerful host of white folk believe but do not plainly say in Melbourne, New Orleans, San Francisco, Hongkong, Berlin, and London.

The words of Smuts in the recent Imperial Conference were transcribed as follows: "The tendencies in South Africa, just as elsewhere, were all democratic. If there was to be equal manhood suffrage over the Union, the whites would be swamped by the blacks. A distinction could not be made between Indians and Africans. They would be impelled by the inevitable force of logic to go the whole hog, and the result would be that not only would the whites be swamped in Natal by the Indians but the whites would be swamped all over South Africa by the blacks and the whole position for which the whites had striven for two hundred years or more now would be given up. So far as South Africa was concerned, therefore, it was a question of impossibility. For white South Africa it was not a question of dignity but a question of existence."

This almost naïve setting of the darker races beyond the pale of democracy and of modern humanity was listened to with sympathetic attention in England. It is without doubt today the dominant policy of the British Empire. Can this policy be carried out? It involves two things—acquiescence of the darker peoples and agreement between capital and labor in white democracies.

This agreement between capital and labor in regard to colored folk cannot be depended on. First of all, no sooner is colored labor duly subordinate, voiceless in government, efficient for the purpose and cheap, than the division of the resultant profit is a matter of dispute. This is the case in South Africa and it came as a singular answer to Smuts. In South Africa white labor is highly paid, can vote, and by a system of black helpers occupies an easy and powerful position. It can only retain this position by vigorously excluding blacks from certain occupations and by beating their wages down to the lowest point even when as helpers they are really doing the prohibited work. It is to the manifest interest of capitalists and investors to breach if not overthrow this caste wall and thus secure higher profits by cheaper and more pliable labor. Already South African courts are slowly moving toward mitigating the law of labor caste and in retaliation the white labor unions have joined Smuts' political enemies, the English-hating Boer party of independence, and have overthrown the great premier.

But how curious are these bedfellows—English capital and African black labor against Dutch home-rulers and the trades unions. The combinations are as illogical as they are thought-producing, for after all if South Africa is really bent on independence she must make economic and political peace with the blacks; and if she hates Negroes more than she hates low wages she must submit even more than now to English rule.

Now what is English rule over colored folk destined to be? Here comes the second puzzling result of the Smuts philosophy. I was in London on the night of the Guild Hall banquet when the Prime Minister spoke on "Empire Policy and World Peace" and gave a sort of summing up of the work of the Imperial Conference. It was significant that in the forefront of his words, cheek by jowl with Imperial "foreign policy," stood the "intensity of feeling in India on the question of the status of British Indians in the Empire." What indeed could be more fundamental than this in the building of world peace? Are the brown Indians to share equally in the ruling of the British Empire or are they an inferior race? And curiously enough, the battle on this point is impending not simply in the unchecked movement toward "swaraj" in India but in Africa—in the Union of South Africa and in Kenya.

In South Africa, despite all Imperial explanations and attempts to smooth things out, Smuts and the Boers have taken firm ground: Indians are to be classed with Negroes in their social and political exclusion. South Africa is to be ruled by its minority of whites. But if this is blunt and unswerving, how much more startling is Kenya. Kenya is the British East Africa of pre-war days and extends from the Indian Ocean to the Victoria Nyanza and from German East Africa to Ethiopia. It is that great roof of the African world where, beneath the silver heads of the Mountains of the Moon, came down in ancient days those waters and races which founded Egypt. The descendant races still live there with fine physique and noble heads —the Masai warriors whom Schweinfurth heralded, the Dinka, the Galla, and Nile Negroes—the herdsmen and primitive artisans of the beautiful highlands. Here was a land largely untainted by the fevers of the tropics and here England proposed to send her sick and impoverished soldiers of the war. Following the lead of South Africa, she took over five million acres of the best lands from the 3,000,000 natives, herded them gradually toward the swamps and gave them, even there, no sure title; then by taxation she forced sixty percent of the black adults into working for the ten thousand white owners for the lowest wage. Here was opportunity not simply for the great land-holder and slave-driver but also for the small trader, and twenty-four thousand Indians came. These Indians claimed the rights of free subjects of the empire—a right to buy land, a right to

exploit labor, a right to a voice in the government now confined
to the handful of whites.

Suddenly a great race conflict swept East Africa—orient and
occident, white, brown and black, landlord, trader and landless
serf.   When the Indians asked rights the whites replied that
this would injure the rights of the natives.   Immediately the
natives began to awake.   Few of them were educated but they
began to form societies and formulate grievances.   A black
political consciousness arose for the first time in Kenya.   Immediately the Indians made a bid for the support of this new force
and asked rights and privileges for all British subjects—white,
brown and black.   As the Indian pressed his case, white South
Africa rose in alarm.   If the Indian became a recognized man,
landholder and voter in Kenya, what of Natal?

The British Government speculated and procrastinated and
then announced its decision: East Africa was primarily a
"trusteeship" for the Africans and not for the Indians.   The
Indians, then, must be satisfied with limited industrial and
political rights, while for the black native—the white Englishman spoke!   A conservative Indian leader speaking in England
after this decision said that if the Indian problem in South
Africa were allowed to fester much longer it would pass beyond
the bounds of domestic issue and would become a question of
foreign policy upon which the unity of the Empire might founder
irretrievably.   The Empire could never keep its colored races
within it by force, he said, but only by preserving and safe-
guarding their sentiments.

Perhaps this shrewd Kenya decision was too shrewd.   It preserved white control of Kenya but it said in effect: "Africa for
the Africans!"   What then about Uganda and the Sudan, where
a black leadership exists under ancient forms; and above all,
what about the educated black leadership in the West Indies
and West Africa?   Why should black West Africa with its industrial triumphs like Nigeria be content forever with a Crown
Government, if Africa is for the Africans?

The result has been a yielding by England to the darker world
—not a yielding of much, but yielding.   India is to have a revision of the impossible "diarchy;" all West Africa is to have a
small elective element in its governing councils; and even the
far West Indies have been visited by a colonial undersecretary
and parliamentary committee, the first of its kind in the long

history of the islands. Their report is worth quoting in part: "Several reasons combine to make it likely that the common demand for a measure of representative government will in the long run prove irresistible. The wave of democratic sentiment has been powerfully stimulated by the war. Education is rapidly spreading and tending to produce a colored and black intelligentsia of which the members are quick to absorb elements of knowledge requisite for entry into learned professions and return from travel abroad with minds emancipated and enlarged, ready to devote time and energy to propaganda among their own people."

Egypt is Africa and the Bilad-es-Sudan, Land of the Blacks, has in its eastern reaches belonged to Egypt even since Egypt belonged to the Sudan—ever since the Pharoahs bowed to the Lords of Meroe. Fifty times England has promised freedom and independence to Egypt and today she keeps her word by seizing the Sudan with a million square miles, six million black folk and twenty million dollars of annual revenue. But Egypt without the Sudan can never be free and independent and this England well knows, but she will hold the Sudan against Egypt as "trustee" for the blacks. That was a fateful step that the new Conservatives took after the Sirdar was murdered by hot revolutionists. Its echo will long haunt the world.

If now England is literally forced to yield some measure of self-government to her darker colonies; if France remains steadfast in the way in which her feet seem to be tending; if Asia arises from the dead and can no longer be rendered impotent by the opium of international finance, what will happen to imperialistic world industry as exemplified in the great expansion of the nineteenth and early twentieth centuries?

LABOR IN THE SHADOWS

This is the question that faces the new labor parties of the world—the new political organizations which are determined to force a larger measure of democracy in industry than now obtains. The trade union labor movement dominant in Australia, South Africa and the United States has been hitherto autocratic and at heart capitalistic, believing in profit-making industry and wishing only to secure a larger share of profits for particular guilds. But the larger labor movement following the war envisages through democratic political action real democratic power of the mass of workers in industry and commerce.

Two questions here arise: Will the new labor parties welcome the darker race to this industrial democracy? And, if they do, how will this affect industry?

The attitude of the white laborer toward colored folk is largely a matter of long continued propaganda and gossip. The white laborers can read and write, but beyond this their education and experience are limited and they live in a world of color prejudice. The curious, most childish propaganda dominates us, by which good, earnest, even intelligent men have come by millions to believe almost religiously that white folk are a peculiar and chosen people whose one great accomplishment is civilization and that civilization must be protected from the rest of the world by cheating, stealing, lying, and murder. The propaganda, the terrible, ceaseless propaganda that buttresses this belief day by day,—the propaganda of poet and novelist, the uncanny welter of romance, the half knowledge of scientists, the pseudo-science of statesmen,—all these, united in the myth of mass inferiority of most men, have built a wall which many centuries will not break down. Born into such a spiritual world, the average white worker is absolutely at the mercy of its beliefs and prejudices. Color hate easily assumes the form of a religion and the laborer becomes the blind executive of the decrees of the masters of the white world; he votes armies and navies for "punitive" expeditions; he sends his sons as soldiers and sailors; he composes the Negro-hating mob, demands Japanese exclusion and lynches untried prisoners. What hope is there that such a mass of dimly thinking and misled men will ever demand universal democracy for all men?

The chief hope lies in the gradual but inevitable spread of the knowledge that the denial of democracy in Asia and Africa hinders its complete realization in Europe. It is this that makes the Color Problem and the Labor Problem to so great an extent two sides of the same human tangle. How far does white labor see this? Not far, as yet. Its attitude toward colored labor varies from the Russian extreme to the extreme in South Africa and Australia. Russia has been seeking a *rapprochement* with colored labor. She is making her peace with China and Japan. Her leaders have come in close touch with the leaders of India. Claude McKay, an American Negro poet traveling in Russia, declares: "Lenin himself grappled with the question of the American Negroes and spoke on the subject before the Second

Congress of the Third International. He consulted with John Reed, the American journalist, and dwelt on the urgent necessity of propaganda and organization work among the Negroes of the South."

Between these extremes waver the white workers of the rest of the world. On the whole they still lean rather toward the attitude of South Africa than that of Russia. They exclude colored labor from empty Australia. They sit in armed truce against them in America where the Negroes are forcing their way into ranks of union labor by breaking strikes and under-bidding them in wage.

It is precisely by these tactics, however, and by hindering the natural flow of labor toward the highest wage and the best conditions in the world that white labor is segregating colored labor in just those parts of the world where it can be most easily exploited by white capital and thus giving white capital the power to rule all labor, white and black, in the rest of the world. White labor is beginning dimly to see this. Colored labor knows it, and as colored labor becomes more organized and more intelligent it is going to spread this grievance through the white world.

THE SHADOW OF SHADOWS

How much intelligent organization is there for this purpose on the part of the colored world? So far there is very little. For while the colored people of today are common victims of white culture, there is a vast gulf between the red-black South and the yellow-brown East. In the East long since, centuries ago, there were mastered a technique and philosophy which still stand among the greatest the world has known; and the black and African South, beginning in the dim dawn of time when beginnings were everything, have evolved a physique and an art, a will to be and to enjoy, which the world has never done without and never can. But these cultures have little in common, either today or yesterday, and are being pounded together artificially and not attracting each other naturally. And yet quickened India, the South and West African Congresses, the Pan-African movement, the National Association for the Advancement of Colored People in America, together with rising China and risen Japan—all these at no distant day may come to common consciousness of aim and be able to give to the labor parties of the world a message that they will understand.

THE COLOR LINE

My ship seeks Africa. Ten days we crept across the Atlantic; five days we sailed to the Canaries. And then, turning, we sought the curve of that mighty and fateful shoulder of gigantic Africa. Slowly, slowly we creep down the coast in a little German cargo boat. Yonder behind the horizon is Cape Bojador, whence in 1441 came the brown Moors and black Moors who, through the slave trade, built America and modern commerce and let loose the furies on the world. Another day afar we glide past Dakar, city and center of French Senegal. Thereupon we fall down, down to the burning equator, past Guinea and Gambia, to where the Lion Mountain glares, toward the vast gulf whose sides are lined with silver and gold and ivory. And now we stand before Liberia—Liberia that is a little thing set upon a hill—thirty or forty thousand square miles and two million folk. But it represents to me the world. Here political power has tried to resist the concentration in the power of modern capital. It has not yet succeeded, but its partial failure is not because the republic is black but because the world has failed in this same battle; because the oligarchy that owns organized industry owns and rules England, France, Germany, America, and Heaven. And it fastens this ownership by the Color Line. Can Liberia escape the power that rules the world? I do not know. But I do know that unless the world escapes, world democracy as well as Liberia will die: and if Liberia lives it will be because the world is reborn as in that vision splendid that came in the higher dreams of the World War.

And thus again in 1925, as in 1899, I seem to see the problem of the Twentieth Century as the Problem of the Color Line.

¶ REFLECTIONS ON THE QUESTION OF WAR GUILT

by Thomas G. Masaryk   (July, 1925)

*In 1925, when President Thomas Garrigue Masaryk of Czechoslovakia pub-
lished his article "Reflections on the Question of War Guilt," the German
effort to shift the responsibility for the war to the shoulders of the Allies was
in full cry.*

*Masaryk, born the son of a coachman in Moravia in 1850, knew Pan-Ger-
manism well. Long before 1914, he had perceived that Austria-Hungary was
fated to be the tool of German expansion, and it was precisely in the name of
necessary opposition to Pan-Germanism that he had declared for the breaking
up of that corrupt and decrepit Empire. His belief that a free Czechslovak state
was an essential factor in creating a free and liberal Europe, as well as his
insight into the nervous irritation and suicidal mania that underlay German
militarism, were to be given deadly corroboration, for a second time, fifteen
years after he composed the article that follows.*

*To many students of history, Masaryk, the Professor of Philosophy at
Prague, who, with his young assistant Dr. Beneš and with the extraordinarily
close and confident cooperation of the Czech and Slovak people, created the
Czechoslovak state, was one of the truly great men of his time and one of the
wisest statesmen in history. This brief essay suggests the quality of his mind.
Thought and action in Masaryk seemed exactly in balance. Although his judgments and aims were clear, he never pretended that the conditions that gave rise
to great political developments were simple. "Policy, i.e., the principle of the
politics of states, is complicated," he wrote. He knew that the outburst of
German militarism that the world had just fought off was a particularly
deadly manifestation of the cultural crisis that existed everywhere in modern
civilization. His remedy, however, was not that modern men should turn their
backs on freedom and civilization. He had only condemnation for absolutisms
of any kind. He proposed "a calm, direct analysis and criticism of our culture
and its elements . . . by thinking people." Not the least remarkable aspect of
Masaryk's achievements was that he accomplished his prodigies of practical
politics by emphasizing his ideals, not by sacrificing them.*

REFLECTIONS ON THE QUESTION OF WAR GUILT

By Thomas G. Masaryk

WHAT is the significance of the World War? What is the meaning of this enormous common manifestation in the history of Europe and of humanity?

The Marxian interpretation of war will not hold. Not that a specifically capitalistic interpretation of economic history is entirely wrong; but it is one-sided, incomplete, and uncertain. The conception of capitalism itself is vague; there were certainly wars before capitalism—and nobody has demonstrated the extent to which capitalism is responsible for the genesis and development of this latest war. Are we to understand by "capitalism" a whole and complete economic system or, specifically, finance? Or great industrial development? And in what countries? Capitalism is to be found in all countries, and capitalism has always opposed capitalism. Which capitalism is the deciding factor? We always return to one main question: Which of the combatant parties was conducting an offensive war, and which a defensive?—for this distinction is of great importance in estimating the character of the war.

Nobody doubts that economic interests have always been an important reason for making wars. But there are, in addition, other deciding factors. Historians are always teaching (as are also the historical Marxists) that in modern times wars are made in order that states, their rulers and their statesmen may increase their power and prestige, that they may extend their sway over portions of neighboring countries, and that they may get colonies. They talk much about imperialism, especially in the case of large states. The proponents of this point of view stress ambition, the desire to dominate, greed, and racial and national hatred as the motives for a military offensive.

An interpretation of the World War in the light of nationalism is likewise one-sided and vague. Nationalism differs in various countries, and again the question is raised as to what sort of nationalism was responsible. Who began the offensive, and who was on the defensive? What is implied by this "nationalism"? Certainly, nationalist quarrels and disputes were one of the causes of the war. But the war cannot be regarded as exclusively a war of nationalities. Nations are not yet quite synonymous with states; the states were at war, the nations only so indirectly, or as far as they were organized by their states and were represented in them. Moreover, the policy of the states was not merely national. Policy, *i.e.*, the principle of the politics of states, is complicated. It is affected by dynasties, governments, influential statesmen and politicians, journalists, parliaments, parties, and by intellectual and moral movements. To define scientifically exactly who conducted, and was responsible for, the policy of a given state—who, in a given instance, made the decision and why—who had greater and who less influence upon it—this is a task for genuine history and the philosophy of history. It is impossible to say that wars are nationalist, that is, nationalist only. England and America certainly did not take part in the war for reasons of nationalism, at any rate nationalism of the type common on the Continent, although they recognized the principle of nationality and especially the rights of small nations in Europe to be free and independent. It cannot, therefore, be said that the war was a contest between the Germans and Slavs, or between the Germans and the Romance peoples. It was a World War. The genesis and development of the war clearly demonstrate that nationality— at times national Chauvinism—was only one factor among others.

The war has sometimes been regarded as an ecclesiastical and religious quarrel between the Orthodoxy of Russians and Serbs and the Catholicism of Austria, the Protestantism of the Germans and the Catholicism of the French. These religious influences were also factors, but again only factors among others.

The character of this war can to a certain extent be realized by a comparison of the military aims of the contestants and their programs; that of the West, leading the enormous majority of mankind, and that of Germany, leading a minority composed of the Central Powers. This division had more than a temporary military significance; it expressed the whole situation. Ideas faced each other in a life and death struggle.

In modern times, the independence of states and peoples has been substituted for the mediaeval theocracy which centered in the spiritual leadership of the Papacy as an international authority. The Reformation, humanism, science, art and philosophy laid down new spiritual and moral ideals as the foundation for the organization of a new society. A great revolution was prepared in England, France and America. In this revolution the enormous gain was that the state and the church (or rather the churches) became independent of one another. With the passage of time, state and church have become more and more separated in the West, that is, in Europe and America, not to the detriment of religion but on the contrary to its gain, as also to the gain of political life. And as the state gradually became emancipated from ecclesiastical influence all institutions and strata of society—science, together with philosophy, education and morality—became emancipated also.

In the state which after the Reformation took over the leadership of society and, following the example of the church, became absolutist, the French Revolution proclaimed the great watchword "Liberty, Equality, Fraternity." The rights of man and of citizens were enunciated and codified, France and America became republics, England, and for a time France also, constitutional monarchies. Against the old aristocratic system—for monarchy is but a form of aristocracy—democracy developed in different forms and degrees. The revolutionary process was not exhausted by the French Revolution. A succession of revolutions followed, and we are still in the midst of them. It may even be that in the World War we not only overthrew the old régime but also the earlier stages of revolution.

The ideal of the whole revolution was humanity. Morally, this signified mutual sympathy and respect between individuals, and the recognition of the principle that one man must not be used by another as a tool. Politically and socially, it meant the equality of all citizens in the state, the alliance of nations and states, and through them the coming together of the whole of humanity. This idea of natural right was an old one which we had inherited from the Greeks and Romans, and in some respects it had been consecrated by the church and by the churches, though the social and political content of this natural right was only gradually formulated. Closely allied to this ideal of humanity was the conception of enlightenment, expressed in a striving for knowledge and education. From this grew, in the last century, the universal recognition of science and the attempts to develop a new philosophy with a scientific basis, as also the continual efforts to organize general education, to make attendance at schools obligatory, to popularize science, and to develop journalism, publicity and the press generally.

The revolution, and the great changes which it wrought in the outlook on life, fixed the idea and the ideal of progress in all branches of human effort, and spread the faith that nations as well as humanity in general would gradually, through their own efforts, reach a higher and higher degree of achievement and satisfaction.

These, it seems to me, are the dominating ideas of Western Europe. I say Western Europe, although I am chiefly thinking of France, since the West (France and the adjoining nations, England and America, and Italy and the other Romance nations) forms a cultural whole, as is clearly demonstrated by the history of the reciprocal influences exerted by the various nations mentioned.

During the Middle Ages, Germany also belonged to the cultural body of Europe. But in modern times she has steadily separated herself, more and more, in her culture. Prussia, an aggressive state from the very beginning, strengthened by the Reformation, came to dominate Germany. A noticeable *étatisme* also prevailed in the West, but there the state grew to be the organ of Parliament and of public opinion, while in Germany a monarchistic state was deified and its absolutism generally recognized. Not till the end of the World War did the Prussian King, as German Emperor, decide for the parliamentarization of the government. Prussia and Germany were really an organized Caesarism; certainly Frederick the Great, Bismarck and the Wilhelms in contrast to Napoleon were Caesars and Tsars. The soldier, the Prussian officer, was for the Germans the standard of social organization, in fact of the organization of the world. The soldier and war became institutions. In Germany the Reformation, humanism, science, art and philosophy did not expel theocracy as thoroughly as they did in the West; the German people accepted the Reformation only in part, and in its German form (Lutheranism) adapted it to Catholicism. A kind of Caesaro-Papism arose, although different from the Russian Caesaro-Papism. The humanitarian ideals of Lessing,

Herder, Goethe, Kant, and Schiller, derived from observing and from collaborating in the development of the West and of the world in general, came to be replaced by a pan-Germanic imperialism. The Berlin-Bagdad scheme was characteristic of the effort to dominate Europe and Asia and Africa—an effort in which is to be seen the ideal of the ancient world! Germany maintains and develops the ideal of the Roman *imperium.*

In contrast with this, the ideal of the West is the organization of the whole of humanity,—the alliance (before everything) of Europe with America, and by this means the alliance of the other parts of the world. The World War furthered this unification.

Pan-Germanism did not recognize the rights of peoples to independence. It wished to be the sole leader and ruler of all. In its arrogance it announced that the ideal was a multi-national state. It rejected natural right and substituted for it historical right. Kant is certainly recognized as a leading philosopher; but his inclination towards natural right and Rousseau was rejected by Germany, as were humanitarian ideals in general. Historical right was strengthened with the aid of Darwinism, through the theory of mechanical evolution, guaranteeing success to the strongest. War and the making of war became divine institutions. Prussian militarism utilized the theory of the English naturalist to strengthen its military aristocracy, which proclaimed as its chief dogma the so-called *Realpolitik,* the notion that all right is born of might. Power and force were identified.[1] The German nation was described as a nation of born rulers.

The results of Prussianism can be seen not only in politics, but also in German philosophy, science, art and, of course, in theology. When in a nation the leading men and classes begin to rely upon power and force, eschewing sympathy, people cease to have any interest in finding out about the feelings and thoughts of those who are near to them, and finally of foreigners; for all contact with them is made through the state mechanism. They cease to think freely, and knowledge becomes devoid of living ideas.

[1] The proof of this Pan-German identification of right and might is given by Professor Schafer in "Staat und Gesellschaft," 1922 (*i.e.,* after the war). He shows that right is only an expression of conditions of power, particularly external right; but under his hands power becomes force. "The thing cannot be otherwise, force and power can create right" (p. 264).

This is an interpretation of the great errors of German history and of German thought before and after the war. Bismarck, with his use of force in his relations with the people near to him, is the type of the domineering Prussian spirit. I should describe the development schematically as follows: Goethe, Kant, Frederick the Great, Hegel, Lagarde, Marx, Moltke, Bismarck, William II.

In Hegel we see the synthesis of both tendencies of German culture; he accepted the Prussian idea of the state, namely that it is the chief expression of nationality and the leader of all society. By his pantheism and his imaginative philosophy he constitutes a transition from Goethe, and in the practical domain a transition to Prussianism and its mechanism, materialism and force. Not for nothing was Hegel originally a theologian—even in this connection he formulated the principles of the Prussian theocracy. Bismarck and Wilhelm were always calling on God, of course the Prussian God; Hegel, with his "absolute idealism," served the "authoritism" of the Prussian state, abandoned humanity and the universal outlook of Goethe and Kant, and laid a foundation for the theoretical and practical employment of force. Bismarck and Bismarckism absorbed Goethe—the Prussian state became the infallible leader of the nation and the arbiter of its spiritual and cultural efforts.

Marx, having passed through the philosophy of Feuerbach ("a man is what he eats"), turned Hegel's pantheism and absolute idealism into materialism and accepted the mechanism of Prussian organization and *étatisme* (all-powerful centralization), although he made the state subject to economic laws. The fact that during the war the German Marxians, in spite of their socialism and revolutionary tendencies, accepted without criticism the Prussian policy and remained so long in alliance with the Pan-Germans, is due to their relationship with them in method and tactics. The undemocratic conception regarding the necessity of large economic units corresponds to the Prussian theory of super-humanity. Marx himself had the same view of the Slav peoples as Treitschke and Lagarde.

German thought, beginning with Kant, took a wrong road. Kant set opposite the one-sided English empiricism, and especially the skepticism of Hume, the one-sided intellectualism of so-called pure creative reason. He constructed a whole system of *a priori* eternal truths and thus began the reign of German subjectivism, leading inevitably to solipsistic isolation and egoism, to an aristocratic individualism and a super-humanity based on force. This metaphysical titanism necessarily led the German subjectivists to moral isolation. The phantasy of Fichte and Schelling gave birth to the nihilism and pessimism of Schopenhauer. The titans became wrathful, ironical—and anger and irony and titanism are a *contradictio in adjecto*—and finally desperate. Hegel and Feuerbach sought a refuge in the police state and in materialism, through which they avoided metaphysical imagination; they submitted to the régime of Prussian "corporalism," for which Kant had given strong justification by his categorical imperative. The German universities became the spiritual barracks of this philosophical absolutism, which reached its consummation in the idea of the Prussian state and kingdom, deified by Hegel. Hegel created absolutism for the state, and justified right by strength and force. Nietzsche, like Schopenhauer, rejects this development, but only in words; in reality Nietzsche became a philosophical prophet of the Hohenzollern parvenus and of Pan-German absolutism. Nietzsche is the type of the modern hair-splitting scholastic, intoxicating and satisfying himself with big words.

Hegel proclaimed not only the infallibility of the state, but the "self-saving" quality of war and militarism; Lagarde and his followers then conceived a philosophy and policy of panGermanism. This it was which was defeated in France. With the Prussian regiments there fell the philosophy which stood for the doctrines "exterminate the Poles" (von Hartmann); "break the thick skulls of the Czechs" (Mommsen); "destroy the decadent French and the haughty English." Prussian panGermanism was overthrown by the war.

In rejecting the one-sidedness of German thought which was initiated by Kant I do not say that German philosophy is entirely faulty, nor do I say that it is superficial or uninteresting. On the contrary, German philosophy is interesting and profound, but profound for the reason that it is not, and can not be, free. It is a scholasticism of the mediaeval type, ready-made, a predetermined official creed. Like the Prussian state and Prussianism generally, German philosophy, and also German idealism, is absolutist, violent, unjust to the greatness of free united humanity.

In my first work, "Suicide as a Collective Social Phenomenon in Modern Civilization" (1881), I attempted to interpret the surprising and terrible fact that in modern times, from the end of the eighteenth century, the number of suicides has increased everywhere in Europe and in America, and particularly amongst the most enlightened peoples, and this to such an extent that it is necessary to speak of suicide as a pathological condition of modern society. This tendency to suicide in the modern individual is allied to his increasing psychism. Through a detailed analysis of the causes and motives of isolated suicides I was forced to the recognition of the fact that the instigating, and often the deciding, factor in suicide is a weakening of character through the loss of religion. Seen in historical perspective, modern suicide and psychism appear as the result of the precocity or crudity of the new conception of the world and the inadequate organization of the society inhabiting it.

Mediaeval Catholic theocracy consolidated throughout Christendom a unified conception of the world and, corresponding to it, a moral and political régime; but the power of the Catholic theocracy in modern times (and this is what makes them modern!) decreased, and is still decreasing. Revolution—scientific, philosophical, artistic, religious, political and social—characterized the transition from the Middle Ages. Hume and Kant, skepticism and the attempt to overcome skepticism, are both characteristic of modern times. Against infallibility, absolutism and inquisition, mankind protested and revolted; there developed a revolutionary and excessive individualism and subjectivism, leading to spiritual and moral isolation, to general anarchy instead of the previous catholicity. Skepticism, criticism, irony and negation have forced faith into the background, man has become uneasy, inconstant, restless, nervous; through his very energy, often artificially increased, he has fallen into Utopianism; through his continual searching and enterprise he has been deceived again and again; the idealist has plunged himself into gluttony, but has not found satisfaction; pessimism, not only theoretical, but also practical, has become widespread—as also joylessness and anxiety, hate and despair, and from these exhaustion, nervousness, psychism and suicide. Modern society is pathologically irritated, torn, disintegrated—always in one transition after another. In the number of suicides we find a direct arithmetical measure of this psychic sickness, at once moral and psychological.

The psychological opposite of suicide and the suicidal mania is murder. Suicide is violence done by the soul to itself and is intrinsically egocentric and subjective; murder is violence to the soul, turned outwards—it is abnormal objectivization. Subjectivistic individualism, reaching a higher stage in solipsism and titanic equality with God, is unendurable to man—finally he uses force, either on himself or on somebody near him: suicide and murder are degrees of the same violence.

Modern militarism, especially Prussian militarism, is a violent flight from morbid subjectivity and the suicidal mania. I repeat, modern militarism; for, psychologically and morally, the bellicosity of the savage, the barbarian, and even of the mediaeval knight and mercenary, are different from the scientifically calculated military system of the modern absolutist states. The savage and the barbarian fight from original savagery; but in the World War, there were to be found in the trenches disciples of Rousseau and Kant, Goethe and Herder, Byron and Musset! If Sombart praises German militarism in the spirit of Hegel, and is proud of the fact that Fausts and Zarathustras are fighting in the trenches, he does not realize that he is thus condemning the bloodthirstiness of German and European civilization.

The warfare of these modern civilized peoples is in actuality a violent flight from the narrow conditions imposed by the conception of the superhuman "I." For this reason the intelligentsia, as far as bellicosity went, were not eclipsed by countrymen and laborers, but on the contrary took a leading part in the war. In modern war the opponents do not stand opposite to one another, eye to eye; it is not a battle, as it used to be; they destroy one another at a distance, abstractly, one man not seeing the other, killing one another through ideas and in ideas— German idealism turned into "Kruppism." The *natural* man knows nothing of suicide from modern reasons of exhaustion, nervousness and boredom; only in isolated instances does he commit suicide from anger at the lack of recognition or from general failure of his energy. The *modern* man, through exhaustion and narrow conditions due to spiritual and moral isolation, from a fruitless desire for greatness, and from "superhumanism," suffers from a morbid desire for suicide. Militarism is the attempt of this superman to flee from his malady, but it only constitutes an aggravation of it. It is a nation of thinkers and philosophers which has had the greatest number of suicides, which has produced the most perfected militarism, and which was responsible for the World War.

I am of the opinion that this connection between the modern suicidal mania and Prussian militarism is very real. The World War was a war of peoples. Not the old, permanent armies were opposed to one another, but new armies created through a universal obligation to military service, armies consisting chiefly of reserves. Not many of the soldiers engaged on opposing sides were soldiers by profession, though, of course, the Kaiser and the military leaders, as well as a portion of the *personnel*, were soldiers of the old type. The fact, however, that the World War was conducted on a huge scale gave it a peculiar stamp— the characteristics of the combatant peoples themselves were made manifest. The character of the war depends on the character of the soldiers. If the war, as the pacifists assure us, let loose all the evil forces such as hate, ill-will, and bellicosity, then these qualities did not arise only in the war, but were characteristic of the people before the war; the devils of the year 1914 were not the angels of 1913. The World War had, as has been said, an abstract, scientific quality. It was the preeminence of scientific military industry and the mathematical employment of great masses which finally brought victory.

I am of the opinion that the moral significance of the World War as an attempt at objectivization after excessive subjectivism is plain enough; the war and the method of making war arose from this moral and spiritual condition of the modern man and of his whole culture, as I have briefly set it forth. The modern contest between objectivization and subjectivization, expressed in literature and philosophy, and therefore in life, is a protracted historical process and expressed itself in the war also and particularly in its long duration. The war demonstrated what the modern man is capable of and what he would be capable of if he were to rid himself of his desire for domination and did not suppress in himself that love for his neighbor which is innate in every man.

The German historian, Lamprecht, in endeavoring so enthusiastically and energetically to justify the Germans in the war, supports my analysis in spite of himself. In his history of modern Germany, written before the war,[2] he rightly characterizes the time as an epoch of nervous irritation (he coined the

---

[2] "Zur jungsten deutschen Vergangenheit," 1904.

word "Reizsamkeit"), and quotes not only Wilhelm but also Bismarck as types of this neurosis. In fact, the German superman, the titan, is nervous and seeks either for death or war as an acute excitement in the place of chronic excitement.

This applies to all nations, but before everything to the German nation. In their spiritual isolation the German philosophers and scientists, historians and politicians, declared German civilization and culture to constitute the zenith of human development, and in the name of this self-appointed eminence Prussian Pan-Germanism announced the right of conquest and the right generally to subdue by power and force. The Prussian state, its army and militarism, became a corrective to morbid subjectivism; Prussian Pan-Germanism is responsible for the World War, is the moral cause of it.

The crisis of the modern man is a general one; it is a crisis of the whole man in his whole spiritual existence. Modern life, our institutions, our views on the world, must be revised. The internal disintegration and disharmony of the modern man and his life, the disintegration and disharmony of society and the general spiritual anarchy, the contest between the present and the past, between fathers and children, the war between the churches and science, philosophy, art and the state, these penetrate the whole of modern culture. We are seeking for the peace of our own souls—how and where shall we find it? In our effort to attain spiritual freedom we fell into an excessive individualism and subjectivity, which were the source of this general spiritual and moral anarchy. Many of us gave ourselves up to materialism and mechanics. We have cultivated intellectualism one-sidedly and have forgotten the harmonious cultivation of all our spiritual and physical powers and qualities. In opposing the churches and religion, we have contented ourselves with doubt and denial, we have snatched at revolutionary politicism, although we have convinced ourselves that at least in the primary conceptions of life and of the world a permanent social organization is impossible without harmony. We have revolted against the discipline of the church, but we have become slaves to programs and to the principles of parties and factions. To talk about and to demand morality and moral discipline is considered to be an exhibition of old-world moralizing. Restlessness, anxiety, skepticism, exhaustion, pessimism, hate, despair, suicide, militarism, going to war—that is the end of the modern man, the modern super-man.

The post-war situation led many to the conviction that Europe and the civilization of peoples were declining, declining definitely. Before the war, the Pan-Germans often announced the decline of the Romance peoples, especially of the French; now the German philosophers of history (Spengler) talk about the decline of the Germans and of the whole of the West. Some, on the other hand, hope for salvation from Russia or even from further east, although Russia fell in the war just as did Germany and Austria.

I do not believe in a general and definite degeneration and decadence. As a consequence of the war we are living through an acute and chronic crisis. Not we alone are responsible for this crisis, but our forefathers also. We could not refrain from altering what they left us; but the alterations we made were erroneous, and we continue to err. However, an honest recognition of a mistake is the beginning of improvement. The war and its horrors upset all of us—we stand helpless before a tremendous historical mystery, faced with an occurrence of a type which has never been known before in the history of humanity. But perturbation is not a program. We need a calm, direct analysis and criticism of our culture and its elements, and we must decide upon a concrete improvement in every sphere of thought and action. In all the enlightened nations there are enough thinking people to carry out this reform in concert.

¶ CURZON

by Harold Nicolson   (January, 1929)

This is a profile of one of the most formidable and cantankerous of modern statesmen, yet, as the reader will see, one for whom his close personal assistant, Sir Harold Nicolson, had a grudging affection. Lord Curzon played almost every role in British politics except that of prime minister, and his influence was exerted in many directions, most importantly, perhaps, as Viceroy of India and at the Lausanne Conference, which tried to settle the Turkish question after World War I.

In this essay, Harold Nicolson is at his most brilliant. It was one of the first—if not the first—of his articles to be published in an American periodical. The Editor of Foreign Affairs *was led to invite him to do this article by a description of Lord Curzon's valet in one of Nicolson's early books. It was so delicious that the idea arose at once to persuade him to follow it with a profile of Curzon himself. The result was spectacularly good.*

More recently, Nicolson's volumes of diaries, published posthumously, have been a literary sensation. His main works include a life of his father, Lord Carnock, which had as a subtitle A Study on the Old Diplomacy, *and a book about the Paris Peace Conference of 1919, too optimistically, as he himself would have admitted, entitled* Peacemaking.

CURZON

By Harold Nicolson

THE LIFE OF LORD CURZON. BY THE RT. HON. THE EARL OF RONALD-
SHAY. London: Benn. New York: Horace Liveright. 3 vols. 1928.

WE live today in an age of catch-words and the edges
of our daily awareness are blunted to uniformity.
We employ these slogans with democratic indolence,
scarcely realizing that they possess an affective quality which dis-
turbs our reason. "Imperialist" we say, not pausing to consider
what we mean by the expression, too lazy even to discount the
depreciatory effect which the word produces. "Reactionary" we
say again, confident that we are implying something discreditable,
confident that progress is good absolutely, that to be retrograde
is absolutely to be bad. Such habits of thought and expression are
perhaps inevitable: we are too busy, in this lively world of ours, to
resist the temptation of verbal fore-shortening, to struggle against
the intellectual label. At times, however, something occurs to arrest
our attention: these familiar words, with their trite emotional
connections, are by some sudden alteration of lighting, thrown
into relief: we see them with fresh eyes, we are bewildered by the
altered angle of familiarity, even as we are puzzled for a moment
by an envelope which we have addressed to ourselves. "Imperialist" we again murmur, and the word detaches itself from
its background; it becomes the symbol of something wider and
deeper; it awakes enquiry; it makes us pause and think.

Some such sudden readjustment of values is occasioned in any
unbiassed reader by the admirable biography which Lord Ronaldshay has just completed on Lord Curzon of Kedleston. On reading
this tragic human history, even the most inveterate victim of the
slogan-habit would feel that the scarlet label of "imperialist"
was no adequate explanation of the problem; that Lord Curzon's
passionate and idealistic conviction of his own mission constituted
a psychological mystery at once so vivid and so complex that it
imposes upon any honest enquirer some reëxamination of what he
means by imperialism, some recognition that this particular
political emotion is not necessarily vicious, and not necessarily in-
humane. Clearly, and Curzon is there to prove it, imperialism in
the twentieth century is highly inexpedient. For that reason it is
doomed, at least in its political form, to disappear. But the honest

enquirer, on reading this enthralling book, will come to appreciate that a political theory, even if outworn, can still be a subject of living scientific interest; and he will feel grateful to Lord Ronaldshay for having displayed this specimen with such care, such vivid detail and such intelligence.

The task of Lord Curzon's biographer was not an easy one. In the first place, he was faced by an almost overwhelming mass of detail. The actual correspondence which Lord Curzon either amassed or emitted was stupendous; then there were his pencil notes, scattered in portfolios, rammed untidily into official envelopes, scored on the margins of letters; hopes, fears, disappointments, bitterness — all were recorded in that large and flowing hand; recorded in pencil, written down, kept. Behind all these personalia existed a great mass of official records and documents, needing to be read and digested, needed to be fitted proportionately into the whole. No wonder that a slight atmosphere of exhaustion hangs about the last of the three volumes: and fittingly so, since it was in an atmosphere of dynamic exhaustion that Lord Curzon passed the last years of his life. Not only has Lord Ronaldshay been hampered by a plethora of papers, but he has been careful not to offend those who are still alive. Lord Curzon would at moments lash himself into fierce vituperative passions against people who, he imagined, had offended him, and these outbursts have rightly been suppressed. Unpublishable also are many of the broad rabelaisian sallies with which he would season his letters, and which formed so pungent a constituent of his conversation and his style. A great deal of Curzon has thus escaped from these volumes, but what remains (and it is essential) is sufficient to give us what is one of the best English standard biographies, and to provide those interested in political problems with a very durable subject of discussion.

What, in fact, was the nature of Curzon's political doctrine? Was his essential failure due to some inner defect in his own character, or merely to some fault in the circumstances of his life? If the latter, then is the tragedy of Lord Curzon to be regarded as a criticism of democratic institutions, as implying that in democracy only the mediocre can prevail? What again was the quality of his intelligence and imagination? How far did the ideals that he stood for proceed from the springs of his conviction? How far were they but the surface stirrings of his emotionalism and conceit? Such are the questions which this book arouses and such are the questions to which I should propose an answer. It is easy enough to explain away Lord Curzon as an anachronism strayed out of the eighteenth century. The whole story is far more poignant and more complicated than that. It is a strange story of which we today can scarcely grasp the meaning. A hundred years from now students of social history may see in Lord Curzon one of the most arresting figures of our age. They may, for all we know, regard him as the last defender of a disappearing order; on the other hand they may, for all we know, honor him as one of the few statesmen of the twentieth century who had the audacity not only to see, but to say, what was going wrong.

I do not think myself that the failure of Lord Curzon to reach the highest pinnacle of office can by any honest enquirer be attributed to the short-comings of the democratic system. I feel that there were certain flaws in his personal character and intelligence which vitiated his immense abilities, and which were responsible for onsets of blind unreason, and for sudden weakenings of his domineering will. Lord Ronaldshay hints as much in his biography, but does not analyze either the causes or the effects of this strange warping of an essentially noble character and an essentially brilliant brain. And yet it is in this problem that the inner tragedy of Lord Curzon is to be sought.

Let me illustrate the problem at the outset by an incident in my own experience, an incident on which I often look back with interested and puzzled scrutiny. It was during the Lausanne Conference. Lord Curzon, that morning, had been rude, excessively rude, to a tiresome but harmless member of one of the Allied delegations. His victim on this occasion was a little old man, somewhat like Philip II in appearance, who had interrupted the progress of one of Curzon's harangues. He had raised his wizened hand aloft like a school-boy in class and had piped out some foolish interruption. Curzon paused and stared. He stared at Philip II with the eyes of a pained basilisk. The latter, who was not only courageous but convinced, continued to babble his inconsequences. Lord Curzon, in a voice of ice, told him to hold his tongue. "Voulez-vous bien," were the words he used, "vous taire." At which the old gentleman (who incidentally considered himself of great European importance) tottered from the room twittering with rage and mumbling imprecations. Lord Curzon, monumental in the presidential throne, gulped slightly, and then continued his discourse. That evening I was asked to extract an apology from my chief. This was no easy task. I appealed to his magnanimity, to his regard for old age, to his regard for distinguished statesmen who had rendered great services to the Allies, to the actual expediency of not embittering relations on so small a point. Lord Curzon was obdurate: the little old man had interrupted him: he was not only irritating but foolish: the sooner he left Lausanne the better: an apology might encourage him to stay: besides, he, Curzon, never apologized. I was in despair: I then appealed to his emotion: I said that it made me unhappy to see my chief rendering himself disliked: I begged him, as a return for the real affection that I felt for him (and God knows I still feel it), to render me this small service. A wave of sentiment descended upon him. "You are very kind," he said, "Of course...." he said, "Of course....." He pulled a sheet of paper towards him, and dashed off a letter, resting the writing pad upon his knee. No letter of apology has ever been conceived with such grace and kindliness. I thanked him. He sat there hunched in his chair with his leg thrust out upon the green-baize foot-rest. "Ah yes," he sighed, "I will tell you something which will surprise you. Every morning when I say my prayers, I ask God that he will grant me not to be disagreeable during the coming day. And do you know? Every evening when I look back upon my day I am forced to confess that I have been disagreeable to five, or sometimes even six, different people!" He said this with a puzzled seriousness which it is impossible to convey. It was only when I laughed, that he allowed his own face to relax from the earnest, and indeed religious, expression which it had assumed.

In this incident you have concentrated the essential enigmas of Lord Curzon's character. His initial cruelty and insensitiveness: his refusal to admit he was in the wrong: his obdurate resistance to all reasonable arguments: his lavish collapse before an emotional argument: his ultimate generosity: and the amazingly naïve commentary by which the incident was closed. For Curzon was hard in the wrong places and soft in the wrong places. He had the mentality of an adolescent. His character became ossified at the age of nineteen.

I do not think Lord Ronaldshay has paid sufficient attention to the early influences by which Lord Curzon's nature was warped. There was that austere and lovely house at Kedleston. The vast rooms and terraces, the cold alabaster columns in the hall, the bell, that echoed through those cold corridors announcing morning prayers. Little Curzon ran, fearful of being late; little Curzon knelt there listening to his father reading the Old Testament, imbibing the conception of a cold and revengeful Jehovah. Then there was Miss Paraman, the governess into whose care those wretched children were entrusted. Deeply did she impress upon those pliant minds her own theories of God and Hell and parsimony and discipline. Her anger was terrible, her punishments ingenious in their cruelty. She wore, Lord Curzon would relate, a large greasy skirt, the bottom of which was trimmed with six broad bands of braid. One of her punishments was to force the children to unpick those bands of braid, and to stitch them on again. Little Curzon, weeping in the big cold house, stitching at Miss Paraman's unpleasant skirt. Then there came Mr. Dunbar, the assistant master at the Rev. Cowley Powle's private school at Wixenford. Mr. Dunbar was violent and sensitive. He believed with passionate fervor in the value of accuracy. Detail was his God. He also destroyed whatever sense of values little Curzon might himself have evolved. Then his mother, Lady Scarsdale, died when he was just sixteen. Three years later he developed curvature of the spine. From that moment he was isolated from his kind by a curtain of suffering and exhaustion. The character which he possessed at eighteen was thereafter incased, as his body was incased, in a cage of steel. Through the interstices of this rigidity, his human qualities escaped but rarely, and then in the shape of emotionalism. He retained throughout his life the "larme facile" of his puberty: I have never known a man cry so frequently or so easily as Curzon cried.

Such then were the early influences which twisted his character into contorted forms. Miss Paraman had taught him the importance of parsimony, and throughout his life his attitude towards money matters was lacking in charm. Miss Paraman had taught him cruelty, anger, suspicion, resentment: these lessons remained with him till the end. Mr. Dunbar, for his part, had impressed upon his then receptive mind the vital necessity of attending to detail: Lord Curzon's passion for detail was to ruin his career. A grandiose and chilly childhood, softened by scant humanity, troubled by fears of God and Miss Paraman and what happened to people who failed to know about the Treaty of Amiens. And beneath it all, emerging while he was still at Eton, a determined egoism, a consciousness that with so uncertain a body, so uncertain a will, great efforts would be necessary if he were to realize his vast ambition. He set his teeth and made those efforts: he tackled every circumstance in his life with torrential energy; immense generators, vast dynamos, were employed to thread a needle; and in the last resort energy, efficiency, accomplishment, became ends in themselves, irrespective of the purposes to which they were devoted. Miss Paraman and Mr. Dunbar had left their mark. Lord Curzon at the age of sixteen had fallen into the fallacy of confusing energy with strength of mind.

It is legitimate, I think, thus to assume that Curzon's character was warped in childhood, and that his spinal affection, although sometimes exaggerated by himself and his biographer, did in fact account for much of the psychological obtuseness which marred his high abilities. Scarcely less important, however, was the comparative disaster of his career at Oxford, where he failed to obtain a first class in the schools. "Now," he wrote, "I shall devote the rest of my life to showing the examiners that they have made a mistake." Curzon was always far more affected by his failures than by his successes. From that moment his ambition became embittered by the poison of his academic defeat, it became ruthless, inelastic, unremitting. The God of success, an amiable deity, loomed for him as Jehovah, demanding blood and human sacrifice. He gave it, and in vain, all that it desired.

It is absurd, of course, to contend that Lord Curzon obtained from his God no rewards for such devotion. He was Viceroy at 39: he was Foreign Secretary at a time of vast historical importance: he possessed riches and titles and many great houses and the glitter of the Garter at his knee. He rode on elephants whose trappings were of gold and emeralds, he sat on alabaster thrones while potentates bowed jewelled heads before him, he walked on the wide lawns of English homes, he purchased castles and palaces, and he won the love of two of the most lovely women of our age. Yet all these were for him but a temporary solace in great bitterness. He did not get a first at Oxford; he did not get the better of Lord Kitchener, or of Mr. Lloyd George; and it was Mr. Baldwin, not George Curzon, who was appointed Prime Minister at the death of Mr. Bonar Law. These three disappointments remained for him the essential facts of his existence. His victories were for him but evidence of the injustice of his defeats.

It is not, I think, correct to dismiss Lord Curzon as a materialist who failed through lack of any directing idea. He had his ideas and his ideals. That they were somewhat old-fashioned bears, to

my mind, but scant relation to the problem. His imperialism, for
instance, was in no sense a despicable thing. There was much
about it, of course, that was vain and flashy. "No Englishman,"
he wrote at the age of 28, "can land in Hongkong without feeling
a thrill of pride for his nationality. Here is that furthermost link
in that chain of fortresses which from Spain to China girds half
the globe." "The sight," he wrote on the same journey, "of these
successive metropolises of England and the British Empire in
foreign parts is one of the proudest experiences of travel." This
of course is wrong and silly. But the imperialism of Curzon was
made of stuff far more serious than mere national showing-off.
Americans may smile at the Britisher's belief in his own mission,
and indeed this facile theory is apt to cover many selfish sins.
But to those who have seen British imperialism in action it is not
wholly ridiculous to feel that in the administration of alien
peoples the Anglo-Saxon genius finds its fullest expression. To
Curzon this theory was an article of faith. He believed that God
had bestowed on England a divine mission to administer what he
called "backward races." This mission which had been "for
some peculiar and inscrutable reason entrusted to her by Providence" entailed upon Great Britain "that supreme idea without
which Imperialism is only a sounding brass and a tinkling cymbal,
namely the sense of sacrifice and the idea of duty." "If," he said
while Viceroy, "I felt that we were not working here for the good
of India in obedience to a higher law and a nobler aim, then I
would see the link that holds England and India together severed
without a sigh."

Lord Curzon, of course, was not of those who believe that self-
government is in every case better than good government. "Efficiency of administration," he wrote, "is in my view a synonym
for the contentment of the governed. It is the only means of
affecting the people in their homes and of adding only an atom
perhaps, but still an atom, to the happiness of the masses." It
never occurred to him that, except for a "handful of agitators" the
people of India might really prefer their own warm muddles to
the chilly efficiency of English rule. He sincerely dreaded the
extent of human suffering which would be caused in India by any
sudden relaxation of our dominion. He insisted, however, that
that rule, though alien, should be just. "I do not know," he
wrote to the Secretary of State for India in connection with
some cases of ill-treatment of natives, "I do not know what you

think of these cases. They eat into my very soul." In writing that Curzon was absolutely sincere, and the whole burden of his doctrine and his ideal is contained in the magnificent farewell speech which he made on leaving India. "A hundred times," he said on that occasion, "have I said to myself, 'Oh that to every Englishman in this country, as he ends his work, might be truthfully applied the phrase, *Thou hast loved righteousness and hated iniquity.*' No man has, I believe, ever served India faithfully of whom that could not be said. All other triumphs are tinsel and sham. Perhaps there are few of us who make anything but a poor approximation to that ideal. But let it be our ideal all the same — to fight for the right, to abhor the imperfect, the unjust or the mean, to swerve neither to the right hand not to the left, to care nothing for flattery or applause or odium or abuse, never to let your enthusiasm be soured or your courage grow dim, but to remember that the Almighty has placed your hand on the greatest of His ploughs, in whose furrow the nations of the future are germinating and taking shape, to drive the blade a little forward in your time, and to feel that somewhere among these millions you have left a little justice or happiness or prosperity, a sense of manliness or moral dignity, a spring of patriotism, a dawn of intellectual enlightenment or a stirring of duty where it did not exist before — that is enough, that is the Englishman's justification in India. It is good enough for his watchword when he is here, for his epitaph when he is gone. I have worked for no other aim. Let India be my judge." There will be sceptics, of course, who will dismiss this fine finale as mere rhetoric: they would be wrong: these words represented the very essence of Lord Curzon's faith: there have been faiths more peccant and more harmful; there have been few faiths which have done such practical good.

But again we are brought back to the original conundrum. How came it that a man who had been given such talents and opportunities, who was inspired by such high ambition, such dogged energy, such burning faith, should have missed the main object of his ambitions, should have been worsted in the struggle by lesser minds, should have failed, ultimately, to make good? The explanation, as I have already indicated, may well lie in that strange rigidity which came over his character at the age of nineteen. Other men have been egoistic, but Lord Curzon's egoism was of so inelastic a character as to render him dangerously impervious to what was really going on. He was apt to allow his judgment to be affected by purely personal considerations. His anti-Turkish bias, for instance, dates from the inconvenience to which he had been subjected by the Turkish customs officials in 1889. His dislike of France, and the low opinion he held of French statesmen, could be traced back to his early contempt for the French officials he had met in Cochin China and to the irritation caused him by the incident at Muscat. His scant sympathy for the cause of Greece is to be attributed not merely to his dislike of M. Venizelos, but also the fact that he had been severely heckled on the Cretan question when Under Secretary of State. This personal aspect frequently vitiated his sense of proportion. "If only," he wrote in 1899, "I could transfer a little of the misplaced anxiety about the Transvaal to Persia and the Persian Gulf. ..." That, in 1899, was an excessively foolish thing to say.

A further, and most unfortunate element in Lord Curzon's egoism, was the extreme combativeness, often on petty matters, which it provoked. It was, as Lord Ronaldshay remarks, "with the utmost difficulty that he subordinated his views to those of other people." He was continually being diverted from the object he was pursuing by some personal slight or suspicion; often by the mere desire to triumph over his adversaries upon some wholly secondary point. His comparative insuccess as Foreign Minister is implicit in a passage of a letter written in 1900: "I never," he wrote, "spend five minutes in enquiring whether we are unpopular. The answer is written in red ink on the map of the globe. Neither would I ever adopt Lord Salisbury's plan of throwing bones to keep the various dogs quiet. ... They devour your bone and then turn round and snarl for more. No; I would count everywhere on the individual hostility of all the Great Powers, but would endeavour so to arrange things that they were not *united* against me. And the first condition in such a policy is, in my opinion, the exact inverse of your present policy: for I would be as strong in small things as in big." Here, in a phrase, lies the secret of Lord Curzon's failure to realize the great hopes and opportunities of his tenure of the Foreign Office. "As strong in small things as in big," — Curzon was so busy being "strong" about the little things that he had no time left to deal with the really important problems which called for solution.

This native egoism was, for the conduct of negotiations, rendered even more unpalatable to his colleagues or opponents by Curzon's unfortunate passion for marshalling facts. This was the fault of Mr. Dunbar at Wixenford who had insisted somewhat unduly on accuracy of detail. Lord Curzon became so intoxicated by his own ability to present a case that his every remark became an oration, and that he adopted the manner, as Labouchère had observed even before he went to India, "of a Divinity addressing blackbeetles." "The pleasure," writes Lord Ronaldshay, "which he derived from speech and writing made him a great master of language; but it tended to broaden rather than deepen his mind. He absorbed knowledge rather than evolved it." Hence arose an unfortunate prolixity, and much irritation, boredom and resentment on the part of those to whom these diatribes were addressed. M. Poincaré, for one, did not appreciate Lord Curzon's rhetoric in the least.

Curzon, for his part, was amazed at his own efficiency. He was proud of what he called "my middle-class method," or "my remorseless scrutiny into everything." "The goal," writes Lord Ronaldshay, "at which he aimed can be described compendiously as achievement, — the bringing of things to a conclusion, the multiplication and accumulation of bundles of acts of accomplishment, across whose respective dockets might be written with a flourish of satisfaction *res gestae*." The amount of unnecessary business with which Curzon obstructed his daily life was almost incredible. His conviction that only he himself could do a job to his own satisfaction was a very unfortunate element in his character and one which when he came to office did him untold harm. He was so overwhelmed by unimportant matters which he refused to entrust to other hands that he had no time to think of anything important. His official life was a hurricane of trivialities. I have seen him, during a serious European crisis, writing invitations to a dinner party with his own hand for fear lest his wife or secretary might make some mistake. And I have heard from his daughter the story of the lawn at Hackwood which is so extraordinary that it merits to be retold. In the first place Hackwood was not his own home, but a house which he had rented for a term of years. In the second place the lawn at Hackwood is about half a mile square. Lord Curzon observed that the lawn was disfigured by the presence of several dock-leaves or plantains. He ordered the gardener to remove these unsightly objects. This was before luncheon. By three o'clock the lawn was black with gardeners removing docks. Lord Curzon came to watch. He said that the gardeners were doing it all wrong, that they were leaving holes where the docks had been extracted. They answered, with all respect, that if one removes a large dock from a piece of lawn, a slight abrasion is bound, for a day or two, to be left on the surface. "*But not at all,*" said Lord Curzon, "*not at all.* As usual you do not know your job. I see that as usual I shall have to do it myself." The gardeners were then told never to touch the lawn again. And during the next few months Lord Curzon spent his Sunday afternoons extracting docks from the Hackwood lawn, a task he loathed. They would lunch early and hurriedly. Lord Curzon would then approach the lawn, preceded by a footman carrying a leather cushion, and followed by his three daughters carrying baskets into which the docks were thrown upon extraction. Lord Curzon would kneel slowly down upon the cushion and proceed slowly from dock to dock while his daughters and the footman followed behind. At tea time they would return exhausted to the house, leaving the lawn pitted with the excavations in which Lord Curzon had indulged. Nor did it occur to him for one instant that gardeners were perhaps better at docks than he was, or that there might be something less exhausting and less trivial that he and his daughters could have done on Sunday afternoons.

Such blindness, such evasions of reality, diminished his efficiency as Minister for Foreign Affairs. During his first tenure of that high office he was irked by the inevitable dominance of the Prime Minister, during the second period his labors were nullified by the antagonism of M. Poincaré. He choked himself with a mass of detail and in the intricacies of personal polemics, and in one notable instance, that of Persia, he failed completely to realize that the world had altered somewhat since 1899. But he was almost a great Foreign Secretary, and we are too apt to forget that it was Curzon who was the real originator of the Dawes Plan, and that it was he who in the face of immense difficulties restored British credit at the first Conference of Lausanne. His failure was the failure of adaptability. He was ruined by the rigidity of his own temperament. And in the ultimate resort there was a flaw in the steel. His will-power, so dominating, so ruthless up to the last moment, would suddenly collapse. The essential Curzon was not a strong man. From this there came apparent inconsistencies and betrayals: what Lord Ronaldshay with great kindness calls "his new-found pliancy;" and thus one cannot wholly excuse his sudden abandonment of loudly proclaimed principles as in such questions as the House of Lords Reform, the Woman Suffrage problem, and the Montagu-Chelmsford report. Had he been less inconsistent, he might have died Prime Minister of England. But he hesitated and made excuses to himself: and people realized that he did not in fact possess that strength of character which alone would have justified his egoism and his obstinacy.

Let it not be thought, however, that Curzon was a little man. He had faults of pettiness and vulgarity, he was often unkind. His intellect and his imagination were marred by curious limitations. But he possessed a soaring sense of duty, a deep intrinsic humanity, and above all a passionate love of truth. "Let me," he wrote, "side with those who abhor the diplomatic lie." And it was truth and duty which inspired what Lord Ronaldshay rightly calls "the breathless activity of his days."

Then there was his charm. Even in the most querulous of his moments, even on what he called his "angry days," the fascination of the man, his "cheery and boisterous energy," held one entranced. He was such a boy. So simple, so petty, so human. He was so amused and hospitable; so interested in every manifestation of reality or life. Lord Ronaldshay speaks of his lack of consideration to his subordinates. I think this is exaggerated. He had little sense of time and would keep one waiting about. But then there was champagne to follow. There was always that champagne feeling when one worked with Curzon, and it was worth it. While behind it all was the immense pathos of his later life. One's heart went out to this sick and querulous man, a man at one moment radiant at some unexpected compliment or triumph, at another cast into the depths of gloom by some unkindly criticism or misfortune. Lord Ronaldshay tells of how, when the days of disappointment and disillusion were already upon him, he discovered in a drawer at Kedleston a collection of his school reports, in which his masters had unanimously predicted for him a great future. Had these forecasts proved correct? Lord Curzon summed up his impressions of his own career in a note of great pathos evoked by these faded school reports. "I never seem," he wrote, "to get any credit for anything nowadays. No one accuses me of any definite errors or blunders of statesmanship. But there seems to be a general tendency to run me down, or completely to ignore what I am doing or have done. If one looks at the record of this in any book of reference it is very substantial, as varied, and in a way successful, as that of any

Englishman of my age living. And yet it does not seem to count for much, and I am treated as though I were rather a back number. Well, perhaps I am. I suppose one gets what one deserves and I daresay the fault lies somewhere in me. And yet, how I have worked and toiled and never spared myself, while I see others treating work as a jest and life as a holiday."

For reasons such as these posterity will look back upon Lord Curzon, not as on some arrogant proconsul who gloried in the honors he obtained, but as on a man of superhuman energy and great gifts who, by the irony of fate, had been robbed of the gift of adaptability. Curzon did not fit. But in the end, after that agonizing interview with Lord Stamfordham of May 22, 1923, after a night of bitter weeping, he attained to real moral greatness, and accorded to the man who had won the prize for which he himself had yearned since childhood his unswerving loyalty and his unstinted support. The story of Curzon's life is a drama of disappointed ambition. And his biographer has rendered it with all the skill and dignity that it deserves.

¶ THE GREAT DEPRESSION

by Edwin F. Gay   (July, 1932)

The fundamental assumption of the American people and of American foreign policy at the end of the 1920's—that, in and of itself, the strength of the United States was impregnable—had by the early 1930's suddenly and surprisingly vanished, not under the impact of weapons of war but because of the working of the impalpable acid of economic decay. The corrosive filled the world. But where it came from, what produced it, and what, indeed, it was, Americans did not understand. In bewilderment, anger, and bitterly divided counsels, but also in renewed vigor and determination, there began the re-examination of the basic premise of self-sufficiency—the "great debate"—that set the tone of American life for the next ten years and resulted in a sweeping political and economic reorientation of American foreign policy.

The first response of Americans to the dissolution of the barriers that had been counted on to fence out the problems of a less fortunate world was, not unnaturally, a blind effort to build them stronger. Politically, this took the form of the drive for neutrality. Economically, its expression was the Smoot-Hawley tariff. In 1931 came a corresponding endeavor by nations everywhere to seal off their preserves against the universal malady—culminating in the abandonment by Great Britain of its traditional free-trade policy. Every man for himself.

Even at the height of the panic of economic nationalism, voices of reason were heard. One that was influential in the United States was that of Edwin F. Gay, Professor of Economic History at Harvard and the first Dean of the Harvard Graduate School of Business Administration. The article by him is especially noteworthy because Gay wrote little—yet, as has been said, "through teaching and guidance of research he dominated economic history as very few American scholars have ever dominated any major academic field." It is interesting to note that Gay also played an important, if unpublicized, part in practical affairs. He was called one of the "miracle men" of 1917, for his part in finding shipping to transport American troops to France: As head of the Import Bureau of the War Trade Board, he made a million tons of additional shipping available by rearranging imports.

THE GREAT DEPRESSION

By Edwin F. Gay

A RECENT statement by Mr. Justice Brandeis has been widely quoted. "The people of the United States," he said, "are now confronted with an emergency more serious than war. Misery is widespread, in a time, not of scarcity, but of overabundance. The long-continued depression has brought unprecedented unemployment, a catastrophic fall in commodity prices and a volume of economic losses which threatens our financial institutions."

The economic losses both of the World War and the present depression, in their full volume and extent, are incalculable, but it is not only of such losses that Mr. Justice Brandeis was speaking. The gravity of the present situation lies not merely in the widespread suffering, vast as that is, but in the questions it excites concerning the fundamental strength and character of our economic structure and in the series of decisions which must be made, indeed are now in process of making. These decisions are much more difficult than those of war. In war the chief problem is clearly set and calls for immediate action, unifying in its effect. In such a depression as this the problem is infinitely complex, decisions are beset by doubt, action seems always too late or has effects contrary to what were expected, and disunion and disruption have spread as each centrifugal force, seeking to strengthen itself, weakens the whole. War stimulates the full expansion of productive energy, but the deep depression cripples every economic process and discourages even the most sanguine business leaders. There are many confusing prescriptions offered from all sides. But no one, however skilled, really knows the character of or the specific cure for what some practitioners diagnose as a wasting disease.

Whether or not a phenomenon regularly recurring, though at unequal intervals and with varying intensity, may properly be called a disease is questionable. A continuous succession of wave-like fluctuations, each with its phases of rising business activity, boom, recession and depression, may more properly be regarded as the result of the normal functioning of a competitive economy. Multitudes of business men, each making his individual calculation of gain in a future market, but each affected by the contagious movement of contemporary business hopes or fears, unconsciously coöperate in creating the fluctuations known as business cycles. In this ebb and flow, however, there is more than the repeated concurrence of a mass of individual plans and expectations. Physical determinants are clearly present in other types of contemporary fluctuations, such as those affecting agriculture and the short seasonal swings. Monetary and other technological factors enter largely into the long secular trends. All the different types of fluctuations interact. It is possible, in the present instance, that a business cycle has been intensified by an agricultural cycle and by greater seasonal fluctuations, and then prolonged by the impact of a longer downward-moving secular trend in prices. There are also to be considered the stresses and strains which may result when the normally uneven operation of the economic forces in the business cycle, never fully balanced, develops from time to time a state of acute disequilibrium. And, in addition to these and many other disturbing factors, come the irregular influences named by the economists, rather inadequately, as "random perturbations," such as cyclones, earthquakes, widespread visitations of disease, and wars. The economists find the analysis of business cycles no simple thing, and the present deep depression, transcending in depth and extent the usual amplitudes and intensities of business cycles, is still more difficult to explain.

It is generally recognized, however, that the World War has had serious effects upon the economic conditions of the post-war period, such as the depletion of man-power, the stimulus to overcapacity of some essential industries, including American agriculture, the forcing process in the industrial development of regions cut off from their former sources of supply and of the newly-created states, the widespread monetary disorders, and the staggering burden of internal debts and foreign obligations. The World War left deep wounds, but they could be healed. As Sir

Arthur Salter has just pointed out in his admirable book, "Recovery, the Second Effort," the war — except in Russia — meant
not the destruction but the dislocation of the economic structure.
This seemed to be demonstrated by the remarkable economic
recovery in the decade after the war, and especially after 1924,
even in ravaged Europe. But now we are wondering whether
this recovery was not simply a respite rather than a cure.

The range of the great depression is unprecedentedly wide. Past
crises have affected many countries simultaneously; but, despite
the growing economic international interdependence, even in
previous major crises some important countries have been little
affected. The timing of the business cycles as between countries
has not been parallel, nor their incidence equal. At the close of
1929, when the crash came in the United States, about half the
countries for which statistical evidence is available were already
suffering a decline in prosperity. But thereafter the process
continued, with brief deceptive pauses, until after the middle of
1931 the disastrous, deepening depression had become world-
wide. The depression is also unprecedentedly deep. Experience
as measured in statistics of prices, production, foreign and domestic trade, and unemployment, shows nothing comparable in
intensity. The United States has suffered bitterly during former
depressions, notably in the years following 1837, and 1873, and
1893, but it then had free land to absorb its unemployed and an
expanding European market for its increased agricultural production. During those former crises banks failed and specie
payments ceased to an extent which the present experience has
not equalled, but this was the habitual behavior of a young and
rapidly growing country. Finally, after the crisis of 1907, when the
banks had again been prostrated, the Federal Reserve System
was created to put an end to an intolerable weakness. Now, despite strong banks in the leading countries, despite a productive
equipment in materials and men unmatched in the world's
history, deep business depression is universal.

That the World War and the World Depression are intimately
linked, as fundamental cause and ultimate effect, is beginning to
be realized. There are other coöperating causes of our present
distress, some antedating the war and some coming in its wake;
but the war accentuated the prior trends of change and was
largely responsible for the later dislocations. The economists
in 1930 at first looked for the familiar signs of a business cycle.

There seemed in 1929 to be no such accumulation of inventory in the hands of producers as in 1920, but in the form of goods bought on credit, installment purchases, housing and the like, a great inventory was being carried by consumers. In many lines of productive activity, both industrial and agricultural, it appeared that an excess capacity was facing a saturated market. "Cumulative disequilibria" of various sorts were seen to have strained the economic system: the increase in the consumer's spending power had not kept pace with the increase in productive power, the wage-earner's income had not grown as rapidly as that of the entrepreneur, and the flow of savings toward investment in capital goods and in durable consumption goods was exceptionally great. The technological advance had been more rapid than the growth of the market demand for new or cheaper products, so that, despite the great mobility of the working population, there was a steady increase of unemployment. These and similar unbalancing elements, it was thought, went far to explain the break in the economic mechanism with its slackening business activity and increasing unemployment. But as the depression was prolonged and intensified through the first half of 1931 it became clear that changes of greater range and longer duration were operating than those ordinarily engendered by business cycles. The economists looked farther afield. They noted the shift in monetary gold supply and the demonstrable alterations in the money markets of the world; the declining birth rate; the rise in the standard of living and the changes in habits of consumption tending to make the market more sensitive to fluctuations; the increasing mechanization which was revolutionizing agriculture and affecting many other industries; the development of large-scale organizations in industry, banking.and labor; and the spread of price agreements and market controls which tended to introduce dangerous rigidities into the flexible system of free competition.

Then came the collapse of the Austrian Kredit Anstalt in May 1931, the breakdown of the German financial system in June, England's abandonment of the gold standard in September, followed promptly by many other countries, the cessation of international lending, and the further and alarming deepening of depression everywhere. The factors producing business cycles and the changes in long-time trends have exerted their influence upon the depression, but the specialists in the study of business fluctuations, after arraying the factors and weighing those which are measurable, acknowledge that their accustomed methods of analysis are inadequate. A more incalculable force seems to be at work. The situation suggests that the credit economy, not alone of nations as separate units but of all, is involved; and that recovery demands both separate and common efforts.

"We have still inadequately realized," writes Sir Arthur Salter, "how deeply the foundations of the system of credit have been undermined." The World Depression reveals many related causes at work, but it now is evident that the break in the stream of credit should be especially emphasized and carefully studied. The sapping process, undermining credit, goes back to the war, to the huge unproductive debts which it created and which, by the financial illusions engendered, have been continually extended. The war was fought with determination through four interminable years; and the confidence of all its participants was buoyed up, and in turn supported an enormous inflation of credit. The exaltation of war made possible the incredible toll it exacted. Unmindful of post-war consequences, the contestants piled mountainously high their demands upon the future and thus mobilized for war's exigent present the productive resources of the world. To the people of the United States especially the war revealed possibilities of credit expansion which seemed boundless; the whole world shared in the illusion, but not so riotously in the exploitation of it. The military contribution of the United States in the war's concluding year was of decisive character, but the country's primary function was the furnishing of supplies, in the first two years paid for largely by shipments of gold from Europe and the repatriation of American securities, and in the last two supported by great domestic credits, which financed the production of war materials both for the American armies and for their associates.

The war fervor, aided and inflamed by energetic organization, placed government bonds in the hands of millions of people who never before had possessed such instruments of credit. They were not thereby educated in the use of credit; they simply received a new vision of its possibilities. The basis was thus laid for the vast and credulous post-war market for credit which culminated in the portentous speculation of 1928 and 1929. Great enterprises learned that they could distribute their shares and bonds by direct sale to the public, and smaller enterprises were recapitalized by busy investment houses to float new securities in a national market canvassed by high-pressure bond salesmen. Despite the heavy inflow of gold to the United States, particularly during the first half of the decade, despite the easy money policy of the Federal Reserve Board, especially in 1927, and despite the large repayments by the United States Treasury of the principal of the domestic debt, prices of commodities did not rise. Instead, after 1924, they showed a slight tendency downward, in consonance probably with the more pronounced price-fall outside the United States. It was perhaps because the pressure for a rise was checked in this section of the elastic tissue of the price system that it burst forth with such redoubled vigor in the stock market. Here was presented the greatest scene in the history of speculation. Stock values were pyramided again and again as they soared to heights out of all rational relationship to earnings present or prospective. The mania spread in unexampled breadth; where millions had bought Liberty Bonds, tens of millions now were buying shares or speculating on margin at the new brokerage offices springing up everywhere.

Below these paper values, the easy credit was stimulating actual production. American economic progress during the post-war period was rapid but uneven. Certain regions, whose old staple industries or agricultural products were in competition with the new mechanization or with virgin land, lagged in the race; but the pace was set by relatively new industries like the electrical or chemical industries, with the giant automobile industry far in the lead both in methods of mass production and in volume of mass sales. The construction industry in all its branches, and the machine-tool industry, especially in its export trade, grew amazingly. Spending (though toward the close it showed signs of "sales resistance," even though reinforced by abundant consumers' credit) seemed on the whole to be holding its place with production. Public spending by governmental agencies — federal, state and municipal — likewise mightily increased. The fructifying stream, attracted by high interest rates, overflowed in foreign loans, which in turn financed the growth in exports. Foreign states, towns and business concerns, especially those of Germany and Latin America, sought, or were sought by, the American investment houses and banks, until the total volume of private post-war loans surpassed, or on a net reckoning fully equalled, the public war loans.

All this was the work of credit, of which the war had taught the lesson of apparently unlimited expansion. Credit on the great scale is a modern invention, an instrument of immense power, comparable with the prime-movers in the physical field for whose introduction through the industrial revolution it had prepared the way. Together these new powers are transforming the world. But the engineers of credit know far less about the limitations and control of their new organ than the engineers of steam and electricity do about theirs. Credit is a social force, operating upon masses of people through its own specialized institutions. It has become robust and resilient and yet sensitively flexible, adjusting itself to daily repeated shocks. Its outer limits of expansion and contraction are not ordinarily reached and tested, and hence in part the reason for our lack of scientific knowledge. Nevertheless, as historical experience if not yet economic theory has demonstrated, it has limits in both directions. Its essential form is that of a continuous stream of debts, constantly renewed, flowing where profitable enterprise beckons. Since these debts or advances rest upon a conglomerate of human estimates of future gains, some near and more certain, others distant and more speculative, wastage is inevitable, and so long as it is not excessive this does not check the stream. It flows confidently on and draws new volume from its watershed of supply.

The continuous and excessive waste of credit by unproductive use was initiated by the war, and has been continued under the habit inherited from the war of drawing freely upon the future for the immediate enhancement of productive power and of living standards. Credit has been used in unprecedented volume, but it has also been abused, in a manner not indeed different in kind but enormously increased in degree as compared with earlier experiences. When finally (as in the time of John Law's great speculative venture, a period of inflated credit in many respects like our own) the *realisateurs* commenced to cash in on their paper gains, the swollen stream contracted and for the first time the great body of investors became aware that it was fed by inadequate earnings. Then panics began. The domestic and foreign capital which had been drawn into the maelstrom by the lure of high call-rates was hastily withdrawn. The stream of American credit which had been diverted to the speculative market suddenly left the foreign debtors stranded, and their distress today adds to the depression. Abroad some of the unproductive debts cannot pay their interest; at home extravagantly invested funds, supplied by credit, fail to pay dividends or rent. Investors widely come to feel that the public trust which credit implies has been betrayed and their confidence abused. People complain of the paradox that poverty appears in the midst of abundance. It is no paradox; abundance is freighted on credit and credit stretched beyond its limits of safety must withdraw.

While America has been experiencing the elation and suffering of excessive overconfidence, bred from the war's extravagance and its after-effects, Europe has not been immune. She was left shattered by the war. The monetary systems of combatants and neutrals were tottering. Some of these systems succumbed utterly, in the case of others the fall was checked. But by the middle of the post-war decade order had been restored, the bulk of the work of reconstruction seemed to have been accomplished, and Europe was turning hopefully to the modernization of her industries and to the redemption of her pledges, expressed or tacit, to make her lands fit for heroes to live in. The strong desire for social betterment, running from peasant land allotments to recreation facilities, was matched, on the part of peoples who had during the war seen money poured out like water, by a belief that a material improvement in the conditions of life was attainable. The same miraculous rock could be tapped again; and in fact the stream of credit did again flow. Furthermore, since the menace of social upheaval is a reality in Europe (where an example lies close on her eastern border), her rulers feel that measures of social amelioration are more than desirable: they are necessary. The debts for reconstruction added to the war debts were crushing, but in many countries they have been greatly alleviated by the devaluations of currency, shifting part of the loss to the *rentier* class and the recipients of fixed incomes. When the currencies had been re-stabilized new hope made possible new credits.

But it now becomes apparent that the war left a legacy of fundamental insecurity to the continent of Europe. To the manifestly continuing political insecurity has been added a persistent undercurrent of economic insecurity, which has made itself felt in repeated emergencies and in various ways. The nervousness of European investors, great and small, has been shown in the more conspicuous episodes of the successive "flights" from the mark, the franc or other currencies; it has been allayed for periods, but still has been instant to take alarm. Largely for this reason the flow of capital from country to country has tended to be spasmodic and unpredictable; investors have sought security by shifting funds from one financial centre to another without primary regard to differences in interest rates. They have thus contributed to impede the quasi-automatic operation of the mechanism of foreign exchange which before the war, when security was taken for granted, affected national price levels and regulated the international movements of goods and gold.

In the quest for security, especially during the respite afforded by the relative improvement in economic conditions for a few years after 1925, many countries, anxious to stabilize their disordered currencies, adopted an equivalent for the gold standard. Their equivalent was the gold exchange standard which permitted them to place bills of exchange in their portfolios instead of gold bullion in their vaults. This gave them rights to call on gold held in the great Central Banks, but the innovation not only laid an increased load of responsibility on the Central Banks, especially during periods of sudden emergency, but it acted as another impediment to the normal regulating flow of foreign exchange. Meanwhile the Central Banks were sweeping up gold from private holdings, and much of this, together with the newly-mined monetary gold (because of the abnormally functioning forces of the period) flowed into two great reservoirs — before 1925 mainly to the Federal Reserve System of the United States, and since that date the larger portion to the Bank of France. By the end of 1931 a substantial part (probably a fifth) of the banking reserves of the world was in the exposed form of foreign exchange, the "cushion" of domestic circulating gold had everywhere disappeared, and about three-quarters of the world's monetary stock of gold had been so withdrawn as to intensify the downward movement of world commodity prices. Monetary security was sought, but on an unstable basis; and since England, the first establisher and maintainer of the gold standard, has departed from it, monetary insecurity and difficult experimentation with "managed" currencies have again returned.

The effort to maintain stability in the agitated post-war world has been the underlying motive for the renewal of the great movement not merely toward large-scale business organizations but toward combinations, cartels and similar agreements for the maintenance of prices or the division and control of markets. The combination movement has been long-continued, for in industry it commenced its first great operations in the eighties and nineties of the last century, after the railroads had shown the way; it is world-wide; it is paralleled by an analogous growth of social organizations in many other fields, such as labor and agricultural and consumers' coöperatives; it shows variety, adaptiveness, and increasing strength; in short, it is an organic development of revolutionary importance. For it has begun to modify profoundly the system of free competition and the social attitudes which accompanied that blindly "automatic" system. A free system which in a community of small competitive producers worked satisfactorily for the mass of consumers, since it furnished its products at the lowest price compatible with adequate remuneration to the more efficient producers and ruthlessly discarded the less efficient, was bound ultimately to force the strongest or most adaptable producers to increase their scale of operations. And the larger and better organized these operations become, the more inevitable it is that the small group of great producers, accustomed to order and discipline in their factories, should combine to regulate the disorderly, crisis-ridden market. It seems apparent that this tendency toward a planned economy, already initiated each in its own sphere by a growing number of the great industries, sponsored governmentally by the necessities of the Great War, and now filling men's minds, should proceed further. It obviously faces great difficulties both in organization and in public control; and stability, if it is gradually attained, is likely to entail a slowing up of technical progress and a degree of social regimentation for which perhaps the public's mind is already being prepared. The process of re-adaptation of the economic system is likely to be long and full of unexpected disappointments, but the successes and failures of the various nations already experimenting with economic planning will be instructive.

Meantime, the post-war developments of industrial planning have served to add to our present difficulties rather than to aid in solving them. They have taken mainly the form of stabilizing, by price or market agreements, a number of the great raw material producers, some of them with governmental aid and supervision, like the Brazilian valorization schemes or the Stevenson plan for rubber, others, like the international organization of copper producers, by private agreements. Some of them failed or were in process of failure before the depression, some have succumbed or seem about to succumb under the pressure of the disastrous fall in prices. Only two great raw material industries, both practically monopolies, nickel and sulphur, have thus far maintained prices in the face of serious decreases in production. There is evident danger of intensifying the stresses and strains in the system of prices if the fixity of great sections increases the fluctuations of the unorganized remainder, but the danger would be much less if the attempt were made to obtain stability by intelligent and timely price adjustments instead of to obtain rigidity by price maintenance. The great difficulty of a price maintenance policy, supposing all the producers, national and international, to be combined, is not only its possible repercussions on the price system and therefore the economic system in general, but its almost certain inability to restrain producers from overproductions and to check the entrance of new competitors into the profitable field, not to speak of the competition of substitute commodities. By mistaking rigidity for stability most of the post-war so-called stabilization plans have thus far failed to give the security so ardently desired.

If in this outline of some of the economic consequences of the World War in their bearing on the World Depression only cursory mention has been made of reparations and war debts, it is because they have become matter even more for political than for economic discussion. The two payments, while theoretically distinct, are in European opinion and practice so closely connected as to form practically one problem in two phases — receiving from Germany in order to pay to the United States. Since the cessation of American lending to Germany and since the rise of nationalist propaganda, Germany has come passionately to believe, and her political leaders declare, that an end must be made of reparation payments. Indeed, it seems highly probable that no government could stand which proposed to continue these payments. In the interest not merely of European but of world appeasement and of the economic recovery which depends thereupon, some settlement must promptly be arrived at. An extended moratorium, which in any case must be granted, seems likely only to prolong the disquiet, not to allay it. France, pressed by her own economic insecurity, may prefer to take the best obtainable terms which Germany can now offer rather than run the risk of another Ruhr occupation and the even graver risk of thereby unsettling further an economic world already in peril. The United States, then, must come to grips with the related problem of the war debts. Will it prefer a radical revision of the debts to meet the radically changed position of the debtors, or will it prefer a futile and embittered altercation, charged with national animosities? A reasonable end to the debt problem would not, indeed, at once stop the World Depression, but it would be a great step toward the appeasement which is necessary for recovery. The steady exacerbation of international feelings resulting from a settlement of reparations and debts which was not a settlement reveals in a clearer light the fundamental error of continuing the economic war after peace had been signed. It has only added continuously to post-war insecurity.

What has especially aggravated the European feeling about the war debts has been the American tariff. This has been held responsible for the relative decline in the imports from the European debtors to the United States. Supplementary causes may be found for the general decline in imports of European commodities into the United States, from the 48 percent of total imports in 1913 to the 30 percent of recent years. And there has been an offset, which should be taken into account, in the increase of expenditures by American tourists abroad. But the fact remains that the narrowly nationalistic policy of the United States, as exemplified again in the tariff of 1930 — inexcusable from an economic point of view and definitely harmful from a broader national standpoint — has been one of the great complicating and accelerating factors in the cumulation of abnormal unbalances and rigidities which brought the world to the Great Depression.

A time must come when the United States as a powerful world state and a great creditor nation, hence vitally interested in world trade and world prosperity, will face the realities of its new position. It will realize that a policy of self-sufficiency is not only impossible, but that a policy which presupposes it to be possible is stultifying and impoverishing. To say, as one frequently heard it said, that because the value of American exports is less than 10 percent of the total American production, we may therefore go our own way regardless of foreign trade or international responsibilities is to misinterpret the plain facts. The whole network of domestic prices and domestic credit in the United States is bound indissolubly with the system of world prices and with the stream of world credit. A dislocation anywhere in the fabric is now felt everywhere. The World War affirmed the international political responsibilities of the United States; the World Depression demonstrates the economic interdependence of the United States with other states. It cannot be a hermit nation.

¶ OF LIBERTY

by Benedetto Croce   (October, 1932)

Have the ideas of half a century of history, described in these pages by men who often were their protagonists and, indeed, leaders in some of the major events of their time, resolved themselves into any discernible pattern? There seems at least one fixed point of reference: The constant is man's need for freedom. It was in relation to this fixed point that Benedetto Croce drew a balance sheet of postwar society in 1932. He evaluates the three disastrous "ideals" of the early 1930's: the trend toward authoritarian truth through rule imposed from above, the philosophy of "action for action's sake," and the manifestation of communism as autocracy.

During a quarter of a century of close combat, the standard that Benedetto Croce raised, as senator, Minister of Public Instruction, historian, and philosopher, was never lowered. Even during Mussolini's regime, he did not fear to send out of Italy a great and confident statement like this article for Foreign Affairs. *"There are those who question the future of the ideal of freedom," he said. "To them we answer that it has more than a future: it has eternity." In his own life, Benedetto Croce showed the meaning of his greatest philosophical truth: Freedom is a fighting faith.*

OF LIBERTY

By Benedetto Croce

BETWEEN the orderly Europe that we used to know and the distracted Europe of today is fixed the great gulf of the World War. We remember the old Europe with its riches, its flourishing trade, its abundance of goods, its ease of life, its bold sense of security; we see today the new Europe — impoverished, discouraged, crisscrossed with high tariff walls, each nation occupied solely with its own affairs, too distraught to pay heed to the things of the spirit and tormented by the fear of worse to come. Gone is the gay international society once the pride of Europe's capitals; extinct, or almost so, is the old community of thought, art, civilization. How many astounding changes there have been in frontiers and in political relationships! In the place of the Germany of the Hohenzollerns we see the German Republic; Austria-Hungary has been dismembered and cut up into new states; French sway has been reëstablished over the provinces lost in 1870, and the Italian frontiers now include the unredeemed territories and extend to the Brenner; Poland has been reconstituted; Russia is ruled, not by the Tsars but by the Soviets; and the United States has become a dominant factor in European policy.

Yet if we pass from externals to essentials and try to identify the controlling forces now at work, we soon discern that these two Europes, so dissimilar in appearance, have continuity and homogeneity. When we leave out superficial impressions and make a careful analysis we detect the same characteristics in both, though in the Europe of today they have been exaggerated by the war. The same proclivities and the same spiritual conflicts are there, though aggravated by the general intellectual decay which was to be expected after a war which counted its victims by the millions, accustomed its survivors to violence, and destroyed the habit of critical, constructive and concentrated mental labor.

Nationalistic and imperialistic impulses have seized the victorious nations because they are victors, and the vanquished because they are vanquished; while the new states add new nationalisms, new imperialisms to the list. Impatience with free institutions has led to open or masked dictatorships, and, where dictatorships do not exist, to the desire for them. Liberty, which before the war was a faith, or at least a routine acceptance, has now departed from the hearts of men even if it still survives in certain institutions. In its place is an atavistic libertarism which more than ever ponders disorder and destruction, gives rein to extravagant impulses, and produces spectacular and sterile works. Indifferent and contemptuous, its followers scorn meditative and loving labor, labor with a reverent affection for the past and a courageous mastery of the future. They scorn actions which spring from the heart and speak to the heart, speculations which hold the germs of truth, history based on a realization of all that man has achieved by painful struggle, poetry which is beautiful.

Under the name of socialism, communism had already been introduced into the political life and institutions of Europe before the war. Now it has reappeared, crude and disruptive. Liberalism it ridicules as something naïvely moralistic. Like atavism, into which it often blends, this communism is a sterile thing that kills thought, religion and art: seeking to subjugate them to its own purposes, it can only destroy them. All the distortions and decrepit sophistries of historical materialism have reappeared in the current opinions and theories of the day as if they were new and full of promise, although any man with a slight knowledge of criticism and the history of ideas passed judgment upon them long ago. They have taken on an air of novelty and modernness merely because, although originally introduced by Europe to Russia, they now come out of Russia; if anything they are more immature and shallow than ever; but in this age of unprecedented callowness and crudity they gain unprecedented credence. Catholicism, moreover, which before the war sought to draw new strength from the forces of irrationalism and mysticism, has been gathering into its fold many weak and bewildered souls. Thus once again is heard that chorus of pessimism and decadence which echoed through pre-war literature, this time announcing the decline of western civilization and of the human race itself. According to these prophets it is about to sink back to the level of beasts after having failed to reach the estate of man.

All these are facts, and it is useless to deny them or to say that they are true only of certain people in certain countries. Like the situation from which they spring they are common to all Europe and all the world. And since they are facts, they must have a function to fill in the development of the human spirit and in social and human progress — if not as direct creators of new values, then at least as resources and stimuli for the deepening and broadening of old values. This function, whatever it may be, will be understood and described only by the future historian. He will have before him as a completed story the movement in which we are now involved and its subsequent developments. We cannot understand it or even attempt to describe it as a whole because we are part of it. Being in it, moving with it, we can, it is true, observe and understand many of its aspects, but that is all.

And what practical moral is there for each of us in the fact that we cannot know the future? This: that we must take part in what is going on about us, and not waste our forces in the contemplation of the unknowable, that we must act, to the degree that each of us can, as our conscience and duty command. Those who in disregard of the ancient admonition of Solon strive to understand and judge a life "before it is finished," and who lose themselves in conjecture and surmise, should be on their guard lest these digressions into the unknown prove a snare set by a bad demon to keep them from their goal.

Not "a history of the future" (as the old thinkers used to define prophecy), but a history of the past which is summed up in the present, is what we need for our work, for our action. And what we need most at the moment is to examine, or at least to review, those ideals which are generally accepted today. We must discover whether they contain the power to dissolve or surpass or correct the ideals which we ourselves hold; so that thereafter we may change or modify our ideals, and in any event reëstablish them upon a surer, sounder foundation.

The ideal of a transcendental system of truth, and, corollary to it, of a system of government from on high, exercised on earth by a vicar and represented by a church, has not yet acquired the intellectual proof which past ages found it to lack. Like all obvious statements this one runs the risk of seeming ungenerous. None the less, it is a fact that the spiritual impulse which has prompted many

persons to return to Catholicism or to take refuge in it (or in similar
if less venerable and authoritative havens) is merely a craving,
amid the turmoil of clashing and changing ideals, for a truth that is
fixed and a rule of life that is imposed from above. In some cases
it may have no nobler basis than fear and renunciation, a childish
terror in the presence of the perception that all truth is absolute
and at the same time relative. But a moral ideal cannot conform
to the needs of the discouraged and the fearful.

Nor can a moral ideal conform to the purposes of those who are
drunk with action for action's sake; for action thus conceived
leaves only nausea, a profound indifference toward all that has
stirred the human race, and an incapacity for objective work. Humanity has drunk deep of nationalism and imperialism and the
taste of them is already bitter as gall: *inveni amariorem felle*. Those
who love action for its own sake still rage on. But where is their
serenity of soul, their joy in life? The best of them are enveloped
in gloom; the great mass of them are merely raw and stupid.

Communism, it is the fashion to claim, has passed from theory
to practice and is being applied in Russia. But it is being practised
not as communism but — in keeping with its inner contradiction
— as a form of autocracy, as its critics had always predicted would
be the case. Under it the people of Russia are denied even that
faint breath of freedom which they managed to obtain under the
autocracy of the Tsars. The abolition of the State, that "transition
from the régime of necessity to the régime of liberty" about
which Marx theorized, has not taken place. Communism has not
abolished the State — it could not and never will be able to do so
— but, as irony would have it, has forged for itself one of the most
oppressive state systems which it is possible to imagine. In saying
this we are not trying to deny that perhaps there were circumstances which forced the Russian revolutionists to choose the
course they did and no other. Neither do we wish to detract from
the immensity of their endeavors to develop, under these circumstances, the productive forces of the country. Neither do we minimize the importance of the lessons to be learned from their endeavors, or fail to admire the mystic enthusiasm, materialistic
though it be, which inspires them and keeps them from sinking
beneath the load which they have put on their own backs. It is
this enthusiasm which gives them courage to trample on religion,
thought, poetry, on everything in a word which we in the West
revere as sacred or noble.

Nevertheless the Russian Communists have not solved, nor will their violent and repressive methods ever enable them to solve, the fundamental problem of human society, the problem of freedom. For in freedom only can human society flourish and bear fruit. Freedom alone gives meaning to life: without it life is unbearable. Here is an inescapable problem. It cannot be eliminated. It springs from the very vitals of things and stirs in the souls of all those countless human beings whom the Communists are trying to control and reshape in accordance with their arbitrary concepts. And on the day that this problem is faced, the materialistic foundations of the Soviet structure will crumble and new and very different supports will have to be found for it. Then, even as now, pure communism will not be practised in Russia.

Outside of Russia this pseudo-communism has not gained much ground in spite of the fascination that always attaches to things remote in time and space — as the old adage has it, *maior e longinquo reverentia*. Two conditions present in Russia are indeed lacking in Western and Central Europe: the Tsarist tradition and mysticism. Miliukov was not far from the truth when he wrote of Lenin some twelve or more years ago that "in Russia he was building on the solid foundations of the good old autocratic tradition, but that as far as other countries were concerned he was merely building castles in the air." Even if such experiments should develop in other parts of Europe, the fact that other countries differ so from Russia in religion, civilization, education, customs, traditions — in historical background, in short — would produce something quite new, whatever its name and appearance; or else, after an indeterminate period of blind groping and struggle, there would sooner or later emerge that liberty which is only another name for humanity.

For liberty is the only ideal which unites the stability that Catholicism once possessed with the flexibility which it could never attain, the only ideal which faces the future without proposing to mould it to some particular form, the only ideal that can survive criticism and give human society a fixed point by which from time to time to reëstablish its balance. There are those who question the future of the ideal of freedom. To them we answer that it has more than a future: it has eternity. And today, despite the contempt and ridicule heaped upon it, liberty still endures in many of our institutions and customs and still exercises a beneficent influence upon them. More significant still, it abides in the hearts and minds of many noble men all over the world, men who though scattered and isolated, reduced to a small but aristocratic *res publica literaria*, still keep faith with it, reverently hallow its name, and love it more truly than ever they did in the days when no one denied or questioned its absolute sovereignty, when the mob proclaimed its glory and contaminated it with a vulgarity of which it is now purged.

And not only does freedom abide in such men, and not only does it exist and persist in the constitutions of many important countries and in institutions and customs. Its virtue is operative in things themselves and is gradually opening a way through many difficulties. We see it at work in the present wish for a truce in suspicions, a reduction in armaments and a peaceful settlement among the nations of Europe. That this is true is apparent in the general feeling that somehow these nations must contrive to harmonize their plans and efforts if they are to retain not their political and economic supremacy only, but even their leadership as creators of civilization and the aptitudes for this unending task which they have acquired through centuries of labor and experience.

Disarmament and world peace are the only statesmanlike projects among the many put forward since the war which have not faded out or been dissipated; rather are they gaining ground from year to year and converting many who were once antagonistic or incredulous or faint-hearted. We are entitled to hope that they will not be allowed to fail but will be carried forward to fulfilment in the face of all opposition. It is true that the World War, which future historians may well regard as the *reductio ad absurdum* of nationalism, has embittered the relations of certain states as a result of an unjust and foolish peace treaty; but it also has made the peoples aware in their innermost consciousness that they have common virtues and defects, common strengths and weaknesses, that they share a common destiny, are inspired by the same affections, afflicted by the same sorrows, glory in the same patrimony of ideals. This explains why already in all parts of Europe we are witnessing the birth of a new consciousness, a new nationality — for nations are not, as has been imagined, data of nature but results of conscious acts, historical formations. Just as seventy years ago the Neapolitans and the Piedmontese decided to become Italians, not by abjuring their original nationality but by exalting and merging it in the new one, so Frenchmen and Germans and Italians and all the others will rise to becoming

Europeans; they will think as Europeans, their hearts will beat
for Europe as they now do for their smaller countries, not forgetting them but loving them the better.

This process of amalgamation is directly opposed to competitive nationalism and will in time destroy it entirely; meanwhile
it tends to free Europe from the psychology of nationalism and its
attendant habits of thought and action. If and when this happens,
the liberal ideal will again prevail in the European mind and re-
sume its sway over European hearts. But we must not see in this
rebirth of liberalism merely a way to bring back the "old times"
for which the Romantics idly yearn. Present events, those still
to take place, will have their due effect; certain institutions of
the old liberalism will have to be modified and replaced by ones
better adapted to their tasks; new governing classes, made up of
different elements, will arise; and experience will bring forth new
concepts and give a new direction to the popular will.

In this new mental and moral atmosphere it will be imperative
to take up again the so-called "social" problems. They are certainly not of recent making; thinkers and statesmen have struggled with them for centuries, dealing with them as they arose, case
by case and in the spirit of the times. During the nineteenth
century they were the object of deep attention and most heroic
remedies, and were dealt with in such a way as to improve greatly
the conditions of the working classes, to raise their standards of
living and to better their legal and moral status. "Planned"
economy, as it is now being called, although it holds a foremost
position in talk today is not essentially new; and the question
cannot be seriously raised of finding a collective substitute for
individual economy or free individual initiative, both of themselves necessary to human life and economic progress. Discussion
can turn only on the proportions, great or small, to be assigned to
one form of economic organization rather than to another, differing with different means, places, times and other circumstances.
This is primarily a question for technical experts and statesmen,
who will have to devise solutions suitable to the times and favorable to an increase of wealth and its more equitable distribution.
It is a question for experts and statesmen; but they will be unable
to fulfil their function or attain their ends unless liberty be there
to prepare and maintain the intellectual and moral atmosphere
indispensable to labors so arduous, and to quicken the legal systems within which their duties must be performed.

¶ IMPERIALISM AND COMMUNISM
by Nikolai Bukharin   (July, 1936)

Nikolai Bukharin was one of the great theoreticians of Marxism, the author of The ABC of Communism *and* Historical Materialism, *chief of the editorial board of* Izvestia, *one of Lenin's early colleagues in the Bolshevik movement, and a member of the Politburo from 1918 to 1929. In this article, he gives a classic presentation of the communist creed that war is simply a form of capitalist competition.*

Besides having a command of Marxist theory, Bukharin—like most old Bolsheviks a European as well as a Russian—was a master of the art of pamphleteering. But, though Soviet publicists no longer quote French and Latin, and the present fashion of vituperation is less beguiling than Bukharin's witty dogmatism, the major propositions of his argument nonetheless have a strikingly contemporary sound. Only the social and economic system of capitalism (of which the fascist countries were exemplars) can be "imperialist." Tsarist imperialism was merely a product of Tsarist capitalism. The Soviet Union can by definition have no expansionist desires—in regard to the Baltic states or Turkey, for instance. If, however, these (or any) states become proletarian states, they logically will join with the Russian proletarian state. Finally, in a "unified Communist society," the state will disappear and there will be peace. There is no possibility that communism can be expansive and aggressive, but there is likewise no possible doubt that it can fail to embrace the world.

The contradictions of communism seem not to have ended with the public confession of error Bukharin made before he was executed in March, 1938. But Westerners can hardly congratulate themselves upon their own perspicacity at that time. It was the era of appeasement of Germany. In 1935, Hitler had openly included in the Reichswehr the secret aviation force the Versailles Treaty had forbidden. Great Britain's reply was the signing (without consultation with France) of the Anglo-German Naval Treaty of June, 1935, which legitimized the construction of a German navy. The attempts to apply League of Nations sanctions against Italian aggression in Ethiopia, in 1935 and 1936, were a total fiasco, sabotaged in the last instance by Laval. In the offing were Hitler's occupation of the Rhineland, the policy of "nonbelligerence" toward the Fascist conquest of Spain, and the capitulation at Munich.

IMPERIALISM AND COMMUNISM

By N. Bukharin

IT IS well known that people have sometimes talked prose without having the least idea what it is. This holds true not only of characters in French literature but also of professional politicians. Thus at the present time a regular epidemic of discussion is raging in certain sections of the capitalist press in the effort to find explanations for the acts of aggression which again threaten to rack the world with war. And they are being discovered in natural factors — territory, raw materials, growth of population. These are considered quite apart from the economic form of society and the political superstructure in which it finds expression. In this parlance, Germany, Italy, Japan are "nations without land." The natural growth of the population of these states necessarily leads to a hunt for new land and more raw materials. Here, according to this view, lie the roots of the future war. It is fate, historical destiny. And the only salvation lies in a redivision of territory.

A plan of this sort was proposed by the late Frank H. Simonds in an article entitled "The 'Haves' and 'Have-Nots'" in *The Fortnightly*.[1] *The Economist* [2] published detailed tables showing the distribution of land and raw materials among the various countries in order to prove Great Britain's right to the *status quo*. In France, the fascist proponents of a rapprochement with Germany at the expense of Soviet Ukraine are highly indignant over the vast territories of the Soviet Union and the comparative sparseness of its population. In Germany itself, imperialism is frankly proclaimed as the sacred right of "Aryans" suffocating for lack of "space" ("*Volk ohne Raum*"). Needless to say, the required "space" is sought in the Soviet Union, the government of which is moreover accused of continuing the foreign policy of the Tsars. In Italy and Japan analogous theories have become the creed of the ruling classes, which preach them *ex professo*. The basis of all these arguments — though most of their authors are unaware of the fact — is the so-called theory of "Geopolitik," now particularly fashionable in fascist Germany. It is with this geopolitical "prose" that we shall commence our analysis.

[1] London, June 1935. [2] London, October 26, 1935.

I. "GEOPOLITICS" IN THEORY AND PRACTICE

It need hardly be said that the forerunners of geopolitics, *e.g.* the English historian Buckle, were in their day on a far higher level scientifically than their contemporaries who adhered to theological conceptions of the historical process; they were able to explain much by material factors that could not be explained by heavenly illusions. In Germany this peculiar brand of geographic materialism, or rather geographical naturalism, was developed by the founders of so-called "political geography," especially by Richthofen and above all Ratzel. The latter declared that the explanation of the historical process and of all politics lay in the size, position and frontiers of a given territory; in the form of the earth's surface and the soil, with its vegetation, water resources, etc.; and, finally, in the relation of the territory in question to other parts of the earth's surface. He maintained "that the attributes of the state are composed of those of the people and of the land" ("dass sich die Eigenschaften des Staates aus denen des Volkes und des Bodens zusammensetzen"). Before him, Richthofen had also introduced the race factor, in addition to factors of a geophysical order. The present-day school of "geopoliticians" (a name invented by the Swedish imperialist and political theorist R. Kjellén), who are grouped around the German magazine *Zeitschrift für Geopolitik* and its editor, Professor Haushofer, reiterate substantially the same ideas.

But while the views of Buckle (in so far as we are discussing the influence of climate, etc.) were progressive in their day, now, after the historical materialism of Marx, the writings of contemporary geopoliticians seem so much childish prattle (that is, logically; politically they are far from that).

In effect, geopolitics flatly denies all history. Relatively constant factors such as territory, soil, climate (and racial attributes which biological sociologists also consider as constant) cannot serve to explain historical and social changes. "Politics" does not grow out of the "land" at all, but first and foremost out of economic relations. The "land" undoubtedly influences the historical process; but it does so primarily through the process of labor and through economics, and these in their turn exercise a decisive influence on politics. The territory and the racial attributes of the British Isles have changed very little since the nineties of the last century, and they cannot possibly be made to explain, let us say, Great Britain's rapid change from free trade to a high protective tariff. The existence of a foreign trade monopoly in the U. S. S. R. cannot be explained by the "Russian steppes" or by the so-called "Slavic soul." But Great Britain's change to a high protective tariff can very well be explained by the transition of her economic system to monopoly capitalism, with its trusts and syndicates; and the foreign trade monopoly in the U. S. S. R. can very easily be explained by the peculiarities of the socialist economic system, with its plan, and by the relationship of this system to the outside world. Arguments about space and territory *per se* remind one— if the adherents of these theories will excuse the remark — of people hunting for differential tariffs among crabs or for paper money on wheat fields.

But however ridiculous geopolitics is from the point of view of logic, it nevertheless plays a very active reactionary rôle *in practice*. It supplies an excuse for bellicose fascism, a justification for war and imperialism; it preaches new conquests and wars of intervention. The essence of the matter lies here, not in the quasi-moralistic poetized sophistry with which imperialists often veil their prose.

II. "PERPETUUM MOBILE" IN WARS

In his article which I have already mentioned the late Mr. Simonds, after sharply (and to a great extent correctly) criticizing the League of Nations, draws the conclusion that foreign territory and raw materials are indispensable to Germany, Italy and Japan; that any attempt to persuade these countries to the contrary would be absurd; and that the League of Nations must adopt the rule of economic parity and make an equitable distribution of the world's resources of territory and raw materials. This will avert a world tragedy.

Indeed? But what will come of this plan objectively, that is, apart from the subjective intentions of its authors? Let us analyze this plan of the new "levellers."

First. Who are to be the *subjects* of this deal? Alas! These do not include such countries as Egypt or China or India. Nor do they include any of the small independent states like Czechoslovakia. The subjects of the deal are to be the biggest capitalist powers.

Second. Who are to be the *objects* of the deal? Apparently the U. S. S. R. and a number of small independent countries such as

Lithuania (for the author of the scheme seeks to justify German fascist aspirations), China (for Japan's policy is similarly "justified") and the colonies (Italy's policy also finds "justification" in this scheme). Thus in effect it is proposed: (1) to cut up the U. S. S. R.; (2) to destroy the independence of small countries, such as Ethiopia; (3) to partition China; (4) to divide up the colonies again, like so much small coin thrown in to complete a bargain. In other words, the entire plan is aimed against: (a) the workers (the U. S. S. R.); (b) the masses in densely populated China (*i.e.*, the semi-colonies); (c) the colonial masses. *Cui prodest?* The biggest capitalist powers. Such is the scheme's "justice" and "morality."

Third. Let us assume that by some miracle or other the idea has been carried into effect. The great capitalist powers have divided up the spoils among themselves (the others, as we have seen, are *quantités négligeables*) on a "basic principle" of super-aristocratic world "parity." But what will happen the day after? That is the question.

It is not hard to answer. The mere fact that in different countries there are different levels of productive power, different quantities of skilled labor power, will lead to different results in the struggle for the world market. No amount of "autarchy" will save a country from having resort to this world market, the more so as the capitalist system will inevitably lead to overproduction. The search for new markets and spheres for capital investment will necessitate new re-divisions of land and resources. And since tariff barriers, trusts, armies and fleets will not disappear, the war song will break out afresh. Thus what is proposed is nothing more nor less than the continuing reproduction of wars, a *perpetuum mobile* of annihilating catastrophes. The picture is truly horrifying.

Fourth. Aside from all this, the plan recalls the verse about Roland's horse:

> *Wunderschön war diese Stute,*
> *Leider aber war sie tot.*

It is just another Utopia. The more powerful groups of capitalists wielding state power will not surrender their colonies for the benefit of their poorer relatives. If Germany, Japan and Italy cannot be persuaded to abandon their expansionist policy, then there is just as little expectation of philanthropy on the part of

Great Britain, the United States or France. As regards the workers of the U. S. S. R., they can see absolutely no reason for surrendering their common property to their bitterest class antagonists.

Fifth. Capitalist states might ask themselves whether this levelling scheme does not have in it the germs of what Japanese diplomats would call "dangerous thoughts." For mankind is divided not only horizontally into states, but also vertically into classes. (By the way, this idea of a redivision, and of a blow at the maxim "Beati possidentes," calls to mind the whole class which is made up of the "possidentes." Here, however, it is not a question of re-dividing the factories and distributing the machines among the workers, but of common ownership of the means of production. And this is the course which history will take.)

III. WHAT IS IMPERIALISM?

So we may put the question as follows: Is the present tendency to violent expansion now being displayed so strikingly in Japan, Germany and Italy a purely natural function of land and race, or is it a function of the social-economic system?

The question can be most easily considered by taking the example of Japan. The density of population in Japan is great. There is little land per capita. Emigration has always been very considerable. The German professor, Paul Berkenkopf, in his recent work "Sibirien als Zukunftsland der Industrie," uses the very fact of overpopulation ("Druck der japanischen Übervölkerung") to explain Japanese imperialist expansion, assuming, however, that this expansion will proceed primarily in the direction of Australia and the Philippines. And thus it would seem that here as nowhere else the bare laws of geopolitics are the determining factor. But in that case how can we explain the crisis of overproduction? And how can we explain the paradox that this strange profusion of products is constantly impelling Japan's ruling classes to more intensive expansion? What becomes, then, of all the primitive argumentation that where there is little land, nothing to eat, and too many people, *ergo*, new territory is needed? It simply goes to pieces. Obviously the matter is not at all so simple. In reality, it is a bastard form of *fin de siècle* monopoly capitalism coupled with considerable survivals of feudal barbarism: savage exploitation of the workers and peasants, land-hunger on the part of the latter, exorbitantly high rents, poverty, and consequently low purchasing power of the masses — all leading to the paradox of plenty and poverty, overproduction and the quest for new territories. And are not these things peculiar to capitalism as a whole? Is not the hunt for markets, coupled with over-production and under-consumption, a characteristic feature of the special capitalist "mode of production?"

Or take Germany. We hear the chorus that it is absolutely essential for her to steal new territory from the U. S. S. R., since she, Germany, is starved for raw materials. We shall not speak here about the German war industry, which has swelled to gigantic proportions, which swallows up vast quantities of raw materials, and which does not in any way "grow" out of the properties of the German "soil." Nor shall we talk about the stocks of raw materials for war at the expense of consumption, nor about the sabotage on the part of the peasants. We only put the following elementary question: Why should not Germany *buy* raw materials from the U. S. S. R.? Does the latter want a high price? No, on the contrary. Many persons have shouted at the top of their voices that the U. S. S. R. is practising dumping — so favorable to the purchaser are the prices at which the U. S. S. R. has sold raw material. But German monopoly capital wants to have monopoly ownership of Ukrainian raw materials for military-economic autarchy, which in its turn is a weapon for further world struggle. "Territory," "space" (fascist philosphers have raised the category of "space" five heads higher than that of "time") do not produce any policy *by themselves*. It is definite social-historical conditions that lead to wars.

Mr. Simonds quoted Signor Mussolini's dictum: "For us Italians the choice is between foreign expansion and domestic explosion." And he added: "And that is why Italy and Germany, like Japan, are preparing for war." About Germany he spoke still more clearly: either a war of conquest, or communism.

Let us assume that this is so. But what does it signify? It simply signifies that communism can live without wars, whereas the other social form, capitalism, through the mouths of its own politicians and ideologists, declares: Better a war of conquest than communism. This only serves to corroborate the proposition that a war of conquest is a function of the social order, that it is not a non-historical category connected directly with geophysical and biological factors.

The structure of modern capitalism must be analyzed scientifically, soberly and without prejudice. The Italian fascists claim that there is no capitalism in Italy, but a special kind of order which is neither capitalism nor socialism. Herr Hitler's followers declare that in their country they have national socialism. Mr. Araki and the other ideologists of Japanese aggression speak about the "imperial path," about Japan's peculiar traditions and her celestial mission: God himself points out definite strategic and tactical plans to Mr. Araki. Camouflage and juggling with words constitute one of the distinguishing features of profound social decadence. But fact remains fact. In none of the above-mentioned countries has one hair fallen from the head of the finance-capital oligarchy. Herr Fried in his book, "Das Ende des Kapitalismus," painted a very graphic picture of this oligarchy. But Hitler's régime has left it in complete immunity; these oligarchs have only been converted (in words) into "leaders of industry" on the basis of "public service." If we recall that fascism's most outstanding philosopher, Spengler, considered the Hohenzollern Officers' Corps and the Prussian Government officials as the epitome of "socialism" there is really no need for surprise. Has it not been said that "man was given a tongue to hide his thoughts?"

The same kind of camouflage is observable in another form even in capitalistic countries with democratic régimes. Not so long ago, for example, Mr. Thomas Nixon Carver, an indiscreet Pindar of "prosperity," proclaimed *urbi et orbi* that in the United States every worker is a capitalist. The subsequent spread of the crisis and of so-called "technical unemployment" have given a tragic refutation of this capitalist optimism.

What is in fact the real state of affairs? And why does this real state of affairs give rise to imperialist wars?

Since the eighties of the last century, as a result of the triumph of large-scale production and the centralization of capital, the form of capitalism has changed. From the previous stage of industrial capitalism, with its freedom of competition, its individualism, its principle of *laissez faire, laissez passer*, it entered the stage of monopoly capitalism (trusts, intergrowth of banking capital and industrial capital, monopoly prices). The partition of the world led to accentuated competition; to the policy of dumping (the losses incurred were compensated for by high monopoly prices in the home market); and to the system of a high protective tariff. In its turn, protectionism intensified the export of capital (in place of commodity exports, now hampered by tariff barriers).

The monopolistic possession of markets, raw materials and spheres of capital investment, together with the whole system of monopoly exploitation, tariffs, etc., based on the already accomplished partition of the so-called "free lands" (which meant putting an end to the principle of the Open Door), led capitalist competition on the world market to acquire more and more clearly the character of forcible pressure (*Machtpolitik*). The diminished possibilities of "peaceful penetration" were remedied by the brutal policy of armed force.

Accordingly, the state power of capital, its "interference" in economic life, acquires increased significance. We witness the militarization of the economic system and an extreme intensification of the tendency to economic autarchy, which is also important militarily and politically in determining the *Machtposition* in the arena of world struggle. Here the inner motive is represented by the interests of profit, which on the one hand maintain the purchasing power of the working masses at an extremely low level (even in Ricardo's day it was a well-known fact that profit stands in inverse proportion to wages), and which on the other hand continually force commodities and capital beyond the bounds of the given state, compelling a constant search for fresh markets, fresh sources of raw materials and fresh spheres for capital investment. The greater the contradiction between the productive forces of capitalism and the mass impoverishment which is immanent in this system, the more intensive grows world competition, the more acute becomes the problem of war.

Imperialist war is an expression of the expansionist policy of monopoly capitalism. Such is the specific, historically limited, significance of imperialist wars. On the one hand, monopoly capitalism acts as a check on the development of the productive forces (the decay of capitalism); on the other, it leads to catastrophes of the most devastating kind.

Thus not every sort of war, not even every predatory war, is an imperialist war. Slave-owning forms of society waged wars for slaves; feudal lords fought for land; merchants and traders fought for markets and for exploitation through trade and plunder ("Handel und Piraterie," as Goethe called it); and so forth. Imperialism wages wars to extend the domination of one country's finance capital, for the monopoly profits of trusts and banks. Its wars are universal (for the whole world is already divided up); its wars confront all mankind with the dilemma: either death or socialism. *Hic Rhodus! Hic salta!*

IV. IMPERIALISM AND THE U. S. S. R.

From the above it will be clear how senseless it is to talk about the "imperialism" of the U. S. S. R., as is done *con amore* by fascist theoreticians and by "researchers" of the type of Herr von Kleinow. A phrase like "the imperialism of the U. S. S. R." is a contradiction in terms, like "dry water" or "square circles."

But it may be asked: Will not the U. S. S. R. pursue an aggressive policy, not in favor of finance capital, but against it? Will it not fight for the expansion of socialism? Here again let us begin with an example.

As is well known, the Empire of the Tsars formerly occupied present territory of the Soviet Union, plus Poland, plus Finland, etc. It possessed even more territory and more "natural wealth" than does the U. S. S. R. But it was continually engaged in wars of conquest. On the eve of 1914 it dreamed of seizing Constantinople and the Dardanelles and of subjugating all Turkey, of seizing the whole of Galicia from Austria-Hungary, of dealing Germany a blow and of concluding a trade agreement with her on onerous terms; and so on. What, under Tsarism, drove not only the landlords but also the bourgeoisie (even before they had a share in the government) to these adventures? First and foremost, the weakness of the home market. The peasant was fleeced to the skin by the landlord, the worker's wages were meagre. Hence the policy which the Tsar's minister Vyshnegradsky characterized in the words: "We'll go hungry but we'll export." Hence the Far Eastern adventure — and the "Russo-Japanese War," during which, by the way, all sections of Russian society except the landlord aristocracy desired the Tsarist Government's defeat. Hence, too, Russia's participation in the World War, with a frenzied imperialist program (here the grain exporters played the biggest part).

Now let us take the U. S. S. R. One does not need to be a genius to observe that in the U. S. S. R. *the demand is not less but greater than the supply.* In our country we have a tremendously strong home market. Despite the enormous scale of production there is a shortage of commodities, there are still too few goods on sale.

The socialist system contains within itself much greater possibilities for productive forces to develop, for labor to increase its productivity and for technique to progress. But in the Soviet Union, be it noted, this cannot result either in unemployment or in overproduction. Our national economy is conducted not with a view to profits for a capitalist class, but to satisfy the requirements of the masses. This means that when production of necessary articles is increased their consumption is proportionately raised, and not lowered into the sea like Brazilian coffee. If completely superfluous articles are produced — a highly improbable contingency — corrections can be made in the production process itself. Under planned economy it is easy to redistribute the productive forces; they can be transferred to new sectors, engendering new requirements and supplying the masses with new lines of production. There will never be any threat of unemployment, and a universal rise in labor productivity will only lead to a growth of plenty, shorten the working day, and leave more scope for cultural development.

Thus the motive inherent in the very nature of the capitalist system, which begets surplus value and prevents its realization — the motive which is most glaringly manifested in the era of imperialism and impels the ruling classes to war — is reduced in a socialist society to absolute nonsense.

This was why beggarly Tsarist Russia, where the "upper ten thousand" of landlords and bourgeois lived in splendor while the masses starved, pursued a policy of wars of conquest. And that is why the U. S. S. R., which is rapidly growing rich in the sense that well-being is spreading throughout the entire mass of the people while social wealth is concentrated in the hands of the socialist state, pursues an exactly opposite policy, the policy of peace. The U. S. S. R. is not interested in conquests in any direction whatever. But it is interested, very deeply and lastingly interested, in peace. What, then, remains of the celebrated argument that the U. S. S. R. "is continuing the policy of the Tsars?"

There is another piece of geopolitical sophistry in circulation which goes more or less as follows. Fact remains fact: in 1914 Russia was in conflict with Japan in the Far East; in 1914–18 she was in conflict with Germany; the same thing is happening again, *mutatis mutandis*, and the fundamental geophysical laws are again breaking their way through all obstacles.

What is the reply to this piece of sophistry?

First, even the facts themselves are distorted. For example, in 1914 and the years following Japan was in league with Russia against Germany; now Japan is in league with Germany against the U. S. S. R. The Japanese Samurai have even been proclaimed oriental Prussians of Aryan extraction.

Second, the question must be stated more clearly. What, in effect, is under discussion? What we are discussing is not the mere fact of a conflict (for a conflict presupposes at least two parties — our object in this case not being to analyze the inner struggles of a Hamlet), but the policy of one party and the policy of another. After this logical dissection the question becomes perfectly clear. In Japan power is in the hands of approximately the same classes as before, and Japan is continuing its policy of imperialist aggression, heading for war. The U. S. S. R. is not Tsarist Russia and the radical change of the country's economic system demands an exactly opposite policy, the policy of peace. Nevertheless war *may* break out, for the situation is not determined by the one-sided will to peace of the Soviets. War may be forced upon us. Contiguity of frontiers and territory certainly have an influence here, but not directly, and the war guilt will lie not with "the land" but with Japanese imperialism.

Finally, there is one other argument with which the opponents of the U. S. S. R. try to discredit Soviet foreign policy. It is trotted out regularly by Herr Hitler and his ideological agents. It runs, roughly speaking, as follows: National Socialism is based on "nationality" ("Volkstum," "Volksgemeinschaft"); its business is with the domestic, internal affairs of Germany; National Socialism is *national* socialism, and is not super- or supra-national. Accordingly it never meddles in "other folks' affairs," but speaks exclusively *pro domo sua*. Conversely, Sovietism — bolshevism, communism — has a super- and supra-national orientation; it is an international force, dreaming of world domination; it is the *spiritus rector* of all sedition and unrest.

Clearly this argument is intimately connected with our theme.

First of all, a few words about the Germany of Herr Hitler. The German fascists, it is true, are idolaters of the fetish of so-called "race purity;" they even castrate those who are not pure Aryans and imprison people for the "crime" of sexual intercourse with non-Aryan men and women. They propagate economico-national autarchy, as a vessel containing the holy and precious body and blood of the "Nordic Aryan race." But it would be a childish absurdity to suppose that this leads to a policy of "non-interference." Quite the contrary. Fascist action is most energetic in all foreign countries. And this is easy to understand, for their very "national narrowness" is nothing more nor less than the clenching of the military-economic and ideological fist. Their orientation is towards world hegemony, entailing the crushing and enslavement of all other nations. No, to be sure, they are not internationalists. But they are potential nationalistic oppressors of all other nations (those of "low degree"). It is precisely from this point of view that the Nazis meddle in the internal affairs of all other states. It is worth knowing, for instance, that even in the case of the United States the Nazis count on the millions of citizens of German blood to act against the Anglo-Saxon and other elements. In fact, it is to fear of a German revolt that Herr Colin Ross ascribes the unfavorable attitude of Americans towards National Socialism.[3] Setting out from the premise that "present-day America is tired and old, amazingly old" ("*das heutige Amerika ist müde und alt, erstaunlich alt*") the author threatens a national upheaval of millions of "self-knowing" Germans. Approximately the same arguments ("salvation" of the Ukraine or of the Volga Germans) are employed by Herr Rosenberg in his appeals for war against the U. S. S. R. It is thus quite futile for the Nazis to pose as offended children, occupied in the washing of purely domestic linen. That argument is mendacious.

However, *revenons à nos moutons*. Do we believe in the worldwide triumph of socialism? Of course we do. Moreover, we know for sure that this will undoubtedly come, as a result of the inner contradictions of capitalism, through the victory of the historically progressive forces within it. We know that our diagnosis and prognosis are scientific and exact. But does this mean that the U. S. S. R. should interfere in the affairs of other states or pursue a policy of conquest? Of course not. For the best "propaganda" of all is the very fact of the existence and uninterrupted development of the new economic relations and the new culture. It would be sheer stupidity to interrupt this process.

Hence it follows that not only from the economic but also from the purely political standpoint — not only from the standpoint of the U. S. S. R. proper but also from that of the ultimate worldwide victory of socialism — it is utterly senseless to think of a policy of war being adopted by the proletarian state. And as regards the "last days" and the "world rule of communism," history will settle this question. "*Que les destinées s'accomplissent!*"

---

[3] *Zeitschrift für Geopolitik*, XII Jahrg., 3 Heft. p. 135: "Idee und Zukunftsgestaltung der Vereinigten Staaten von Amerika."

However, in the interests of full scientific clarity we cannot leave unanswered one further argument against the Marxist presentation of the question concerning the destinies of society. It is set forth in an article in *The Round Table* (No. 99) entitled "Economics and War." The author asserts that Marxism is wrong, because:

> If, as its disciples hold, the existing economic system leads inherently to the class war, which of its nature cuts across national boundaries, then surely it cannot also lead inherently to the war between nations, in which all classes are ranged side by side against their fellows of another country. . . . For experience amply proves that war is the great opportunity of the forces of the Left to overthrow the established régime. The calculating communist, far more than the calculating capitalist, ought to foment war.

I regret to say that the author errs on every point. War "between nations" (or rather between capitalist states) formally unites classes, but only to aggravate class antagonisms still further later on and speed up the revolutionary process. So it was in Germany and Austria, so it was in Russia, where the revolutionary party was able to carry things through to the end. It is precisely for this reason that war enables "the forces of the Left" to "overthrow the established régime." But they are able to do so for the further reason that they rally the masses against war. It is as the force of peace, the only consistent force of peace, that they are victorious — not as the fictitious and silly-clever "calculating communist" imagined by *The Round Table*. As regards the capitalists, they are driven on by the blind, supra-rational, elemental forces of an unorganized society. One of the characteristic features of this society is that people get results quite different from those intended: thus none of the capitalists wanted the crisis, but the crisis is the result of their actions. This is the so-called law of the heterogeneity of aims, characteristic of irrational (capitalist) society and non-existent in rational, organized (socialist) society. Thus, the peace policy of the socialist state is not just a passing "juncture" for it, not a temporary zigzag in policy, not an opportunist compromise. It expresses the very essence of the socialist system.

We are not obliged to think for the capitalists. But, contrary to *The Round Table's* advice, we stand and will continue to stand for peace, peace and yet again peace. And precisely for this reason we shall conquer in a war if the imperialists force one on us.

V. THE SYSTEM OF PROLETARIAN STATES:
COMMUNISM AND WAR

Now it will be easy to answer the question as to whether wars between proletarian states will be possible — wars for markets, for raw materials, for spheres of capital investment — and whether wars will be possible under communism, *i.e.*, in the subsequent stage of mankind's evolution, after it has already taken to socialism.

Basic actuating motives are represented by definite interests. The world economic system of the capitalist régime is broken up into "national" economic units with conflicting interests (we put the word "national" in quotation marks, for the term includes bourgeois states composing many nationalities). The most acute form of conflict in which this clash of interests finds expression is war between these states. War is a special form of capitalist competition, peculiar to the capitalist world as such. The question of relations between proletarian states is altogether different.

Logically: there is no clash of real interests between proletarian states whatsoever; on the contrary, their real interest is in maximum coöperation. From the very start this real interest is realized as the actuating motive of all activity, for it is commensurate with the whole system of rationally organized labor with the ideology of the revolutionary proletariat.

Genetically: the very process of the struggle waged by the proletarian states for their existence will knit them together in a still closer bond. There can be no doubt that after a certain stage of development tremendously powerful centripetal tendencies will be revealed — tendencies toward a state union of proletarian republics.

Empirically: the experience of the U. S. S. R. fully confirms these considerations. Tsarist Russia collapsed as an integral whole, and in those parts where the bourgeoisie remained in power (Finland, Estonia, Lithuania, Poland) it has split apart and now forms mutually antagonistic elements (*cf.* Poland versus Lithuania). On the other hand, in those places where the workers were victorious they have joined the Union of proletarian republics, united by a single economic plan and a centralized government, but organized in a federation. The constituent nations have full rights, and their various cultures, national in form and socialist in content, are flourishing now as never before. This, of course, is far from being an accident; it is a manifestation of the most profound historical law, linked with a new social structure.

With the further flowering of proletarian states throughout the entire world war will become unnecessary. War will be impossible in a system of unified communist society, where there are no classes and even — *horribile dictu* — no coercive state power nor armies. This society will really "turn swords into ploughshares" and release gigantic masses of energy for national creative work for the benefit of all mankind. If even the first historical phases of socialist development in our country have already produced such brilliant creative results as the Stakhanov movement, and the heroic feats accomplished by our youth in all fields of culture, then what abundant sources of social wealth will pour forth in the splendid fraternal society of communism!

This, it will be said, is utopian. But we know very well that Aristotle was no fool, that he was one of the greatest men of all times. Yet he held that society was inconceivable without slaves. Not so long ago the planters of the southern states held that Negroes are innate slaves. So today the bourgeois and their little "Aristotles" hold that society would be as inconceivable without war as without wage slavery, and that the U. S. S. R. is a *lapsus historiæ*. Let them think so. *Qui vivra verra*.

¶ THE PROBLEM CHILD OF EUROPE
by Dorothy Thompson   (April, 1940)

*The following article by Dorothy Thompson, the famous journalist, was pub-
lished in April, 1940, at the last moment before the shattering explosion of
German power. The Soviet-German ten-year nonaggression pact was signed
for the U.S.S.R. by Foreign Commissar Molotov and for the Third Reich by
Foreign Minister Ribbentrop in Moscow on August 24, 1939. It was accompanied by a secret agreement dividing Eastern Europe between the great Slav
and Teuton powers, whose enmity for one another, and whose attraction for
one another, had supplied the major design in the pattern of European relationships since World War 1. A week later, on September 1, Germany invaded
Poland. Great Britain and France declared war on Germany on September 3,
following the expiration of an ultimatum demanding the withdrawal of German troops from Poland. In a broadcast on the same date, President Franklin
D. Roosevelt said to the American people, "You must master at the outset a
simple but unalterable fact in modern foreign relations. When peace has been
broken anywhere, peace of all countries everywhere is in danger."*

*On September 17, Russian troops entered Poland "to protect Russian in-
terests." Polish resistance collapsed. Because Soviet forces did not reach the line
of the Vistula, as contemplated in the treaty of August 24, a second secret
agreement compensated the U.S.S.R. by including Lithuania in its zone. On
October 6, Hitler told the Reichstag that he was ready to discuss peace and
declared that Germany and the Soviet Union would cooperate in the establishment of a new order in Eastern and Southern Europe. On October 31,
Foreign Commissar Molotov praised the German effort for peace, criticized
the United States for lifting the arms embargo, and denounced Great Britain
and France for waging an ideological war against Germany. For five more
months, the period of the "phony" war, the outward appearance of the old
Europe remained unchanged. Then the German tank-plane team struck in the
west and it disappeared forever. The merger of the fascist and communist revolts against European civilization had precipitated a world revolution.*

*The article has been called one of the best things Miss Thompson ever wrote
and one of the most perspicacious examinations ever made of the German character.*

THE PROBLEM CHILD OF EUROPE

By Dorothy Thompson

WHEN a drastic revolution occurs in a society the change in atmosphere and behavior is so overwhelming that one cannot believe one's eyes and ears. This is not the society with which one was familiar, the place where one felt so much at home. The old society had a face which one knew and trusted. Suddenly it is gone. Another face is there — a strange, foreign face. One thinks, "This is a nightmare." One closes one's eyes and pinches oneself, naïvely expecting that with another look the distorted vision will have passed, and the old familiar face will be there again. The first impression which a revolution gives anyone not a part of it is that it will certainly pass, and almost immediately. One says to oneself, comfortingly, "These people are not like that! I have known them for years!"

This attitude greatly contributes to the success and expansion of the revolution. For even the classes and groups hostile to it lend it collaboration, in the optimistic certainty that it is not really representative. This is inevitable, because all groups and individuals who have long enjoyed social power consider themselves, and themselves alone, as representative. They have a complacent conviction they can "handle" the situation. They need merely enter the revolutionary ranks, and in a short time the features of the revolution will conform to their own features. For *our* face, they argue, is the "true" face of this society.

The powers about to be dispossessed feel also that they enjoy an advantage in occupying a defensive position. They are fighting on home soil, against invaders. And actually, a drastic revolution does resemble a foreign invasion. I was in Germany when the 1933 Nazi revolution occurred. I remember standing with a fellow-journalist on the Grosse Stern in Berlin in April of 1933, watching a regiment of Storm Troopers march by. Their feet beat the ground rhythmically, their faces were grim, and in short, sharp barks they were repeating with a horrible monotony, "*Judah Verrecke! Judah Verrecke!*" — left, right — "*Judah Verrecke!*" — the cry giving the tact to their march. The sight of several thousand grown-up Germans marching in broad daylight to the words "Perish the Jews" seemed almost funny. One had, of course, seen these Storm Troopers marching before, but not in this manner of complete confidence. They had been mavericks, no more representative than the Christian Front in this country — merely more numerous. "Crazy people," was the usual comment, "when times are hard some people get like that."

Of course, what had happened was that a numerous but hitherto invisible class had risen to the surface. One thought, "Where, in heaven's name, did these people come from?" Yet possibly that man there had waited on you in the restaurant the night before; perhaps that one was the concierge who had unlocked the door to usher you to the elevator in a friend's house; that boy may have delivered the groceries in the morning. Hitherto they had been anonymous, the anonymous and indistinguishable mass. Suddenly they were very visible indeed. But still, one thought — or more accurately, felt — they are not representative. "They can't last."

By and by one begins to discern in the strange new mass-face of a revolutionized society certain familiar features. But they are distorted almost beyond recognition. One then has a feeling that society has gone insane. This realization is accompanied by a feeling of pity. A madman is a sad spectacle. Pity also assists the "madman." One must not treat the revolution too roughly. A revolution is like an hysterical woman. The best thing is to give her her way until she snaps back into normalcy. Normalcy, of course, is the previous society, the society to which one belongs oneself. One still feels sovereign and superior.

The Nazi revolution was assisted by this attitude, and the person of Adolf Hitler helped to cultivate it. The psychopathy of Hitler is obvious, and the Nazi revolution was made in his image. To the candid eye he is immediately inferior. Above all, of inferior race and breeding. His fulminations about the great superior Germanic, Nordic or Aryan race brought a smile to the humorous lips of any handsome, virile Jew. "Is this the face to launch a thousand ships in a race war?" one bantered.

It would have been more pertinent to inquire why this person had acquired such power over the masses. Clearly, he was a frustrated and even sick individual. Even a layman's eye diagnosed some pituitary disturbance, some masculine deficiency. The Leader of Men is not at all a masculine type. Then, all his talk about the masses being like a Woman; his treatment of audiences — brutalizing and seductive, and culminating in orgiastic outbursts that were distinctly uncomfortable and embarrassing to the detached spectator. What frustrations must be in this man, one thought — so sensitive, so cruel, so weak, and so aggressive! And those fantastic characters around him — perverts and adventurers, frustrated intellectuals who could not hold a job on any good newspaper or get their plays produced or their books published. And his own background — *"Lumpenproletariat"* — not even a casualty of the economic depression; one of the permanent class of unemployables, caught up briefly into the common adventure of war, taking refuge the rest of the time in a dream-world; a man whom nobody "understood," full of envy, furtive hatred, frustrated creative power.

One dismissed him, still clinging to the concept of "normal," not wondering what might happen if such a man, surrounded by others with a capacity for organization, should come to the surface in a *society* which shared his own symptoms, a society which was also frustrated and sick. "Can the blind lead the blind?" is an open question. Do not societies make gods in their own images? The tendency of history to employ disreputable characters is lost sight of in "normal" times.

A psychopath is a person unable to exercise conscious discipline over his unconscious urges. A drunkard achieves release from inhibitions by means of a stimulant. But all psychopaths and all drunkards do not behave in the same way. Nothing comes out of the released unconscious that is not there. Some men are aggressive when they are drunk, and some are amorous; some are garrulous, and some morose. Many go crazy, but not everybody goes crazy in the same way.

Release from the inhibitions and disciplines imposed by habit, tradition, reason, and fear comes also in dreams. Freud says, "Tell me what you dream and I will tell you what you are." It would seem that not only individuals but whole societies have an unconscious life, a dream life, which differs from the unconscious and dream life of other societies. A revolution releases the unconscious; it destroys inhibitions. The result is a caricature of the society, as an individual in a psychopathic state is an aberration of himself and no one else: as a drunk is a caricature of himself sober.

And so, gradually, one comes to observe in the distorted Nazi face of Germany certain familiar German features. The face is more representative than we thought in the first shock of surprise. The patient will be quieter one of these days; this is certainly not his permanent condition; he will recover. But meanwhile he has revealed more of himself than he ever would have shown us, sober. It is worth watching this society released from its inhibitions. For we hope to live on good terms with it when it is well again, if we are well ourselves. And we shall understand it better hereafter.

But we have also had an opportunity to watch revolutionary developments in an urbanized middle-class society in the twentieth century. In the distorted features of this case we can discern more than German features. The behavior is not German only; it is, in many ways, twentieth century. Let us try to separate two sets of symptoms: symptoms peculiar to *Homo Germanicus*, and symptoms somewhat characteristic of all decaying middle-class society. We may learn something from both.

II

The German revolution did not begin in 1933, with Hitler. It began in 1918, with the loss of the war and the collapse of the Hohenzollern state. It has gone through many phases and will go through more before it is over. In all its phases it is "German" — the Weimar Republic as well as the Nazi dictatorship. The German revolution and the Russian revolution coincided at their births, and, for a brief time, collaborated. It is not certain that they will not end in a close embrace.

The German revolution of 1919 occurred after a lost war in a world in which the middle class was the most representative class, and bourgeois values generally accepted. It occurred, however, in a society in which middle-class civilization had never had the authority that it has exercised in France or Great Britain. Germany was a country where the social and political ideas of the French Revolution did not take permanent root; and it had escaped almost entirely the English Revolution which preceded the French. The belief in the individual and in democracy lacked the authority which the spilling of blood for a cause lends to it. Germany had no Magna Charta, no Declaration of the Rights of Man, no Declaration of Independence, no popular cult of Liberty around which a moral unity could be built.

The ideal of individual autonomy had never had a real hold in Germany. There was a feudal Germany, an industrial Germany, and a workers' Germany. Feudal Germany was already in conflict with industrial Germany, and in that conflict seemed to come out on top. Actually, feudal Germany was closer to proletarian Germany, which was not democratic and individualistic, but Socialist.

Although radical Socialism was given no official encouragement and much official suppression under the monarchy, the form of the German state encouraged the tendency to Socialism rather than the tendency to individualism. The German state, from Bismarck's time on, was a *"Fürsorgestaat"* — literally translated, a "caring-for-you state," the state in the rôle of Providence. By the close of the war the economic organization of Germany had already brought about a strict social dependency. In the ensuing years Germany became urbanized to the point where only about a third of the population lived on the land; and in the east these lived on great estates as tenants and laborers. A quarter of the population lived in small towns, forty percent in large towns, a fourth of these in cities of over 100,000. A breakdown of the population into social classes would have shown that only a quarter of the population could be regarded as economically independent; three-quarters of all of them were tied to the "system." [1] The basis for liberal democracy — the democracy of individualism, thrift, and middle-class morality — was not there. The drift toward Socialism, Communism, National Socialism, or some other expression of an urbanized, industrial, socially dependent society was inevitable.

The revolt against middle-class values had started before the war, especially in the Youth Movement. This movement of twentieth century minnesingers was anti-bourgeois, anti-respectable, against pedantry, materialism, and what they called "tradesman morality." It was a revolt against all conventions, including those surrounding sex. But it was not a revolt in the direction of economic liberalism. It was a search after a more coherent social life, not dominated by the idea of personal profit. It affirmed the war,

[1] See Pierre Viénot, "Incertitudes Allemandes" (Paris: Valois, 1931).

for the war represented heroism, sacrifice, and the spirit of the front — comradeship and mutual affection in danger.

The solidity of the Hohenzollern structure rested upon the Army, the Bureaucracy, the Church, the Junker Estates, the Great Industries. The organization was impressive and powerful. The Benevolent State could point with pride to the fact that Germany had no slums like those of Glasgow and Birmingham, no slaughtered forests as in the United States, no plutocratically controlled culture, but order, discipline, and strength. The organization was so impressive and powerful that it held the world at bay for four years. Then it collapsed. The world's best army lost the war; the All-Highest fled to Holland; the masses of the people were hungry. At a blow Authority had been destroyed, the authority of the Emperor and his caste.

The fall of Hohenzollern Germany was a psychological shock to a generation of Germans from which they never recovered. One must bear in mind that Germany, in the modern sense, the Germany created by Bismarck, had never fought a great war until 1914, and had never lost any war. England and France had waged many and lost several — and still lived and adjusted themselves. The lost war confronted Germany with a reality for which she was unprepared by previous experience. It was the incredible. If that could happen anything could happen. It made no difference that the Weimar Republic put down mob risings, dissolved bolshevism, and restored order in a remarkably short time. Gone was Faith in an Order. What had happened once could happen again.

The shock gave enormous impetus to the idea of historic relativism. Obviously there were no enduring values. Nothing was permanent except change.

The second shock to which the German mind was subjected was the Inflation. This cannot be overrated. In the inflation money *disappeared*. It simply vanished. It became utterly and completely valueless — a dollar was worth a billion marks. The effect of the total collapse of all money values upon an ill-founded and already weakened middle-class society cannot adequately be described. The German youth, who had lyrically denounced money values in the days when those values were very solid, saw that they really could disappear in the course of a few weeks. Germans ceased to believe in money. Ceasing to believe in money, they ceased to believe in thrift, or in any kind of individual security.

The entire economic structure of society came into question. If wages, the savings of a lifetime, pensions, bonds, the most gilt-edged securities could all disappear overnight, were not the standards which had encouraged those savings worthless also?

The Inflation brought about rapid changes in classes. A whole breed of parvenus and *nouveaux riches* speculators cropped up to become the targets of hatred. The spendthrift and the speculator were rewarded, the sober man punished. To be rich was contemptible.

Two such overturns of values in the course of five years induced an acute feeling of crisis. But people in some curious way managed to survive. Life, then, was not the Emperor, or the finely organized caste-state, or the financial and economic system. Life was — life. A new money was made, the *Rentenmark* based on grain and not on metal. But why try to hold on to this money, either? Perhaps it too would go. Foreign money began pouring into Germany. It was welcome. Entire urban districts were rebuilt with it, industries rationalized, there was an era of intense economic activity in which Germany built the finest civil aviation service in Europe and launched the best and fastest ships on the sea. But the feeling of crisis never diminished. "This, too, will pass," was in everyone's mind. Since it will pass, let us live while we live.

The sense of living in a crisis induces a feverish self-analysis. A society that constantly analyzes its own symptoms becomes hypochondriac. The Communists saw in everything a prophecy come true. Since the next thing to come would certainly be Communism, the wisest thing to do was to push the careening society further along the escalator. The Social Democracy was loyal to the Republic, but in a half-hearted manner, for what the Socialists desired was not liberal democracy but Socialism. The Republic represented no ultimate value, but only a bridge to something else.

This concept of the existing order as only a stopping place on the road to something else — something ahead or something behind — was reflected in all the political parties. The idea that political parties are one means of approximating that balance of interests which is called "the General Welfare" never existed in Germany. The Socialists and Communists were not interested in the General Welfare. Marxian and class-conscious, they sought the welfare of the industrial proletariat alone. The

German Nationalists were wholly interested in the reëstablishment of the caste state. The Democratic Party was liberal in the interests of the capitalists. Each party was a sort of sovereign state representing a specific interest and all coalitions were precarious. The party system tended to eternal divisions rather than to the repeated striking of an average. The political structure was therefore brittle, not elastic.

In 1929 came the third great shock, and again within five years: the world-wide depression. The over-expanded plant, over expanded on borrowed money, poured out, not goods, but wageless workers. The Providential state fed them, but at a table that became increasingly meager. The solidarity of the workers was broken. For there was not one working class of the proletariat, but a working class and an out-of-work class of the proletariat. The more privileged, the skilled, and those protected by the strong trades unions, were better off than the twice-dispossessed small bourgeoisie, and excited their envy and hatred. The Social Democrats, defending the Republic, held on to the privileged workers. The unemployed and the desperate small tradespeople, peasants, and white collar workers joined the Communists or the Nazis, looking for a radical solution. The Youth sat in employment offices, or took their various insurance cards to be punched. They had time on their hands — time to go to meetings, or march in parades. Soothsayers arose and the crop of mystic prophets who perennially rove the German countryside increased, to tell the people from crystals or stars or cabalistic books or out of their own visions that the world was going to collapse or that the Redeemer was at hand.

Characteristic of this time was that almost no one — but, precisely, almost no one — believed in capitalism. The little capitalists went broke for the second time in five years; the big ones also went broke but were salvaged by the state, which in instance after instance became the chief shareholder. The sons of all the Thomas Lamonts were Corliss Lamonts.

Marxian Socialism preached materialism, and it failed to excite the youth because they had long since ceased to believe in material values. To a great extent, Communism is based upon envy. But can an unemployed man really envy a bankrupt capitalist? Hitler offered to youth fellowship in a mystic community. "No one else wants you, but I want you. I need you. And I promise you that as long as I live you shall belong to me and I shall belong to you." In the ranks of the Storm Troopers there was a uniform and fellowship. It was the "front spirit" all over again, the front spirit of which the youth had heard their elders talk, but which they had missed.

The next phase in the revolution was Hitler's dictatorship. It cannot be wholly or even chiefly attributed to the Treaty of Versailles. It was the response to the 1929 depression, to the third shattering psychological shock in half a generation.

The revolution was gathering momentum, in a kind of psychological vacuum from which all values had been obliterated — belief in the old régime, belief in the economic order, belief in the present régime, belief in middle-class morality, belief in Communism. There was belief in *nothing*. If there is belief in nothing, one cause is as good as another. The most amazing thing about the success of the Nazi revolution is that most of its followers did not believe in most of its dogmas. In the years 1930–1934 I met scores of members of the Nazi Party but I never met a 100-percent Nazi in my life — except Hitler. They only believed in the crisis, and in the certainty that "Something Must Happen," that "It Can't Go on Like This."

Those who followed Hitler did not believe, they did not have convictions; they had faith. They *had* to have some faith. Only the very strong can bear to live in a world utterly devoid of absolute values, which was what the bourgeois middle-class world had become. The rock-bottom of faith in life is "blood and soil."

Hitler came, mind you, as the Redeemer of precisely that middle-class world. But he could not save it. It was in the Euphoria of death when it elected him.

III

I have what the Germans would call *"eine unglückliche Liebe"* for Germany — a frustrated love. Germany is the only foreign civilization in which I have ever attempted to plunge myself. The word "plunge" slipped out on the typewriter and is revelatory. One would not think of "plunging" oneself into France. One enters the life of France step by step, and has to undergo an examination before every new door. The French tolerate foreigners but they do not welcome them. One has to prove oneself, by sheer merit. One would not dream of trying to "plunge" oneself into England. It would be a very uncomfortable experience.

But Germany invites the plunge. The German mind, the German psyche, has about it something oceanic and boundless. Despite the xenophobia that rules under the Nazis, despite all the talk about "German art," "German science," "German this" and "German that," the odd fact is that no people seem constantly to pursue the universal and to seek the generality as do the Germans. It is a much less compact society than the French, and there is nothing of the finely differentiated hierarchical structure of the British. The German mind seems constantly to struggle between a tendency to be open to all the winds that blow — open on all borders, north, south, east and west — and to make convulsive gestures to close those borders and dam the ocean between rigid dykes.

Whereas the French and the British social structures represent a fine equilibrium between freedom and order and seem to have some organic cohesion, German society always seemed to me to represent an attempt to enclose chaos in the strait jacket of a rigid organization. This chaos exercises an enormous attraction. It is something like the primordial chaos out of which came Creation. It gives one the feeling that something great might come out of Germany, something greater than anything that has ever been, if only for the reason that it might be *anything*.

The German mind has never been able to make itself up. Most importantly, it has never been able to choose, once and for all, between the East and the West. Dominant Prussia undoubtedly pulls it north and east; Bavaria and the Rhinelands pull it south and west; Austria and the new Slavic territories acquired will pull it south and east. If there is anything in the call of the blood, then that call comes from all directions too. For Germany is a land of the most mixed bloods — Slavic, Tartar, Nordic and Danubian, the latter being itself a description of mixture.

It is characteristic of the German that he is likely to find his spiritual home somewhere else. Goethe and Nietzsche both despised Germany. Goethe, however, loved the Mediterranean and western civilization. Nietzsche's blood pulled him eastward, for he was of Polish ancestry. Yet he incorporates the German longing for the West, the longing for form; and, because he is paradoxical he is the more German. The desire of Germans to escape from themselves may account for the fact that they make first class colonists. Germany has to keep their loyalty to the Fatherland by all sorts of propaganda and organization. But it still is easier to make an American out of a German than out of a Frenchman.

The Nazi leaders, who insist so strongly on Germanism, were to a quite remarkable extent born abroad. For them Germanism seems to be a kind of Zionism. Hitler was born in the Austria of the Hapsburgs and loathed it. He looked wistfully across the borders into the German promised land. Hess was born in Cairo; Darré was born in the Argentine; Rosenberg was born in Estonia. Ernst Bohle, head of the "Service for Foreign Germans," was born in England. I am sure that there is something significant in this. For to these men Germany is not a place, an existing organized society, but an idea. And that also is along the German line, for the Germans are the most idealistic people on earth, with a passion for the abstract.

The thinkers whom they have accepted, the men who have most strongly influenced their intellectual life, were idealistic philosophers and deductive thinkers, or else chaotic and explosive poets, like Wagner and Nietzsche. Hegel, who elevated the state into an ideal of total order and total virtue, is hardly more characteristic than Nietzsche, who was the total nihilist as far as the state is concerned, despising all forms of bureaucratic society as the enemy of the creative will. This polarity of the German soul (which Nietzsche said was a chronic indigestion) accounts for a great deal, particularly the German discipline and the pedantically organized order. The German does not accept discipline because of a neat love of order. He accepts it the way a drunkard delivers himself into a sanitarium. He wants someone to impose it on him, because he cannot impose it on himself. He is anguished, divided, at loose in the cosmos. Even prison, since it means four walls and a routine, may be attractive to him. But inside the four walls he wants to get out again, into the cosmos. It was probably a great mistake to put Hitler into prison, for in prison he dreamed of "*Lebensraum*," the cosmos of the whole world which he would conquer and dominate.

Goethe said "Zwei Seelen wohnen ach, in dieser Brust," and Goethe probably understated it. At least two souls dwell in the German bosom. The polarity accounts for the amazing German sentimentality. German feeling is to an immeasurable extent *imagined* feeling, and the German temperament unreckonable. Germany is the only country where I have seen "strong" men weep for what would seem to an Anglo-Saxon the most trivial

reasons. Observers under the Nazi régime have been amazed to
see Germans cruelly beat some poor Jew one moment and pick
up and comfort a stray kitten the next. It may also account for
the curious lack of what other peoples consider loyalty. "*Deutsche
Treue*" (German loyalty) has been a very odd thing from the
Nibelungen onward. In twenty years we have seen the whole
German people desert from the régime of the Kaiser to the régime
of the Republic to the régime of the Nazis with a unanimity that
is amazing. Each time they desert they have a plausible rationale
for doing so.

But the Germans are also one of the most purely rational of
peoples. It is a rationalism unhampered by common sense, a quality that the Germans, in their duality and profound inner individualism, possess less than any European people. They are
rational but not reasonable. There is no "common" sense in Germany. The Germans do not speak of common sense or even of
common aim, but of a common destiny. The lack of empiricism
leads them to the rationalization even of their vices. Other societies have homosexuals; it remains for the Germans to make a
systematic apologia for homosexuality. Xenophobia exists almost
everywhere, and anti-Semitism. It remains for the Germans to
make a rationale of anti-Semitism and elevate it into a cosmic explanation of the world. This in no way prevents Nietzsche, who
loathed Christianity as a "slave religion" foisted upon the human
race by the Jews, from greatly admiring the Jews for denying their
own child, and from proclaiming them to be the most aristocratic
of peoples, since they had learned how to live dangerously.

The German duality of feeling finds expression in many words
in the German language. Take "*Schadenfreude*." There is no one
word to translate this; it means literally "injury-joy" — joy in
the injury of someone else. Now, this combination of emotions is
known to all of us; it is the basis, for instance, of slapstick
comedy. But some instinct warns other peoples to separate the
concepts into different words. The fusion is dangerous. We see
the same fusion of opposites in the word "*Liebestod*" — love-
death — love, the assertion of life and creation, and death its
opposite!

The very structure of the German language seems to indicate
the desire to escape limitations. It is the greatest language in
the world in which to express emotions. It is also the most useful
in which to avoid an issue. French compels intellectual precision.

English, the preëminent language of the verb, impels to action.
The French language constantly pulls us back to reality. The
German language pushes us out, if we are not very careful, into
a no man's land. In the French, English and Italian languages
the noun — the thing or the concept — is tied as closely as
possible to the verb, the word that acts. We say, "Father has
built us a beautiful home." The Germans say, "Father has us a
beautiful home built." You have father, the concept of beauty,
and home, before you know what father has done about it —
whether he has built it or set it on fire. It is a language of un-
signed or revocable treaties. The German passion for the concept and the abstract is equal to the German fear of the fact.
The verb postponed is the fact postponed — the fact being reality.

This plurality and boundlessness, so attractive and so repellent,
so intemperate, immoderate and profoundly unclassical, gives
German spiritual life its vitality and its anguish. The one thing
that no German poet could ever have written about his race and
his nation are the words of John of Gaunt in Richard II: "This
happy breed of men, this *little* world." To be German is to be divided, perplexed, longing for form, aggressively saying "I am"
because one is not quite sure whether one is; and one is sure that,
whether one is or not, one is something-beyond-Germanism.
With all this goes a remarkable notion of world mission, but a
remarkable uncertainty of what that world mission may be.

IV

"Mein Kampf" is one of the most illuminating books ever
written. In it can be read the content of the German mind in a
degenerate and plebeianized form. There is nothing at all in "Mein
Kampf," except the description of propaganda, that has not been
part of German intellectual wares for a long time. I do not mean
to put Mr. Hitler's scholarship at issue. It is of no consequence
whether he ever read Hegel or Nietzsche, or Marx or Luther.
These four men have so influenced the German mind that their
ideas have become part of the German collective unconscious, including the unconscious of Hitler himself.

Martin Luther made a Protestant church divorced from the
idea of political freedom, commanding complete obedience to
the state in everything but theology. His counterpart today is the
Reverend Martin Niemoeller, who, being imprisoned for his defense of the rights of the Church in theological affairs, neverthe-

less, and from prison, offered his services to Hitler as a submarine commander.

Hegel saw the glorified state and the possible total sweep of its character. He gave it a moral and intellectual meaning that nobody before him had thought to contribute. The concept of the state as encompassing all of life was never reached more clearly than in Hegel.

Nietzsche who hated the state and thought of life as torrential creative power, in which good and evil each had polar and equal functions, affirmed force, youth and violence.

Marx, who was a great deal more of a German than he was a Jew, was profoundly influenced by Hegel; he was a Hegelian scholar and took his famous dialectic intact from Hegel, using it, however, in the economic rather than the philosophical field. He is enormously important to the mental life of Germany, for Germany is the only country in the world in which the entire industrial proletariat was to some extent intellectualized, and in which all of it has been dominated by Marx. What Marx conveyed to the German workers was the *inevitability* of revolution, revolution according to inescapable law. Marxism combines the idea of will with the idea of predestination. It is therefore exceedingly powerful, for it puts a guarantee of success behind the will of men. The processes of history are inexorable and apart from human will; the human will can, however, expedite the processes. To be a Marxist is to be convinced that one is in an active alliance with inexorable history.

To hold these four men responsible for Naziism is, of course, absurd. Hegel, a profound moralist, must be turning in his grave at the thought of a frame such as the state which he conceived, filled with such bestial power. Nietzsche must be exploding in his, at the sight of *bureaucratized* violence. A "boiling soul of the people" organized to boil at the pressing of a button! And Marx's revolution is not going as he plotted it, either. That pedantic and embittered soul must be having one of his interminable arguments in purgatory.

But these men enlarged the psychological boundaries of the German mind. Naziism has usurped its content, and, of course, has indigestion. It is a fusion of perhaps unfusible concepts. The Nazi state is totalitarian and in that sense Hegelian, but it is also dynamic; and German "dynamism," which has direct roots back to Nietzsche, is rapidly turning the totalitarian state into totalitarian and perpetual revolution, which is another way of saying perpetual war. The word "state" is connected with the Latin "stet;" so are the words "status," "stay" and "static," which means something that stays put. Hitler's state is a runaway state, which would seem to be a contradiction in terms. He has turned the state into a "*Bewegung*" — a movement — and even adopted as its symbol the Swastika, the wheeling cross. Instead of the Movement coming to rest, with the conquest of power, in the state, the state has become an enormous juggernaut to propel the Movement. The state and the Movement are in the relationship of the body of a motor car and the engine. All Germany rides in the body of the car (the state), but passively. The Movement is the propelling power, and the chauffeur is the Leader, who chooses the roads arbitrarily. This is the totalitarian state in one sense, but it is certainly not Hegelian.

Hegel is one of the most abstruse of philosophers. He is quoted as saying, "One man has understood me and he has not." It is pretentious for someone not a philosophical scholar to discuss him. But what is important is the residue of his philosophy in the minds of the intelligentsia, who have passed it on in a sloganized form to the masses. The idea of the *Volkstaat* is certainly to be found in Hegel. He conceived the individual as finding himself only in the society of which he is an organic member; religion was not universal, but the spontaneous development of the national conscience; the artist was not an individual but a concentration of the passion and the power of the whole community. The deformation of these ideas is part of Naziism. The organic state is the Nazi ideal, in spite of the fact that Naziism destroyed what is organic. For one cannot create an organism by *Gleichschaltung* — switching into line — an idea not derived from biology but from mechanics.

Reading Hegel, and observing the relationship in Nazi Germany between state and Movement, one can see how easy would be a jump to the conception of the state as a proselytizing church, an idea which possessed Byzantium and the Eastern Church, and which is given expression in Dostoevski's novels. In "The Brothers Karamazov" he makes Father Paissy say: "The Church is not to be transformed into the State. That is Rome and its dream. On the contrary, the State transformed in the Church will ascend and become a church over the whole world — the glorious destiny ordained. . . . This star will rise in the East."

I quote Dostoevski here because the sympathy between the German idealistic philosophers and the great nineteenth century Russian novelists is constantly apparent. The Russian Communist state is certainly not the state dreamed of by Dostoevski who, at the end of his life at least, was deeply Christian; but it is a state that is, at the same time, a secular religion with a mission of world salvation. And so is the Nazi state. And with this it stops being a state in any Western sense of the word.

The attraction between Germany and Russia is enormous, and always has been. The Russian revolution was made in Germany — it grew out of German idealism via Marx — and Russia has contributed to it, and to the German mind as well, the spirit of Byzantium. That these two revolutions, the German and the Russian, would one day merge has been anticipated by many people. It is interesting that in 1931, two years before Hitler, the German Kaiser gave an interview at Doorn in which he expressed his scorn for any pan-Europeanism that would link Germany in an economic and spiritual alliance with Western Europe, above all with France and England. In fact, he made the statement, startling from a conservative at that time, that Germany's next of kin was Russia. "Western culture has reduced itself to mere utilitarianism, but the pendulum of civilization is switching to Eastern Europe and its way of life. We are not Westerners. . . . We cling with all our roots to the East."

The German belief that the West is decadent reached its clearest expression in Spengler. Utilitarianism is interpreted as a sure sign of decadence. Except in the East — to which Germany belongs — idealism is dead. The West has lost its biological vitality, its will to life and power. So run the arguments. The Nazis' revolt towards paganism as a spring from which Life can be renewed, and their systematic anti-intellectualism, are both reflections from Nietzsche, who denounced the concepts of "the good, the true, and the beautiful" as arresters of Life. Good, true, and beautiful, are only relative. They are the values of impotent, humble, feeble men with slave minds. The morality of bold, vigorous, healthy men is different. Their ethic is an ethic of strength, cruelty, combativeness, vigor and joy. Caution, humility, cleverness, pacifism, are only virtues for slaves, who can best advance themselves by the cultivation of these qualities.

Every one of Hitler's ideas of the "master race" is in Nietzsche, who, like Dostoevski, prophesied what has happened. "The democratization of Europe is an involuntary preparation for the rearing of tyrants." "A daring ruler race is building itself up on the foundation of the intelligent mass." "Man's fate depends on the success of its highest types." "The twentieth century will be a classical era of great wars and revolutions." "There is no moral code for the generality of men. I am a law only for my own." That this master race should be bred according to a stud farm formula, as Walter Darré has conceived it, and that it would be formed in a society where fierce pride is more likely to land you in a concentration camp than anywhere else, was certainly not in Nietzsche's mind, any more than that the master-race idea should be made actual in a régime headed by a man overcompensating for severe inferiority. But Nietzsche himself foresaw "unwanted disciples."

The point is that the idea of a total transvaluation of values occurs over and over again in only two literatures: the German and the Russian. It reaches its summit in Nietzsche and Dostoevski. The latter, in the scene of the Grand Inquisitor in "The Brothers Karamazov," makes the most brilliant defense of Satan against Jesus, demolishing the idea of freedom and substituting for it the idea of equality, and affirming the "spirit of the earth," which demands bread and not freedom. Dostoevski was obsessed with the idea that the masses crave equality, that equality must mean slavery, and that the élite, the lovers of freedom, must rule as a priesthood and as vicarious sufferers taking upon themselves the sins of the masses. The idea is completely formulated in the description of Shigalovism in "The Demons." Both Dostoevski and Nietzsche could face and affirm nihilism — the return of civilization to primordial chaos, its rebirth in slime and corruption, and the emergence of a new society. In Dostoevski, a society "redeemed."

Even Marx with all his intellectualism has something apocalyptic about him. Social and economic power is to be centered in the "Dictatorship of the Proletariat." The state is to be an executive committee for managing the affairs of the proletariat, and for crushing their opponents. This accomplished, it is to wither away. Wither away into what? One asks — and comes again to the idea of the state as a Church or as a Movement. In Communist Russia as in Nazi Germany essential functions of the state are supplanted by the Party. In this sense, the state has already withered away in both countries; its power has withered.

It does not legislate, it does not plan, it does not direct. It does not even judge, except in minor matters. Power in Russia is not in the Council of Commissars but in the Politburo; and in Germany also the direction and decision regarding crucial affairs are not in the state at all, but in the Party. And the Party — whether Communist or Nazi — is built along the lines of a religious order. It is a Leader and a following, a priesthood and a flock. To call either of these phenomena the super-state is false. They represent the anti-state.

But these parties came into being in both cases as instruments of war — of class war or race war. The Party is at once a proselyting and a fighting body, a flaming sword and a missionary society. It is concerned with the Propagation of the Faith, and obviously must place enormous importance upon the Propaganda Ministry, which in Germany as in Russia is attached to the Party not the state. The Party's purpose is to administer a war which has no foreseeable end, since in the one case the superior race, and in the other the class whose time has come in history (the proletariat), must first obtain their sway over the whole world.

For a long time the Western world made the mistake — a mistake that may be fatal — of believing that there was no possible synthesis between the Russian and German revolutions. The possibility of synthesis was implicit from the beginning. Hitler always spoke of Germany as a "proletarianized nation." This slogan was invented by the German Communists, and stolen by Hitler. It was they who first said that Germany was the coolie of international finance capitalism. Marx believed that Germany would be the first workable Communist state, and the natural Communist Mecca for good Marxians ought to be Berlin. The idea of the Master Class and the idea of the Master Race that embodies and leads that class are not incompatible. We are already getting hints from Dr. Robert Ley, leader of the Nazi Labor Front, who is advising the workmen of the world to unite, throw off their chains, and, obviously, accept German leadership.

Western civilization, so runs the argument, is commercialistic, utilitarian, bourgeois, and decadent. Karl Marx himself denounced the Jews and said they could only be emancipated when they were freed from *Judaism*, which he identified with commercialism. Translated into terms of "Communaziism," the war against the Jews is therefore a war against commercialism and the West, especially England. When the Nazis say that England represents world Jewry, only the more gullible among them mean it in the sense of an Elders of Zion plot. The others mean it as a concept — that recurrent German abstraction! They mean that Judaism = Commercialism = England, and things equal to the same thing are the same.

One can imagine a slogan for the merged revolutions: "Proletariat of the world and all Have-Not nations unite under the Stakhanovite workers of Germany, and with your pure blood unspoiled by bourgeois marriages made for money, and your vital instincts to will and power uncorrupted by Christianity and Jewish Commercialism, throw off your chains! *Rot Front! Sieg Heil!*" This is not said as a joke.

v

In Nazi Germany and Communist Russia, the Party, having caught up into itself the powers of the state, is, at the same time, a caricature of the ugliest forms of the state — arbitrary force, which is terror, and arbitrary and self-appointed leadership, which is tyranny. The Party-state does not govern, because it is incapable of directing its actions by law. The state does not make laws, and the Party cannot make them. The state merely executes the aims of the Party, according to criteria which neither have predictability nor offer any security. That this condition of affairs will, in time, produce its own antithesis and new synthesis, one is compelled to believe, whether according to Hegelian dialectic or according to historic experience.

But it is a mistake not to recognize certain things that will probably remain in Germany, whatever new synthesis may take place. One is forced to conclude that whatever changes occur, Germany will remain, in however modified a form, a socialist society. The nineteenth century middle-class order based upon individual economic liberty never had strong roots in Germany, and the roots and the plants have died or been destroyed. That flower will not grow again in German soil.

Furthermore, as long as the West represents what to average Germans is a dead or rapidly dying middle-class civilization, it will exercise no attractive power for them, just as it exercises none for the Russians. Herein lies the greatest weakness of the French and British approach to the German people. For the French and British representatives of middle-class economics and morality are trying to sell the German people something that they have lived through or given up, whether they are Nazis, or Communists, or neither. The whole of Germany is convinced that the epoch represented by the economics, moral values, and social forms developed since the eighteenth century is over. They never liked it much, and they believe that the future does not belong to individualism and bourgeois ideas, but to some form of coherent and organic community in which the vitalizing forces rise from the masses. The German mind was already groping in this direction before the war, and the German revolution through all its phases has emphasized the tendency.

Actually, moreover, this German and Russian tendency exercises an attraction for the West, for the West has already discovered in itself advanced symptoms of the decay of middle-class forms and values and also has become conscious of explosive forces rising from the masses, the unemployed, and the youth. This attraction over the West exercised by Nazi Germany and Soviet Russia is, to be sure, a kind of horrible fascination. But it is a fascination. The problem of the West is to effect the transition from one form of society to another without the appalling aberrations and boundless exaggerations and horrors of the Russian and German experiences.

The growing crisis of Western middle-class civilization is one of the greatest assets possessed by Hitler and Stalin, and they both count shrewdly upon it as a war potential. It is Hitler's "secret weapon." For he and Stalin know that the war will enormously accelerate that crisis. At present it is being pushed ahead in Great Britain and France by the policies of the most conservative middle-class society left on this planet — that of the United States of America. Our credit policy toward the Allies in the present war is forcing them into economic totalitarianism faster than they need otherwise go. The fact, curiously, is unobserved by our political representatives of capitalism, who preach laissez-faire domestically and simultaneously egg on state-controlled economics throughout the world.

Nevertheless, Hitler and Stalin probably exaggerate the results upon the conduct of the war of the rapid transition being made in France and Britain to a controlled economy and a form of military-socialist organization. (I am compelled to use the word "socialist" in a rather loose sense, as the opposite of individualism.) There is far more inner unity and spontaneous patriotism in England and France than there ever was in Germany. If in the business of winning the war they find that they must dispense with capitalism, in the nineteenth century meaning of that word, they probably will simply accept the fact and pay the price. Even if they find they must erect the Moloch totalitarian state they will accept it and plan that it will be temporary and that after the war they will be able to make an adjustment closer to their own traditions and genius. The very fact that the war is going on will produce collaboration until the war is over.

And whatever changes occur in the organization of social and economic life in the Western democracies, the pattern that will emerge will not be the same as the German and Russian — unless the Germans and Russians win the war and impose it by force.

The German and Russian phenomenon that has emerged is military, messianic, despotic. It has a mass base. Its sources were latent in German and Russian thought and society. Both the Nazi and the Russian Communist movements are fusions between the army and the masses, forced by the Party. One must never forget that the modern German Reich — the Reich founded by Bismarck — was to an enormous extent the creation of the Prussian Army. Under the Hohenzollerns, the army had a symbolic value and moral authority that it does not have in France or in England. The French and English societies are civilian, and the army is their instrument. Soviet Russia is also very largely the creation of the Red Army, which established the Communist régime in the civil wars and the foreign invasions following the Great War. Russia never had had a middle-class of any strength, and feudalism was extirpated by the Bolshevists. The Party state which emerged is, like the Nazi Party state, despot-led — army plus masses.

By a succession of purges, both in Russia and Germany, the army has been transformed more and more into an instrument of the Party, that is to say of the Movement. Hitler had Roehm murdered for wanting precisely this function for the army. But the fact that a man is murdered does not necessarily mean that his policies will not be adopted by his assassin. Stalin exiled Trotsky and executed Tukhachevsky, but he adopted ideas from both.

To what extent the German Army actually has become one with the Party is still disputable. Some of the strongest moral values in postwar Germany were there, and it is difficult to believe that they have been wholly obliterated. The Elite Guards and the *Gestapo* may render the Army politically impotent. But there are grounds for believing that it still has a primary loyalty to the German nation rather than to the Nazi Party, that it differentiates between them in its mind. Nobody can say that its aid may not one day be a factor in rehabilitating Germany and restoring to her an organic social order.

At any rate, the Eastern and Mohammedan-like concept is foreign to the whole spirit of Western civilization. We certainly shall have a form of military Socialism in France and England during the war, but one cannot conceive of it as permanent. The social and economic structures of both countries, and indeed of all Western countries, including our own, will certainly be profoundly modified before this great revolutionary period is over. But though German dynamism and Russian messianism have much in common, nothing in the tradition of England or France indicates a corollary there to the German and Russian experience. One can imagine a more controlled state economy there, and Socialism, and even dictatorship; but one cannot imagine oriental despotism or a mystique of despotism. One cannot picture the dictator in a halo, elevated to Godhead. The French had Jeanne d'Arc, but they burned her, and only canonized her when she had been dead a long time.

Because freedom in Germany was never so well rooted in political institutions as it was elsewhere in the West, and because it was never so universally associated with economic liberalism, is not proof that the Germans do not love freedom. They merely love it in a different way. The German universities, before Hitler, were as free as any on earth. Nothing so eager and paradoxical as the German mind can be wholly regimented and subdued. And the violent expression of the many ill-digested elements in that mind may bring about a great catharsis. The fact of another war, and within a generation, confronts the Germans with a check to that sense of illimitability which I have spoken of as so characteristic. A moving body moves until it meets an obstacle. The war is that obstacle. Germany cannot move now with the exuberance of a year ago. There must be something sobering for her in the recognition that other people also have force and that they can apply it. The German mentality is compelled again to recognize that there are limits, and if Germany is to belong to Western civilization that is the lesson she has to learn. With the recognition of limits will come the possibility of making a truly organic and civilized society.

Docile acceptance of the unquestioned authority of the state, traditional in Germany, may be broken when Germans have had a sufficiently long and intimate experience of what the state, transformed into a militant messianic Movement, can become and do. Whatever may go on in the national mind, individual people remain individuals. They want to breathe and eat and make love according to their own tastes, have children and keep them around them, and die, eventually, in their beds. The *Gestapo*, the terror, the strangling red tape, the unceasing and horribly boring propaganda, the profound psychological insecurity of a country without law, the thousand and one petty irritations which this kind of system requires of the individual, may pull Germany out of the maze of abstractions and back to some simple realities. Freedom in the Western democracies dominated by the middle-class has been institutionalized in bourgeois forms, and is so wholly taken for granted that it is tarnished. Quite possibly it may find its rebirth in a socialist Germany in the form of something as real, intimate and necessary as daily bread, deeply personal, alive, and human, and founded not on middle-class economic ideas but on a profound and religious respect for the human soul. With the German transition into humanism the German prophesy may come true: "An Deutschem Wesen soll die Welt genesen" (The world will be redeemed by Germany).

If the state is to be transformed into the church, in Dostoevski's sense, then it must rest on moral foundations, and (since no one yet has invented anything approximately as aesthetically perfected and humanized) upon *Christian* foundations. Dostoevski came to this conclusion before he died; and Nietzsche died mad, trying to avoid the same conclusion. Satanism is not a permanent religion. The life of love is the affirmative life, releasing every creative instinct. The ethical content of Communism and Naziism is beneath contempt, and certainly beneath that great moralist Hegel. It was the German poet Schiller who said, in the words of the Marquis Posa to Philip II, "Man is greater than you esteem him." Germany is greater than Hitler esteems her to be and Russia is greater than Stalin esteems her.

One cannot avoid recognizing that the West confronts the

greatest danger in her whole history. But the recognition should lead us to the realization of what a renascence is demanded. If the West is to survive it must throw off, in its own way, the musty and outworn values of nineteenth century individualism. It was a great century, but it is over.

If the West is to be true to its eternal spirit, it must transform these values, if need be under a changed economic and social system, into the humanist and personalist values which have always been the source of its greatest strength. I use the word "personalist" rather than "individualist" to indicate that a civilized society requires that the natural man, born an individual, develop into a person, a socially conscious and coöperative human being, whose "rights" are in direct ratio to his obligations. The West must find the way simultaneously to feed men and to liberate them, to adjust the social system to the reality of social interdependency without reëstablishing slavery. When it has achieved this, the pull of the German soul will be Westward again. Or, if Germany finds the solution first, the pull of the West will be towards Germany.

Meanwhile, the West must save itself from destruction. Its awakening may accompany or follow the war. It has not yet come. But we who love the West, and yearn for a Germany integrated with the West, have faith that it will.

¶ PACIFISM AND DEMOCRACY
by Julien Benda   (July, 1941)

The British Government was in flabby hands and the French Government was in the hands of a scoundrel in October, 1935, when Italy invaded Ethiopia and the League of Nations made its great but abortive effort to bring fascist aggression to a stop. But it would be unbecoming for Americans to omit a further element in assessing responsibilities for the supine behavior of the democracies then and in the years down to 1939. For about fifteen years, the majority of Americans, including an overwhelming majority of the members of Congress, had been telling Englishmen and Frenchmen that, if they took part in another war, the United States would wash its hands of the whole affair. In other words, no program of resistance to fascism was to count on any help from the most powerful of the democratic nations.

In the neutrality acts of 1935, 1936, and 1937, the United States made a series of efforts, each more intense than the last, to avoid involvement in the war that had ended in 1918. As late as January, 1940, the U.S. Government was protesting to Great Britain against the blockade measures it was trying to enforce against Germany, and the American republics were insisting that British warships should not interfere with German merchantmen within a "security zone" of three hundred miles around the Americas. And in August, 1941, the House of Representatives, by a majority of but one vote, renewed the Selective Service Act and thereby decided not to disband the U.S. Army four months before Pearl Harbor.

Behind this American weakness of will was more than the propaganda of xenophobes like Hearst and McCormick or of communists who, from the signing of the Soviet-Nazi pact to Hitler's attack on the U.S.S.R., proclaimed the undesirability of opposing the fascist powers, and more than that the belief that American participation in World War I had been a mistake and that a better peace would have resulted from a stalemate than from an Allied victory. An even more profound cause of the American weakness of will was the belief of many good but foolish people that, because a democrat hated militarism, he must be a pacifist. Such a confusion of values was democracy's greatest danger, for it rendered nerveless the hands of many of the very people who should have been dedicated to its defense.

That was the issue to which the French philosopher Julien Benda, famous author of The Treason of the Intellectuals, *addressed himself in this article.*

PACIFISM AND DEMOCRACY

By *Julien Benda*

IN all countries there are democrats who maintain that a democratic state must, because it is democratic, refuse any kind of war — a war of defense just as much as a war of conquest. Their thesis is that a democracy must abstain from any international action which is liable to cause war. In short, it must be for peace at any price.

Those who take this position do not always say so frankly. They are embarrassed to admit that they refuse even a defensive war. They therefore claim that what is being presented to them as a defensive war is really an offensive war, planned by politicians or industrialists who expect to derive power or profits from having men kill one another. I once asked one of them whether he thought that the Greeks were right to have stood out against Xerxes rather than become his Helots. He did not reply. If he had stuck to his thesis he would have had to answer that they acted wrongly. Not long ago a citizen of a certain great democracy exclaimed: "This policy of our President means that we shall have war, and one out of every four of our sons will be killed." He should have been told that his own policy meant that all four of them risked becoming slaves. Maybe subconsciously he really preferred this prospect; but he probably would not have admitted it, even to himself.

Others are more outspoken. They endorse a slogan which a group of French Socialists adopted a few years ago: "Servitude rather than war!" Or one that we used to hear from certain French intellectuals: "In our eyes *nothing* justifies war." [1] In most cases this position is based simply on a desire to avoid fighting, camouflaged as well as possible under doctrinal reasons.

---

[1] Manifesto sponsored by Alain and signed by a group of students of the Ecole Normale Supérieure at the time of the Italo-Ethiopian war.

The desire is normal enough, and especially today when war has become the thing we know it to be and when the whole nation is involved in it. Sometimes, however, the position is based on sincere ideological convictions. Those who adopt it often are veterans of the last war.[2] It is the position of these perfectly sincere people which we shall consider here, particularly the ones who maintain that the theory of peace at any price is an integral part of the definition of democracy.

DEMOCRACY'S "HIGHEST GOOD"

The mistake of thinking that peace at any price has anything to do with democracy comes from a confusion of essential values. It is imagined that democracy's paramount concern is human life, whereas it is human liberty. Human life deprived of liberty is worthless. Therefore the democrat, in order to preserve the advantages of democracy for his children, admits and sanctifies the sacrifice of life.[3] Over and over again in the course of history democracy has proved this to be its supreme law. If our pacifists were consistent, they would have to condemn the French revolutionaries who were willing to shed human blood to win their liberties, and the Americans who preferred war to remaining the servants of George III. As a matter of fact, some of them do. The question is how they can then pretend to be democrats.

They should meditate the words of George Washington, who was not a bad democrat. In his Farewell Address he weighed the advantages, in various circumstances, of neutrality, and did not hesitate to say that "we may choose peace or war, as our interest, guided by justice, shall counsel." We shall be told in reply that war has become something very different from what it was in 1796. But the question of principle has not become different.

The mistake also arises from a confusion between the *fact* of war and the *love* of war. Democracy may accept the one and condemn the other. War may be imposed upon men who have no love for it whatsoever.[4] The ideal of democracy is, certainly, to suppress the fact of war. But the effective way to attain this goal

---

[2] For example Alain, who was a volunteer in the World War.

[3] Jean Giono declares distinctly that the supreme value, the only one, is human life. "There is no glory," he says, "in being French. There is only one glory: it is to be alive." ("Jean le Bleu," p. 303.) But Giono makes no pretense of being a democrat.

[4] "What does one condemn in war?" says St. Augustine. "Is it the fact that it kills men who all must some day die? Faint-hearted men may blame war for this, but not religious men. What one condemns in war is the desire to harm, implacable hate, the fury of reprisals, the passion for domination."

is to hold in check the people who worship war. This entails accepting the fact of war, under the democratic slogan "War on war."

SAVING PEACE AND ESTABLISHING PEACE

There is a distinction, though it is scarcely ever made, between *saving* peace and *establishing* peace. To save peace is to ward off war in some particular moment of great excitement. There is no leading motive, no general idea. To establish peace is to act deliberately to prevent war in accordance with a thought-out plan, in a time when no particular fear of war exists because those who might wish to disturb the peace have been temporarily deprived of the power to do so. At Munich in 1938 the British and French ministers saved peace. We all know that they did not establish it. At Versailles, the victors of 1918 were in a position to establish peace, maybe because four years earlier they had been willing not to save it.

Two profoundly distinct conceptions of peace are here involved. According to one, peace is based on respect for contracts between nations and on sanctions against violators. This is the *legal* conception. The other, the *sentimental* conception, expects love between men to bring about peace, all idea of contracts or sanctions aside. The first conception puts justice before peace, or at least states that it is respect for justice which must bring peace. This is displeasing to the sentimentalists who, naturally, place love above justice. At the time of the Italo-Ethiopian war, the Archbishop of Canterbury startled some persons by declaring that he, a churchman, favored the use of sanctions against the aggressor. When told that sanctions were liable to cause war, he answered: "My ideal is not peace, but justice." He was only repeating the words of his divine Master: "I came not to send peace, but a sword" — *i.e.*, to make war against evil.

A few examples of the purely sentimental conception of peace might help my readers to measure its intellectual worth.

A famous author, I read recently, was visiting in the Engadine. As he stood looking at the landscape he uttered some words which were much admired by the newspaperman who reported them. "Facing so much beauty," he said, "how is it possible not to think that men ought to love and not hate one another!" Laments of this sort seem to me quite childish. Men should be loved when they deserve to be loved, when they show justice and loyalty and respect for the rights of others. I am under no compulsion to love them when they violate elementary rules of moral conduct. Instead, I have to protect myself from them — even if, later on, I try to change them. Landscapes have nothing to do with it.

Recalling pleasant memories of his youth, my compatriot Jean Guéhenno writes: "We were twenty years old. It was a serene July and the sun shone over Europe. . . . Our thoughts, like the earth, were ripening. . . . And then, all of a sudden, there was war, because an Austrian Archduke, whose name no one remembers any more, had been killed at Sarajevo." What does all this signify? It may also have been a beautiful morning at Marathon, at Valmy, at Saratoga. Would that have been a reason to give in to Xerxes, to Brunswick, to Burgoyne?

Again, many of my readers probably saw a film depicting the wife of a German peasant who had been killed in the war giving a kind welcome to an escaped French prisoner. She lets him stay in her house several weeks and watches him depart with regret. The film's name, "Grande Illusion," obviously was chosen to show the error of believing that war between nations implies hatred between peoples. But this question is not related to the question whether or not France in 1914 was right to resist the German invasion.

The really significant thing, however, is that many of my readers will be disgusted that, confronted with such touching pictures, I persist in continuing to use my powers of reason.

NOT DEMOCRATS, BUT ANARCHISTS

One of the ways the absolute pacifists have of arguing is to challenge their opponents: "You call yourself a democracy, that is, a government of the people by the people, and yet you send me to war without consulting me, in spite of myself." Thus we find a character in Roger Martin du Gard's book "The Thibaults" declaring that if the French people had been consulted in 1914 eighty percent of them would have rejected war. This statement rests upon the hope — apparently justified, I must admit — that most men, even in most democracies, still have so little political education that, if consulted individually, they will refuse to make the sacrifices necessary for the preservation of the whole. Now it is arguable that no true democracy as yet exists — in the sense of being completely a government of the people and by the people. But is not the reason precisely because men find such difficulty in forgetting their individual conveniences in favor of the collective good? If they were consulted separately, how many citizens would offer spontaneously to pay taxes? Yet even "absolute democrats" probably admit that taxes are indispensable for the State.

"Absolute democrats" also contend not only that there should be a referendum on war, but that only those who voted "yes" should then have to go to war. This is a denial of national solidarity. Yet such people certainly accept some of the advantages of national solidarity. If they are civil servants, for example, they want to be paid salaries which some (perhaps many) of their fellow-citizens might, if they were consulted, refuse to grant. If they are interested in art, they might find that many tax-payers, consulted in the same way, would veto appropriations to maintain the museums. The fact is that these intellectuals would be more truthful — or, let us say, more enlightened about their own natures — if instead of pretending to be pure democrats they called themselves pure individualists or pure anarchists.[5]

Another sophistry often is uttered in the name of democracy. It consists in rejecting even a defensive war on the ground that it will require the surrender of full powers to the governing body, and that this surrender will spell "the end of democracy." They forget that among the basic democratic principles it is formally inscribed that in exceptional circumstances a nation may grant full powers to the governing body. During its famous meeting of September 9, 1793, the Convention declared that it accepted the idea of dictatorship for times of crisis. This doctrine meant, of course, that popular control would be suspended only temporarily and that it would be restored as soon as the emergency had passed. "Revolutionary France," says the historian Mathiez, "would never have accepted the dictatorship of the Convention if she had not been convinced that victory was impossible without the suspension of her liberty."

Two occurrences in French history show democracy accepting dictatorial powers because it is necessary, and discarding them as soon as the necessity is past — the rise and fall of Robespierre,

---

[5] The American States, though always jealous of their autonomy, conferred upon the Federal Government, as early as 1787, the exclusive power to declare war and the right to promulgate the laws necessary for the "common defense."

and the rise and fall of Clemenceau. The fall of each occurred when victory was at hand and the danger which the dictatorship had been created to repel seemed safely over. I say "seemed" because France was far from being out of danger on November 11, 1918, and it would have been better for the country if the war government had continued for a while longer.

FORCE, BUT FOR JUSTICE

There is still another side to the argument of the "absolute democrats." They say that when democracy resorts to force it denies its essential character and becomes similar to the very systems which it affects to despise. This is a formalist argument. It forgets that one can inquire on whose behalf force is to be used. To use force on behalf of justice is not the same thing as to use it for aggression. This being so, the democratic system which uses force for justice cannot be assimilated to opposite systems which use force for aggression.

There also seems to be a widespread conception that democracy is a sort of celestial body, aloof and, by definition, scornful of mundane necessities of self-defense. This idea, like the total condemnation of force regardless of the purpose for which it is used, plays straight into the hands of those who wish to use force for aggression. It thus becomes itself an agent of immorality.

At the bottom of these erroneous conceptions of democracy we discern what some would call a Christian idea, namely that it is the fit and necessary lot of the righteous to be weak and to suffer. If the righteous ever becomes strong enough to demand justice, apparently he ceases, for this school of thought, to be righteous. If Socrates had resisted his executioners, for example, he would no longer symbolize righteousness. Carry the argument one step further, and it will be the executioners who, having become the victims, incarnate righteousness. This obviously was the sort of feeling which obsessed many persons in 1918, when a violent nation had at last been compelled to cease from violence and listen to reason.

In such matters, democratic doctrine, like the doctrine of one great school of Catholic thought,[6] considers that the righteous are entitled to "the right of the sword" when they use it in a just cause and without regard for personal profit. Democracy

---

[6] The so-called scholastic doctrine of war, enunciated by Thomas Aquinas. See my "Trahison des Clercs" (edition in English, entitled "The Treason of the Intellectuals," p. 130).

merely remains true to its dogma when it reminds absolute pacifists that there are angels who go armed; and that because Lohengrin draws his sword and strikes the felon down, he is not thereby
any the less Lohengrin and has not become Attila.

Pascal said: "Justice without force is powerless." I should like
to add: "It is essential for democracy that justice shall have
power so long as there are men determined to ignore it." Contrary
to those who pretend that, by very reason of its democratic principle, the democratic State must be deprived of arms, I contend
that by very reason of its democratic principle it must be better
armed than any other State, in order that it may be respected by
States which might otherwise be tempted to ignore justice and
strike across its borders.

HOW ABSOLUTE PACIFISM EVADES THE ISSUE

To be consistent, non-resisters must accept the prospect that
their country may be annihilated. André Gide wonders: "What
would have happened in 1914 if France had offered no resistance
to Germany?" Everyone knows what would have happened.
When he says that France would have been invincible if she had
used only spiritual force against Germany, instead of opposing
force to force, he forgets to inform his fellow-citizens that there
is nothing incompatible between the "invincibility" which he
speaks of and the erasure of their country from the map.[7]

Others go even further and find that non-resistance to evil is
a practical doctrine, the only one which will bring peace to the
world. Tolstoi in his "Intimate Diary" says that when a wall
stands up to blows it causes the aggression to continue, whereas if
it gives in it "absorbs the movement" and causes it to stop. By
analogy, war would be suppressed if people never resisted any
group which was greedy to expand at their expense. Tolstoi omits,
however, to tell us that in "absorbing the movement" the wall
ceases to exist, that is to say, loses its life, which, oddly enough,
it might wish to keep.

NON-INTERVENTION

It is absolutely contrary to the democratic ideal to watch from
a distance, without interfering, while a strong nation crushes a

---

[7] "Journal," p. 1320–1321. The author adds that though Germany "could swallow France, she could not have digested her." There are no grounds for this assertion. Moreover, it is a most cruel experience merely to be swallowed.

weaker one and deprives it of its liberty. Non-intervention may be forced upon democracies because they happen not to be strong enough to give material help to the nation which is being abused and oppressed. But if they are true to themselves, they must deplore their weakness and inertia. To some extent they must feel disgraced, as a European minister felt disgraced when, in answer to a call for help from a small country whose independence was being threatened, he replied: "*Flere possumus, juvare non.*" To set up non-intervention as a principle, to feel almost proud of it, is to undermine democratic morality. Selfishness may be a necessity. It cannot be a democratic dogma.

A democracy which rejects the idea of intervention usually declares that it has adopted this attitude in order to "save peace." The truth is that its passiveness encourages the aggressor. He not only attacks the state which has appealed in vain for help, but some day he will perpetrate an act which even the laggard democracy cannot condone and which therefore causes war a second time. Thus the war of 1914 was brought on by the inertia of the democratic governments which did not care to interfere with Austria in Bosnia-Herzegovina in 1908. A statesman of one of the Central Empires told us in 1920: "It is you who were responsible for the war. You yielded to us for so many years that you led us to think that we could do anything with impunity." It is unnecessary to cite more recent examples.

It is not by accident that those who disturb the peace of the world are almost always the heads of autocratic states. A man who mocks ordinary standards of justice at home sees no reason to act differently abroad. For that reason democracy should be prepared to intervene within a foreign state when its head flagrantly violates the rights of his people. This is what Mr. Herbert Morrison, a member of the British Parliament, meant when he said on November 27, 1939: "We must cling to an ideal of government, whatever its actual form, as something which exists to serve peoples and not to dominate them; and we must remember that this is no mere internal question, since the governments which dominate at home are often the peace-breakers abroad." In the past few years the democracies have usually refrained from this kind of intervention. But their course has not been determined, as some would like to have us believe, out of regard for democratic principle, but simply because democracy has come to worship peace and quiet. So far as I know, there is no principle inscribed in its statutes providing for, or excusing, that form of worship.

OF "DEMOCRATIC ANTI-MILITARISM"

Another aspect of the pacifist democracy which we are here discussing is that democrats often display a sort of systematic hostility to their country's military institutions. They haggle over the number of men there ought to be in the army, the number of years they should serve, how much money should be voted to cover their expenses. They claim that this "anti-militaristic" attitude suits the real spirit of democracy.

In a true democracy the military element should be subordinate to the civilian. Once this principle has been established, we need merely see to it that the military machine is powerful enough to perform its tasks and so to enable the democratic State to survive. One looks in vain through the great declarations of democratic principle, in any time or country, for a single text advocating a weak army. There are plenty of statements about the ideal future world in which this kind of institution will no longer be required. But there is no statement that makes weakness a virtue.[8] Once again we find that an idea which never had any connection with democracy has been added to its concept and has falsified it.

We saw in France, a few years ago, what harm the doctrine of peace at any price can do to democracy. Its devotees maintained that the best defense against a neighbor's greed was disarmament. They even went so far as to advocate a general strike in case war came. Recently in several countries the enemies of democracy exploited the doctrine of peace at any price in order to prevent a war which, though necessary for the salvation of the State, menaced the interests of their particular class. In France men of this sort who for years had berated the working class for their pacifism, suddenly found that same pacifism beautiful and called on labor to oppose the war which lay ahead.

Pacifism, in the sense I have described it here, is a parasite on democracy. It has nothing to do with democratic doctrine. Democracy must repudiate it.

[8] In his "Histoire de Belgique" the great historian, Henri Pirenne, shows how systematic anti-militarism made it impossible for Belgium to avoid war in 1914.

¶ THE GENERAL ASSEMBLY

by John Foster Dulles   (October, 1945)

*Militarily, politically, and psychologically, a new chapter of world history
began in the spring and summer of 1945. Organized German resistance in
Berlin ended on May 8, 1945. Two weeks before that, American and Russian
troops had met on the Elbe River; three days later, they were to meet in
Czechoslovakia. There were mountains of smoke and flame over Hiroshima
and Nagasaki on August 6 and August 9—terrible exclamation points for the
end of a page of history—and the capitulation of the Japanese homeland, without invasion and with 5 million Japanese soldiers still under arms, took place
on August 14. The San Francisco Conference, which put into final form a
plan for a new world organization, had adjourned on June 26, 1945. The
Senate had ratified the treaty establishing U.S. membership in the United
Nations Organization, 89 to 2, on July 28. The period of American neutrality
had ended.*

*John Foster Dulles had been one of the advisers to the U.S. delegation at
San Francisco and had a background of experience as counsel to the American
Commission to Negotiate Peace, 1918–19; American representative at the
Berlin debt conference, 1933; and representative in 1944 of the Republican
Presidential candidate, Thomas E. Dewey, in fixing the basis for a bipartisan
approach to foreign policy. He subsequently became Secretary of State in 1953
under President Eisenhower, a position he held until his death in 1959. In
this article, we can see Dulles' drive to erect bulwarks against threats to America's peace—a course he pursued throughout his career.*

*The analysis of the past had (provisionally at least) been made; its lessons
(it was hoped) learned. The machinery devised at San Francisco made action
to enforce peace against the threat of an aggressor nation depend upon action
by the five great powers—in the first instance by their acting in unanimity,
in the second instance (under Article 51 of the Charter) by "individual or
collective self-defense" outside the Security Council if necessary. It was intended that the peace would be kept by these means, while agencies to change
the conditions that produce wars set to work.*

THE GENERAL ASSEMBLY

By John Foster Dulles

"GOVERNMENT," said Alexander Hamilton, "ought to contain an active principle." Political institutions which advance the welfare of their human constituents achieve an internal state which is cohesive and dynamic and produce an external environment which is sympathetic and receptive. Those are the conditions needed for survival and growth.

The United Nations Organization is charged with positive tasks. That at least gives it a chance to be potent in the world. Whether the chance is realized will depend primarily upon the General Assembly. The rôle of the Security Council is predominantly negative. Its task is to stop the nations from public brawling. But it has no mandate to change the conditions which make brawls likely.

By contrast, the General Assembly, directly or through its Economic and Social Council, is charged: to promote international coöperation in economic, social, cultural, educational and health fields; to assist in the realization of human rights and fundamental freedoms for all, without distinction as to race, sex, language or religion and, in this connection, to establish a Commission on Human Rights; to promote higher standards of living, full employment and conditions of economic and social progress and development; to coördinate the policies and activities of what the Charter calls "specialized agencies," such as the World Bank and the Food and Agriculture Organization; to promote the development and codification of international law; to recommend measures for the peaceful adjustment of any situation likely to impair the general welfare or friendly relations among nations; to deal with colonial trusteeships for non-strategic areas; and, generally, to discuss any matter within the scope of the Charter — thus assuming the rôle of a "town meeting of the world," where public opinion is focused as an effective force.

The foregoing list is not complete, but it is enough to give an impression of the vast range of opportunities opened up to the Assembly. Also, it is enough to make apparent that the Assembly is given a tempting invitation to chase rainbows.

The Assembly will have to pick its way carefully if it is to justify the responsibility which the Charter places upon it. It cannot afford the luxury of dabbling pleasurably in experimentation while looking to the Security Council to keep the peace. The tasks given it are, indeed, the primary means to peace. They must be undertaken with sober realization of such basic facts as these:

The Organization as now set up lacks the political powers usually relied upon to assure civic order. It would, therefore, be reckless to let peace depend upon the political functioning of the Organization.

The Organization's lack of political power is a semi-permanent fact. It is not due to an oversight or incompetence on the part of the authors but to basic conditions which the Charter meritoriously reflects.

Peace, accordingly, will depend primarily upon there being such fellowship among the member nations as will prevent the occurrence of a major war, while advancing the time when the Organization can be made into a more adequate political instrument.

Fellowship based on a war coalition usually disintegrates after the enemy's defeat. The way to prevent this from happening to the United Nations is to continue them in combat against the material and spiritual enemies of human welfare. To organize that combat is the primary responsibility of the General Assembly, and to do it successfully calls for a high order of statesmanship.

II

The political inadequacy of the United Nations Organization is obvious. Any political order which eliminates major violence over a long period of time must depend largely on laws defining, concretely and acceptably, what conduct is admissible and what is not. They need to be changed frequently so as to adapt the basic judgments they express to constantly changing conditions and so as to assure an acceptable balance among members of the society who incline to pull in different directions. The achievement of such a body of laws calls for a lawmaking process. And to enforce them there is required, in addition to the pressure of public opinion, a judicial system and a police force which will act automatically as the law directs.

At San Francisco these political goals could not be realized. The Charter itself does not establish rules of conduct which the Organization is committed to enforce. It does set forth certain general principles; but these are expressed as self-denying ordinances, not as law which the Organization enforces. The Security Council is under no injunction to move against violators. Some consideration was given to a possible prohibition of "aggression." But, as Mr. Eden observed at San Francisco, aggression is a concept without any precise agreed content. Some expansions and contractions of zones of national influence are reprehensible and some may be desirable. It is not easy to find words which would define and prohibit such exploits as the initial acts of Hitler and Hirohito and yet permit the expansion of the U.S.S.R. from the low ebb to which Russia fell under the Tsars and authorize Great Britain to "erase the sore spots in Europe" as now proposed by Professor Laski.

Of course, there are always people who would like to make change in the world illegal. Some are satisfied and selfish, some are morally shocked at the injustices which too often accompany change. That point of view prevailed in 1919, with the result that the Covenant of the League of Nations, by Article 10, went far toward identifying peace and morality with the maintenance of the status quo. Elihu Root, when he saw that proposed Article, said:

> It would be an attempt to preserve for all time unchanged the distribution of power and territory made in accordance with the views and exigencies of the Allies in this present juncture of affairs. It would necessarily be futile. . . . It would not only be futile; it would be mischievous. Change and growth are the law of life, and no generation can impose its will in regard to the growth of nations and the distribution of power, upon succeeding generations.

The point of view thus expressed by Root prevailed at San Francisco. The Conference abstained from seeking to legislate perpetual peace by a single Article sanctifying for all time things as they are. Yet after that deceptively easy way had been rejected, the problem of legislating was seen as immensely difficult. The nations represented at San Francisco had not yet reached the position where they constituted a true community with common judgments about conduct. Also, many of them did not want the establishment of any law which would be superior to their own particular will and conscience. Wisely, then, the Conference did not attempt to write laws for the Organization to enforce. But it recognized that the omission to do this represented a grave inadequacy in the Organization as constituted.

The San Francisco Conference also failed to establish a body to make laws hereafter. There is to be an international court; but courts do not, or at least should not, legislate. The Assembly is directed to encourage the development and codification of international law. But neither it nor the Security Council is given any authority to enact law. The Security Council, although not intended to be a legislating body, might conceivably build up a body of international common law through its reasoned action in dealing with international disputes. In view, however, of the difficulty of the Security Council's taking any action at all, under its voting procedure, it is not likely that an adequate body of law could develop in this way in time to meet the necessities which will face the world.

Obviously, neither the Assembly nor the Security Council was qualified to be a legislating body. The voting procedure in both is so artificial that it could not be relied upon to reflect the predominant will of the world community. In the Assembly, where each state has one vote regardless of size, a small minority of the people in the world could impose its will on the great majority. In the Security Council, a single great state could block action desired by all the others. At San Francisco much was said about the inequity of a big Power like the United States or Soviet Russia having a right of veto. Very little was said about Liberia and Luxembourg, for example, having equal voting power in the Assembly with the United States and Soviet Russia. The fact is, the small powers as well as the big ones are still tenacious of special privileges. So long as that is so, the Organization cannot be politically mature. This was a second grave inadequacy to which the Conference felt it must reconcile itself.

Since the San Francisco Conference was unable either to write rules of conduct into the Charter or to establish a lawmaking process, it could not establish any effective enforcement procedure. Neither courts nor policemen can do much without an adequate body of law behind them. A police force ought to work automatically, as previously instructed by law. With no laws, and with no body to make them, an international force cannot perform in the manner of a police force. No act of violence, however flagrant, will enable the military contingents of the

World Organization to go into action immediately. In every case they must await the decision of the Security Council. The reaching of that decision is a quasi-legislative process, something like passing a special law which will be retroactive. Many political factors will have to be considered and, finally, the five Permanent Member States will have to concur.

In view of this, many persons at San Francisco felt that the Security Council might prove rather impotent so far as concerned its use of force. That was a third grave inadequacy to which the Conference felt it had to reconcile itself.

III

The political inadequacies described above are not of a kind that can be quickly remedied. It is not a matter of rewording the Charter. Underlying conditions caused the Charter to be what it is. Many went to San Francisco hoping for a Charter worded differently from the one which emerged. Few, at the end, would have had it very different from what it is.

The present Charter represents a conscientious and successful effort to create the best world organization which the realities permit. Of course, anyone who is free to disregard realities and to act only in the realm of theory can write a "better" Charter. A reasonably intelligent schoolboy could do that. The task of statesmanship, however, is to relate theory to reality. Political institutions ought to come as close to theoretical perfection as is consonant with their vigorous survival in the existing environment. Orchids may be the perfect flower. But it is a waste of time to plant orchids in Iceland. That is what many peace planners would do.

The merit of the present Charter is not disclosed if one judges it merely as an abstract political document. That, as we have seen, discloses its inadequacies. The merit of the present Charter lies in the fact that its words correspond with the realities. What in the abstract are defects become in reality merits. The Charter was deliberately made to mirror the hopes and fears, the trusts and distrusts, the strength and infirmities of the human environment in which it must live and work.

Never before has such a project been tested on so tough a proving ground. The Holy Alliance was the exclusive handiwork of three rulers and their personal advisers. Its noble words bore no relation to realities. The Covenant of the League of Nations was essentially the work of five or six men. It was adopted after a committee of 20, made up of two representatives from each of five states and one representative of each of ten states, had held 14 meetings. At San Francisco, 12 Committees, each composed of 50 delegates and about 100 advisers and technical assistants, met regularly over a two-month period. Literally hundreds of proposals were considered and every avenue of action was explored. The discussion took place in an atmosphere of freedom and in a spirit of responsibility. There was no compulsion and no veto except that imposed by the good judgment of the delegates.

The result is an honest document. Under present conditions it could not advantageously be made materially different. But some day it ought to be different. The delegates at San Francisco were almost unanimous about that. They gave much thought to how and when the Charter should be revised. Indeed, that was the most debated topic of the Conference. But the most earnest proponents of easy amendment did not want an immediate special Conference to review the Charter. About ten years should elapse, they felt, before a first review of the Charter could usefully be attempted. That was because they realized that what was needed could not be brought about by changing words, but only by changing the conditions which had made the present words inevitable. Such a change of conditions, they saw, would require well-directed efforts over a period of time.

IV

The present war has caused an unprecedented exhaustion, both human and material, and the end has not yet been reached. Even now that Japan has been beaten there may still be an aftermath of disturbances as peoples and régimes seek new equilibriums, internal and external. But the time will probably come when the dominant craving of men everywhere will be for a chance to recuperate and when no important group will tolerate a government whose policies risk a major war. During such a period even an inadequate organization can keep the peace. Exhaustion and fear will be its allies. But, judging by reason and experience, this will be merely an interlude between wars unless the time is used to good advantage.

The San Francisco Conference succeeded in transforming a war alliance into a political association containing the potentialities of growth. As we have seen, however, it was not able to establish an Organization possessing the political powers usually depended on to maintain civic order, because the United Nations are not yet sufficiently aware of their continuing interdependence, sufficiently homogeneous and sufficiently trustful of each other to delegate such powers to a new political organism.

We must not accept that condition as permanent. There are certain risks which only an adequate political institution will be able to eliminate. To seek the increased trust and sense of unity which will make the attainment of a more adequate political instrument possible should therefore be the major goal of the next era. Human nature is still such, however, that unity is achieved easily only through common effort for a common advantage. That is why external perils create coalitions and why those coalitions disintegrate when the common enemy is vanquished. That is why the present unity of the United Nations will vanish unless we find new enemies to fight together.

The great merit of the Charter is that it faces up to this reality. It creates an Organization which has "active principles." It brands intolerance, repression, injustice and economic want as common enemies of tomorrow, just as Nazi Germany and Imperial Japan have been the common enemies of yesterday. It proposes to its members that they stay united to wage war against those evils.

If this new call to battle arouses the enthusiasm of the peoples of the United Nations, and if they commit their best abilities to waging it successfully, the normal trend toward disintegration can be halted and a trend toward a greater sense of unity and greater friendship can be substituted. Thus can be gradually created the store of trust and confidence which must precede any adequate delegation of power to a world organization.

v

It is the General Assembly which will have to plan the campaign of the United Nations against their newly proclaimed enemies. The Charter offers many possible objectives, not all of which can be pursued immediately. The Assembly must make an orderly choice, and it must take into account not merely the relative merits of the goals themselves but the degree to which the pursuit of them will produce the by-products of increased fellowship between the member nations. Various considerations will need to be weighed in this connection.

It is very important, for example, particularly during the first years when the war coalition will tend to disintegrate, that the

Assembly choose projects which are likely to succeed. The possibility of preserving unity between the United Nations will depend above all upon a quick practical demonstration that, by staying together, they can accomplish desired results which otherwise would be impossible. A joint success brings co-workers to a generous appreciation of each other, while a failure leads to recrimination and disunity. Therefore, it is of the utmost importance that the Organization in its early stages should embark on undertakings where success is likely.

It is important, too, that the goals first chosen by the Assembly should include some which will arouse popular interest and backing. Much technical work can usefully be done on an international basis, but the compilation of scientific data on meteorological and hydrographic matters does little to promote the fellowship of peoples. Though such tasks should of course continue to be undertaken, they are no substitute for activities which will develop the enthusiastic loyalty and support of the peoples of many lands and afford a peaceful outlet for their dynamic impulses. The Assembly should seek psychological substitutes for military warfare. It must do some things that will be dramatic.

The Charter recognizes in Article 55 that "conditions of stability and well-being are necessary for peaceful and friendly relations among nations." Economic distress and social maladjustments give evil men the opportunity to gain leadership and to menace the peace of the world. In choosing its objectives, therefore, the Assembly should utilize its grant of authority and act to ameliorate the economic and social conditions which help to breed war.

Future peace depends above all upon accord between the Great Powers. The Charter recognizes this by forbidding the Security Council to take any enforcement measures unless the "Big Five" are in agreement. But while this emphasizes the importance of harmony, it does not assure that harmony will exist. Of course, the Great Powers themselves will primarily determine the character of their relations with each other; but the Assembly can contribute to the accord between them which is necessary if the Security Council is to function. Negatively, it can refrain from using its privileges, notably that of discussion, in a way to exploit and magnify the minor differences which will inevitably arise among the Great Powers. Affirmatively, it can select tasks upon which the Great Powers can readily unite.

Since the smaller nations control the Assembly, there will be a natural tendency for them to organize its social and economic activities so as to benefit themselves at the expense of the larger members. Of course, the strong must help the weak, if only because their self-interest is served by preventing anarchy. But such help, of which UNRRA is an example, should be left to the initiative of the strong powers. The Assembly should consciously sponsor activities which bring the larger powers to like an international way of life and thereby promote harmony between themselves and the small powers. It will succeed in this if it chooses activities of a kind which will be affirmatively advantageous to all.

Other factors which the Assembly should consider in deciding on its initial program could be mentioned. But even the above tests show how hard its choice will be if it is to be successful. To illustrate:

One mandatory task of the General Assembly is to encourage the development and codification of international law. This is of extreme importance, since, as we have seen, lack of law is a principal weakness of the present situation. However, to achieve a body of written law enforceable against states as such is a most difficult project. "The Federalist" said that thinking men would at once dismiss it "as idle and visionary;" and added: "The principle of legislation for sovereign States, supported by military coercion, has never been found effectual. It has rarely been attempted to be employed, but against the weaker members."

There is, however, an alternative to legislation for states, namely, the adoption of laws to operate upon individuals. This avenue of development is being explored today, when considerations of justice have brought the United Nations to postulate the existence of an international law enforceable against individual Germans. The time is thus propitious to begin to frame international law which will not be merely applicable retroactively but which will operate in the future to deter individuals anywhere from wilfully or maliciously plotting or inciting international disorder. Also, once individual duties are made a subject of international law, it becomes logical also to define the international aspects of individual rights. By promoting that development the General Assembly could begin to give practical content to the affirmation by the peoples of the United Nations of their "faith in fundamental human rights, in the dignity and worth of the human person."

If an effort were made to develop international law for individuals rather than for states, then the criteria we have mentioned could largely be met. There would be a good chance of some success. The effort would be dramatic and would awaken popular interest. A cause of war might be curbed. The effort would be one in which the nations, large and small, could be expected ʻto work together in harmony. It was the sponsoring Powers which, at San Francisco, by one of their "four-power amendments," unhesitatingly and enthusiastically determined that a major purpose of the Organization should be to promote and encourage "respect for human rights and fundamental freedoms for all without distinction as to race, sex, language, or religion."

Another task for the General Assembly is the solution of international problems of an economic character. The conditions of trade and finance ought to be such that nations can acquire, on a fair exchange basis, the food, raw materials and other products which do not lie within their own resources and which they need for the maintenance of tolerable standards of living. The Bretton Woods plan for a World Bank and Monetary Fund is an effort to solve this problem primarily through its financial aspects. That approach alone will be inadequate, for neither credit nor monetary arrangements can permanently substitute for a near balance in the exchange of goods and services. The Assembly can undertake a broader and sounder approach. The effort probably would not arouse popular enthusiasm. Also it might frighten, even though needlessly, the more productive countries. Nevertheless, a practical success can be achieved along this line, and it ought to be possible to achieve it on a basis advantageous to all. A success here would do much to eliminate some of the underlying causes of war.

The General Assembly is authorized to promote international coöperation in the field of health. Of course, disease is not in a primary sense a cause of war. Indeed, a cynic might say that to reduce mortality from disease increases the risk of war from population pressures. On the other hand, a successful combat against disease, particularly the epidemics which inspire general dread, can arouse popular interest and give a practical demonstration of the advantages of international action. The Rockefeller Foundation, now in its thirty-third year, works in various fields — health, natural sciences, social sciences and the humanities. Its labors which have produced the most tangible results and have brought it world-wide good will have been those in the field of international health. The Assembly could, with advantage, consider that experience in deciding what lines of effort can be expected to produce a demonstrable success. The field is one where all the Powers could advantageously work together, pooling for peace the achievements of their scientists, as they pooled them in war to produce the atomic bomb.

Such are some of the problems which the Assembly will face in planning its contribution to peace. The San Francisco Conference was, in a sense, the first meeting of the Assembly. It will now approach its concrete tasks with zeal born of a first success and with discretion born of responsibility. The meeting at San Francisco went far to assure a successful transition from the unity of war to a new unity of peace. Trust and confidence, somewhat in suspense during the early days of the Conference, developed strongly toward the end. Hard, competent work resulted in a good start being made. The Conference can be said to have done much to reverse the normal trend toward postwar disintegration.

It cannot be taken for granted, however, that future meetings of the Assembly will be like that of San Francisco. Success there was due above all to the millions of individuals throughout the world who directed upon that Conference the power of their spirit. They put the immediate participants under the strongest possible moral pressure not to fail. Without that constant pressure the Conference might have broken up on any one of several issues, or it might have ended with merely perfunctory results.

The present danger is that the millions who compelled the achievements of San Francisco will now relax, feeling that the battle has been won and the Organization can carry on alone from this point. That would be disastrous. Organizations are incorporeal; they have no will, no mind, no soul. They live only through human beings who implement them. The individuals whose wills and brains and spirits will animate the Assembly of the United Nations will need the same sort of stimulus that made the San Francisco Conference a success. Their task will not be mechanistic. It will be to select, plan, organize and lead great works of human betterment. They can do that successfully only in response to the expressed wishes and demands of their fellows. Thus, in the final analysis, the peoples of the world will decide their own fate.

¶ The Nuremberg Trial: Landmark in Law

by Henry L. Stimson   (January, 1947)

For the first time in history, at Nuremberg, Germany, in 1946, individual citizens of a state were convicted of the crime of planning and waging aggressive war. So great an advance in the field of international law, of course, produced differences of opinion. That the Nazi ringleaders had been brought to account for their crimes was accepted as wise and just by American public opinion generally and by most of the American press. Though some publicists sneered at the "Nuremberg novelty," most laymen saw in the Nuremberg trial welcome evidence that law had at last caught up with the sentiment of the civilized world.

For the most part, however, the controversy as to the justice of the trials was confined to legal experts, and in the main to one count in the indictment—that of crimes against peace. Thoughtful and responsible lawyers noted that, despite the Kellogg-Briand Pact of August 27, 1928, and such other formal documents as the Geneva Protocol of 1924 for the Pacific Settlement of International Disputes, the Resolution of the Eighth Assembly of the League of Nations of 1921, and the Resolution adopted by the twenty-one American Republics at the Sixth Pan-American Conference, held at Havana in 1928, international law included no clear statute that could be cited by the prosecution at Nuremberg. Great popular movements can, after all, be in error, and some lawyers were uncomfortable, doubting not that justice in substance had been done but that the legal procedure had been impeccable.

It was to such doubts as these that Henry L. Stimson, Secretary of War under President Taft, Governor-General of the Philippines under President Coolidge, Secretary of State under President Hoover, Secretary of War under President Franklin D. Roosevelt, one of America's great public servants and a great international lawyer, turned his attention in the following pages, written for the January, 1947, issue of Foreign Affairs. *The issue takes on a renewed importance today, after new war-crimes trials have resulted from atrocities committed in Vietnam. It had been hoped that the Nuremberg trial would have been* sui generis *rather than serve as precedent.*

THE NUREMBERG TRIAL:
LANDMARK IN LAW

By Henry L. Stimson

I N THE confusion and disquiet of the war's first aftermath, there has been at least one great event from which we may properly take hope. The surviving leaders of the Nazi conspiracy against mankind have been indicted, tried, and judged in a proceeding whose magnitude and quality make it a landmark in the history of international law. The great undertaking at Nuremberg can live and grow in meaning, however, only if its principles are rightly understood and accepted. It is therefore disturbing to find that its work is criticized and even challenged as lawless by many who should know better. In the deep conviction that this trial deserves to be known and valued as a long step ahead on the only upward road, I venture to set down my general view of its nature and accomplishment.

The defendants at Nuremberg were leaders of the most highly organized and extensive wickedness in history. It was not a trick of the law which brought them to the bar; it was the "massed angered forces of common humanity." There were three different courses open to us when the Nazi leaders were captured: release, summary punishment, or trial. Release was unthinkable; it would have been taken as an admission that there was here no crime. Summary punishment was widely recommended. It would have satisfied the immediate requirement of the emotions, and in its own roughhewn way it would have been fair enough, for this was precisely the type of justice that the Nazis themselves had so often used. But this fact was in reality the best reason for rejecting such a solution. The whole moral position of the victorious Powers must collapse if their judgments could be enforced only by Nazi methods. Our anger, as righteous anger, must be subject to the law. We therefore took the third course and tried the captive criminals by a judicial proceeding. We gave to the Nazis what they had denied their own opponents — the protection of the Law. The Nuremberg Tribunal was thus in no sense an instrument of vengeance but the reverse. It was, as Mr. Justice Jackson said in opening the case for the prosecution, "one of the most significant tributes that Power has ever paid to Reason."

The function of the law here, as everywhere, has been to insure fair judgment. By preventing abuse and minimizing error, proceedings under law give dignity and method to the ordinary conscience of mankind. For this purpose the law demands three things: that the defendant be charged with a punishable crime; that he have full opportunity for defense; and that he be judged fairly on the evidence by a proper judicial authority. Should it fail to meet any one of these three requirements, a trial would not be justice. Against these standards, therefore, the judgment of Nuremberg must itself be judged.

I. PUNISHABLE CRIMES

In our modern domestic law, a man can be penalized only when he has done something which was authoritatively recognized as punishable when he did it. This is the well-known principle that forbids *ex post facto* law, and it accords entirely with our standards of fair play. A mistaken appeal to this principle has been the cause of much confusion about the Nuremberg trial. It is argued that parts of the Tribunal's Charter, written in 1945, make crimes out of what before were activities beyond the scope of national and international law. Were this an exact statement of the situation we might well be concerned, but it is not. It rests on a misconception of the whole nature of the law of nations. International law is not a body of authoritative codes or statutes; it is the gradual expression, case by case, of the moral judgments of the civilized world. As such, it corresponds precisely to the common law of Anglo-American tradition. We can understand the law of Nuremberg only if we see it for what it is — a great new case in the book of international law, and not a formal enforcement of codified statutes. A look at the charges will show what I mean.

The Charter of the Tribunal recognizes three kinds of crime, all of which were charged in the indictment: crimes against peace, war crimes, and crimes against humanity. There was a fourth charge, of conspiracy to commit one or all of these crimes. To me personally this fourth charge is the most realistic of them all, for the Nazi crime is in the end indivisible. Each of the myriad transgressions was an interlocking part of the whole gigantic barbarity. But basically it is the first three that we must consider. The fourth is built on them.

Of the three charges, only one has been seriously criticized. War crimes have not greatly concerned the Tribunal's critics; these are offenses well understood and long generally recognized in the law or rules of war. The charge of crimes against humanity has not aroused much comment in this country, perhaps because this part of the indictment was not of central concern to the American prosecutor. The Tribunal's findings on this charge are significant, but not such as to raise much question of their legal validity, so I defer my comment to a later section of this article.

There remains the charge of crimes against peace, which has been the chief target of most of the honest critics of Nuremberg. It is under this charge that a penalty has been asked, for the first time, against the individual leaders in a war of aggression. It is this that well-intentioned critics have called "*ex post facto* law."

It is clear that until quite recently any legal judgment against a war-maker would have been absurd. Throughout the centuries, until after World War I, the choice between war and peace remained entirely in the hands of each sovereign state, and neither the law nor the ordinary conscience of humanity ventured to deny that right. The concept of just and unjust wars is of course as old at least as Plato. But in the anarchy of individual sovereignties, the right to fight was denied to no people and the right to start a fight was denied to no ruler. For the loser in a war, punishment was certain. But this was not a matter of law; it was simply a matter of course. At the best it was like the early law of the blood feud, in which the punishment of a murderer was the responsibility of the victim's family alone and not of the whole community. Even in 1914 the German violation of Belgian neutrality was regarded as a matter for action only by those nations directly concerned in the Treaties of 1839. So far indeed was this sovereign right of war-making accepted that it was frequently extended to include the barbarous notion that a sovereign ruler is not subject to the law.

In the face of this acceptance of war as a proper instrument of sovereign national policy, the only field for the early development of international law lay in restricting so far as possible the brutalities of warfare. In obedience to age-long instincts of chivalry and magnanimity, there were gradually developed international standards for the conduct of war. Civilians and neutrals were given protecting rights and privileges, the treatment of prisoners was prescribed, and certain weapons were outlawed. It is these long established and universally accepted standards, most of them formally included in the internal law of Germany, that are covered by the charge of war crimes in the Nuremberg indictment.

The attempt to moderate the excesses of war without controlling war itself was doomed to failure by the extraordinary scientific and industrial developments of the nineteenth and twentieth centuries. By 1914 the world had been intertwined into a single unit and weapons had been so far developed that a major war could shake the whole structure of civilization. No rules of warfare were sufficient to limit the vast new destructive powers of belligerents, and the First World War made it clear that old notions must be abandoned; the world must attack the problem at its root. Thus after 1918 repeated efforts were made to eliminate aggressive war as a legal national undertaking. These efforts reached their climax in the Kellogg-Briand Pact of 1928, in which 63 nations, including Germany, Japan and Italy, renounced aggressive warfare. This pact was not an isolated incident of the postwar era. During that period the whole world was at one in its opinion of aggressive war. In repeated resolutions in the League of Nations and elsewhere, aggression was roundly denounced as criminal. In the judgment of the peoples of the world the once proud title of "conqueror" was replaced by the criminal epithet "aggressor."

The progress made from 1918 to 1931 was halting and incomplete, but its direction was clear; the mandate for peace was overwhelming. Most tragically, the peoples who had renounced war were not sufficiently alert to their danger when in the following years the ruling groups of three great nations, in wanton denial of every principle of peace and civilization, launched a conspiracy against the rest of the world. Thus it happened that in the ten years which began with the invasion of Manchuria the principles of the Kellogg Pact were steadily under attack, and only as the danger came slowly home to each one of them individually did the peace-loving nations take action against aggression. In early 1945, as it became apparent that the long delayed victory was at hand, the question posed itself directly: Has there been a war of aggression and are its leaders punishable? There were many then, as there are some now, who argued that there was no law for this offense, and they found their justification in the feebleness and acquiescence of other nations in the early aggression of the Axis. Other counsels prevailed, however, and by the Charter of the Nuremberg Tribunal the responsible leaders of aggressive war were subjected to trial and conviction on the charge of crimes against peace.

Here we come to the heart of the matter. Able lawyers and honest men have cried out that this aggressive war was not a crime. They have argued that the Nuremberg defendants were not properly forewarned when they made war that what they did was criminal.

Now in one sense the concept of *ex post facto* law is a strange one to apply here, because this concept relates to a state of mind on the part of the defendants that in this case was wholly absent. That concept is based on the assumption that if the defendant had known that the proposed act was criminal he would have refrained from committing it. Nothing in the attitude of the Nazi leaders corresponds to this assumption; their minds were wholly untroubled by the question of their guilt or innocence. Not in their aggression only but in their whole philosophy, they excluded the very concept of law. They deliberately put themselves below such a concept. To international law — as to the law of Germany — they paid only such respect as they found politic, and in the end they had smashed its every rule. Their attitude toward aggressive war was exactly like their attitude toward murder — both were useful instruments in a great design. It is therefore impossible to get any light on the validity of this charge of aggressive war by inspecting the Nazi mind. We must study rather the minds of the rest of the world, which is at once a less revolting and a more fruitful labor.

What did the rest of us think about aggressive war at the time of the Nazi attacks? This question is complex, but to that part of it which affects the legality of the Nuremberg trial we can give a simple answer. That we considered aggressive war wicked is clear; that we considered the leaders of an aggressive war wicked is equally clear. These opinions, in large part formally embodied in the Kellogg Pact, are the basis for the law of Nuremberg. With the detailed reasoning by which the prosecution has supported the law set forth in the Charter of the International Military Tribunal, we cannot here concern ourselves. The proposition sustained by the Tribunal is simple: if a man plans aggression when aggression has been formally renounced by his nation, he is a criminal. Those who are concerned with the law of this proposition cannot do better than to read the pertinent passages in the opening address of Mr. Justice Jackson, the closing address of Sir Hartley Shawcross, and the opinion of the Tribunal itself.

What really troubles the critics of Nuremberg is that they see no evidence that before 1945 we considered the capture and conviction of such aggressors to be our legal duty. In this view they are in the main correct, but it is vitally important to remember that a legal right is not lost merely because temporarily it is not used. What happened before World War II was that we lacked the courage to enforce the authoritative decision of the international world. We agreed with the Kellogg Pact that aggressive war must end. We renounced it, and we condemned those who might use it. But it was a moral condemnation only. We thus did not reach the second half of the question: What will you do to an aggressor when you catch him? If we *had* reached it, we should easily have found the right answer. But that answer escaped us, for it implied a duty to catch the criminal, and such a chase meant war. It was the Nazi confidence that we would never chase and catch them, and not a misunderstanding of our opinion of them, that led them to commit their crimes. Our offense was thus that of the man who passed by on the other side. That we have finally recognized our negligence and named the criminals for what they are is a piece of righteousness too long delayed by fear.

We did not ask ourselves, in 1939 or 1940, or even in 1941, what punishment, if any, Hitler and his chief assistants deserved. We asked simply two questions: How do we avoid war, and how do we keep this wickedness from overwhelming us? These seemed larger questions to us than the guilt or innocence of individuals. In the end we found an answer to the second question, but none to the first. The crime of the Nazis, against *us*, lay in this very fact: that their making of aggressive war made peace here impossible. We have now seen again, in hard and deadly terms, what had been proved in 1917 — that "peace is indivisible." The man who makes aggressive war at all makes war against mankind. That is an exact, not a rhetorical, description of the crime of aggressive war.

Thus the Second World War brought it home to us that our repugnance to aggressive war was incomplete without a judgment of its leaders. What we had called a crime demanded punishment; we must bring our law in balance with the universal moral judgment of mankind. The wickedness of aggression must be punished by a trial and judgment. This is what has been done at Nuremberg.

Now this is a new judicial process, but it is not *ex post facto* law. It is the enforcement of a moral judgment which dates back a generation. It is a growth in the application of law that any student of our common law should recognize as natural and proper, for it is in just this manner that the common law grew up. There was, somewhere in our distant past, a first case of murder, a first case where the tribe replaced the victim's family as judge of the offender. The tribe had learned that the deliberate and malicious killing of any human being was, and must be treated as, an offense against the whole community. The analogy is exact. All case law grows by new decisions, and where those new decisions match the conscience of the community, they are law as truly as the law of murder. They do not become *ex post facto* law merely because until the first decision and punishment comes, a man's only warning that he offends is in the general sense and feeling of his fellow men.

The charge of aggressive war is unsound, therefore, only if the community of nations did not believe in 1939 that aggressive war was an offense. Merely to make such a suggestion, however, is to discard it. Aggression is an offense, and we all know it; we have known it for a generation. It is an offense so deep and heinous that we cannot endure its repetition.

The law made effective by the trial at Nuremberg is righteous law long overdue. It is in just such cases as this one that the law becomes more nearly what Mr. Justice Holmes called it: "the witness and external deposit of our moral life."

With the Judgment of Nuremberg we at last reach to the very core of international strife, and we set a penalty not merely for war crimes, but for the very act of war itself, except in self-defense. If a man will argue that this is bad law, untrue to our ideals, I will listen. But I feel only pity for the casuist who would dismiss the Nazi leaders because "they were not warned it was a crime." They were warned, and they sneered contempt. Our shame is that their contempt was so nearly justified, not that we have in the end made good our warning.

II. FAIR TRIAL

Next after its assertion of the criminality of aggressive war, the triumph of Nuremberg rests in the manner and degree to which it has discharged with honor the true functions of a legal instrument. The crimes charged were punishable as we have seen — so clearly punishable that the only important suggested alternative to a trial was summary execution of the accused. It is in its pursuit of a different course that the Nuremberg Tribunal has demonstrated at once the dignity and the value of the law, and students of law everywhere will find inspiration and enlightenment in close study of its work. In its skilful development of a procedure satisfying every traditional and material safeguard of the varying legal forms of the prosecuting nations, it represents a signal success in the field of international negotiation, and in its rigid fidelity to the fundamental principles of fair play it has insured the lasting value of its work.

In their insistence on fairness to the defendants, the Charter and the Tribunal leaned over backwards. Each defendant was allowed to testify for himself, a right denied by Continental law. At the conclusion of the trial, each defendant was allowed to address the Tribunal, at great length, a right denied by Anglo-American law. The difference between Continental and Anglo-American law was thus adjusted by allowing to the defendant his rights under both. Counsel for the defendants were leading German lawyers and professors from the German universities, some of them ardent and unrepentant Nazis. Counsel were paid, fed, sheltered and transported at the expense of the Allies, and were furnished offices and secretarial help. The defense had full access to all documents. Every attempt was made to produce desired witnesses when the Tribunal believed that they had any relevant evidence to offer. In the summation of the trial the defense had 20 days and the prosecution three, and the defense case as a whole occupied considerably more time than the prosecution.

The record of the Nuremberg trial thus becomes one of the foundation stones of the peace. Under the most rigid safeguards of jurisprudence, subject to challenge, denial and disproof by men on trial for their lives and assisted by counsel of their own choosing, the great conspiracy has been unmasked. In documents unchallenged by the defense and often in the words of the defendants themselves, there is recorded the whole black history of murder, enslavement and aggression. This record, so established, will stand as a demonstration, on a wholly new level of validity and strength, of the true character of the Nazi régime. And this is so not in spite of our insistence upon law, but because of it.

In this connection it is worth noting that the trial has totally exploded many of the strange notions that seem to lurk in the minds of some who have expressed their doubts about Nuremberg. Some of the doubters are not basically concerned with "*ex post facto* law" or with "vengeance." Their real trouble is that they did not think the Nazis could be proved guilty. To these gentlemen I earnestly commend a reading of the record. If after reading it they do not think there was in fact aggressive war, in its most naked form, then I shall be constrained to believe that they do not think any such thing exists or can exist.

III. FAIR JUDGMENT

Not having made a study of the evidence presented in the case with special reference to each defendant, I am not qualified to pass judgment on the verdicts and sentences of the Tribunal against individuals and criminal groups. I have, however, heard no claim that these sentences were too severe. The Tribunal's findings as to the law are on the whole encouraging. The charge of aggressive war was accepted and ably explained. The charge of war crimes was sustained almost without comment. The charge of crimes against humanity was limited by the Tribunal to include only activities pursued in connection with the crime of war. The Tribunal eliminated from its jurisdiction the question of the criminal accountability of those responsible for wholesale persecution before the outbreak of the war in 1939. With this decision I do not here venture to quarrel, but its effect appears to me to involve a reduction of the meaning of crimes against humanity to a point where they become practically synonymous with war crimes.

If there is a weakness in the Tribunal's findings, I believe it lies in its very limited construction of the legal concept of conspiracy. That only eight of the 22 defendants should have been found guilty on the count of conspiracy to commit the various crimes involved in the indictment seems to me surprising. I believe that the Tribunal would have been justified in a broader construction of the law of conspiracy, and under such a construction it might well have found a different verdict in a case like that of Schacht.

In this first great international trial, however, it is perhaps as well that the Tribunal has very rigidly interpreted both the law and the evidence. In this connection we may observe that only in the case of Rudolf Hess, sentenced to life imprisonment, does the punishment of any of the defendants depend solely on the count of aggressive war. All of those who have been hanged were convicted of war crimes or crimes against humanity, and all but one were convicted of both. Certainly, then, the charge of aggressive war has not been established in international law at the expense of any innocent lives.

The judgment of the Tribunal is thus, in its findings of guilt, beyond challenge. We may regret that some of the charges were not regarded as proven and some of the defendants not found clearly guilty. But we may take pride in the restraint of a tribunal which has so clearly insisted upon certain proof of guilt. It is far better that a Schacht should go free than that a judge should compromise his conscience.

IV. THE MEANING OF NUREMBERG

A single landmark of justice and honor does not make a world of peace. The Nazi leaders are not the only ones who have renounced and denied the principles of western civilization. They are unique only in the degree and violence of their offenses. In every nation which acquiesced even for a time in their offense, there were offenders. There have been still more culpable offenders in nations which joined before or after in the brutal business of aggression. If we claimed for Nuremberg that it was final justice, or that only these criminals were guilty, we might well be criticized as being swayed by vengeance and not justice. But this is not the claim. The American prosecutor has explicitly stated that he looks uneasily and with great regret upon certain brutalities that have occurred since the ending of the war. He speaks for us all when he says that there has been enough bloodletting in Europe. But the sins of others do not make the Nazi leaders less guilty, and the importance of Nuremberg lies not in any claim that by itself it clears the board, but rather in the pattern it has set. The four nations prosecuting, and the 19 others subscribing to the Charter of the International Military Tribunal, have firmly bound themselves to the principle that aggressive war is a personal and punishable crime.

It is this principle upon which we must henceforth rely for our legal protection against the horrors of war. We must never forget that under modern conditions of life, science and technology, all war has become greatly brutalized, and that no one who joins in it, even in self-defense, can escape becoming also in a measure brutalized. Modern war cannot be limited in its destructive methods and in the inevitable debasement of all participants. A fair scrutiny of the last two World Wars makes clear the steady intensification in the inhumanity of the weapons and methods employed by both the aggressors and the victors. In order to defeat Japanese aggression, we were forced, as Admiral Nimitz has stated, to employ a technique of unrestricted submarine warfare not unlike that which 25 years ago was the proximate cause of our entry into World War I. In the use of strategic air power, the Allies took the lives of hundreds of thousands of civilians in Germany, and in Japan the destruction of civilian life wreaked by our B-29s, even before the final blow of the atomic bombs, was at least proportionately great. It is true that our use of this destructive power, particularly of the atomic bomb, was for the purpose of winning a quick victory over aggressors, so as to minimize the loss of life, not only of our troops but of the civilian populations of our enemies as well, and that this purpose in the case of Japan was clearly effected. But even so, we as well as our enemies have contributed to the proof that the central moral problem is war and not its methods, and that a continuance of war will in all probability end with the destruction of our civilization.

International law is still limited by international politics, and we must not pretend that either can live and grow without the other. But in the judgment of Nuremberg there is affirmed the central principle of peace — that the man who makes or plans to make aggressive war is a criminal. A standard has been raised to which Americans, at least, must repair; for it is only as this standard is accepted, supported and enforced that we can move onward to a world of law and peace.

¶ THE SOURCES OF SOVIET CONDUCT
by X (George F. Kennan)   (July, 1947)

The pseudonymous author of this famous article was later identified as the Soviet expert George F. Kennan, who became U.S. Ambassador to Russia in the early 1950's. The article was at once widely recognized as being of quite exceptional interest, both as an analysis of Russian policy and as a statement of the attitude the United States would be wise to adopt in consequence. In view of the apparently remorseless division of "One World" into a "Western" half and a communist half, and the awesome dangers such a development brought in its train, the problems here considered were, perforce, the major concern of every foreign office. This concern was and is shared by the public, as is indicated by the extent to which the article has been used in classrooms and reprinted over the years in books, newspapers, and periodicals, both in the United States and abroad. The term "containment," which originated here, has become common parlance in discussing the cold war, for political analyst and layman alike. Although much has changed in twenty-five years—the situation in the Soviet Union as well as Kennan's views—this article retains its importance for the strong formative influence it exerted on American foreign policy for nearly two decades.

THE SOURCES OF SOVIET CONDUCT

By X

THE political personality of Soviet power as we know it to-day is the product of ideology and circumstances: ideology inherited by the present Soviet leaders from the movement in which they had their political origin, and circumstances of the power which they now have exercised for nearly three decades in Russia. There can be few tasks of psychological analysis more difficult than to try to trace the interaction of these two forces and the relative rôle of each in the determination of official Soviet conduct. Yet the attempt must be made if that conduct is to be understood and effectively countered.

It is difficult to summarize the set of ideological concepts with which the Soviet leaders came into power. Marxian ideology, in its Russian-Communist projection, has always been in process of subtle evolution. The materials on which it bases itself are extensive and complex. But the outstanding features of Communist thought as it existed in 1916 may perhaps be summarized as follows: (a) that the central factor in the life of man, the factor which determines the character of public life and the "physiognomy of society," is the system by which material goods are produced and exchanged; (b) that the capitalist system of production is a nefarious one which inevitably leads to the exploitation of the working class by the capital-owning class and is incapable of developing adequately the economic resources of society or of distributing fairly the material goods produced by human labor; (c) that capitalism contains the seeds of its own destruction and must, in view of the inability of the capital-owning class to adjust itself to economic change, result eventually and inescapably in a revolutionary transfer of power to the working class; and (d) that imperialism, the final phase of capitalism, leads directly to war and revolution.

The rest may be outlined in Lenin's own words: "Unevenness of economic and political development is the inflexible law of capitalism. It follows from this that the victory of Socialism may come originally in a few capitalist countries or even in a single capitalist country. The victorious proletariat of that country, having expropriated the capitalists and having organized Socialist production at home, would rise against the remaining capitalist world, drawing to itself in the process the oppressed classes of other countries."[1] It must be noted that there was no assumption that capitalism would perish without proletarian revolution. A final push was needed from a revolutionary proletariat movement in order to tip over the tottering structure. But it was regarded as inevitable that sooner or later that push be given.

For 50 years prior to the outbreak of the Revolution, this pattern of thought had exercised great fascination for the members of the Russian revolutionary movement. Frustrated, discontented, hopeless of finding self-expression — or too impatient to seek it — in the confining limits of the Tsarist political system, yet lacking wide popular support for their choice of bloody revolution as a means of social betterment, these revolutionists found in Marxist theory a highly convenient rationalization for their own instinctive desires. It afforded pseudo-scientific justification for their impatience, for their categoric denial of all value in the Tsarist system, for their yearning for power and revenge and for their inclination to cut corners in the pursuit of it. It is therefore no wonder that they had come to believe implicitly in the truth and soundness of the Marxian-Leninist teachings, so congenial to their own impulses and emotions. Their sincerity need not be impugned. This is a phenomenon as old as human nature itself. It has never been more aptly described than by Edward Gibbon, who wrote in "The Decline and Fall of the Roman Empire": "From enthusiasm to imposture the step is perilous and slippery; the demon of Socrates affords a memorable instance how a wise man may deceive himself, how a good man may deceive others, how the conscience may slumber in a mixed and middle state between self-illusion and voluntary fraud." And it was with this set of conceptions that the members of the Bolshevik Party entered into power.

Now it must be noted that through all the years of preparation for revolution, the attention of these men, as indeed of Marx himself, had been centered less on the future form which Socialism [2] would take than on the necessary overthrow of rival power which, in their view, had to precede the introduction of Socialism. Their views, therefore, on the positive program to be put into

[1] "Concerning the Slogans of the United States of Europe," August 1915. Official Soviet edition of Lenin's works.

[2] Here and elsewhere in this paper "Socialism" refers to Marxist or Leninist Communism, no to liberal Socialism of the Second International variety.

effect, once power was attained, were for the most part nebulous, visionary and impractical. Beyond the nationalization of industry and the expropriation of large private capital holdings there was no agreed program. The treatment of the peasantry, which according to the Marxist formulation was not of the proletariat, had always been a vague spot in the pattern of Communist thought; and it remained an object of controversy and vacillation for the first ten years of Communist power.

The circumstances of the immediate post-revolution period — the existence in Russia of civil war and foreign intervention, together with the obvious fact that the Communists represented only a tiny minority of the Russian people — made the establishment of dictatorial power a necessity. The experiment with "war Communism" and the abrupt attempt to eliminate private production and trade had unfortunate economic consequences and caused further bitterness against the new revolutionary régime. While the temporary relaxation of the effort to communize Russia, represented by the New Economic Policy, alleviated some of this economic distress and thereby served its purpose, it also made it evident that the "capitalistic sector of society" was still prepared to profit at once from any relaxation of governmental pressure, and would, if permitted to continue to exist, always constitute a powerful opposing element to the Soviet régime and a serious rival for influence in the country. Somewhat the same situation prevailed with respect to the individual peasant who, in his own small way, was also a private producer.

Lenin, had he lived, might have proved a great enough man to reconcile these conflicting forces to the ultimate benefit of Russian society, though this is questionable. But be that as it may, Stalin, and those whom he led in the struggle for succession to Lenin's position of leadership, were not the men to tolerate rival political forces in the sphere of power which they coveted. Their sense of insecurity was too great. Their particular brand of fanaticism, unmodified by any of the Anglo-Saxon traditions of compromise, was too fierce and too jealous to envisage any permanent sharing of power. From the Russian-Asiatic world out of which they had emerged they carried with them a skepticism as to the possibilities of permanent and peaceful coexistence of rival forces. Easily persuaded of their own doctrinaire "rightness," they insisted on the submission or destruction of all competing power. Outside of the Communist Party, Russian society was to have no rigidity. There were to be no forms of collective human activity or association which would not be dominated by the Party. No other force in Russian society was to be permitted to achieve vitality or integrity. Only the Party was to have structure. All else was to be an amorphous mass.

And within the Party the same principle was to apply. The mass of Party members might go through the motions of election, deliberation, decision and action; but in these motions they were to be animated not by their own individual wills but by the awesome breath of the Party leadership and the overbrooding presence of "the word."

Let it be stressed again that subjectively these men probably did not seek absolutism for its own sake. They doubtless believed — and found it easy to believe — that they alone knew what was good for society and that they would accomplish that good once their power was secure and unchallengeable. But in seeking that security of their own rule they were prepared to recognize no restrictions, either of God or man, on the character of their methods. And until such time as that security might be achieved, they placed far down on their scale of operational priorities the comforts and happiness of the peoples entrusted to their care.

Now the outstanding circumstance concerning the Soviet régime is that down to the present day this process of political consolidation has never been completed and the men in the Kremlin have continued to be predominantly absorbed with the struggle to secure and make absolute the power which they seized in November 1917. They have endeavored to secure it primarily against forces at home, within Soviet society itself. But they have also endeavored to secure it against the outside world. For ideology, as we have seen, taught them that the outside world was hostile and that it was their duty eventually to overthrow the political forces beyond their borders. The powerful hands of Russian history and tradition reached up to sustain them in this feeling. Finally, their own aggressive intransigence with respect to the outside world began to find its own reaction; and they were soon forced, to use another Gibbonesque phrase, "to chastise the contumacy" which they themselves had provoked. It is an undeniable privilege of every man to prove himself right in the thesis that the world is his enemy; for if he reiterates it frequently enough and makes it the background of his conduct he is bound eventually to be right.

Now it lies in the nature of the mental world of the Soviet leaders, as well as in the character of their ideology, that no opposition to them can be officially recognized as having any merit or justification whatsoever. Such opposition can flow, in theory, only from the hostile and incorrigible forces of dying capitalism. As long as remnants of capitalism were officially recognized as existing in Russia, it was possible to place on them, as an internal element, part of the blame for the maintenance of a dictatorial form of society. But as these remnants were liquidated, little by little, this justification fell away; and when it was indicated officially that they had been finally destroyed, it disappeared altogether. And this fact created one of the most basic of the compulsions which came to act upon the Soviet régime: since capitalism no longer existed in Russia and since it could not be admitted that there could be serious or widespread opposition to the Kremlin springing spontaneously from the liberated masses under its authority, it became necessary to justify the retention of the dictatorship by stressing the menace of capitalism abroad.

This began at an early date. In 1924 Stalin specifically defended the retention of the "organs of suppression," meaning, among others, the army and the secret police, on the ground that "as long as there is a capitalist encirclement there will be danger of intervention with all the consequences that flow from that danger." In accordance with that theory, and from that time on, all internal opposition forces in Russia have consistently been portrayed as the agents of foreign forces of reaction antagonistic to Soviet power.

By the same token, tremendous emphasis has been placed on the original Communist thesis of a basic antagonism between the capitalist and Socialist worlds. It is clear, from many indications, that this emphasis is not founded in reality. The real facts concerning it have been confused by the existence abroad of genuine resentment provoked by Soviet philosophy and tactics and occasionally by the existence of great centers of military power, notably the Nazi régime in Germany and the Japanese Government of the late 1930's, which did indeed have aggressive designs against the Soviet Union. But there is ample evidence that the stress laid in Moscow on the menace confronting Soviet society from the world outside its borders is founded not in the realities of foreign antagonism but in the necessity of explaining away the maintenance of dictatorial authority at home.

Now the maintenance of this pattern of Soviet power, namely, the pursuit of unlimited authority domestically, accompanied by the cultivation of the semi-myth of implacable foreign hostility, has gone far to shape the actual machinery of Soviet power as we know it today. Internal organs of administration which did not serve this purpose withered on the vine. Organs which did serve this purpose became vastly swollen. The security of Soviet power came to rest on the iron discipline of the Party, on the severity and ubiquity of the secret police, and on the uncompromising economic monopolism of the state. The "organs of suppression," in which the Soviet leaders had sought security from rival forces, became in large measure the masters of those whom they were designed to serve. Today the major part of the structure of Soviet power is committed to the perfection of the dictatorship and to the maintenance of the concept of Russia as in a state of siege, with the enemy lowering beyond the walls. And the millions of human beings who form that part of the structure of power must defend at all costs this concept of Russia's position, for without it they are themselves superfluous.

As things stand today, the rulers can no longer dream of parting with these organs of suppression. The quest for absolute power, pursued now for nearly three decades with a ruthlessness unparalleled (in scope at least) in modern times, has again produced internally, as it did externally, its own reaction. The excesses of the police apparatus have fanned the potential opposition to the régime into something far greater and more dangerous than it could have been before those excesses began.

But least of all can the rulers dispense with the fiction by which the maintenance of dictatorial power has been defended. For this fiction has been canonized in Soviet philosophy by the excesses already committed in its name; and it is now anchored in the Soviet structure of thought by bonds far greater than those of mere ideology.

II

So much for the historical background. What does it spell in terms of the political personality of Soviet power as we know it today?

Of the original ideology, nothing has been officially junked. Belief is maintained in the basic badness of capitalism, in the inevitability of its destruction, in the obligation of the proletariat to assist in that destruction and to take power into its own hands. But stress has come to be laid primarily on those concepts which relate most specifically to the Soviet régime itself: to its position as the sole truly Socialist régime in a dark and misguided world, and to the relationships of power within it.

The first of these concepts is that of the innate antagonism between capitalism and Socialism. We have seen how deeply that concept has become imbedded in foundations of Soviet power. It has profound implications for Russia's conduct as a member of international society. It means that there can never be on Moscow's side any sincere assumption of a community of aims between the Soviet Union and powers which are regarded as capitalist. It must invariably be assumed in Moscow that the aims of the capitalist world are antagonistic to the Soviet régime, and therefore to the interests of the peoples it controls. If the Soviet Government occasionally sets its signature to documents which would indicate the contrary, this is to be regarded as a tactical manœuvre permissible in dealing with the enemy (who is without honor) and should be taken in the spirit of *caveat emptor*. Basically, the antagonism remains. It is postulated. And from it flow many of the phenomena which we find disturbing in the Kremlin's conduct of foreign policy: the secretiveness, the lack of frankness, the duplicity, the wary suspiciousness, and the basic unfriendliness of purpose. These phenomena are there to stay, for the foreseeable future. There can be variations of degree and of emphasis. When there is something the Russians want from us, one or the other of these features of their policy may be thrust temporarily into the background; and when that happens there will always be Americans who will leap forward with gleeful announcements that "the Russians have changed," and some who will even try to take credit for having brought about such "changes." But we should not be misled by tactical manœuvres. These characteristics of Soviet policy, like the postulate from which they flow, are basic to the internal nature of Soviet power, and will be with us, whether in the foreground or the background, until the internal nature of Soviet power is changed.

This means that we are going to continue for a long time to find the Russians difficult to deal with. It does not mean that they should be considered as embarked upon a do-or-die program to overthrow our society by a given date. The theory of the inevitability of the eventual fall of capitalism has the fortunate connotation that there is no hurry about it. The forces of progress can take their time in preparing the final *coup de grâce*. Meanwhile, what is vital is that the "Socialist fatherland" — that oasis of power which has been already won for Socialism in the person of the Soviet Union — should be cherished and defended by all good Communists at home and abroad, its fortunes promoted, its enemies badgered and confounded. The promotion of premature, "adventuristic" revolutionary projects abroad which might embarrass Soviet power in any way would be an inexcusable, even a counter-revolutionary act. The cause of Socialism is the support and promotion of Soviet power, as defined in Moscow.

This brings us to the second of the concepts important to contemporary Soviet outlook. That is the infallibility of the Kremlin. The Soviet concept of power, which permits no focal points of organization outside the Party itself, requires that the Party leadership remain in theory the sole repository of truth. For if truth were to be found elsewhere, there would be justification for its expression in organized activity. But it is precisely that which the Kremlin cannot and will not permit.

The leadership of the Communist Party is therefore always right, and has been always right ever since in 1929 Stalin formalized his personal power by announcing that decisions of the Politburo were being taken unanimously.

On the principle of infallibility there rests the iron discipline of the Communist Party. In fact, the two concepts are mutually self-supporting. Perfect discipline requires recognition of infallibility. Infallibility requires the observance of discipline. And the two together go far to determine the behaviorism of the entire Soviet apparatus of power. But their effect cannot be understood unless a third factor be taken into account: namely, the fact that the leadership is at liberty to put forward for tactical purposes any particular thesis which it finds useful to the cause at any particular moment and to require the faithful and unquestioning acceptance of that thesis by the members of the movement as a whole. This means that truth is not a constant but is actually created, for all intents and purposes, by the Soviet leaders themselves. It may vary from week to week, from month to month. It is nothing absolute and immutable — nothing which flows from objective reality. It is only the most recent manifestation of the wisdom of those in whom the ultimate wisdom is supposed to reside, because they represent the logic of history.

The accumulative effect of these factors is to give to the whole subordinate apparatus of Soviet power an unshakeable stubbornness and steadfastness in its orientation. This orientation can be changed at will by the Kremlin but by no other power. Once a given party line has been laid down on a given issue of current policy, the whole Soviet governmental machine, including the mechanism of diplomacy, moves inexorably along the prescribed path, like a persistent toy automobile wound up and headed in a given direction, stopping only when it meets with some unanswerable force. The individuals who are the components of this machine are unamenable to argument or reason which comes to them from outside sources. Their whole training has taught them to mistrust and discount the glib persuasiveness of the outside world. Like the white dog before the phonograph, they hear only the "master's voice." And if they are to be called off from the purposes last dictated to them, it is the master who must call them off. Thus the foreign representative cannot hope that his words will make any impression on them. The most that he can hope is that they will be transmitted to those at the top, who are capable of changing the party line. But even those are not likely to be swayed by any normal logic in the words of the bourgeois representative. Since there can be no appeal to common purposes, there can be no appeal to common mental approaches. For this reason, facts speak louder than words to the ears of the Kremlin; and words carry the greatest weight when they have the ring of reflecting, or being backed up by, facts of unchallengeable validity.

But we have seen that the Kremlin is under no ideological compulsion to accomplish its purposes in a hurry. Like the Church, it is dealing in ideological concepts which are of long-term validity, and it can afford to be patient. It has no right to risk the existing achievements of the revolution for the sake of vain baubles of the future. The very teachings of Lenin himself require great caution and flexibility in the pursuit of Communist purposes. Again, these precepts are fortified by the lessons of Russian history: of centuries of obscure battles between nomadic forces over the stretches of a vast unfortified plain. Here caution, circumspection, flexibility and deception are the valuable qualities; and their value finds natural appreciation in the Russian or the oriental mind. Thus the Kremlin has no compunction about retreating in the face of superior force. And being under the compulsion of no timetable, it does not get panicky under the necessity for such retreat. Its political action is a fluid stream which moves constantly, wherever it is permitted to move, toward a given goal. Its main concern is to make sure that it has filled every nook and cranny available to it in the basin of world power. But if it finds unassailable barriers in its path, it accepts these philosophically and accommodates itself to them. The main thing is that there should always be pressure, unceasing constant pressure, toward the desired goal. There is no trace of any feeling in Soviet psychology that that goal must be reached at any given time.

These considerations make Soviet diplomacy at once easier and more difficult to deal with than the diplomacy of individual aggressive leaders like Napoleon and Hitler. On the one hand it is more sensitive to contrary force, more ready to yield on individual sectors of the diplomatic front when that force is felt to be too strong, and thus more rational in the logic and rhetoric of power. On the other hand it cannot be easily defeated or discouraged by a single victory on the part of its opponents. And the patient persistence by which it is animated means that it can be effectively countered not by sporadic acts which represent the momentary whims of democratic opinion but only by intelligent long-range policies on the part of Russia's adversaries — policies no less steady in their purpose, and no less variegated and resourceful in their application, than those of the Soviet Union itself.

In these circumstances it is clear that the main element of any United States policy toward the Soviet Union must be that of a long-term, patient but firm and vigilant containment of Russian expansive tendencies. It is important to note, however, that such a policy has nothing to do with outward histrionics: with threats or blustering or superfluous gestures of outward "toughness." While the Kremlin is basically flexible in its reaction to political realities, it is by no means unamenable to considerations of prestige. Like almost any other government, it can be placed by tactless and threatening gestures in a position where it cannot afford to yield even though this might be dictated by its sense of realism. The Russian leaders are keen judges of human psychology, and as such they are highly conscious that loss of temper and of self-control is never a source of strength in political affairs. They are quick to exploit such evidences of weakness. For these reasons, it is a *sine qua non* of successful dealing with Russia that the foreign government in question should remain at all times cool and collected and that its demands on Russian policy should be put forward in such a manner as to leave the way open for a compliance not too detrimental to Russian prestige.

III

In the light of the above, it will be clearly seen that the Soviet pressure against the free institutions of the western world is something that can be contained by the adroit and vigilant application of counter-force at a series of constantly shifting geographical and political points, corresponding to the shifts and manœuvres of Soviet policy, but which cannot be charmed or talked out of existence. The Russians look forward to a duel of infinite duration, and they see that already they have scored great successes. It must be borne in mind that there was a time when the Communist Party represented far more of a minority in the sphere of Russian national life than Soviet power today represents in the world community.

But if ideology convinces the rulers of Russia that truth is on their side and that they can therefore afford to wait, those of us on whom that ideology has no claim are free to examine objectively the validity of that premise. The Soviet thesis not only implies complete lack of control by the west over its own economic destiny, it likewise assumes Russian unity, discipline and patience over an infinite period. Let us bring this apocalyptic vision down to earth, and suppose that the western world finds the strength and resourcefulness to contain Soviet power over a period of ten to fifteen years. What does that spell for Russia itself?

The Soviet leaders, taking advantage of the contributions of modern technique to the arts of despotism, have solved the question of obedience within the confines of their power. Few challenge their authority; and even those who do are unable to make that challenge valid as against the organs of suppression of the state.

The Kremlin has also proved able to accomplish its purpose of building up in Russia, regardless of the interests of the inhabitants, an industrial foundation of heavy metallurgy, which is, to be sure, not yet complete but which is nevertheless continuing to grow and is approaching those of the other major industrial countries. All of this, however, both the maintenance of internal political security and the building of heavy industry, has been carried out at a terrible cost in human life and in human hopes and energies. It has necessitated the use of forced labor on a scale unprecedented in modern times under conditions of peace. It has involved the neglect or abuse of other phases of Soviet economic life, particularly agriculture, consumers' goods production, housing and transportation.

To all that, the war has added its tremendous toll of destruction, death and human exhaustion. In consequence of this, we have in Russia today a population which is physically and spiritually tired. The mass of the people are disillusioned, skeptical and no longer as accessible as they once were to the magical attraction which Soviet power still radiates to its followers abroad. The avidity with which people seized upon the slight respite accorded to the Church for tactical reasons during the war was eloquent testimony to the fact that their capacity for faith and devotion found little expression in the purposes of the régime.

In these circumstances, there are limits to the physical and nervous strength of people themselves. These limits are absolute ones, and are binding even for the cruelest dictatorship, because beyond them people cannot be driven. The forced labor camps and the other agencies of constraint provide temporary means of compelling people to work longer hours than their own volition or mere economic pressure would dictate; but if people survive them at all they become old before their time and must be considered as human casualties to the demands of dictatorship. In either case their best powers are no longer available to society and can no longer be enlisted in the service of the state.

Here only the younger generation can help. The younger generation, despite all vicissitudes and sufferings, is numerous and vigorous; and the Russians are a talented people. But it still remains to be seen what will be the effects on mature performance of the abnormal emotional strains of childhood which Soviet dictatorship created and which were enormously increased by the war. Such things as normal security and placidity of home environment have practically ceased to exist in the Soviet Union outside of the most remote farms and villages. And observers are not yet sure whether that is not going to leave its mark on the over-all capacity of the generation now coming into maturity.

In addition to this, we have the fact that Soviet economic development, while it can list certain formidable achievements, has been precariously spotty and uneven. Russian Communists who speak of the "uneven development of capitalism" should blush at the contemplation of their own national economy. Here certain branches of economic life, such as the metallurgical and machine industries, have been pushed out of all proportion to other sectors of economy. Here is a nation striving to become in a short period one of the great industrial nations of the world while it still has no highway network worthy of the name and only a relatively primitive network of railways. Much has been done to increase efficiency of labor and to teach primitive peasants something about the operation of machines. But maintenance is still a crying deficiency of all Soviet economy. Construction is hasty and poor in quality. Depreciation must be enormous. And in vast sectors of economic life it has not yet been possible to instill into labor anything like that general culture of production and technical self-respect which characterizes the skilled worker of the west.

It is difficult to see how these deficiencies can be corrected at an early date by a tired and dispirited population working largely under the shadow of fear and compulsion. And as long as they are not overcome, Russia will remain economically a vulnerable, and in a certain sense an impotent, nation, capable of exporting its enthusiasms and of radiating the strange charm of its primitive political vitality but unable to back up those articles of export by the real evidences of material power and prosperity.

Meanwhile, a great uncertainty hangs over the political life of the Soviet Union. That is the uncertainty involved in the transfer of power from one individual or group of individuals to others.

This is, of course, outstandingly the problem of the personal position of Stalin. We must remember that his succession to Lenin's pinnacle of preëminence in the Communist movement was the only such transfer of individual authority which the Soviet Union has experienced. That transfer took 12 years to consolidate. It cost the lives of millions of people and shook the state to its foundations. The attendant tremors were felt all through the international revolutionary movement, to the disadvantage of the Kremlin itself.

It is always possible that another transfer of preëminent power may take place quietly and inconspicuously, with no repercussions anywhere. But again, it is possible that the questions involved may unleash, to use some of Lenin's words, one of those "incredibly swift transitions" from "delicate deceit" to "wild violence" which characterize Russian history, and may shake Soviet power to its foundations.

But this is not only a question of Stalin himself. There has been, since 1938, a dangerous congealment of political life in the higher circles of Soviet power. The All-Union Congress of Soviets, in theory the supreme body of the Party, is supposed to meet not less often than once in three years. It will soon be eight full years since its last meeting. During this period membership in the Party has numerically doubled. Party mortality during the war was enormous; and today well over half of the Party members are persons who have entered since the last Party congress was held. Meanwhile, the same small group of men has carried on at the top through an amazing series of national vicissitudes. Surely there is some reason why the experiences of the war brought basic political changes to every one of the great governments of the west. Surely the causes of that phenomenon are basic enough to be present somewhere in the obscurity of Soviet political life, as well. And yet no recognition has been given to these causes in Russia.

It must be surmised from this that even within so highly disciplined an organization as the Communist Party there must be a growing divergence in age, outlook and interest between the great mass of Party members, only so recently recruited into the movement, and the little self-perpetuating clique of men at the top, whom most of these Party members have never met, with whom they have never conversed, and with whom they can have no political intimacy.

Who can say whether, in these circumstances, the eventual rejuvenation of the higher spheres of authority (which can only be a matter of time) can take place smoothly and peacefully, or whether rivals in the quest for higher power will not eventually reach down into these politically immature and inexperienced masses in order to find support for their respective claims? If this were ever to happen, strange consequences could flow for the Communist Party: for the membership at large has been exercised only in the practices of iron discipline and obedience and not in the arts of compromise and accommodation. And if disunity were ever to seize and paralyze the Party, the chaos and weakness of Russian society would be revealed in forms beyond description. For we have seen that Soviet power is only a crust concealing an amorphous mass of human beings among whom no independent organizational structure is tolerated. In Russia there is not even such a thing as local government. The present generation of Russians have never known spontaneity of collective action. If, consequently, anything were ever to occur to disrupt the unity and efficacy of the Party as a political instrument, Soviet Russia might be changed overnight from one of the strongest to one of the weakest and most pitiable of national societies.

Thus the future of Soviet power may not be by any means as secure as Russian capacity for self-delusion would make it appear to the men in the Kremlin. That they can keep power themselves, they have demonstrated. That they can quietly and easily turn it over to others remains to be proved. Meanwhile, the hardships of their rule and the vicissitudes of international life have taken a heavy toll of the strength and hopes of the great people on whom their power rests. It is curious to note that the ideological power of Soviet authority is strongest today in areas beyond the frontiers of Russia, beyond the reach of its police power. This phenomenon brings to mind a comparison used by Thomas Mann in his great novel "Buddenbrooks." Observing that human institutions often show the greatest outward brilliance at a moment when inner decay is in reality farthest advanced, he compared the Buddenbrook family, in the days of its greatest glamour, to one of those stars whose light shines most brightly on this world when in reality it has long since ceased to exist. And who can say with assurance that the strong light still cast by the Kremlin on the dissatisfied peoples of the western world is not the powerful afterglow of a constellation which is in actuality on the wane? This cannot be proved. And it cannot be disproved. But the possibility remains (and in the opinion of this writer it is a strong one) that Soviet power, like the capitalist world of its conception, bears within it the seeds of its own decay, and that the sprouting of these seeds is well advanced.

IV

It is clear that the United States cannot expect in the foreseeable future to enjoy political intimacy with the Soviet régime. It must continue to regard the Soviet Union as a rival, not a partner, in the political arena. It must continue to expect that Soviet policies will reflect no abstract love of peace and stability, no real faith in the possibility of a permanent happy coexistence of the Socialist and capitalist worlds, but rather a cautious, persistent pressure toward the disruption and weakening of all rival influence and rival power.

Balanced against this are the facts that Russia, as opposed to the western world in general, is still by far the weaker party, that Soviet policy is highly flexible, and that Soviet society may well contain deficiencies which will eventually weaken its own total potential. This would of itself warrant the United States entering with reasonable confidence upon a policy of firm containment, designed to confront the Russians with unalterable counter-force at every point where they show signs of encroaching upon the interests of a peaceful and stable world.

But in actuality the possibilities for American policy are by no means limited to holding the line and hoping for the best. It is entirely possible for the United States to influence by its actions the internal developments, both within Russia and throughout the international Communist movement, by which Russian policy is largely determined. This is not only a question of the modest measure of informational activity which this government can conduct in the Soviet Union and elsewhere, although that, too, is important. It is rather a question of the degree to which the United States can create among the peoples of the world generally the impression of a country which knows what it wants, which is coping successfully with the problems of its internal life and with the responsibilities of a World Power, and which has a spiritual vitality capable of holding its own among the major ideological currents of the time. To the extent that such an impression can be created and maintained, the aims of Russian Communism must appear sterile and quixotic, the hopes and enthusiasm of Moscow's supporters must wane, and added strain must be imposed on the Kremlin's foreign policies. For the palsied decrepitude of the capitalist world is the keystone of Communist philosophy. Even the failure of the United States to experience the early economic depression which the ravens of the Red Square have been predicting with such complacent confidence since hostilities ceased would have deep and important repercussions throughout the Communist world.

By the same token, exhibitions of indecision, disunity and internal disintegration within this country have an exhilarating effect on the whole Communist movement. At each evidence of these tendencies, a thrill of hope and excitement goes through the Communist world; a new jauntiness can be noted in the Moscow tread; new groups of foreign supporters climb on to what they can only view as the band wagon of international politics; and Russian pressure increases all along the line in international affairs.

It would be an exaggeration to say that American behavior unassisted and alone could exercise a power of life and death over the Communist movement and bring about the early fall of Soviet power in Russia. But the United States has it in its power to increase enormously the strains under which Soviet policy must operate, to force upon the Kremlin a far greater degree of moderation and circumspection than it has had to observe in recent years, and in this way to promote tendencies which must eventually find their outlet in either the break-up or the gradual mellowing of Soviet power. For no mystical, Messianic movement — and particularly not that of the Kremlin — can face frustration indefinitely without eventually adjusting itself in one way or another to the logic of that state of affairs.

Thus the decision will really fall in large measure in this country itself. The issue of Soviet-American relations is in essence a test of the over-all worth of the United States as a nation among nations. To avoid destruction the United States need only measure up to its own best traditions and prove itself worthy of preservation as a great nation.

Surely, there was never a fairer test of national quality than this. In the light of these circumstances, the thoughtful observer of Russian-American relations will find no cause for complaint in the Kremlin's challenge to American society. He will rather experience a certain gratitude to a Providence which, by providing the American people with this implacable challenge, has made their entire security as a nation dependent on their pulling themselves together and accepting the responsibilities of moral and political leadership that history plainly intended them to bear.

¶ THE CRISIS IN OUR CIVILIZATION
by Harold J. Laski   (October, 1947)

"Every civilization is in serious danger when, as in ours, there is a grave disproportion between the growth of material power and the growth of that spiritual and intellectual insight which makes possible common agreement about the use of that power." According to this definition set down twenty-five years ago by Harold Laski, our civilization remains on the brink of disaster.

Laski was the intellectual pride and sometimes considered the nuisance of the British Labour Party. In this article, his socialist outlook provides the premises for most of his conclusions, but many are valid regardless of how one arrives at them. His complaint about the gap between the interest of the people and the will of the state is widely shared. It is generally agreed that our world is one of contrasts and inequities that are alike fantastic and unforgivable. Yet Laski's arguments in favor of world government were not then, and still are not, universally accepted. National sovereignty remains a cherished concept, though there have been some recent attempts to deal with supranational problems on a supranational level, namely, the European communities. The success of these attests to their political and economic feasibility, but Laski pointed up the higher conception of citizenship, which becomes possible as well.

A thoughtful reading of "The Crisis in Our Civilization" continues to provide ideas that may hasten the coming of the equilibrium Laski envisioned, in which peace and reason become the habitual instruments of action.

THE CRISIS IN OUR CIVILIZATION

By Harold J. Laski

THE world has been very near to disaster, and it is far from apparent that its direction is now set to clear waters. I address myself here principally to the responsibilities for this situation which rest on the inheritors of the western capitalist tradition. We have built an interdependent world economy, but we have hardly sought in any serious way to build the institutions that are appropriate to its governance. Our science and its technology have opened to us the prospect of material well-being upon a scale no generation has previously known; but our relations of production halt us at the very entrance to the riches of Aladdin's cave. At the very center of our civilization there still lie hates and envies, ignorance and blindness, which cast a grim shadow over our future. Our world is one of contrasts that are alike fantastic and unforgivable. Here immense wealth, and there a grinding poverty. Here a culture that penetrates to the innermost secrets of nature, and there a tragic superstition that is born of an illiteracy which fetters the mind to ignorance. Here there is the dignity that is the elder child of freedom, while there whole nations toil under the curse of a slavery not less bitter because we have appeased our conscience by giving to its chains another name. In western society the use of medical science gives men and women at least the high prospect of life which may reach the allotted span; in other areas youth has hardly passed before death inexorably beckons. No doubt it is the right of all mankind to put Utopia upon its maps; but there are few organized peoples whose rulers have yet pointed to its presence save as a figure of rhetorical speech which binds most men and women afresh to the endless renewal of an exhausting round of toil.

The United Nations have won a global war waged in the name of freedom and democracy; but we are far from agreement upon what we mean by our great wars. We have founded a vast international organization that the peace may be kept and that the minds and bodies of men may be safeguarded from ignorance and credulity, from want and disease; but we have founded it upon a principle of national sovereignty that is on any rational showing wholly incompatible with the fulfilment of its purposes. Two years have passed since open hostilities ceased; but there is hardly an area of the world in which secret hostilities, made bitter by the darkness and conspiracies which surround them, do not continue with intensity and vigor. We tell one another that it requires only an effort of will to overcome the differences which divide the world; but we do little to organize the conditions under which that effort of will is likely to be made. There is no mask that is not used to cover the face of social injustices the remedies for which men seek to avoid. Sometimes we invoke the mythology of nationalism, as though we have not seen its problems continuously transcended in the war from which we have just emerged. Sometimes a social philosophy, already completely outmoded, is evoked to protect the habitual routine of past privilege against the innovating claims of men who deny the validity of some obsolete pattern of political and economic order. There is no injustice in our time which does not use the power of religion, the authority of custom, or the grim hand of state or mob coercion to safeguard its perpetuation. And each injustice, be it racial or national, religious or economic, rationalizes the claims it embodies by sheltering under a half-examined metaphysic of values, set, if it be possible, in a context made familiar by tradition, and so rooted in precious memories that faith may guard it from exposure by the keen sword of rational analysis. To the maintenance of that faith, techniques of propaganda are now devoted which condition the minds of millions against the right of reason to consideration before even the discussion of the validity of the faith has seriously commenced. Nearly 200 years ago Rousseau said that mankind ran to meet its chains; now it is our gravest danger that we should regard as our enemies the forces, human and impersonal alike, which strive by their interaction to liberate us from their burden.

It is, moreover, urgent for us in the west to remember that the technological conditions of our time make the power of those who control the instruments of production far greater than in any previous age. Our Alexanders and Caesars and Napoleons are no longer the great military captains who hack their way to empire; they have become half-impersonal but mighty business corporations, at whose bid a trackless desert may become the scene of battles for which the steel workers of Pittsburgh and Coventry, or the miners of the Ruhr and Silesia, may be mobilized to settle the decision, not only without knowing the end for which their effort is being employed, but in the passionate conviction that they labor for America or Britain, for Germany or Poland, and that their freedom from tyranny depends upon their effort. They toil in the light of a hope that is a half-promise from their masters that, if they endure till victory, tomorrow will begin the fulfilment of dreams beyond their horizon today. Security is to be theirs, a little of the ease that gives life its color and its dignity, freedom from the frustration of their trivial insignificance and from the haunting fear that their old age will be made mean and ugly by a stark poverty against which they cannot provide. But, even when victory has crowned their effort, they hear that the promise is beyond their rulers' power to fulfil since its redemption would disturb confidence or provoke disorder or transfer the power of government to men whose exercise of its authority would involve all in a common ruin because these lack the gift or the habitation which makes likely its successful operation. So the hope slowly fades, until all sense is lost of those common purposes of mind and heart which lead the citizens of some given society to believe that they can discuss how they may reach the new goal by methods which permit the accommodation where peace has freedom as its eldest child. Cannot we in the west yet see, even in the shadowed light of so profound a tragedy as we have just experienced, that a civilization built like ours upon so massive and so ruthless an exploitation of man by man must either move to the ending of that exploitation or perish in the bloody violence of fratricidal revolution?

II

Let us at least be sure that we have reached the end of that road, first fully opened by American independence and the Revolution of 1789, in which the aristocrat and the bourgeois combined to organize individual opportunity for those whose rise was not dependent merely upon the labor power they had to sell. That road had ceased to be a highway when the last American frontier had been overpassed. Thenceforward, gates were steadily closed which could have been kept open only if the men who ruled the United States had been willing to accept a vertical instead of a horizontal expansion of their well-being. Once they chose the latter, they not only chose to pattern their own society upon the model of Europe, with values which, however different the outward form in which they were clothed, had nevertheless the same inner essence; but they also imprisoned most of Europe within a frame of power increasingly difficult to adjust in any peaceful way because it had been driven to accept pressures beyond its capacity to contain. The multiform Europe of the twentieth century was a variegated mosaic in which the productive possibilities were always being defeated by historic and social relations which prevented their adequate use of technological possibilities. It was economically pluralistic, where its obvious need was set in monistic terms. Its cultural evils set the residuary legatees of medieval theocracy alongside the imaginative ardor of the men who thought in terms of what the outcome of tomorrow's scientific thinking might reveal. Its nationalist obsessions made political exclusiveness retard and even deny the felt implications of economic necessity. If, in some sudden crisis like 1832 or 1848, its privileged classes paid to democracy and freedom the hypocritical homage that vice has always paid to virtue, it was upon the assumed condition, never frankly stated but always secretly resolved, that the concession could be cancelled by some hidden device. So that when, after the close of the First World War, the combined impact of the Russian Revolution and that counter-revolution of which Hitler and Mussolini are the ugly symptoms forced the secret revolution of privilege throughout Europe into the open, by making its validity the basis of what was virtually an immense international civil war, men faced the question they can never avoid when they reach some vital crossroads of their historical experience: the question of whether they are to make their systems of property systems which at once increase the quantum of material well-being and distribute it with what can be recognized as a genuine concern for equity, or whether they will leave the issue of adjusting their systems of property to the arbitrament of pressures on either side, which are bound to entail violence as their influence is exerted more closely upon one another.

The answer to that question, moreover, was both more complicated and more important because, given the technological conditions of a world economy, expansion that was horizontal and not vertical, alike in the United States and Europe, meant that Asia and Africa, as well as the half-known potentialities of the Australasian continent, were bound to become quite vital elements in the equation which had to be solved. The bombing airplane made frontiers obsolete since it virtually annihilated distance. The discovery of atomic fission brought into hazard the industrial potential of any state which could not destroy its enemy before it was itself destroyed. The vast changes which the application of science had forced upon the world meant either that matters of common concern must be decided in common and freely, or that Hobbes' picture of the relations between states as a *bellum omnium contra omnes* was, quite inescapably, a literal description of obvious fact. Would statesmen, to whom those premises of action we term Machiavellianism seem obvious postulates, realize in time that, from these postulates, there now followed, unmistakably, the destruction of all principles of civilized living? Or, could they so overcome the heavy inertia of inherited tradition as to embark upon great experiments proportionate to the necessity they faced, of overcoming the anachronistic contradictions the mere continuance of which spelled the ruin of the world they were ceasing to comprehend, much less to govern?

III

The contradictions of our present situation can be illustrated by a quite simple example. When, as the United States reached its last internal frontier, its rulers chose horizontal, instead of vertical, expansion, its whole future was bound up with its ability to become a great exporting power. Its "manifest destiny" now became, not the Jeffersonian dream of a virtually self-sufficient, if mighty, nation of agrarian and not commercial, complexion, but that of a powerful competitor for the purchasing power of the world's markets, with a prosperity dependent upon its ability to satisfy effective demand more adequately than its rivals. But there it was bound to meet the search of other nations in a similar position, to increase their well-being by similar means. And, at every point, this struggle for external trade was matched by an internal struggle, from which none of them was free, by means of which their workers sought a larger share in well-being in their effort to pass beyond the mere subsistence-level of life. But, once the problem of a nation's ability to become a great exporting Power became a major need, two other unavoidable problems arose. The first was that, as a general rule, the greater the material well-being conceded to the workers by their employers especially where their labor was directly relevant to export, the higher would be the price of the commodity they produced, the more difficult, therefore, to sell it in the face of competition from their rivals. The second was that it was difficult alike for employers not to demand, and for statesmen not to offer, the assistance of the state power, both to industry and commerce, to safeguard that export trade upon which so much of any given national well-being had come, by our own time, to depend.

Nothing illustrates more incisively this second problem than the position of Great Britain today. It literally has the choice between an immense expansion of its exports and a swift, perhaps a catastrophic, reduction in its standard of life. If it fails to expand its export capacity, the share of well-being it can allot to its workers is bound to shrink, at a time when those workers have so organized their collective power that a reduction of their share is bound to seem to them an unacceptable denial of legitimate expectation. Great Britain, therefore, must within the framework of her present social and economic order either greatly expand her exports or call upon employers and workers, perhaps upon both alike, to give up the hope of increased well-being.

What is true of the United States and of Great Britain is also true, if in different degrees, of all the major industrial countries. And their position is complicated by the fact that the backward countries in an industrial sense, like India and China in Asia, or like Rumania and Jugoslavia in Europe, can advance the standard of life of their citizens only by taking large and rapid strides to industrialization. But, as they do so in this age of horizontal expansion, they intensify the difficulties of the well-established industrial Powers or they run the grave danger of accepting aid for their economic development in such a way as to become a political dependency of the Power from which they accept it. This is why the immense productive capacity of the United States drives it to seek for open markets abroad, while its manufacturers and merchants who live by its domestic market seek, almost with frenzy, to prevent the entry of foreign goods into territory they regard as their own. That is why, also, Jugoslavia seeks to prevent its nascent industrialism from being subjected to the pressure of more powerful, and often more efficient, competitors from outside. The Jugoslav fear of economic exploitation is shared by other states in eastern and central Europe whose political affiliations with Soviet Russia are close; and, indeed, an objective observer might reasonably argue that these affiliations have also their economic consequences. What emerges is the grave difficulty that none of these secondary states may safely be able, in view of the disagreements between the major states, to make choices based upon considerations of its own economic welfare.

It has, moreover, been the fear of entanglement in foreign finance-capitalism which made Soviet Russia, until the beginning of the Second World War, seek to develop its own industrial development with capital deliberately taken from a national level of production which has not yet provided for its workers a standard of life seriously comparable with that of the American worker, the Swedish, the Swiss, the British or the citizen of New Zealand. The market economy, in brief, which is the essential condition of an operative capitalist society, has now in terms of technological possibilities reached a stage where it has become an impossible hindrance to our capacity to produce. If it were to regain the status which once made its principles an aid to progress, it would rapidly reduce all weaker competitors, in the struggle it postulates, to a condition of helpless dependency on the stronger Powers or to a permanent poverty from which they could escape only by the grace of an allotment of some place in the economic sun they were unable to win by their own effort. Since no nation is ready to acquiesce in a status that is bound to lead to violent conflict within its own boundaries, it becomes increasingly involved in the obligation to deny the validity of the market economy. The plain lesson of our situation is the obsolescence of Adam Smith's "simple system of natural liberty," and indeed, further, of any of those more sophisticated versions of its substance that in one form or another now constitute applications of equilibrium-economies. We have reached the point where vertical expansion is necessary for the safety of the world. But vertical expansion means public ownership of the means of production that planned distribution may secure an equitable share for the members of the community. The age of *laissez-faire* has, on every plane of living, drawn to its close. Either we go forward to Socialism or we must go back to an industrial feudalism in which the maintenance of a privileged aristocracy of predatory capitalists involves the destruction alike of freedom and democracy.

IV

That is the issue posed to us upon the economic plane. It is, of course, an issue inseparable from its political context, and in that aspect it sets us a problem as decisively simple in its principles as it is decisively complex in their application. A world economy means a world government; and we cannot achieve a world government so long as the operating unit of political administration is the sovereign national state. That became very evident during the recent hostilities when every major plan of the United Nations in the western theater of war demanded, and largely achieved, the transcendence of sovereignty. Indeed, it is reasonable to argue that the difficulties between Russia and the western Powers in the postwar period have largely arisen because, during the conflict itself, the contrast in the implications of their economic systems never permitted that transcendence to emerge by a full coöperation. I do not think it is an exaggeration to say that the Britain of Mr. Churchill and the America which gave President Roosevelt its support on the vital condition that he abandon the New Deal welcomed partnership with Russia as a means to the defeat of their enemies, but without enthusiasm for the new status victory would bring to Russia. It is, of course, not less true that Russia's wartime alliance with Great Britain and the United States was an essential condition for its liberation from the threat to its existence of Nazi Germany and Fascist Japan; but the rulers of Russia were never under the illusion that America, at any rate, would travel upon the road they had chosen once the common enemy had been vanquished.

That is why the Charter of the United Nations was bound to be built upon the preservation of the national sovereign state, and bound, therefore, to be an unsatisfactory compromise disproportionate to the scale of the problem it was intended to meet. For it applies to the political requirements of a world economy those concepts of Grotius which he devised for a society which existed 300 years ago. He was writing in a mercantilist epoch, when the bourgeoisie had only begun its dramatic rise to power and when the use of the state authority to organize the nation, both for production at home and for markets abroad, coincided with a massive increase in the forces of production, and a creative adjustment of the system of ownership to the possibilities involved in that massive increase. The outlook of Grotius is intelligible enough until some such period as the end of the American Civil War. After its close, the sovereignty of the national state imposed an increasing strain upon the implications of a world economy. For as it was utilized to protect or to further the vested interests of the owners in the industry and commerce of any national community, it was essentially an attempt to protect the past against the future, an old technology against a new, the claims of new men and new nations, to alter the historic dispositions of power that they, too, might advance in well-being. Once the Charter of San Francisco made the principle of national sovereignty its basis, the constituent members of the United Nations could coöperate only to the degree that their governments were prepared to sacrifice or to adjust the claims of the vested interests it was the function of each of them to protect, to some larger common welfare which reached so clearly beyond those claims that no vested interest within the territory it controlled would dare to challenge its decision.

Even in the 30 months that have passed since the Charter was signed, it is clear how narrow is the room for manœuvre permitted by this limitation. The really vital decisions taken in the international field since the spring of 1945 have been taken outside and not inside the United Nations organization. That was true of the principles laid down at Potsdam. It was true of the Anglo-American loan. It was true of the aid given to Greece and Turkey by the United States even though, as an afterthought, Senator Vandenberg thought it was wise to make a graceful bow in the direction of Lake Success. Even Secretary Marshall's offer, in June 1947, of collective aid from the United States to Europe takes no account of that European Economic Commission of the United Nations which would seem as though it had been founded for precisely the purpose Mr. Marshall had in mind. To this must be added that, so far, what attempts have been made to utilize the new body do not suggest that it is free from any of the major difficulties — all hinging upon the sovereignty of its members — which wrecked the League of Nations. The veto power means, in effect, that the Security Council is a platform for discussion and not an organ for command, and that, as the Albanian incident showed in the spring of 1946, even where the obligations of a small Power may be concerned. Great Britain has asked for and obtained an investigation into the Palestinian Mandate by the Assembly of the United Nations; but its representative there has been emphatic that acceptance of any proposals the Assembly may agree to make is contingent upon approval of them by the British Government.

If Egypt and Iran make appeals to the Security Council, it is less in the hope that a decision may be made in their favor than because of their awareness that there alone can they so state their case that they may hope for more consideration than in private diplomacy. Nor must we miss the significance of the facts, first, that the vital rearming by the American Government of the reactionary forces behind Generalissimo Chiang Kai-shek in China was done without discussion with or consent from the United Nations; and that, on acquiring the innumerable islands of the South Pacific, some of which have considerable strategic importance, the American Government refused to be accountable for them to the Trusteeship Council. Nor is it without importance that no reference was made to the views of the United Nations when the American Government obtained its air base in Iceland by a treaty which the Icelandic legislature was far from eager to ratify; it is, indeed, at least possible that, without the pressure of the British Foreign Office on behalf of the United States, the request for the base would have been refused by the Government of Iceland.

The political problem that has emerged from the Second World War is not likely to be solved by the half-measures to which, like its predecessor, the United Nations organization is confined. That is to be set in the background of the absence of Russia from most of its supplementary institutions, above all from the Food and Agricultural Organization, from UNESCO and from the International Monetary Fund. Without full Russian coöperation each of these institutions is bound to be halting and inconclusive. Given as we are given a world economy, any international government which, like the U.N., is fragmentary and interstitial, and possessed only of conditional law-making powers, is profoundly unsatisfactory because so profoundly disproportionate to the issues before it. We cannot rest content until we have a genuine world government expressing, through the direct choice of peoples, in a parliament responsible to them, the will of the common folk, instead of being dependent, like the United Nations, upon the sovereign wills of nation states which express, in all vital matters, the purposes of their ruling classes and subordinate to those purposes the interests of the common peoples. International peace which maximizes creative opportunity is the supreme end of which the common people take account.

The difficulty is that we do not live in a world in which the basic economic principles of social organization are viewed in a similar way by all governments. That is, no doubt, the reason why, at San Francisco, Soviet Russia was not less insistent than the United States that the principle of national sovereignty was the heart of the Charter and why, therefore, it insisted upon the veto as the instrument which would express that sovereignty in the operation of international decisions. It is important to realize that this was a reiteration, in a different form, of that insistence upon the rule of unanimity which was closely connected with the weakness of the League of Nations.

For a considerable period, the principle of national sovereignty — and therefore the veto — is likely to remain. It is useless to deny that it hampers any big move toward genuine world government, not only because it prevents decisions being made after discussion, but, even more, because the fear that it may be used acts as a kind of prenatal control over issues which ought to be discussed. The one way round what is, otherwise, a grave handicap to any serious move toward world government would seem to lie in the growth of a functional as distinct from a territorial federalism. If nation states could agree to pool their interests in certain areas of action, as in a single European railway system, or a single system of aviation for the American continent, if there could be joint ownership and control of electric power, say in the Danubian Valley, or an internationally governed irrigation and power authority in the Middle East, we should begin to think in supranational terms about problems which are not only in themselves supranational, but are rarely capable of being satisfactorily solved if they are dealt with always on the national level. The work of the Combined Staffs Committee during the war, and of UNRRA after its close, has shown that this functional federalism can succeed if those who operate it have good faith and imagination and energy. This is a field in which experiment is urgently required. For it is only by transcending a principle the obsolescence of which hinders international coöperation at every turn that we can begin to make men realize that the little platoon which now demands their exclusive loyalty is in fact only a part of the great regiment of mankind. To get that regiment to strike its tents is the first of the duties before us. That is the condition which alone will make it possible for humanity to move forward to a higher conception of citizenship than is permitted by the narrow horizons of the nation state.

V

If we are honest, we must admit that everywhere there is an important gap between the interest of the people and the will of the state, as this is expressed by the government which exercises sovereignty over a nation. The gap is not easy to define, though it is always there. We can see it in the mutual interpenetration of purposes between the Nazi Party and the German Army under the Hitler régime, or between I.G. Farben and those who, under Hitler, made the ultimate decisions about the German economy. We can see it again in the interaction between the American oil interests and the State Department, as the policy of the United States is made in the Middle East; in this aspect, there is high interest in the contrast between President Truman's claims for the Jews in Palestine, and the curious relations between the Middle East Division of the State Department and the similar division of the British Foreign Office. Or, again, it emerges in the impact of the electric power interests in the United States, both upon the federal government and the governments of the different states.

The gap was grimly clear in France in the protection offered by the Government to the Army during the Dreyfus case, and in that creeping paralysis of will which afflicted the French Government at least from Munich onward; and, indeed, in the fantastic domination of Vichy by Laval, whose allegiance was always coincident with his bank balance. It is the same, too, in Great Britain. A great deal of British agricultural legislation is, right down to our own day, the outcome of a partnership between landowner and farmer and the government, with the general public and the farm laborer bearing the burden of that partnership. The peculiar configuration of landowner, house-property owner, the building industry and the government has always stood in the way of any drastic attempt to grapple with the British housing problem in the interest of the common people; it is only since the general election of 1945 that Mr. Sartorius'[1] daughter has begun to feel uneasy about the unearned increment of her grandchildren. Nor do I doubt for one moment that in any single-party state the very fact that criticism is so swiftly regarded as sedition or treason, that the boundary is so thin between opposition and conspiracy, is proof that there also, even when the instru-

[1] *Cf.* Bernard Shaw's play, "Widowers' Houses."

ments of production are publicly owned, it is by no means inevitable that the gap is bridged.

I do not need to multiply examples. It is no more than a commonplace to insist that most governments exercise the state power in national communities in the service of the ruling class of the time. They do not do this out of conscious malevolence; they do this because, as Marx said in a classic sentence, "the ruling ideas of an age are the ideas of its ruling class." But this clearly implies that an international organization, based upon governments representing sovereign nation states, reproduces, in the sphere of world affairs, the gap I have described which exists in the domestic affairs of each national community. If we accept the principle that we cannot transcend the sovereignty of the nation state, we are, in fact, saying that the gap cannot be closed in world affairs. We are then arguing that what I have elsewhere termed cosmopolitan lawmaking is ruled out as impossible, even when we know that there are areas of behavior where the need for it is both obvious and urgent. I take one example only. Nothing has done more to poison international relations in the last two years than the revelation of the terrifying destructive power of the atomic bomb. That the principle of national sovereignty should hinder us from being able to prevent its use as an instrument of state policy is the gravest single reason I know for pessimism about the future of mankind. That its manufacture should threaten the integrity of that public and free knowledge within the international community of science, which has been so largely responsible for the conquest of nature, is only less tragic in its possible consequences. So long as we build a world order on sovereignty, when the facts about us have made that principle a clear anachronism, our world order, as a going political concern, is a pretty thin and insubstantial thing, a veil which will be torn aside when the member states in that world order confront their first crisis of serious magnitude. The principle that the nation state must, at all costs, preserve its sovereignty, belongs to and maintains an age of economic scarcity in which privilege is concerned to preserve by force claims which it could not defend by reason. To continue the authority of that principle into an age when we might advance to the economics of abundance is to sacrifice the future to the past, to maintain scarcity because privilege is afraid to buy off its fears by pursuing exactly the same policy which a century ago made 1848 inevitable.

This is the clue to the First World War, to the inevitability of the Russian Revolution, to the acceptance of Hitler as the executioner of Weimar Germany, and thence, by a logic which the historical pattern has so often repeated, to the Second World War.

Politically, on the international plane, we have not yet taken a single step which proves that we have learned the lessons of this second catastrophe. Europe lies about us maimed and scarred; there is wide divergence of opinion about its restoration to health. We cannot agree upon either the shape or the character of the new Germany; and the longer we delay in reaching that agreement, the deeper the Nazi poison takes hold of its heart. We had an Italy in our hands as early as 1943 which could have been a genuine *Risorgimento* had we possessed the capacity of instant magnanimity; we threw the chances away lest, in exorcising its demon, we injure a pattern of historic relations and promote innovations our rulers cannot bring themselves to regard as desirable, even though they suspect that they may prove to be inevitable. There was the same failure in Greece, a more profound and tragic failure, because we broke liberal hopes in the service of our vested interests. Even the France of the Liberation seems not to have understood all that is implied in the disaster of 1940 and its aftermath in the régime of Vichy — that it is time for France to accept the great Revolution, and to complete the translation of its principles into the fabric of the French nation. If the meaning of so vast an experience as the Revolution of 1789 can still leave mankind in doubt and deep division, it becomes the less remarkable that an event as near us as the Russian Revolution should still have the power to divide men into hostile and angry camps, each of which can hardly speak a language that the other can understand.

Is it possible that the war for freedom and democracy has left us unable to understand what is involved in their fulfilment? Are we so crippled by the burden of our heritage, and so fatigued by our exertions for victory, that we have lost the power to make those innovations in civilized living which any realistic imagination can see are inevitable? Is our western statesmanship so bankrupt that it does not know that the essential wisdom in the art of politics is to abridge the birth-pangs of our emerging order? These are the questions we are bound to ask in this tortured world; and we have to answer them because it is the foundations of our civilization that are in peril.

For the Second World War was, above everything, the proof of a mortal sickness in the way of life by which we sought to preserve the security of those foundations. Every civilization is in serious danger when, as in ours, there is so grave a disproportion between the growth of material power and the growth of that spiritual and intellectual insight which makes possible common agreement about the use of that power. We could hold social relationships in an uneasy equilibrium so long as faith in some supernatural compensation for earthly inequalities seemed to mitigate their harshness. When that faith declined so swiftly, we were driven to the impossible task of finding a rational explanation for differences which were mostly inexplicable save in terms of laws intended themselves to maintain those differences. And this task was the more hopeless to the degree that it was attempted in a society which, over wide areas, announced its allegiance to democratic principles. In their turn, these depend on the preservation of that freedom of discussion which alone preserves the empire of reason over the minds of men.

The fatal contradiction in the ethos of western civilization is the obvious one that the greater the power it possessed over material things, the more it seemed to call upon the masses to renounce the prospect of the well-being and grace and dignity which it provided for those who owned and operated the instruments of production; and the less able it was to persuade the masses to accept the religious sanction under which that renunciation had been previously imposed. The masses sought, on every plane of political activity, to use the democratic power of numbers to mitigate the results of social and economic inequality; yet each new method they used, from universal suffrage to direct government, always seemed in the end to maintain the configuration of a world in which, both within and between nation states, the growth of material power brought no proportionately juster distribution of the well-being it made possible. That is why, at a pace which has never ceased to grow swifter since the French Revolution and especially since the immense events in Russia in 1917, men's thoughts have turned from political to economic changes, as the effective basis upon which the masses can achieve what they regard as social justice. They have thus been driven to reconsider the legal relations which are implied in a capitalist system of ownership, and in so doing to attempt the readjustment of every aspect of organization, national and international alike, in which the legal relations of capitalist ownership are involved. This has brought the vital problem of property into the central field of discussion. About no problem are men more likely to make their reason the slave of their passions; none, therefore, is less easily discussed in a democratic society whose safety depends upon the triumph of reason over passion. As always, when the foundations of social order come into view, primitive emotions are released in both men and nations which make tolerance and reflection too pale a mental climate in which to fulfil the ends for which we are reaching.

We shall not reach a new equilibrium in which peace and reason become the habitual instruments of action until we realize that, in itself, the material control over nature is not an assurance of a civilized way of life. That power must be matched by a proportionate capacity to use our insight into the processes of nature, to offer more spiritual dignity and a higher level of intellectual satisfaction, to the underprivileged citizens in every nation state. And it must be able to offer greater adequacy, also, to the nation states which now fight among themselves for what well-being there is. For it has become common knowledge that well-being is limited less by the depth of our insight than by the boundaries within which the prevalent economic order forces it to remain confined. We have created all over the world fear and envy and anger in human relations by the restraints we have seemed to impose upon men's access to a richer civilization; we have even fought world wars to impose those restraints through one channel rather than through another. We shall not persuade men to go down a third time into the abyss to rescue a way of life that decays before their eyes.

Our supreme need, therefore, is to find that common faith which enables us all to coöperate in casting off those restraints. Our history will become an ever more tragic drama until, by the discovery of that faith, we become able to persuade the world that we are consciously devoting alike our knowledge and our power to affirm, and not to deny, the yearning of the common man for creative fulfilment. It is, moreover, urgent to realize with all the speed we may that in this epoch time is no longer on our side.

¶ KEYNES IN RETROSPECT

by Herbert Feis   (July, 1951)

A whole generation knows Herbert Feis only as a historian. But when this article appeared in 1951, as he was approaching sixty, most of the impressive series of volumes about the diplomacy of World War II and its aftermath were still ahead of him. Behind him was a career as one of the leading American economists concerned with international affairs. His classic, Europe, the World's Banker: 1870–1914, *was published in 1930, and the next year Secretary of State Henry L. Stimson made him his economic adviser. For a time, almost all the economic issues that came to the State Department passed through his hands, except perhaps the management of Secretary Hull's favorite trade-agreements program.*

Feis was a fine choice to write for Foreign Affairs *about Keynes. Like the Englishman, he was an economist touched by the humanities, loving language and willing to take the dissenting or idiosyncratic position—indeed, rather relishing it. Both liked to put their ideas in a broad setting of history, even if, following the famous passage quoted at the beginning of this article, Feis wrote* sub specie temporis. *After two decades, Feis's sympathetic appraisal stands up well.*

The economist-turned-historian had a feeling for the great economist who once attracted attention as a semihistorian—though not necessarily a judicious one, as Feis's strictures on Keynes's account of Versailles suggest. Feis tells us in his volume 1933 *that his study of Keynes had made him "reserved about the lilting reassurances that were diffused" by the Hoover Administration in promising to end the Depression. His own prescriptions for the postwar world —in* The Sinews of Peace, *published in 1944—were, if not notably Keynesian, quite compatible with Keynes's. He was clear about the great differences between the "neatly planted and attractive bed" of classical economics, as he called it, and the needs of a modern, partly Keynesian, world in which governments would be expected to guide economies so as to ensure the full use of resources. Both Keynes and Feis were acutely aware of the difficulty of balancing national freedom of action with the need for international cooperation, and they both saw the vital importance of American policy in that regard. For a guiding principle, Feis went back to Keynes's analysis of Versailles, which, he tells us in this article, teaches "that regard for the economic fortune of other countries is not merely an act of kindness, but an essential of good relations, and perhaps of peace."*

KEYNES IN RETROSPECT

By Herbert Feis

Economists must leave to Adam Smith the glory of the Quarto, must pluck the day, fling pamphlets into the wind, write always *sub-specie temporis,* and achieve immortality by accident, if at all.
—*John Maynard Keynes, in his essay on Alfred Marshall*

AT THE whisper of an economic issue Keynes leaps among us with brightening opinion and advice. He will continue to do so. That is immortality.

The publication of Roy Harrod's "Life"[1] stirs the impulse to inspect his title to remembrance. That is not easy. For his mind and spirit both were always on the move. Those who travel with them will appreciate, even if they do not approve, the wry comment of Sir Eyre Crowe: ". . . he, Keynes, only sees for the time being, the point he sets himself to prove, and regardless of the fact he has proved something very different yesterday, and is very likely to prove something different still tomorrow. . . . He can bring a converging series of arguments to bear upon a single point so that he succeeds in making everything else seem to have a minor interest to other persons, and it is doubtful if it even has a subordinate interest for Keynes himself. His opinions are in a perpetual state of progress, and therefore of apparent flux. . . ."

In this flux there were many themes. Of these I shall pursue but three: his assault upon the Peace Treaty with Germany (1919); his examination of international monetary matters; and his inquiries into our economic system.

II

"The Economic Consequences of the Peace" appeared in the late autumn of 1919. It cried woe. The book transported its readers to Bedlam (a spot of which Keynes was often reminded when visiting the realm of statesmanship).

His censure touched all features of the Treaty. But it centered on economic terms, particularly the reparation demands imposed on Germany. These, he argued in an analytical brief that impressed the world, were hugely beyond Germany's capacity to pay. The refusal of the Allies to fix a terminal time for the obligation would, moreover, kill any impulse to try to pay. Such a

[1] "The Life of John Maynard Keynes," by R. F. Harrod. New York: Harcourt, Brace, 1951.

reparation policy, Keynes predicted, would condemn Germany to misery, reduce her to servitude, and must fail. It would work havoc everywhere, destroy forever the interests which sustained and held Western Europe together, and rob the newly created states of a chance to live. As summarized in a letter to Austen Chamberlain in May: "The Prime Minister is leading us all into a morass of destruction. The settlement which he is proposing for Europe disrupts it economically and must depopulate it by millions of persons. The New States we are setting up cannot survive in such surroundings. Nor can the peace be kept or the League of Nations live."

These verdicts more deeply shocked because of his interpretation of the making of the Treaty. A most sensitive and disturbed artist had been in the conference room along with the Treasury expert; and around the grim statistics he wrote a tale of scorn and horror. Such excusing historic reasons as there were for the Treaty were, in his telling, subdued. The tensions and hatred that had forced the creation of new states and inspired the wish that Germany be made to pay appeared in a wanton light. Passion, fear, hurt, the wish for independence—none of these is granted right to satisfaction. Ruin was being prepared because nations were acting like rabble and ignoring the compulsive facts of economics. And this was so because the leaders of the victorious allied countries—Lloyd George, Clemenceau and Woodrow Wilson—were, each in his own way, so failing in purpose or character. The decisions are dramas of personal traits and responsibility. One might think almost that the Treaty was distilled out of Lloyd George's waywardness, Wilson's stubbornness and Clemenceau's grey gloves.

Of the three, it was Wilson's standing among men that suffered most, and the cause for which Wilson fought. Keynes struck him hardest—from his own disappointment and hurt, probably. For he had hoped for little wise or fair of the other two, but of Wilson he had. In his eyes the American President forsook the good which he had avowed. He who had once spoken of a "peace without victory" had consented to a harsh victor's peace; and then, self-deceiving, denied the fact. Thus Keynes found him wholly wanting: a rigid, nebulous, ill-informed fraud. Also irritating to Keynes was the "Wilsonian dogma which exalts and dignifies the divisions of race and nationality above the bonds of trade and culture."

Around the mistakes and injustice his denunciation whirled. Keynes' analysis soon proved itself. It became quickly evident that the reparations were, as he had argued, destructive and unenforceable. But the economic consequences were not as calamitous or lasting as those Keynes foresaw. For after the troubles and defaults of the kind that he predicted, the burden was reduced and payment made easier. Keynes' assault hastened the failure and prepared opinion for the needed revisions. In that way he himself revoked the sentence of doom which he had pronounced. By 1929 Germany had recovered. Her production, exports and imports were as great as before the war. Unemployment was less than half of that in Britain. Had the great depression not begun, reparations would soon have become a secondary feature of international economic life. Those who thought Keynes' excitement extreme may thus maintain that they were right. But they were not, because the erosion by which the settlement was dissolved did great harm. It left a miasmic pond of misery which awaited Hitler's image.

The mark left by Keynes' polemic spread far beyond the particulars of the reparations settlement. It sharpened perception over a wide area of experience; and it refreshed lessons that had been forgotten or ignored. First, that the victors in war are not usually able to make the losers pay for or repair their losses; and that sustained attempts to make them do so will increase rather than lessen the damage. Only slavery and sack—as practised by the Romans and Russians—can qualify this conclusion greatly. Second, that statesmen must give heed to economic consequences when settling frontiers, transfers of territory, issues of statehood. Third, that regard for the economic fortunes of other countries is not merely an act of kindness, but an essential condition of good relations, and perhaps of peace. Fourth, that peacemaking is not apt to be a consistent exercise in the application of some general principle, or moral idea. It is apt rather to be a savage struggle, swayed by prejudice among conflicting desires for advantage, safety and power, until and unless we have a strong international system of order permeated by morality.

As against these points of instruction—commonplaces now— a heavy bill of consequences lies against Keynes. Proof of this opinion cannot be given here. Such as there may be is diffused through the millions of pages and in one's memories and those of friends. Many came to think, under the influence of his words, that the war of 1914–18 was a struggle without meaning; that the Allies were as responsible for it as Germany; that the whole Treaty imposed upon Germany was cruelly unjust; that Germany would be well justified in destroying it as soon as she could; that the small new states had no future. Nor in his view did Europe have much future. Did not he write that we were hearing "the fearful convulsions of a dying civilization?"

These versions of events and prospects, toward which he persuaded many, had, as I have said, consequences. Of these, two surged with enough force against the structure of peace built at Versailles to be reckoned among the causes of its crumbling. Germans (and many others) could, on this authority, trace the source of the misery that beset them to the Treaty, not only in the early twenties, but in the depression years. It became easier to forget that the war itself did more permanent damage to Germany's economic condition than the Treaty, and to suppress the fact that Bruening's policy of drastic deflation in the midst of world-wide depression contributed much to the mass unemployment of the early thirties. Keynes, so far as I know, made no effort to prevent such deductions from his work. Hitler's screams about the *Diktat* of Versailles could travel down an authorized road.

Those Americans who wanted to keep clear of Europe and its conflicts were also given sanction for their views. Wilson had been a solemn innocent abroad; France and Britain—sterile and grasping—had made it almost inevitable that war in Europe would soon come again; we could not clear up this mess; the League of Nations was a trap. Toward judgments of this sort many Americans were drawn on reading Keynes. Harrod points out that the American Senate had rejected the Treaty, as presented, before the "Economic Consequences" appeared in print. Therefore, he concludes, "Keynes can be entirely exempted from any shadow of responsibility for the great American decision, which was to have such vast effect on the working of the European settlement." That is so. But that was not the last of the issues of our relationship with Europe and the League. Keynes made it seem futile, if not fatal, to engage American fortune with theirs.

Judgments and phrases such as his are remembered long after they are read. Taunts survive long after their objects are dead. This was no masque, no ballet that ended of an evening. The wind in which he tossed his pamphlet had course and currents with which he, in his despair, did not wisely reckon. His theme was sound. His revolt against the Treaty justified. But now, looking back, it seems that his reasoning proved too much, his scorn was too corrosive, and his compassion was badly shared as between Germany and the countries that had to live next her. His gift for exposing error was greater than his power to guide the world toward balanced harmony. In judging treaties, tolerance is to be prized more than wit; for most of them are but mauled children of forced consent.

III

Keynes' attention gradually turned away from the turmoil of adjusting economic realities and political actions in the countries of Europe. For a while he followed these subjects as observer and reporter. But his comment became less declamatory, more hopeful. His soaring, sterilizing mind reverted to matters on which it had been engaged before.

His effort was purposeful. The world possessed the means and knowledge to live decently and securely; why did it not manage to do so? It had need of the labor of all, but many were idle, decayingly idle. It endured poverty while in sight of plenty, anxious misery next to great riches. What interests, attitudes or forms were responsible? Or what faults of understanding, or errors of policy? He went in search of the explanation; and, when he thought he had located the trouble, in search of the remedies. His answers qualify him for place among the greatest physicians of our public affairs.

His concern struck first against the prevailing international monetary system. Conditions spurred his pen. There was then— in the twenties—persistent unemployment in Britain and stiffness in the joints of her economy. No longer could it with ease make the adjustments required of a faithful adherent to the international gold standard, with a fixed gold value for sterling. It was essential, his traveling mind concluded, that Britain (and other countries) withdraw from these bonds, in order to do what must be done to invigorate economic life.

His scrutiny of the gold standard system broke its authority. A despot king gold had been. Keynes, at the start, thought it could be tolerated as a constitutional monarch. But at the end it was deposed: the currency rulers regarded it merely as their treasure, to be managed like any other asset.

The charges he pressed against the gold standard were several. Each was a shock to most of the world of finance. He showed the irrationality of allowing the trend of money incomes and prices throughout the world to be influenced by changes in the total supply of gold, and the still greater irrationality of allowing the rate of economic activity in any individual country to vary with the quantity of that metal in its possession. And most irrational of all was the toleration of unemployment and misery because the supply of gold in any country ran short, or the toleration of unhealthy expansion because the supply grew greatly. None of this, he urged, was a necessary feature of a sound and serviceable currency system, either national or international. All of it was wasteful and socially unjust.

Events were moving with his opinions, but not as rapidly. He anticipated rather than recorded fact when in 1923 he wrote that passage which teased his antagonists: "In truth, the gold standard is already a barbarous relic. . . . A regulated non-metallic standard has slipped in unnoticed. It exists. While economists dozed, the academic dream of a hundred years, doffing its cap and gown, clad in paper, has crept into the world by means of the bad fairies, always so much more potent than the good—the wicked Ministers of Finance."

Keynes recognized, except when the imp of controversy tickled his hand, that there was need for some form of order and restraint in the monetary relations among nations. He was aware that unless there were some kind of commonly endorsed international rules all countries might be the worse off. There was a danger, he appreciated, that the freedom gained by discarding the gold standard might turn into a riot of loose national financing, debased currencies, unhealthy surges of capital across frontiers, and unsettling trade reversals—as the supporters of the gold standard said it must. And there was danger too that this abuse of freedom might in the end bring clamping controls upon all trade and enterprise. In answer he urged regulatory management. "We should," it was his reiterated plea, "rid ourselves of deep distrust of regulation of the standard of value by deliberate decision."

But how? By what means and principles? On these questions he wavered. Anyone who now rereads the proposals he made during 20 years will find them a lexicon of many variations. His views were supple—and subject to abrupt change—particularly as regards the question whether management should be national or international. Should each country do its own managing, or was there need for a system conducted internationally? His views on this revolved with his judgment as to which of the two methods was, at the moment, more likely to stimulate economic expansion.

Thus in 1923 he opposed the idea of joint management with the United States, since it would make Britain too dependent on the policy of the Federal Reserve Board. He was sure that Britain at that time needed a policy that would increase money values as an alternative to poverty and collapse; the United States was not then subject to the same necessity. Hence his conclusion: "I see grave objections to reinstating gold in the pious hope that international coöperation would keep it in order." This also dictated the judgment he passed upon Britain's decision in 1925 to return to gold at the old parity; "a triumph of unreasoning prejudice," he called it. In short, international management could be beneficial only if there were assurances that it would not, in effect, restrict in the way that gold does. This is the consistency, I think, behind his inconsistency. It was the conditioning factor in his quest.

But by 1930 all countries were in the same plight. Here was the time to strike, he thought, and strike he did (in a "Treatise on Money"). At the end of that most stimulating and comprehensive analysis of monetary matters, he proposed the creation of an International Monetary Authority to manage the value of gold. It was to be the center of a cluster of national systems which would try to regulate the price level. This meant an active, coördinated effort to raise the level of prices, and to stimulate investment till all had work. Each government was to make borrowing easy and cheap, and each, if necessary, was to subsidize or direct domestic schemes of capital investment.

No government was ready for a program such as this. Each country, as the slump grew worse, thought and fought for itself alone. Keynes swung with the tide: if such individual effort, then, was the only way managed expansion could be attained, he was ready to acclaim that method. Thus when Britain left the gold standard in 1931 he wrote: "There are few Englishmen who do not rejoice at the breaking of our gold fetters." And when Roosevelt in 1933 rejected the flexible stabilization accord prepared in London, he hailed the decision as "magnificently right." Others will disagree with this opinion, as I do, even though they share Keynes' belief that it was essential at that time that money values should keep on the rise. But the difference of judgment about this decision cannot be argued here.

Ten years later (1943) his thought came to logical fullness. In a plan for an International Clearing Union his mind flung itself into most brilliant exposition of a plan of universal expansion. This time his ideas were approved by the British Government. His design was to harmonize monetary intentions by underwriting a simultaneous effort by all countries to engage in fullest economic activity.

Each country was to allow all others to draw upon it for such amounts of its currency—up to a high limit—as they might need. This would enable each and all, he reckoned, to expand investment, production and employment without quick or close regard for its balance of payments. Debits and credits between members of the Union were to be adjusted in good time by the responsible effort of each and all. Relative values of currencies were to be left fluid, but subject to international scrutiny.

The proposal smashed against two main objections. Keynes proposed that as much as 25 or 30 billions (dollar equivalent) should be available as needed. All knew it would be dollars that would be most wanted. Such a sum was then deemed by the American Government outside of reason. There was another objection, also tough. Would not this scheme—providing credit for the asking, almost—be misused and abused? Would it not support the lazy, the corrupt and selfish among nations at the expense of the industrious and honest? That it would have seems beyond dispute.

The Bretton Woods Agreements were the compromise. These acknowledged lesser purposes and provided strictly limited funds. Keynes seemed to reconcile himself to the stingy substitute. Some reasons why he did may be surmised. These agreements made some extra dollars available to Britain and others in a time of great need. They subordinated gold, though to the superficial observer they did not seem to do so. They contemplated easy adjustment of exchange rates. They admitted, in the scarce-currencies provision, that creditors had joint responsibilities with debtors for disequilibrium in the international accounts. And they endorsed the reasonableness of the goal of full employment. Keynes' conceptions had been recognized, though the means of satisfying them had not, then and there, been provided.

These features were enough to turn Keynes, for the first time (and only for a short time), into an almost uncritical friend of the American financial authorities. But his satisfaction was brief. At the inaugural meeting of the International Fund at Savannah, it became clear that the sponsors had not, at Bretton Woods, really agreed as to how it should operate. Keynes ran squarely into the question of *who* would do the managing. The American Government, speaking through Mr. Vinson, made it plain that it intended to assert its power as provider. American wishes would be most influential if not dominant. Further, the task was not to be left to sheltered experts and officials. It might be taken over by untutored politicians. To make the issue still graver, Keynes perceived that the Americans thought that the Fund should exert severe censorship over the monetary policies of its members. This was contrary to his previous understanding and wish. Keynes recoiled, and on his return trip to Washington, his heart failed.

But his work in this field was transforming. He had scented events and emerging pressures clearly, and his arguments had changed prevailing thought and practice. Stability at a high level of activity was raised to first place among the aims of national and international monetary policy. Free convertibility of currencies remained a desirable objective but was no longer regarded as essential. The obligation to maintain fixed gold values of currencies took a subordinate place in prevailing economic thought. The idea of deliberate management of international monetary relations displaced the belief that economic tides should be allowed to run their course. Whether governments know enough to manage well, whether they will act decently enough, time will tell. Keynes did more than any man of his time to instruct us as to how they may act wisely.

IV

In his studies of monetary policy, Keynes was seeking freedom to use monetary measures to correct economic deformities. But unless the causes of the trouble were more certainly identified, and more thoroughly known, even the best prescription could be only an inspired guess.

Classical economic theory, as taught at Cambridge, proffered explanations. But these Keynes found unsatisfactory. They seemed to him in some respects in conflict with experience, in others indifferent to it. The logic of these theories, he concluded, needed rearrangement, its equilibriums needed reëxamination, and its application needed correction. His writings on these matters were more crucial than all else he did. For here he was dissecting the heart of the system of free private enterprise. At the end of his work he had created a system of economic analysis which much improved our understanding. But it is doubtful whether he managed fully to solve (or dissolve) the main problem which he exposed.

The older doctrine concluded that, under the conditions assumed, the system of private enterprise could and would take care of itself well, and tended toward equilibrium with employment for all. If all participants in production bowed to the decisions of the market (thus allowing flexible money wage rates, prices and interest rates) there could be no persisting flaw: payments for production would provide the purchasing power needed to buy the product and keep all productive elements well employed. After examining the propensities and institutions which governed the flow and use of purchasing power, Keynes reached quite contrary conclusions. First, that our economy might arrive at, or come to rest in, many other situations besides full employment; "equilibrium" (for he clung to that abstraction) could be reached in any situation. Second, that marked fluctuations were probable, and the period of slump not necessarily transient. The reasoning which led to these conclusions was conducted with cold, technical logic. But he spelled out their meaning boldly; posted it in plain and large letters for the world to read as it ran—downhill.

As a portrayal of the characteristics of our economy, his analysis has won acceptance. Not as the whole and invariable truth; but as a more discerning and profound report on the pattern and behavior of the forces at work than any other. Our economic system may fail badly and stubbornly to yield full measure for our resources and effort. It does so at times; and much of the time it comes close to doing so. It must—and this was Keynes' plea— be made to do so all of the time.

Many, myself among them, who accept the main course of his reasoning, find his exposition murky or inconclusive in two important ways. First: the analysis of the cause of the failure of purchasing power does not seem complete. Second: he seems to have no answer to the question of proportionality over the long run between accumulated investment and the size of national income. This—if it be so—means that his prescriptions may bring only transient cures, need larger and larger doses, and in the end necessitate complete control of the patient.

Vast as it is, the interpretative literature on his theories does not seem to clear up these perplexing points. That should not cause surprise. For Keynes shared the revolving course of his cogitations too soon with his readers. He changed his formulations in successive works, correcting himself without remorse and with only curt apology.

Loosely it may be said that in all versions of his work he located the main cause of malfunctioning of the system to failure of "effective demand." This he traced to faulty use of income—as between spent income, saved income and invested income. But on what a turntable of logic and definition his analysis went round! In 1929 he wrote with blunt finality, "When investment runs ahead of saving, we have a boom, intense employment, and a tendency to inflation. When investment lags behind we have a slump and abnormal unemployment." His concepts seemed ordinary, his definitions usual, his meaning simple. In his next work, "Treatise on Money" (1930), he seemed to leave his basic dictum unaltered: ". . . disequilibrium between savings and investment is the mainspring of change." But in this book different and novel meanings were assigned to the terms "savings" and "investment." They were used by Keynes from then on not as names of familiar acts, but as symbols for deduced abstractions. He came to regard them as determinates within the economic system, not determinants.

This was a novel form of statement rather than a revolutionary conclusion. But it seemed to be so. For by his rearranged treatment of economic behavior he lifted attention away from the acts of saving and investment in their evident and familiar sense; he fixed attention instead upon the propensities which, over a period of time, determined how much saving and how much investment *were actually realized*. By this turn of exposition he brought into startling prominence certain ideas previously left in the background. For example, that the amount a country could save was not governed by the part of its income its people tried to put aside, but by the flow of effective demand, as sustained by investment.

These ideas remained in his next and greatest book, "The General Theory of Employment, Interest and Money." But as a result of the further changes in the cage of definition within which his reasoning was conducted, Keynes now insisted that savings and investment must come out equal and even. It is no wonder that ever since his thought has had to make its way through confusion. To the searcher for his meaning a quotation used in the "Treatise" may well recur: "The wild duck has dived down to the bottom—as deep as she can get—and bitten fast hold of the weed and tangle and all the rubbish that is down there, and it would need an extraordinary clever dog to dive and fish her up again."

Keynes stated the practical inferences of his analysis in propellant phrases, to the following effect:

1. Unless necessary measures are taken, the capitalist system may destroy itself.

2. Since consumption lags behind income, employment cannot increase unless new investment increases; hence there can be prolonged unemployment. And ". . . moreover the richer the community, the wider will tend to be the gap between actual and potential production; and therefore the more obvious and outrageous the defects of the economic system. For its propensity to consume will be weaker and the opportunities for investment less —unless the interest rate falls enough." Here is the frightening ghost of "stagnation" which during the thirties roamed through American economic texts.

3. A too vigorous attempt on the part of too many to save was apt to have bad results, and be self-defeating.

4. A redistribution of income will favor economic progress.

5. Governments must see to it that "effective demand" is sufficient to keep the productive system fully employed. To this end interest rates should usually be kept low. But since this and related measures might not serve, a comprehensive socialization of investment might prove to be the only means of securing an approximation to full employment.

v

What can be said of these in the light of past wisdom and recent experience? Five brief and inadequate comments may be ventured. One: this counsel is surely in the right direction and its prospect of progress is invigorating. Two: any general theory of economic behavior is of necessity abstract. Even though the type of economic system is the same in, say, two countries, the operative tendencies will be in degree different in each. Hence even though the same general prescription may be sound for all, the proper dose for each, and the proper mode of administering it, will be different for each. Keynes' prescription fitted Britain best. Three: its bent against deliberate saving—that is to say, thrift—is excessive. Such severe disparagement could be justified only on the supposition that much or most saving is hoarded. Four: the thesis may not give due place to the stimulus of invention. Five: the intense emphasis on investment as a cure may easily be taken for a cure-all. That certainly it can never be.

Unless social relations within a community are good, and there is enough flexibility (of all kinds) within the economic system, investment, no matter how well subsidized or sustained, will not bring stable and full activity. Inflation will be cumulative, and the effort will end either in collapse or thorough control or both.

Keynesian ideas have had great subsurface effect in the international field—first of shock, then of reassurance. For they were infused with certainty that if the Western capitalist or semi-Socialist democracies are alert and flexible, they can perform well and can assure a better and more secure economic life than ever before. Keynes tells us that if necessary measures are taken, their best time lies before them, not behind.

This was the emerging answer to the Marxian prophecies of inanition and collapse. Keynes summarily rejected the Marxian exposition of our economic system. Marx argued that the extension of the private capitalist system, by which it accumulates and uses more and more capital, condemns it to collapse. Keynes, in contrast, conceived capital accumulation (investment) as the means by which the whole society can improve its condition without end —provided (and the provisos were all-important) it took the proper means and measures. Thus he carefully distinguished his analysis from the theories of "over-saving" or "under-consumption." These, he pointed out, argue that the distribution of wealth leads to over-investment—"an entirely different terrain than my theory; inasmuch as on my theory it is a large volume of saving which does *not* lead to a corresponding large volume of investment (not one which *does*) which is at the root of the trouble." Again, and later, he emphasized the focal point of difference; that the troubling factor in our economy is not excessive saving, causing excessive accumulation of capital, but the propensity to save more income than is attracted into investment. In the Marxian analysis the course of capital growth itself creates an impasse; in the Keynesian, capital growth can bring mounting advantage.

Keynes' ideas stimulated a revision of international economic attitudes and expectations. The poorer, capital-lacking countries took them up eagerly. They were soon translated into requests for foreign aid, and into proposals for the international maintenance of investment. Capital has been made not only the key to prosperity, but also a test of international friendship. Formerly power to repay (to transfer) seemed an accepted limit to the advisable flow of capital across frontiers. Now the prevalent attitude justifies the investment in face of obscure transfer prospects, on the theory that the resultant full use of resources will provide the solution. It is ironic that Keynes, whose first great work centered on the difficulties of transfer payments across frontiers, in the end sowed the belief in the expansibility of transfer capacity.

It is to the United States above all that other nations look for the realization of the promise of a better economic life that Keynes' work holds out. The responsibility is a proper consequence of American economic strength. It will be, as we are learning, neither cheap nor easy. But it may be greatly rewarding.

To his last days the remark Keynes made in 1926 to the Manchester Reform Club remained true: "The Republic of my imagination lies on the extreme left of celestial space." The world has been fascinated by his flight over the vast regions between here and there. Since he is gone, we must do for ourselves the job of correcting, as we coldly test, those trails which his genius found.

¶ THE FUTURE OF DEMOCRACY IN LATIN AMERICA
by Frank Tannenbaum   (April, 1955)

In this century, in most Latin American countries, political and military dictatorships have alternated with periods of revolutionary upheaval and sporadic pursuit of the chimera of constitutional democracy. Despite real economic growth, the lot of most Latin Americans has not shown comparable improvement. Since Frank Tannenbaum wrote this article in 1955, changes affecting much of the Southern Hemisphere have taken place. Nationalism, expressed particularly in a movement for economic independence from the United States, has provided at least a superficial bond among various strata of society. But his analysis of the causes of political instability in Latin America remains valid today, and his prescription for an important role by local administration strikingly prefigures the now fashionable concept of decentralization.

Frank Tannenbaum was one of a small band of American historians with firsthand knowledge of Latin America; his own experience was mostly of Mexico. He had faith in democracy (in indigenous form) for Latin America. In the city neither the middle class, the labor unions, nor the intellectuals could muster the power to counterbalance the army, the oligarchy, and the Church, while in the country no organization of interests replaced the local leadership. Thus, many Latin Americans are excluded from the political process.

If rural people are to participate, Tannenbaum asserted, they must do so as members of their communities rather than as individuals, for the rural folk in the Andean area, Central America, and Mexico are communal rather than individualistic. He proposed a scheme that seemed rather utopian at the time but that is very similar to ideas widely endorsed by today's urban and regional planners as "decentralization" and "local control." He emphasizes the need for local communities to be accepted as self-sufficient entities with their own integrated value systems and for their administration and education to be geared to their own needs and resources. "The program of the school," he wrote, "is how to discover the ways to the good life within the place where the community is located and with the available resources—for there are no others."

THE FUTURE OF DEMOCRACY IN LATIN AMERICA

By Frank Tannenbaum

THERE is no reason for believing that political stability in Latin America is greater in the nineteen-fifties than it was a hundred years ago. Revolutions in the last 30 years have been as frequent, dictatorships as numerous, durable and oppressive as they were a century ago. It may, of course, be argued that the reasons for instability have changed, and the contention may or may not be true. But the fact of revolution versus dictatorship has remained constant. It cannot even be said that the contemporary revolutions are less bloody or that the tyrannies are more humane. What happened in Colombia between 1946 and 1954 is sufficient to disprove that thesis. Democratic government has remained an unfulfilled hope in spite of the many interesting constitutions that have been written during the last century. The aspiration to achieve the ideal of legality has failed. I shall seek here to suggest some reasons for the failure and to argue for a way out of the dilemma posed by the dream of representative democracy and the fact of revolution or dictatorship.

Contemporary Latin American political difficulties cannot be divorced from their historical past. The Spanish tradition is authoritarian, bureaucratic and centralized. The tradition is to leave political responsibility to the government and expect it to do everything. The extreme individualism of the Spanish character and the authoritarian tradition of the Spanish government seem to go hand in hand. The bureaucratic colonial administration controlled every agency of political administration—with the exception of the *cabildo* (township), and the township government was immersed in petty localisms. It was aristocratic in character and incompetent to become the base of a national government. The descendants of the Spaniards, the *criollos*, who led the independence movements, were inexperienced in politics and possessed no clear concepts of nationality. The nation was in the future, something to be forged, molded and solidified. This was true territorially as well as ideologically. There was either no American tradition to appeal to, or it was nebulous and fanciful —such as the attempt to resurrect the Incaic past. There was certainly a sense of identity of the American as against the Spaniard or the European, but the form and substance of this something new upon which the future political life of the people was to be reared had not been molded and the process of integration remains incomplete.

The character of the Latin American people is still being formed and a sense of inner identity and unity such as characterizes the Italian, the French or the English people is something that lies in the future. The king and crown of the Spanish past were unacceptable, and the local milieu, as Bolivar so clearly saw, would not tolerate an American monarchical system. But the milieu proved recalcitrant to all other forms of government. If it visibly rejected the rule of the absolute king, it also resisted and found unpalatable the ideas that derived from the French *philosophes* and United States constitutionalism.

The bitter and disorganized wars of independence, that had no central guidance, no official date of termination, and ended in no peace treaty, had shattered a great empire and stable government and led to a political vacuum and social disorganization. The end of the wars found Latin America divided in many separate countries, each in turn fractured into regional provinces governed by municipal oligarchies and ruled by local military *caudillos*. The king as the symbol of government had disappeared without leaving as substitute any other universally accepted idea around which a common loyalty could be evoked and in the name of which government could be carried on. The magic words of liberty, equality and fraternity fell on deaf ears and had a hollow sound, for the society remained stratified, and divided in *castas*. Neither the sacrifice nor the heroism of the wars of independence made the ideals of the French *philosophes* and American constitutionalism operative. For what had happened was that, of the two great public institutions—the crown and the church—the first had been destroyed and the second had been seriously weakened. The traditional sources of recognized authority were no longer sufficient. They were substituted for, because authority there has to be, by the informal and legally non-recognized rule of the plantation family associated with the local military. The hacienda with its control of acreages sometimes greater than a European principality became the effective source of local political power. The fact that the power it exercised had no basis in law was irrelevant to its effective rule of its own domain. With the hacienda went the control of hundreds and sometimes thousands of people. These retainers and *peones* provided a personal militia useful for defense and, if need be, for attack. By intermar-. riage, by the institution of *compradazgo* (godfatherhood), by alliances forged of mutual dependence and neighborliness, the plantation system ruled the region, and the leading landowner was "king of all he surveyed." The independence movement had substituted this locally effective but legally nonexistent means of rule and governance for the authority of the king it had destroyed.

The national governments in the early days were so busy try-ing to stay in power that they had little time to "govern." When there is a new rebellion to suppress every month, and when for many years there is annually a new "national" administration brought in by a new revolution, it is idle to talk about the de-tails of governing—that fell naturally to those that had both sta-bility and power locally. Someone had to protect the locality, its families and its animals, and they who could do that were in fact the governors even if not graced by the name or sanctioned by the requisite legal formula. A detailed description of the life of the older plantations would show it to be both a society and a government; and so it had to be, and so it remained during the nineteenth century, and to some extent so it is, or was until 1910 if not until 1930. There have been some changes—by revolution in Mexico, by the effect of new means of communication, indus-trialization, social theories, movements and agitation. But the plantation was until the day before yesterday, or the year before last, an economic, a social and a political system with powers of local rule and governance and with a powerful rôle in controlling the provincial and the national political systems. Only in Chile was this substantial fact recognized for what it was—a political force—and a government frankly designed to rest on the planta-tion family gave to that country peace and quiet through the years when the rest of Latin America was trying to build govern-ment upon an individualism that did not exist and upon ideas that had no local relevance.

The splintering of political authority and the rule of the local *caudillo* were fortified by a social stratification that has persisted in spite of the racial tolerance characteristic of Latin America. Certainly since the Independence, if not before, it has been pos-sible, at least in some countries, for the pure-blooded Indian, like Juarez, to reach the highest office. There has been room for the exceptional individual who, by some magic, had shed his Indian ways and taken on the outlook and interests of the *criollo* (descendant of the Spaniards). It was possible for him to become a respected member of the non-Indian community. Very much the same thing may be said of the Negro. An age-old law defined him as a legal person and the rule of the Catholic Church identified him as a moral person. This made manumission relatively easy, and kept the social system sufficiently flexible to permit the abolition of slavery without violence and to allow for the acceptance of the ex-slave as a freeman rather than a freedman. This tolerance opened the doors to cultural participation and made possible important contributions by the Negro and the mulatto to art, architecture, music and literature. Latin American society has certainly been friendly to the non-European, and the Negro, at least, has long felt himself identified with the people in Latin America. This is in sharp contrast to the fear and isolation that for so long beset the Negro in many parts of the United States. But after all this has been said, it has to be added that Latin American society has remained stratified, immobile and, if a colonial expression may be used, divided into *castas*. These are relative statements, but compared to the United States there is noticeably less vertical mobility in Latin America. The countries vary among themselves. There is more mobility in Argentina, Southern Brazil and Cuba than there is in Ecuador or Colombia, and a great deal more than in Peru. But the rôle of the important family, the barrier made by wealth, race and occupation, is markedly obvious in its effect upon social mobility.

More important perhaps than the above sources of social stratification is division between country and city, between urban and rural. The city belongs to one world and the country to another. The capital of the country, like Mexico, Guatemala or Lima, will have all the modern conveniences, newspapers and universities, electric lights and refrigeration. But the little village in the country will in all likelihood have neither literacy nor shoes nor electric lights—it may not even have the Spanish language. More than that, the rural communities may have value systems of their own; their own inner hierarchy, their own sense of propriety, make them a world apart from the city, nation, state or government. A village of Trique Indians in Oaxaca, a Cakchiquel village in Guatemala, a Quetcha Indian village high in the mountains in the province in Ayacucho, has little in common with the world to which it officially belongs, and the political life of the "nation" remains an unrevealed mystery. They do not know the meaning of the activity called politics.

For these and many other reasons political leadership has been regional and personal. The local *caudillo* was secure from outside interventions and beyond the need of support from a "political party" because his power rested in the loyalty of an extended family, rich in lands and sure of the coöperation of neighboring towns entwined economically and socially with the dominant hacienda ownership. This leader was the "political party" in his region. The people were his. The phrase went "people of Don Pancho" or "of Don Pedro," or "of General Contreras;" there were no other people in the region—and the region might be larger than a good-sized state in the United States. In that area there was only one politician, one party, one loyalty. Everyone belonged to him, and all affairs, even the most personal, the most trivial, were brought to him for settlement and adjudication. He knew and tolerated no opposition, and no stranger could travel in the country without his explicit or implicit consent, for he controlled all the agencies of government, in so far as there were such agencies, including the tax gatherer, the judge, the sheriff, the schoolteacher and the local militia. He was the patron, the father, the judge, the protector of all "his people" and they were loyal to him. If he wanted to run for office, he could always be elected unanimously—for it would occur to no one to oppose him —and his politics did not matter. If he did not wish to run for office, his blessing was sufficient to elect anyone it was bestowed upon. In fact, his mere consent was equivalent to an election— with or without a counting of the votes. This *caudillo* could die but he could not be removed. He could be murdered, or driven from power by armed force coming from another part of the country under another *caudillo,* or by the national army controlled at the time by his enemies. But short of these exceptional circumstances, he enjoyed lifelong tenure and his place was secure and his rule absolute.

Under these and similar circumstances, the government could rest only upon the army, and the political party could be only personal. Admittedly, this is a somewhat overdrawn description if taken as applying universally to all parts of Latin America— but not so overdrawn as to be misleading. Admittedly, too, this is a picture of rural rather than urban social, economic and political structure. But Latin America is rural, and the urban has been deeply influenced by this leadership design of the countryside. In the smaller mestizo towns and cities this influence is immediate and visible—because the "family" and its many ramifying alliances fill the important places and are conspicuous in the economic and social life of the community. To an extent hard for New Yorkers to understand, but not so difficult for people in Charleston, South Carolina, or Richmond, Virginia, the important families rule the state, and not only socially. Lima and Quito are good examples of what I am trying to say. But Popayan, Mendoza and Bahia would be even better examples of a rule over the town by families whose roots are in the country. National politics were shaped by the antagonisms and alliances among these regional *caudillos* and their extended families.

Since 1910 a number of influences have tended to change this picture. Better communication, increased literacy, a growing industry, a larger middle class, a trade union movement, the impact of such exotic ideas as Fascism and Communism, the great rôle of a strident nationalism, the criticisms of and legislative attacks upon the *latifundia,* the very rapid expansion of the large cities with their tendency to dissolve the older family loyalties and dependencies, the wealth produced in some places by oil, minerals and large investments in agricultural enterprises—these have, taken together, weakened the rôle of the regional *caudillo* and the dominion of his imperious family. Another reason for his lessening power and prestige has been the acquisition of more efficient arms by the government in power. This has tended to weaken the "democratic" impact of regions against the national *caudillo* who has the machine guns, the tanks and the airplanes so generously provided him by the United States on the assumption that it was in the interest of the defense of continental democracy—but for the time being helping to perpetuate the self-elected ruler in the control of the government. Under the circumstances, political parties continue to be personal.

The trade unions have made some differences, but they, too, are largely dominated or controlled by the government in power. Presumably, the middle class has interests of its own and would —or should—have independent political aspirations that manifest themselves in political activity. But the middle class, like the trade unions, is so much under the thumb of the administration and so beholden to the government for favors received that it has in fact no effective means of opposing the administration. The mass of the people in most places are beyond the political horizon —they do not vote, are indifferent to the election, and in many instances, especially in the Andean countries, unaware of the nature and meaning of the political process. It must by now be clear that the government rests upon the army and why it can in fact rest upon nothing else. In the Andean countries at least, the local leadership, which was the natural foundation of political power in the past, has not been adequately substituted for. From some points of view, the political foundations in Latin America are weaker and less stable than they were, because nothing so clearly representative of a region or a class or an interest has replaced the local leadership.

Under the circumstances, the president of the country must be the author of his own political party and must unite about himself the group with which he governs. Once in office, he can brook no opposition because disagreement is a challenge to the power of the president and not to his policies. All dissent leads in the direction of revolution, and criticism is taken as a prelude to political violence. The president must make all the decisions, even the most trivial. He must rule the army, the civil service, the judiciary, the legislature, the universities and the economy. And with the current penchant for increasing governmental participation in the economic affairs of the nation, the president is ever more competent to favor his supporters and to punish his opponents. He must and does control the national and the local elections. No governor of a state can come to office against his will or remain in office against his wishes. The frequent use of the constitutional provision for "intervention" in Argentina and Brazil, and the equally effective powers exercised through the permanent committee of the congress in Mexico, make that clear enough. What holds true of a governor also applies to the election of members of congress and of the Senate. The power of the president is pervasive and nothing escapes it completely, not even the judiciary.

In addition, the president must decide who is going to succeed him, and he must be able to enforce that decision or face a revolution. This is true whether there is an official governmental party, as in the case of Mexico and Argentina, or not. The president will either choose his successor and place him in power, even if he decides to succeed himself, or someone else will make that choice and overthrow the régime to make sure of the election.

This is the most important political decision of the president and will affect his ability to pass on the executive powers peacefully to his successor. The more peaceful the election, the larger the officially announced vote, the quieter and the more democratic the electoral process seems, the more effectively has the original decision been carried out. Doubtful governors will have been removed, the police heads changed, the army's loyalty made sure of, the control of the voting machinery securely placed in proper hands and the final result known long before the formal decision-making process has been set in motion. That is why opposition parties frequently refuse to participate in the voting. They, like everyone else, know the outcome in advance and have no desire to lend moral sanction to an executive decision by taking part in the election. If, however, they do participate, it is in the hope that some accident—a rebellion or division of the army—will upset the official plan and a revolution will pave the way for their own candidate. One could point to Costa Rica, Uruguay, Chile and possibly Brazil as exceptions, but both Chile and Brazil have relatively recent histories that would neatly fit into the electoral process just described. The recent history of Bolivia is in some ways an exception. The government in power failed because of ineffective executive leadership to produce an electoral majority, the army took over the government, and a revolution based upon the miners and the urban workers ousted the army. But the entire electoral apparatus as revealed in the election of 1951 involved for all parties only 50,000 voters out of a population of more than 3,500,000. The parties do not represent the people—they represent the leaders.

In fact, party organization does not attempt to embrace the mass of the people and there is no experience that would lead a political party to the idea that it needs to be based upon the local communities, representing local interests meeting together to hammer out national policy. If one excepts Colombia, Chile, Uruguay and Cuba, it might be questioned whether there are, in fact, any political parties in Latin America that fit any meaningful definition. The APRA is a movement rather than a party. The Fascist and the Communist "organizations" are exotic groupings that may have significant political consequences but they are not describable as political parties; they are organized from the top down, have centralized control and discipline, and lack the local spontaneity so essential to representative political activity. The intellectuals in Latin America are an important political influence but they are not organized, have no power and serve a purely critical and negative function.

II

This bleak political panorama leaves little room for an optimistic formula on how to establish democratic and representative government in Latin America. What then is to be done—if anything effective can be done—in the face of a personal leadership tradition and a tenaciously stratified social system? The first need is to draw the people into political activity, and these are mainly rural rather than urban folk. In most of the countries, 50 to 80 percent of the people live in country villages, and many of the seemingly urban communities are essentially rural in their outlook, interest and activities. More important is the fact that the rural folk are, in the Andean area, in Central America and in Mexico, *communal* rather than individualistic. The concept of the individual as the base of the political party system, so characteristic of the United States, is not really applicable to vast areas in Latin America. If we are going to talk of effective participation in politics by the mass of the people in most of Latin America, we must recognize that we are talking about isolated and often highly integrated rural communities possessed of an internally tenacious value system. These communities must become part of the political party system if the parties are to represent the mass of the people or become instruments of effective democratic governments. But it will be hard to come by these aims.

In the Andean countries, with the possible exception of Venezuela, in Central America and in Mexico, the special character of Latin American rural organization, so largely neglected by intellectuals and politicians, hampers the easy development of effective political parties. The individual peasant-*ranchero* is a relatively rare specimen; perhaps not more than 5 percent of the total rural population and certainly not as high as 10 percent live on individual small farms which they own. One needs to make an exception here of Costa Rica and the highlands of Venezuela and parts of Colombia, but in countries like Mexico, Guatemala, Ecuador, Peru, Bolivia, Chile, and to a lesser extent in other places, the people live either in hacienda communities or in free villages. And these villages, as suggested above, are isolated from the nation politically, socially and to a very considerable extent culturally. In vast areas they are Indian rather than European, and even the mestizo villages are often immersed in an Indian rather than European cultural milieu. These rural communities live on the fringe of the monetary economy. They build their own houses, weave their own clothes, raise their own food, make their own utensils, and what they secure from the outside comes through a parochial market from other villages and frequently by barter. Many have little or no knowledge of the Spanish language, they are illiterate, and those who can read have neither newspapers nor books. They are in fact nonparticipants in the affairs of the nation.

These communities are the actual base of the nation, whatever city folk may think of the matter, and the future of the Latin American countries will be largely shaped by the changes that occur in these little human groupings. Mexico alone has over 100,000 rural villages. In countries where the hacienda system remains in full vigor, the problem is complicated by the fact that a majority of these villages may be located within the confines of the plantation and have no possibilities for independent political life and no room for initiative in their own community affairs. They can neither build a school, hire a teacher nor freely shape their own agricultural activities. We have no statistics for the distribution of the rural communities between the free and the plantation, but it would require great boldness to suggest that less than 50 percent of the inhabited places in Ecuador, Peru, Bolivia and Guatemala, not to mention other countries, are not located within hacienda boundaries. The point is worth stressing because it complicates the attempt to integrate the rural folk into the political life of the nation. To bring these communities to participate in the active political parties is difficult enough and the plantations make it more so—perhaps make it impossible. The preliminary to the growth of peaceful and representative government in Latin America is the disintegration of the present hacienda system. This may for many reasons prove neither possible nor practical. If so, then hopes for democratic government in Latin America are dim indeed.

But the plantation system is not the only thing that stands in the way. The cultural isolation of the rural community is equally effective as an obstacle to the growth of national representative government. This isolation, as the people working on the Point Four program know, makes the community apathetic and indifferent, almost unaware of the nation. The major single issue in the political destiny of Latin America is to bridge this gap between the rural Indian and mestizo community and the nation. This can be done only with an adequate system of rural education. At best, it will take—even with heroic effort—generations of unremitting devotion to the task.

The successful pursuit of this task requires a new vision of the nation itself—a nation of thousands of free, economically competent and culturally developed rural communities. The stability and well-being of the nation must be seen as depending upon the initiative and leadership shown by these villages. Latin American nations—at least the nations facing the Pacific—are multicellular, and each cell is frequently a community with its own value system. These communities have to be developed as such. The emphasis has to be on the group and not on the individual in the group. The needs of the community determine the school curriculum. The available resources are the raw materials which the school must use in its program, for in the long run it has no others. It needs to be remembered that a rural community has a fixed habitat—the mountains, the woods, the earth, the spring, brook, river or lake are given, and little can be done to change them. If the community is to achieve the good life, it must do so in *that* place—for there is no magic to move the mountain or change the course of the river. The climate, too, is given. The heat, moisture and rain are what they are, and man must find the skills and the wisdom to abide in comfort within the limitations nature has provided. Literacy may be useful, but habits, techniques, practical wisdom that derives from experience, and the special knowledge modern science can offer, are more immediately effective.

The question to be resolved is how to fit what modern science has to offer into this specific and limited environment. How to use and conserve the resources, how to keep the soil from eroding, how to purify the water, how to drain the swamp, or how to irrigate the land with the available waters and with the little means at the disposal of the community, how to make two blades of wheat grow where only one was grown before, how to increase the yield from the stalk of corn, how to select the new fruits that could thrive in the specific place, how to prune the tree, how to protect it from disease, how to conserve and use the fruit, how to build a good house out of the available stone, clay or bamboo, how to improve the diet by growing vegetables that will not wither or die, how to tap the underground for water in a desert area, how to make new uses of the local fibres, how to improve the weaving, how to design and cut a dress, how to improve the cooking, how to breed good pigs, how to smoke, salt or otherwise conserve the meat, how to improve the cattle of the village and how to adapt the hundred different possible uses of milk. All of these activities and a thousand more are the legitimate curricula of the rural school, not to mention the town band, the arts and crafts, and, if one lets his imagination go, the reading of good fiction and poetry.

The program of the school is how to discover the ways to the good life within the place where the community is located and with the available resources—for there are no others, and even the best of governments can do little to substitute for what nature has provided. The emphasis must be on creativity rather than on book learning. The school becomes the House of the People that is open from sunrise to the middle of the night. For the life of the community itself is mirrored in the school's activities. The children are there, but so are the women folk who use the school sewing machine or school medicine chest or consult the teacher who is a practical nurse; and the men are there when not at work to learn how to read or to use the tools from the school carpenter shop, or to discuss one of the many questions that arise every day of the year. The emphasis is upon the development of local leadership and the tapping of the tradition of coöperation imbedded in the rural community. Everything is done coöperatively. The school is built by the community with its own labor, all taking part, including the women and children. And every activity has to have its committee, its mutual responsibility, its special leadership, its special discussion. The school has to be built and largely maintained by the community, for the simple fact is that the governments do not have the financial resources out of which to build the schools, equip them and pay the teachers as well. *If it cannot be done by the communities it will remain undone.* Even in Mexico, where such heroic efforts have been made to develop a rural school system, at least half the children of school age are not going to school, and this is probably an understatement. In fact, the villages must learn to build and maintain their rural schools as they once built and maintained their rural churches; otherwise, the dream of a matured and self-confident rural community will remain a dream and representative democracy an unfulfilled hope.

III

It is easy enough to pose the issue in these—shall I say, romantic?—terms. It is difficult to visualize a realistic effort to meet the challenge the rural community represents. For one thing, this kind of program requires an almost religious devotion to the idea of an independent and mature rural community. Such a devotion to a rural ideal is hard to find and difficult to generate. Latin American intellectuals are urban and not rural minded. They are filled with the ideal of literary rather than practical education, and they simply do not know their own rural community and are on the whole indifferent to it. They do not see that the strength of the society and its stability requires a healthy and vigorous rural basis which in the Andean areas means thousands of self-sufficient rural villages.

What is true of the intellectuals is in most cases even truer of the governments. The government bureaucracy is urban minded and preoccupied with the large city. The capital of the country crowds all other communities to the very thin edge of the bureaucratic conscience. And equally serious is the fact that such a program cannot be developed in a country where the large plantation is the dominant rural institution. Unless the government has an effective agrarian policy, it cannot have an effective program of rural education—and the first may, for political reasons, be impossible and the second appear undesirable.

But even where the intellectuals—or some of them and the government as well—have a commitment to building a healthy multi-cellular nation based upon rural communities, the difficulties are so great as to seem almost insurmountable. The program of bringing these commitments and their leadership into the nation will require many years of continuing effort in the *same* direction. There is, to begin with, the lack of funds—a chronic state of affairs and, except for a windfall as in the case of Venezuela, not visibly remedial. But even with funds, where are the teachers to come from? The ordinary teachers' training courses do not prepare for the thousand needs and skills essential for the rural community. And worst, perhaps, teachers raised in an urban environment, unless moved by missionary zeal, find the rural community—where no Spanish is spoken, where there are no electric lights, no moving picture houses, and no newspapers—a place of exile. To be a rural schoolteacher in these surroundings calls for a high degree of self-sacrifice and devotion to an ideal. The Mexicans have tried to meet this difficulty by developing the Cultural Mission which, by periodically bringing the poorly trained rural schoolteachers together, gives them a renewed stimulus, additional training and a feeling of working on a task of national importance. A fully staffed and wisely administered rural normal school so placed as to train teachers for a given rural environment with similar problems would meet part of the difficulty, but only if it succeeded, which is almost impossible, in imparting many skills without so changing the habits and attitudes of its students as to make them wish for an escape to the city, which unfortunately is too often the case.

But all these obstacles are perhaps secondary to what is after all the major difficulty—to make the educational efforts constructive rather than disruptive of the life of the rural community, where prejudices are tenacious, values noncommercial and noncompetitive, and where the local mores are something apart from the urban and sophisticated world whence the educational impulse must come in the first instance. To be useful, the teacher, the administrator, must learn respect for the idiosyncratic cultural traits of the rural folk as a preliminary to the acceptance and trust without which nothing useful can be done. The emphasis must be upon building new habits, attitudes and institutions inside the rim of an older culture complex and not against it. It must always be borne in mind that the new habit or institution must make its way and be absorbed by the community, that changes must come from the inside, from accommodation, and not be forced. That if this can be accomplished, then there are vast resources of possible coöperation, initiative and leadership to be had. But confidence and good will must first be won, and they can be had only if the administrators and the teachers can accept the communities as moral entities with their own integrated value systems.

We have had some useful experience in this matter, most of it in Mexico where the rural education endeavor dates back to at least 1923. Here, however, the original impulse derived from a social upheaval that emphasized the needs of the rural community and the worthwhileness of the rural population. But even here some of the original impulse has been lost: impatience and too much sophistication have, as they always do, borne their usual fruit—skepticism and indifference. But the experience did show that when given the opportunity, thousands of rural communities not only built their own schools but took on, with an almost childlike faith, the many new responsibilities that the school brought.

It still remains a question whether such a program is sufficient for the purpose of bringing the communities into the political life of the nation. In some way the leadership developed in the rural communities must become related to or identified with the leadership of the larger world, and the schoolteachers and the inevitably bureaucratic personnel of a Department of Education are not the real leaders of either the community or the nation as a whole. General Lazaro Cardenas has recently initiated a voluntary effort by active people in the region about Uruapan, in the state of Michoacan, each of whom adopted a rural community as his special interest and responsibility. The individual in a sense is elected as the *padrino*-godfather of the village and takes on the rôle, establishing contact for the community with the larger world. He is the adviser and consultant, the guide and the counselor of his village, and tries to help it work out its own problems. This is an initial effort. It is nongovernmental. There are about 40 such individuals, each of whom has adopted and been accepted by a community. The undertaking has to remain nonpolitical, nonbureaucratic, and take on a missionary flavor. A meeting of these 40 people represents a cross section of the best available skills and scientific knowledge in the region. The group contains doctors, lawyers, engineers, chemists, agronomists, foresters, specialists in cattle, in fruit culture, and so on. The scientific and cultural resources of the group are impressive. And at the meeting which I attended it was interesting to see that these men would call on each other for help. One man said to another, "I have a water problem that my village does not know how to deal with. You know about these things. Could you come and spend a day with me?" It was evident that here were substantial resources that could be tapped in behalf of any one community. Equally important, here were possible contacts with the active leaders of the larger world.

If one could assume that the effort will persist, that it will not become bureaucratized, that it will develop into a kind of missionary movement, then perhaps we have the opening of a way towards bridging the gap between the rural community and the nation. But so many unresolved questions face the project that it will be a miracle if it fulfills even part of the promise it carries.

And any such program, difficult in itself, would have to hurdle two stubborn "states of mind" so deeply imbedded that they are likely to survive whatever political changes the winds may blow across Latin America. It would require the toleration of increased local independence and the devolution of the tax system so as to give the localities an increasing measure of income. As things stand at present, and have stood from time immemorial, the central government absorbs most of the available income and leaves a pittance to the states and the municipalities. Everyone expects it to be that way and local officials beg hat in hand as a favor what they could have had on their own if the tax were differently distributed. I would like to believe myself wrong in this characterization—for it will largely determine the prospect of political stability in Latin America—but the one revolution that has no advocates, no parties and no prospects is the one that would strengthen the parish, the township, the county and the state at the expense of the central government. And yet without such a change, neither the rural education we have been suggesting nor the political party to which it is antecedent can fully make its way.

The other "state of mind" is the well-nigh universal expectancy of centralized control and guidance of the economic and social life of the nation. The tradition of governmental regulation and "planning" antedates the Independence and is so much part of the milieu that all political credos take it for granted. The idea of planning, seemingly so new and so revolutionary, is congenial even to the most conservative Latin Americans, for to them the notion is old and inevitable. The government must do everything, for no one else will. That is the conviction and the expectancy. The friends of Latin American democracy who look to the planning of the economy as a means towards political stability and representative democracy will, to their disillusionment, discover that they have strengthened the central political machine at the expense of the localities and increased the barriers to representative government and political stability. The route out of the dilemma lies in the growth of local and national institutions with resilience enough to survive the all-absorbing tendency of the central government. But that growth will be slow and painful.

¶ REFLECTIONS ON AMERICAN DIPLOMACY

by Henry A. Kissinger   (October, 1956)

Henry A. Kissinger's article describes some of the pitfalls into which an American statesman may stumble when his antagonists belong to a different political order—a revolutionary order—and are concerned not with adjustments within a given framework but with the destruction of the framework itself. In a legitimate order, diplomacy seeks to compromise disagreements; in a revolutionary order, adjustments have primarily a tactical significance—that is, the aim is to prepare positions for the next test of strength.

Since the time of the article, Kissinger has assumed a predominant role in the formation of American foreign policy as Assistant for National Security Affairs to President Nixon and has been the chief strategist in arranging the President's visits to Peking and Moscow. The changes in his political philosophy are striking. In 1956, he wrote that the Soviets were offering peaceful coexistence not in order to solidify the status quo *but as a maneuver to subvert the existing order and substitute a communist order. And he quoted Chairman Mao as saying, "In the world, from now on, neutrality is only a word for deceiving people."*

Those warnings of a professor of history have not deterred him as a political practitioner from becoming involved in intense negotiations with the leaders of the Soviet Union and the People's Republic of China, embodiments of the world revolutionary order. One comment in his article may explain the disparity between earlier theory and later conduct. "Policy," he wrote, "exists in time as well as in space," meaning that measures are correct only if they can be carried out at the proper moment. What might not be possible in 1956 might, he hopes, become possible in 1972.

REFLECTIONS ON AMERICAN DIPLOMACY

By Henry A. Kissinger

"POLICY," wrote Metternich, the Austrian minister who steered his country through 39 years of crisis by a tour de force perhaps never excelled, "is like a play in many acts which unfolds inevitably once the curtain is raised. To declare then that the play will not go on is an absurdity. The play *will* go on either by means of the actors or by means of the spectators who mount the stage. . . . The crucial problem [of statesmanship], therefore, resides in the decision of whether to assemble the audience, whether the curtain is to be raised and above all in the intrinsic merit of the play."

There can be little doubt that the foreign policy of the United States has reached an impasse. For several years we have been groping for a concept to deal with the transformation of the cold war from an effort to build defensive barriers into a contest for the allegiance of humanity. But the new Soviet tactics, coupled with the equally unassimilated increase in the destructive potential of the new weapons technology, have led to a crisis in our system of alliances and to substantial Soviet gains among the uncommitted peoples of the world.

It would be a mistake, however, to ascribe our difficulties to this or that error of policy or to a particular administration, although the present Administration has not helped matters by its pretense of "normalcy." To return to Metternich's metaphor: It can be argued that our policy has reached an impasse because of our penchant for happy endings; the Soviet rulers have been able to use negotiations to their advantage because we insisted on reading from an old script. As in all tragedies, many of our problems have been produced in spite of our good intentions and have been caused, not by our worst qualities, but by our best. What is at issue, therefore, is not a policy but an attitude.

It is with this attitude and its consequences in the conduct of negotiations and our policy of alliances that this article seeks to deal.

II

It is understandable that a nation which for a century and a half had been preoccupied with its domestic affairs should seek to apply the pattern of these to international affairs. But the very success of the American experiment and the spontaneity of our social institutions have served to emphasize the dilemma faced at some stage by every country: how to reconcile its vision of itself with the vision of it as seen by others. To itself, a nation is an expression of justice, and the more spontaneous has been the growth of its social institutions the more this is true; for government functions effectively only when most citizens obey voluntarily and they will obey only to the extent that they consider the demands of their rulers just. But to other nations, a state is a force to be balanced. This is inevitable because national strategy must be planned on the basis of the other side's capabilities and not merely a calculation of its intentions. There exists a double standard, therefore, in all foreign policy: internally, foreign policy is justified like all other policy in terms of an absolute standard; but abroad, what is defined as justice domestically becomes a program to be compromised by negotiation. If the institutions and values of the states comprising the international order are sufficiently similar, this incommensurability may not become apparent. But in a revolutionary period like the present, it affects profoundly relationships among states.

Foremost among the attitudes affecting our foreign policy is American empiricism and its quest for methodological certainty: nothing is "true" unless it is "objective" and it is not "objective" unless it is part of experience. This makes for the absence of dogmatism and for the ease of social relations on the domestic scene. But in the conduct of foreign policy it has pernicious consequences. Foreign policy is the art of weighing probabilities; mastery of it lies in grasping the nuances of possibilities. To attempt to conduct it as a science must lead to rigidity. For only the risks are certain; the opportunities are conjectural. One cannot be "sure" about the implications of events until they have happened and when they have occurred it is too late to do anything about them. Empiricism in foreign policy leads to a penchant for *ad hoc* solutions; the rejection of dogmatism inclines our policy-makers to postpone committing themselves until all facts are in; but by the time the facts are in, a crisis has usually developed or an opportunity has passed. Our policy is therefore geared to dealing with emergencies; it finds difficulty in developing the long-range program that might forestall them.

A symptom of our need for methodological certainty is the

vast number of committees charged with examining and developing policy. The very multiplicity of committees makes it difficult to arrive at decisions in time. It tends to give a disproportionate influence to subordinate officials who prepare the initial memoranda and it overwhelms our higher officials with trivia. Because of our cult of specialization, sovereign departments negotiate national policy among each other with no single authority able to take an over-all view or to apply decisions over a period of time.[1] This results in a hiatus between grand strategy and particular tactics, between the definition of general objectives so vague as to be truistic and the concern with immediate problems. The gap is bridged only when a crisis forces the bureaucratic machinery into accelerated action, and then the top leadership has little choice but to concur in the administrative proposals. In short, we are trying to cope with political problems by administrative means.

The temptation to formulate policy administratively is ever present in a government organized, as ours is, primarily for the conduct of domestic affairs. But the spirit of policy and that of bureaucracy are fundamentally opposed. Profound policy thrives on creativeness; good administration thrives on routine—a procedure which can assimilate mediocrity. Policy involves an adjustment of risks; administration an avoidance of deviation. The attempt to formulate policy administratively leads to the acceptance of a standard which evaluates by mistakes avoided rather than by goals achieved. It is no accident that most great statesmen were opposed by the "experts" in their foreign offices, for the very greatness of the statesman's conception tends to make it inaccessible to those whose primary concern is with safety and minimum risk.

Our methodological doubt makes for vulnerability to Soviet manœuvres in two ways: on the one hand, every Soviet change of line is taken at least in part at face value, for we cannot be certain that the Soviets may not "mean" it this time until they have proved they do not; and they will try their best not to prove it until the tactic has served its purpose. On the other hand, we have found it difficult to adjust our tactics to new situations, so that we always tend to speak in the categories of the most recent

---

[1] This is true despite the National Security Council. Since the N.S.C. is composed mainly of department heads overwhelmed with administrative responsibilities, all the pressures make for a departmental outlook and a concern with immediate problems.

threat but one. The paradoxical result is that we, the empiricists, appear to the world as rigid, unimaginative and even somewhat cynical, while the dogmatic Bolsheviks exhibit flexibility, daring and subtlety. This is because our empiricism dooms us to an essentially reactive policy that improvises a counter to every Soviet move, while the Soviet emphasis on theory gives them the certainty to act, to manœuvre and to run risks. The very fact of action forces us to assume the risks of countermoves and absorbs our energies in essentially defensive manœuvres.

The willingness to act need not derive from theory, of course. Indeed, an overemphasis on theory can lead to a loss of touch with reality. In many societies—in Great Britain, for example—policy developed from a firmly held tradition of a national strategy. Throughout the nineteenth century it was a tenet of British policy that Antwerp should not fall into the hands of a major Power. This was not backed by an elaborate metaphysics but simply by a tradition of British sea power whose requirements were so generally understood that they were never debated. It is the absence of a tradition of foreign policy which exaggerates the biases of our empiricism and makes it difficult to conduct our policy with a proper regard for the timing of measures. It causes us to overlook the fact that policy exists in time as well as in space, that a measure is correct only if it can be carried out at the proper moment. To be sure, our cumbersome administrative mechanism adds immeasurably to the problem. But in addition, our deliberations are conducted as if a course of action were eternally valid, as if a measure which might meet exactly the needs of a given moment could not backfire if adopted a year later. For this reason our policy lacks a feeling for nuance, the ability to come up with variations on the same theme, as the Soviets have done so effectively. We consider policy-making concluded when the National Security Council has come to a decision. And in fact, the process of arriving at a decision is so arduous and a reappraisal is necessarily so "agonizing" that we are reluctant to reëxamine policies after they have outlived their usefulness.

But a written statement of policy is likely to amount to a truism; the real difficulty arises in applying it to concrete situations. And while we have often come up with the proper measures, we have not found it easy to adapt our approach to the requirements of the situation over a period of time. The different uses made by the Soviets of the time interval between the "summit conference" and the Geneva conference of foreign ministers illustrates this point. The Soviets established diplomatic relations with the German Federal Republic and thus placed themselves in position to deal directly with both German governments; they used the peace offensive to undermine the cohesiveness of NATO and concluded the arms deal with Egypt. By the time we returned to Geneva, we found ourselves confronted by a series of *faits accomplis* and the conference foredoomed.

Another factor shaping our attitude toward foreign affairs is our lack of tragic experience. Though we have known severe hardships, our history has been notably free of disaster. Indeed, the American domestic experience exhibits an unparalleled success, of great daring rewarded and of great obstacles overcome. It is no wonder, therefore, that to many of our most responsible men, particularly in the business community, the warnings of impending peril or of imminent disaster sound like the Cassandra cries of abstracted "egg-heads." For is not the attribute of the "egg-head" his lack of touch with reality, and does not American reality show an unparalleled wealth coupled with an unparalleled growth?

There has been much criticism of Secretaries Humphrey and Wilson for their defense economies. But in fairness the psychological background of their decisions should be understood; despite all the information at their disposal, they simply cannot believe that in the nuclear age the penalty for miscalculation may be national catastrophe. They may know in their heads, but they cannot accept in their hearts, that the society they helped to build could disappear as did Rome or Carthage or Byzantium, which probably seemed as eternal to their citizens. These characteristics make for an absence of a sense of urgency, a tendency to believe that everything can be tried once and that the worst consequence mistakes can have is that we may be forced to redouble our efforts later on. The irrevocable error is not yet part of the American experience.

Related to this problem is our reluctance to think in terms of power. To be sure, American expansion both economic and geographical was not accomplished without a judicious application of power. But our Calvinist heritage has required success to display the attribute of justice. Even our great fortunes, however accumulated, were almost invariably held to impose a social obligation; the great foundation is after all a peculiarly American phenomenon. As a nation, we have used power almost shamefacedly as if it were inherently wicked. We have wanted to be liked for our own sakes and we have wished to succeed because of the persuasiveness of our principles rather than through our strength. Our feeling of guilt with respect to power has caused us to transform all wars into crusades, and then to apply our power in the most absolute terms. We have rarely found intermediary ways to apply our power and in those cases we have done so reluctantly.

But international relations cannot be conducted without an awareness of power relationships. To be sure, the contemporary revolution cannot be managed merely by an exercise of force. But unless we maintain at least an equilibrium of power between us and the Soviet bloc we will have no chance to undertake any positive measures. And maintaining this equilibrium may confront us with some very difficult choices. We are certain to be confronted with situations of extraordinary ambiguity such as civil wars or domestic coups. Every successful Soviet move makes our moral position that much more difficult: Indochina was more ambiguous than Korea; the Soviet arms deal with Egypt more ambiguous than Indochina; the Suez crisis more ambiguous than the arms deal. There can be no doubt that we should seek to prevent such occurrences. But once they have occurred, we must find the will to act and to run risks in a situation which permits only a choice among evils. While we should never give up our principles, we must also realize that we cannot maintain our principles unless we survive.

Consistent with our reluctance to think in terms of power has been our notion of the nature of peace. We assume that peace is the "normal" pattern of relations among states, that it is equivalent to a consciousness of harmony, that it can be aimed at directly as a goal of policy. These are truisms rarely challenged in our political debate. Both major political parties maintain that they work for a lasting peace, even if they differ about the best means of attaining it. Both make statements which imply that on a certain magic day, perhaps after a four-power conference, "peace will break out."

No idea could be more dangerous. To begin with, the polarization of power in the world would give international relations a degree of instability even if there were no ideological disagreement, and the present volatile state of technology is likely to compound this sense of insecurity. Moreover, whenever peace—conceived as the avoidance of war—has become the direct objective of a Power or a group of Powers, international relations have been at the mercy of the state willing to forego peace. No statesman can entrust the fate of his country entirely to the continued good will of another sovereign state, if only because the best guarantee for the will remaining good is not to tempt it by too great a disproportion of power. Peace, therefore, cannot be aimed at directly; it is the expression of certain conditions and power relationships. It is to these relationships—not to peace—that diplomacy must address itself.

It is obviously to the interest of the Soviet Union to equate peace with a state of good feeling unconnected with power relationships or past usurpations, for such an attitude ratifies all its gains since World War II. By the same token, it is to the interest of the United States to leave no doubt that the tension of the cold war was produced not only by the intransigence of the Soviet tone but also by the intransigence of their measures. As long as the Soviets can give the impression that conciliatory statements by themselves are a symptom of peaceful intentions, they can control the pace of negotiations and gain the benefits of the advocacy of peace without paying any price for its achievement. If the Soviets are given the privilege of initiating negotiations when it suits their purpose and of breaking them off without any penalty, diplomacy will become a tool of Soviet propaganda. And the variety of Soviet manœuvres will in time erode the cohesion of the free world.

III

With this we have reached one of the major problems confronting current American diplomacy: the changed nature of negotiations in a revolutionary political order. An international order, the basic arrangements of which are accepted by all the major Powers, may be called "legitimate;" a system which contains a Power or group of Powers which refuses to accept either the arrangements of the settlement or the domestic structure of the other states is "revolutionary." A legitimate order does not make conflicts impossible; it limits their scope. Wars may arise, but they will be fought in *the name* of the existing system and the peace will be justified as a better expression of the agreed arrangements. In a revolutionary order, on the other hand, disputes do not concern adjustments within a given framework, but the framework itself.

There can be little doubt that we are living through a revolutionary period. On the physical plane, the power of weapons is out of balance with the objectives for which they might be employed; as a result, at a moment of unparalleled strength we find ourselves paralyzed by the implications of our own weapons technology. On the political plane, many of the newly independent Powers continue to inject into their international policies the revolutionary fervor that gained them independence. On the ideological plane, the contemporary ferment is fed by the newly awakened hopes and expectations of hitherto inarticulate peoples and by the rapidity with which ideas can be communicated. And the Soviet bloc, eager to exploit all dissatisfactions for its own ends, has given the present situation its revolutionary urgency.

This is true despite the conciliatory statements of the Twentieth Party Congress. For "peaceful coexistence" was not advanced as an acceptance of the *status quo*. On the contrary, it was justified as the most efficient offensive tactic, as a more effective means to subvert the existing order. The Soviet leaders gave up neither the class struggle with its postulate of irreconcilable conflict, nor the inevitable triumph of Communism with its corollary of the dictatorship of the proletariat. To be sure, war was held to be no longer inevitable, but only because soon the U.S.S.R. would possess preponderant strength. Should the policy of "peaceful coexistence" prove less fruitful than expected, we can look for other tactics. "In the world from now on," Mao has said, "neutrality is only a word for deceiving people."[2]

These have been hard lessons to come by. Lulled by a century and a half of comparative tranquillity and without experience with disaster, we have been reluctant to take at face value the often-repeated Soviet assertion that they mean to smash the existing framework. We have tended to treat Soviet protestations as if their intent were merely tactical—as if the U.S.S.R. overstated its case for bargaining purposes or were motivated by specific grievances to be assuaged by individual concessions. There is a measure of pathos in our effort to find "reasonable" motives for the Soviets to cease being Bolshevik: the opportun-

---

[2] Quoted in Richard Walker, "China Under Communism" (New Haven: Yale University Press, 1955), p. 272.

ity to develop the resources of their own country, the unlimited possibilities of nuclear energy or of international trade. We reveal thereby a state of mind which cannot come to grips with a policy of unlimited objectives. Our belief that an antagonist can be vanquished by the persuasiveness of argument, our trust in the efficacy of the process of negotiation, reflect the dominant rôle played in our diplomacy by the legal profession and their conception of diplomacy as a legal process.

But the legal method cannot be applied in a revolutionary situation, for it presupposes a framework of agreed rules within which negotiating skill is exercised. It is not the process of negotiation as such which accounts for the settlement of legal disputes, but a social environment which permits that process to operate. This explains why conciliatory American statements have so often missed their mark. To the Soviets, the key to their ultimate triumph resides in their superior understanding of "objective" forces and of the processes of history.[3] Even when they accept the "subjective" sincerity of American statesmen, they still believe them powerless to deal with the "objective" factors of American society which will ultimately produce a showdown. Conciliatory American statements will appear to the Soviet leaders either as hypocrisy or stupidity, ignorance or propaganda. It is therefore futile to seek to sway Soviet leaders through logical persuasion or by invocations of abstract justice. Soviet statesmen consider conferences a means to confirm an "objective" situation. A Soviet diplomat who wishes to make concessions can justify them at home only if he can demonstrate that they resulted from a proper balancing of risks.

In short, diplomacy has a different function in a revolutionary international order. In a legitimate order, diplomacy seeks to compromise disagreements in order to perpetuate the international system. Adjustments occur because agreement is itself a desirable goal, because of a tacit agreement to come to an agreement. In a revolutionary order, on the other hand, adjustments have primarily a tactical significance: to prepare positions for the next test of strength. Negotiations in a legitimate order have three functions: to formulate by expressing agreements or dis-

---

[3] There is no little exasperation in the Soviet replies to our repeated assertion that a change of tactics on their part implies a surrender of Marxism. Khrushchev has said (September 17, 1955), "If anyone believes that our smiles involve abandonment of the teaching of Marx, Engels and Lenin he deceives himself poorly. Those who wait for that must wait until a shrimp learns to whistle."

cords in a manner that does not open unbridgeable schisms; to perpetuate by providing a forum for making concessions; to persuade by stating a plausible reason for settlement. But in a revolutionary period, most of these functions have changed their purpose: diplomats can still meet, but they cannot persuade, for they have ceased to speak the same language. Instead, diplomatic conferences become elaborate stage plays which seek to attach the uncommitted to one or the other of the contenders.

Nothing is more futile, therefore, than to attempt to deal with a revolutionary power by ordinary diplomatic methods. In a legitimate order, demands once made are negotiable; they are put forward with the intention of being compromised. But in a revolutionary order, they are programmatic; they represent a claim for allegiance. In a legitimate order, it is good negotiating tactics to formulate maximum demands because this facilitates compromise without loss of essential objectives. In a revolutionary order, it is good negotiating tactics to formulate minimum demands in order to gain the advantage of advocating moderation. In a legitimate order, proposals are addressed to the opposite number at the conference table. They must, therefore, be drafted with great attention to their substantive content and with sufficient ambiguity so that they do not appear as invitations to surrender. But in a revolutionary order the protagonists at the conference table address not so much one another as the world at large. Proposals here must be framed with a maximum of clarity and even simplicity, for their major utility is their symbolic content. In short, in a legitimate order, a conference represents a struggle to find formulae to achieve agreement; in a revolutionary order, it is a struggle to capture the symbols which move humanity.

The major weakness of U.S. diplomacy has been the insufficient attention given to the symbolic aspect of foreign policy. Our positions have usually been worked out with great attention to their legal content, with special emphasis on the step-by-step approach of traditional diplomacy. But while we have been addressing the Soviets, they have been speaking to the people of the world. With a few exceptions we have not succeeded in dramatizing our position, in reducing a complex negotiation to its symbolic terms. In major areas of the world the Soviets have captured the "peace offensive" by dint of the endless repetition of slogans that seemed preposterous when first advanced, but which have become common currency through usage. The Power which has added 150 million people to its orbit by force has become the champion of anti-colonialism; the state which has developed slave labor as an integral part of its economic system has emerged in many parts of the world as the champion of human dignity. Neither regarding German unity nor Korea nor the satellite orbit have we succeeded in mobilizing world opinion. But Formosa has become a symbol of American intransigence and our overseas air bases a token of American aggressiveness. We have replied to every Soviet thrust like a pedantic professor sure of his right-eousness; but the world is not moved by legalistic phrases, at least in a revolutionary period. This is not to say that negotia-tion should be conceived as mere propaganda; only that by failing to cope adequately with their psychological aspect we have given the Soviets unnecessary opportunities.

As a result, the international debate is carried on almost en-tirely in the categories and at the pace established by the Soviets; the world's attention is directed toward the horror of nuclear weapons but not toward the fact of aggression which would un-leash them. The Soviets negotiate when a relaxation of tension serves their purpose and they break off negotiations when it is to their advantage, without being forced to shoulder the onus for the failure. We were right to agree to the summit conference and the subsequent meeting of the foreign ministers. But it was not necessary to permit the Four-Power meetings to become an effort to turn the Soviets respectable; or for the President to give the Soviet Union a certificate of good conduct by assuring Bul-ganin he believed in his peaceful intentions. Nor was it wise to let the Soviet leaders build up a distinction between the President and the rest of the United States Government, so that any in-crease in tensions will be ascribed to the fact that the President succumbed to the pressures of his advisors or to the operation of the "objective" factors of the U.S. economy or to a change of administration. Because of our inability to raise the negotiations above the commonplace, they were conducted in a never-never land where a Soviet smile was considered to outweigh the fact of the perpetuated division of Germany and where problems were evaded simply by denying that they existed.

IV

But could we have carried our allies and the uncommitted

along on a different policy? Perhaps the best way to approach a discussion of our system of alliances is to analyze the historic rôle of coalitions. In the past, coalitions have generally been held together by a combination of three motivations: (1) To leave no doubt about the alignment of forces and to discourage aggression by assembling superior power—this in effect is the doctrine of collective security. (2) To provide an obligation for assistance. Were the national interest unambiguous and unchangeable, each Power would know its obligations without any formal pact. But the national interest fluctuates within limits; it must be adapted to changing circumstances. An alliance is a form of insurance against contingencies, an additional weight when considering whether to go to war. (3) To legitimize the assistance of foreign troops or intervention in a foreign country.

An alliance is effective, then, to the extent that its power appears formidable and its purpose unambiguous. If an alliance is composed of too many disparate elements or if its members pursue too varying aims it will not survive a real test. The legal obligation by itself will not suffice if the coalition has no common purpose or is incapable of giving its purpose a military expression. The French system of alliances between the two wars, however imposing on paper, could not survive the conflicting interests of its components and its lack of a unifying military doctrine. It is not the fact of alliance which deters aggression but the application it can be given in any concrete case.

If we examine the structure of the present system of alliances created by the United States we discover that most of the historic conditions for coalitions no longer apply, or apply in a different sense. From the point of view of power relationships none of our alliances, save NATO, adds to our effective strength. And NATO is in difficulty because we cannot give it a military doctrine which makes sense to our NATO partners. Our interest in the alliance is twofold: a, to prevent Eurasia from being controlled by a hostile Power, because if the United States were confined to the Western Hemisphere it could survive, if at all, only through an effort inconsistent with what is now considered the American way of life; b, to add to our over-all strength vis-à-vis the U.S.S.R. by obtaining overseas facilities, particularly air bases. Our empiricist bias has, however, caused us to place these objectives in the framework of a specific threat—that of overt Soviet military aggression—and to look at this threat only in

terms of the total strategic relationship between us and the
Soviet bloc. In these terms, Eurasia is protected not by our capability for local defense, but by our strategic superiority in an
all-out war, and we have therefore tended to justify our alliances
because of the overseas air bases they afford us.

An alliance is useless, however, unless it expresses a mutuality
of interest between the partners. Our military policy is increasingly based on a strategy of "revenge," the objective of which is
to retaliate with greater destruction than we suffer. But in all
situations short of all-out war (and perhaps even then) deterrence is produced not by a capability to inflict *disproportionate*
losses, but a capability to inflict losses *unacceptable* in relation
to specific objectives in dispute. The Soviet successes in the
postwar period demonstrate that in certain circumstances even
an inferior retaliatory capability can produce deterrence. Despite
our strategic superiority we refused to intervene in Indochina or
expand the war in Korea, because Korea and Indochina did not
seem "worth" an all-out war and because we had inadequate
alternative capabilities to make the Soviet calculus of risks seem
unattractive. An all-out strategy, moreover, not only increases
our own inhibitions but runs counter to a coalition policy. Our
allies realize that in all-out war they will add to our effective
strength only by supplying facilities; they see no significance in
a military contribution of their own. As long as our military
doctrine threatens to transform every war into an all-out war,
our system of alliances will be in jeopardy.

Our policies have, moreover, been inhibited by the notion of
collective security drawn from the lessons of the 1930s, when a
united front might well have deterred Hitler, and by our historical bias in favor of federal structures. We base our coalitions
on the assumption that unless all allies resist any aggression anywhere no effective resistance is possible at all. But this notion
of collective security has the paradoxical result of paralyzing the
partner capable of resisting alone. For governments hard pressed
to act in areas of direct concern to them cannot be brought to
run risks outside that area, so that the effort to obtain NATO
support in Asia tends to undermine the cohesiveness of NATO
in Europe. Even within the purely regional alliances the combinations of purposes are extremely various. Pakistan desires arms
more for their effect on India than for the protection they afford
against the U.S.S.R. or China; Iraq is interested in the Baghdad

Pact primarily for the military advantages it gives over Saudi Arabia and Egypt. And in neither SEATO nor the Baghdad Pact are we associated with partners with whom we share the degree of common purpose conferred by the cultural heritage that we share with our European allies.

The problems of our system of alliances can be summed up under two headings: either the alliances add little to our effective strength or they do not reflect a common purpose, or both. In such circumstances a system of collective security leads in fact to a dilution of purpose and to an air of unreality in which the existence of an alliance, and not the resolution behind it, is considered the guarantee of security. Thus, we speak of plugging gaps in defenses as if a treaty instrument were itself a defense. We will not be able to overcome these difficulties until we develop a new approach to our coalition policy, above all until we set less ambitious goals. We must confine our alliances to the purposes we and our allies share.

But can such a coalition policy be developed? The implications of the growing Soviet nuclear capability would seem to impose a measure of harmony between the interest of the United States in an over-all strategy and our allies' concern with local defense. For with the end of our immunity from nuclear attack the nature of deterrence has altered. A deterrent is effective only to the degree that it is plausible and as the Soviet nuclear stockpile grows our willingness to run the risk of an all-out war for any objective save a direct attack on the continental United States will diminish. In such a situation, deterrence with respect to the issues most likely to be in dispute is above all achieved by a capability for local defense.[4] In the face of the horrors of thermonuclear war, it is in our interest to seek to defend Eurasia by means other than all-out war: to devise a strategy which will allow us to inflict the minimum amount of damage consistent with deterrence. The justification for our alliances, therefore, is less that they add to our over-all strength than that they give us an opportunity to apply our power subtly and with less fearful risks.

From the military point of view, our alliances should be conceived as devices to organize local defense and our assistance as a means to make local defense possible. We should make clear to our allies that their best chance of avoiding thermonuclear war resides in our ability to make local aggression too costly.

[4] See the author's "Force and Diplomacy in the Nuclear Age," *Foreign Affairs*, April 1956.

They should understand that they cannot avoid their dilemma by neutrality or surrender, for if we are pushed out of Eurasia they will bring on what they fear most. Confined to the Western Hemisphere, we would have no choice but to fight an all-out war. To be sure, the Soviets have skillfully fomented neutralism by giving the impression that local resistance must inevitably lead to all-out war. But the Soviets can be no more interested than we in total war; the fear of thermonuclear extinction would provide a powerful sanction against expanding a conflict.

The corollary to a regional system of alliances, however, is willingness on our part to act alone if the over-all strategic balance is imperiled. None of our allies, with the exception of Great Britain, has the capability or the willingness to act outside its own geographical area. To ask them to do so will only undermine the domestic position of already weak governments and demoralize them further. It will lead to subterfuges and to the dilution of common action behind the form of joint communiqués. We have to face the fact that only the United States is strong enough domestically and economically to assume worldwide responsibilities and that the attempt to obtain the prior approval by all our allies of our every step will lead not to common action but to inaction. To be sure, whenever there exists a community of purpose, as for example with Great Britain in the Middle East and perhaps in Southeast Asia, we should concert our efforts. But we must reserve the right to act alone, or with a regional grouping of Powers, if our strategic interest so dictates. We cannot permit the Soviets to overturn the balance of power for the sake of allied unity, for whatever the disagreement of our allies on specific measures their survival depends on our unimpaired strength.

The military point of view must not supply the sole motivation for our system of alliances, however. In fact, in many areas, particularly those newly independent, our emphasis on the military factor is the cause of our failure to develop a sense of common purpose. We are undoubtedly right in our belief in the Soviet menace. But revolutions are not logical and the Asian revolution is interested more in internal development than in foreign affairs. Our insistence that they focus some of their energies outward appears to them as an irritating interruption of their primary concern and lends color to Soviet peace offensives. Moreover, the military contribution of both the Baghdad Pact and SEATO does not compensate for the decision of Egypt and India to stand apart and for the domestic pressures these instruments generated in some of the signatory countries.

The primary function of these pacts is to draw a line across which the U.S.S.R. cannot move without the risk of war, and to legitimize intervention by the United States should war break out. But the line could have been better drawn by a unilateral declaration. Behind this shield we could then have concentrated on the primary problem of creating a sense of common purpose by emphasizing shared objectives, primarily by striving for the grouping of Powers to assist in economic development. Had we emphasized these nonmilitary functions of SEATO, it would have been much more difficult for India or Indonesia to stay aloof. As these political groupings gain in economic strength, their own interest would dictate a more active concern for common defense; at least it would provide the economic base for a meaningful defense. A powerful grouping of states on the Russian borders is against the interests of the Soviet Union regardless of whether the purpose of this grouping is primarily military. And by the same token, such a grouping is desirable from the American point of view even if it does not go along with our every policy.

The problem of the uncommitted states cannot be solved, however, merely by an economic grouping of Powers. It is related to the whole U.S. posture. Anti-Americanism is fashionable today in many parts of the globe. As the richest and most powerful nation, we are the natural target for all frustrations. As the Power which bears the primary responsibility for the defense of the free world, we are unpopular with all who are so preoccupied with the development of their own countries that they are unwilling to pay sufficient attention to foreign threats. We should, of course, seek to allay legitimate grievances, but we would be wrong to take every criticism at face value. Many of our most voluble critics in Southeast Asia would be terrified were our military protection suddenly withdrawn. Nehru's neutrality is possible, after all, only as long as the United States remains strong. A great deal of anti-Americanism hides a feeling of insecurity both material and spiritual. Popularity is a hopeless mirage in a situation which is revolutionary precisely because old values are disintegrating and millions are groping for a new orientation. For this reason, it is impossible to base policy solely on an inquiry into what people desire; a revolutionary situation is distinguished by its dissatisfactions, which join in protest against the existing order but can propose no clear substitute. This is the reason why most revolutions have been captured by a small minority which could give a sense of direction to popular resentments. In the uncommitted areas popularity may therefore be less important than respect.

In its relations with the uncommitted, the United States must develop not only a greater compassion but also a greater majesty. The picture of high American officials scurrying to all quarters of the globe to inform themselves on each crisis as it develops cannot but make an impression of uncertainty. The nervousness exhibited in our reactions to Soviet moves must contrast unfavorably with what appears to be the deliberate purposefulness of the Soviets. Moreover, for understandable reasons, many of the uncommitted nations are eager to preserve the peace at almost any price. Because of what appears to them as vacillation and uncertainty, they choose in every crisis to direct pressure against us as the more malleable of the two super-Powers. To the degree that we can project a greater sense of purpose, some of these pressures may be deflected on the Soviet bloc. A revolution like Egypt's or even India's cannot be managed by understanding alone; it also requires a readiness on our part to bear the psychological burden of difficult decisions.

v

We thus return to our original problem: the adequacy of American attitudes for dealing with the present crisis. This is above all a problem of leadership. For nations learn only by experience; they "know" only when it is too late to act. But statesmen must act *as if* their intuition were already experience, as if their aspiration were truth. The statesman is, therefore, like one of the heroes of classical tragedy who has had an intuition of the future, but who cannot transmit it directly to his fellowmen and who cannot validate its "truth." This is why statesmen often share the fate of prophets, that they are without honor in their own country and that their greatness is usually apparent only in retrospect when their intuition has become experience. The statesman must be an educator; he must bridge the gap between a people's experience and his vision, between its tradition and its future. In this task his possibilities are limited. A statesman who too far outruns the experience of his people will not be able to sell his program at home; witness Wilson. A statesman who limits his policy to the experience of his people will doom himself to sterility; witness French policy since World War I.

One of the crucial challenges confronting a society is therefore the capacity to produce a leadership group capable of transcending the experience of that society. And here our sudden emergence as the major Power in the free world presents particular difficulties. The qualities of our leadership groups were formed during the period when our primary concerns were domestic. Politics was considered a necessary evil and the primary function of the state was the exercise of police powers. Neither education nor incentives existed for our leadership groups to think in political or strategic terms. This was compounded by our empiricism with its cult of the expert and its premium on specialization. The two groups which are most dominant in the higher levels of government, industry and the law, can serve as an illustration. The rewards in industry, particularly large-scale industry, are for administrative competence; they therefore produce a tendency to deal with conceptual problems by administrative means, by turning them over to committees of experts. And the legal profession, trained to think in terms of discrete individual cases, produces a penchant for *ad hoc* decisions and a resistance to the "hypothetical cases" inherent in long-range planning. Our leadership groups are therefore better prepared to deal with technical than with conceptual problems, with economic than with political issues. Projected on the Washington scene, they often lack the background to cope with a developing political and strategic situation: each problem is dealt with "on its merits," a procedure which emphasizes the particular at the expense of the general and bogs down planning in a mass of detail. The absence of a conceptual framework makes it difficult for them even to identify our problems or to choose effectively among the proposals and interpretations with which our governmental machinery is overloaded.

This explains many postwar Soviet successes. Whatever the qualities of Soviet leadership, its training is eminently political and conceptual. Reading Lenin or Mao or Stalin, one is struck by the emphasis on the relationship between political, military, psychological and economic factors, the insistence on finding a conceptual basis for political action and on the need for dominating a situation by flexible tactics and inflexible purpose. And the internal struggles in the Kremlin ensure that only the most iron-nerved reach the top. Against the Politbureau, trained to think in general terms and freed of problems of day-to-day administration, we have pitted leaders overwhelmed with departmental duties and trained to think that it was a cardinal sin to transgress on another's field of specialization. To our leaders, policy is as a series of discrete problems; to the Soviet leaders it is an aspect of a continuing political process. As a result, the contest between us and the Soviets has had many of the attributes of any contest between a professional and an amateur: even a mediocre professional will usually defeat an excellent amateur, not because the amateur does not know what to do, but because he cannot react sufficiently quickly or consistently. Our leaders have not lacked ability, but they have had to learn while doing and this has imposed too great a handicap.

To be sure, many of the shortcomings of our leadership groups reflect the very qualities which have made for the ease of relationships in American society. The condition for our limited government has been the absence of basic social schisms, the regulation of many concerns not by government fiat but by "what is taken for granted." A society can operate in this fashion only if disputes are not pushed to their logical conclusions, and if disagreements are blunted by the absence of dogmatism. And in fact the fear of seeming dogmatic permeates our social scene. Most opinions are introduced with a disclaimer which indicates that the proponent is aware of their contingency and also that he claims no superior validity for his own conclusions. This produces a preference for decisions by committee, because the process of conversation permits disagreements to be discovered most easily and adjustments made before positions have hardened. Our decision-making process is therefore geared to the pace of conversation; even departmental memoranda on which policy decisions are ultimately based are written with an eye to eventual compromise and not with the expectation that any one of them will be accepted in its entirety.

It would be wrong to be too pessimistic. No one would have believed when World War II ended that the United States would assume commitments on such a world-wide scale. Our shortcomings are imposing only because of the magnitude of the threat confronting us. Moreover, the performance of the United States, for all its failings, compares favorably with that of the other nations of the non-Soviet world. Our difficulties in foreign policy are therefore only a symptom—and by no means the most obvious —of an inward uncertainty in the free world. To be sure, democracies by the nature of their institutions cannot conduct policy as deviously, change course as rapidly or prepare their moves as secretly as dictatorships. But the crisis of the non-Soviet world is deeper. The tragic element in foreign policy is the impossibility of escaping conjecture; after the "objective" analysis of fact there remains a residue of uncertainty about the meaning of events or the opportunities they offer. A statesman can often escape his dilemmas by lowering his sights; he always has the option to ignore the other side's capabilities by assuming it has peaceful intentions. Many of the difficulties of the non-Soviet world have been the result of an attempt to use the element of uncertainty as an excuse for inaction. But certainty in foreign policy is conferred at least as much by philosophy as by fact; it derives from the imposition of purpose on events.

This is not to say that we should imitate Soviet dogmatism. A society can survive only by the genius that made it great. But we should be able to leaven our empiricism with a sense of urgency. And while our history may leave us not well enough prepared to deal with tragedy, it can teach us that great achievement does not result from a quest for safety. Even so, our task will remain psychologically more complex than that of the Soviets. As the strongest and perhaps the most vital Power of the free world we face the challenge of demonstrating that democracy is able to find the moral certainty to act without the support of fanaticism and to run risks without a guarantee of success.

¶ THE SILENCE IN RUSSIAN CULTURE
by Isaiah Berlin   (October, 1957)

To the West, one of the most puzzling features of Soviet development has been the recurrent ebb and flow of tension and partial relaxation throughout the life of the Soviet body politic. One reflection of this process is the complex and variable blending of attraction and hatred in the Soviet attitude to the West.

In the totalitarian system for which Lenin laid the groundwork, and which Stalin then elaborated into an all-directing structure of power, the activating force is the dictatorial party or its leader. This force denies to any actual or potential competitor the right to act, or even to think contrary thoughts. Using the "engineers" of philosophy, science, literature, and the arts as mere instruments of its will, the custodian of "Truth"—the self-appointed leadership of the monopolistic party—reserves to itself the sole right to define both the purposes and the direction of its acts.

Stalin's death in March, 1953, was followed by a partial but marked release of the overtaut spring. Within a few months, his successors made several significant shifts. The arbitrary power of the secret police was curbed. Plans to improve the supply of consumer goods, food, and housing were proclaimed with loud fanfare. The demand for "sincerity," that is, for some limited right of individual judgment, was raised by some writers and artists. Though checked after some time, the first "thaw" of 1953–54 and its reversal have been followed by two or perhaps three later periods of relaxation.

Does this mean that Russia will henceforth move inevitably and more or less continuously toward a condition of genuine personal and intellectual freedom? Or are these convulsive movements a prolongation of the previous Soviet pattern of the purposeful alternation of tensions and relaxations? On the basis of his long study of Russian life and thought, Sir Isaiah Berlin traces in "The Silence in Russian Culture" the historical roots of Soviet totalitarian Messianism.

President of Wolfsin College, Oxford, and Chichele Professor of Social and Political Theory since 1957, Berlin has also been deeply involved in affairs of state. In World War II, he rendered important services as a member of the British embassies in Washington and Moscow. Among his principal studies are Karl Marx, The Hedgehog and the Fox, *and* Two Concepts of Liberty.

THE SILENCE IN RUSSIAN CULTURE

By Isaiah Berlin

ONE of the most arresting characteristics of modern Russian culture is its acute self-consciousness. There has surely never been a society more deeply and exclusively preoccupied with itself, its own nature and destiny. From the eighteen-thirties until our own day the subject of almost all critical and imaginative writing in Russia is Russia. The great novelists, and a good many minor novelists too, as well as the vast majority of the characters in Russian novels, are continuously concerned not merely with their purposes as human beings or members of families or classes or professions, but with their condition or mission or future as Russians, members of a unique society with unique problems. This national self-absorption is to be found among novelists and playwrights of otherwise very different outlooks. An obsessed religious teacher like Dostoevsky, a didactic moralist like Tolstoy, an artist regarded in the West as being dedicated to timeless and universal psychological and aesthetic patterns like Turgenev, a "pure" unpolitical writer, careful not to preach, like Chekhov, are all, and throughout their lives, crucially concerned with the "Russian problem." Russian publicists, historians, political theorists, writers on social topics, literary critics, philosophers, theologians, poets, first and last, all without exception and at enormous length, discuss such issues as what it is to be a Russian; the virtues, vices and destiny of the Russian individual and society; but above all the historic rôle of Russia among the nations; or, in particular, whether its social structure—say, the relation of intellectuals to the masses, or of industry to agriculture—is *sui generis*, or whether, on the contrary, it is similar to that of other countries, or, perhaps, an anomalous, or stunted, or an abortive example of some superior Western model.

From the eighties onwards a vast, now unreadably tedious,

mass of books, articles, pamphlets began to flood upon the Russian intelligentsia, mostly concerned to prove either that Russia is destined to obey unique laws of its own—so that the experience of other countries has little or nothing to teach it—or, on the contrary, that its failures are entirely due to an unhappy dissimilarity to the life of other nations, a blindness to this or that universal law which governs all societies, and which Russians ignore at their peril. The writers of Western countries, as often as not, produce their works of art or learning or even day-to-day comment (even in America where there exists similar self-consciousness, though not on so vast a scale) without necessarily tormenting themselves with the question whether their subject matter has been treated in its right historical or moral or metaphysical context. In Russia, at any rate since the second half of the nineteenth century, the reverse obtained. There no serious writer could think of taking a step without concerning himself with the question whether his work was appropriately related to the great ultimate problems, the purposes of men on earth. The duty of all those who claimed to have the insight to understand, and the moral courage to face, their personal or social or national condition was always the same: in the first place to relate the relevant problems to the path which the given society (*i.e.* Russian; and only after that, human) was inexorably pursuing (if one was a determinist), or should be pursuing (if one thought one had freedom of choice), at the particular historical (or moral or metaphysical) stage of its development.

No doubt the Romantic doctrines, particularly in Germany, with their emphasis on the unique historical missions of different groups of men—Germans, or industrialists, or poets—which dominated European literature and journalism in the eighteen-thirties and forties, are partly responsible for this pervasive Russian attitude. But it went further in Russia than elsewhere. This was partly due to the fact that the effective advance of Russia to the center of the European scene (after the Napoleonic wars) coincided with the impact of the Romantic Movement; it derived partly from a sense of their own cultural inferiority which made many educated Russians painfully anxious to find a worthy part of their own to play—worthy, above all, of their growing material power in a world that was apt to look down upon them, and cause them to look down upon themselves, as a dark mass of benighted barbarians ruled by brutal despots and good only for crushing other freer, more civilized peoples. Again there may be, as some writers maintain, a strong craving for teleological and indeed eschatological systems in all societies influenced by Byzantium or by the Orthodox Church—a craving that the Russian priesthood, lacking as it conspicuously did the intellectual resources and tradition of the Western churches, could not satisfy, at any rate in the case of the better educated and critically inclined young men.

Whatever the truth about its origins, the state of mind of virtually all Russian intellectuals in the nineteenth and early twentieth centuries (there were some exceptions) was dominated by the belief that all problems are interconnected, and that there is some single system in terms of which they are all in principle soluble; moreover, that the discovery of this system is the beginning and end of morality, social life, education; and that to abandon the search for it in order to concentrate upon isolated or personal ends, say, the pursuit of knowledge, or artistic creation, or happiness, or individual freedom for their own sakes, is willful, subjective, irrational, egoistic, an immoral evasion of human responsibility. This attitude is characteristic not merely of the left-wing Russian intelligentsia, but of the outlook of civilized Russians of all shades of political opinion, spread widely both in religious and in secular, in literary and in scientific circles. Almost any philosophical system that affected to give a comprehensive answer to the great questions found a marvellously, indeed excessively, enthusiastic welcome among these eager, over-responsive, idealistic, impeccably consistent, sometimes only too rigorously logical thinkers.

And the systems were not slow in arriving. First came German historicism, particularly in its Hegelian form, which conceived of history as the essential, indeed the only genuine science. True, Hegel looked on the Slavs with contempt as "unhistorical," and declared that (like the "extinct" Chinese civilization) they had no part to play in the march of the human spirit. This part of Hegel was quietly ignored, and adequate room made in the universal schema for the Slavs in general, and (on the authority of Hegel's formidable rival, Schelling) for the Russians in particular. After the infatuation with Schiller, Fichte, Hegel and other German Idealists came a similar faith in French social prophets— Saint-Simon, Fourier and their many disciples and interpreters, who offered cut-and-dried "scientific" plans of reform or revolution for which some among their Russian disciples, with their will to believe in literal inspiration, were ready to lay down their lives. This was followed by many another *Lebensphilosophie*—inspired by Rousseau, by Comtian Positivism, Darwinism, neo-mediæval-ism, Anarchism, which in Russia went far beyond their Western prototypes. Unlike the West where such systems often languished and declined amid cynical indifference, in the Russian Empire they became fighting faiths, thriving on the opposition to them of contrary ideologies—mystical monarchism, Slavophil nostal-gia, clericalism, and the like; and under absolutism, where ideas and daydreams are liable to become substitutes for action, bal-looned out into fantastic shapes, dominating the lives of their dev-otees to a degree scarcely known elsewhere. To turn history or logic or one of the natural sciences—biology or sociology—into a theodicy; to seek, and affect to find, within them solutions to agonizing moral or religious doubts and perplexities; to transform them into secular theologies—all that is nothing new in human history. But the Russians indulged in this process on a heroic and desperate scale, and in the course of it brought forth what today is called the attitude of total commitment, at least of its modern form.

Over a century ago Russian critics denounced European civil-ization for its lack of understanding. It seemed to them character-istic of the morally desiccated, limited thinkers of the West to maintain that human activities were not all necessarily intercon-nected with each other—that what a man did as a writer was one thing and what he did as a citizen was another; that a man might be a good chemist and yet maltreat his family or cheat at cards; that a man might compose profound music and yet hold stupid or immoral political views that were no business of the critics or of the public. This notion of life, according to Russians of almost all shades of opinion, was artificial and shallow and flew to pieces before the deeper insight of the all-embracing view, according to which the life of individuals and the life of their institutions was one and indivisible. Every faculty and element in the individual were in a state of constant interplay; a man could not be one thing as a painter and another as a citizen, honest as a mathematician and false as a husband; it was impossible to draw frontiers be-tween any aspects of human activity, above all between public and private life. Any attempt to insulate this or that area from the invasion of outside forces was held to be founded upon the radical fallacy of thinking that the true function and purpose of a human being does not penetrate every one of his acts and relationships—or worse still, that men had, as men, no specific function or purpose at all. It followed that whatever most fully embodies this ultimate total human purpose—the State, according to the Hegelians; an élite of scientists, artists and managers, according to the followers of Saint-Simon or Comte; the Church, according to those who leaned towards ecclesiastical authority; an elected body of persons embodying the popular or national will, according to democrats or nationalists; the class designated by "history" to free itself and all mankind, according to Socialists and Communists—this central body had a right to invade everything. The very notion of the inviolability of persons, or of areas of life, as an ultimate principle was nothing but an effort to limit, to narrow, to conceal, to shut out the light, to preserve privilege, to protect some portion of ourselves from the universal truth—and therefore the central source of error, weakness and vice.

The doctrine that there is one truth and one only, which the whole of one's life should be made to serve, one method, and one only, of arriving at it, and one body of experts alone qualified to discover and interpret it—this ancient and familiar doctrine can take many shapes. But even in its most idealistic and unworldly forms, it is, in essence, totalitarian. Even those critical versions of it which permit doubts about the nature of the central truth, or about the best method of its discovery, or the title of its preachers, allow none about the right and the duty, once it is established, to make everyone and everything obey it; they allow no intrinsic virtue to variety of opinion or conduct as such; indeed, the opposite. For there can be no more than one truth, one right way of life. Only vice and error are many. Consequently, when Marxism finally came to Russia in the seventies and eighties it found an almost ideal soil for its seeds.

II

Marxism contained all the elements which the young *révoltés* in Russia were looking for. It claimed to be able to demonstrate the proper goals of human existence in terms of a pattern of history of which there was "scientific" proof. The moral and political values which it preached could, so it claimed, be determined "objectively," that is to say, not in terms of the subjective and relative and unpredictable attitudes of different individuals or classes or cultures, but in terms of principles which, being "founded" on the "objective behavior of things," were absolute and alone led to the salvation and liberation of all men to the degree to which they were rational. It preached the indissoluble oneness of men and institutions. It claimed, just as the eighteenth century French philosophers had in effect claimed, that all real, that is to say soluble, problems were fundamentally technological; that the ends of man—what human beings could be, and, if they knew their true interests, would necessarily want to be—were given by the new scientific picture of the universe. The only problem was how to realize these ends. This was not a moral or political problem but a technical task: that of finding and using the right means for the "demonstrably" valid, universal goal; a problem of engineering.

Stalin's famous and most revealing phrase about intellectuals as "engineers of human souls" was faithfully derived from Marxist premises. The duty of intellectuals was to elucidate the correct social goals on the basis of a "scientific" analysis of society and history; and then, by means of education, or "conditioning," so to attune the minds of their fellow citizens that they grasped demonstrated truths and responded accordingly, like the harmonious constituents of a properly regulated and efficiently functioning mechanism. The simile which Lenin used in one of his most famous statements of political doctrine—*State and Revolution*—according to which the new free society, liberated from the coercion of one class by another, would resemble a factory or workshop in which the workers did their jobs almost out of mechanical habit, was a piece of imagery drawn from this technocratic view of human life. The watchwords were efficiency, tidiness, security, freedom for the good to do what they wanted; this last being necessarily one and the same goal for all those who were rational and knew the truth, not freedom to do anything whatever, but only what is right—the only thing which any rational being can wish to do—that which alone will make for true, everlasting universal happiness. This is an old Jacobin doctrine, and indeed much older—in its essentials as old as Plato. But no one, perhaps, had believed it quite so naïvely or fanatically in any previous age.

During the decade that followed the October Revolution these principles—the moral and metaphysical foundations of totalitarianism—were genuinely accepted, at any rate by some among the Communist leaders. Whatever the personal shortcomings of Trotsky or Zinoviev or Bukharin or Molotov or the heads of the secret police, and perhaps even of Stalin at this stage, there is no reason for doubting the sincerity or depth of their convictions or principles. A great many disagreements arose, of course, but they were concerned not with ends but with means; when they went sufficiently far they were stigmatized as deviations. Thus Trotsky thought that there was a danger of a too-well-entrenched bureaucracy which would function as a brake—like all vested interests—upon the progress of the Revolution which needed agents who were more imaginative, more bloody, bold and resolute—men not tempted to stop halfway on the path of the world revolution. The so-called Workers' Opposition objected to the concentration of authority in the hands of the Central Committee of the Communist Party, and wanted more equality, and more democratic control exercised by workers' organizations. The Right-Wing Deviationists thought that over-rapid collectivization of agriculture would produce a degree of economic dislocation, pauperization and ruin likely to be more damaging to the Soviet economy than the adoption of a slower pace in the harsh process of liquidating peasant property and its defenders together with other so-called survivals of the capitalist régime; and advocated a less urgent tempo and milder measures. There were disagreements as to how far the army might be used in the regimentation of industry. There were memorable disagreements about foreign policy and the policy towards Communists abroad.

The acutest of all disagreements occurred, perhaps, on the cultural front: there were those who thought that any "slap in the face" (as it used to be called) to the bourgeois culture of the West, in whatever form—aggressive futurism and modernism in the arts, for example, or any violent revolt against tradition—was *eo ipso* an expression of Bolshevism, in so far as it was a blow at the Western establishment, lowered its morale and undermined its moral and aesthetic foundations. A good deal of experiment, sometimes bold and interesting, at other times merely eccentric and worthless, occurred at this time in the Soviet Union in the guise of cultural warfare against the encircling capitalist world. This was the "Cultural Bolshevism," particularly popular in Germany, against which Communist policy later so sternly set its face. For one thing the audacities of the cultural Bolsheviks were, as might be expected, the personal acts of individual artists and therefore found little favor in the eyes of those members of the Party for whom Communism meant belief in the task of creating a specifically proletarian culture by means of collective action, and for whom the aberrations of the *avant garde* poets, painters and producers were merely so much individualist eccentricity— an *outré* and decadent perversion of the very bourgeois civilization which the Revolution was out to destroy. Lenin, be it noted, disliked all forms of modernism intensely: his attitude to radical artistic experiment was bourgeois in the extreme. But he made no attempt to enforce his aesthetic views, and, under the benevolent patronage of the Commissar of Education, Lunacharsky, a failed critical playwright but a sincere opponent of open barbarism, the controversies continued unabated. There were splits within factions: the champions of "proletarian" culture could not agree on whether it was to be produced by individual men of gifts who distilled within themselves the aspirations of the proletarian masses, actual and potential, acting, as it were, as their mouthpieces or rather megaphones; or whether, as the extremer ideologists proclaimed, individuals as such had no part at all to play in the new order, for the art of the new collectivist society must itself be collective. These latter in effect believed that works of art must be written collectively by groups, and criticism—reviews, essays, directives—by squads of critics, bearing collective responsibility for their work, each member being an anonymous component of a social whole. Again, some maintained that the business of proletarian art was to present the new reality in an intenser form, to heighten it if necessary by the inventions of the socialism-impregnated imagination; others thought that the business of artists was strictly utilitarian: to help with the making of Communist society by documentary reportage of the new life— the building of factories, collective farms, power stations, the destruction of the old installations, the production of the essentials of the socialist economy—tractors, combines, uniform food, identical clothing, mass-produced houses, books, above all good, happy, uncomplicated, standard human beings.

One could go on to multiply examples; the point I wish to make is that these "programmatic" controversies were, in the first place, genuine; that is to say, the contending parties, on the whole, believed what they were saying, and the disagreements between them could justly be described as real differences in the interpretation of an accepted Marxist doctrine. Moreover they were, to some degree, carried on in public; and, most important of all, they were differences not about ends but about means. The ends had become universally accepted since the opponents and doubters had been eliminated or silenced. The intransigence of the Comintern in dealing with foreign Communist and still more Socialist parties, and the merciless heresy hunts, probably derived, for the most part, from the honest belief that these parties might compromise on the central truth—on the dogma of what constituted the desired society—or else that they had chosen, or might choose, paths that could lead away, however imperceptibly at first, from these sacred and undisputed goals.

It was its own conception of itself that divided Bolshevism so sharply from its parent, Western Marxism—a conception which made it not merely a set of political or social or economic beliefs or policies, but a way of life, all-penetrating and compulsory, controlled absolutely by the Party or the Central Committee of the Party in a way for which little authority can be found even in the most extreme pronouncements of Marx or Engels. This was the "Tsarism in reverse," which Herzen in the early fifties had gloomily and accurately predicted that Communism in Russia would become, and which it owes primarily to the personality of Lenin himself. No doubt the conditions of Russian life, which molded both him and it, in part created the need for religious certainty and messianic doctrine which Marxism provided. But the authoritarian element is among Lenin's specific contributions—the conception of the Party as a sect ruled ruthlessly by its elders and demanding from its members the total sacrifice upon its altar of all that they most cherished (material goods, moral principles, personal relationships), the more defiant and horrifying to tender-minded morality the better. It was this streak of stony fanaticism enlivened by a sardonic humor and vindictive trampling upon the liberal past that unnerved some of Lenin's socialist colleagues and attracted such disciples as Stalin and Zinoviev.

It was part and parcel of this vision of the millennium, disguised as a rational doctrine, to ignore the fact that as a scientific theory, claiming to be able to explain and predict social and economic change, Marxism had, by the beginning of the twentieth century, been decisively refuted by events in ways which have been described too often and too fully to be worth recapitulation. In the West, efforts to save the theory from intellectual bankruptcy, some orthodox, some heretical, were from time to time made by conscientious socialists and others. In Russia this was, by and large, not required. In Russia, especially after the October Revolution, Marxism had become a metaphysics, professedly resting on an analysis of history but stubbornly ignoring all awkward facts, designed by force or persuasion to secure conformity to a set of dogmatic propositions with its own esoteric, half-intelligible terminology, its own "dialectical" techniques of argument, its own clear and rigid *a priori* notions of what men and society must, at whatever cost, be made to be.

One of the most striking differences between the Soviet Union and the West was (and is) that in Russia those who were defeated in these internal Soviet controversies were liable from the very beginning of the régime—even before the official beginning of the terror—to be at best silenced, at worst punished or executed. Yet even these Draconian measures did not make the controversies less real. Indeed they had the opposite effect—the fact that the fruit of victory was power, and of defeat elimination, added an element of violent excitement to the duels in which the antagonists had so much to lose or win. I do not mean to assert that all or even the majority of those engaged in these febrile and perilous controversies were persons of integrity or moved by disinterested motives; a great deal of ruthless or desperate fighting for position or survival, with little regard for the professed principles of Marxism, was evident enough in Russia in the twenties. But at least some sort of wage was paid by vice to virtue; the protagonists in these struggles still felt traditionally obliged to advance some kind of theoretical justification for their conduct, and since some of them seemed to believe deeply in what they said, the issues were at times matters of genuine principle. This was most obviously the case on the "cultural front," which has at all times yielded the most reliable symptoms of what was going on in other spheres of Soviet life. Moreover, among the controversialists, men of remarkable gifts and temperament were to be found, and their attitudes, whether honest or opportunist, were those of exceptional human beings. Lunacharsky, Vorovsky, Averbakh were not, by any possible standard, critics of the first water, but they possessed a genuine revolutionary eloquence; Bukharin, Trotsky, Radek were as thinkers negligible, but one of them was a man of genius, and the others were at the very least gifted agitators. And among the creative writers and artists there still were some figures of the first rank who had not emigrated, or had returned. This alone made the twenties memorable, not only in Russian history but in Russian culture.

To all this Stalin put an abrupt end, and a new phase began.

III

The ideological policy of Stalin's régime is a fascinating topic, deserving separate study to itself, which no one has yet attempted seriously, and towards which I should like only to make one or two suggestions.

Once it had become clear to Stalin and his henchmen that an early world revolution was not to be expected, and that the doubtless inevitable fulfillment of Marxist prophecies in the capitalist world might take place at a time and in ways very different from those which the earlier, more optimistic founding fathers had prophesied, he concentrated upon three interconnected purposes. Firstly, the perpetuation of the Bolshevik régime, and in particular of those of its leaders who were prepared to accept his own authority. Secondly, the maintenance and increase of Soviet power, political, economic and military, in a hostile world, by every possible means short of those entailing a radical change in the Soviet system itself. And thirdly, the elimination of all factors, whether at home or abroad, likely to jeopardize either of these two central purposes, whether or not such elimination was consistent with Marxism, Socialism or any other ideological attitude.

Stalin has at times been compared to Napoleon. It is, on the whole, a fanciful and misleading comparison. Stalin did not suppress or pervert the Bolshevik Revolution as Napoleon "liquidated" the Jacobins. There never was a Thermidor (still less a Brumaire) in the Russian Revolution: neither in the mid-twenties (where Trotsky naturally placed it), nor after the assassination of Kirov, nor after the death of Stalin. But there is something also in this analogy that is illuminating. To ask whether Stalin was a faithful Marxist or even a faithful Leninist is like asking whether Napoleon believed in the ideals or ideas of the French Revolution. Napoleon was sufficiently a child of the Revolution to be instinctively opposed to everything connected with the pre-revolutionary régime, and to wish to come to terms with some of its survivals solely for limited periods and for reasons of expediency. Just as Napoleon took it for granted that the relics of feudalism in Europe were doomed beyond recall, that the dynastic principle was not worth respecting, that nationalism was a force that must be used, that centralization and uniformity were policies favorable to his rule and the like, so it may be assumed that Stalin was Marxist and Leninist enough to believe that capitalism was inescapably doomed to be destroyed by its own "internal contradictions," although it might here and there engage in a desperate struggle for survival, whether it realized this or not and however useless such a struggle might be. Similarly Stalin probably accepted the tactical corollary that wherever such "contradictions" reached an acute stage, those who wished to survive and inherit the earth must seek to exacerbate these critical situations and not to palliate them; whereas in situations where these contradictions had not yet reached a critical point the path of prudence on the part of the members of the new society, *i.e.* the Communists, was not to promote premature risings but to bore from within and concentrate on Popular Fronts and Trojan horses of various kinds. It is clear that he genuinely believed that the future of human society was inevitably collectivist and not individualist; that the power of religion and the churches was collapsing; that control of economic power was more important (*i.e.* capable of effecting greater changes or stopping them) than, say, nationalist sentiment or political power; and in all these respects he was, of course, a true, if exceedingly crude follower of Marx. But if it be asked whether he was a Marxist in the sense in which Lenin undoubtedly was one—*i.e.* of believing that as the result of the dreadful birth pangs a new world would be born in which men would in some sense be freer than before, capable of developing their faculties on a vastly more productive scale, living in a world without wars, starvation and oppression, it seems doubtful whether he troubled himself with such questions any more than the Emperor Napoleon reflected about the ultimate validity of any of the ideals of the French Revolution. And, to his intellectual credit be it said, Stalin paid little enough regard—even by way of lip service—to the many utopian elements in Lenin's outlook.

It is, perhaps, a second point of similarity with Napoleon that Stalin firmly grasped a truth which perhaps Napoleon was the first among secular rulers fully to realize and act upon, namely that discussion of ideas—disputes about issues apparently remote from politics, such as metaphysics or logic or aesthetics—was, by promoting the critical spirit, in principle more dangerous to despotic régimes engaged in a struggle for power than belief in any form of authoritarianism. Napoleon's open hostility to the *Idéologues*—the empiricists and positivists of his day—is well known. He openly preferred the implacable legitimist and ultramontane Bonald, who abused him and would have no truck with him, to the politically mild and conformist liberal, Destutt de Tracy. Similarly Stalin, when he felt himself securely in power, decided to put an end to all ideological controversy as such in the Soviet Union. He did this by proclaiming one school to be victorious over all others (it does not historically matter which). The new directive was that the business of the intelligentsia—writers, artists, academics and so forth—was not to interpret, argue about, analyze, still less develop or apply in new spheres, the principles of Marxism, but to simplify them, adopt an agreed interpretation of their meaning and then repeat and ingeminate and hammer home in every available medium and on all possible occasions the selfsame set of approved truths. The new Stalinist values were similar to those proclaimed by Mussolini: loyalty, energy, obedience, discipline. Too much time had been wasted in controversy, time which could have been spent in promoting enforced industrialization or educating the new Soviet man. The very notion that there was an area of permissible disagreement about the interpretation of even unquestioned dogma created the possibility of insubordination; this, beginning indeed in spheres remote from the centers of power—say musical criticism or linguistics—might spread to more politically sensitive areas and so weaken the drive for economic and military power for which no sacrifice was too great or too immoral. The celebrated Marxist formula—the unity of theory and practice—was simplified to mean a set of quotations to justify officially enunciated policies. The methods taken to suppress the least symptom of independence on the part of even the most faithful Stalinist intellectuals (let alone so-called deviationists or unreconstructed relics of older dispensations)—and, let it be added, the success of these methods—are a phenomenon without parallel in the recorded history of human oppression.

The result has been a long blank page in the history of Russian culture. Between 1932 and, say, 1945 or indeed 1955, it would not be too much to say that—outside natural science—scarcely any idea or piece of critical writing of high intrinsic value was published in Russia, and hardly any work of art—scarcely anything genuinely interesting or important in itself and not merely as a symptom of the régime or of the methods practised by it, that is to say, as a piece of historical evidence.

This policy was, perhaps, chiefly due to Stalin's personal character. He was a half-literate member of an oppressed minority, filled with resentment against superior persons and intellectuals of all kinds, but particularly against those articulate and argumentative socialists whose dialectical skill in the realm of theory must have humiliated him often both before the Revolution and after it, and of whom Trotsky was only the most arrogant and brilliant representative. Stalin's attitude towards ideas, intellectuals and intellectual freedom was a mixture of fear, cynical contempt and sadistic humor that took the form (a touch of Caligula) of discovering to what grotesque and degrading postures he could reduce both the Soviet and foreign members of his cowering congregation. After his death this policy has on occasion been defended by his heirs on the ground that when an old world is being destroyed and a new world brought into being, the makers and breakers cannot be expected to have time for the arts and letters, or even ideas, which must, at any rate for the moment, suffer what befalls them without protest.

It is interesting to ask how such absolute subservience, and for so long a period, could have been secured on the part of an intelligentsia which had after all not merely contributed the very term to the languages of Europe, but had itself played so prominent and decisive a rôle in bringing about victory of the Revolution. Here was a body of persons the blood of whose martyrs had been the seed of the entire revolutionary movement, a body to which Lenin, far more than Marx, had assigned a leading rôle in the task of subverting the old order and of keeping the new one going; and yet, when it was crushed, not a mouse stirred: a few indignant voices abroad, but inside the Soviet Union silence and total submission. Mere intimidation, torture and murder should not have proved sufficient in a country which, we are always told, was not unused to just such methods and had nevertheless preserved a revolutionary underground alive for the better part of a century. It is here that one must acknowledge that Stalin achieved this by his own original contributions to the art of government—inventions that deserve the attention of every student of the history and practice of government.

IV

The first invention has been called by Mr. Utis "the artificial dialectic."[1] It is well known that according to the systems of Hegel and of Marx events do not proceed in direct causal sequence but by means of a conflict of forces—of thesis and antithesis—ending in a collision between them, and a Pyrrhic victory, in the course of which they eliminate each other, and history takes "a leap" to a new level, where the process, called dialectical, begins once again. Whatever may be the validity of this theory in any other sphere, it has a very specific applicability to revolutionary situations.

As every student of the subject must know, the principal practical problem before those who have successfully brought off a large-scale revolution is how to prevent the resultant situation from collapsing into one of two opposed extremes. The first—let us, following Mr. Utis, call it Scylla—is reached when the zealots of the revolution, observing that the new world which the revolution was meant to create has somehow not yet come to pass, seek for explanations, culprits, scapegoats, blame it on criminal weakness or treachery on the part of this or that group of their agents or allies, declare the revolution in mortal peril and start a witch hunt which presently develops into a terror, in the course of which various groups of revolutionaries tend to eliminate each other successively, and social existence is in danger of losing the minimum degree of cohesion without which no society can continue to be. This process tends to be checked by some form of counter-revolution, which is brought on by a desperate effort on the part of the majority, whose security is threatened, to preserve itself and achieve stability, an instinctive social recoil from some imminent-looking collapse. This is what occurred during the great French Revolution, to some extent during the Commune of 1871, in some parts of Eastern Europe in 1918, and might have occurred in 1848 had the extreme left-wing parties begun to win. The mounting spiral of terror was, in fact, what Trotsky was suspected of wishing to promote.

The opposite extreme—Charybdis—is subsidence into a weary indifference. When the original impetus of the revolution begins after a time to ebb, and people seek a respite from the terrible tension of the unnatural life to which they have been exposed,

[1] See "Stalin and the Art of Government," by O. Utis, *Foreign Affairs*, January 1952.

they seek relief, comfort, normal forms of life; and the revolution slides by degrees into the ease, *Schlamperei,* moral squalor, financial chicanery and general corruption of the kind which marked, for example, the French Directoire; or else subsides into some conventional dictatorship or oligarchy, as has happened so often in Latin America and elsewhere. The problem for the makers of the revolution, therefore, is how to keep the revolution going without falling foul of either the Scylla of utopian fanaticism or the Charybdis of cynical opportunism.

Stalin should be credited with having discovered and applied a method which did, in fact, solve this particular problem in a certain sense. Theoretically, history or nature (as interpreted by Hegel or Marx) should, by pursuing its own dialectical process, cause these opposites to collide at the crucial stage, forcing reality to ascend a creative spiral instead of collapsing into one-sided forms of bankruptcy. But since history and nature evidently tend to nod, man must from time to time come to the aid of these impersonal agencies. The government, as soon as it sees signs of the fatal hankering after the fleshpots of the older life, must tighten the reins, intensify its propaganda, exhort, frighten, terrorize, if need be make examples of as many conspicuous backsliders as may be required to stop the rout. Malingerers, comfort-lovers, doubters, heretics, other "negative elements" are eliminated. This is the "thesis." The rest of the population, duly chastened, dominated by terror rather than hope or desire for gain or faith, throw themselves into the required labors, and the economy bounds forward for a while. But then the élite of the revolutionary purists, the fanatical terrorists, the simon-pure heart of the Party, who must be genuinely convinced of the sacred duty of cutting off the rotten branches of the body politic, inevitably go too far. If they did not, if they could stop in time, they would not have been the kind of people to perform the task of inquisition with the desperate zeal and ruthlessness required; hypocrites, half-believers, moderates, opportunists, men of cautious judgment or human feeling are of no use for this purpose, for they will, as Bakunin had warned long ago, compromise halfway. Then the moment arrives when the population, too terrorized to advance, or too starved, becomes listless, downs tools, and efficiency and productivity begin to drop off; this is the moment for clemency. The zealots are accused of having gone too far, they are accused of oppressing the people, and—always a popular move—they are in their turn publicly disciplined, that is, in Stalin's heyday, purged and executed. Some small increase of freedom is allowed in remote fields—say, that of literary criticism or poetry or archæology, nothing so near the center of things as economics or politics. This is the "antithesis." The people breathe again, there is optimism, gratitude, talk of the wisdom of their rulers now that their eyes have been opened to the "excesses" of their unfaithful servants, hope of further liberties, a thaw; production leaps up, the government is praised for returning to some earlier, more tolerant ideal, and a relatively happier period ensues.

This once more leads to the inevitable relaxation of tension, slackening of discipline, lowering of productive effort. Once more there is (the new thesis) a call for a return to ideological purity, for the reëstablishment of fundamental principles and loyalties, for the elimination of the parasitical saboteurs, self-seekers, drones, foreign agents, enemies of the people who have in some way managed to creep into the fold. There is a new purge, a new spurt of ideological fanaticism, a new crusade, and the heads of the counter-revolutionary hydra (the new antithesis) have to be cut off once again.

In this way the population is, as it were, kept perpetually on the run, its development proceeds by a zigzag path, and individual self-preservation depends on a gift for perceiving at which precise moment the central authority is about to order a retreat or an advance, and a knack for swiftly adjusting oneself to the new direction. Here timing is all. A miscalculation, due to inertia or political insensitiveness or, worse still, political or moral conviction, causing one to linger too long on a road that has been condemned, must almost always, particularly if persisted in, mean disgrace or death.

It cannot be denied that by this deliberate policy of carefully timed purges and counter-purges of various intensities, of contraction and expansion, Stalin did manage to preserve in being a system that cannot be actively approved or felt to be natural by most of those concerned, and indeed to keep it going for a longer period than that for which any other revolution has, thus far, managed to survive. There is a full discussion of the method in the article by Mr. Utis already cited. Although, as the author there maintains, the method, to be successful, requires the master hand of its inventor, it appears to have survived him. Despite the grave shocks to the system caused by the struggle for power

among Stalin's successors, the emergence into the open of conflicts and factions, the risings of oppressed peoples in the West
totally unforeseen in Moscow, what Mr. Utis calls the "artificial
dialectic" appears to be functioning still. The succession, in strict
sequence, during the last five years, of "liberal" and repressive
moves by the Soviet rulers, both at home and abroad, although no
longer conducted with the virtuosity (or the deep personal
sadism) of Stalin, has too much regularity of pattern to be unin-
tended. The hypothesis advanced by the author to explain only
Stalin's own methods of government seems to fit his successors.

The method is an original political invention, and Stalin deserves full credit for it. One of its deliberate by-products has been
the total demoralization of what is still in the U.S.S.R. called the
intelligentsia—persons interested in art or in ideas. Under the
worst moments of Tsarist oppression there did, after all, exist
some areas of wholly free expression; moreover, one could always
be silent. This was altered by Stalin. No areas were excluded from
the Party's directives; and to refuse to say what had been ordered
was insubordination and led to punishment. "Inner emigration"
requires the possibility of the use of one's mind and means of expression at least in neutral ways. But if one's chances of sheer
survival have been made dependent on continuous active support
of principles or policies which may seem absurd or morally ab-
horrent; and if, moreover, the whole of one's mental capacity is
taxed by the perpetual need to chart one's course in fatally dangerous waters, to manœuvre from position to position, while one's
moral fiber is tested by the need to bow one's head low not to one
but to many capricious, unpredictably changing divinities, so
that the least inattention, slackness or error costs one dear—then
there is less and less possibility of thinking one's own thoughts, or
of escaping into an inner citadel in which one can remain secretly
heterodox and independent and know what one believes. Stalin
went further. He forbade more than a minimum degree of official
intercommunication between one academic faculty and another,
between laboratory and institute, and successfully prevented the
growth of any center of intellectual authority, however humble
and obedient, however fraudulent and obscurantist. No priesthood of dialectical materialism had been allowed to arise, because
no discussion of theoretical issues was permitted; the business of
the Academy of Sciences or the Institute of Red Professors or the
Marx-Engels Institute was to quote Marx in supporting Stalin's

acts: the *doctrine* he, or some other member of the Politbureau (certainly not a professor), would supply for himself.

Where there is an official church or college of augurs, with its own privileges and mysteries, there is a relatively fenced-off area, with walls within which both orthodoxy and heresy can flourish. Stalin set himself to repress ideas as such—at a very high cost, be it added, not merely in terms of the basic education of Soviet citizens (not to speak of disinterested intellectual activity, "pure" research and so on), but even in the useful and applied sciences which were gravely handicapped by the lack of freedom of discussion and suffered an abnormally high admixture of adventurers, charlatans and professional informers. All this was effective in stifling every form of intellectual life to a far greater degree than was realized by even the most hostile and pessimistic observers in the West, or, for that matter, by Communist Parties outside the Soviet orbit. To have created such a system is a very striking achievement on Stalin's part, whose importance should not be underrated. For it has crushed the life out of what once was one of the most gifted and productive societies in the world. At any rate for the time being.

v

There is yet a second consequence of this system which is worthy of remark, namely that most of the standard vices so monotonously attributed by Marxists to capitalism are to be found in their purest form only in the Soviet Union itself. Most readers of this journal will be familiar with such stock Marxist categories as capitalist exploitation, the iron law of wages, the transformation of human beings into mere commodities, the skimming off of surplus value by those who control the means of production, the dependence of the ideological superstructure on the economic base, and other Communist phrases. But where do these concepts best apply?

Economic exploitation is a phenomenon familiar enough in the West; but there is no society in which one body of men is more firmly, systematically and openly "exploited" by another than the workers of the Soviet Union by their overseers. True, the benefits of this process do not go to private employers or capitalists. The exploiter is the state itself, or rather those who effectively control its apparatus of coercion and authority. These controllers —whether they act as Party officials or state bureaucrats or both

—act far more like the capitalists of Marxist mythology than any living capitalists in the West today. The Soviet rulers really do see to it that the workers are supplied with that precise minimum of food, shelter, clothing, entertainment, education and so forth that they are thought to require in order to produce the maximum quantity of the goods and services at which the state planners are aiming. The rest is skimmed off as surplus value far more conveniently and neatly than it can ever have been detached in the unplanned West. Wages are regulated in the most "iron" way possible—by the needs of production. Economic exploitation here is conducted under laboratory conditions not conceivable in Western Europe or America.[2] It is again in the Soviet Union that official professions of "ideology"—principles, slogans, ideals—correspond least to actual practice. It is there, too, that some intellectuals can most truly be described as lackeys (some sluggish and reluctant, others filled with a kind of cynical delight and pride in their own virtuosity) of the ruling group. It is there, far more obviously than in the West, that ideas, literature, works of art act as "rationalizations" or smoke screens for ruthless deeds, or means of escape from the contemplation of crimes or follies, or as an opium for the masses. It is there that the state religion—for that is what the dead and fossilized "dialectical materialism" of the official Soviet philosophers has, in effect, more or less avowedly become—is nothing but a consciously used weapon in the war against the enemy, within and without; and lays no claim to "objective" truth.

The materialist theory of history teaches us that the primary factors that determine the lives of individuals and societies are economic, namely the relationships of human beings in the productive system; while such cultural phenomena as their religious, ethical, political ideas, their judicial and political institutions, their literature, arts, scientific beliefs and so forth belong to various tiers of the "superstructure," that is, are determined by—are a function of—the "base." This celebrated and justly influential doctrine, embodying as it does a great deal that is new, important, illuminating and by now very widely accepted, has, nevertheless, never been easy to fit in detail to any given society or

---

[2] Mr. Milovan Djilas corroborates this forcibly in his book, "The New Class" (New York: Praeger, 1957). Whether the system is to be called state capitalism (the state being anything but a democracy) or a "degenerate workers' state" or a naked autocracy is a question of the most appropriate label. The facts themselves are not in doubt.

period of history in the past. Every attempt to apply it narrowly[3] always encountered too many exceptions: if these were to be explained away, they usually had to be stretched till the theory became too vague or encrusted with too many qualifications to retain any utility. But it holds only too faithfully of Soviet society. There it is absolutely clear to everyone what is part of the base and what is part of the superstructure. Writers and architects can have no illusions about which level of the pyramid they constitute. Economic, military and other "material" needs really do wholly determine—because they are deliberately made to determine—ideological phenomena, and not vice versa. It is not nature nor history that has produced this situation, but a piece of highly artificial engineering, by which Stalin and his officials have transformed the Russian Empire.

It is an extraordinary irony of history that categories and concepts invented to describe Western capitalism should turn out to fit most closely its mortal enemy. But this is scarcely an accident, a *lusus historiae*. Every student of the Russian Revolution knows that the issue that divided the Bolsheviks most deeply from the orthodox Marxists—the Mensheviks—was the practicability of an immediate transition to socialism. The Mensheviks maintained that according to any interpretation of Marx, genuine socialism could be established only in a society which had reached a high degree of industrialization—where the organized proletariat formed the majority of the population, and was, through the working of the "inexorable" and mounting "contradictions" of economic development, in a position to "expropriate the expropriators" and initiate socialism. No one could maintain that this stage had yet been reached in the Russian Empire. But the Bolsheviks, mainly under Trotsky's inspiration, claimed that instead of semi-passively waiting for capitalism (a bourgeois republic) to do the job, leaving the workers insufficiently protected from the free play of "history," "nature," etc.—this process could be controlled by a proletarian dictatorship; Russia could be made to go through the stages demanded by the "dialectic of history" under hothouse conditions regulated by the Communist Party. This was to be the famous "transitional" period of the dictatorship

[3] Say, to demonstrate that the writings of Thomas Love Peacock could not possibly have arisen save in the economic conditions of early nineteenth century England; and that these in their turn made some such writings as those of, let us say, Aldous Huxley (or others like him) quite inevitable a century later.

of the proletariat—the artificial or controlled equivalent of "natural" capitalist development in the West: two roads leading equally to full-blown Communism, but the Russian corridor less painful because not left to the vagaries of "nature," but planned by men in control of their own fate owing to their possession of the "scientific" weapon of Marxist theory and able, therefore, to "shorten the birth pangs" by a well executed revolution. If, like Lenin, one begins with fanatical faith in the truth of the Marxist analysis of history, the fact that it does not too well fit even the capitalist West, which it was designed to describe, will make little difference. If the pattern does not correspond to the facts, the facts must be made to tally with the pattern. There was relatively little capitalism, and a feeble proletariat, in Russia in 1917. But the dialectic of history cannot be cheated. Unless Marxism rested on a gigantic fallacy there *could* be no salvation without the equivalent of the capitalist phase. Hence the corresponding phenomena had to be synthetically produced—made to emerge by artificial means.

This can sometimes be done with success, as in Japan, for example. But the Japanese followed the light of reason and experience. They modernized themselves by the methods that seemed to work best, without being chained to a dogmatic theory. They achieved their purpose not without brutalities, but rapidly and with spectacular success. This course was not open to Lenin and his followers. They were compelled by their fidelity to the Marxist classics to subordinate their practical judgment to the demands of theory: the social and economic development of Russia had to proceed by fixed steps whose order was laid down by the Marxist manuals. This created fantastic handicaps that were overcome at a terrible human cost. Russia *had* to go through phases which, according to Marx, Western capitalism passed during and after its industrial revolution. Russian reality had to be altered to resemble a model constructed, not too competently, to account for the progress of a society very unlike itself. A society was vivisected, as it were, to fit a theory which began life as no more than the explanation of its evolution. Something which began as descriptive became normative: a theory intended to account for the development and behavior of Western Europe in the nineteenth century had been turned into a blueprint for Eastern Europe in the twentieth.

Actions founded upon errors of social observation do not necessarily end badly. There is, for all to see, that part of American constitutional development which was inspired by Montesquieu's mistaken interpretation of British political theory and practice. Lenin's error proved more costly. Russia was precipitated into unheard-of horrors of industrialization largely because Marx had drawn a dark picture of Western capitalism and said that no society could escape something analogous. The imposition of the Bolshevik system upon an economically retarded country is a unique and monstrous monument to the power of a few men's wills and their sovereign contempt for history and empirical evidence; and a bloodcurdling interpretation of the Unity of Theory and Practice.

VI

Faced with crises and the possibility of collapse, Lenin executed a partial retreat. And his successors, under the pressure of events, substituted various practical makeshifts and realistic devices and policies in place of the extravagant utopian design which dominates Lenin's thinking. Nevertheless the violent break with reality that is at the heart of the Bolshevik Revolution can evidently not be eliminated without causing the régime to collapse; at any rate no serious attempt to do so has ever been made. For this reason Soviet society is not, in the normal sense, a civil society at all.

The purpose of normal human societies is in the first place to survive; and, after that, to satisfy what Mill called "the deepest interests of mankind," that is to say, to satisfy at any rate a minimum number of men's normal desires after their basic needs are satisfied—say, for self-expression, happiness, freedom, justice. Any government which realizes these values to a reasonable degree is held to fulfill its function. These are not the principal ends of Soviet society, or of its government. Conditioned by its revolutionary origins, it is organized to achieve objectives, to respond to challenges, win victories. Like a school, a team of players, still more like an army on the march, it is a specialized institution designed for specific purposes that must be made explicit to its members by the leaders. Soviet life is constructed to strive for goals. It makes little difference what the particular goals may be —military or civil, the defeat of the enemy within or without, or the attainment of industrial objectives—announced goals there must be, if Soviet society is to continue to be. The leaders understand this well, and whether or not they are to be regarded as prisoners of their own system, they know that they must continue to exhort their subjects to greater and greater endeavors if they are to avoid the disintegration of the régime. They are in the position of army commanders in a war, who realize that unless their troops see a minimum amount of active service, the discipline, the esprit de corps, the continued existence of the armies as fighting units cannot be guaranteed.

The leaders of the Soviet Union, for all we know, may by now be secretly hankering after the peaceful existence, to abandon the exiguous splendors and unending cruelties and miseries of the régime and subside into "normal" existence. If they harbor any such desires, they know that in the short run, at least, this is not practicable. For Soviet society is organized not for happiness, comfort, liberty, justice, personal relationships, but for combat. Whether they wish it or not the drivers and controllers of this immense train cannot now halt it or leap from it in mid-course without risk of destruction. If they are to survive and above all remain in power, they must go on. Whether they can replace parts of it while it is moving, and so transform it (themselves) into something less savage, less dangerous to themselves and mankind, remains to be seen. At any rate that must be the hope of those who do not think war inevitable.

In the meanwhile this caricature of *dirigisme* has discredited the tradition of social idealism and liquidated the intelligentsia connected with it, perhaps more decisively than unaided persecution could have done. Nothing destroys a minority movement more effectively than the official adoption and inevitable betrayal and perversion of its ends by the state itself. There are cases where nothing succeeds less well than success.

¶ THE PRESIDENT

by Dean Rusk   (April, 1960)

When John F. Kennedy was elected President, Dean Rusk was President of the Rockefeller Foundation. Rusk had served as Deputy Undersecretary of State in 1949–50 and as Assistant Secretary of State for Far Eastern Affairs in 1950–51. In April, 1960, he wrote this piece on the Presidency. "Not presumptuously, I hope, but as a restraint upon partisanship, I try to think of these comments as being addressed to the next administration." Without any premonition on his part, the suggestion worked. It was largely on the basis of his article that President Kennedy named Rusk Secretary of State.

This is an analysis of the magnitude, the transformations, the risks, and the ultimate loneliness of the office of the President. While illusions of omnipotence must be avoided, the influence of the President of the United States can sometimes come close to being absolute, especially in times of crisis. The exercise of this power and responsibility is clearly an awesome burden.

Rusk notes that two major historical changes have expanded the President's constitutional role—massive involvement of the federal government in the economic and social life of the nation, and the revolutionary changes in the world and America's place in it. He must weld a greatly increased bureaucracy into an effective national effort. He must engage in personal diplomacy at the summit, which in this jet age can be anywhere. Yet "the crucial, indispensable contribution which the President can make to the conduct of our foreign affairs is to enter fully into his office, to use its powers and accept its responsibilities, to lead a people who are capable of responding to the obligations of citizenship."

Rusk is to Presidents what Machiavelli is to princes.

THE PRESIDENT

By Dean Rusk

THE United States, in this second half of the twentieth century, is not a raft tossed by the winds and waves of historical forces over which it has little control. Its dynamic power, physical and ideological, generates historical forces; what it does or does not do makes a great deal of difference to the history of man in this epoch. If realism requires us to avoid illusions of omnipotence, it is just as important that we not underestimate the opportunity and the responsibility which flow from our capacity to act and to influence and shape the course of events. Involved is not merely a benign concern for the well-being of others but the shape of the world in which we ourselves must live. The range within which the nation can make deliberate choices is wide; if we do not make them deliberately, we shall make them by negligence or yield the decisions to others, who will not be mindful of our interests. When the emphasis of discussion falls too heavily for my taste upon the limitations on policy, I recall from early childhood the admonition of the circuit preacher: "Pray as if it were up to God; work as if it were up to you."

The foreign policy of the United States since World War II, seen in broad historical terms, has been responsible and constructive. Surely we can say, quietly among ourselves, that it is a matter of no small moment that a nation with so much power has used it with restraint and toward the purposes which dominate this great democracy. If there are occasional suspicions abroad about our motives, they arise in part from the difficulty of compre-

Editor's Note: This article is based on one of the Elihu Root lectures delivered recently at the Council on Foreign Relations, New York. The lectures are to be published later this year in book form.

hending so strange a phenomenon. On the other hand, a very high standard of policy and conduct is imposed upon us by our power and hopes, by the expectations of others, and by the necessities of our situation. But we are not likely to achieve significant improvement in the conduct of our foreign relations simply by thinking up new ideas but rather by serious attention to the manner in which we make policy and translate it into action. Men of long experience in both the Executive and Legislative branches of government have serious doubt about whether our present procedures are adequate to the conduct of the public business in our foreign relations over the next quarter century. It is my own view that there is much which can be done within existing constitutional arrangements and that our first task is to exhaust these possibilities before diverting our energies into deeply divisive debates about constitutional change.

The foregoing remarks take on added significance because we are already in a period of more rapid and fundamental change than we have yet experienced as an American nation. A sense of crisis is a recurrent phenomenon in human affairs but at least two factors suggest that our own period may lay special claim to breathlessness. The one is the rate of change in science and technology. The other is the emergence of scores of independent nations not yet firmly set upon their course and the multiplication of those who must be taken into account in our thinking.

These three premises compel a fourth, namely, that our tasks, our unique constitutional arrangements and the external environment place a special premium upon leadership. I have more confidence than some commentators do in the wisdom of our people and their capacity for understanding the essentials of policy. But public opinion can neither devise policy nor carry it out. It cannot debate it effectively unless the issues are framed and presented for discussion, accompanied by the factual background. It cannot even follow and support, in our kind of society, unless it knows where we are trying to go. The President, with the aid of his Secretary of State and the support of the Congress, supplies the leadership in our foreign relations. Criticisms, direct or implied, are inevitable in discussing this matter, but the problems are bipartisan. Not presumptuously, I hope, but as a restraint upon partisanship, I try to think of these comments as being addressed to the next administration, whatever its political complexion.

II

While Mr. Truman's remark, "The President makes foreign policy," is not the whole story, it serves very well if one wishes to deal with the matter in five words. Most of us have long understood that the powers and responsibilities of the Presidency have grown significantly since 1789 by constitutional interpretation, statute, custom and changing circumstance. What many of us have not fully recognized is the extent to which the office has been transformed during the past three decades under the impact of two historical changes. The one is the massive involvement of the federal government in the economic and social life of the nation, an involvement to which both political parties are committed. The other is the revolutionary change in the world about us and in our own place in it. Although men like Jackson, Lincoln, Theodore Roosevelt and Wilson helped to reduce the shock of the change when it came, the modern Presidency under Franklin Roosevelt, Truman and Eisenhower has become an office of almost unbearable responsibility.

Since even the old and familiar words carry so much new meaning, it might be revealing to recall briefly the burdens undertaken when a man swears that he "will faithfully execute the office of President of the United States." To save time and to look at the full sweep of the office all at once, let us paint with a light and fast-moving brush, taking for granted much of the detail which is or ought to be the common possession of an educated citizenry.

The President is our Chief of State, the formal and symbolic head of the American nation. To the rest of the world he embodies the dignity and sovereignty of the Federal Union and has much to do with the image of America projected beyond our borders. He leads our solemn observances and sets the tone of our national life. Whether we move with zest and confidence in our public and private affairs or plod along in apathy or bewilderment turns in large part upon the morale which flows from the White House. The deference instinctively paid to the office and to the man who holds it is itself a source of power and influence and enhances his ability to act, to persuade and to mediate.

The President is the Chief Executive of the Government of the United States, the administrative head of its ten departments and dozens of independent agencies, staffed by almost two and a quarter million civil servants. Charged by the Constitution to "take care that the laws be faithfully executed," he must recruit competent leadership for the vast machinery of government and, through evidences of his own interest and concern, inspire the federal service with devotion, pride and a passion for good performance. Since the chain of administrative command cannot, for both good and bad reasons, keep him fully informed about how things are going, he must take advantage of other lines of communication as well—his personal staff, the flow of mail to the White House, the press, observations of members of Congress and of his party colleagues. To counteract the inertia of large organization, he keeps it alive and alert by pertinent questions to Cabinet colleagues, by the unexpected phone call, the scribbled note of commendation or criticism, a comment at a press conference.

He soon finds that making policy is not the end of his task, that policy can be negated by what Elihu Root gently called "unwilling subordinates." He will discover attitudes and practices in the bureaucracy which become unconfessed laws of public administration. One, for example, is that where an exaggerated emphasis is placed upon delegation, responsibility, like sediment, sinks to the bottom. Now that Professor Parkinson is in this country, he might accept as his own the law that in any large organization the proportion of time spent upon central tasks varies inversely with elevation in the bureaucracy. Another is the law, which has semi-respectable roots, that no department or agency can be coördinated by a parallel department or agency; it is *infra dig* to defer horizontally rather than vertically. Still another is the law that everyone affected by a decision must participate in making it.

The departments and agencies of government are each concerned about a part of the whole. The President, assisted by his White House staff and the Executive Office, must weld the parts into an effective national effort. He cannot hope to achieve nice consistency in leading a vigorous and diverse people concerned with conflicting interests and aspirations, but he can try to achieve a broad political consistency in the main directions of movement and to limit the waste and frustration which occur when one hand tears down what the other is laboriously trying to build.

The Constitution provides that "The President shall be Commander-in-Chief of the Army and Navy of the United States."

Borrowed from the powers of colonial governors and probably influenced by the prospect that George Washington would be the first President, the provision is an independent source of constitutional authority and places the President in direct personal command of the armed forces. Although Woodrow Wilson did not, Lincoln, Franklin D. Roosevelt and Truman assumed personal charge of what has come to be called "the higher direction of war." The nation looks to the President to play the primary role in deciding the types and scale of military power it needs to defend itself and to support its policy. He cannot escape the crucial task of weighing risks and burdens, of finding the elusive and hazardous line between too little and too much. He must look to the morale of our fighting men, assure them of the nation's appreciation and support, and build their pride in their exacting service. On the other hand, he must firmly assert the principle that the first mission of a man in uniform is to do what he is told to do, regardless of the number of stars on his shoulder, and that the military establishment is an instrument, not the master, of policy. Only the President can resolve inter-service rivalries and disputes about their respective roles and he, working with the Congress, must seek to restrain the growth of independent political constituencies in support of particular services as deeply repugnant to our constitutional system. As Commander-in-Chief the President can deploy the armed forces and order them into active operations. In an age of missiles and hydrogen warheads, his powers are as large as the situation requires and the contingencies perhaps the most awful with which he has to live. In a period when men are groping toward the control of armaments and the nature of war has changed beyond recognition, the role of the President as Commander-in-Chief has entered a new phase.

The President is the head of his political party. Indeed, his election is its principal raison d'être as a national party, and has been since the time of Jefferson. Our federal structure and our constitutionally prescribed terms of office deprive party leadership of some of the instruments of party discipline known to parliamentary systems. Once the moment of quadrennial unity has passed, our parties tend toward aimlessness and factions arise out of regional or special interests and the accidents of personal ambition. But the party to which the President belongs can expect a measure of leadership. His party is drawn together by a common interest in the public response to his performance and a common aversion to the thought that the rascals across the aisle might name his successor. The President can persuade and cajole, threaten and scold, and offer occasional morsels of political advantage. But the vigor of his partisanship is often restrained by his need to cross the aisle and seek support for his policies from among the opposition, especially when the latter controls one or both houses of Congress.

The President is our Chief Legislator. His proposals make up the central agenda of Congress. Important bills are drafted by or in close consultation with the Executive departments and the Bureau of the Budget. The box scores on "must" legislation which appear toward the end of a Congressional session are used to judge the Congress as well as the President. His veto power, his party leadership and his ability to mobilize public support for his point of view make him a formidable partner in the legislative process.

The President is our Chief Budget Officer. Congress acts upon the budget he proposes and, when all the hubbub is over, passes it with changes of a few percentage points. The Federal budget, about a fifth of the national income, and the fiscal and monetary policies of the government deeply affect the economic and social life of the country—its incentives, its priorities, its directions of growth and of public and private investment, even the nature and extent of its voluntary effort.

The Founding Fathers saw clearly that the health and stability of our political arrangements would turn upon the President's role as the Protector of the Constitution. They singled him out for a prescribed oath that he will to the best of his ability "preserve, protect, and defend the Constitution of the United States." He controls the raw power of the state—the armed forces, the F.B.I., the C.I.A., the Secret Service, the U.S. marshals. Congress may pass laws, even over the President's veto, but the President must look to their prudent and impartial application. The Supreme Court may sustain the Constitution in deciding between the adversaries before it, but the President must conform the conduct of government to the Court's interpretation of the basic law. A national respect for constitutional process is the glue which holds us together and is properly the brooding concern of the man who holds our highest office. In a constitutional system which cannot possibly work unless those who exercise its powers are determined to make it work, the President must anticipate constitutional crises and bring all the resources of his office to the prevention of situations for which there can be no tolerable answer. President Franklin D. Roosevelt was effectively rebuked by the nation for resorting to a ward heeler's device to settle his difficulties with the Supreme Court; President Eisenhower failed to use the possibilities of his office to forestall the necessity for bayonets in Little Rock.

In a unique sense the President is the custodian of the national interest. Elected by a national constituency, he speaks to Congress and to the people on the needs of the nation seen as a whole. His audience is understandably more intimately concerned with personal, local or regional affairs and needs his help to understand what is required of citizens of the United States.

But the modern Presidency cannot limit itself to a national interest narrowly defined. Recorded in solemn treaties and rooted in common interest and circumstance, we are a partner in great coalitions which now include more than 40 nations. Our power has reduced our sovereignty and our decisions must take into account the needs and hopes of those whose fates are linked with ours. If the President fails to meet the demands of leadership of a nation-in-coalition, a reluctant or resistant United States cannot be dragged along by others and coalitions as now constituted would rapidly disintegrate.

I have been describing the powers and responsibilities of the highest office in a nation which acts and moves by consent. In only a limited sense is the President in a position to command; it is the essence of our system that the Constitution confers upon him a license to lead. If we are inclined to think of the President as an executive who sits at his desk and strikes off great decisions, we must balance it by the picture of the President as our chief servant who, somewhat as a sheep dog, must round up a free people and persuade them to move in a given direction for a sufficiently long period to make it possible to act upon a policy. This does not mean that he is limited by public opinion as he finds it, or fears it to be. The people who elect him are capable of understanding and concern and are likely to be responsive to his lead. If the issues are critical and there are marginal doubts, many are resolved when the President goes to the country and asks for its support. When we assess the possibilities of action in terms of public opinion it is crucial to understand the difference between desultory impressions and responses to vigorous leadership.

The powers and responsibilities we have been discussing are those which engage the thought, time and energy of the President himself. By statute and executive order provision can be made for large delegations of function, but ultimate responsibility comes back to the office which has led some to call ours a "presidential system" of government. He is indispensable, even if he is not irreplaceable.

III

Against this background of what we have called unbearable responsibility, the question arises as to whether the President of the United States can wisely undertake the burdens and hazards of personal diplomacy at the summit. This is not a moment when it is easy to discuss the problem with detachment. But it needs discussion. Earlier American skepticism and reluctance about summit diplomacy have apparently been brushed aside with the warm approval of public opinion here and abroad. The prospect is for a series of summit meetings during 1960 and beyond. The next President of the United States may find himself limited in his freedom to determine how he is to discharge his awesome duties by commitments made by his predecessor in the closing phase of an eight-year administration. If the President of the United States is to assume an active role in negotiations, this will have a serious bearing upon proposals for the reorganization of the higher echelons of the Executive branch of the government. Indeed, it may affect the definition of the circumstances under which the "inability" of the President should open the way for the Vice President to discharge the duties of the office. Meanwhile, public opinion is moved by desperate hope and the fascinations of the spectacular, and we shall face the problems of distinguishing form from substance and of avoiding the slippery slope of relaxed effort which can lead to disillusionment and critical danger.

To put my readers on an equal footing with me immediately, let me anticipate my conclusion. The President, as Chief of State of the United States, can and ought to undertake a limited and carefully planned program of state visits, short in duration and aimed at the exchange of courtesy and respect as a tangible expression of the good will of the American people. But negotiation at the chief-of-government level is quite another matter. It is not easily accommodated among the peculiarities of our constitutional system; it diverts time and energy from exactly the point at which we can spare it least; it does not give us effective negotiation; such experience as we have had with summit diplomacy does not encourage the view that it contributes to the advancement of American interests. For reasons to which we shall now turn briefly, I conclude that summit diplomacy is to be approached with the wariness with which a prudent physician prescribes a habit-forming drug—a technique to be employed rarely and under the most exceptional circumstances, with rigorous safeguards against its becoming a debilitating or dangerous habit.

It is not surprising that the reasons for American reluctance to go to the summit have not been fully explained, either to our own people or to our friends or enemies abroad. Some we could not expect a President to confess; others would appear tactless to our friends; still others would concede certain tactical advantages to our adversaries. In any event, understanding would be difficult for those who have only the most casual or inaccurate knowledge of our political system, which includes almost everyone beyond our borders. The result is that we are under periodic pressure to appear at the summit ("Isn't negotiation a Good Thing?") and our oversimplified defense ("We must have prior proof that a meeting would be worth while") appears a bit lame. Perhaps an irresponsible private citizen may risk offense by observations which are denied to responsible statesmen.

Why the reluctance? It rests upon an interlacing of political and constitutional factors with notions about effective diplomacy. The first difficulty is that the President of the United States can take the time to prepare himself as a negotiator on serious subjects only by deferring or neglecting some of his central constitutional and political responsibilities.

The principal negotiator must be much more than a mouthpiece for the sheets of paper put in front of him by a staff, however competent the latter might be. Questions worth discussing at the summit are presumably important questions; if so, they require the full involvement of the negotiator before he reaches the table. He must understand the full scope of the issues, and their innermost detail. He must gnaw at his own position and become familiar with its strengths and weaknesses. If he is to use obscure words, he must understand why he does so and in which directions he can afford to clarify. He must know intimately the positions of others who are to be present, especially where a common front among allies is a major objective of policy. He must be aware of the impact of the issues upon nations not present at the table and upon American interests in all parts of the world. Prudence requires that he anticipate as best he can the most probable attitude of his principal adversary and the range of alternatives with which his opponent might confront him. He must think carefully about his conduct away from the table itself—the social arrangements, his informal conversations, and, very important, his relations with the press and public opinion. Staff can render invaluable assistance, particularly if by staff we mean the Secretary of State and three or four Assistant Secretaries; but the principal negotiator is in the position of a task force commander who cannot be well served unless he himself fully grasps the situation and knows where he wants to come out. The type of commitment which is required for important high-level negotiation is illustrated by the handling of the first Berlin blockade by Ambassador Philip C. Jessup, the negotiation of the Japanese Peace Treaty by then Ambassador John Foster Dulles, and the development of the Austrian settlement by Ambassador Llewellyn E. Thompson.

But, it will be replied, this is surely not the type of negotiation which occurs at the summit. Exactly. Let us concede in passing that the summit may have other uses, such as to celebrate or confirm agreement already reached through other channels, or as an arena to contest for propaganda advantage, or to "keep talking" to postpone the precipitation of a dangerous issue. If one would add that the summit is conducive to agreement in principle," it might be well to ponder the remark of Secretary George Marshall to a colleague, "Don't ask me to agree in principle; that just means that we haven't agreed yet."

The physical absence of the President from his post in Washington is of enough consequence to be placed upon the scale. The President is as mobile as a jet aircraft, but it is not clear that the Presidency is equally so. One can accept the pleasant and necessary fiction that the White House is wherever the President happens to be and still recognize that prolonged absences from Washington impair the effective performance of the office. Unless the President is accessible, decisions on important matters are postponed by sympathetic subordinates or settled at the level of the common denominator among the departments and agencies concerned. On his own side, the President will be partially cut off from his Cabinet officers, his personal staff, his usual flow of information, the leaders of Congress and of his own party. In addition, he cannot act with regard to many of the formal and informal aspects of his office which we have earlier discussed. A President must be free to leave Washington, on business or on vacation, but the effect of his absence is greater than his personal staff would have him believe. The Presidency is not quite the same in Warm Springs or Cairo, Key West or Potsdam, Augusta, Moscow, Kabul or Santiago, as it is in Washington, D.C.

We are not concerned here about purely technical problems. In the autumn of 1943, Roosevelt, Churchill and Stalin had an extended exchange about the site of a Big Three meeting. Mr. Stalin preferred Iran and cited his duties in the conduct of the war on the Eastern front. Mr. Roosevelt preferred North Africa and repeatedly insisted that he must be sufficiently close to Washington to be able to deal with legislation sent to him by Congress within the ten days prescribed by the Constitution. His objection to Tehran was that uncertain flying conditions at that season might seriously interfere with this constitutional duty. Stalin refused to budge, even as far as Basra, and the meeting was held in Tehran. In finally yielding, Mr. Roosevelt told Stalin, "You will be glad to know that I have worked out a method whereby, if I receive word that there has been passed by the Congress and forwarded to me a bill requiring my veto, I will fly to Tunis to meet it and then return to the Conference." The charming solution must have confirmed to Stalin that the point had not been serious. It should not be difficult to arrange with Congressional leaders, as a matter of constitutional comity, that bills not be forwarded to the President when he is out of the country or, failing that, to insist that the ten-day meter does not begin to run until the bill reaches the President, wherever he might be. Such problems will not bear the freight which Mr. Roosevelt attempted to load upon them; the real issues are more substantial.

Some of us recall that time was of the essence in the decision to interpose American forces against aggression in Korea. Had the series of decisions been postponed on a scale of, say, 24 hours, we should have faced a wholly different situation on the Korean peninsula. President Truman, in Missouri when the first report of the attack reached Washington, could nevertheless authorize immediate reference of the matter to the Security Council and arrive in Washington on the following afternoon to assume full charge of the situation. Jet transport has reduced the difference between Missouri and, say, Western Europe, but guided missiles and alert bombers have almost obliterated the other side of the time equation. Since constitutional arrangements are designed to cover many contingencies which happily never arise, it is not necessarily a sign of panic to suggest that the present strategic situation places a considerable premium upon the immediate availability of the President and Commander-in-Chief. His absence from the United States, in a personal situation which he himself cannot surely control, suggests a contingent "inability to discharge the powers and duties" of his office and revives under new circumstances the discussion of the same point which arose at the time of Wilson's visit to Europe. It is not unreasonable to consider, if eventually to reject, the possibility of providing by statute that the Vice President shall serve as Acting President during the absence of the President from the United States, leaving it to the two of them to determine which matters, short of great emergency, would be forwarded to the President for an indication of his wishes or held for his return. The great departments of government make provision for acting responsibility during the absence of department heads, and the practice is common with private corporations and institutions. However remote one hopes the contingency might be, it is difficult to shake off an underlying uneasiness that one of the most critical duties of the President might be suspended by his inaccessibility, frustrated by the failure of his chief subordinates to agree to act in unison, or usurped by a politically irresponsible general. A provision that the Vice President serve as Acting President during the absences of the President abroad would, of course, mean that Presidents would go abroad only on the rarest occasions—to me one of its most appealing features.

Returning to summit meetings and their capacity to yield constructive agreements, there are lessons from the rich lore of diplomatic experience which are neither controlling nor negligible. The parties can be expected to come to the table in the hope of obtaining an agreement, each on its own terms. The crucial question is whether these terms fit or can be made to fit each other, opening up the possibility of an agreement which each might find advantageous or at least more tolerable than the status quo. To explore this question is the chief purpose of negotiation; if it be known in advance that there is no such possibility then the proceedings, whatever they are called, are not negotiation.

The experienced diplomat will usually counsel against the direct confrontation of those with final authority. Negotiation *ad referendum* offers greater opportunity for feeling out the situation, exploring the opposing points of view, trying out alternative approaches without commitment, testing general propositions by meticulous attention to detail. The process needs time, patience and precision, three resources which are not found in abundance at the highest political level. The direct confrontation of the chiefs of government of the great powers involves an extra tension because the court of last resort is in session. The costs of error or misunderstanding are multiplied by the seriousness of the issues and the power of those present.

Picture two men sitting down together to talk about matters affecting the very survival of the systems they represent, each in position to unleash unbelievably destructive power. Note that the one is impulsive in manner, supremely confident as only a closed mind can be, tempted to play for dramatic effect, motivated by forces only partially perceived by the other, possibly subject to high blood pressure; the other deeply committed to principles for which his adversary has only contempt, weighted down by a sense of responsibility for the hundreds of millions who have freely given him their confidence and whose fates are largely in his hands, a man limited by conscience and policy in his choice of tactics and argument, a man with a quick temper and a weak heart. Is it wise to gamble so heavily; are not these two men who should be kept apart until others have found a sure meeting ground of accommodation between them? Is there not much to be said for institutionalizing their relationship?

The skepticism of the diplomat about the blessings of togetherness among heads of government and foreign ministers is well known. The fifteenth century advice of Philippe de Comines that "Two great princes who wish to establish good personal relations should never meet each other face to face but ought to communicate through good and wise ambassadors" is matched in our own century by Sir Harold Nicolson's reservations about the "habit of personal contact between the statesmen of the world." Discounting generously for wholesome professional bias, their views point us toward a well-grounded generalization. Thinking broadly and over the long run, the course of wisdom lies in reducing the impact which accidents of personality have upon the relations among nations. We may recall with satisfaction the personal harmony in which George Marshall, Ernest Bevin and Robert Schuman labored for allied unity and may try to forget the painful results of the personal difficulties between Anthony Eden and John Foster Dulles. But neither friendship nor aversion is an adequate basis for high policy. Personalities change, sometimes rapidly; but the great tasks of building a tolerable world order endure and national interests reach far beyond the idiosyncracies of holders of public office.

I must confess to idle speculation about the extent to which the course of world affairs may have been affected by illness among those holding high public office since, say, the time of Woodrow Wilson. I say "idle" because it would probably be impossible to isolate the effects of illness and we cannot know what might have been. But the international list of those who have carried great responsibility while ill is a long one and there are fleeting glimpses of decisions which good health might have turned another way. The point is mentioned because one of the purposes of diplomacy, including its elaborate formality and high style, is to exclude from great affairs of state the many irrelevancies which spring from human frailty.

If personalities make for complications, these are magnified by the circumstances of a summit meeting. When the Big Three consulted about wartime meetings they seemed much less concerned about getting away from the Germans than about getting away from the press. Apart from the harrowing insistence of the most competitive of the professions, the general atmosphere is that of the football stadium. Is our team winning? Did our man throw him for a loss? Who wins the most valuable player award? But beneath the surface lie the desperate hopes that tensions will be eased, that somehow things will get better. The result is a pervasive pressure toward the creation of illusions—at worst an illusion of victory, at best the pretense of accomplishment where none was achieved.

I must confess that I do not see my way through the inevitable entanglement of summit diplomacy with domestic politics. Can there be any doubt that a summit meeting in the spring and the visit of the President to the Soviet Union in June will give Mr. Khrushchev a chance to influence significantly our coming presidential election? Were not some of us just a bit embarrassed when Mr. Macmillan announced a general election almost before the vapor trails of the President's jet had dissolved into British skies? Is the President of the United States to be caught up personally in the difficult task of satisfying General de Gaulle's appetite for grandeur? Can we not anticipate cables from still other quarters reading, "My government will fall unless you come to see us"? And how shall we handle the chain reactions which prestige factors will set off if summitry becomes a habit—the demands of other NATO partners to have a share, the need to show that the exclusive club is not limited to white nations and great powers, the resentment in Latin America if left at the bottom of our interest and concern?

One of the arguments made in behalf of summit meetings is that heads of government can talk things over directly with freedom of action and power to come to agreements promptly and decisively. But the President of the United States is subject to what might be called the Woodrow Wilson Effect—he must keep in mind his ability to make good on his commitments when he gets home. If the summit means bold diplomacy for some, it may well mean timidity for us. A President in Washington, in direct touch with his departments and Congressional and party leaders may be able to react more promptly and more confidently than if he himself were present at the table.

A formidable argument for summit diplomacy is the one endorsed by President Eisenhower and repeated by Ambassador Charles Bohlen and others, to the effect that "If you wish to negotiate with the Soviet Union you must talk to Mr. Khrushchev." Standing alone, the argument is not wholly persuasive. Is there point in allowing the Soviet Union to set the style of international negotiation at the cost of disrupting the established political arrangements of other nations? Have we not already made a major concession in yielding to a procedure which works to his advantage and our disadvantage? If he insists upon having a Foreign Minister to whom he does not wish to give his confidence, is he to impose the same ignominious status upon the Secretary of State of the United States? Can we not insist that it is up to each nation to determine for itself who its highest ranking negotiator is to be? Or cannot Mr. Khrushchev find even *one* high-ranking colleague whom he can trust to represent him loyally and effectively?

IV

Something else has to be thrown into the scale—and because that "something else" may be present, I have been unwilling to criticize the exchange of visits between the President and Mr. Khrushchev and the one summit meeting now firmly arranged. It is just possible that significant changes are taking place in the directions of Soviet policy. It may be that the frightfulness of modern war has made itself felt, that the severities of a police state have revealed their dead end and that public opinion is exerting a moderating influence upon Soviet policy by shifting its priorities. It may be that the Communist revolution is reaching the point which other revolutions have reached, where the dogma is enshrined but not very much is done about it. It could even be that Mr. Khrushchev "needs" summit diplomacy to enable him to bring about certain changes in policy within his own system. If there is substance in these speculations, I would suppose that none of us would regret the President's effort to find out about them. But the risks are as high as the stakes. We are moving into the period in which we have anticipated that we would be at a temporary disadvantage in the strategic field. We are presenting the periodic uncertainty and confusion of a presidential year. In so far as the public record is concerned, there is little to make us think that Soviet objectives have changed, and much to remind us of the growing strength through which they can pursue them. Dissension weakens the unity of the free world. The President is entitled, on the basis of all the information available to him, to take the risks but one can hope that he will be alert to the dangers of illusion. A democratic people can generate their own false hopes very efficiently; the task of leadership is to confront us with our duties in the light of unpleasant reality.

Let me sum up briefly. What we say and how we should like to appear are of transient importance compared with how we conduct the public business in our domestic and foreign affairs. No propaganda is so effective as an earned reputation as a vital society, offering expanding opportunities for its own citizens and basing its relations with the rest of the world upon mutual respect and underlying decency. If we are entitled to a measure of self-confidence, there are insistent problems which demand our attention: the solidarity of our alliances, our relations with newly independent peoples, the suitability of our armed forces for our needs, the orderly growth of our economy, the competitive position of our products abroad, our desperate needs in education, deterioration in our transportation and our great urban centers, the acceptance of our minorities as full-fledged citizens, and, in every vocation, profession or service, our shortage of competent men for leadership. Each can make his own list.

The crucial, indispensable contribution which the President can make to the conduct of our foreign affairs is to enter fully into his office, to use its powers and accept its responsibilities, to lead a people who are capable of responding to the obligations of citizenship. He holds a unique office in a unique constitutional system, which offers him vast powers in exchange for leadership —powers which are as large as the situation requires. With deep compassion we can acknowledge that his are burdens which no man ought to be asked to bear, that the problems before him may reach beyond the capacity of the mind of man, and we can be grateful that there are men with the temerity to seek the office. It is respect for the Presidency which leads one to believe that visits to 20 or more countries in the course of a few months, interspersed by periods of preparation and rest, take too much out of the man and his office. A presidential system cannot easily adjust to an interregnum; a nation moving with such great mass and velocity needs the engineer at the throttle.

Finally, the President must prepare himself for those solemn moments when, after all the advice is in from every quarter, he must ascend his lonely pinnacle and decide what we must do. There are such moments, when the whole world holds its breath and our fate is in his hands. Then every fragment of his experience, all that he has read and learned, his understanding of his own nation and of the world about him, his faith, conscience and courage are brought to bear. It is in this realization, not in petty criticism, that we can be jealous of his time and energy and resistant to every influence which comes between the man and his burdens.

¶ FORTY YEARS ON

by the Earl of Avon (Anthony Eden)   (October, 1962)

Lord Avon looks back over four decades of international relations from a unique vantage point, for he had a direct part in most of the great decisions that were made during that period. As Anthony Eden, he held in succession many of the pivotal ministerial posts in the British Government, beginning as far back as 1935 as Minister for League of Nations Affairs. He became Foreign Secretary in 1951 and four years later succeeded Winston Churchill as Prime Minister.

Lord Avon notes that, even in the interwar years, "all was not folly." And, though he concedes that man's capacity for making the same mistakes over and over has no limit, he maintains that the accomplishments of the period provide workable concepts for future progress.

In what Lord Avon calls a "series of ruthless onslaughts against the ideas and practices of freedom," it has become clear that to sacrifice principles and obligations to expediency is self-defeating. Unjust concessions are no substitute for concerted action to defeat aggression.

The development of nuclear weapons has created a horror of destruction that gives pause to even a dictator, but the risk of accidental war remains, and it increases as more nations acquire a nuclear capability. Lord Avon urges the creation of an international political general staff to provide for consultation on arms limitation and other problems. He sees the development of a closely unified and integrated West as essential and urges that the opportunity to join together be seized before the option is foreclosed.

FORTY YEARS ON

By the Earl of Avon

FOR those who were close to international events in the nine-teen twenties and took a part in the errors and shortcomings of the next decade, there is a fascination in contrasting the two world wars with the experience of the present time. If we can learn from a generation ago and apply the lessons of that period to our present problems, we might render a useful service, for even then all was not folly.

The casualty lists of the First World War were cruel and horrifying. They were also much heavier in proportion for France and for the British Commonwealth than those of the longer Second World War. The few survivors of my own age soon grew used to hearing themselves referred to as the missing generation. The tag was true, and the extent of the holocaust created an in-tense determination to prevent its return. The claim that we were fighting "the war to end war" was sincerely accepted, to an extent which it may be difficult for a more sophisticated modern public to believe. The will to make a repetition of these experiences un-realizable, to create and impose a rule of law to halt or fend them off, was widely and even passionately shared. In my library I have a beautifully produced French annual review entitled *L' Armoire de Citronnier*. This little book was devoted to litera-ture and the arts and had no direct concern with politics; yet, at the end, when I looked for the date, I found it expressed in these words: "In the year one of the League of Nations." In that sense we were all revolutionaries, intent on our new era.

The young League of Nations had need of all this faith and fervor to set against its besetting weakness, the lack of universal-ity. In its beginnings a League of allied and associated powers, eight years had to pass after the armistice before Germany could be admitted to membership, as a sequel to the Locarno Treaties. Revolutionary Russia had to wait eight years more until Barthou found her a place; and meanwhile Japan's aggression in China had compelled her withdrawal. None of these events, however, was comparable in significance with the misfortune which dogged the League of Nations from the outset of its career: the decision of the United States not to ratify the Anglo-American guarantee to France or to take up membership in the League.

The Covenant, which was the League's charter, was well drafted and was on the whole a fair and balanced document. But its association, even though in part technical, with the terms of the peace settlement, gave Hitler a grievance he was always ready to exploit. The fact that Germany had entered the League, after the Locarno Treaty, on equal terms with the victorious allied powers, and enjoyed the same rights to a permanent seat on the Council, was the answer to Hitler's complaints. It remained true that, for the majority of powers around the Council table, it was an important obligation to uphold the peace settlement and, by so doing, to ensure that Germany was not in a position to become again a menace to Europe.

This conviction was strongly held in France, which had suffered most in life, less so in Britain and the countries of the Commonwealth, where, though the casualties had been very heavy, the sense of historic sequence was not so acute. There was a pardonable but not prudent willingness to shake hands and hope that all would be well. At times this was tinged with impatience against those in Europe whose suspicions were not so easily allayed. The further from the fire, the more tolerant the generosity, with the result that there were soon three circling rings of apprehension spaced from the German center. France, and her immediate allies of the Little Entente in the closest ring, Britain and the British Commonwealth in the next, the United States and some of the more remote powers, including those of South America, in the third.

The connection of the Covenant with the peace settlement was not, in my opinion, the misfortune it has often been dubbed. It expressed a reality: a revival of German military power was something to be feared and guarded against. Nor were the terms of the settlement so harsh, except for the reparation demands, which made little sense and had rapidly to be scaled down anyway. One consequence of the link between the Covenant and the peace settlement was to enjoin, among many members of the League of Nations, a convinced adherence to existing treaties and a respect for them. This was not so baleful an influence as well-meaning Anglo-Saxons often pretended.

There were many to argue that if the defeated nations played their part peaceably in upholding an international order, they were entitled to some relaxation of the terms of the engagements they had made. This might be so, but it was not the whole story. It remained healthy and desirable that if peace were to be upheld, international engagements must be respected. Observing our own experience in recent years, I would contend that a growing weakness of the United Nations has been its failure to uphold just this principle. There has been too much neutrality between respect for the pledged word and the ambitions of growing nationalism. There has been too much accommodation between the fire brigade and the fire.

The United Nations must be law-abiding and support those who wish to uphold the law, and not base its conduct solely on what seems at the time expedient, or excusable, because, as an afterthought, the international engagement itself may not seem everything that it should be. There can often be strong arguments for the revision of existing engagements by agreement. There is none for allowing them to be torn up. The League of Nations was certainly firmer on the side of the enforcement of international law so far as it could be defined. The United Nations has too often preferred to look the other way if the international cause were unpopular, with consequences which history has shown to be inevitable.

The widely held respect for written engagements which the Covenant of the League enjoined had consequences even among what we should today call neutral opinion. All other things being equal, there was an inclination to accept that the existing order deserved respect and even support. I do not think that it is an accident, or otherwise an influence for peace, that "neutral" opinion today is so blatantly ready to find pretexts for the misconduct of the Communist powers, as in the matter of Russia's sudden resumption of nuclear tests, and so ready to blame the United States because it could not accept to give the Soviets this stolen advantage indefinitely.

In another respect the League of Nations attempted, until the lawlessness of Hitler smashed this and much else besides, to uphold a certain standard. International property or the property of foreign nationals in a nation's midst was not something which could be seized with impunity and kept without apology. Material grab was not encouraged, even though part of the motive for this resistance to predatory appetites was that those who had the power also had the possessions. This state of affairs was, none the less, an influence for peace.

The actual machinery of the League of Nations was not complicated and it worked well; failings in universality and later in will were in no sense its fault. The regular quarterly meetings of the Council, almost always attended by the Foreign Secretaries of the principal powers, were a valuable practice. These men got to understand each other, knew when they would meet and could prepare with regularity the topics they had to discuss. They did so and, in the years of their authority which immediately succeeded Locarno, they created as serviceable a piece of diplomatic machinery as I have ever known. It had evident advantages over the present practice, when our Secretaries of State and Foreign Ministers have to span the world for meetings of NATO, CENTO and SEATO, while those who meet at the Security Council of the United Nations are usually not the men with chief responsibility for the conduct of their countries' foreign affairs. In part this is a consequence of the Soviet abuse of the veto which has crippled the effectiveness of the Security Council. The tendency to bypass its authority in favor of the Assembly, which cannot take its place or do its work, has only heightened confusion and multiplied weakness, until the United Nations has become an instrument ready to the hand of the prejudiced propagandist, but not always so pliant to the patient toiler for peace, through fortifying confidence in engagements given.

The principal lesson of the nineteen thirties, therefore, remains the significance which must be attached to respect for treaties and the dire consequences which result from denying them. U Thant tells us that history does not repeat itself. I do not think that there is much danger that the nations will heed past lessons too closely. On the contrary, there seems a determination to learn from anything except experience, and there is certainly no limit to man's capacity for making the same mistakes over and over again.

II

The existence of nuclear power and the shattering destructive force its weapons can command have created dismay in many a land. Parades and calls for the abolition of such devastating engines of war are held in many countries, including my own, and it is certainly true that if nuclear war were once loosed, the world would be destroyed. Yet I do not believe that these well-meaning persons are aiming at the right objective.

The very horror of the destruction which must be caused by a nuclear war will give pause to even the most hardened dictator in his search for plunder. All our recent would-be conquerors, down to and including Hitler, embarked upon their careers of aggrandizement believing that, on balance, victory in arms would increase their power. None, except perhaps Hitler at his last gasp, would have deliberately brought destruction on all, himself included. Yet this we now know must be the consequence of nuclear war.

It is further possible to argue that the existence of the nuclear deterrent has been the most powerful influence for the maintenance of peace since the day of the Nazi surrender. Most of us are convinced that it was the knowledge of the preponderant power of the West in this arm which stayed Soviet ambitions in the immediate postwar phase. Certainly, there was no other barrier of force between Soviet arms and the Channel ports, and he would be a bold man or a careless one who accepts that any other influence could halt a Communist power in any plan it wished to execute. It is true that as familiarity with nuclear secrets spreads more widely among the nations, the risk of foolishness or accident which might trigger off the employment of these weapons must inevitably grow. Even so, the boldest and most thoughtless can be expected to hesitate before destruction which must include himself and his land.

Another danger seems to me more likely to spread widening confusion, with perilous consequences. This stems from the small part the United Nations has played in upholding international order. Foreign affairs are a continuing process; they cannot be divided up into chapters, closed and put comfortably away. There is surely a connection between the facility with which President Nasser could seize the Suez Canal by force and threaten Israel, and the impunity with which, less than a year later, Indonesia took possession of Dutch shipping with no presentable offer of compensation. This practice was perfected by Dr. Castro in Cuba, where the scale of the theft of American properties surpassed any attempted before. Others have followed in his wake again, until in Indonesia plans are pointedly prepared for the "liberation" of territories in Western New Guinea, which are administered by the Netherlands and occupied by native populations having no racial connection with the country which would now make them part of a new colonial empire. These depredations vary in character but unless they are checked their cumulative effect can be serious. Anarchy may be a greater danger even than the nuclear bomb.

Certain remedies can be employed. The International Bank wisely declines to give financial aid to any country which is still in default upon its payments to foreign creditors. It would be reasonable to include another condition, that the country to be helped must first have concluded arrangements to compensate foreign powers or foreign nationals for the seizure of their properties within its territories. This is not interference in the internal affairs of any land, any more than is the request that foreign debts should be paid. But such a practice would set a standard and check license which otherwise will certainly grow.

There is another reason for insisting that this maxim of conduct should be enforced. If the underdeveloped countries are to be helped economically on a scale and at a speed which bears relation to their needs, a formidable financial effort will be called for from those powers which have the necessary resources. It is not going to be easy, it is not even easy now, yet the effort must be made. If those who must try to afford it are to be encouraged to make it, they are entitled for their security to know that they or their nationals are not going to be singled out in any revolutionary process by the theft of their property; or at the least if they are, that these deeds will not be passed over when the country which has permitted them asks once again for international financial help. Neither good political relations nor economic plans for mutual help among the nations can develop except in an atmosphere of confidence in which respect for engagements holds first place.

The situation in Western New Guinea on which negotiations have been concluded between the United Nations, the United States, the Netherlands and Indonesia calls for comment. Some uneasy precedents have been set in this business. It is necessary to recall that the territory of New Guinea was expressly excluded from the Agreement of November 1949 when Indonesia became a state. The Agreement stipulated only that the "political status" of West New Guinea was to be determined through "further negotiations." Pending an outcome of such negotiations, there could have been no pretense that Indonesia had a legitimate claim to control Western New Guinea. It therefore seems strange that the Acting Secretary-General of the United Nations should refuse to send observers to report on events in New Guinea, following on Indonesian parachute landings and other inroads into the territory. The Netherlands Government made this request and it was not met, on the pretext that it would be a departure from neutrality to send observers unless both parties agreed that this should be done. This doctrine could mean that both the aggressor and the victim have to agree before the United Nations can send observers to the scene of an alleged aggression. That is not a tenable doctrine on any basis of international equity.

The Netherlands has now, under pressure from the United States and the United Nations, yielded its trusteeship in Western New Guinea, first to the United Nations and then to Indonesia. Only after seven years of Indonesian administration are the native inhabitants to be allowed to decide by plebiscite what their future should be. Yet a vote in such conditions can hardly carry confidence.

It has sometimes been urged in defense of such an arrangement that Soviet Russia is encouraging Indonesia to the early use of force against Western New Guinea, hoping thereby to embroil Indonesia with the West and fortify the appeal of the already formidable Communist Party in that country. This may well be the Soviet intention, yet the consequences for the free nations of sponsoring a solution which is not itself just can be grave; a little present ease may be gained, but probably at the expense of greater trouble thereafter. In the history of the last 30 years it has not proved wise to seek to assuage excessive appetites by unjust concession.

Since the Second World War there have been occasions when the temptation to yield to a dictator who is imposing unreasonable demands has had to be resisted. In Iran after Mosaddeq's accession to power and the seizure of the Anglo-Iranian oil fields, suggestions were made that this ruler should be given financial aid and comfort in the hope of staving off worse consequences. The supporters of this policy were influenced by the fear that the succession to Mosaddeq might be Communist rule, the same possibility as influences Western opinion toward Indonesia today. Yet fortunately the temptation was resisted in Iran, and Mosaddeq was not bolstered to an extent which would have enabled him to claim that he had triumphed through the methods he had employed. Even the risk of Communist rule as a consequence of this refusal was accepted. In the outcome, and after a delay which admittedly carried its dangers, a responsible government succeeded to Mosaddeq's. A settlement was reached with this government which has proved to the financial advantage of Iran. The Consortium Agreement of 1954 still operates and it is clear in retrospect that the firmness shown then did not give the victory to Communism, but resulted in a check to its growing power in that country. Iran gained by obtaining much larger sums through the joint development of the oil fields than Mosaddeq could ever have obtained by his methods; and the world witnessed a salutary lesson.

III

A contrast between conditions today and those of the 1920s, when the League of Nations was still in fair health, is to be found in the means for the close development of relations between the Western powers. Though the world has become smaller since then and the decisions correspondingly more urgent, our machinery is still ineffective. NATO, officially at least, deals only with Europe, while the problems we have to meet together are world-wide. This caused me a year ago to appeal for an international political general staff; and in the intervening period it has become even more necessary.

While nuclear weapons are a powerful deterrent, it will be foolish not to accept that the development of nuclear armament creates other difficulties which must increase in complexity with the passage of time. We should do well to begin considering some of them now and to try to bridge the strategic problems they are already creating. These will not become easier to solve by merely ignoring them. They should be discussed between the Western allies and particularly between the United States, Britain and France. Britain and the United States may still be the only two nuclear powers in the West. If so, this does not seem likely to last much longer. France appears determined to be among them. When I write France, I refer not only to General de Gaulle and the present French Government, but to their predecessors and quite possibly to their successors.

There is nothing to be gained by sulking over this situation; it is better to face the dilemmas. Should active help be given to the French Government at the stage of development which it has now reached, or is it to continue at very heavy cost to cover unaided the ground which the Americans and ourselves have already covered? It seems to me that the present situation, whereby they do this, is unreal and unreasonable. If, however, a solution is to be found, we are brought up at once against another question. If France is to be helped to obtain more quickly scientific knowledge which, in any event, she can gain in time and which the Communist world has already, we must reach agreement on the joint employment of our knowledge and production on behalf of the free world. Perhaps the final answer is a European atomic striking force, including American, British and French contributions. However that may be, a determination of our policies in this regard is becoming urgent.

Recently we have again heard the proposal, made this time, I think, by the United States, that Western defense needs stronger NATO conventional forces in Europe. If this is to be carried through, we must be clear about the purpose of the greater effort entailed. If it is merely to strengthen the defensive screen in Europe, personally I should doubt if its usefulness would justify this extra effort. If on the other hand it is intended to decrease the need for nuclear defense, I would regard that as a dangerous delusion. But here again is subject matter for close examination and decision by the highest authorities in the West, together. A related problem—what the joint policy should be on tactical weapons in the defense of the West—is also one which requires further probing and resolution. So, too, is the question whether means can be found of limiting the danger of destruction upon the civil population in the event of any outbreak of nuclear war. Frankly I am skeptical about this, and if there is no certainty in the matter, I would regard it as dangerous to hold illusions which could have as their consequence a lessening of the fear of nuclear war, because that fear is itself a deterrent and a factor for peace.

It would not be difficult to add other items to this list, which is already a formidable one. Enough has been written to show how necessary is some improvement in the methods of consultation between the Western powers at the levels where decisions can be taken. Better machinery by means of an international political general staff could, I believe, help toward this result. It is quite true that the heads of governments meet each other from time to time, but they do it two by two. Never are there meetings among three or four of them to attempt to straighten out differences which are today tiresome but could tomorrow become dangerous. The outlook would be healthier if we could prepare for such a meeting with a fair chance of success. It is true that the leading Communist powers are at cross-purposes too; but we should forbear from too much cheering on that account and concentrate on mending our own affairs. Certainly we must be under no illusions about the character, intentions and determination of the Communist leaders. The hopes of the lovers of peace in the last 40 years have not been frustrated only because the machinery of international coöperation has been inadequate. Deliberate evil intent has prevailed over all our efforts.

My lifetime has seen a series of ruthless onslaughts against the ideas and practices of freedom. Many nations could have been saved from servitude if their law-abiding partners had combined their resources early enough. The West now faces from without a threat carefully organized and centrally directed. It can meet it only by an idealist faith in its cause and with plans which are closely unified and integrated. In combined strength we are far more powerful than international Communism, but our survival, let alone victory, will depend upon ability to see the realities with unclouded eyes. The scope is there, and the opportunity.

¶ THE UNDERDEVELOPED AND THE OVERDEVELOPED
by Margaret Mead   (October, 1962)

*In the early 1960's, both the aid-giving countries and the newly independent
nations were relatively buoyant about the prospects for economic development
in the poorer nations; there was little propensity to doubt either the goal
or the likelihood of their "catching up." And it was often implicitly assumed
that among the prerogatives conferred by sovereignty was the right to economic development, that is, prosperity.*

*Since then, the problems of the developing countries have come to seem
both more complicated and more intractable. While many have shown de-
cidedly respectable rates of growth in GNP, population increases have often
diminished or nullified their effect. In fact, the creation of a modern sector
in their economies has fostered inequality by setting one small highly paid group
of workers apart from the rest of both urban and rural working populations.
And rising expectations have brought job-seekers flooding into the crowded
cities.*

*In view of this, questions are being raised about the primacy of economic
growth measured in terms of GNP for the developing countries. In regard
to aid, should we leave them largely to their own devices, perhaps to develop
according to values that differ radically from ours? Or should we continue
to offer aid—but through multilateral channels?*

*In 1962, Margaret Mead suggested many of these questions in this article.
With her highly developed sense of the wide divergencies between the norms
of different cultures, Mrs. Mead was naturally opposed to judging all nations
on a single scale referring to standard of living and ultimately to the extent
of industrialization. As she pointed out, poverty is often relative to one's expectations, and the newly inflated expectations of the poor countries could add
to their problems. Too, she argued, the widespread notion that poverty is a
consequence of underdevelopment and therefore remediable—because every
country is capable of development, or a rising level of production—constituted a promise that could not easily be fulfilled under the present international
system. Only in a new worldwide framework might the earth's resources and
modern technology be employed on a scale that could lead to the eradication of
poverty. Here, Mrs. Mead presaged the contemporary notion of multilateral
channels for aid-giving. Finally, she underlined the necessities for different
standards of measurement and for each nation to preserve its own identity.*

THE UNDERDEVELOPED AND
THE OVERDEVELOPED

By Margaret Mead

THIS pair of phrases sums up the new, conflicting and contradictory assumptions that underlie the highly unsatisfactory climate of opinion in today's world. The use of the word "underdeveloped" in connection with a country implies that the most significant dimension of measurement in the world today is standard of living and that standard of living should be measured in terms of those indices that are inextricably linked with industrialization. Countries that are unindustrialized and depend primarily on agriculture and other primary industries are poor. Countries that are industrialized are rich. Richness and poverty are unequivocal terms. They relate to a single scale and provide one set of measurements in accordance with which all countries can be placed.

Economists grant that the problem of weighting is a difficult one. It is perfectly clear that, in a country in which 90 percent of the population can raise little more food than they need for their own consumption, very little will be left over to satisfy other and more complicated needs. If, for example, there is just enough extra food to take to a nearby market to sell for the few things that must be bought there—salt, candles, tea or coffee, tobacco, woven cloth—and the sellers always walk to market, then when bicycles are introduced, there will be no funds to buy them unless a change takes place. But in a relatively rich underdeveloped country like old Bali, where food was plentiful and there was a large surplus which could be spent on cremations, it was possible to cut down on cremations and to buy bicycles instead. When this happens, the standard of living is said to be higher. The culture has been impoverished and the country is not yet developed, but a first step in development has been taken—at cultural expense only. But where, as in most underdeveloped countries, the population lives at the subsistence level without a surplus of any kind, where the only source of animal protein is the ox or the pig consumed at a feast, the desire to own a bicycle can be realized only at the expense of something that is absolutely essential to subsistence as well as to a full and rewarding life. So, once the people of any country have learned to want manufactured objects that they cannot buy out of an existing surplus, because there is no such surplus, they are immediately defined by themselves and others as underdeveloped and therefore poor.

The term "underdeveloped" is used technically to place a country in terms of industrialization, real and potential, on a scale which implies that industrial development can, should and will take place. The term "poor," however, is not used to place a country on a continuum of technical change. It is used rather to describe its relative consumption position—or the relative consumption position of the majority of its citizens—in comparison with other countries. Poor can mean not knowing where the next meal is coming from, as it does for many of the urban poor, or it can mean not being able to buy a bicycle, a jeep or a truck. It has no absolute connotation, in this context.

A group of primitive Eskimo, caught between winter and summer, their snow house melting above their heads but the time not yet come when summer hunting and fishing have brought in new supplies of food, or, at the opposite season, caught by the terrible autumnal storms that for days on end make hunting impossible, sitting together starving and the lamps gone out for lack of oil, until in desperation some hunter braves the storm and the punishing supernaturals—these people can be described as in danger of death but not as poor. They had the same equipment as the other Eskimo for meeting the harsh realities of their environment. They knew how to build snow houses, they had dogs, sleds, harpoons, soapstone lamps, bone needles, clothes of skin and fur. In those desperate situations when, in order to stay alive, they had to eat their dogs and then had to go on living without the means to make a living, they might be considered unfortunate. Or a man who, for some reason, had no wife to cook for him and dress his skins might be considered temporarily unfortunate. But these losses were potentially retrievable. His misfortune was a temporary lack of equipment or the lack of a working partner as compared with his fellow Eskimo. For an isolated individual or family group the lack might well be fatal; in other circumstances recoupment was possible. In the early days of contact, Europeans in the Arctic had to adopt Eskimo equipment in order to survive; the Eskimo were not then, by comparison, poor. But later, when modern equipment suitable for the Arctic was developed, the Eskimo did become poor in comparison with Europeans.

Poverty appears only when some people are organized into

groups from which they themselves have no means of escape or of self-betterment, because of ignorance, or government regulation, or lack of a culturally derived belief that escape is possible. So they are immobilized and do without necessities that others have, or they do without some of the luxuries that others have. Moreover, the more egalitarian the society, the more important is the concept of poverty. Where only the chief or the feudal lord lives in a large house and all other men in houses which are small and mean, the distinction is not between richness and poverty but between privilege and absence of privilege in a system based on rank or caste or class. But when it is possible for a majority of the population to have some given thing—a tin roof, a well, a pump, inside plumbing, a donkey, a team of horses, two teams of horses, a bicycle, a tractor, a truck, a station wagon—then the smaller number who cannot acquire it do not regard themselves, and are not regarded by others, as members of a different or a lesser breed. Instead they come to feel, and others come to feel, that they are simply poor.

While the term underdeveloped implies occupation of a place on a continuum that is defined in terms of technological per capita capacity to produce, the term poor implies placement at the bottom of the scale of consumption, having less than others—less, usually, than most others. When the two ideas are combined, and emphasis is laid on the relative presence or absence of technical productive capacity, all this is changed.

In older discussions of the condition of the poor, the poor at home or abroad, it was emphasized that it would do little good to divide up the riches of the wealthy few in an attempt to alleviate the poverty of the myriads of poor. Then it was possible for the rich to sit at overweighted tables while the poor pressed their noses against the windows in envious contemplation. If the rich were generous in a time of famine or flood, if they built hospitals or endowed schools so that a few more individuals could escape from misery, they could go their way without too bad a conscience. However wealth was rationalized—as the reward of individual effort or parental effort, as the necessary support of high birth—it was necessarily only for the few; the fortunate should be individually generous and should improve their position in heaven. If they did so, they had no special reason to feel guilty; they could enjoy their wealth.

But acceptance of the assumption that technological development is possible for all and, therefore, that improvement of consumption is possible for all meant that it was no longer morally acceptable to let the majority of the peoples of the world live in poverty. From an economy of scarcity—in which, if one person got more, someone else got less and no redistribution of the rubies and emeralds of the rich could, in the long run, help more than a handful of beggars—we have moved, by definition, to an economy of plenty. Riches are no longer somebody's disproportionate, though legitimate, share of a scarce supply; poverty is no longer the consequence of someone else having a large proportion of the existing supply. Stated simply, as between the peoples of the world, poverty is the consequence of being underdeveloped. According to this doctrine, wealth is not given but is produced and every country is capable of an ever-rising rate of production; therefore poverty, defined as the present state of low consumption of most of the peoples of the world, is remediable. A people need not be poor; development will cure their poverty.

Systematic change from the older to the newer position has its difficulties, but there is a further complication. For, in the present position, poverty is defined in two different ways—relative and absolute. In the relative sense, poverty is defined as having less than others. In the absolute sense, there is a minimum standard below which no human beings should fall; when this minimum standard is attained by all the peoples of the world, when the now developed nations have helped the underdeveloped countries to develop, then everyone will be well off. This complication, arising from the discrepant definitions of poverty as relative and as absolute, is as seldom worked out in discussions about countries as it is in relief situations in the United States, where the relief agency attempts to meet standards of nutrition, medical care, shelter and so on, on an absolute scale of health and decency, while the recipients of relief experience profound and humiliating poverty on a relative standard.

A further consequence of the confusion between these two definitions of poverty is the effect it has on the planning and expectations of countries that are, by definition, rich. By implication, "closing the gap" between underdeveloped and developed countries means that the developed countries are, in fact, developed (or, as Myrdal puts it, are "now developed"[1]) and, essentially,

[1] Gunnar Myrdal, "Beyond the Welfare State: Economic Planning and Its International Implications." New Haven: Yale University Press, 1960.

should develop no further; that is, the standard of living should rise no further. Instead, such countries should use the surplus that could go into further development to "close the gap" by supplying the undeveloped countries with capital already accumulated in the rich countries through the sweat and toil of the poor of other generations.

If, on the contrary, the rich countries continue to develop their already enormous productive capacities for their own use, and existing discrepancies in birth rates are maintained, then the underdeveloped countries will become poorer, relative to the rich countries, but poverty in the other sense—the absolute sense—will also result, *i.e.* deprivation of basic subsistence goods.

Thus advocacy of "closing the gap" includes, implicitly, a demand that developed countries should either arrest consumption or arrest the motivating force in their productive development—the desire for a rising consumption standard.

A second very widely accepted assumption is that our capacity —based on our tremendous command of technology—to feed, clothe, shelter, educate and medicate the peoples of the world should be shared among the peoples of the world seen not as individual human beings with human needs, but as citizens of nation states. The vision that no one need be hungry or cold, illiterate and ignorant, or suffer from an illness for which there is a cure coincided with the contemporary implementation of ideals of self-determination, especially for colonial peoples. Both are aspects of anti-colonialism, as an ethic and as a political tool which has been exploited in the cold war and by ambitious local leaders, hungry for power.

So, on the one hand, our new conception of technical development is geared to a twentieth-century understanding of the relationship between technology, productivity and the determination and satisfaction of minimal human needs. But on the other hand, our conception of how these needs are to be met is geared to an obsolescent conception of what nation states, of whatever size, shape, resources, population and so on, can accomplish as full, complete and sufficient units for the implementation of new forms of satisfaction of human needs. The focus is not on hungry *people,* wherever they may be, but on underdeveloped *countries,* which should be able to feed, clothe and educate their citizens. The combination of these two ethics—the right of human beings to the satisfaction of their basic needs and the right to national autonomy of any group of people who have come to regard themselves as a group because of the institution of colonialism or the accidents of political treaties—has resulted in an extraordinary degree of obfuscation.

For centuries the lack of equal resources, natural or man-made, has been compensated for by migration of some kind. The poor peasant went to the city or another country, or worked as a coolie overseas. Younger sons of the landed gentry or the wealthy went abroad to make their fortune. Inlanders went to sea. Opportunity was conceived of as localized and people as movable within a region, within a country, between nations or areas of the world. But today, possibly in reaction to the stress of millions of refugees —people who left their homes unwillingly—we have created a new right, the right to stay at home under one's own apple tree and have light industry brought to one's own backyard. This implication of bringing development to underdeveloped countries has gone almost unnoticed. Americans have been subjected to so much compulsory moving since the beginning of World War II, and have developed such a phobia about shifting their children from one school to another, that it seems to them a quite reasonable demand that everyone should be allowed to stay in his own country and have the comforts of civilization brought within his reach. Moreover, various fortuitous circumstances attendant on the wars and revolutions of the twentieth century have effectively obscured some of the serious consequences of taking the position that it is the right of every *nation,* new or old, rich or poor, large or small, no matter where located or how technically competent, to be developed and to become, if not rich, at least as well off as every other nation, with as high a standard of living for its people and as large and as conspicuous marks of national prestige in the way of embassies, airlines, armies and so on.

Today the idea of the nation state as the unit of development is the more easily supported because a very important part of the planning for underdeveloped nations has been done by those who come from small developed nation states, in which state intervention and planning for a welfare state are already far advanced. If extensive intervention by government has made it possible for such countries as Sweden, Switzerland, Denmark, Norway, Holland, Belgium, West Germany and the United Kingdom to maintain an optimum standard of living, then government appears to be the appropriate instrument for benevolent economic change;

the welfare of peoples is thought of as inextricably related to activities of government, and the focus is on the nation state—which has a government—as the appropriate unit in developing the means of improving the well-being of a people.

Thus, just at the moment in history when most of the paraphernalia of the nation state, postulated on the political protection of citizens whose economic lot it was powerless to ameliorate, is becoming obsolete (for it can no longer protect its citizens, and their economic lot can be more efficiently ameliorated in larger or smaller units), the nation state has been transformed into a highly valued and highly inefficient instrument for the equalization of opportunity and the optimization of the good life. At a time when there is a crying need for transnational organizations, whether it be for the sharing of scarce or unevenly distributed natural resources, the eradication of disease, or the use of scarce intellectual resources, most of the efforts of the world have gone into the construction of mechanisms that are not transnational but intergovernmental.

In a new nation the poverty of its people and the prestige of its day- or month- or year-old national identity become intertwined. The poverty of the people represents a moral claim on the conscience of the world, which can be enforced in political terms, manipulated for political purposes, sometimes promoting but more often defeating the satisfaction of the very needs in the name of which the manipulation is done. While Germaine Tillion pled for the maintenance of the tie between France and Algeria for the sake of the hungry people of Algeria,[2] political considerations made this impossible. In China, millions are on the verge of starvation and there is urgent need for materials and tools essential for mere subsistence. Yet to supply them, under present circumstances, would mean crossing a national boundary and, in addition, crossing an ideological line defined by the cold war and breaching Mainland China's new inviolability. Coupled with our enormously enhanced ability to feed the peoples of the world, technically, is a definite crippling of our ability to do so organizationally. While valid in themselves, the arguments in favor of national pride, self-determination, autonomy and dignity essentially fail to recognize—even as they have been used to decry bilateral aid and to promote internationally organized aid—the

[2] Germaine Tillion, "Algeria: The Realities," translated by Ronald Matthews. New York: Knopf, 1958.

ways in which nation states, all nation states, have become economically and technically irrelevant. There are two continuous
reminders of the irrelevancy of the old borders, as lines drawn on
the ground. One is our technical ability to feed the peoples of the
world, disregarding boundaries; the other is the presence of the
satellites of the United States and the Soviet Union, circling
overhead.

II

In the context of the foregoing discussion, the term "overdeveloped" is anomalous. If technical development is good because it produces a higher standard of living, how can there be an
overdeveloped country? It should be recognized that the phrase
has been used most frequently to undo the damage done by placing all countries on a single scale. The term was brought into use
collaboratively by members of underdeveloped and more developed countries, acting out of patriotism, ambition or humani-
tarianism. Only by playing up the underdeveloped state of the
underdeveloped countries, by calling them poor, did it seem possible to create the climate of opinion that was being sought. But
when this resulted in a single scale, on which all countries could be
set up in a hierarchy, it became clear that a low position—on a
scale of development—was necessarily invidious and odious. The
underdeveloped countries wanted to gain every benefit from having their position so defined; especially they wanted high priority
in every form of economic aid. At the same time the inappropriate association between economic need and national prestige
meant that it was insulting to be called underdeveloped. With a
display of the kind of good manners by which a hostess, to put at
ease the guest who has dropped a plate, proceeds to break a
platter, internationalists, guilty over colonialism and preventable
human suffering on the one hand, and their own conspicuous,
wasteful consumption on the other, responded to the touchiness
of members of less industrialized countries by calling the old,
rich, industrialized countries "overdeveloped." Seen simply in
these terms, it is a piece of good manners in rather poor taste.

But the term overdeveloped also permits several questions to
be raised about what is the position of industrialized countries in
a world which has been reorganized in accordance with pre-industrial ideas of nationalism. Are they, for example, overdeveloped in
terms of over-consumption? This judgment is expressed in the

accusation that enough paper is wasted every day in the United States to provide the newsprint necessary to save freedom in some new country. Or it is said that the power wasted in the average electrified home would be enough to bring food and water to a village of several hundred people, or that by eliminating the duplication of radios and television sets in American homes a great many villages could be supplied with modern communications. In these terms, can a country like the United States be said to have passed the point of optimum development? This question, in turn, can lead to the advocacy either of arrest or of curtailment of standards of consumption in the developed nations—or at least to a growing fear that other nation states will not long tolerate their have-not position vis-à-vis the have nations.

But those who use the term overdeveloped may go even further. They may point to indices of social disorganization in those industrial countries in which political democracy and welfare-state organization have gone further than elsewhere—the indices of crime, delinquency, suicide, divorce, alcoholism and homicide. These are the current costs of overdevelopment—of becoming rich without abolishing poverty, however high the level of that poverty is in comparison with the poverty of the average Indian or Mestizo resident of a Latin American city or an average resident of Calcutta.

Futhermore, use of the term raises the question of whether the continuum of technical development, which is assumed to be a good thing, may not in fact be something which should not be pursued indefinitely or something which should not be pursued at all, or at least so singlemindedly. It emphasizes the price paid by human beings in industrial countries—both the price paid by those who suffer in their own person through neglect that leads to crime, alcoholism, family disorganization and so on, and the price paid by the apparent beneficiaries of industrialization through lack of space, leisure and privacy and through the exchange of peace of mind for a greater number of material possessions. It stresses the values of a pre-industrial (or just possibly a post-industrial) form of society, in which standard of living may be seen as having optimum but not maximum value. It refocuses attention on the values of other countries of the world, poor only by a recent definition of what is the right of a nation state, and stresses values which are intangible. Coupled with an emphasis on the intangibles of faith and a delight in life, there may be, as in Theobald's work,[8] a sophisticated recognition of how difficult it is to transform the motivations of people who have worked all their lives for what they regard as enough into a restless quest for more, because this is part of their newly acquired sense of national identity.

In fact, the world has been manœuvred into a situation which is not technically, economically or politically feasible. The association of national identity with industrial development is no less ridiculous on a world scale than it would be on a national scale if some group of developers (in the United States, for example) were to say: Every town in the United States, of whatever size, location or composition, needs a modern factory that can give steady employment to five hundred people and will adjust constructively to changes in world demand. We will lend you the money to build it, supply you with the name of a distributor who will provide you with the equipment, lend you more money if you get in trouble, and control the world market so that your product will always be salable. It is up to you to decide whether the unit of control is to be an unincorporated borough or a section of a metropolitan area, etc. It is also up to you to decide whether the board of managers is to be composed of the D.A.R., the Chamber of Commerce, ten elementary schoolteachers, the Fire Department, a local of an international union, the top 10 percent of the senior class in high school, a representative sample of families who have lived in the area for a hundred years, Catholics, Baptists, Jehovah's Witnesses, a random selection of engineers educated at M.I.T., former employees of the F.B.I., at least 10 percent American Indians, and so on. We want you to have a high standard of living. We are sure that a manufacturing plant will make it possible for you to improve your health and your educational facilities and to share in the general benefits of an affluent society. But, the developers would have to add, be certain that all this, however you organize it, will result in support of our political position and will not help our rivals. All other considerations—technical, economic and social—are to be subordinated to this end. It is true we and our political rivals agree that you must have a series of benefits in the way of food, housing, medical care, education and security; there is no argument about this. And of course you are free to choose the size and shape of the unit within which you

[8] Robert Theobald, "The Rich and the Poor: A Study of the Economics of Rising Expectations." New York: Clarkson N. Potter, 1960.

want to work. What really is at stake is that in doing this you stay on our side. But our aim is for you as a community—regardless of whether you are a village, a city or a suburban housing development—to catch up with the highest standard of living that can be shown to exist anywhere.

In effect, the idea of world-wide economic development on a single scale is a case where our ethic for human welfare and human dignity has outrun our ethic for group relevance, where political rivalry, in terms of the 1960s, still permits an efflorescence of economically irrelevant units within which economic development is expected to occur.

What we need urgently today is a set of new propositions which are congruent, one with the other:

1. The technical skills and resources exist; no one in the world need be hungry or cold, unclothed, uneducated or unmedicated. Standards can be set below which no people anywhere should be allowed to fall. What help is needed to bring their living standard up to the minimum can be introduced in ways that are appropriate, whether by the export of natural resources, by migration, immigration or resettlement, regional planning or world-wide organization.

2. The nation state, which historically was concerned primarily with warding off attack and with attacking others, is an imperfect unit for the administration of human welfare and is an even more imperfect one for the administration of economic development. There is a need for a new kind of nationhood within which every people may find dignity and take responsibility in certain ways for their fellow citizens and in other ways for all other peoples.

3. Any single scale of development is invidious and leads inevitably to conflict, humiliation and hurt pride. Our present roster of nations has in common only nationhood; in other respects the widest discrepancies exist—in size, age, wealth, tradition, degree of internal homogeneity, natural resources, rate of growth, racial composition, legal practice, level of skill. So it is important to phrase nationhood in terms of what a nation can accomplish in the way of assigning dignity, responsibility and recognized world-wide status to all peoples of this planet. Citizenship, so phrased, is independent of age, sex, size, intelligence, experience, wealth, beauty, past glory or future expectations. Any attempt to alter this position, in regard to individual citizenship, would—and should—be opposed with vigor. Yet we are allowing the world

to drift toward a position in which all nations will fail to find the dignity they seek if, as is now the case, nationhood is joined to planning for economic development in inappropriate ways. Single-scale development, under these circumstances, will inevitably result in a hierarchy of citizenship as well as of nations.

We need to develop a new framework within which to meet people's basic needs and all world-relevant needs, *i.e.* for transportation, communications, currency, the allocation of medical supplies, and so on. All these should be dealt with in other than national or simple intergovernmental frameworks. Simultaneously, those countries which are now called underdeveloped could be encouraged to develop their own distinctive identities within the modern world—to cherish their local languages while all children also learned a world language, to develop their own architecture, their own poetry, their own style of life.

With the development of new contexts, it would immediately become apparent that there is nowhere an "overdeveloped" country. The price paid, in delinquency, crime, suicide and disorganization, by those who live in politically democratic, industrialized countries is high because they themselves have failed to realize their own economic potential. This in turn hinders the development of a world-wide viable economy.

Nations are, and should be, different from one another. Units of economic development should meet technical, not national, criteria. What we need to work out is a series of overlapping structures which are so acephalous that it will be as difficult for any member to destroy them as it will be unprofitable for any member to withdraw.

¶ THE PARTY SYSTEM AND DEMOCRACY IN AFRICA

by Tom J. Mboya   (July, 1963)

In trying to see Africa whole—as it is and may come to be—one of the hardest things for a Westerner is to avoid parochialism, on the one hand, and, on the other, a kind of easygoing tolerance of the African, which is in fact patronizing. We cannot avoid forming estimates and expectations of the Africans' capacity to govern, based to some extent on our own ideals and institutions, and yet we know that even the very imperfect democracy we have achieved depends on education and the long cultivation of restraint and countervailing powers within the society—elements largely missing in Africa. We know, too, whatever Africa adopts from the West will be sifted and shaped in ways that are not yet clear. How, then, are we to judge an African leader who infringes rights we deem to be fundamental to democracy? Is he to that extent an autocrat and would-be dictator? Does he correctly comprehend that his people are incapable of making democracy work? Or is he intelligently adapting Western institutions to the environment and traditions of Africa?

"The Party System and Democracy in Africa" is addressed to one aspect of this problem—the one-party system that is now the predominant form of government in African countries where parliamentary democracy is still operative. Anyone who has compared the one-party system of, say, Tanganyika to the two-party system of Kenya (at least as each has worked so far) must concede great advantages to the former in terms of free political expression, as well as stability. A multiparty system in an unsophisticated society often seems to encourage political irresponsibility, with each party trying to outdo the other in proposing heaven on earth to the voters. In Kenya, as in most of Africa where more than one party exists, political division is between groups of tribes with ancient fears and animosities, not between those with differing concepts of the national interest.

Tom Mboya, who was assassinated in 1969, was quite possibly the most capable politician in all of Africa. Gifted, self-confident, and poised, he commanded the respect even of the white settlers in Kenya who hated him, and his effectiveness in London made him the architect of Kenyan self-government more truly than any other African. Next to Jomo Kenyatta, the Prime Minister, he was the most influential politician in Kenya, and he was active in the cause of East African union. This perceptive article reveals how much, with his death, Africa lost in intelligent leadership.

THE PARTY SYSTEM
AND DEMOCRACY IN AFRICA

By Tom J. Mboya

Practically nobody in these islands understands the Party System. Britons do not know its history. They believe that it is founded in human nature and therefore indestructible and eternal . . . by the immutable law of political human nature.
—BERNARD SHAW, in "Everybody's Political What's What?"

. . . if you were to ask . . . an American concerning the two great parties of his own country . . . , a bewildered look would probably cross his face; he would scratch his head and murmur something about tariffs. You would be puzzled. If you asked five Americans you would be five times as puzzled.
—VIRGINIA COWLES, in "How America Is Governed"

MANY people believe there is some special connection between the democratic form of government and the party system, so that one cannot exist without the other. This belief is strengthened by the fact that the freedom to form as many parties as people want is seen to be incompatible with a totalitarian régime. An ideal Communist government is run by a single party composed of the working class; a Fascist government is similarly run by one party in the interests of the capitalist class.

This type of thinking is based on a misconception of the true nature of democracy. It confuses cause and effect. There were parties before the advent of democracy. The first political parties in Britain, for example, are believed to have come into being in the reign of Charles II. This was long before the Reform Act of 1832, which was the bare beginning of change in the direction of democracy.

At present there are political parties in countries which do not even admit the correctness of the thinking behind democracy. Has not the U.N.'s 17-nation committee on colonialism ruled that there is no self-government— let alone full democracy—in Southern Rhodesia because of the denial of equal voting rights to Africans? And yet Southern Rhodesia has political parties which fight and win elections and form governments. South Africa also has parties which have been governing the country for over 50 years against the will of the majority of the people. No one can suggest South Africa enjoys anything like democracy.

The same conclusion is reached if we look at the circumstances which bring parties into being. In Britain there was an attempt to exclude James, Duke of York, from the succession to the throne because he was a Roman Catholic. Some people sympathized with him and started agitating in his favor. Their opponents called them Tories (which was the name popularly given to Irish pirates). Tories returned the compliment by calling their opponents Whigs (which was the name given to highwaymen in Scotland).

In giving such names to each other, the parties seem to have suggested that there was not much to choose between them. In my own country, Africans were united in a single political organization which put up a united front at the 1960 Constitutional Conference. Then, independence came into sight and politicians started dreaming of loaves and fishes. The Kenya African National Union (KANU) was created as soon as Africans were permitted to form national political organizations. The Kenya African Democratic Union (KADU) followed three months later, but it had no separate program and found it difficult to justify its existence until somebody's brain wave came up with the platform of "Regionalism." This fitted in with the traditional regard shown by British politicians and the press for the interests of the so-called downtrodden minority tribes or communities.

A great deal of political confusion and weakness in dependent countries has resulted from this sort of practice. A national movement starts sooner or later in every country seeking independence. It has a universal appeal and quickly gathers strength. This alarms the ruling race which tries to find forces to counteract nationalism. Agencies of propaganda (the press, the radio) are fully used, but they alone are hardly equal to the task of convincing world opinion that nationalism is wrong. What is really needed is an indigenous opposition to the nationalist movement. Because no foreign government could possibly succeed in setting up a completely artificial opposition party, the policy is adopted of giving every encouragement to disgruntled politicians, especially if they belong to a different religious denomination, tribe, race or area from that of the main body of leaders of the nationalist movement. Such disgruntled elements are sought out and supported.

India, for example, had one nationalist party at the beginning of its political struggle for independence. Later, props were offered to the leaders of a minority group. This induced other minority groups to demand special representation, and in every case the demand was acceded to. This process continued until the whole population was divided into warring sections. The same sort of thing has been seen recently in Kenya, where KANU originally represented the national front. Then KADU was formed and received the fullest support from the local press, which is largely European-owned. The European population generally, and also certain sections of the Asian community, joined it. In the first general election KANU received 67 percent of the African votes cast; KADU received 17 percent. But the constituencies had been so formed as to give KANU 19 seats and KADU 15.

The European press and radio have always been willing to give full publicity to new, dissident groups, although their policies seldom reflect a national outlook; they are sectional or tribal groups whose only effect—if not their purpose—is to delay the coming of freedom. Parties are formed because they are free to form, not because there is need for them. In our country a new trade union may not be formed if there is already one which serves the interests of workers in that field. No similar test of need is laid down for political parties. Anyone who feels like starting a political party can do so. The more sensational and unnecessary its program, the more publicity it will receive in the European press.

The worst of it is that in dependent countries imperialism has managed to keep the level of illiteracy and ignorance high so that every person who takes it into his head to become a leader can find some followers in his own district or tribe or religious denomination. No wonder that the parties in dependent, or erstwhile dependent, countries are not divided on ideological lines. There is generally one party which presses—and whose leaders suffer for—the nationalist cause. Other parties exist because the law allows them to, and because their alien sympathizers give them limelight, encouragement and sometimes money.

II

It is quite clear that the party system can exist without democracy. The only question is whether the converse is also true. To put it more strongly—and I hope agreeably to those brought up in the traditions of the West—we must ascertain whether democracy can function fully and fruitfully without a party system.

Here, a further distinction is necessary. There are states which allow the fullest freedom for the formation and working of political parties but where the multi-party system (which is what we really mean by the expression "party system") fails to flourish.

In Tanganyika it has, in the past, been possible for anyone to start a political party. At least two parties have in fact existed there. Nevertheless, one of the parties (the Tanganyika African National Union led by Mr. Julius Nyerere) was able to win 70 seats out of a total 71 in a straight, completely free, general election. To all intents and purposes, therefore, Tanganyika has had a single-party system. Does it cease on that account to be a democracy?

To take another illustration, India has a multiplicity of political parties and there is freedom to form more if the people so desire. The country has had three general elections during the 15 years or so of her freedom, and each of them was vigorously contested. One of the parties (the Indian National Congress led by Mr. Jawaharlal Nehru) has won all three elections and still occupies a more or less unchallengeable position. Is India not to be called a democracy because of this?

The only conclusion one can draw from the political experience of newly freed countries in Asia and Africa is that the party system is not a necessary part of democracy, which is truly concerned with the views, wishes and interests of the individuals making up the nation. Democracy is not fundamentally or necessarily concerned with the existence or well-being of parties, which may represent either sections or cross-sections of the population.

A good, relevant definition of democracy is suggested by the late Dr. C. E. M. Joad:

> If we define democracy as a method of government under which every citizen has an opportunity of participating, through discussion, in an attempt to reach voluntary agreement as to what shall be done for the good of the whole, we shall conclude that in offering to its members opportunities to shape its policy and to realize in action the policy they have shaped, it offers them also opportunities for the development of their nature. . . . It enables the individual to realize himself in service to the State, while not forgetting that the true end of the State must be sought in the lives of individuals.[1]

Even those who believe that there is a connection between democracy and the party system must therefore agree that what is necessary is the freedom to form parties. It is not necessary that more than one should in fact exist and function effectively.

Let us take the argument one step further. The chief theoretical justification for the party system is that it increases the force and effectiveness of the people's views. It is an instrument, a means to

[1] "Guide to the Philosophy of Morals and Politics," London: Gollancz, 1938, p. 807.

an end, not the end itself. If the end can be achieved by an alternative means, there is no reason why that alternative should not be adopted. And as in democratic theory the people are sovereign, they can, of course, decide to achieve their ends by another means. A sovereign legislature parts with its sovereignty to the parliament of a new state (say in Africa) which was hitherto a dependency. In the same way, the sovereign people may decide to forego their right to form parties and decree that there shall in future be only one party in the country.

Now, it can be argued that no people will ever do that, but the theoretical possibility is there. And can anyone question the competence of the sovereign people to make such a decision? The only condition is that the decision should be voluntary, and arrived at after free and frank discussion. But, it will be objected, dictators in the early years of their rule always command a persuasive tongue; will they not misuse the weapon of a single party which has been placed in their hands? Have they not in fact misused it in the past?

Perhaps the single-party system will be misused. But has anyone the right or power to stop the sovereign people from decreeing such a system? At the most, we can insist on two things. First, the original decision should be completely voluntary and without any coercion. Secondly, the people should be able, if they so desire, to restore the multi-party system by a further amendment of the constitution. Nevertheless, it should be said that if the people have the right to take a revocable decision to establish a single-party system, they also have the right to say that that decision shall be irrevocable. It is this unfettered right of the people which is difficult to exclude or outlaw.

Now, the people can either express themselves in the words of a constitutional amendment or by their conduct. Suppose Mr. Nyerere's party in Tanganyika repeats its electoral performance once, twice, thrice. Can anyone then doubt what are the wishes of the people? My view, therefore, is that the question whether a country is to have a single party or several parties is to be answered not in terms of any preconceived ideas of "democracy" but in the concrete terms of the wishes of the people.

III

It is unfortunate that the intentions and declarations of African leaders are so often misunderstood. Immediately the people of a country feel a need to strengthen their central government and take steps in that direction, there is a hue and cry in the West that a dictatorship is being created. The fears expressed may in some cases turn out to be justified, but the readiness with which they are expressed shows that the critics start with preconceived notions.

Only a short while ago, Mr. Julius Nyerere of Tanganyika made a public announcement on the subject of party organization in his country. Most newspapers noticed in his long, carefully prepared speech nothing but a determination to put an end to the party system. His essential arguments were carefully excluded from newspaper reports. I should like to quote only a few passages from the speech, omitting the general arguments against the multi-party system which can be found in any good political textbook:

In Tanganyika . . . we adopted the Westminster type of representative democracy. . . . But it soon became clear to us that, however ready we leaders might have been to accept the theory that an official Opposition was essential to democratic government, our own people thought otherwise . . . in spite of our having only one party, we were very democratic. But we were more democratic within the Party. . . . In Parliament it is no longer permissible for each Member to express his own personal opinion. . . . There is a party line to be followed . . . where there is no Opposition party, there is no reason why the debate in Parliament should not be as free as the debate in the National Executive. . . . It seems at least open to doubt, therefore, that a system which forces political parties to limit the freedom of their members is a democratic system, and that one which can permit a party to leave its members their freedom is undemocratic. . . .

The existence of a Two-Party system in the older democracies is best explained by reference to the history of those countries. . . . the genesis of the Two-Party system was a class society. . . .

Our own parties had a very different origin. They were not formed to challenge any ruling group of our own people, they were formed to challenge the *foreigners* who ruled over us. They were . . . nationalist movements.

. . . where there is *one* party—provided it is identified with the nation as a whole—the foundations of democracy can be firmer, and the people can have more opportunity to exercise a real choice, than where you have two or more parties. . . . we can conduct our elections in a way which is genuinely free and democratic. . . .

. . . a National Movement is open to all. . . . Those forming the Government will, of course, be replaced from time to time; that is what elections are for. The leadership of our Movement is constantly changing. . . . since such a National Movement leaves no room for the growth of discontented elements excluded from its membership, it has nothing to fear from criticism and the free expression of ideas. . . . Any member of the Movement . . . would be free to stand as a candidate if he so wishes . . . the voters would be able to make their choice freely from among these candidates.

To elaborate briefly on the ideas expressed by Mr. Nyerere, there are circumstances in Africa which favor emergence of single parties, or systems in which there are many parties but with one in a dominating position. Those circumstances can now be listed.

First, the new states of Africa have hardly got out of the woods. In the days of struggle against a foreign nation or against a racial minority placed in power by a foreign nation, the minds of the people are preoccupied with their political troubles. They experience these troubles not as individuals but as a racial group, all of whom suffer the same disabilities and indignities. There are no exceptions made in favor of anyone. Therefore, when the victims of discrimination combine to form a single party, it tends to be based on race. Small "moderate" groups may be formed here and there, but they are of no consequence. The essential point is that all opposition to foreign rule or a mono-racial rule comes from what is to all intents and purposes a single political party. As the tempo of struggle against racial policies rises, this political party becomes better organized and more widely based. In time, it becomes the mouthpiece of an oppressed nation, a possible successor to the alien government.

Secondly, this party or movement comes to have a leader who, by reason of his sincere and effective advocacy of the national cause and by reason of his sacrifices in that cause, is regarded by the masses as *the* leader, the hero, the father of the nation. He is a symbol of national unity. He is identified in the mind of the people and the outside world with the party, with the nation. This serves to solidify the foundations of the political organization and the general movement for unity.

Thirdly, this movement for unity continues after independence. The original party which fought for, and brought about, freedom continues in being—maybe as the government of the country. The same leader with the same group of collaborators is now the leader of both the people and the government. This in itself works against the emergence of a multi-party system. Again, the problems facing the new government are serious and urgent. It was easy in the pre-independence days to blame the foreign or the racial minority government for the poverty, the ignorance and the poor health of the people. Now, these causes of backwardness have to be removed—a process which requires planning, money and popular enthusiasm. This is the time when the government feels it must somehow persuade the people to give it all the support possible. The opposition parties, which were always small and weak, try to justify themselves by increasing their opposition to government measures—opposition largely for its own sake. This irritates the government which is engaged in the work of nation-building. At this stage, two courses are possible: either the government acts as a steamroller, ignoring the existence of the opposition, or it takes steps to put an end to opposition for its own sake—completely and permanently.

There is another force which militates against the establishment of a multi-party democracy of the Western type. The majority party in a dependent country—that is, the party which represents the nationalist movement—comes into conflict with the ruling race almost from the start. To establish a counterweight the rulers choose dissident individuals and groups and build them up. When the nationalist majority, naturally, demands a one-man-one-vote democracy on the Westminster model, the favorite minorities oppose it and ask for safeguards against majority rule. The rulers side with the minorities and a democratic system crippled by a crop of entrenched clauses is ultimately introduced. The majority party has to agree to this crippling in order to get rid of the foreign rule.

Our own experience in Kenya serves as an illustration. The African community was united in its demand for freedom and had the support of many of the Asians and some of the Europeans. At the Constitutional Conference in London in 1960, the African Elected Members presented a unanimous demand, speaking as one single party led by one leader. This Conference accepted two aims of constitutional development in Kenya: "first, to build a nation based on parliamentary institutions on the Westminster model and enjoying responsible self-government under certain traditional conditions; and secondly, a general acceptance by all of the right of each community to remain in Kenya and play a part in public life."

In pursuance of the second of these aims, the majority party (that is, KANU) proposed a comprehensive Bill of Rights guaranteeing full and equal political, economic and social rights to members of all races. As regards the first aim, the memorandum presented by KANU to the 1962 Constitutional Conference stated: "We understand this to mean majority rule, with the majority party, for the time being, running the Government, and the acceptance of an opposition party or parties who—on their part—

accept parliamentary rules and methods as the means of advancing their policies and in pursuance of their political activities."

Can anyone in the face of these clear statements maintain that the majority party wanted to establish either a dictatorship or a one-party system? Nevertheless, we did not get the necessary backing from the British Government and many British papers were hostile to us.

IV

I think it will be useful if I now summarize my conclusions in a few brief paragraphs:

1. Democracy is government of the *people,* by the *people,* for the *people.* The supporters of the party system argue as though the word "people" in this definition read "party."

2. A government which gives all citizens the right to vote, the right to contest elections and the right to express themselves freely inside and outside parliament is not undemocratic.

3. The current aims of, and the history behind, the parties in the older countries of the West are different from the aims and history of the parties (or national movements) in the countries of Africa.

4. The responsibility for the emergence in African countries of a single political party or of one strong and several weak parties must be laid at the door of imperialist nations which created the conditions militating against the establishment of democracy based on two or more political parties.

5. The imperialist nations of the West and the Western press continue their traditional attitude of encouraging and actively instigating disgruntled, dissident elements which oppose the establishment of a parliamentary system of government (implying one-man-one-vote and majority rule). The Western statesmen and their representatives in Africa never tire of asserting that majority rule suits the countries of the West but that in Africa the minority tribes and races stand in need of special protection against majorities.

6. The countries of Africa emerging from political subjection are entitled to modify, to suit their own needs, the institutions of democracy as developed in the West. No one has the right to cavil at this so long as all citizens—irrespective of their racial, tribal or religious affiliations—are treated alike.

¶ DE GAULLE: POSE AND POLICY

by Herbert Lüthy   (July, 1965)

Charles de Gaulle was the last of a generation of great Western leaders, and, although France was not really in the first rank in economic or military power, he was perhaps the most resplendent of them all. After having served briefly as a symbol of unity and courage for the French people immediately after World War II, he returned from retirement in 1958 to bring order where there had been political chaos and eventually to extricate his country from its debilitating colonial struggle in Algeria. This article was written three years after de Gaulle had freed France from internal and external strife so that it could express what he felt was its unique destiny in international affairs. This he would continue to do for four more years, giving his nation a decade of security and self-confidence.

In the opening passage of The War Memoirs, *de Gaulle wrote, "France cannot be France without* la grandeur." *It was his overriding aim—personally, politically, indeed in every respect—to provide his country with that grandeur. He made himself its incarnation, "as a historical phenomenon distinct from his individual person," according to Lüthy. It was the role of the ideal king sacrificing his ego to his royal function.* Noblesse oblige.

Herbert Lüthy, Professor of History at the Swiss Federal Institute of Technology, in Zurich, and author of France Against Herself, *emphasizes that one cannot separate de Gaulle's perceptions from his policies. Both stemmed from the idea that France must always be in the first rank. Symbols, not facts, were of the essence; attitudes mattered more than actions.*

When de Gaulle resigned and retired to Colombey-les-deux-Églises to write, a leading Gaullist, Georges Pompidou, became the President of France. Despite the extreme personalization of de Gaulle's rule, much of the grandeur he strove for survives in France. But Lüthy raises the question of whether the majesty of his vision will be enough to sustain France far into the future.

DE GAULLE: POSE AND POLICY

By Herbert Lüthy

A S long as French foreign policy is nothing else than the personal policy of President de Gaulle, any analysis of it depends essentially on an understanding of his personal psychology. While his psychology is not that of the ordinary political leader, there is nothing impenetrable or mysterious about it. Even the sphinx-like pose which he is fond of assuming is deliberate and calculated; from his earliest writings, he has been consciously creating the ideal portrait of *le grand chef,* who must, as he wrote in 1927, "possess something indefinable, mysterious . . . remain impenetrable to his subordinates, and in this way keep them in suspense." According to a more recent formulation of his, this mystery resides, too, in the political art of "not crystalizing in words that which the future is going to demonstrate," of not defining goals before being assured of their success, and then always appearing to have desired what comes to pass.

This is the A.B.C. of the art of politics. De Gaulle's mastery of *mystère,* which is above all the art of ambiguity and of Pythian formulas, permitted him, when faced with the gravest problem he ever had to meet—the Algerian War—to manœuvre among the reefs for four years, to envisage in turn every possible or impossible solution and to see them all miscarry. First there was the offer made to the Algerians to become "whole-share French citizens;" then the mission given the army to "integrate the souls" of the Algerian people; then the grand vision of an African California grouping Algeria and French Black Africa in a zone of prosperity around the oil of the Sahara; then the still ambiguous concept of an "Algerian Algeria," independent but associated— all leading finally to the collapse of French colonization in North Africa and the accords of Evian, now hardly more than a scrap of paper. At the end of this tortuous course, the wisdom of the statesman has been "to accept things as they are," to respect the Evian Agreements on his side and to accept unflinchingly the violation of them by the other side, in order to show that he is satisfied—and to keep the future open.

The extent of de Gaulle's success in this tragic imbroglio is shown by the fact that the whole world is convinced that from the outset he wanted in his secret heart to end up exactly where he did. This is an improbable hypothesis and, above all, terribly unjust, for it supposes that de Gaulle willfully deceived and betrayed all those who carried him to power in 1958; but the reputation for being a man of unfathomable cunning does not displease him, and in any case he prefers it to the contrary hypothesis—truer but less grandiose—that, unable to do what he wished, he wished for what he could do. The essential is that the prestige of the leader be preserved; the rest counts for little.

Charles de Gaulle is not a man of mystery. The air of mystery is part of the character which he has created, by calculation as much as by inclination, because it allows him to feint, to manœuvre in front of the obstacle and to withdraw, if need be, without losing face. What distinguishes his political style, and what makes him unique, is precisely that he knows how to be an opportunist without appearing to be one, and how to compromise without compromising himself. He believes profoundly in a fate which is stronger than men; and he knows how to take advantage of unforeseen events. His fatalistic side becomes stronger with the wisdom of age: "Regarding the stars, I am imbued with the insignificance of things." But his realism is limited by a number of fundamental ideas, which are unarguable and beyond compromise; they give his policies not only their content but their style. These constants consist of his conception of the world and of politics, the system of coördinates within which his thought evolves, and outside which he refuses to venture: a world of symbols rather than of realities. Before searching in his acts or in his words for hidden designs, we must grasp this basic point; from it all else follows.

The vision of the political world—the *Weltanschauung*—of General de Gaulle is a matter of individual psychology only in so far as his own predestined role in it is concerned. Apart from this crucial detail, it is a vision so imbued with French traditions of the most classic sort that individual psychology plays a lesser part than collective psychology; hence the power of suggestion

which his vision holds for Frenchmen. Through de Gaulle a venerable and glorious France takes on the splendor of a spectacular
sunset.

II

The biography of Charles de Gaulle (and especially his own
version of it) is so well known that we can easily trace the origin
of the elements that make up his vision. He was born into an
exemplary family in which the father was a teacher of history,
literature and classical languages at a Jesuit school in Paris, and
in which the cult of France and nostalgia for the legitimate
monarchy—*Dieu et le Roi!*—were celebrated with a religious
fervor. Reading was in the classics and the lives of heroes: Alexander the Great, Hannibal, Caesar, Joan of Arc, the kings and
marshals of France. He grew up among history books in which the
world was illumined exclusively by the deeds of France—"nation
of heroes and saints"—and among little lead soldiers with which
the de Gaulle children reconstructed glorious battles of the past.
Like most right-thinking families of the time, the de Gaulles
abhorred the Republic and all the régimes which followed 1789,
and from childhood Charles learned to make that distinction
which for him remains fundamental: the sublime idea of France,
predestined leader of the world as soon as she found incarnation in
a legitimate sovereign or God-sent hero; and the mass of flesh-
and-blood Frenchmen, dedicated to mediocrity, confusion and
sterile partisan struggles when lacking the guidance of an anointed
leader.

Nothing of the historical imagery and political convictions
acquired in childhood was shaken by the years in a Catholic
lycée, nor, evidently, by his education at the Ecole de Guerre. In
World War I, the "ambition to serve France" was hardly satisfied
by nearly three years of frustration as a prisoner in Germany, during which time he saw continental empires collapse on all sides.
In 1927, at the age of 37, the thought of the young Commandant
de Gaulle was summed up in a series of lectures given at the Ecole
de Guerre, under the presidency of Marshal Pétain, then his idol
and patron: "Military Action and the Leader," "On Prestige,"
"On Character." All were in the heroic and classic style inspired
by Plutarch, Caesar and Machiavelli. In them de Gaulle portrayed his ideal of the leader born to command, a vocation to
which he clearly felt called.

All this—the naïve faith of childhood and the authoritarian conception of history forged by the military profession—passed into the grand design of his mature thought and took shape in "The War Memoirs" written during the period of his "withdrawal to the desert," 1952–1958. Actually, it is neither history nor recollections of war, but the monumental self-portrait of the solitary man who made himself the champion and knight-servant of "Our Lady France." Each sentence must be taken word for word—even (and indeed especially) in the rhetorical passages and the patriotic clichés—beginning with the celebrated passage at the opening of the Memoirs: "All my life I have thought of France in a certain way . . . like the princess of fairy stories . . . dedicated to an exalted and exceptional destiny. . . . Providence has created her for complete successes or for exemplary misfortunes. . . . France is not really herself except in the first rank. . . . In short, to my mind, France cannot be France without *la grandeur*"; and, from early childhood, "I did not doubt that France would have to go through gigantic trials, that life's interest would consist in one day rendering her some signal service, and that I would have that opportunity."

All this still adds up to nothing more than the makings of a first-rate officer of the old French school. What has been joined to the faith which was instilled in the cradle, and what has differentiated de Gaulle from the intellectual environment in which he grew up, is something that at first appears very banal, but which has been decisive: namely, that very early he added to the glories of ancient France the glories of the revolutionary and Napoleonic armies. A monarchist by instinct and molding, he ceased to be one by ideology; indeed, with one stroke he **dis**encumbered himself of all ideology, in order "to serve **only** France." This explains why, in the years when the menace of the Third Reich was mounting, he broke with the disciples of Maurras, who, disgusted with the France of the Popular Front and entranced by the Fascist dictators, put their ideological sympathies above the interests of France.

For de Gaulle, the philosophy of history and political philosophy are one. The generals of the Revolution and of the Empire "served France well," just as later the Communists in the Resistance and Maurice Thorez (as long as he was a minister under de Gaulle) "served France well." "Is it simply political tactics? The answer is not for me to unravel. For me it is enough that

France is served." This ideological indifference, which springs not from opportunism but from unqualified nationalism, is what separated de Gaulle most sharply from all "party men" and what distinguished him as well from most of the leaders of the French army. It made it possible for him to decide in 1940 to break all traditions of discipline, to revolt against the authority and legitimacy of Marshal Pétain, and to proclaim that legitimacy now rested with him, the solitary soldier who picked up "from the mud" and raised anew the flag which had fallen from the hands of his superiors.

He was not anti-Fascist; little did it matter to him who ruled Germany: he refused to admit the defeat of France, and personally, in 1940–1945, he was much less at war with Germany than with the Anglo-Saxon allies who considered that "France was gone." Nor was he anti-Communist when, in 1947, convinced of the imminence of war between Russia and the West, he founded a party whose only ideology was to rally France around himself. He then excluded from the national community all those who put faith in Soviet Russia above patriotism, and in order to point out that this was not a question of ideology, he labeled them, not Communists, but "separatists," or "those who do not play the game of France." In the same way today he never speaks of the Soviet Union, but only of Russia, signifying that in his eyes what matters is the eternal Russia, so many times the ally of France and perhaps an ally again some day; and that ideologies are only a veil covering the timeless politics of national power.

Read in the last volume of "The War Memoirs" his portrayal of Stalin: ". . . astute and implacable champion of a Russia exhausted by suffering and tyranny but afire with national ambition . . . mightier and more durable than any theory, any régime . . . to unite the Slavs, to overcome the Germans, to expand in Asia, to gain access to open seas: these were the dreams of Mother Russia, these were the despot's goals." But also read the fascinated passage in which de Gaulle wrote of the suicide of Hitler ("So as not to be bound, Prometheus cast himself into the abyss") : "the terrible greatness of his combat and his memory," the "superhuman and inhuman attempt" of that "Titan who tries to lift the world," and whom Germany had "served with greater exertions than any people has ever offered any leader." Each was the embodiment of his nation and played the game of national ambition, as it is the role of great statesmen to do.

What is true for Hitler or Stalin is also true for Churchill or Roosevelt. In the same "Memoirs" de Gaulle examines Roosevelt's conception of how the postwar world should be organized, with its Directory of the Big Four, *i.e.* Roosevelt, Stalin, Churchill and Chiang Kai-shek, of whom the last two, he remarked, were dependent "clients" of the United States. De Gaulle's analysis is one of the most perspicacious that has been made—not only because he had reason to resent the American effort to discount France as a great power, but even more because of his haughty disdain of the ideological and idealistic aspects of Roosevelt's grand design. "As is human," de Gaulle wrote, "idealism here dresses up the will to power." International politics is and will remain what it has been since there have been rival states in the world—a game of power politics; and all the rest, ideologies and contrivances of international organizations, is nothing but masquerade and illusion. In this game, it is imperative that France play her cards well and sustain her role.

This view of international politics which, for all its apparent simplicity, is capable of every Machiavellian refinement, has at bottom always been the view taken by the man in the street following in his newspaper the endless conflicts of the "powers," whose leaders clash as often over precedence and prestige as over concrete conflicts of interest. The Gaullist version of this concept springs from European history, or rather from the dramatized, nationalistic version of it which, in the service of patriotic education, the history books of every European nation have imparted to generations of studious youths. It is a complicated history of an equilibrium which was forever in question among powers and coalitions of powers divided one against the other on a narrow continent, where each nation always had to guard its bridges against the enemy of the moment—and against the ally of the moment, who could be the adversary of tomorrow—and where, according to the historiographers who poisoned the minds of generations of Europeans, the increased status of one nation was always paid for by the decline of others.

The United States, which has dominated a vast continent almost from its birth, never knew the problem of "balance of power" until very recently, and then on a global scale. It is this very different historical experience which has resulted in so many misunderstandings between America and Europe, from Versailles to Yalta. But was Roosevelt's reasoning very different when he sought to found the postwar world on the basis of a personal entente among the Big Four of that time? That is the irrational way in which children imagine the world is ruled, and in this respect great statesmen and children are very much alike; nor is their view further from reality than the complicated models of political scientists. Even in the science of international law, until quite recently, Europe could not conceive of international relations except in allegorical terms—as relations between legitimate heads of state. When Europeans of General de Gaulle's generation were growing up, international relations were, in fact and in law, relations between dynastic sovereigns, equal in rank if not in power; and Frenchmen with family traditions such as those of de Gaulle suffered to see Republican France, and France alone in Europe, deprived of dynasty—that is, of personification, continuity and dignity.

The postulate of a single strong authority as head of state does not, for de Gaulle, spring from considerations of domestic social order or ideologies; it is an imperative imposed by the realities of international life, which demand that a country be "represented." He was enough of a modernist and a realist to resign himself to the fact that France was no longer a hereditary monarchy, but in his innermost self he never doubted that France needed a monarch—that is to say, an uncontested *chef*—in order to make her voice heard; and the course of events (and his will) finally permitted him to present a monarch to France: himself. His truly monarchical sense of the dignity of the head of state is what strikes one most in his ceremony, in his oratorical style and in his attention to precedence; but this is often misinterpreted. It requires perhaps a feeling for royal tradition to understand how a man can, in all humility, so venerate himself as the incarnation and symbol of his country, as a historical phenomenon distinct from his individual person and of different clay from ordinary men, and subordinate himself so entirely to the "heavy burden" of this self-imposed role which prevents him from ever descending to the level of simple humans; so must the ideal king sacrifice his ego to his royal function. Indeed, de Gaulle has pushed the distinction between himself, "the poor mortal," and Charles de Gaulle, who is invested by history with national legitimacy, to the point of grammatically separating "me" and "de Gaulle," whom he invokes in the third person. In the plebeian world of today, this aspect of his personality is doubtless as uncommon as the appearance of a dinosaur among post-diluvian fauna; and one of the worst mistakes is to confuse him with the vulgar demagogues and rabble-rousers who abound throughout the present-day world. He plays this royal role to perfection and he knows the power of its attraction. There are few Frenchmen, even among those who are irritated by him or who make fun of him, who are not secretly under his spell and who do not experience at least an esthetic satisfaction in seeing France so regally represented after having seen it led so long by men of little stature.

III

What, then, are de Gaulle's policies? They have only one common and consistent thread: to "maintain his status," his and France's, the two being synonymous, "as long as God lends him life." In the key chapter of his Memoirs, programmatically entitled *Le Rang,* the words which endlessly recur are "rank," "prestige," "honor," "dignity," "power" and "greatness." As a retrospective exposition of his "great national aims," this apologia of de Gaulle's postwar policy is rather disappointing, and its concrete objectives are now only bad memories: the dismemberment of Germany, the extension of the French frontier to the Rhine, the annexation of the Saar and of some Italian territory, and the stubborn maintenance of the French imperial position in Asia and Africa. The alliance with Stalin, as a stratagem against "the Anglo-Saxon hegemony," remained utterly sterile, and the lofty vision—now revived—of an "association of Slavs, Germans, Gauls and Latins," uniting Europe "from the Atlantic to the Urals," has never meant anything definable. We know only that the aim is to transform the continent into "one of the three planetary powers" which "one day, if necessary, could arbitrate between the Soviet and the Anglo-Saxon camps." Where, then, are the Urals? The common denominator of so many vague or contradictory projects was the high-minded determination to see France "act boldly, achieve stature, and nobly serve the interests of herself and of mankind."

To uphold status is an aristocratic ideal which can fill the life of a man and of a nation. What that ideal requires has less to do with actions than with attitudes. The criteria are simple and easy to understand. "France is only France when she is in the first rank;" she can never accept less; never recognize a hegemony other than her own; never join a group as less than equal with the greatest; never integrate—or rather, "dissolve herself"—in a supranational organization where her veto power would no longer come into play. The Atlantic Alliance may be a good thing, but an "integrated" Atlantic organization under command other than de Gaulle's is unacceptable. A European confederation under French leadership may be desirable, but a United States of Europe in which France might have to give in to the will of the majority is inconceivable. Partnership with the United States is something to be wished for, but an *Atlantic* partnership, in which the United States' partner would not be France, but an integrated Europe, can only be rejected. A United Nations in which France has an assured veto power and a seat in the supreme directory can be useful, but an international organization in which a majority can overrule her is an abomination. Instinctively de Gaulle resists all the bright organizers, all the "technocratic robots" who threaten to depersonalize international relations, just as he instinctively tends to return to the pre-1914 rules of the game, to classical diplomacy, classical alliances, national armaments and the gold standard. Political scientists may debate whether or not these notions are anachronisms in the modern world. But to try to make de Gaulle give in on any of them is to knock one's head against a wall. Those who have to deal with him had better discard in advance any such thoughts as far as France is concerned.

It is true, then, that Gaullist policy—or political style—is more easily defined by what it rejects in contemporary Western politics than by its concrete objectives or constructive proposals. To say "no" is one of the rare things that one can do all alone. Then, too, history is unforeseeable—"the future lasts a long time and anything can happen one day"—and the wise statesman keeps his hands free to deal with any eventuality; he does not commit himself to anything irrevocable. As long as the symbolic attributes of great-power status are preserved, no material catastrophe can engulf a country. It is the symbols that matter, not the facts: this is the summary of de Gaulle's wartime experience and the essence of his policy. Immediate goals, as well as the means to attain them, can be endlessly adjusted to "the changing nature of things."

When France was faced with the Algiers *putsch* in May 1958, and only de Gaulle's return seemed able to avert a civil war, did he know what he was going to do with the almost unlimited powers he had obtained as a condition for his return? In France, in Algeria and in the French possessions overseas, he called for a vote on a new constitution making him president of the "French Community," and he excommunicated the one territory which did not give him a majority, Guinea. He certainly did not envisage the demise of the Community within two years, without its institutions ever having functioned. Nor did he foresee the loss of Algeria after four years of tortuous manœuvres, riots, pronunciamentos and, finally, the exodus of the French population under the worst possible conditions. But he knew how to submit gallantly to what he could not prevent, and so to enhance France's prestige in the eyes of the Third World. Nor did he imagine that he would fall heir to the European policies of Jean Monnet, Robert Schuman and Guy Mollet, on which he had always showered sarcasm; but he knew how to forge those policies into an instrument of *French* policy, reducing the Common Market to a technical organization from which his ministers were able to draw every advantage for the French economy, while chopping down the political hopes of its creators.

De Gaulle knew how to play every card and keep the public guessing. But in no domain, either domestic or European, has he created anything which is assured of surviving him. The constitution he has given France, with its "president-arbiter" and its "separation of powers," has never functioned and he has not hesitated to recast it or to disregard it when it got in his way, with the result that no one can say how France will be governed after he goes.

If "de-colonizer" de Gaulle retains a sort of moral presence in what was the French Community, it is because after the unhappy Guinea experience he consented to finance it on generous terms without ever testing its loyalty—just as he has consented to finance socialist Algeria without insisting on the Evian Agreements. But again, no one can say what Franco-Algerian and Franco-African relations will be like when de Gaulle has gone and France perhaps tires of the high cost of prestige. As for Europe, having blocked political integration in the name of national sovereignty and the admission of Britain in the name of political integration, and having attempted to impose a Franco-German directorate (which was bound in advance to fail), he has left the political construction of Europe in an impasse from which it will not emerge so long as he rules, if ever.

The same is true of the Atlantic Alliance. It has been at logger-
heads since September 1958 when de Gaulle, just returned to
power, proposed a three-power directorate for the global strategy
of the West. Implied, of course, was a request for allied support
for France's still undefined policy in Africa and Algeria. All the
vicissitudes since then have done nothing to reduce the stumbling-
block created by ill-humor; but neither has the ill-humor been
pushed to the point of rupture. The most obvious result, thus far,
is that for the sake of status symbols, de Gaulle has reduced
France's potentially great influence inside the Alliance to a mere
sulky negativism which has simply to be discounted in advance
by her partners. Still, in his eyes, the Alliance is necessary "for
a long time to come" in order to maintain equilibrium in the
world and in Europe and to cover his retreat while he explores
the foggy perspectives of a "European Europe" equilibrated between Paris and Moscow.

In this Gaullist policy of simple ideas and complicated games,
everything is provisional; and everything is based on his personal
reign, which can last six more months or seven more years. The
only certainty is that there will be no one to carry on. Whether
the presidency will go to a Pompidou or a Defferre, or whether
France will return to parliamentary government or whatever, his
successors will have to search for another style and other ways.
As with Bismarck, who was successful in everything except assuring the continuation of his work, de Gaulle's policies and per-
sonalized rule will end with him. France's partners can no more
count on de Gaulle lasting forever than they can avoid living with
him while he stays.

But is it really more difficult for France's allies to live with de
Gaulle than it was to live with the Fourth Republic, from Bidault
to Pflimlin, with its feeble central power, enormous world-wide responsibilities and torn conscience? When we make up a tentative
balance-sheet for the first seven years of the Fifth Republic, at
least one item is certain: with all its jolts and dramatic repudia-
tions, the reign of General de Gaulle has succeeded in drawing
France back within her natural boundaries, removing the burden
of her imperial heritage which had become too heavy to carry,
and making her a European nation, without world-wide involvement—political or strategic. It may not be what he wished, nor
what was hoped for by those who carried him to power and who
are today in prison, in exile or, in the case of those like Michel

Debré who were most faithful to his person and myth, in melancholy retirement. The cost to France—and to Algeria—of the misunderstanding which it took four years to dispel may have been appalling, but the liquidation has been radical and has left nothing but a hangover of sterile rancors. It is futile to speculate whether, if the phenomenon of de Gaulle had never existed to confuse all the issues, the parliamentary republic would in the end have done better or worse in amputating its former North African province: this would be to suppose French history other than it has been since 1940, perhaps less colorful, perhaps more normal. However that may be, it is done; and miraculously de Gaulle has succeeded in transforming into a personal triumph what under any other régime would have appeared to be a catastrophe, and what perhaps no other régime could have survived. Never does the grand manner matter so much as in misfortune; the art of the glorious retreat is the most difficult in war or in politics. Thanks to de Gaulle, thanks to his majestic bearing in times of adversity and to the magic of his language, the régime which "sold out the empire" is in French minds the reign that reëstablished the ranking position of France and made the world sit up and take notice.

France's partners would be wrong to take offense. These manifestations of pride are often annoying, but it may be more important that for the first time in centuries, if not indeed since "France became France," her *amour-propre* can find satisfaction solely in prestige. Thanks to the second reign of General de Gaulle, France is without territorial claims, without grievances which menace world peace, and without strategic positions to defend outside France proper. (Djibouti, Martinique, Réunion and the New Hebrides are not strategic positions, but souvenirs and curiosities.) In fact, since 1962, France has had no dramatic problems on her horizons; and no decisions are rending or pressing her.

De Gaulle may make a triumphant tour of Latin America and embrace dreams of a "Latin world" opposed to the "Anglo-Saxon hegemony," but this does not affect the equilibrium or disequilibrium of that continent. He may raise his voice on the boiling issues of Southeast Asia, recognize China and cause his name to be applauded in Pnompenh on a par with those of Castro and Sukarno as the "champions of national independence," but he has no stake in the game. He can give his advice on the affairs of central Africa, condemn subversive plots and disapprove—with excellent reasons—the botched-up action recently led by the United Nations in the Congo; but he no longer has the means to prevent Brazzaville, the most insignificant of his clients, from serving as a relay station for the subversion of which he disapproves. One may regret that France, freed of her imperial burden and enjoying the fruits of European prosperity, applies these gains less to giving durable institutions to herself and to Europe than to throwing herself into vain competition for status symbols—from the *force de frappe* to supersonic jet transports and the recruiting of clients in the Third World. But if de Gaulle is often uncoöperative, in fact his behavior weighs less heavily on Western politics than, for example, the uncertainty of Germany or the confusion of Italy. And, in the last analysis, does not the West gain more than it loses by General de Gaulle's show of independence, by the demonstration to the world—the Third World as well as Eastern Europe—of the reality of the pluralism which it so proudly claims for itself? For whatever may be his sometimes disconcerting positions, no one can ever doubt that de Gaulle belongs to the West—or rather, as he would say with a slightly anti-American bias, to the most classical Occident.

¶ AMERICAN INTELLECTUALS AND FOREIGN POLICY
by Irving Kristol   (July, 1967)

The "credit" for the movement to discredit the Vietnam War must go largely to those American liberal intellectuals who began fairly early to register their discontent with their country's involvement in Southeast Asia. Irving Kristol examines the assumptions and traditions that enable this segment of society to claim moral authority over political acts—and then judges the validity of their claim.

The United States continues to suffer from deep internal divisions, and American troops and POWs are still in Indochina, five years after Kristol wrote that disaffected intellectuals who no longer offer guidance but denounce and mock American policy are performing a disservice. While policy-makers must necessarily deal daily with immediate contingencies, abstractions constitute the lifeblood of intellectuals. From such different standpoints, one cannot expect complete coincidence of views.

Whether domestic dissent has in fact prolonged the war or in any way undermined the U.S. position in Southeast Asia will no doubt continue to be a topic of considerable controversy for many years. Kristol incurred the wrath of many "intellectuals" for this article, although, as Executive Vice-President and Senior Editor of Basic Books and as Coeditor of The Public Interest, *he must, nonetheless, be acknowledged by them as "one of their own."*

AMERICAN INTELLECTUALS
AND FOREIGN POLICY

By Irving Kristol

A recent letter to *The New York Times,* complaining about the role of the academic community in opposing President Johnson's Viet Nam policy, argued that "it is not clear why people trained in mathematics, religion, geology, music, etc., believe their opinions on military and international problems should carry much validity." And the letter went on: "Certainly they [the professors] would oppose unqualified Pentagon generals telling them how to teach their course."

One can understand this complaint; one may even sympathize with the sentiments behind it. The fact remains, however, that it does miss the point. For the issue is not intellectual competence or intellectual validity—not really, and despite all protestations to the contrary. What is at stake is that species of power we call moral authority. The intellectual critics of American foreign policy obviously and sincerely believe that their arguments are right. But it is clear they believe, even more obviously and sincerely, that *they* are right—and that the totality of this rightness amounts to much more than the sum of the individual arguments.

An intellectual may be defined as a man who speaks with general authority about a subject on which he has no particular competence. This definition sounds ironic, but is not. The authority is real enough, just as the lack of specific competence is crucial. An economist writing about economics is not acting as an intellectual, nor is a literary critic when he explicates a text. In such cases, we are witnessing professionals at work. On the other hand, there is good reason why we ordinarily take the "man of letters" as the archetypical intellectual. It is he who most closely resembles his sociological forbear and ideal type: the sermonizing cleric.

Precisely which people, at which time, in any particular social situation, are certified as "intellectuals" is less important than the fact that such certification is achieved—informally but indisputably. And this process involves the recognition of the intellectual as legitimately possessing the prerogative of being moral guide and critic to the world. (It is not too much of an exaggeration to say that even the clergy in the modern world can claim this prerogative only to the extent that it apes the intellectual class.

It is the "writing cleric," like the "writing psychoanalyst," who achieves recognition.) But there is this critical difference between the intellectual of today and the average cleric of yesteryear: the intellectual, lacking in other-worldly interests, is committed to the pursuit of temporal status, temporal influence and temporal power with a single-minded passion that used to be found only in the highest reaches of the Catholic Church. Way back in 1797, Benjamin Constant observed that "in the new society where the prestige of rank is destroyed, we—thinkers, writers, and philosophers—should be honored as the first among all citizens." The only reason Constant did not say "we intellectuals" is that the term had not yet come into common usage.

It is simply not possible to comprehend what is happening in the United States today unless one keeps the sociological condition and political ambitions of the intellectual class very much in the forefront of one's mind. What we are witnessing is no mere difference of opinion about foreign policy, or about Viet Nam. Such differences of opinion do exist, of course. Some of the most articulate critics believe that the United States has, through bureaucratic inertia and mental sloth, persisted in a foreign policy that, whatever its relevance to the immediate postwar years, is by now dangerously anachronistic. They insist that the United States has unthinkingly accepted world responsibilities which are beyond its resources and that, in any case, these responsibilities have only an illusory connection with the enduring national interest. These men may be right; or they may be wrong. But right or wrong, *this* debate is largely irrelevant to the convulsion that the American intellectual community is now going through— even though occasional references may be made to it, for credibility's sake. One does not accuse the President of the United States and the Secretary of State of being "war criminals" and "mass murderers" because they have erred in estimating the proper dimensions of the United States' overseas commitments. And it is precisely accusations of this kind that are inflaming passions on the campus, and which are more and more coming to characterize the "peace movement" as a whole.

What we are observing is a phenomenon that is far more complex in its origins and far-reaching in its implications. It involves, among other things, the highly problematic relationship of the modern intellectual to foreign affairs, the basic self-definition of the American intellectual, the tortured connections between

American liberal ideology and the American imperial republic, and the role of the newly established academic classes in an affluent society. Above all, it raises the question of whether democratic societies can cope with the kinds of political pathologies that seem to be spontaneously generated by their very commitment to economic and social progress.

II

No modern nation has ever constructed a foreign policy that was acceptable to its intellectuals. True, at moments of national peril or national exaltation, intellectuals will feel the same patriotic emotions as everyone else, and will subscribe as enthusiastically to the common cause. But these moments pass, the process of disengagement begins, and it usually does not take long for disengagement to eventuate in alienation. Public opinion polls generally reveal that the overwhelming majority of ordinary citizens, at any particular time, will be approving of their government's foreign policy; among intellectuals, this majority tends to be skimpy at best, and will frequently not exist at all. It is reasonable to suppose that there is an instinctive bias at work here, favorable to government among the common people, unfavorable among the intellectuals.

The bias of the common man is easy to understand: he is never much interested in foreign affairs; his patriotic feelings incline him to favor his own government against the governments of foreigners; and in cases of international conflict, he is ready to sacrifice his self-interest for what the government assures him to be the common good. The persistent bias of intellectuals, on the other hand, requires some explaining.

We have noted that the intellectual lays claim—and the claim is, more often than not, recognized—to moral authority over the intentions and actions of political leaders. This claim finds concrete rhetorical expression in an ideology. What creates a community of intellectuals, as against a mere aggregate of individuals, is the fact that they subscribe—with varying degrees of warmth, or with more or less explicit reservations—to a prevailing ideology. This ideology permits them to interpret the past, make sense of the present, outline a shape for the future. It constitutes the essence of their rationality, as this is directed toward the life of man in society.

Now, it is the peculiarity of foreign policy that it is the area of public life in which ideology flounders most dramatically. Thus, while it is possible—if not necessarily fruitful—to organize the political writings of the past three hundred years along a spectrum ranging from the ideological "left" to the ideological "right," no such arrangement is conceivable for writings on foreign policy. There is no great "radical" text on the conduct of foreign policy —and no great "conservative" text, either. What texts there are (*e.g.* Machiavelli, Grotius, in our own day the writings of George Kennan and Hans Morgenthau) are used indifferently by all parties, as circumstance allows.

And we find, if we pursue the matter further, that the entire tradition of Western political thought has very little to say about foreign policy. From Thucydides to our own time, political philosophy has seen foreign affairs as so radically affected by contingency, fortune and fate as to leave little room for speculative enlightenment. John Locke was fertile in suggestions for the establishment and maintenance of good government, but when it came to foreign affairs he pretty much threw up his hands: "What is to be done in reference to foreigners, depending much upon their actions and the variation of designs and interests, must be left in great part to the prudence of those who have this power committed to them, to be managed by the best of their skill for the advantage of the Commonwealth."

The reasons why this should be so are not mysterious. To begin with, the very idea of "foreign policy" is so amorphous as to be misleading. As James Q. Wilson has pointed out, it is not at all clear that a State Department can have a foreign policy in a meaningful sense of that term—*i.e.* one "policy" that encompasses our economic, military, political and sentimental relations with nations neighborly or distant, friendly or inimical. Moreover, whereas a national community is governed by principles by which one takes one's intellectual and moral bearings, the nations of the world do not constitute such a community and propose few principles by which their conduct may be evaluated. What this adds up to is that ideology can obtain exasperatingly little purchase over the realities of foreign policy—and that intellectuals feel keenly their dispossession from this area. It is not that intellectuals actually believe—though they often assert it—that the heavy reliance upon expediency in foreign affairs is intrinsically immoral. It is just that this reliance renders intellectuals as a class so much the less indispensable: to the extent that expediency is a necessary principle of action, to that extent the sovereignty of intellectuals is automatically circumscribed. It is only where politics is ideologized that intellectuals have a pivotal social and political role. To be good at coping with expediential situations you don't have to be an intellectual—and it may even be a handicap.

It is this state of affairs that explains the extraordinary inconsistencies of intellectuals on matters of foreign policy, and the ease with which they can enunciate a positive principle, only in the next breath to urge a contrary action. So it is that many intellectuals are appalled at our military intervention in Southeast Asia, on the grounds that, no matter what happens there, the national security of the United States will not be threatened. But these same intellectuals would raise no objection if the United States sent an expeditionary force all the way to South Africa to overthrow apartheid, even though South Africa offers no threat to American security. So it is, too, that intellectual critics are fond of accusing American foreign policy of neglecting "political solutions" in favor of crude military and economic action—thereby demonstrating their faith that, if foreign policy were suffused with sufficient ideological rationality, it would dissolve the recalcitrance that mere statesmen encounter. And when the statesman candidly responds that he is coping, not with problems, but with an endless series of crises, and that he really has no way of knowing beforehand what "solution," if any, is feasible, he is simply reinforcing the intellectual's conviction that the managers of foreign affairs are, if not more wicked than he is, then certainly more stupid. Usually, he will be willing to think they are both.

Charles Frankel has written that "international affairs are peculiarly susceptible to galloping abstractions"[1] and has stressed that "intellectuals, more than most other groups, have the power to create, dignify, inflate, criticize, moderate or puncture these abstractions." In the event, intellectuals rarely moderate or puncture, but are diligent in inflation. Abstractions are their life's blood, and even when they resolutely decide to become "tough-minded" they end up with an oversimplified ideology of Realpolitik that is quite useless as a guide to the conduct of foreign affairs and leads its expounders to one self-contradiction after another. But the important point is not that intellectuals are

---

[1] Charles Frankel, "The Scribblers and International Relations," *Foreign Affairs*, October 1965.

always wrong on matters of foreign policy—they are not, and could not possibly be, if only by the laws of chance. What is striking is that, right or wrong, they are so often, from the statesman's point of view, irrelevant. And it is their self-definition as ideological creatures that makes them so.

III

In the United States, this ideological self-definition has taken on a very special form, and the relation of the American intellectual to foreign policy has its own distinctive qualities. Just how distinctive may be gathered from asking oneself the following question: Is it conceivable that American intellectuals should *ever* disapprove of *any* popular revolution, anywhere in the world —whatever the express or implicit principles of this revolution? One can make this question even sharper: Is it conceivable for American intellectuals ever to approve of their government suppressing, or helping to frustrate, any popular revolution *by poor people*—whatever the nature or consequences of this revolution? The answer would obviously have to be in the negative; and the implications of this answer for American foreign policy are not insignificant. This policy must work within a climate of opinion that finds the idea of a *gradual* evolution of traditional societies thoroughly uninteresting—which, indeed, has an instinctive detestation of all traditional societies as being inherently unjust, and an equally instinctive approval, as being inherently righteous, of any revolutionary ideology which claims to incorporate the people's will.

As a matter of fact, even though official policy must obviously be based on other considerations, the makers of policy themselves find it nearly impossible to escape from this ideological framework. The State Department, for example, is always insisting that the United States is a truly revolutionary society, founded on revolutionary principles and offering a true revolutionary promise—as contrasted with the communists' spurious promises. The intellectual critics of American foreign policy deny that any such revolutionary intention or program exists—but think it ought to. There are precious few people in the United States who will say aloud that revolutionary intentions are inconsistent with a prudent and responsible foreign policy of a great power. Oddly enough, to hear this point made with some urgency these days, one has to go to the Soviet Union.

The American intellectual tradition has two profound commitments: to "ideals" and to "the people." It is the marriage of these two themes that has made the American mind and given it its characteristic cast—which might be called *transcendentalist populism*.

The "transcendentalist" theme in American thought is linked to a disrespect for tradition, a suspicion of all institutionalized authority, an unshakable faith in the "natural" (what once was called "divine") wisdom of the sincere individual, an incorruptible allegiance to one's own "inner light." The American intellectual sees himself as being in perpetual "prophetic confrontation" with principalities and powers. (That very phrase, "prophetic confrontation," has lately been used by Hans Morgenthau to define the proper stance of the intellectual vis-à-vis his government's policies.) Tell an American intellectual that he is a disturber of the intellectual peace, and he is gratified. Tell him he is a reassuring spokesman for calm and tranquillity, and he will think you have made a nasty accusation.

This transcendentalist "protestantism" of the American intellectual derives from the history of American Protestantism itself —as does his near-mystical celebration of "the people." Indeed, the two themes have evolved as part of one historical process, which has been concisely described by the historian, Russell B. Nye:

> From the mid-18th century to the mid-19th in American thought . . . the accepted version of the individual's power to grasp and interpret God's truth underwent a complete change—from Calvin's dependence on the Bible . . . to Deism's grant to man of equal sovereignty in a universe of reason, to Channing's transfer of sovereignty from Bible and church to man, and finally to the *self*-reliance of Emerson, Parker, and Thoreau. The lines of thought moved from Mather's distrust of man, to Jefferson's qualified confidence in him, to Emerson's and Jackson's deep and abiding faith in his capacity to find out and act upon divine truth.[2]

This evolution, which might be called the democratization of the spirit, has created an American intellectual who is at one and the same time (a) humble toward an idealized and mythical prototype of the common man (if the people have a quasi-ecclesiastical function, to oppose them in any consistent way partakes of heresy) and (b) arrogant toward existing authority, as presumptively representing nothing but a petrified form of

[2] Russell B. Nye, "The Search for the Individual, 1750–1850," *The Centennial Review*, Winter 1961.

yesteryear's vital forces. It has also had a peculiar effect upon the politics of American intellectuals, which is more often than not a kind of transcendentalist politics, focusing less on the reform of the polity than on the perfection and purification of self in opposition to the polity. Just as the intellectual opposition to slavery in the 1830s and 1840s paid little attention to the reform of particular institutions but focused primarily on the need for the individual to avoid being compromised and contaminated by this general evil, so in the 1960s what appears most to torment our academic intellectuals is the morality of their own actions— whether they should coöperate with Selective Service, accept government contracts, pay taxes, etc. At both times, the issue of individual, conscientious "civil disobedience" has become acute. It is instructive to note that, though the British Labor Party bitterly opposed British imperialism for over five decades, its opposition never took any such form. This is some measure of the difference between a political tradition and one that transcends mere politics.

The United States, to be sure, does have its own political tradition. And though the American intellectual tradition has suffused all areas of American life, it has never completely overwhelmed the political. This latter, mainly the creation of American Whiggery, is incarnated in our major institutions and finds its literary expression in such documents as the Constitution, the Federalist Papers, some presidential addresses, judicial decisions, etc. This tradition is still very much alive in our law schools and helps explain why these schools play so singular a role in our political life. But among intellectuals it has never enjoyed much favor, being thought to be inherently conservative and non-democratic. The American intellectual of today is far more comfortable listening to a "protest folk song"—the truly indigenous art form of transcendental populism—than he is listening to a grave and solemn debate over a matter of policy. Witness the way in which the one genre has overwhelmed the other in the "teach-in."

Precisely what an American intellectual does *not* believe was most elegantly expressed by Sir Thomas More, in the discussion of an intellectual's obligation in his "Utopia":

> If evil persons cannot be quite rooted out, and if you cannot correct habitual attitudes as you wish, you must not therefore abandon the commonwealth. . . . You must strive to guide policy indirectly, so that you make the best of things, and what you cannot turn to good, you can at least make less

bad. For it is impossible to do all things well unless all men are good, and this I do not expect to see for a long time.

There have been, of course, some American intellectuals who have followed Sir Thomas More's direction. For their efforts and pains, they have been subjected to the scorn and contempt of the intellectual community as a whole. (Arthur Schlesinger, Jr., Eric Goldman and John Roche could provide us with eloquent testimony on this score.) This community, unlike Sir Thomas More, is quite convinced that all men are indeed good and that any such modest and compromising involvement with political power can represent only a corruption of the spirit.

IV

The transformation of the American republic into an imperial power has sharply exacerbated the relations between the intellectual and the makers of foreign policy. The term "imperial power" is merely a synonym for "great power" and is not necessarily the same thing as "imperialistic" power. But there would seem to be a gain in clarity, and a diminution of humbug, in insisting on the use of the more provocative phrase. There are a great many people who appear to think that a great power is only the magnification of a small power, and that the principles governing the actions of the latter are simply transferrable—perhaps with some modification—to the former. In fact, there is a qualitative difference between the two conditions, and the difference can be summed up as follows: a great power is "imperial" because what it does *not* do is just as significant, and just as consequential, as what it does. Which is to say, a great power does not have the range of freedom of action—derived from the freedom of inaction—that a small power possesses. It is entangled in a web of responsibilities from which there is no hope of escape; and its policy-makers are doomed to a strenuous and unquiet life, with no prospect of ultimate resolution, no hope for an unproblematic existence, no promise of final contentment. It is understandable that these policy-makers should sometimes talk as if some particular redirection of policy, of any great power, is capable of terminating the tensions inherent in this imperial condition. But it is foolish for us to believe them; and it is even more foolish for them to believe themselves. It is no accident that all classical political philosophers, and all depicters of utopia, have agreed that, to be truly happy, a human community should be relatively small and as isolated as possible from foreign entanglements.

Indeed, this utopian ideal is a major historic theme of American foreign policy, being at the root of what we call "isolationism." And so long as the United States was not a great power, it was not entirely utopian. The American republic, until the beginning of the twentieth century, was genuinely isolationist, and isolationism made both practical and idealistic sense. Practical sense, because the United States was geographically isolated from the main currents of world politics. Idealistic sense, because the United States could feel—and it was no illusion—that it served as a splendid and inspiring example to all believers in popular government everywhere, and that this exemplary role was more important than any foreign actions it might undertake, with the limited resources at its command. True, at the same time that the United States was isolationist, it was also expansionist. But there is no necessary contradiction between these two orientations, even though some modern historians are shocked to contemplate their coexistence. Most of the territories that the United States coveted, and all that were acquired, prior to the Civil War, were thinly populated—there was no subjugation of large, alien masses. And the intent of this expansion was always to incorporate such territories into the United States on absolutely equal terms, not to dominate them for any reasons of state. The idea of "manifest destiny" was therefore easily reconcilable to the isolationist idea. This reconciliation became troublesome only when expansion threatened to disturb the regional balance of power within the republic. Thus, the opposition to the Mexican War among some Northerners was intense, because it meant a possible accretion to the power of the "slavocracy." But there would otherwise have been little opposition to westward and southwestern expansion; and, once the war was over, no one thought for a moment of giving these territories back to Mexico or permitting them to evolve into independent national entities.

In the end, of course, "manifest destiny" did write an end to American isolationism, by establishing the material conditions for the emergence of the United States as a great power. But the isolationist idea, or at least crucial aspects of it, survived—not simply as some kind of "cultural lag," but by reason of being so intimately conjoined to "the American way of life," and to the American intellectual creed. This way of life insisted upon the subordination of public policy to private, individual needs and concerns. It had little use for the idea of military glory, which Abraham Lincoln called "that attractive rainbow that rises in showers of blood—that serpent's eye that charms to destroy." It was intensely patriotic, but allergic to all conceptions of national *grandeur*. The United States was tempted to a brief fling at European-style imperialism under Presidents McKinley and Theodore Roosevelt, but found the experience disagreeable, and that enterprise was gradually liquidated. When the American democracy entered World War I, it was in no imperial frame of mind. On the contrary, the whole point of the Wilsonian "crusade" was to rid the world of imperial politics. One can almost say that this crusade was a penultimate outburst of the isolationist spirit, in that its goal was a happy, self-determined existence for all the individuals on this earth—*une vie à l'Américaine*—without any further cruel violations of it by international power politics.

The disillusionment consequent upon this crusade prepared the way for the United States to enter history as an imperial power. To be sure, its most immediate effect was to stimulate a purely geographic isolationism that was shot through with streaks of xenophobia. But this attitude simply could not withstand the pressure of events and the insistent demands of world realities. In retrospect, the spectacle of the United States entering World War II has an almost dreamlike, fatalistic quality. There was never, prior to Pearl Harbor, any literal threat to the national security of the United States. And there was no popular enthusiasm, except among a small if influential group of "internationalists," for the United States' accepting responsibility for the maintenance of "world order." It all just seemed inescapable, and the alternative—retiring into a Fortress America—just too unmanly. The dominant mood was resignation, tinged with outrage at the Japanese bombardment of American soil. And resignation —sometimes sullen, sometimes equable—has remained the dominant popular mood ever since.

Strangely enough, this resigned acceptance of great-power responsibilities by the American people has been accompanied by a great unease on the part of the intellectuals. It is strange, because one had expected the reverse of this situation. During the two postwar decades, many commentators expressed doubt whether the American people could sustain the frustrations and sacrifices inherent in an imperial role. Such doubts were given point by the upsurge of extremist sentiments associated with the late Senator McCarthy, and unquestionably incited by popular resentment at the Korean War. But Korea can now be seen to have been a kind of baptism-by-fire; and the war in Viet Nam has been borne with greater patience than might have been expected. It is not a popular war—how could it be?—but the general feeling is that it has to be endured. It is among the intellectuals—including some of the aforementioned commentators—that extreme dissatisfaction, sometimes extremist dissatisfaction, is rife. It is among American intellectuals that the isolationist ideal is experiencing its final, convulsive agony.

Though this dissatisfaction affects only a minority, it is nevertheless a most serious matter. It is much to be doubted that the United States can continue to play an imperial role without the endorsement of its intellectual class. Or, to put it more precisely: since there is no way the United States, as the world's mightiest power, can avoid such an imperial role, the opposition of its intellectuals means that this role will be played out in a domestic climate of ideological dissent that will enfeeble the resolution of our statesmen and diminish the credibility of their policies abroad.

What is to be done? It is always possible to hope that this intellectual class will come to realize that its traditional ideology needs reformation and revision. It is even possible to argue plausibly that, in the nature of things, this is "historically inevitable." One can go so far as to say that, on intellectual grounds alone, this intellectual class will feel moved to desist from the shrill enunciation of pieties and principles that have little relevance to the particular cases our statesmen now confront, and to help formulate a new set of more specific principles that will relate the ideals which sustain the American democracy to the harsh and nasty imperatives of imperial power. All of this is possible. But one must add that none of these possibilities is likely to be realized in the immediate or even near future.

It is unlikely for two reasons. The first is that the burden of guilt such a process would generate would be so great as to be insupportable. It took three centuries to create the American intellectual as we know him today; he is not going to be recreated in one generation. He is committed in the most profound way to a whole set of assumptions and ideas that are rooted in the "isolationist" era of American history, and he cannot depart from these assumptions and ideals without a terrible sense of self-betrayal.

Our State Department may find it necessary, if disagreeable, to support military dictatorships in certain countries, at certain times. It is hard to see our intellectuals swallowing this necessity. They might agree in the abstract that alternatives are not available. They might even grant to certain dictatorships the kind of dispensation that is often extended to heathens by an otherwise dogmatic orthodoxy. But they will gag at extending such a dispensation to "our" dictators—this would be too subversive of the dogmas by which they define their existence as a class. The furthest that American intellectuals can go toward coping with the realities of imperial power is to erect a double standard that undermines the moral basis of American diplomacy.

Secondly, this crisis of the intellectual class in the face of an imperial destiny coincides with an internal power struggle within the United States itself. Our intellectuals are moving toward a significant "confrontation" with the American "establishment" and will do nothing to strengthen the position of their antagonist. Which is to say that the American intellectual class actually has an interest in thwarting the evolution of any kind of responsible and coherent imperial policy. Just what this interest is, and what this confrontation involves, we are only now beginning to discern. Behind the general fog that the ideology of dissent generates, the outlines of a very material sociological and political problem are emerging.

V

It has always been assumed that as the United States became a more highly organized national society, as its economy became more managerial, its power more imperial and its populace more sophisticated, the intellectuals would move inexorably closer to the seats of authority—would, perhaps, even be incorporated en masse into a kind of "power élite." Many writers and thinkers—and not only on the political left—have viewed this prospect with the greatest unease, for it seemed to them to threaten the continued existence of intellectuals as a critical and moral force in American life.

Well, it has happened here—only, as is so often the case, it is all very different from what one expected. It is true that a small section of the American intellectual class has become a kind of permanent brain trust to the political, the military, the economic authorities. These are the men who commute regularly to Washington, who help draw up programs for reorganizing the bureau-cracy, who evaluate proposed weapons systems, who figure out ways to improve our cities and assist our poor, who analyze the course of economic growth, who reckon the cost and effectiveness of foreign aid programs, who dream up new approaches to such old social problems as the mental health of the aged, etc., etc. But what has also happened, at the same time, is that a whole new intellectual class has emerged as a result of the explosive growth, in these past decades, of higher education in the United States. And these "new men," so far from being any kind of élite, are a mass—and have engendered their own mass movement.

As a matter of courtesy and habit, one refers to these professors as "intellectuals." Some of them, of course, are intellectuals, in the traditional sense of the term. The majority unquestionably are not—no population, no matter how elevated, could produce *that many* intellectuals. Professor Robert Nisbet, as shrewd an ob-server of the academic scene as we have, has estimated that "at the present time not less than sixty percent of all academics in the universities in this country have so profound a distaste for the classroom and for the pains of genuine scholarship or creative thought that they will seize upon anything . . . to exempt them-selves respectably from each."[3]

In most instances, whether a man these days ends up a college professor or, say, a social worker or a civil servant is largely a matter of chance. Nevertheless, this academic mass has taken over not only the political metaphysics of the American intel-lectual, but also his status and prerogatives. Americans have al-ways had a superstitious, if touching, faith in the importance of education. And the American people have quickly conceded to the professoriat of our affluent society the moral authority that intellectuals have always claimed as their peculiar endowment.

Now, this new intellectual class, though to outsiders appearing to be not at all badly off, is full of grievance and resentment. It feels discriminated against—opinion polls reveal that professors, especially in the social sciences and humanities, invariably tend drastically to underestimate the esteem in which public opinion (and, more particularly, the opinion of the business community) holds them. It feels underpaid; you'll not find any credence on the campus for the proposition (demonstrably true) that the salaries of professors do not compare unfavorably with the salaries of bank

[3] Robert A. Nisbet, "What Is An Intellectual?" *Commentary*, December 1965.

executives. It feels put upon in all sorts of other familiar ways. The symptoms are only too typical: here is a new class that is "alienated" from the established order because it feels that this order has not conceded to it sufficient power and recognition.

The politics of this new class is novel in that its locus of struggle is the college campus. One is shocked at this—we are used to thinking that politics ought not to intrude on the campus. But we shall no doubt get accustomed to the idea. Meanwhile, there is going to be a great deal of unpleasant turbulence. The academic community in the United States today has evolved into a new political constituency. College students, like their teachers, are "new men" who find the traditional student role too restrictive. Students and faculty therefore find it easy to combine their numbers and their energies for the purpose of social and political action. The first objective—already accomplished in large measure—is to weaken control of the administration and to dispossess it of its authoritative powers over campus activities. From this point the movement into politics proper—including elections—is about as predictable as anything can be.

Just what direction this movement into politics will follow it is too early to say with certainty. Presumably, it will be toward "the left," since this is the historical orientation of the intellectual class as a whole. It is even possible that the movement will not be calmed until the United States has witnessed the transformation of its two-party system to make room for a mass party of the ideological left, as in most European countries—except that its "grass roots" will be on the campus rather than in the factory. But what is certain is that the national prestige and the international position of the United States are being adversely affected by this *sécession des clercs*. Imperial powers need social equilibrium at home if they are to act effectively in the world. It was possible to think, in the years immediately after World War II, that the United States had indeed achieved this kind of equilibrium—that consensus and equipoise at home would permit our statesmen to formulate and pursue a coherent foreign policy. But the "academic revolution" of the 1950s and 1960s raises this issue again, in a most problematic and urgent way.

VI

Though there is much fancy rhetoric, pro and con, about "the purpose of American foreign policy," there is really nothing esoteric about this purpose. The United States wishes to establish and sustain a world order that (a) ensures its national security as against the other great powers, (b) encourages other nations, especially the smaller ones, to mold their own social, political and economic institutions along lines that are at least not repugnant to (if not actually congruent with) American values, and (c) minimizes the possibility of naked, armed conflict. This is, of course, also the purpose of the foreign policies of such other great powers as Soviet Russia and Maoist China. Nor could it be otherwise, short of a fit of collective insanity on the part of the governing classes of these powers. Without the conflict, tension and reconciliation of such imperial purposes there would be no such thing as "foreign affairs" or "world politics," as we ordinarily understand these terms.

But for any imperial policy to work effectively—even if one means by that nothing more than doing the least possible mischief—it needs intellectual and moral guidance. It needs such guidance precisely because, in foreign affairs, one is always forced to compromise one's values. In the United States today, a relative handful of intellectuals proffers such guidance to the policymaker. But the intellectual community en masse, disaffected from established power even as it tries to establish a power base of its own, feels no such sense of responsibility. It denounces, it mocks, it vilifies—and even if one were to concede that its fierce indignation was justified by extraordinary ineptitude in high places, the fact remains that its activity is singularly unhelpful. The United States is not going to cease being an imperial power, no matter what happens in Viet Nam or elsewhere. It is the world situation —and the history which created this situation—that appoints imperial powers, not anyone's decision or even anyone's overweening ambition. And power begets responsibility—above all, the responsibility to use this power responsibly. The policy-maker in the United States today—and, no doubt, in the other great powers, too—finds this responsibility a terrible burden. The intellectuals, in contrast, are bemused by dreams of power without responsibility, even as they complain of moral responsibility without power. It is not a healthy situation; and, as of this moment, it must be said that one cannot see how, or where, or when it will all end.

¶ ASIA AFTER VIET NAM
by Richard M. Nixon   (October, 1967)

When Foreign Affairs *published "Asia After Viet Nam," Richard M. Nixon was an aspirant for the Republican Presidential nomination. The article received considerable attention at the time and was considered to be a rather moderate foreign-policy statement on the part of the former Vice-President, a noted anticommunist. After Nixon's nomination, however, and his election as President in 1968, the piece began to be examined as an important source on the President's thinking.*

Perhaps most significantly, it can be seen as an early manifestation of his changing China policy. While Nixon still viewed Communist China as nursing "imperial ambitions" and intent upon "foreign adventures," he stated that "taking the long view, we simply cannot afford to leave China forever outside the family of nations, there to nurture its fantasies, cherish its hates and threaten its neighbors." America's aim, in his view, should be to induce China to change, to turn inward "toward the solution of its own domestic problems." President Nixon's approach to China, in fact, came rather sooner than he advocated in this article, where he said that we should begin our dialogue with that country only when the nations of noncommunist Asia have become strong enough to take care of themselves and no longer offer tempting targets for Peking.

Some rudiments of what has become known as the "Nixon Doctrine" can also be found in this article. If the doctrine is understood as an intention to reduce U.S. involvement abroad while depending on America's allies to do more, President Nixon was applying the notion, if not the formulation, to Asia in this article when he called upon the nations threatened by China to form an "indigenous Asian framework for their own future security." And he said further that, before Asian nations ask the United States for aid against communist threats, those nations ought to make a collective effort to deal with the aggressor themselves. The essence of this attitude is contained in his forthright statement that "the role of the United States as world policeman is likely to be limited in the future."

ASIA AFTER VIET NAM

By Richard M. Nixon

THE war in Viet Nam has for so long dominated our field of vision that it has distorted our picture of Asia. A small country on the rim of the continent has filled the screen of our minds; but it does not fill the map. Sometimes dramatically, but more often quietly, the rest of Asia has been undergoing a profound, an exciting and on balance an extraordinarily promising transformation. One key to this transformation is the emergence of Asian regionalism; another is the development of a number of the Asian economies; another is gathering disaffection with all the old isms that have so long imprisoned so many minds and so many governments. By and large the non-communist Asian governments are looking for solutions that work, rather than solutions that fit a preconceived set of doctrines and dogmas.

Most of them also recognize a common danger, and see its source as Peking. Taken together, these developments present an extraordinary set of opportunities for a U.S. policy which must begin to look beyond Viet Nam. In looking toward the future, however, we should not ignore the vital role Viet Nam has played in making these developments possible. Whatever one may think of the "domino" theory, it is beyond question that without the American commitment in Viet Nam Asia would be a far different place today.

The U.S. presence has provided tangible and highly visible proof that communism is not necessarily the wave of Asia's future. This was a vital factor in the turnaround in Indonesia, where a tendency toward fatalism is a national characteristic. It provided a shield behind which the anti-communist forces found the courage and the capacity to stage their counter-coup and, at the final moment, to rescue their country from the Chinese orbit. And, with its 100 million people, and its 3,000-mile arc of islands containing the region's richest hoard of natural resources, Indonesia constitutes by far the greatest prize in the Southeast Asian area.

Beyond this, Viet Nam has diverted Peking from such other potential targets as India, Thailand and Malaysia. It has bought vitally needed time for governments that were weak or unstable or leaning toward Peking as a hedge against the future—time which has allowed them to attempt to cope with their own insurrections while pressing ahead with their political, economic and military development. From Japan to India, Asian leaders know why we are in Viet Nam and, privately if not publicly, they urge us to see it through to a satisfactory conclusion.

II

Many argue that an Atlantic axis is natural and necessary, but maintain, in effect, that Kipling was right, and that the Asian peoples are so "different" that Asia itself is only peripherally an American concern. This represents a racial and cultural chauvinism that does little credit to American ideals, and it shows little appreciation either of the westward thrust of American interests or of the dynamics of world development.

During the final third of the twentieth century, Asia, not Europe or Latin America, will pose the greatest danger of a confrontation which could escalate into World War III. At the same time, the fact that the United States has now fought three Asian wars in the space of a generation is grimly but truly symbolic of the deepening involvement of the United States in what happens on the other side of the Pacific—which modern transportation and communications have brought closer to us today than Europe was in the years immediately preceding World War II.

The United States is a Pacific power. Europe has been withdrawing the remnants of empire, but the United States, with its coast reaching in an arc from Mexico to the Bering Straits, is one anchor of a vast Pacific community. Both our interests and our ideals propel us westward across the Pacific, not as conquerors but as partners, linked by the sea not only with those oriental nations on Asia's Pacific littoral but at the same time with occidental Australia and New Zealand, and with the island nations between.

Since World War II, a new Asia has been emerging with startling rapidity; indeed, Asia is changing more swiftly than any other part of the world. All around the rim of China nations are becoming Western without ceasing to be Asian.

The dominant development in Asia immediately after World War II was decolonization, with its admixture of intense nationalism. But the old nationalist slogans have less meaning for today's young than they had for their fathers. Having never known a "colonialist," they find colonialists unconvincing as scapegoats for the present ills of their societies. If dissatisfied with conditions as they see them, the young tend to blame those now in power.

As the sharp anticolonial focus blurs, the old nationalism is evolving into a more complex, multi-layered set of concepts and attitudes. On the one hand are a multitude of local and tribal identifications—the Montagnards in Viet Nam, the Han tribes in Burma, the provincial and linguistic separatisms that constantly claw at the fabric of Indian unity. On the other hand, there is a reaching-out by the governing élites, and particularly the young, for something larger, more like an Asian regionalism.

The developing coherence of Asian regional thinking is reflected in a disposition to consider problems and loyalties in regional terms, and to evolve regional approaches to development needs and to the evolution of a new world order. This is not excessively chauvinistic, but rather in the nature of a coalescing confidence, a recognition that Asia can become a counterbalance to the West, and an increasing disposition to seek Asian solutions to Asian problems through coöperative action.

Along with the rising complex of national, subregional and regional identification and pride, there is also an acute sense of common danger—a factor which serves as catalyst to the others. The common danger from Communist China is now in the process of shifting the Asian governments' center of concern. During the colonial and immediately post-colonial eras, Asians stood opposed primarily to the West, which represented the intruding alien power. But now the West has abandoned its colonial role, and it no longer threatens the independence of the Asian nations. Red China, however, does, and its threat is clear, present and repeatedly and insistently expressed. The message has not been lost on Asia's leaders. They recognize that the West, and particularly the United States, now represents not an oppressor but a protector. And they recognize their need for protection.

This does not mean that the old resentments and distrusts have vanished, or that new ones will not arise. It does, however, mean that there has been an important shift in the balance of their perceptions about the balance of danger, and this shift has important implications for the future.

One of the legacies of Viet Nam almost certainly will be a deep reluctance on the part of the United States to become involved once again in a similar intervention on a similar basis. The war has imposed severe strains on the United States, not only militarily and economically but socially and politically as well. Bitter dissension has torn the fabric of American intellectual life, and whatever the outcome of the war the tear may be a long time mending. If another friendly country should be faced with an externally supported communist insurrection—whether in Asia, or in Africa or even Latin America—there is serious question whether the American public or the American Congress would now support a unilateral American intervention, even at the request of the host government. This makes it vitally in their own interest that the nations in the path of China's ambitions move quickly to establish an indigenous Asian framework for their own future security.

In doing so, they need to fashion arrangements able to deal both with old-style wars and with new—with traditional wars, in which armies cross over national boundaries, and with the so-called "wars of national liberation," in which they burrow under national boundaries.

I am not arguing that the day is past when the United States would respond militarily to communist threats in the less stable parts of the world, or that a unilateral response to a unilateral request for help is out of the question. But other nations must recognize that the role of the United States as world policeman is likely to be limited in the future. To ensure that a U.S. response will be forthcoming if needed, machinery must be created that is capable of meeting two conditions: (*a*) a collective effort by the nations of the region to contain the threat by themselves; and, if that effort fails, (*b*) a collective request to the United States for assistance. This is important not only from the respective national standpoints, but also from the standpoint of avoiding nuclear collision.

Nations not possessing great power can indulge in the luxury of criticism of others; those possessing it have the responsibility of decision. Faced with a clear challenge, the decision not to use one's power must be as deliberate as the decision to use it. The consequences can be fully as far-reaching and fully as irrevocable.

If another world war is to be prevented, every step possible must be taken to avert direct confrontations between the nuclear powers. To achieve this, it is essential to minimize the number of occasions on which the great powers have to decide whether or not to commit their forces. These choices cannot be eliminated, but they can be reduced by the development of regional defense pacts, in which nations undertake, among themselves, to attempt to contain aggression in their own areas.

If the initial response to a threatened aggression, of whichever type—whether across the border or under it—can be made by lesser powers in the immediate area and thus within the path of aggression, one of two things can be achieved: either they can in fact contain it by themselves, in which case the United States is spared involvement and thus the world is spared the consequences of great-power action; or, if they cannot, the ultimate choice can be presented to the United States in clear-cut terms, by nations which would automatically become allies in whatever response might prove necessary. To put it another way, the regional pact becomes a buffer separating the distant great power from the immediate threat. Only if the buffer proves insufficient does the great power become involved, and then in terms that make victory more attainable and the enterprise more palatable.

This is particularly important when the threat takes the form of an externally supported guerrilla action, as we have faced in Viet Nam, as is even now being mounted in Thailand, and as could be launched in any of a half-dozen other spots in the Chinese shadow. Viet Nam has shown how difficult it is to make clear the distinction between this and an ordinary factional civil war, and how subject the assisting power is to charges of having intervened in an internal matter. Viet Nam's neighbors know that the war there is not internal, but our own allies in Europe have difficulty grasping the fact.

The fragmenting of the communist world has lent credence to the frequently heard argument that a communist advance by proxy, as we have seen attempted in Viet Nam, is of only peripheral importance; that with the weakening of rigid central control of the communist world, local fights between communist and non-communist factions are a local matter. This ignores, however, the fact that with the decentralization of communist control has come an appropriately tailored shift in communist tactics. National communism poses a different kind of threat than did the old-style international communism, but by being subtler it is in some ways more dangerous.

SEATO was useful and appropriate to its time, but it was Western in origin and drew its strength from the United States and Europe. It has weakened to the point at which it is little more than an institutional embodiment of an American commitment, and a somewhat anachronistic relic of the days when France and Britain were active members. Asia today needs its own security undertakings, reflecting the new realities of Asian independence and Asian needs.

Thus far, despite a pattern of rapidly increasing coöperation in cultural and economic affairs, the Asian nations have been unwilling to form a military grouping designed to forestall the Chinese threat, even though several have bilateral arrangements with the United States. But an appropriate foundation-stone exists on which to build: the Asian and Pacific Council. ASPAC held its first ministerial-level meeting in Seoul in June 1966, and its second in Bangkok in July 1967. It has carefully limited itself to strengthening regional coöperation in economic, cultural and social matters, and its members have voiced strong feelings that, as Japan's Foreign Minister Takeo Miki put it at the Bangkok meeting, it should not be made "a body to promote anticommunist campaigns."

Despite ASPAC's present cultural and economic orientation, however, the solidifying awareness of China's threat should make it possible—if the need for a regional alliance is put in sufficiently compelling terms—to develop it into an alliance actively dedicated to concerting whatever efforts might be necessary to maintain the security of the region. And ASPAC is peculiarly well situated to play such a role. Its members (South Korea, Japan, Taiwan, Thailand, Malaysia, South Viet Nam, the Philippines, Australia and New Zealand, with Laos as an observer) all are acutely conscious of the Chinese threat. All except Malaysia have military ties with the United States. It has the distinct advantage of including Australia and New Zealand, which share the danger and would be able to contribute substantially to its strength, without an unbalancing great-power presence.

I do not mean to minimize the difficulties of winning acceptance of such a concept. In Japan, public opinion still lags behind official awareness of military needs. The avowedly neutralist nations under China's cloud would be reluctant, at present, to join any such grouping. But looking further down the road we can project either an erosion of their neutralism or the formation of their own loose association or associations, which might be tied into a militarily oriented ASPAC on an interlocking or coöperative basis. One can hope that even India might finally be persuaded to

give its support, having itself been the target of overt Chinese
aggression, and still cherishing as it does a desire to play a substantial role beyond its own borders.

III

Military security has to rest, ultimately, on economic and political stability. One of the effects of the rapidity of change in the
world today is that there can no longer be static stability; there
can only be dynamic stability. A nation or society that fails to
keep pace with change is in danger of flying apart. It is important
that we recognize this, but equally important that in trying to
maintain a dynamic stability we remember that the stability is as
important as the dynamism.

If a given set of ends is deemed desirable, then from the standpoint of those dedicated to peace and an essential stability in
world order the desideratum is to reach those ends by evolutionary rather than revolutionary means. Looking at the pattern
of change in non-communist Asia, we find that the professed aims
of the revolutionaries are in fact being achieved by an evolutionary process. This offers a dramatic opportunity to draw the
distinction between the fact of a revolutionary *result* and the
process of revolutionary change. The Asian nations are showing
that evolutionary change can be as exciting as revolutionary
change. Having revolutionized the aims of their societies, they are
showing what can be achieved within a framework of dynamic
stability.

The "people," in the broadest sense, have become an entity to
be served rather than used. In much of Asia, this change represents
a revolution of no less magnitude than the revolution that created
the industrial West, or that in the years following World War II
transformed empires into new and struggling nations. It is precisely the promise of this reversal that has been at the heart of
communist rhetoric, and at the heart of the popular and intellectual appeal which that rhetoric achieved.

Not all the governments of non-communist Asia fit the Western
ideal of parliamentary democracy—far from it. But Americans
must recognize that a highly sophisticated, highly advanced political system, which required many centuries to develop in the
West, may not be best for other nations which have far different
traditions and are still in an earlier stage of development. What
matters is that these governments are consciously, deliberately

and programmatically developing in the direction of greater liberty, greater abundance, broader choice and increased popular involvement in the processes of government.

Poverty that was accepted for centuries as the norm is accepted no longer. In a sense it could be said that a new chapter is being written in the winning of the West: in this case, a winning of the promise of Western technology and Western organization by the nations of the East. The cultural clash has had its costs and produced its strains, but out of it is coming a modernization of ancient civilizations that promises to leap the centuries.

The process produces transitional anomalies—such as the Indian woman squatting in the mud, forming cow-dung patties with her hands and laying them out to dry, while a transistor radio in her lap plays music from a Delhi station. It takes a long time to bring visions of the future to the far villages—but time is needed to make those visions credible, and make them achievable. Too wide a gap between reality and expectation always produces an explosive situation, and the fact that what the leaders know is possible is unknown to the great mass of the peasantry helps buy time to make the possible achievable. But the important thing is that the leaders do know what is possible, and by and large they are determined to make it happen.

Whether that process is going to proceed at a pace fast enough to keep one step ahead of the pressure of rising expectations is one of the great questions and challenges of the years ahead. But there is solid ground for hope. The successful Asian nations have been writing extraordinary records. To call their performance an economic miracle would be something of a semantic imprecision; it would also be a disservice. Precisely because the origins and ingredients of that success are not miraculous, it offers hope to those which have not yet turned the corner.

India still is a staggering giant, Burma flirts with economic chaos, and the Philippines, caught in a conflict of cultures and in search of an identity, lives in a precarious economic and social balance. But the most exciting trends in economic development today are being recorded by those Asian nations that have accepted the keys of progress and used them. Japan, Hong Kong, Taiwan, Thailand, Korea, Singapore and Malaysia all have been recording sustained economic growth rates of 7 percent a year or more; Japan has sustained a remarkable average of 9 percent a year since 1950, and an average 16.7 percent per year increase in exports over the same period. Thailand shifted into a period of rapid growth in 1958 and has averaged 7 percent a year since. South Korea, despite the unflattering estimates of its people's abilities by the average G.I. during the Korean War, is shooting ahead at a growth rate that has averaged 8 percent a year since 1963, with an average 42 percent a year increase in its exports.

These rapidly advancing countries vary widely in their social traditions and political systems, but their methods of economic management have certain traits in common: a prime reliance on private enterprise and on the pricing mechanisms of the market as the chief determinant of business decisions; a pacing of monetary expansion to match growth in output; receptivity to private capital investment, both domestic and foreign, including such incentives as tax advantages and quick government clearance of proposed projects; imaginative national programs for dealing with social problems; and, not least, a generally restrained posture in government planning, with the government's role suggestive rather than coercive. These nations have, in short, discovered and applied the lessons of America's own economic success.

IV

Any discussion of Asia's future must ultimately focus on the respective roles of four giants: India, the world's most populous non-communist nation; Japan, Asia's principal industrial and economic power; China, the world's most populous nation and Asia's most immediate threat; and the United States, the greatest Pacific power. (Although the U.S.S.R. occupies much of the land map of Asia, its principal focus is toward the west and its vast Asian lands are an appendage of European Russia.)

India is both challenging and frustrating: challenging because of its promise, frustrating because of its performance. It suffers from escalating overpopulation, from too much emphasis on industrialization and not enough on agriculture, and from too doctrinaire a reliance on government enterprise instead of private enterprise. Many are deeply pessimistic about its future. One has to remember, however, that in the past five years India has fought two wars and faced two catastrophic droughts. On both the population and the agricultural fronts, India's present leaders at least are trying. And the essential factor, from the standpoint of U.S. policy, is that a nation of nearly half a billion people is seeking ways to wrench itself forward without a sacrifice of basic freedoms; in exceedingly difficult circumstances, the ideal of evolutionary change is being tested. For the most populous representative democracy in the world to fail, while Communist China—surmounting its troubles—succeeded, would be a disaster of worldwide proportions. Thus the United States must do two things: (1) continue its aid and support for Indian economic objectives; and (2) do its best to persuade the Indian Government to shift its means and adjust its institutions so that those objectives can be more quickly and more effectively secured, drawing from the lessons not only of the United States but also of India's more successful neighbors, including Pakistan.

Japan has been edging cautiously and discreetly toward a wider leadership role, acutely conscious at every step that bitter memories of the Greater East Asia Co-Prosperity Sphere might rise to haunt her if she pressed too hard or too eagerly. But what would not have been possible ten, or even five, years ago is becoming possible today. Half the people now living in Asia have been born since World War II, and the new generation has neither the old guilts (in the case of the Japanese themselves) nor the old fears born of conquest.

The natural momentum of Japan's growth, the industry of her people and the advanced state of her society must inevitably propel Japan into a more conspicuous position of leadership. Japan's industrial complex, expanding by 14 percent annually since 1950, already is comparable to that of West Germany or the United Kingdom. Japan's gross national product ($95 billion) is substantially greater than that of mainland China, with seven times the population. Japan is expected soon to rank as the world's third-strongest economic power, trailing only the United States and the Soviet Union. Along with this dramatic economic surge, Japan will surely want to play a greater role both diplomatically and militarily in maintaining the balance in Asia. As the Prime Minister of one neighboring country put it: "The Japanese are a great people, and no great people will accept as their destiny making better transistor radios and teaching the underdeveloped how to grow better rice."

This greater role will entail, among other things, a modification of the present terms of the Japanese Constitution, which specifically provides that "land, sea and air forces, as well as other war potential, will never be maintained." (Japan's 275,000 men presently under arms are called "Self-Defense Forces.") Twenty years ago it was considered unthinkable that Japan should acquire even a conventional military capability. Five years ago, while some Japanese thought about it, they did not talk about it. Today a substantial majority of Japanese still oppose the idea, but it is openly discussed and debated. Looking toward the future, one must recognize that it simply is not realistic to expect a nation moving into the first rank of major powers to be totally dependent for its own security on another nation, however close the ties. Japan's whole society has been restructured since World War II. While there still are traces of fanaticism, its politics at least conform to the democratic ideal. Not to trust Japan today with its own armed forces and with responsibility for its own defense would be to place its people and its government under a disability which, whatever its roots in painful recent history, ill accords with the role Japan must play in helping secure the common safety of non-communist Asia.

Any American policy toward Asia must come urgently to grips with the reality of China. This does not mean, as many would simplistically have it, rushing to grant recognition to Peking, to admit it to the United Nations and to ply it with offers of trade—all of which would serve to confirm its rulers in their present course. It does mean recognizing the present and potential danger from Communist China, and taking measures designed to meet that danger. It also means distinguishing carefully between long-range and short-range policies, and fashioning short-range programs so as to advance our long-range goals.

Taking the long view, we simply cannot afford to leave China forever outside the family of nations, there to nurture its fantasies, cherish its hates and threaten its neighbors. There is no place on this small planet for a billion of its potentially most able people to live in angry isolation. But we could go disastrously wrong if, in pursuing this long-range goal, we failed in the short range to read the lessons of history.

The world cannot be safe until China changes. Thus our aim, to the extent that we can influence events, should be to induce change. The way to do this is to persuade China that it *must* change: that it cannot satisfy its imperial ambitions, and that its own national interest requires a turning away from foreign adventuring and a turning inward toward the solution of its own domestic problems.

If the challenge posed by the Soviet Union after World War II was not precisely similar, it was sufficiently so to offer a valid precedent and a valuable lesson. Moscow finally changed when it, too, found that change was necessary. This was essentially a change of the head, not of the heart. Internal evolution played a role, to be sure, but the key factor was that the West was able to create conditions—notably in the shoring up of European defenses, the rapid restoration of European economies and the cementing of the Atlantic Alliance—that forced Moscow to look to the wisdom of reaching some measure of accommodation with the West. We are still far from reaching a full détente, but at least substantial progress has been made.

During the next decade the West faces two prospects which, together, could create a crisis of the first order: (1) that the Soviets may reach nuclear parity with the United States; and (2) that China, within three to five years, will have a significant deliverable nuclear capability—and that this same China will be outside any nonproliferation treaty that might be signed, free, if it chooses, to scatter its weapons among "liberation" forces anywhere in the world.

This heightens the urgency of building buffers that can keep the major nuclear powers apart in the case of "wars of national liberation," supported by Moscow or Peking but fought by proxy. It also requires that we now assign to the strengthening of noncommunist Asia a priority comparable to that which we gave to the strengthening of Western Europe after World War II.

Some counsel conceding to China a "sphere of influence" embracing much of the Asian mainland and extending even to the island nations beyond; others urge that we eliminate the threat by preëmptive war. Clearly, neither of these courses would be acceptable to the United States or to its Asian allies. Others argue that we should seek an anti-Chinese alliance with European powers, even including the Soviet Union. Quite apart from the obvious problems involved in Soviet participation, such a course would inevitably carry connotations of Europe vs. Asia, white vs. non-white, which could have catastrophic repercussions throughout the rest of the non-white world in general and Asia in particular. If our long-range aim is to pull China back into the family of nations, we must avoid the impression that the great powers or the European powers are "ganging up;" the response should clearly be one of active defense rather than potential offense, and must be untainted with any suspicion of racism.

For the United States to go it alone in containing China would not only place an unconscionable burden on our own country, but also would heighten the chances of nuclear war while undercutting the independent development of the nations of Asia. The primary restraint on China's Asian ambitions should be exercised by the Asian nations in the path of those ambitions, backed by the ultimate power of the United States. This is sound strategically, sound psychologically and sound in terms of the dynamics of Asian development. Only as the nations of non-communist Asia become so strong—economically, politically and militarily—that they no longer furnish tempting targets for Chinese aggression, will the leaders in Peking be persuaded to turn their energies inward rather than outward. And that will be the time when the dialogue with mainland China can begin.

For the short run, then, this means a policy of firm restraint, of no reward, of a creative counterpressure designed to persuade Peking that its interests can be served only by accepting the basic rules of international civility. For the long run, it means pulling China back into the world community—but as a great and progressing nation, not as the epicenter of world revolution.

"Containment without isolation" is a good phrase and a sound concept, as far as it goes. But it covers only half the problem. Along with it, we need a positive policy of pressure and persuasion, of dynamic detoxification, a marshaling of Asian forces both to keep the peace and to help draw off the poison from the Thoughts of Mao.

Dealing with Red China is something like trying to cope with the more explosive ghetto elements in our own country. In each case a potentially destructive force has to be curbed; in each case an outlaw element has to be brought within the law; in each case dialogues have to be opened; in each case aggression has to be restrained while education proceeds; and, not least, in neither case can we afford to let those now self-exiled from society stay exiled forever. We have to proceed with both an urgency born of necessity and a patience born of realism, moving step by calculated step toward the final goal.

v

And finally, the role of the United States.

Weary with war, disheartened with allies, disillusioned with aid, dismayed at domestic crises, many Americans are heeding the call of the new isolationism. And they are not alone; there is a tendency in the whole Western world to turn inward, to become parochial and isolationist—dangerously so. But there can be neither peace nor security a generation hence unless we recognize now the massiveness of the forces at work in Asia, where more than half the world's people live and where the greatest explosive potential is lodged.

Out of the wreckage of two world wars we forged a concept of an Atlantic community, within which a ravaged Europe was rebuilt and the westward advance of the Soviets contained. If tensions now strain that community, these are themselves a by-product of success. But history has its rhythms, and now the focus of both crisis and change is shifting. Without turning our backs on Europe, we have now to reach out westward to the East, and to fashion the sinews of a Pacific community.

This has to be a community in the fullest sense: a community of purpose, of understanding and of mutual assistance, in which military defenses are coördinated while economies are strengthened; a community embracing a concert of Asian strengths as a counterforce to the designs of China; one in which Japan will play an increasing role, as befits its commanding position as a world economic power; and one in which U.S. leadership is exercised with restraint, with respect for our partners and with a sophisticated discretion that ensures a genuinely Asian idiom and Asian origin for whatever new Asian institutions are developed.

In a design for Asia's future, there is no room for heavy-handed American pressures; there is need for subtle encouragement of the kind of Asian initiatives that help bring the design to reality. The distinction may seem superficial, but in fact it is central both to the kind of Asia we want and to the effectiveness of the means of achieving it. The central pattern of the future in U.S.–Asian relations must be American support for Asian initiatives.

The industrial revolution has shown that mass abundance is possible, and as the United States moves into the post-industrial world—the age of computers and cybernetics—we have to find ways to engineer an escape from privation for those now living in mass poverty. There can be no security, whatever our nuclear stockpiles, in a world of boiling resentment and magnified envy. The oceans provide no sanctuary for the rich, no barrier behind which we can hide our abundance.

The struggle for influence in the Third World is a three-way race among Moscow, Peking and the West. The West has offered both idealism and example, but the idealism has often been unconvincing and the example non-idiomatic. However, an industrialized Japan demonstrates the economically possible in Asian terms, while an advancing Asia tied into a Pacific community offers a bridge to the underdeveloped elsewhere. During this final third of the twentieth century, the great race will be between man and change: the race to control change, rather than be controlled by it. In this race we cannot afford to wait for others to act, and then merely react. And the race in Asia is already under way.

¶ ORIGINS OF THE COLD WAR

by Arthur Schlesinger, Jr.   (October, 1967)

"Origins of the Cold War" by Arthur Schlesinger, Jr., has been repeatedly attacked by "revisionist" historians. Apparently, they regard it as the most powerful concise analysis of a period in which they believe that American policy was deliberately aggressive, while Schlesinger, by contrast, refuses to see the cold war as arising out of either Russian aggression and American response or American aggression and Russian response.

According to Schlesinger, the basic Soviet-American conflict after World War II was between the American effort to establish a structure of universalism, as enshrined in the Atlantic Charter, the U.N. Charter, and the Moscow Declaration, and, on the other hand, the opposing Kremlin policy of creating spheres of influence, which included, of course, domination of Eastern Europe. Schlesinger traces with admirable clarity the progression of events that bred mutual suspicion, and then action and counteraction, from Hitler's attack on Russia, June 22, 1941, which made Russia an ally of the Western Allies, to Russia's refusal to join the Marshall Plan for European reconstruction, June 22, 1947. Schlesinger does not argue that the United States was at all times wise in its responses to Soviet actions, but he does not believe that even the most rational American policies would have averted the ideological and material conflict that lasted twenty years and only thereafter showed signs of dissolving.

The tone of the article is eloquent though calm, the documentation impeccable. Reprints have been in continuous demand since its publication in 1967, often for use in college history courses.

ORIGINS OF THE COLD WAR

By *Arthur Schlesinger, Jr.*

THE Cold War in its original form was a presumably mortal antagonism, arising in the wake of the Second World War, between two rigidly hostile blocs, one led by the Soviet Union, the other by the United States. For nearly two somber and dangerous decades this antagonism dominated the fears of mankind; it may even, on occasion, have come close to blowing up the planet. In recent years, however, the once implacable struggle has lost its familiar clarity of outline. With the passing of old issues and the emergence of new conflicts and contestants, there is a natural tendency, especially on the part of the generation which grew up during the Cold War, to take a fresh look at the causes of the great contention between Russia and America.

Some exercises in reappraisal have merely elaborated the orthodoxies promulgated in Washington or Moscow during the boom years of the Cold War. But others, especially in the United States (there are no signs, alas, of this in the Soviet Union), represent what American historians call "revisionism"—that is, a readiness to challenge official explanations. No one should be surprised by this phenomenon. Every war in American history has been followed in due course by skeptical reassessments of supposedly sacred assumptions. So the War of 1812, fought at the time for the freedom of the seas, was in later years ascribed to the expansionist ambitions of Congressional war hawks; so the Mexican War became a slaveholders' conspiracy. So the Civil War has been pronounced a "needless war," and Lincoln has even been accused of manœuvring the rebel attack on Fort Sumter. So too the Spanish-American War and the First and Second World Wars have, each in its turn, undergone revisionist critiques. It is not to be supposed that the Cold War would remain exempt.

In the case of the Cold War, special factors reinforce the predictable historiographical rhythm. The outburst of polycentrism in the communist empire has made people wonder whether communism was ever so monolithic as official theories of the Cold War supposed. A generation with no vivid memories of Stalinism may see the Russia of the forties in the image of the relatively mild, seedy and irresolute Russia of the sixties. And for this same

generation the American course of widening the war in Viet Nam
—which even non-revisionists can easily regard as folly—has
unquestionably stirred doubts about the wisdom of American
foreign policy in the sixties which younger historians may have
begun to read back into the forties.

It is useful to remember that, on the whole, past exercises in
revisionism have failed to stick. Few historians today believe that
the war hawks caused the War of 1812 or the slaveholders the
Mexican War, or that the Civil War was needless, or that the
House of Morgan brought America into the First World War or
that Franklin Roosevelt schemed to produce the attack on Pearl
Harbor. But this does not mean that one should deplore the rise
of Cold War revisionism.[1] For revisionism is an essential part of
the process by which history, through the posing of new problems
and the investigation of new possibilities, enlarges its perspectives
and enriches its insights.

More than this, in the present context, revisionism expresses a
deep, legitimate and tragic apprehension. As the Cold War has
begun to lose its purity of definition, as the moral absolutes of the
fifties become the moralistic clichés of the sixties, some have begun to ask whether the appalling risks which humanity ran during
the Cold War were, after all, necessary and inevitable; whether
more restrained and rational policies might not have guided the
energies of man from the perils of conflict into the potentialities
of collaboration. The fact that such questions are in their nature
unanswerable does not mean that it is not right and useful to
raise them. Nor does it mean that our sons and daughters are not
entitled to an accounting from the generation of Russians and
Americans who produced the Cold War.

II

The orthodox American view, as originally set forth by the
American government and as reaffirmed until recently by most
American scholars, has been that the Cold War was the brave
and essential response of free men to communist aggression. Some
have gone back well before the Second World War to lay open
the sources of Russian expansionism. Geopoliticians traced the
Cold War to imperial Russian strategic ambitions which in the
nineteenth century led to the Crimean War, to Russian penetra-

---

[1] As this writer somewhat intemperately did in a letter to *The New York Review of Books,*
October 20, 1966.

tion of the Balkans and the Middle East and to Russian pressure on Britain's "lifeline" to India. Ideologists traced it to the Communist Manifesto of 1848 ("the violent overthrow of the bourgeoisie lays the foundation for the sway of the proletariat"). Thoughtful observers (a phrase meant to exclude those who speak in Dullese about the unlimited evil of godless, atheistic, militant communism) concluded that classical Russian imperialism and Pan-Slavism, compounded after 1917 by Leninist messianism, confronted the West at the end of the Second World War with an inexorable drive for domination.[2]

The revisionist thesis is very different.[3] In its extreme form, it is that, after the death of Franklin Roosevelt and the end of the

[2] Every student of the Cold War must acknowledge his debt to W. H. McNeill's remarkable account, "America, Britain and Russia: Their Cooperation and Conflict, 1941-1946" (New York, 1953) and to the brilliant and indispensable series by Herbert Feis: "Churchill, Roosevelt, Stalin: The War They Waged and the Peace They Sought" (Princeton, 1957); "Between War and Peace: The Potsdam Conference" (Princeton, 1960); and "The Atomic Bomb and the End of World War II" (Princeton, 1966). Useful recent analyses include André Fontaine, "Histoire de la Guerre Froide" (2 v., Paris, 1965, 1967); N. A. Graebner, "Cold War Diplomacy, 1945-1960" (Princeton, 1962); L. J. Halle, "The Cold War as History" (London, 1967); M. F. Herz, "Beginnings of the Cold War" (Bloomington, 1966) and W. L. Neumann, "After Victory: Churchill, Roosevelt, Stalin and the Making of the Peace" (New York, 1967).

[3] The fullest statement of this case is to be found in D. F. Fleming's voluminous "The Cold War and Its Origins" (New York, 1961). For a shorter version of this argument, see David Horowitz, "The Free World Colossus" (New York, 1965); the most subtle and ingenious statements come in W. A. Williams' "The Tragedy of American Diplomacy" (rev. ed., New York, 1962) and in Gar Alperowitz's "Atomic Diplomacy: Hiroshima and Potsdam" (New York, 1965) and in subsequent articles and reviews by Mr. Alperowitz in *The New York Review of Books*. The fact that in some aspects the revisionist thesis parallels the official Soviet argument must not, of course, prevent consideration of the case on its merits, nor raise questions about the motives of the writers, all of whom, so far as I know, are independent-minded scholars.

I might further add that all these books, in spite of their ostentatious display of scholarly apparatus, must be used with caution. Professor Fleming, for example, relies heavily on newspaper articles and even columnists. While Mr. Alperowitz bases his case on official documents or authoritative reminiscences, he sometimes twists his material in a most unscholarly way. For example, in describing Ambassador Harriman's talk with President Truman on April 20, 1945, Mr. Alperowitz writes, "He argued that a reconsideration of Roosevelt's policy was necessary" (p. 22, repeated on p. 24). The citation is to p. 70-72 in President Truman's "Years of Decision." What President Truman reported Harriman as saying was the exact opposite: "Before leaving, Harriman took me aside and said, 'Frankly, one of the reasons that made me rush back to Washington was the fear that you did not understand, as I had seen Roosevelt understand, that Stalin is breaking his agreements.'" Similarly, in an appendix (p. 271) Mr. Alperowitz writes that the Hopkins and Davies missions of May 1945 "were opposed by the 'firm' advisers." Actually the Hopkins mission was proposed by Harriman and Charles E. Bohlen, who Mr. Alperowitz elsewhere suggests were the firmest of the firm—and was proposed by them precisely to impress on Stalin the continuity of American policy from Roosevelt to Truman. While the idea that Truman reversed Roosevelt's policy is tempting dramatically, it is a myth. See, for example, the testimony of Anna Rosenberg Hoffman, who lunched with Roosevelt on March 24, 1945, the last day he spent in Washington. After luncheon, Roosevelt was handed a cable. "He read it and became quite angry. He banged his fists on the arms of his wheelchair and said, 'Averell is right; we can't do business with Stalin. He has broken every one of the promises he made at Yalta.' He was very upset and continued in the same vein on the subject."

Second World War, the United States deliberately abandoned the wartime policy of collaboration and, exhilarated by the possession of the atomic bomb, undertook a course of aggression of its own designed to expel all Russian influence from Eastern Europe and to establish democratic-capitalist states on the very border of the Soviet Union. As the revisionists see it, this radically new American policy—or rather this resumption by Truman of the pre-Roosevelt policy of insensate anti-communism—left Moscow no alternative but to take measures in defense of its own borders. The result was the Cold War.

These two views, of course, could not be more starkly contrasting. It is therefore not unreasonable to look again at the half-dozen critical years between June 22, 1941, when Hitler attacked Russia, and July 2, 1947, when the Russians walked out of the Marshall Plan meeting in Paris. Several things should be borne in mind as this reëxamination is made. For one thing, we have thought a great deal more in recent years, in part because of writers like Roberta Wohlstetter and T. C. Schelling, about the problems of communication in diplomacy—the signals which one nation, by word or by deed, gives, inadvertently or intentionally, to another. Any honest reappraisal of the origins of the Cold War requires the imaginative leap—which should in any case be as instinctive for the historian as it is prudent for the statesman—into the adversary's viewpoint. We must strive to see how, given Soviet perspectives, the Russians might conceivably have misread our signals, as we must reconsider how intelligently we read theirs.

For another, the historian must not overindulge the man of power in the illusion cherished by those in office that high position carries with it the easy ability to shape history. Violating the statesman's creed, Lincoln once blurted out the truth in his letter of 1864 to A. G. Hodges: "I claim not to have controlled events, but confess plainly that events have controlled me." He was not asserting Tolstoyan fatalism but rather suggesting how greatly events limit the capacity of the statesman to bend history to his will. The physical course of the Second World War—the military operations undertaken, the position of the respective armies at the war's end, the momentum generated by victory and the vacuums created by defeat—all these determined the future as much as the character of individual leaders and the substance of national ideology and purpose.

Nor can the historian forget the conditions under which decisions are made, especially in a time like the Second World War. These were tired, overworked, aging men: in 1945, Churchill was 71 years old, Stalin had governed his country for 17 exacting years, Roosevelt his for 12 years nearly as exacting. During the war, moreover, the importunities of military operations had shoved postwar questions to the margins of their minds. All— even Stalin, behind his screen of ideology—had became addicts of improvisation, relying on authority and virtuosity to conceal the fact that they were constantly surprised by developments. Like Eliza, they leaped from one cake of ice to the next in the effort to reach the other side of the river. None showed great tactical consistency, or cared much about it; all employed a certain ambiguity to preserve their power to decide big issues; and it is hard to know how to interpret anything any one of them said on any specific occasion. This was partly because, like all princes, they designed their expressions to have particular effects on particular audiences; partly because the entirely genuine intellectual difficulty of the questions they faced made a degree of vacillation and mind-changing eminently reasonable. If historians cannot solve their problems in retrospect, who are they to blame Roosevelt, Stalin and Churchill for not having solved them at the time?

III

Peacemaking after the Second World War was not so much a tapestry as it was a hopelessly raveled and knotted mess of yarn. Yet, for purposes of clarity, it is essential to follow certain threads. One theme indispensable to an understanding of the Cold War is the contrast between two clashing views of world order: the "universalist" view, by which all nations shared a common interest in all the affairs of the world, and the "sphere-of-influence" view, by which each great power would be assured by the other great powers of an acknowledged predominance in its own area of special interest. The universalist view assumed that national security would be guaranteed by an international organization. The sphere-of-interest view assumed that national security would be guaranteed by the balance of power. While in practice these views have by no means been incompatible (indeed, our shaky peace has been based on a combination of the two), in the abstract they involved sharp contradictions.

The tradition of American thought in these matters was universalist—*i.e.* Wilsonian. Roosevelt had been a member of Wilson's subcabinet; in 1920, as candidate for Vice President, he had campaigned for the League of Nations. It is true that, within Roosevelt's infinitely complex mind, Wilsonianism warred with the perception of vital strategic interests he had imbibed from Mahan. Morever, his temperamental inclination to settle things with fellow princes around the conference table led him to regard the Big Three—or Four—as trustees for the rest of the world. On occasion, as this narrative will show, he was beguiled into flirtation with the sphere-of-influence heresy. But in principle he believed in joint action and remained a Wilsonian. His hope for Yalta, as he told the Congress on his return, was that it would "spell the end of the system of unilateral action, the exclusive alliances, the spheres of influence, the balances of power, and all the other expedients that have been tried for centuries—and have always failed."

Whenever Roosevelt backslid, he had at his side that Wilsonian fundamentalist, Secretary of State Cordell Hull, to recall him to the pure faith. After his visit to Moscow in 1943, Hull characteristically said that, with the Declaration of Four Nations on General Security (in which America, Russia, Britain and China pledged "united action . . . for the organization and maintenance of peace and security"), "there will no longer be need for spheres of influence, for alliances, for balance of power, or any other of the special arrangements through which, in the unhappy past, the nations strove to safeguard their security or to promote their interests."

Remembering the corruption of the Wilsonian vision by the secret treaties of the First World War, Hull was determined to prevent any sphere-of-influence nonsense after the Second World War. He therefore fought all proposals to settle border questions while the war was still on and, excluded as he largely was from wartime diplomacy, poured his not inconsiderable moral energy and frustration into the promulgation of virtuous and spacious general principles.

In adopting the universalist view, Roosevelt and Hull were not indulging personal hobbies. Sumner Welles, Adolf Berle, Averell Harriman, Charles Bohlen—all, if with a variety of nuances, opposed the sphere-of-influence approach. And here the State Department was expressing what seems clearly to have been the predominant mood of the American people, so long mistrustful of European power politics. The Republicans shared the true faith. John Foster Dulles argued that the great threat to peace after the war would lie in the revival of sphere-of-influence thinking. The United States, he said, must not permit Britain and Russia to revert to these bad old ways; it must therefore insist on American participation in all policy decisions for all territories in the world. Dulles wrote pessimistically in January 1945, "The three great powers which at Moscow agreed upon the 'closest coöperation' about European questions have shifted to a practice of separate, regional responsibility."

It is true that critics, and even friends, of the United States sometimes noted a discrepancy between the American passion for universalism when it applied to territory far from American shores and the preëminence the United States accorded its own interests nearer home. Churchill, seeking Washington's blessing for a sphere-of-influence initiative in Eastern Europe, could not forbear reminding the Americans, "We follow the lead of the United States in South America;" nor did any universalist of record propose the abolition of the Monroe Doctrine. But a convenient myopia prevented such inconsistencies from qualifying the ardency of the universalist faith.

There seem only to have been three officials in the United States Government who dissented. One was the Secretary of War, Henry L. Stimson, a classical balance-of-power man, who in 1944 opposed the creation of a vacuum in Central Europe by the pastoralization of Germany and in 1945 urged "the settlement of all territorial acquisitions in the shape of defense posts which each of these four powers may deem to be necessary for their own safety" in advance of any effort to establish a peacetime United Nations. Stimson considered the claim of Russia to a preferred position in Eastern Europe as not unreasonable: as he told President Truman, "he thought the Russians perhaps were being more realistic than we were in regard to their own security." Such a position for Russia seemed to him comparable to the preferred American position in Latin America; he even spoke of "our respective orbits." Stimson was therefore skeptical of what he regarded as the prevailing tendency "to hang on to exaggerated views of the Monroe Doctrine and at the same time butt into every question that comes up in Central Europe." Acceptance of spheres of influence seemed to him the way to avoid "a head-on collision."

A second official opponent of universalism was George Kennan, an eloquent advocate from the American Embassy in Moscow of "a prompt and clear recognition of the division of Europe into spheres of influence and of a policy based on the fact of such division." Kennan argued that nothing we could do would possibly alter the course of events in Eastern Europe; that we were deceiving ourselves by supposing that these countries had any future but Russian domination; that we should therefore relinquish Eastern Europe to the Soviet Union and avoid anything which would make things easier for the Russians by giving them economic assistance or by sharing moral responsibility for their actions.

A third voice within the government against universalism was (at least after the war) Henry A. Wallace. As Secretary of Commerce, he stated the sphere-of-influence case with trenchancy in the famous Madison Square Garden speech of September 1946 which led to his dismissal by President Truman:

On our part, we should recognize that we have no more business in the *political* affairs of Eastern Europe than Russia has in the *political* affairs of Latin America, Western Europe, and the United States. . . . Whether we like it or not, the Russians will try to socialize their sphere of influence just as we try to democratize our sphere of influence. . . . The Russians have no more business stirring up native Communists to political activity in Western Europe, Latin America, and the United States than we have in interfering with the politics of Eastern Europe and Russia.

Stimson, Kennan and Wallace seem to have been alone in the government, however, in taking these views. They were very much minority voices. Meanwhile universalism, rooted in the American legal and moral tradition, overwhelmingly backed by contemporary opinion, received successive enshrinements in the Atlantic Charter of 1941, in the Declaration of the United Nations in 1942 and in the Moscow Declaration of 1943.

IV

The Kremlin, on the other hand, thought *only* of spheres of interest; above all, the Russians were determined to protect their frontiers, and especially their border to the west, crossed so often and so bloodily in the dark course of their history. These western frontiers lacked natural means of defense—no great oceans, rugged mountains, steaming swamps or impenetrable jungles. The history of Russia had been the history of invasion, the last of which was by now horribly killing up to twenty million of its people. The protocol of Russia therefore meant the enlargement of the area of Russian influence. Kennan himself wrote (in May 1944), "Behind Russia's stubborn expansion lies only the age-old sense of insecurity of a sedentary people reared on an exposed plain in the neighborhood of fierce nomadic peoples," and he called this "urge" a "permanent feature of Russian psychology."

In earlier times the "urge" had produced the tsarist search for buffer states and maritime outlets. In 1939 the Soviet-Nazi pact and its secret protocol had enabled Russia to begin to satisfy in the Baltic states, Karelian Finland and Poland, part of what it conceived as its security requirements in Eastern Europe. But the "urge" persisted, causing the friction between Russia and Germany in 1940 as each jostled for position in the area which separated them. Later it led to Molotov's new demands on Hitler in November 1940—a free hand in Finland, Soviet predominance in Rumania and Bulgaria, bases in the Dardanelles—the demands which convinced Hitler that he had no choice but to attack Russia. Now Stalin hoped to gain from the West what Hitler, a closer neighbor, had not dared yield him.

It is true that, so long as Russian survival appeared to require a second front to relieve the Nazi pressure, Moscow's demand for Eastern Europe was a little muffled. Thus the Soviet government adhered to the Atlantic Charter (though with a significant if obscure reservation about adapting its principles to "the circumstances, needs, and historic peculiarities of particular countries"). Thus it also adhered to the Moscow Declaration of 1943, and Molotov then, with his easy mendacity, even denied that Russia had any desire to divide Europe into spheres of influence. But this was guff, which the Russians were perfectly willing to ladle out if it would keep the Americans, and especially Secretary Hull (who made a strong personal impression at the Moscow conference) happy. "A declaration," as Stalin once observed to Eden, "I regard as algebra, but an agreement as practical arithmetic. I do not wish to decry algebra, but I prefer practical arithmetic."

The more consistent Russian purpose was revealed when Stalin offered the British a straight sphere-of-influence deal at the end of 1941. Britain, he suggested, should recognize the Russian absorption of the Baltic states, part of Finland, eastern Poland and Bessarabia; in return, Russia would support any special British need for bases or security arrangements in Western Europe. There was nothing specifically communist about these ambitions.

If Stalin achieved them, he would be fulfilling an age-old dream of the tsars. The British reaction was mixed. "Soviet policy is amoral," as Anthony Eden noted at the time; "United States policy is exaggeratedly moral, at least where non-American interests are concerned." If Roosevelt was a universalist with occasional leanings toward spheres of influence and Stalin was a sphere-of-influence man with occasional gestures toward universalism, Churchill seemed evenly poised between the familiar realism of the balance of power, which he had so long recorded as an historian and manipulated as a statesman, and the hope that there must be some better way of doing things. His 1943 proposal of a world organization divided into regional councils represented an effort to blend universalist and sphere-of-interest conceptions. His initial rejection of Stalin's proposal in December 1941 as "directly contrary to the first, second and third articles of the Atlantic Charter" thus did not spring entirely from a desire to propitiate the United States. On the other hand, he had himself already reinterpreted the Atlantic Charter as applying only to Europe (and thus not to the British Empire), and he was, above all, an empiricist who never believed in sacrificing reality on the altar of doctrine.

So in April 1942 he wrote Roosevelt that "the increasing gravity of the war" had led him to feel that the Charter "ought not to be construed so as to deny Russia the frontiers she occupied when Germany attacked her." Hull, however, remained fiercely hostile to the inclusion of territorial provisions in the Anglo-Russian treaty; the American position, Eden noted, "chilled me with Wilsonian memories." Though Stalin complained that it looked "as if the Atlantic Charter was directed against the U.S.S.R.," it was the Russian season of military adversity in the spring of 1942, and he dropped his demands.

He did not, however, change his intentions. A year later Ambassador Standley could cable Washington from Moscow: "In 1918 Western Europe attempted to set up a *cordon sanitaire* to protect it from the influence of bolshevism. Might not now the Kremlin envisage the formation of a belt of pro-Soviet states to protect it from the influences of the West?" It well might; and that purpose became increasingly clear as the war approached its end. Indeed, it derived sustenance from Western policy in the first area of liberation.

The unconditional surrender of Italy in July 1943 created the first major test of the Western devotion to universalism. America and Britain, having won the Italian war, handled the capitulation, keeping Moscow informed at a distance. Stalin complained:

The United States and Great Britain made agreements but the Soviet Union received information about the results . . . just as a passive third observer. I have to tell you that it is impossible to tolerate the situation any longer. I propose that the [tripartite military-political commission] be established and that Sicily be assigned . . . as its place of residence.

Roosevelt, who had no intention of sharing the control of Italy with the Russians, suavely replied with the suggestion that Stalin send an officer "to General Eisenhower's headquarters in connection with the commission." Unimpressed, Stalin continued to press for a tripartite body; but his Western allies were adamant in keeping the Soviet Union off the Control Commission for Italy, and the Russians in the end had to be satisfied with a seat, along with minor Allied states, on a meaningless Inter-Allied Advisory Council. Their acquiescence in this was doubtless not unconnected with a desire to establish precedents for Eastern Europe.

Teheran in December 1943 marked the high point of three-power collaboration. Still, when Churchill asked about Russian territorial interests, Stalin replied a little ominously, "There is no need to speak at the present time about any Soviet desires, but when the time comes we will speak." In the next weeks, there were increasing indications of a Soviet determination to deal unilaterally with Eastern Europe—so much so that in early February 1944 Hull cabled Harriman in Moscow:

Matters are rapidly approaching the point where the Soviet Government will have to choose between the development and extension of the foundation of international cooperation as the guiding principle of the postwar world as against the continuance of a unilateral and arbitrary method of dealing with its special problems even though these problems are admittedly of more direct interest to the Soviet Union than to other great powers.

As against this approach, however, Churchill, more tolerant of sphere-of-influence deviations, soon proposed that, with the impending liberation of the Balkans, Russia should run things in Rumania and Britain in Greece. Hull strongly opposed this suggestion but made the mistake of leaving Washington for a few days; and Roosevelt, momentarily free from his Wilsonian conscience, yielded to Churchill's plea for a three-months' trial. Hull resumed the fight on his return, and Churchill postponed the matter.

The Red Army continued its advance into Eastern Europe. In August the Polish Home Army, urged on by Polish-language broadcasts from Moscow, rose up against the Nazis in Warsaw. For 63 terrible days, the Poles fought valiantly on, while the Red Army halted on the banks of the Vistula a few miles away, and in Moscow Stalin for more than half this time declined to coöperate with the Western effort to drop supplies to the Warsaw Resistance. It appeared a calculated Soviet decision to let the Nazis slaughter the anti-Soviet Polish underground; and, indeed, the result was to destroy any substantial alternative to a Soviet solution in Poland. The agony of Warsaw caused the most deep and genuine moral shock in Britain and America and provoked dark forebodings about Soviet postwar purposes.

Again history enjoins the imaginative leap in order to see things for a moment from Moscow's viewpoint. The Polish question, Churchill would say at Yalta, was for Britain a question of honor. "It is not only a question of honor for Russia," Stalin replied, "but one of life and death. . . . Throughout history Poland had been the corridor for attack on Russia." A top postwar priority for any Russian régime must be to close that corridor. The Home Army was led by anti-communists. It clearly hoped by its action to forestall the Soviet occupation of Warsaw and, in Russian eyes, to prepare the way for an anti-Russian Poland. In addition, the uprising from a strictly operational viewpoint was premature. The Russians, it is evident in retrospect, had real military problems at the Vistula. The Soviet attempt in September to send Polish units from the Red Army across the river to join forces with the Home Army was a disaster. Heavy German shelling thereafter prevented the ferrying of tanks necessary for an assault on the German position. The Red Army itself did not take Warsaw for another three months. None the less, Stalin's indifference to the human tragedy, his effort to blackmail the London Poles during the ordeal, his sanctimonious opposition during five precious weeks to aerial resupply, the invariable coldness of his explanations ("the Soviet command has come to the conclusion that it must dissociate itself from the Warsaw adventure") and the obvious political benefit to the Soviet Union from the destruction of the Home Army—all these had the effect of suddenly dropping the mask of wartime comradeship and displaying to the West the hard face of Soviet policy. In now pursuing what he grimly regarded as the minimal requirements for the postwar security of

his country, Stalin was inadvertently showing the irreconcil-
ability of both his means and his ends with the Anglo-American
conception of the peace.

Meanwhile Eastern Europe presented the Alliance with still
another crisis that same September. Bulgaria, which was not at
war with Russia, decided to surrender to the Western Allies while
it still could; and the English and Americans at Cairo began to
discuss armistice terms with Bulgarian envoys. Moscow, challenged by what it plainly saw as a Western intrusion into its own
zone of vital interest, promptly declared war on Bulgaria, took
over the surrender negotiations and, invoking the Italian precedent, denied its Western Allies any role in the Bulgarian Control
Commission. In a long and thoughtful cable, Ambassador Harriman meditated on the problems of communication with the
Soviet Union. "Words," he reflected, "have a different connotation to the Soviets than they have to us. When they speak of
insisting on 'friendly governments' in their neighboring countries,
they have in mind something quite different from what we would
mean." The Russians, he surmised, really believed that Washington accepted "their position that although they would keep us
informed they had the right to settle their problems with their
western neighbors unilaterally." But the Soviet position was still
in flux: "the Soviet Government is not one mind." The problem,
as Harriman had earlier told Harry Hopkins, was "to strengthen
the hands of those around Stalin who want to play the game along
our lines." The way to do this, he now told Hull, was to

> be understanding of their sensitivity, meet them much more than half way,
> encourage them and support them wherever we can, and yet oppose them
> promptly with the greatest of firmness where we see them going wrong. . . .
> The only way we can eventually come to an understanding with the Soviet
> Union on the question of non-interference in the internal affairs of other
> countries is for us to take a definite interest in the solution of the problems
> of each individual country as they arise.

As against Harriman's sophisticated universalist strategy,
however, Churchill, increasingly fearful of the consequences of
unrestrained competition in Eastern Europe, decided in early
October to carry his sphere-of-influence proposal directly to
Moscow. Roosevelt was at first content to have Churchill speak
for him too and even prepared a cable to that effect. But Hopkins,
a more rigorous universalist, took it upon himself to stop the cable
and warn Roosevelt of its possible implications. Eventually

Roosevelt sent a message to Harriman in Moscow emphasizing that he expected to "retain complete freedom of action after this conference is over." It was now that Churchill quickly proposed —and Stalin as quickly accepted—the celebrated division of southeastern Europe: ending (after further haggling between Eden and Molotov) with 90 percent Soviet predominance in Rumania, 80 percent in Bulgaria and Hungary, fifty-fifty in Jugoslavia, 90 percent British predominance in Greece.

Churchill in discussing this with Harriman used the phrase "spheres of influence." But he insisted that these were only "immediate wartime arrangements" and received a highly general blessing from Roosevelt. Yet, whatever Churchill intended, there is reason to believe that Stalin construed the percentages as an agreement, not a declaration; as practical arithmetic, not algebra. For Stalin, it should be understood, the sphere-of-influence idea did not mean that he would abandon all efforts to spread communism in some other nation's sphere; it did mean that, if he tried this and the other side cracked down, he could not feel he had serious cause for complaint. As Kennan wrote to Harriman at the end of 1944:

As far as border states are concerned the Soviet government has never ceased to think in terms of spheres of interest. They expect us to support them in whatever action they wish to take in those regions, regardless of whether that action seems to us or to the rest of the world to be right or wrong. . . . I have no doubt that this position is honestly maintained on their part, and that they would be equally prepared to reserve moral judgment on any actions which we might wish to carry out, i.e., in the Caribbean area.

In any case, the matter was already under test a good deal closer to Moscow than the Caribbean. The communist-dominated resistance movement in Greece was in open revolt against the effort of the Papandreou government to disarm and disband the guerrillas (the same Papandreou whom the Greek colonels have recently arrested on the claim that he is a tool of the communists). Churchill now called in British Army units to crush the insurrection. This action produced a storm of criticism in his own country and in the United States; the American Government even publicly dissociated itself from the intervention, thereby emphasizing its detachment from the sphere-of-influence deal. But Stalin, Churchill later claimed, "adhered strictly and faithfully to our agreement of October, and during all the long weeks of fighting the Communists in the streets of Athens not one word of reproach came from *Pravda* or *Izvestia*," though there is no evidence that he tried to call off the Greek communists. Still, when the communist rebellion later broke out again in Greece, Stalin told Kardelj and Djilas of Jugoslavia in 1948, "The uprising in Greece must be stopped, and as quickly as possible."

No one, of course, can know what really was in the minds of the Russian leaders. The Kremlin archives are locked; of the primary actors, only Molotov survives, and he has not yet indicated any desire to collaborate with the Columbia Oral History Project. We do know that Stalin did not wholly surrender to sentimental illusion about his new friends. In June 1944, on the night before the landings in Normandy, he told Djilas that the English "find nothing sweeter than to trick their allies. . . . And Churchill? Churchill is the kind who, if you don't watch him, will slip a kopeck out of your pocket. Yes, a kopeck out of your pocket! . . . Roosevelt is not like that. He dips in his hand only for bigger coins." But whatever his views of his colleagues it is not unreasonable to suppose that Stalin would have been satisfied at the end of the war to secure what Kennan has called "a protective glacis along Russia's western border," and that, in exchange for a free hand in Eastern Europe, he was prepared to give the British and Americans equally free hands in their zones of vital interest, including in nations as close to Russia as Greece (for the British) and, very probably—or at least so the Jugoslavs believe—China (for the United States). In other words, his initial objectives were very probably not world conquest but Russian security.

V

It is now pertinent to inquire why the United States rejected the idea of stabilizing the world by division into spheres of influence and insisted on an East European strategy. One should warn against rushing to the conclusion that it was all a row between hard-nosed, balance-of-power realists and starry-eyed Wilsonians. Roosevelt, Hopkins, Welles, Harriman, Bohlen, Berle, Dulles and other universalists were tough and serious men. Why then did they rebuff the sphere-of-influence solution?

The first reason is that they regarded this solution as containing within itself the seeds of a third world war. The balance-of-power idea seemed inherently unstable. It had always broken down in the past. It held out to each power the permanent temptation to try to alter the balance in its own favor, and it built this temptation into the international order. It would turn the great powers of 1945 away from the objective of concerting common policies toward competition for postwar advantage. As Hopkins told Molotov at Teheran, "The President feels it essential to world peace that Russia, Great Britain and the United States work out this control question in a manner which will not start each of the three powers arming against the others." "The greatest likelihood of eventual conflict," said the Joint Chiefs of Staff in 1944 (the only conflict which the J.C.S., in its wisdom, could then glimpse "in the foreseeable future" was between Britain and Russia), "... would seem to grow out of either nation initiating attempts to build up its strength, by seeking to attach to herself parts of Europe to the disadvantage and possible danger of her potential adversary." The Americans were perfectly ready to acknowledge that Russia was entitled to convincing assurance of her national security—but not this way. "I could sympathize fully with Stalin's desire to protect his western borders from future attack," as Hull put it. "But I felt that this security could best be obtained through a strong postwar peace organization."

Hull's remark suggests the second objection: that the sphere-of-influence approach would, in the words of the State Department in 1945, "militate against the establishment and effective functioning of a broader system of general security in which all countries will have their part." The United Nations, in short, was seen as the alternative to the balance of power. Nor did the universalists see any necessary incompatibility between the Russian desire for "friendly governments" on its frontier and the American desire for self-determination in Eastern Europe. Before Yalta the State Department judged the general mood of Europe as "to the left and strongly in favor of far-reaching economic and social reforms, but not, however, in favor of a left-wing totalitarian regime to achieve these reforms." Governments in Eastern Europe could be sufficiently to the left "to allay Soviet suspicions" but sufficiently representative "of the center and *petit bourgeois* elements" not to seem a prelude to communist dictatorship. The American criteria were therefore that the government "should be dedicated to the preservation of civil liberties" and "should favor social and economic reforms." A string of New Deal states —of Finlands and Czechoslovakias—seemed a reasonable compromise solution.

Third, the universalists feared that the sphere-of-interest approach would be what Hull termed "a haven for the isolationists," who would advocate America's participation in Western Hemisphere affairs on condition that it did not participate in European or Asian affairs. Hull also feared that spheres of interest would lead to "closed trade areas or discriminatory systems" and thus defeat his cherished dream of a low-tariff, freely trading world.

Fourth, the sphere-of-interest solution meant the betrayal of the principles for which the Second World War was being fought —the Atlantic Charter, the Four Freedoms, the Declaration of the United Nations. Poland summed up the problem. Britain, having gone to war to defend the independence of Poland from the Germans, could not easily conclude the war by surrendering the independence of Poland to the Russians. Thus, as Hopkins told Stalin after Roosevelt's death in 1945, Poland had "become the symbol of our ability to work out problems with the Soviet Union." Nor could American liberals in general watch with equanimity while the police state spread into countries which, if they had mostly not been real democracies, had mostly not been tyrannies either. The execution in 1943 of Ehrlich and Alter, the Polish socialist trade union leaders, excited deep concern. "I have particularly in mind," Harriman cabled in 1944, "objection to the institution of secret police who may become involved in the persecution of persons of truly democratic convictions who may not be willing to conform to Soviet methods."

Fifth, the sphere-of-influence solution would create difficult domestic problems in American politics. Roosevelt was aware of the six million or more Polish votes in the 1944 election; even more acutely, he was aware of the broader and deeper attack which would follow if, after going to war to stop the Nazi conquest of Europe, he permitted the war to end with the communist conquest of Eastern Europe. As Archibald MacLeish, then Assistant Secretary of State for Public Affairs, warned in January 1945, "The wave of disillusionment which has distressed us in the last several weeks will be increased if the impression is permitted to get abroad that potentially totalitarian provisional governments are to be set up without adequate safeguards as to the holding of free elections and the realization of the principles of the Atlantic Charter." Roosevelt believed that no administration could survive which did not try everything short of war to save Eastern Europe, and he was the supreme American politician of the century.

Sixth, if the Russians were allowed to overrun Eastern Europe without argument, would that satisfy them? Even Kennan, in a dispatch of May 1944, admitted that the "urge" had dreadful potentialities: "If initially successful, will it know where to stop? Will it not be inexorably carried forward, by its very nature, in a struggle to reach the whole—to attain complete mastery of the shores of the Atlantic and the Pacific?" His own answer was that there were inherent limits to the Russian capacity to expand— "that Russia will not have an easy time in maintaining the power which it has seized over other people in Eastern and Central Europe unless it receives both moral and material assistance from the West." Subsequent developments have vindicated Kennan's argument. By the late forties, Jugoslavia and Albania, the two East European states farthest from the Soviet Union and the two in which communism was imposed from within rather than from without, had declared their independence of Moscow. But, given Russia's success in maintaining centralized control over the international communist movement for a quarter of a century, who in 1944 could have had much confidence in the idea of communist revolts against Moscow?

Most of those involved therefore rejected Kennan's answer and stayed with his question. If the West turned its back on Eastern Europe, the higher probability, in their view, was that the Russians would use their security zone, not just for defensive purposes, but as a springboard from which to mount an attack on Western Europe, now shattered by war, a vacuum of power awaiting its master. "If the policy is accepted that the Soviet Union has a right to penetrate her immediate neighbors for security," Harriman said in 1944, "penetration of the next immediate neighbors becomes at a certain time equally logical." If a row with Russia were inevitable, every consideration of prudence dictated that it should take place in Eastern rather than Western Europe.

Thus idealism and realism joined in opposition to the sphere-of-influence solution. The consequence was a determination to assert an American interest in the postwar destiny of all nations, including those of Eastern Europe. In the message which Roosevelt and Hopkins drafted after Hopkins had stopped Roosevelt's initial cable authorizing Churchill to speak for the United States at the Moscow meeting of October 1944, Roosevelt now said, "There is in this global war literally no question, either military or political, in which the United States is not interested." After

Roosevelt's death Hopkins repeated the point to Stalin: "The cardinal basis of President Roosevelt's policy which the American people had fully supported had been the concept that the interests of the U.S. were worldwide and not confined to North and South America and the Pacific Ocean."

VI

For better or worse, this was the American position. It is now necessary to attempt the imaginative leap and consider the impact of this position on the leaders of the Soviet Union who, also for better or for worse, had reached the bitter conclusion that the survival of their country depended on their unchallenged control of the corridors through which enemies had so often invaded their homeland. They could claim to have been keeping their own side of the sphere-of-influence bargain. Of course, they were working to capture the resistance movements of Western Europe; indeed, with the appointment of Oumansky as Ambassador to Mexico they were even beginning to enlarge underground operations in the Western Hemisphere. But, from their viewpoint, if the West permitted this, the more fools they; and, if the West stopped it, it was within their right to do so. In overt political matters the Russians were scrupulously playing the game. They had watched in silence while the British shot down communists in Greece. In Jugoslavia Stalin was urging Tito (as Djilas later revealed) to keep King Peter. They had not only acknowledged Western preëminence in Italy but had recognized the Badoglio régime; the Italian Communists had even voted (against the Socialists and the Liberals) for the renewal of the Lateran Pacts.

They would not regard anti-communist action in a Western zone as a *casus belli;* and they expected reciprocal license to assert their own authority in the East. But the principle of self-determination was carrying the United States into a deeper entanglement in Eastern Europe than the Soviet Union claimed as a right (whatever it was doing underground) in the affairs of Italy, Greece or China. When the Russians now exercised in Eastern Europe the same brutal control they were prepared to have Washington exercise in the American sphere of influence, the American protests, given the paranoia produced alike by Russian history and Leninist ideology, no doubt seemed not only an act of hypocrisy but a threat to security. To the Russians, a stroll into the neighborhood easily became a plot to burn down the house:

when, for example, damaged American planes made emergency landings in Poland and Hungary, Moscow took this as attempts to organize the local resistance. It is not unusual to suspect one's adversary of doing what one is already doing oneself. At the same time, the cruelty with which the Russians executed their idea of spheres of influence—in a sense, perhaps, an unwitting cruelty, since Stalin treated the East Europeans no worse than he had treated the Russians in the thirties—discouraged the West from accepting the equation (for example, Italy = Rumania) which seemed so self-evident to the Kremlin.

So Moscow very probably, and not unnaturally, perceived the emphasis on self-determination as a systematic and deliberate pressure on Russia's western frontiers. Moreover, the restoration of capitalism to countries freed at frightful cost by the Red Army no doubt struck the Russians as the betrayal of the principles for which *they* were fighting. "That they, the victors," Isaac Deutscher has suggested, "should now preserve an order from which they had experienced nothing but hostility, and could expect nothing but hostility . . . would have been the most miserable anti-climax to their great 'war of liberation.'" By 1944 Poland was the critical issue; Harriman later said that "under instructions from President Roosevelt, I talked about Poland with Stalin more frequently than any other subject." While the West saw the point of Stalin's demand for a "friendly government" in Warsaw, the American insistence on the sovereign virtues of free elections (ironically in the spirit of the 1917 Bolshevik decree of peace, which affirmed "the right" of a nation "to decide the forms of its state existence by a free vote, taken after the complete evacuation of the incorporating or, generally, of the stronger nation") created an insoluble problem in those countries, like Poland (and Rumania) where free elections would almost certainly produce anti-Soviet governments.

The Russians thus may well have estimated the Western pressures as calculated to encourage their enemies in Eastern Europe and to defeat their own minimum objective of a protective glacis. Everything still hung, however, on the course of military operations. The wartime collaboration had been created by one thing, and one thing alone: the threat of Nazi victory. So long as this threat was real, so was the collaboration. In late December 1944, von Rundstedt launched his counter-offensive in the Ardennes. A few weeks later, when Roosevelt, Churchill and Stalin gathered in the Crimea, it was in the shadow of this last considerable explosion of German power. The meeting at Yalta was still dominated by the mood of war.

Yalta remains something of an historical perplexity—less, from the perspective of 1967, because of a mythical American deference to the sphere-of-influence thesis than because of the documentable Russian deference to the universalist thesis. Why should Stalin in 1945 have accepted the Declaration on Liberated Europe and an agreement on Poland pledging that "the three governments will jointly" act to assure "free elections of governments responsive to the will of the people"? There are several probable answers: that the war was not over and the Russians still wanted the Americans to intensify their military effort in the West; that one clause in the Declaration premised action on "the opinion of the three governments" and thus implied a Soviet veto, though the Polish agreement was more definite; most of all that the universalist algebra of the Declaration was plainly in Stalin's mind to be construed in terms of the practical arithmetic of his sphere-of-influence agreement with Churchill the previous October. Stalin's assurance to Churchill at Yalta that a proposed Russian amendment to the Declaration would not apply to Greece makes it clear that Roosevelt's pieties did not, in Stalin's mind, nullify Churchill's percentages. He could well have been strengthened in this supposition by the fact that *after* Yalta, Churchill himself repeatedly reasserted the terms of the October agreement as if he regarded it, despite Yalta, as controlling.

Harriman still had the feeling before Yalta that the Kremlin had "two approaches to their postwar policies" and that Stalin himself was "of two minds." One approach emphasized the internal reconstruction and development of Russia; the other its external expansion. But in the meantime the fact which dominated all political decisions—that is, the war against Germany—was moving into its final phase. In the weeks after Yalta, the military situation changed with great rapidity. As the Nazi threat declined, so too did the need for coöperation. The Soviet Union, feeling itself menaced by the American idea of self-determination and the borderlands diplomacy to which it was leading, skeptical whether the United Nations would protect its frontiers as reliably as its own domination in Eastern Europe, began to fulfill its security requirements unilaterally.

In March Stalin expressed his evaluation of the United Nations by rejecting Roosevelt's plea that Molotov come to the San Francisco conference, if only for the opening sessions. In the next weeks the Russians emphatically and crudely worked their will in Eastern Europe, above all in the test country of Poland. They were ignoring the Declaration on Liberated Europe, ignoring the Atlantic Charter, self-determination, human freedom and everything else the Americans considered essential for a stable peace. "We must clearly recognize," Harriman wired Washington a few days before Roosevelt's death, "that the Soviet program is the establishment of totalitarianism, ending personal liberty and democracy as we know and respect it."

At the same time, the Russians also began to mobilize communist resources in the United States itself to block American universalism. In April 1945 Jacques Duclos, who had been the Comintern official responsible for the Western communist parties, launched in *Cahiers du Communisme* an uncompromising attack on the policy of the American Communist Party. Duclos sharply condemned the revisionism of Earl Browder, the American Communist leader, as "expressed in the concept of a long-term class peace in the United States, of the possibility of the suppression of the class struggle in the postwar period and of establishment of harmony between labor and capital." Browder was specifically rebuked for favoring the "self-determination" of Europe "west of the Soviet Union" on a bourgeois-democratic basis. The excommunication of Browderism was plainly the Politburo's considered reaction to the impending defeat of Germany; it was a signal to the communist parties of the West that they should recover their identity; it was Moscow's alert to communists everywhere that they should prepare for new policies in the postwar world.

The Duclos piece obviously could not have been planned and written much later than the Yalta conference—that is, well before a number of events which revisionists now cite in order to demonstrate American responsibility for the Cold War: before Allen Dulles, for example, began to negotiate the surrender of the German armies in Italy (the episode which provoked Stalin to charge Roosevelt with seeking a separate peace and provoked Roosevelt to denounce the "vile misrepresentations" of Stalin's informants); well before Roosevelt died; many months before the testing of the atomic bomb; even more months before Truman ordered that the bomb be dropped on Japan. William Z. Foster, who soon replaced Browder as the leader of the American Communist Party and embodied the new Moscow line, later boasted of having said in January 1944, "A post-war Roosevelt administration would continue to be, as it is now, an imperialist government." With ancient suspicions revived by the American insistence on universalism, this was no doubt the conclusion which the Russians were reaching at the same time. The Soviet canonization of Roosevelt (like their present-day canonization of Kennedy) took place after the American President's death.

The atmosphere of mutual suspicion was beginning to rise. In January 1945 Molotov formally proposed that the United States grant Russia a $6 billion credit for postwar reconstruction. With characteristic tact he explained that he was doing this as a favor to save America from a postwar depression. The proposal seems to have been diffidently made and diffidently received. Roosevelt requested that the matter "not be pressed further" on the American side until he had a chance to talk with Stalin; but the Russians did not follow it up either at Yalta in February (save for a single glancing reference) or during the Stalin-Hopkins talks in May or at Potsdam. Finally the proposal was renewed in the very different political atmosphere of August. This time Washington inexplicably mislaid the request during the transfer of the records of the Foreign Economic Administration to the State Department. It did not turn up again until March 1946. Of course this was impossible for the Russians to believe; it is hard enough even for those acquainted with the capacity of the American government for incompetence to believe; and it only strengthened Soviet suspicions of American purposes.

The American credit was one conceivable form of Western contribution to Russian reconstruction. Another was lend-lease, and the possibility of reconstruction aid under the lend-lease protocol had already been discussed in 1944. But in May 1945 Russia, like Britain, suffered from Truman's abrupt termination of lend-lease shipments—"unfortunate and even brutal," Stalin told Hopkins, adding that, if it was "designed as pressure on the Russians in order to soften them up, then it was a fundamental mistake." A third form was German reparations. Here Stalin in demanding $10 billion in reparations for the Soviet Union made his strongest fight at Yalta. Roosevelt, while agreeing essentially with Churchill's opposition, tried to postpone the matter by accepting the Soviet figure as a "basis for discussion"—a formula which led to future misunderstanding. In short, the Russian hope for major Western assistance in postwar reconstruction foundered on three events which the Kremlin could well have interpreted respectively as deliberate sabotage (the loan request), blackmail (lend-lease cancellation) and pro-Germanism (reparations).

Actually the American attempt to settle the fourth lend-lease protocol was generous and the Russians for their own reasons declined to come to an agreement. It is not clear, though, that satisfying Moscow on any of these financial scores would have made much essential difference. It might have persuaded some doves in the Kremlin that the U.S. government was genuinely friendly; it might have persuaded some hawks that the American anxiety for Soviet friendship was such that Moscow could do as it wished without inviting challenge from the United States. It would, in short, merely have reinforced both sides of the Kremlin debate; it would hardly have reversed deeper tendencies toward the deterioration of political relationships. Economic deals were surely subordinate to the quality of mutual political confidence; and here, in the months after Yalta, the decay was steady.

The Cold War had now begun. It was the product not of a decision but of a dilemma. Each side felt compelled to adopt policies which the other could not but regard as a threat to the principles of the peace. Each then felt compelled to undertake defensive measures. Thus the Russians saw no choice but to consolidate their security in Eastern Europe. The Americans, regarding Eastern Europe as the first step toward Western Europe, responded by asserting their interest in the zone the Russians deemed vital to their security. The Russians concluded that the West was resuming its old course of capitalist encirclement; that it was purposefully laying the foundation for anti-Soviet régimes in the area defined by the blood of centuries as crucial to Russian survival. Each side believed with passion that future international stability depended on the success of its own conception of world order. Each side, in pursuing its own clearly indicated and deeply cherished principles, was only confirming the fear of the other that it was bent on aggression.

Very soon the process began to acquire a cumulative momentum. The impending collapse of Germany thus provoked new troubles: the Russians, for example, sincerely feared that the West was planning a separate surrender of the German armies in Italy in a way which would release troops for Hitler's eastern front, as they subsequently feared that the Nazis might succeed in surrendering Berlin to the West. This was the context in which the atomic bomb now appeared. Though the revisionist argument that Truman dropped the bomb less to defeat Japan than to intimidate Russia is not convincing, this thought unquestionably appealed to some in Washington as at least an advantageous side-effect of Hiroshima.

So the machinery of suspicion and counter-suspicion, action and counter-action, was set in motion. But, given relations among traditional national states, there was still no reason, even with all the postwar jostling, why this should not have remained a manageable situation. What made it unmanageable, what caused the rapid escalation of the Cold War and in another two years completed the division of Europe, was a set of considerations which this account has thus far excluded.

VII

Up to this point, the discussion has considered the schism within the wartime coalition as if it were entirely the result of disagreements among national states. Assuming this framework, there was unquestionably a failure of communication between America and Russia, a misperception of signals and, as time went on, a mounting tendency to ascribe ominous motives to the other side. It seems hard, for example, to deny that American postwar policy created genuine difficulties for the Russians and even assumed a threatening aspect for them. All this the revisionists have rightly and usefully emphasized.

But the great omission of the revisionists—and also the fundamental explanation of the speed with which the Cold War escalated—lies precisely in the fact that the Soviet Union was *not* a traditional national state.[4] This is where the "mirror image," invoked by some psychologists, falls down. For the Soviet Union was a phenomenon very different from America or Britain: it was a totalitarian state, endowed with an all-explanatory, all-consuming ideology, committed to the infallibility of government and party, still in a somewhat messianic mood, equating dis-

---

[4] This is the classical revisionist fallacy—the assumption of the rationality, or at least of the traditionalism, of states where ideology and social organization have created a different range of motives. So the Second World War revisionists omit the totalitarian dynamism of Nazism and the fanaticism of Hitler, as the Civil War revisionists omit the fact that the slavery system was producing a doctrinaire closed society in the American South. For a consideration of some of these issues, see "The Causes of the Civil War: A Note on Historical Sentimentalism" in my "The Politics of Hope" (Boston, 1963).

sent with treason, and ruled by a dictator who, for all his quite extraordinary abilities, had his paranoid moments.

Marxism-Leninism gave the Russian leaders a view of the world according to which all societies were inexorably destined to proceed along appointed roads by appointed stages until they achieved the classless nirvana. Moreover, given the resistance of the capitalists to this development, the existence of any non-communist state was *by definition* a threat to the Soviet Union. "As long as capitalism and socialism exist," Lenin wrote, "we cannot live in peace: in the end, one or the other will triumph—a funeral dirge will be sung either over the Soviet Republic or over world capitalism."

Stalin and his associates, whatever Roosevelt or Truman did or failed to do, were bound to regard the United States as the enemy, not because of this deed or that, but because of the primordial fact that America was the leading capitalist power and thus, by Leninist syllogism, unappeasably hostile, driven by the logic of its system to oppose, encircle and destroy Soviet Russia. Nothing the United States could have done in 1944–45 would have abolished this mistrust, required and sanctified as it was by Marxist gospel—nothing short of the conversion of the United States into a Stalinist despotism; and even this would not have sufficed, as the experience of Jugoslavia and China soon showed, unless it were accompanied by total subservience to Moscow. So long as the United States remained a capitalist democracy, no American policy, given Moscow's theology, could hope to win basic Soviet confidence, and every American action was poisoned from the source. So long as the Soviet Union remained a messianic state, ideology compelled a steady expansion of communist power.

It is easy, of course, to exaggerate the capacity of ideology to control events. The tension of acting according to revolutionary abstractions is too much for most nations to sustain over a long period: that is why Mao Tse-tung has launched his Cultural Revolution, hoping thereby to create a permanent revolutionary mood and save Chinese communism from the degeneration which, in his view, has overtaken Russian communism. Still, as any revolution grows older, normal human and social motives will increasingly reassert themselves. In due course, we can be sure, Leninism will be about as effective in governing the daily lives of Russians as Christianity is in governing the daily lives of Americans. Like the Ten Commandments and the Sermon on the

Mount, the Leninist verities will increasingly become platitudes for ritual observance, not guides to secular decision. There can be no worse fallacy (even if respectable people practiced it diligently for a season in the United States) than that of drawing from a nation's ideology permanent conclusions about its behavior.

A temporary recession of ideology was already taking place during the Second World War when Stalin, to rally his people against the invader, had to replace the appeal of Marxism by that of nationalism. ("We are under no illusions that they are fighting for us," Stalin once said to Harriman. "They are fighting for Mother Russia.") But this was still taking place within the strictest limitations. The Soviet Union remained as much a police state as ever; the régime was as infallible as ever; foreigners and their ideas were as suspect as ever. "Never, except possibly during my later experience as ambassador in Moscow," Kennan has written, "did the insistence of the Soviet authorities on isolation of the diplomatic corps weigh more heavily on me . . . than in these first weeks following my return to Russia in the final months of the war. . . . [We were] treated as though we were the bearers of some species of the plague"—which, of course, from the Soviet viewpoint, they were: the plague of skepticism.

Paradoxically, of the forces capable of bringing about a modification of ideology, the most practical and effective was the Soviet dictatorship itself. If Stalin was an ideologist, he was also a pragmatist. If he saw everything through the lenses of Marxism-Leninism, he also, as the infallible expositor of the faith, could reinterpret Marxism-Leninism to justify anything he wanted to do at any given moment. No doubt Roosevelt's ignorance of Marxism-Leninism was inexcusable and led to grievous miscalculations. But Roosevelt's efforts to work on and through Stalin were not so hopelessly naïve as it used to be fashionable to think. With the extraordinary instinct of a great political leader, Roosevelt intuitively understood that Stalin was the *only* lever available to the West against the Leninist ideology and the Soviet system. If Stalin could be reached, then alone was there a chance of getting the Russians to act contrary to the prescriptions of their faith. The best evidence is that Roosevelt retained a certain capacity to influence Stalin to the end; the nominal Soviet acquiescence in American universalism as late as Yalta was perhaps an indication of that. It is in this way that the death of Roosevelt was crucial—not in the vulgar sense that his policy was then reversed by his successor, which did not happen, but in the sense that no other American could hope to have the restraining impact on Stalin which Roosevelt might for a while have had.

Stalin alone could have made any difference. Yet Stalin, in spite of the impression of sobriety and realism he made on Westerners who saw him during the Second World War, was plainly a man of deep and morbid obsessions and compulsions. When he was still a young man, Lenin had criticized his rude and arbitrary ways. A reasonably authoritative observer (N. S. Khrushchev) later commented, "These negative characteristics of his developed steadily and during the last years acquired an absolutely insufferable character." His paranoia, probably set off by the suicide of his wife in 1932, led to the terrible purges of the mid-thirties and the wanton murder of thousands of his Bolshevik comrades. "Everywhere and in everything," Khrushchev says of this period, "he saw 'enemies,' 'double-dealers' and 'spies.'" The crisis of war evidently steadied him in some way, though Khrushchev speaks of his "nervousness and hysteria . . . even after the war began." The madness, so rigidly controlled for a time, burst out with new and shocking intensity in the postwar years. "After the war," Khrushchev testifies,

the situation became even more complicated. Stalin became even more capricious, irritable and brutal; in particular, his suspicion grew. His persecution mania reached unbelievable dimensions. . . . He decided everything, without any consideration for anyone or anything.

Stalin's wilfulness showed itself . . . also in the international relations of the Soviet Union. . . . He had completely lost a sense of reality; he demonstrated his suspicion and haughtiness not only in relation to individuals in the USSR, but in relation to whole parties and nations.

A revisionist fallacy has been to treat Stalin as just another Realpolitik statesman, as Second World War revisionists see Hitler as just another Stresemann or Bismarck. But the record makes it clear that in the end nothing could satisfy Stalin's paranoia. His own associates failed. Why does anyone suppose that any conceivable American policy would have succeeded?

An analysis of the origins of the Cold War which leaves out these factors—the intransigence of Leninist ideology, the sinister dynamics of a totalitarian society and the madness of Stalin—is obviously incomplete. It was these factors which made it hard for the West to accept the thesis that Russia was moved only by a desire to protect its security and would be satisfied by the control of Eastern Europe; it was these factors which charged the debate between universalism and spheres of influence with apocalyptic potentiality.

Leninism and totalitarianism created a structure of thought and behavior which made postwar collaboration between Russia and America—in any normal sense of civilized intercourse between national states—inherently impossible. The Soviet dictatorship of 1945 simply could not have survived such a collaboration. Indeed, nearly a quarter-century later, the Soviet régime, though it has meanwhile moved a good distance, could still hardly survive it without risking the release inside Russia of energies profoundly opposed to communist despotism. As for Stalin, he may have represented the only force in 1945 capable of overcoming Stalinism, but the very traits which enabled him to win absolute power expressed terrifying instabilities of mind and temperament and hardly offered a solid foundation for a peaceful world.

VIII

The difference between America and Russia in 1945 was that some Americans fundamentally believed that, over a long run, a modus vivendi with Russia was possible; while the Russians, so far as one can tell, believed in no more than a short-run modus vivendi with the United States.

Harriman and Kennan, this narrative has made clear, took the lead in warning Washington about the difficulties of short-run dealings with the Soviet Union. But both argued that, if the United States developed a rational policy and stuck to it, there would be, after long and rough passages, the prospect of eventual clearing. "I am, as you know," Harriman cabled Washington in early April, "a most earnest advocate of the closest possible understanding with the Soviet Union so that what I am saying relates only to how best to attain such understanding." Kennan has similarly made it clear that the function of his containment policy was "to tide us over a difficult time and bring us to the point where we could discuss effectively with the Russians the dangers and drawbacks this status quo involved, and to arrange with them for its peaceful replacement by a better and sounder one." The subsequent careers of both men attest to the honesty of these statements.

There is no corresponding evidence on the Russian side that

anyone seriously sought a modus vivendi in these terms. Stalin's choice was whether his long-term ideological and national interests would be better served by a short-run truce with the West or by an immediate resumption of pressure. In October 1945 Stalin indicated to Harriman at Sochi that he planned to adopt the second course—that the Soviet Union was going isolationist. No doubt the succession of problems with the United States contributed to this decision, but the basic causes most probably lay elsewhere: in the developing situations in Eastern Europe, in Western Europe and in the United States.

In Eastern Europe, Stalin was still for a moment experimenting with techniques of control. But he must by now have begun to conclude that he had underestimated the hostility of the people to Russian dominion. The Hungarian elections in November would finally convince him that the Yalta formula was a road to anti-Soviet governments. At the same time, he was feeling more strongly than ever a sense of his opportunities in Western Europe. The other half of the Continent lay unexpectedly before him, politically demoralized, economically prostrate, militarily defenseless. The hunting would be better and safer than he had anticipated. As for the United States, the alacrity of postwar demobilization must have recalled Roosevelt's offhand remark at Yalta that "two years would be the limit" for keeping American troops in Europe. And, despite Dr. Eugene Varga's doubts about the imminence of American economic breakdown, Marxist theology assured Stalin that the United States was heading into a bitter postwar depression and would be consumed with its own problems. If the condition of Eastern Europe made unilateral action seem essential in the interests of Russian security, the condition of Western Europe and the United States offered new temptations for communist expansion. The Cold War was now in full swing.

It still had its year of modulations and accommodations. Secretary Byrnes conducted his long and fruitless campaign to persuade the Russians that America only sought governments in Eastern Europe "both friendly to the Soviet Union and representative of all the democratic elements of the country." Crises were surmounted in Trieste and Iran. Secretary Marshall evidently did not give up hope of a modus vivendi until the Moscow conference of foreign secretaries of March 1947. Even then, the Soviet Union was invited to participate in the Marshall Plan.

The point of no return came on July 2, 1947, when Molotov, after bringing 89 technical specialists with him to Paris and evincing initial interest in the project for European reconstruction, received the hot flash from the Kremlin, denounced the whole idea and walked out of the conference. For the next fifteen years the Cold War raged unabated, passing out of historical ambiguity into the realm of good versus evil and breeding on both sides simplifications, stereotypes and self-serving absolutes, often couched in interchangeable phrases. Under the pressure even America, for a deplorable decade, forsook its pragmatic and pluralist traditions, posed as God's appointed messenger to ignorant and sinful man and followed the Soviet example in looking to a world remade in its own image.

In retrospect, if it is impossible to see the Cold War as a case of American aggression and Russian response, it is also hard to see it as a pure case of Russian aggression and American response. "In what is truly tragic," wrote Hegel, "there must be valid moral powers on both the sides which come into collision. . . . Both suffer loss and yet both are mutually justified." In this sense, the Cold War had its tragic elements. The question remains whether it was an instance of Greek tragedy—as Auden has called it, "the tragedy of necessity," where the feeling aroused in the spectator is "What a pity it had to be this way"—or of Christian tragedy, "the tragedy of possibility," where the feeling aroused is "What a pity it was this way when it might have been otherwise."

Once something has happened, the historian is tempted to assume that it had to happen; but this may often be a highly unphilosophical assumption. The Cold War could have been avoided only if the Soviet Union had not been possessed by convictions both of the infallibility of the communist word and of the inevitability of a communist world. These convictions transformed an impasse between national states into a religious war, a tragedy of possibility into one of necessity. One might wish that America had preserved the poise and proportion of the first years of the Cold War and had not in time succumbed to its own forms of self-righteousness. But the most rational of American policies could hardly have averted the Cold War. Only today, as Russia begins to recede from its messianic mission and to accept, in practice if not yet in principle, the permanence of the world of diversity, only now can the hope flicker that this long, dreary, costly contest may at last be taking on forms less dramatic, less obsessive and less dangerous to the future of mankind.

¶ A VIET NAM REAPPRAISAL
by Clark M. Clifford   (July, 1969)

Clark Clifford took office as U.S. Secretary of Defense on March 1, 1968, when the Vietnam War was at its height, and the Tet offensive of January and February had raised the possibility of greatly increased American troop deployments. One month later, President Lyndon Johnson announced to the nation that what had seemed an almost limitless process of escalation had ended, that the training of Vietnamese to take over the war would be greatly accelerated, and that he was discontinuing the bombing of North Vietnam above the twentieth parallel. This was obviously one of the most important turning points for the United States in Vietnam, and Clifford played a signifi-cant role in breaking the cycle of almost automatic escalation in response to attrition and military setbacks. In this article, he offers a fascinating glimpse into the decision-making processes of the U.S. Government, as well as the de-velopment of his own thinking during the month of March and later in his term of office as Defense Secretary.

When Clifford was appointed to succeed Robert McNamara at the Penta-gon, he was not known for his dovish views on the war. A friend of the Presi-dent and a successful Washington lawyer, he was expected to prosecute the war with new dedication and vigor. He had first become aware of the gravity of the situation in Indochina when he had served as adviser to President Ken-nedy during the transitional period before Kennedy's inauguration in 1961. His first doubts about the U.S. course of action had arisen during an official visit to South Korea, Thailand, the Philippines, Australia, and New Zealand in the summer preceding his appointment as Defense Secretary, when he had found America's Asian allies extremely unwilling to increase their contribu-tions to the war effort, despite their proximity to the conflict.

The Tet offensive, in late January and early February of 1968, was perhaps the major factor in changing Americans' minds about the war. Clifford contra-dicted the long-standing optimism about Vietnam on the part of U.S. military and government officials. The "credibility gap" widened. Fundamental ques-tions kept asserting themselves, until Clifford became convinced that the mili-tary course the United States was pursuing was "not only endless but hope-less." It is fortunate that a man of his strength of mind and intellectual resiliency occupied his influential office at such a crucial time.

A VIET NAM REAPPRAISAL

THE PERSONAL HISTORY OF ONE MAN'S VIEW AND HOW IT EVOLVED

By Clark M. Clifford

VIET Nam remains unquestionably the transcendent problem that confronts our nation. Though the escalation has ceased, we seem to be no closer to finding our way out of this infinitely complex difficulty. The confidence of the past has become the frustration of the present. Predictions of progress and of military success, made so often by so many, have proved to be illusory as the fighting and the dying continue at a tragic rate. Within our country, the dialogue quickens and the debate sharpens. There is a growing impatience among our people, and questions regarding the war and our participation in it are being asked with increasing vehemence.

Many individuals these past years have sought to make some contribution toward finding the answers that have been so elusive. It is with this hope in mind that I present herewith the case history of one man's attitude toward Viet Nam, and the various stages of thought he experienced as he plodded painfully from one point of view to another, and another, until he arrived at the unshakable opinion he possesses today.

Views on Viet Nam have become increasingly polarized as the war has gone on without visible progress toward the traditional American military triumph. There remain some who insist that we were right to intervene militarily and, because we were right, we have no choice but to press on until the enemy knuckles under and concedes defeat. At the other extreme, and in increasing numbers, there are those who maintain that the present unsatisfactory situation proves that our Viet Nam policy has been wrong from the very beginning. There are even those who suggest that our problems in Viet Nam cast doubt on the entire course of American foreign policy since World War II. Both schools share a common and, as I see it, an erroneous concept. They both would make military victory the ultimate test of the propriety of our participation in the conflict in Southeast Asia.

I find myself unable to agree with either extreme. At the time of our original involvement in Viet Nam, I considered it to be based upon sound and unassailable premises, thoroughly consistent with our self-interest and our responsibilities. There has been no change in the exemplary character of our intentions in Viet Nam. We intervened to help a new and small nation resist subjugation by a neighboring country—a neighboring country, incidentally, which was being assisted by the resources of the world's two largest communist powers.

I see no profit and no purpose in any divisive national debate about whether we were right or wrong initially to become involved in the struggle in Viet Nam. Such debate at the present time clouds the issue and obscures the pressing need for a clear and logical evaluation of our present predicament, and how we can extricate ourselves from it.

Only history will be able to tell whether or not our military presence in Southeast Asia was warranted. Certainly the decisions that brought it about were based upon a reasonable reading of the past three decades. We had seen the calamitous consequences of standing aside while totalitarian and expansionist nations moved successively against their weaker neighbors and accumulated a military might which left even the stronger nations uneasy and insecure. We had seen in the period immediately after World War II the seemingly insatiable urge of the Soviet Union to secure satellite states on its western periphery. We had seen in Asia itself the attempt by open invasion to extend communist control into the independent South of the Korean Peninsula. We had reason to feel that the fate averted in Korea through American and United Nations military force would overtake the independent countries of Asia, albeit in somewhat subtler form, were we to stand aside while the communist North sponsored subversion and terrorism in South Viet Nam.

The transformation that has taken place in my thinking has been brought about, however, by the conclusion that the world situation has changed dramatically, and that American involvement in Viet Nam can and must change with it. Important ingredients of this present situation include the manner in which South Viet Nam and its Asian neighbors have responded to the threat and to our own massive intervention. They also include internal developments both in Asian nations and elsewhere, and the changing relations among world powers.

The decisions which our nation faces today in Viet Nam should not be made on interpretations of the facts as they were perceived four or five or fifteen years ago, even if, through compromise, a consensus could be reached on these interpretations. They must instead be based upon our present view of our obligations as a world power; upon our current concept of our national security; upon our conclusions regarding our commitments as they exist today; upon our fervent desire to contribute to peace throughout the world; and, hopefully, upon our acceptance of the principle of enlightened self-interest.

But these are broad and general guidelines, subject to many constructions and misconstructions. They also have the obvious drawback of being remote and impersonal.

The purpose of this article is to present to the reader the intimate and highly personal experience of one man, in the hope that by so doing there will be a simpler and clearer understanding of where we are in Viet Nam today, and what we must do about it. I shall go back to the beginning and identify, as well as I can, the origins of my consciousness of the problem, the opportunities I had to obtain the facts, and the resulting evolution of what I shall guardedly refer to as my thought processes.

II

Although I had served President Truman in the White House from May 1945 until February 1950, I do not recall ever having had to focus on Southeast Asia. Indochina, as it was then universally known, was regarded by our government as a French problem. President Truman was prompted from time to time by the State Department to approve statements that seemed to me to be little more than reiterations of the long-standing American attitude against "colonialism." If any of those provoked extensive discussion at the White House, I cannot recall. For the next decade, I watched foreign affairs and the growing turbulence of Asia from the sidelines as a private citizen, increasingly concerned but not directly involved.

In the summer of 1960, Senator John Kennedy invited me to act as his transition planner, and later as liaison with the Eisenhower Administration in the interval between the election and January 20, 1961. Among the foreign policy problems that I encountered at once was a deteriorating situation in Southeast Asia. Major-General Wilton B. Persons, whom President Eisenhower had designated to work with me, explained the gravity of the situation as viewed by the outgoing Administration. I suggested to the President-elect that it would be well for him to hear President Eisenhower personally on the subject. He agreed, and accordingly General Persons and I placed Southeast Asia as the first item on the agenda of the final meeting between the outgoing and the incoming Presidents. This meeting, held on the morning of January 19, 1961, in the Cabinet Room, was attended by President Eisenhower, Secretary of State Christian Herter, Secretary of Defense Thomas Gates, Secretary of the Treasury Robert Anderson and General Persons. President-elect Kennedy had his counterparts present: Secretary of State-designate Dean Rusk, Secretary of Defense-designate Robert McNamara, Secretary of the Treasury-designate Douglas Dillon, and me.

At President-elect Kennedy's suggestion, I took notes of the important subjects discussed. Most of the time, the discussion centered on Southeast Asia, with emphasis upon Laos. At that particular time, January 1961, Laos had come sharply into focus and appeared to constitute the major danger in the area.

My notes disclose the following comments by the President:

At this point, President Eisenhower said, with considerable emotion, that Laos was the key to the entire area of Southeast Asia.

He said that if we permitted Laos to fall, then we would have to write off all the area. He stated we must not permit a Communist take-over. He reiterated that we should make every effort to persuade member nations of SEATO or the International Control Commission to accept the burden with us to defend the freedom of Laos.

As he concluded these remarks, President Eisenhower stated it was imperative that Laos be defended. He said that the United States should accept this task with our allies, if we could persuade them, and alone if we could not. He added, "Our unilateral intervention would be our last desperate hope in the event we were unable to prevail upon the other signatories to join us."

That morning's discussion, and the gravity with which President Eisenhower addressed the problem, had a substantial impact on me. He and his advisers were finishing eight years of responsible service to the nation. I had neither facts nor personal experience to challenge their assessment of the situation, even if I had had the inclination to do so. The thrust of the presentation was the great importance to the United States of taking a firm stand in Southeast Asia, and I accepted that judgment.

On an earlier occasion, in speaking of Southeast Asia, President Eisenhower had said that South Viet Nam's capture by the communists would bring their power several hundred miles into a hitherto free region. The freedom of 12 million people would be lost immediately, and that of 150 million in adjacent lands would be seriously endangered. The loss of South Viet Nam would set in motion a crumbling process that could, as it progressed, have grave consequences for us and for freedom.

As I listened to him in the Cabinet Room that January morning, I recalled that it was President Eisenhower who had acquainted the public with the phrase "domino theory" by using it to describe how one country after another could be expected to fall under communist control once the process started in Southeast Asia.

In the spring of 1961, I was appointed to membership on the President's Foreign Intelligence Advisory Board. In this capacity, I received briefings from time to time on affairs in Asia. The information provided the Board supported the assessment of the previous Administration, with which President Kennedy concurred. "Withdrawal in the case of Viet Nam," President Kennedy said in 1961, "and in the case of Thailand could mean the collapse of the whole area." He never wavered. A year later, he said of Viet Nam: "We are not going to withdraw from that effort. In my opinion, for us to withdraw from that effort would mean a collapse not only of South Viet Nam but Southeast Asia. So we are going to stay there." I had no occasion to question the collective opinion of our duly chosen officials.

After President Johnson took office, our involvement became greater, but so did most public and private assessments of the correctness of our course. The Tonkin Gulf resolution was adopted by the Congress in 1964 by a vote of 504 to 2. The language was stern: "The United States is, therefore, prepared, as the President determines, to take all necessary steps, including the use of armed force, to assist any member or protocol state of the Southeast Asia Collective Defense Treaty requesting assistance in defense of its freedom."

When decisions were made in 1965 to increase, in very substantial fashion, the American commitment in Viet Nam, I accepted the judgment that such actions were necessary. That fall, I made a trip to Southeast Asia in my capacity as Chairman of the Foreign Intelligence Advisory Board. The optimism of our military and Vietnamese officials on the conduct of the war, together with the encouragement of our Asian allies, confirmed my belief in the correctness of our policy. In the absence at the time of indications that Hanoi had any interest in peace negotiations, I did not favor the 37-day bombing halt over the Christmas 1965–New Year 1966 holiday season. I felt such a halt could be construed by Hanoi as a sign of weakness on our part.

In 1966, I served as an adviser to President Johnson at the Manila Conference. It was an impressive gathering of the Chiefs of State and Heads of Government of the allied nations; it reassured me that we were on the right road and that our military progress was bringing us closer to the resolution of the conflict.

In the late summer of 1967, President Johnson asked me to go with his Special Assistant, General Maxwell Taylor, to review the situation in South Viet Nam, and then to visit some of our Pacific allies. We were to brief them on the war and to discuss with them the possibility of their increasing their troop commitments. Our briefings in South Viet Nam were extensive and encouraging. There were suggestions that the enemy was being hurt badly and that our bombing and superior firepower were beginning to achieve the expected results.

Our visits to the allied capitals, however, produced results that I had not foreseen. It was strikingly apparent to me that the other troop-contributing countries no longer shared our degree of concern about the war in South Viet Nam. General Taylor and I urged them to increase their participation. In the main, our plea fell on deaf ears.

Thailand, a near neighbor to South Viet Nam, with a population of some 30 million, had assigned only 2,500 men to South Viet Nam, and was in no hurry to allocate more.

The President of the Philippines advised President Johnson that he preferred we not stop there because of possible adverse public reaction. The Philippines, so close and ostensibly so vulnerable if they accepted the domino theory, had sent a hospital corps and an engineer battalion to Viet Nam, but no combat troops. It was also made clear to President Johnson that they had no intention of sending any combat personnel.

South Korea had the only sizable contingent of Asian troops assisting South Viet Nam, but officials argued that a higher level of activity on the part of the North Koreans prevented their increasing their support.

Disappointing though these visits were, I had high hopes for the success of our mission in Australia and New Zealand. I recalled that Australia, then with a much smaller population, had been able to maintain well over 300,000 troops overseas in World War II. They had sent only 7,000 to Viet Nam. Surely there was hope here. But Prime Minister Holt, who had been fully briefed, presented a long list of reasons why Australia was already close to its maximum effort.

In New Zealand, we spent the better part of a day conferring with the Prime Minister and his cabinet, while hundreds of students picketed the Parliament Building carrying signs bearing peace slogans. These officials were courteous and sympathetic, as all the others had been, but they made it clear that any appreciable increase was out of the question. New Zealand at one time had 70,000 troops overseas in the various theaters of World War II. They had 500 men in Viet Nam. I naturally wondered if this was their evaluation of the respective dangers of the two conflicts.

I returned home puzzled, troubled, concerned. Was it possible that our assessment of the danger to the stability of Southeast Asia and the Western Pacific was exaggerated? Was it possible that those nations which were neighbors of Viet Nam had a clearer perception of the tides of world events in 1967 than we? Was it possible that we were continuing to be guided by judgments that might once have had validity but were now obsolete? In short, although I still counted myself a staunch supporter of our policies, there were nagging, not-to-be-suppressed doubts in my mind.

These doubts were dramatized a short time later back in the United States when I attended a dinner at the White House for Prime Minister Lee Kuan Yew of Singapore. His country, which knew the bitterness of defeat and occupation in World War II, had declined to send any men at all to Viet Nam. In answer to my question as to when he thought troops might be sent, he stated he saw no possibility of that taking place because of the adverse political effect in Singapore.

Accordingly, I welcomed President Johnson's San Antonio speech of September 30, 1967, with far greater enthusiasm than

I would have had I not so recently returned from the Pacific. I felt it marked a substantial step in the right direction because it offered an alternative to a military solution of the lengthy and costly conflict. Allied bombing of North Viet Nam had by now assumed a symbolic significance of enormous proportions and the President focused his attention on this. The essence of his proposal was an offer to stop the bombing of North Viet Nam if prompt and productive peace discussions with the other side would ensue. We would assume that the other side would "not take advantage" of the bombing cessation. By this formula, the President made an imaginative move to end the deadlock over the bombing and get negotiations started.

I, of course, shared the universal disappointment that the San Antonio offer evoked no favorable response from Hanoi, but my feelings were more complex than those of mere disappointment. As I listened to the official discussion in Washington, my feelings turned from disappointment to dismay. I found it was being quietly asserted that, in return for a bombing cessation in the North, the North Vietnamese must stop sending men and maté-riel into South Viet Nam. On the surface, this might have seemed a fair exchange. To me, it was an unfortunate interpretation that —intentionally or not—rendered the San Antonio formula virtually meaningless. The North Vietnamese had more than 100,-000 men in the South. It was totally unrealistic to expect them to abandon their men by not replacing casualties, and by failing to provide them with clothing, food, munitions and other supplies. We could never expect them to accept an offer to negotiate on those conditions.

III

In mid-January 1968, President Johnson asked me to serve as Secretary of Defense, succeeding Secretary McNamara, who was leaving to become President of the World Bank. In the confirmation hearing before the Senate Armed Services Committee on January 25, I was asked about the San Antonio formula. The interpretation I gave was in accord with President Johnson's intense desire to start negotiations, and it offered a possibility of acceptance which I was convinced did not exist with the extreme and rigid interpretations that so concerned me. I said that I assumed that the North Vietnamese would "continue to transport the normal amount of goods, munitions and men to South

Viet Nam" at the levels that had prevailed prior to our bombing cessation. This was my understanding of what the President meant by "not take advantage."

The varying interpretations of the San Antonio formula raised in my mind the question as to whether all of us had the same objective in view. Some, it seemed, could envision as satisfactory no solution short of the complete military defeat of the enemy. I did not count myself in this group. Although I still accepted as valid the premises of our Viet Nam involvement, I was dissatisfied with the rigidities that so limited our course of action and our alternatives.

I took office on March 1, 1968. The enemy's Tet offensive of late January and early February had been beaten back at great cost. The confidence of the American people had been badly shaken. The ability of the South Vietnamese Government to restore order and morale in the populace, and discipline and esprit in the armed forces, was being questioned. At the President's direction, General Earle G. Wheeler, Chairman of the Joint Chiefs of Staff, had flown to Viet Nam in late February for an on-the-spot conference with General Westmoreland. He had just returned and presented the military's request that over 200,000 troops be prepared for deployment to Viet Nam. These troops would be in addition to the 525,000 previously authorized. I was directed, as my first assignment, to chair a task force named by the President to determine how this new requirement could be met. We were not instructed to assess the need for substantial increases in men and matériel; we were to devise the means by which they could be provided.

My work was cut out. The task force included Secretary Rusk, Secretary Henry Fowler, Under Secretary of State Nicholas Katzenbach, Deputy Secretary of Defense Paul Nitze, General Wheeler, CIA Director Richard Helms, the President's Special Assistant, Walt Rostow, General Maxwell Taylor and other skilled and highly capable officials. All of them had had long and direct experience with Vietnamese problems. I had not. I had attended various meetings in the past several years and I had been to Viet Nam three times, but it was quickly apparent to me how little one knows if he has been on the periphery of a problem and not truly in it. Until the day-long sessions of early March, I had never had the opportunity of intensive analysis and fact-finding. Now I was thrust into a vigorous, ruthlessly frank assessment of our situation by the men who knew the most about it. Try though we would to stay with the assignment of devising means to meet the military's requests, fundamental questions began to recur over and over.

It is, of course, not possible to recall all the questions that were asked nor all of the answers that were given. Had a transcript of our discussions been made—one was not—it would have run to hundreds of closely printed pages. The documents brought to the table by participants would have totalled, if collected in one place—which they were not—many hundreds more. All that is pertinent to this essay are the impressions I formed, and the conclusions I ultimately reached in those days of exhausting scrutiny. In the colloquial style of those meetings, here are some of the principal issues raised and some of the answers as I understood them:

"Will 200,000 more men do the job?" I found no assurance that they would.

"If not, how many more might be needed—and when?" There was no way of knowing.

"What would be involved in committing 200,000 more men to Viet Nam?" A reserve call-up of approximately 280,000, an increased draft call and an extension of tours of duty of most men then in service.

"Can the enemy respond with a build-up of his own?" He could and he probably would.

"What are the estimated costs of the latest requests?" First calculations were on the order of $2 billion for the remaining four months of that fiscal year, and an increase of $10 to $12 billion for the year beginning July 1, 1968.

"What will be the impact on the economy?" So great that we would face the possibility of credit restrictions, a tax increase and even wage and price controls. The balance of payments would be worsened by at least half a billion dollars a year.

"Can bombing stop the war?" Never by itself. It was inflicting heavy personnel and matériel losses, but bombing by itself would not stop the war.

"Will stepping up the bombing decrease American casualties?" Very little, if at all. Our casualties were due to the intensity of the ground fighting in the South. We had already dropped a heavier tonnage of bombs than in all the theaters of World War II. During 1967, an estimated 90,000 North Vietnamese had infiltrated into South Viet Nam. In the opening weeks of 1968, infiltrators were coming in at three to four times the rate of a year earlier, despite the ferocity and intensity of our campaign of aerial interdiction.

"How long must we keep on sending our men and carrying the main burden of combat?" The South Vietnamese were doing better, but they were not ready yet to replace our troops and we did not know when they would be.

When I asked for a presentation of the military plan for attaining victory in Viet Nam, I was told that there was no plan for victory in the historic American sense. Why not? Because our forces were operating under three major political restrictions: The President had forbidden the invasion of North Viet Nam because this could trigger the mutual assistance pact between North Viet Nam and China; the President had forbidden the mining of the harbor at Haiphong, the principal port through which the North received military supplies, because a Soviet vessel might be sunk; the President had forbidden our forces to pursue the enemy into Laos and Cambodia, for to do so would spread the war, politically and geographically, with no discernible advantage. These and other restrictions which precluded an all-out, no-holds-barred military effort were wisely designed to prevent our being drawn into a larger war. We had no inclination to recommend to the President their cancellation.

"Given these circumstances, how can we win?" We would, I was told, continue to evidence our superiority over the enemy; we would continue to attack in the belief that he would reach the stage where he would find it inadvisable to go on with the war. He could not afford the attrition we were inflicting on him. And we were improving our posture all the time.

I then asked, "What is the best estimate as to how long this course of action will take? Six months? One year? Two years?" There was no agreement on an answer. Not only was there no agreement, I could find no one willing to express any confidence in his guesses. Certainly, none of us was willing to assert that he could see "light at the end of the tunnel" or that American troops would be coming home by the end of the year.

After days of this type of analysis, my concern had greatly deepened. I could not find out when the war was going to end; I could not find out the manner in which it was going to end; I could not find out whether the new requests for men and equipment were going to be enough, or whether it would take more and, if more, when and how much; I could not find out how soon the South Vietnamese forces would be ready to take over. All I had was the statement, given with too little self-assurance to be comforting, that if we persisted for an indeterminate length of time, the enemy would choose not to go on.

And so I asked, "Does anyone see any diminution in the will of the enemy after four years of our having been there, after enormous casualties and after massive destruction from our bombing?"

The answer was that there appeared to be no diminution in the will of the enemy. This reply was doubly impressive, because I was more conscious each day of domestic unrest in our own country. Draft card burnings, marches in the streets, problems on school campuses, bitterness and divisiveness were rampant. Just as disturbing to me were the economic implications of a struggle to be indefinitely continued at ever-increasing cost. The dollar was already in trouble, prices were escalating far too fast and emergency controls on foreign investment imposed on New Year's Day would be only a prelude to more stringent controls, if we were to add another $12 billion to Viet Nam spending—with perhaps still more to follow.

I was also conscious of our obligations and involvements elsewhere in the world. There were certain hopeful signs in our relations with the Soviet Union, but both nations were hampered in moving toward vitally important talks on the limitation of strategic weapons so long as the United States was committed to a military solution in Viet Nam. We could not afford to disregard our interests in the Middle East, South Asia, Africa, Western Europe and elsewhere. Even accepting the validity of our objective in Viet Nam, that objective had to be viewed in the context of our overall national interest, and could not sensibly be pursued at a price so high as to impair our ability to achieve other, and perhaps even more important, foreign policy objectives.

Also, I could not free myself from the continuing nagging doubt left over from that August trip, that if the nations living in the shadow of Viet Nam were not now persuaded by the domino theory, perhaps it was time for us to take another look. Our efforts had given the nations in that area a number of years following independence to organize and build their security. I could see no reason at this time for us to continue to add to our commitment. Finally, there was no assurance that a 40 percent increase in American troops would place us within the next few weeks, months or even years in any substantially better military position than we were in then. All that could be predicted accurately was that more troops would raise the level of combat and automatically raise the level of casualties on both sides.

And so, after these exhausting days, I was convinced that the military course we were pursuing was not only endless, but hopeless. A further substantial increase in American forces could only increase the devastation and the Americanization of the war, and thus leave us even further from our goal of a peace that would permit the people of South Viet Nam to fashion their own political and economic institutions. Henceforth, I was also convinced, our primary goal should be to level off our involvement, and to work toward gradual disengagement.

IV

To reach a conclusion and to implement it are not the same, especially when one does not have the ultimate power of decision. It now became my purpose to emphasize to my colleagues and to the President, that the United States had entered Viet Nam with a limited aim—to prevent its subjugation by the North and to enable the people of South Viet Nam to determine their own future. I also argued that we had largely accomplished that objective. Nothing required us to remain until the North had been ejected from the South, and the Saigon government had been established in complete military control of all South Viet Nam. An increase of over 200,000 in troop strength would mean that American forces would be twice the size of the regular South Vietnamese Army at that time. Our goal of building a stronger South Vietnamese Government, and an effective military force capable of ultimately taking over from us, would be frustrated rather than furthered. The more we continued to do in South Viet Nam, the less likely the South Vietnamese were to shoulder their own burden.

The debate continued at the White House for days. President Johnson encouraged me to report my findings and my views with total candor, but he was equally insistent on hearing the views of others. Finally, the President, in the closing hours of March, made his decisions and reported them to the people on the eve-

ning of the 31st. Three related directly to the month's review of
the war. First, the President announced he was establishing a
ceiling of 549,500 in the American commitment to Viet Nam;
the only new troops going out would be support troops previously promised. Second, we would speed up our aid to the South
Vietnamese armed forces. We would equip and train them to take
over major combat responsibilities from us on a much accelerated
schedule. Third, speaking to Hanoi, the President stated he was
greatly restricting American bombing of the North as an invitation and an inducement to begin peace talks. We would no longer
bomb north of the Twentieth Parallel. By this act of unilateral
restraint, nearly 80 percent of the territory of North Viet Nam
would no longer be subjected to our bombing.

I had taken office at the beginning of the month with one overriding immediate assignment—responding to the military request to strengthen our forces in Viet Nam so that we might
prosecute the war more forcefully. Now my colleagues and I had
two different and longer-range tasks—developing a plan for
shifting the burden to the South Vietnamese as rapidly as they
could be made ready, and supporting our government's diplomatic efforts to engage in peace talks.

To assess the rate of progress in the first task, I went to Viet
Nam in July. I was heartened by the excellent spirit and the
condition of our forces, but I found distressingly little evidence
that the other troop-contributing countries, or the South Vietnamese, were straining to relieve us of our burdens. Although
there had been nominal increases in troop contributions from
Australia and Thailand since the preceding summer, the Philippines had actually withdrawn several hundred men. The troop-
contributing countries were bearing no more of the combat
burden; their casualty rates were actually falling.

As for South Vietnamese officials, in discussion after discussion, I found them professing unawareness of shortcomings in
such matters as troop training, junior officer strength and rate
of desertions. They were, I felt, too complacent when the facts
were laid before them. I asked Vice President Ky, for example,
about the gross desertion rate of South Vietnamese combat personnel that was running at 30 percent a year. He responded
that it was so large, in part, because their men were not paid
enough. I asked what his government intended to do. He suggested that we could cut back our bombing, give the money thus

saved to the Saigon government, and it would be used for troop pay. He was not jesting; his suggestion was a serious one. I returned home oppressed by the pervasive Americanization of the war: we were still giving the military instructions, still doing most of the fighting, still providing all the matériel, still paying most of the bills. Worst of all, I concluded that the South Vietnamese leaders seemed content to have it that way.

The North had responded to the President's speech of March 31 and meetings had begun in Paris in May. It was, however, a euphemism to call them peace talks. In mid-summer, substantive discussions had not yet begun. Our negotiators, the able and experienced Ambassador Averell Harriman and his talented associate, Cyrus Vance, were insisting that the Saigon government be a participant in the talks. Hanoi rejected this. President Johnson, rightly and understandably, refused to order a total bombing halt of the North until Hanoi would accept reciprocal restraints. Hanoi refused. With this unsatisfactory deadlock, the summer passed in Paris.

In Viet Nam, American casualty lists were tragically long, week after week. The enemy was not winning but, I felt, neither were we. There were many other areas in the world where our influence, moral force and economic contributions were sorely in demand and were limited because of our preoccupation with our involvement in Southeast Asia.

I returned from a NATO meeting in Bonn on Sunday evening, October 13, to find a summons to a White House meeting the following morning. There had been movement in Paris. There were no formal agreements, but certain "understandings" had been reached by our negotiating team and the North Vietnamese. At last the North had accepted the participation of the South in peace talks. We would stop all bombing of North Viet Nam. Substantive talks were to start promptly. We had made it clear to Hanoi that we could not continue such talks if there were indiscriminate shelling of major cities in the South, or if the demilitarized zone were violated so as to place our troops in jeopardy.

The President outlined the situation to his advisers. We spent a day of hard and full review. The Joint Chiefs of Staff were unanimous in stating that the bombing halt under these circumstances was acceptable. The State Department was authorized to report to Saigon that we had won a seat at the conference table for the Saigon government and to request the earliest possible presence of their delegation in Paris. I felt a sense of relief and hope; we were started down the road to peace.

These feelings were short-lived. The next three weeks were almost as agonizing to me as March had been. The cables from Saigon were stunning. The South Vietnamese Government, suddenly and unexpectedly, was not willing to go to Paris. First one reason, then another, then still another were cabled to Washington. As fast as one Saigon obstacle was overcome, another took its place. Incredulity turned to dismay. I felt that the President and the United States were being badly used. Even worse, I felt that Saigon was attempting to exert a veto power over our agreement to engage in peace negotiations. I admired greatly the President's ability to be patient under the most exasperating circumstances. Each day ran the risk that the North might change its mind, and that months of diligent effort at Paris would be in vain; each day saw a new effort on his part to meet the latest Saigon objection.

To satisfy himself that the bombing halt would neither jeopardize our own forces nor those of our allies, the President ordered General Creighton W. Abrams back from South Viet Nam for a personal report. Finally, on October 31, President Johnson announced that the bombing of North Viet Nam would cease, peace talks would begin promptly and Saigon was assured of a place at the conference table. However, it took weeks to get the Saigon government to Paris, and still additional weeks to get their agreement on seating arrangements.

By the time the various difficulties had been resolved, certain clear and unequivocal opinions regarding the attitude and posture of the Saigon government had crystalized in my mind. These opinions had been forming since my trip to South Viet Nam the preceding July.

The goal of the Saigon government and the goal of the United States were no longer one and the same, if indeed they ever had been. They were not in total conflict but they were clearly not identical. We had largely accomplished the objective for which we had entered the struggle. There was no longer any question about the desire of the American people to bring the Viet Nam adventure to a close.

As Ambassador Harriman observed, it is dangerous to let your aims be escalated in the middle of a war. Keep your objectives in mind, he advised, and as soon as they are attained, call a halt. The winning of the loyalty of villagers to the central government in Saigon, the form of a postwar government, who its leaders should be and how they are to be selected—these were clearly not among our original war objectives. But these were the precise areas of our differences with the Saigon government.

As Saigon authorities saw it, the longer the war went on, with the large-scale American involvement, the more stable was their régime, and the fewer concessions they would have to make to other political groupings. If the United States were to continue its military efforts for another two or three years, perhaps the North Vietnamese and the Viet Cong would be so decimated that no concessions would be needed at all. In the meantime, vast amounts of American wealth were being poured into the South Vietnamese economy. In short, grim and distasteful though it might be, I concluded during the bleak winter weeks that Saigon was in no hurry for the fighting to end and that the Saigon régime did not want us to reach an early settlement of military issues with Hanoi.

The fact is that the creation of strong political, social and economic institutions is a job that the Vietnamese must do for themselves. We cannot do it for them, nor can they do it while our presence hangs over them so massively. President Thieu, Vice President Ky, Prime Minister Huong and those who may follow them have the task of welding viable political institutions from the 100 or more splinter groups that call themselves political parties. It is up to us to let them get on with the job. Nothing we might do could be so beneficial or could so add to the political maturity of South Viet Nam as to begin to withdraw our combat troops. Moreover, in my opinion, we cannot realistically expect to achieve anything more through our military force, and the time has come to begin to disengage. That was my final conclusion as I left the Pentagon on January 20, 1969.

v

It remains my firm opinion today. It is based not only on my personal experiences, but on the many significant changes that have occurred in the world situation in the last four years.

In 1965, the forces supported by North Viet Nam were on the verge of a military take-over of South Viet Nam. Only by sending large numbers of American troops was it possible to prevent this from happening. The South Vietnamese were militarily weak and politically demoralized. They could not, at that time, be expected to preserve for themselves the right to determine their own future. Communist China had recently proclaimed its intention to implement the doctrine of "wars of national liberation." Khrushchev's fall from power the preceding October and Chou En-lai's visit to Moscow in November 1964 posed the dire possibility of the two communist giants working together to spread disruption throughout the underdeveloped nations of the world. Indonesia, under Sukarno, presented a posture of implacable hostility toward Malaysia, and was a destabilizing element in the entire Pacific picture. Malaysia itself, as well as Thailand and Singapore, needed time for their governmental institutions to mature. Apparent American indifference to developments in Asia might, at that time, have had a disastrous impact on the independent countries of that area.

During the past four years, the situation has altered dramatically. The armed forces of South Viet Nam have increased in size and proficiency. The political situation there has become more stable, and the governmental institutions more representative. Elsewhere in Asia, conditions of greater security exist. The bloody defeat of the attempted communist coup in Indonesia removed Sukarno from power and changed the confrontation with Malaysia to coöperation between the two countries. The governments of Thailand and Singapore have made good use of these four years to increase their popular support. Australia and New Zealand have moved toward closer regional defense ties, while Japan, the Republic of Korea and Taiwan have exhibited a rate of economic growth and an improvement in living standards that discredit the teachings of Chairman Mao.

Of at least equal significance is the fact that, since 1965, relations between Russia and China have steadily worsened. The schism between these two powers is one of the watershed events of our time. Ironically, their joint support of Hanoi has contributed to the acrimony between them. It has brought into focus their competition for leadership in the communist camp. Conflicting positions on the desirability of the peace negotiations in Paris have provided a further divisive factor. In an analogous development, increased Soviet aid to North Korea has made Pyongyang less dependent on China. The Cultural Revolution and the depredations of the Red Guards have created in China a situation of internal unrest that presently preoccupies China's military forces. The recent border clashes on the Ussuri River further decrease the likelihood that China will, in the near future, be able to devote its attention and resources to the export of revolution.

These considerations are augmented by another. It seems clear that the necessity to devote more of our minds and our means to our pressing domestic problems requires that we set a chronological limit on our Vietnamese involvement.

A year ago, we placed a numerical limit on this involvement, and did so without lessening the effectiveness of the total military effort. There will, undeniably, be many problems inherent in the replacement of American combat forces with South Vietnamese forces. But whatever these problems, they must be faced. There is no way to achieve our goal of creating the conditions that will allow the South Vietnamese to determine their own future unless we begin, and begin promptly, to turn over to them the major responsibility for their own defense. This ability to defend themselves can never be developed so long as we continue to bear the brunt of the battle. Sooner or later, the test must be whether the South Vietnamese will serve their own country sufficiently well to guarantee its national survival. In my view, this test must be made sooner, rather than later.

A first step would be to inform the South Vietnamese Government that we will withdraw about 100,000 troops before the end of this year. We should also make it clear that this is not an isolated action, but the beginning of a process under which all U.S. ground combat forces will have been withdrawn from Viet Nam by the end of 1970. The same information should, of course, be provided to the other countries who are contributing forces for the defense of South Viet Nam.

Strenuous political and military objections to this decision must be anticipated. Arguments will be made that such a withdrawal will cause the collapse of the Saigon government and jeopardize the security of our own and allied troops. Identical arguments, however, were urged against the decisions to restrict the bombing on March 31 of last year and to stop it completely on October 31. They have proven to be unfounded. There is, in fact, no magic and no specific military rationale for the number of American troops presently in South Viet Nam. The current figure represents only the level at which the escalator stopped.

It should also be noted that our military commanders have stated flatly since last summer that no additional American troops are needed. During these months the number of South Vietnamese under arms in the Government cause has increased substantially and we have received steady reports of their improved performance. Gradual withdrawal of American combat troops thus not only would be consistent with continued overall military strength, but also would serve to substantiate the claims of the growing combat effectiveness of the South Vietnamese forces.

Concurrently with the decision to begin withdrawal, orders should be issued to our military commanders to discontinue efforts to apply maximum military pressure on the enemy and to seek instead to reduce the level of combat. The public statements of our officials show that there has as yet been no change in our policy of maximum military effort. The result has been a continuation of the high level of American casualties, without any discernible impact on the peace negotiations in Paris.

While our combat troops are being withdrawn, we would continue to provide the armed forces of the Saigon government with logistic support and with our air resources. As the process goes on, we can appraise both friendly and enemy reactions. The pattern of our eventual withdrawal of non-combat troops and personnel engaged in air lift and air support can be determined on the basis of political and military developments. So long as we retain our air resources in South Viet Nam, with total air superiority, I do not believe that the lessening in the military pressure exerted by the ground forces would permit the enemy to make any significant gains. There is, moreover, the possibility of reciprocal reduction in North Vietnamese combat activity.

Our decision progressively to turn over the combat burden to the armed forces of South Viet Nam would confront the North Vietnamese leaders with a painful dilemma. Word that the Americans were beginning to withdraw might at first lead them to claims of victory. But even these initial claims could be expected to be tinged with apprehension. There has, in my view, long been considerable evidence that Hanoi fears the possibility that those whom they characterize as "puppet forces" may, with continued but gradually reduced American support, prove able to stand off the communist forces.

As American combat forces are withdrawn, Hanoi would be

faced with the prospect of a prolonged and substantial presence of American air and logistics personnel in support of South Viet Nam's combat troops, which would be constantly improving in efficiency. Hanoi's only alternative would be to arrange, tacitly or explicitly, for a mutual withdrawal of all external forces. In either eventuality, the resulting balance of forces should avert any danger of a blood bath which some fear might occur in the aftermath of our withdrawal.

Once our withdrawal of combat troops commences, the Saigon government would recognize, probably for the first time, that American objectives do not demand the perpetuation in power of any one group of South Vietnamese. So long as we appear prepared to remain indefinitely, there is no pressure on Saigon to dilute the control of those presently in positions of power by making room for individuals representative of other nationalist elements in South Vietnamese society.

Accordingly, I anticipate no adverse impact on the Paris negotiations from the announcement and implementation of a program of American withdrawal. Instead, I would foresee the creation of circumstances under which true bargaining may proceed among the Vietnamese present in Paris. Unquestionably, the North Vietnamese and the National Liberation Front would do so in the hope that any political settlement would move them toward eventual domination in South Viet Nam. But their hopes and expectations necessarily will yield to the political realities, and these political realities are, in the final analysis, both beyond our control and beyond our ken. Moreover, they are basically none of our business. The one million South Vietnamese in the various components of the armed forces, with American logistics, air lift and air support, should be able, if they have the will, to prevent the imposition by force of a Hanoi-controlled régime. If they lack a sense or a sufficiency of national purpose, we can never force it on them.

In the long run, the security of the Pacific region will depend upon the ability of the countries there to meet the legitimate growing demands of their own people. No military strength we can bring to bear can give them internal stability or popular acceptance. In Southeast Asia, and elsewhere in the less developed regions of the world, our ability to understand and to control the basic forces that are at play is a very limited one. We can advise, we can urge, we can furnish economic aid. But American military power cannot build nations, any more than it can solve the social and economic problems that face us here at home.

This, then, is the case history of the evolution of one individual's thinking regarding Viet Nam. Throughout this entire period it has been difficult to cling closely to reality because of the constant recurrence of optimistic predictions that our task was nearly over, and that better times were just around the corner, or just over the next hill.

We cannot afford to lose sight of the fact that this is a limited war, for limited aims and employing limited power. The forces we now have deployed and the human and material costs we are now incurring have become, in my opinion, out of all proportion to our purpose. The present scale of military effort can bring us no closer to meaningful victory. It can only continue to devastate the countryside and to prolong the suffering of the Vietnamese people of every political persuasion.

Unless we have the imagination and the courage to adopt a different course, I am convinced that we will be in no better, and no different, a position a year from now than we are today.

At current casualty rates, 10,000 more American boys will have lost their lives.

We should reduce American casualties by reducing American combat forces. We should do so in accordance with a definite schedule and with a specified end point.

Let us start to bring our men home—and let us start *now*.

¶ MORTGAGING THE OLD HOMESTEAD
  by Lord Ritchie-Calder   (January, 1970)

Although we have been placing inordinate demands on our environment for a number of years, environment as a "problem" seems very new because our realization of the fragility of the ecological balance that sustains us has come very suddenly.

Awareness of the problem may have some positive effects internationally. Because noxious effluents know no national boundaries and cut across ideological barriers, the common struggle to combat them may lead us to create new forms of cooperation among nations, new international institutions. It may also increase the leverage of the developing countries, as their environments become a valuable commodity in the world market place. And it is increasingly accepted that the poor nations must get at least a fair share of our common resource—the oceans.

But, in trying to deal with environmental pollution, we are faced with both a lack of knowledge and institutional inertia. Some environmentalists assert that, to avoid irreparable damage to the earth and its atmospheric envelope, the industrialized nations must restructure their economies to minimize growth and severely limit the use of resources. However, people have always tired easily of those predicting the imminent doom of mankind.

Lord Ritchie-Calder's article is a dramatic attempt to shake people into action on the environment. He successfully bridges the gap between the two cultures, painting for the layman a stark picture of the deleterious effects of lack of foresight on the part of specialists in the scientific community.

MORTGAGING THE OLD HOMESTEAD

By Lord Ritchie-Calder

PAST civilizations are buried in the graveyards of their own mistakes, but as each died of its greed, its carelessness or its effeteness another took its place. That was because such civilizations took their character from a locality or region. Today ours is a global civilization; it is not bounded by the Tigris and the Euphrates nor even the Hellespont and the Indus; it is the whole world. Its planet has shrunk to a neighborhood round which a man-made satellite can patrol sixteen times a day, riding the gravitational fences of Man's family estate. It is a community so interdependent that our mistakes are exaggerated on a world scale.

For the first time in history, Man has the power of veto over the evolution of his own species through a nuclear holocaust. The overkill is enough to wipe out every man, woman and child on earth, together with our fellow lodgers, the animals, the birds and the insects, and to reduce our planet to a radioactive wilderness. Or the Doomsday Machine could be replaced by the Doomsday Bug. By gene-manipulation and man-made mutations, it is possible to produce, or generate, a disease against which there would be no natural immunity; by "generate" is meant that even if the perpetrators inoculated themselves protectively, the disease in spreading round the world could assume a virulence of its own and involve them too. When a British bacteriologist died of the bug he had invented, a distinguished scientist said, "Thank God he didn't sneeze; he could have started a pandemic against which there would have been no immunity."

Modern Man can outboast the Ancients, who in the arrogance of their material achievements built pyramids as the gravestones of their civilizations. We can blast our pyramids into space to orbit through all eternity round a planet which perished by our neglect.

A hundred years ago Claude Bernard, the famous French physiologist, enjoined his colleagues, "True science teaches us to doubt and in ignorance to refrain." What he meant was that the scientist must proceed from one tested foothold to the next (like going into a mine-field with a mine-detector). Today we are using the biosphere, the living space, as an experimental laboratory. When the mad scientist of fiction blows himself and his laboratory skyhigh, that is all right, but when scientists and decision-makers act out of ignorance and pretend that it is knowledge, they are putting the whole world in hazard. Anyway, science at best is not wisdom; it is knowledge, while wisdom is knowledge tempered with judgment. Because of overspecialization, most scientists are disabled from exercising judgments beyond their own sphere.

A classic example was the atomic bomb. It was the Physicists' Bomb. When the device exploded at Alamogordo on July 16, 1945, and made a notch-mark in history from which Man's future would be dated, the safe-breakers had cracked the lock of the nucleus before the locksmiths knew how it worked. (The evidence of this is the billions of dollars which have been spent since 1945 on gargantuan machines to study the fundamental particles, the components of the nucleus; and they still do not know how they interrelate.)

Prime Minister Clement Attlee, who concurred with President Truman's decision to drop the bomb on Hiroshima, later said: "We knew nothing whatever at that time about the genetic effects of an atomic explosion. I knew nothing about fall-out and all the rest of what emerged after Hiroshima. As far as I know, President Truman and Winston Churchill knew nothing of those things either, nor did Sir John Anderson who coördinated research on our side. Whether the scientists directly concerned knew or guessed, I do not know. But if they did, then so far as I am aware, they said nothing of it to those who had to make the decision."[1]

That sounds absurd, since as long before as 1927, Herman J. Muller had been studying the genetic effects of radiation, work for which he was awarded the Nobel Prize in 1946. But it is true that in the whole documentation of the British effort, before it merged in the Manhattan Project, there is only one reference to

[1] "Twilight of Empire," by Clement Attlee with Francis Williams. New York: Barnes, 1961, p. 74.

genetic effects—a Medical Research Council minute which was not connected with the bomb they were intending to make; it concerned the possibility that the Germans might, short of the bomb, produce radioactive isotopes as a form of biological warfare. In the Franck Report, the most statesmanlike document ever produced by scientists, with its percipience of the military and political consequences of unilateral use of the bomb (presented to Secretary of War Henry L. Stimson even before the test bomb exploded), no reference is made to the biological effects, although one would have supposed that to have been a very powerful argument. The explanation, of course, was that it was the Physicists' Bomb and military security restricted information and discussion to the bomb-makers, which excluded the biologists.

The same kind of breakdown in interdisciplinary consultation was manifest in the subsequent testing of fission and fusion bombs. Categorical assurances were given that the fallout would be confined to the testing area, but the Japanese fishing-boat *Lucky Dragon* was "dusted" well outside the predicted range. Then we got the story of radiostrontium. Radiostrontium is an analogue of calcium. Therefore in bone-formation an atom of natural strontium can take the place of calcium and the radioactive version can do likewise. Radiostrontium did not exist in the world before 1945; it is a man-made element. Today every young person, anywhere in the world, whose bones were forming during the massive bomb-testing in the atmosphere, carries this brandmark of the Atomic Age. The radiostrontium in their bones is medically insignificant, but, if the test ban (belated recognition) had not prevented the escalation of atmospheric testing, it might not have been.

Every young person everywhere was affected, and why? Because those responsible for H-bomb testing miscalculated. They assumed that the upthrust of the H-bomb would punch a hole in the stratosphere and that the gaseous radioactivity would dissipate itself. One of those gases was radioactive krypton, which quickly decays into radiostrontium, which is a particulate. The technicians had been wrongly briefed about the nature of the troposphere, the climatic ceiling which would, they maintained, prevent the fall-back. But between the equatorial troposphere and the polar troposphere there is a gap, and the radiostrontium came back through this fanlight into the climatic jet-streams. It was swept all round the world to come to earth as radioactive rain, to be deposited on foodcrops and pastures, to be ingested by animals and to get into milk and into babies and children and adolescents whose growing bones were hungry for calcium or its equivalent strontium, in this case radioactive. Incidentally, radio-strontium was known to the biologists before it "hit the head-lines." They had found it in the skin burns of animals exposed on the Nevada testing ranges and they knew its sinister nature as a "bone-seeker." But the authorities clapped security on their work, classified it as "Operation Sunshine" and cynically called the units of radiostrontium "Sunshine Units"—an instance not of ignorance but of deliberate non-communication.

One beneficial effect of the alarm caused by all this has been that the atoms industry is, bar none, the safest in the world for those working in it. Precautions, now universal, were built into the code of practice from the beginning. Indeed it can be ad-mitted that the safety margins in health and in working condi-tions are perhaps excessive in the light of experience, but no one would dare to modify them. There can, however, be accidents in which the public assumes the risk. At Windscale, the British atomic center in Cumberland, a reactor burned out. Radioactive fumes escaped from the stacks in spite of the filters. They drifted over the country. Milk was dumped into the sea because radio-active iodine had covered the dairy pastures.

There is the problem of atomic waste disposal, which persists in the peaceful uses as well as in the making of nuclear explo-sives. Low energy wastes, carefully monitored, can be safely dis-posed of. Trash, irradiated metals and laboratory waste can be embedded in concrete and dumped in the ocean deeps—although this practice raises some misgivings. But high-level wastes, some with elements the radioactivity of which can persist for *hundreds of thousands* of years, present prodigious difficulties. There must be "burial grounds" (or euphemistically "farms"), the biggest of which is at Hanford, Washington. It encloses a stretch of the Columbia River in a tract covering 575 square miles, where no one is allowed to live or to trespass.

There, in the twentieth century Giza, it has cost more, much more, to bury live atoms than it cost to entomb the sun-god Kings of Egypt. The capital outlay runs into hundreds of millions of dollars and the maintenance of the U.S. sepulchres is over $6 million a year. (Add to that the buried waste of the U.S.S.R., Britain, Canada, France and China, and one can see what it costs to bury live atoms.) And they are very much alive. At Hanford they are kept in million-gallon carbon-steel tanks. Their radioactive vitality keeps the accompanying acids boiling like a witches' cauldron. A cooling system has to be maintained continuously. The vapors from the self-boiling tanks have to be condensed and "scrubbed" (radioactive atoms removed); otherwise a radioactive miasma would escape from the vents. The tanks will not endure as long as the pyramids and certainly not for the hundreds of thousands of years of the long-lived atoms. The acids and the atomic ferments erode the toughest metal, so the tanks have to be periodically decanted. Another method is to entomb them in disused salt mines. Another is to embed them in ceramics, lock them up in glass beads. Another is what is known as "hydraulic fraction": a hole is drilled into a shale formation (below the subsoil water); liquid is piped down under pressure and causes the shale to split laterally. Hence the atoms in liquid cement can be injected under enormous pressure and spread into the fissures to set like a radioactive sandwich.

This accumulating waste from fission plants will persist until the promise, still far from fulfilled, of peaceful thermonuclear power comes about. With the multiplication of power reactors, the wastes will increase. It is calculated that by the year 2000, the number of six-ton nuclear "hearses" in transit to "burial grounds" at any given time on the highways of the United States will be well over 3,000 and the amount of radioactive products will be about a billion curies, which is a mighty lot of curies to be roaming around a populated country.

The alarming possibilities were well illustrated by the incident at Palomares, on the coast of Spain, when there occurred a collision of a refueling aircraft with a U.S. nuclear bomber on "live" mission. The bombs were scattered. There was no explosion, but radioactive materials broke loose and the contaminated beaches and farm soil had to be scooped up and taken to the United States for burial.

Imagine what would have happened if the *Torrey Canyon,* the giant tanker which was wrecked off the Scilly Isles, had been nuclear-powered. Some experts make comforting noises and say that the reactors would have "closed down," but the *Torrey Canyon* was a wreck and the Palomares incident showed what happens when radioactive materials break loose. All those oil-polluted beaches of southwest England and the coasts of Brittany would have had to be scooped up for nuclear burial.

II

The *Torrey Canyon* is a nightmarish example of progress for its own sake. The bigger the tanker the cheaper the freightage, which is supposed to be progress. This ship was built at Newport News, Virginia, in 1959 for the Union Oil Company; it was a giant for the time—810 feet long and 104 feet beam—but, five years later, that was not big enough. She was taken to Japan to be "stretched." The ship was cut in half amidship and a mid-body section inserted. With a new bow, this made her 974 feet long, and her beam was extended 21 feet. She could carry 850,000 barrels of oil, twice her original capacity.

Built for Union Oil, she was "owned" by the Barracuda Tanker Corporation, the head office of which is a filing cabinet in Hamilton, Bermuda. She was registered under the Liberian flag of convenience and her captain and crew were Italians, recruited in Genoa. Just to complicate the international triangle, she was under charter to the British Petroleum Tanker Company to bring 118,000 tons of crude oil from Kuwait to Milford Haven in Wales, via the Cape of Good Hope. Approaching Lands End, the Italian captain was informed that if he did not reach Milford Haven by 11 p.m. Saturday night, he would miss highwater and would not be able to enter the harbor for another five days, which would have annoyed his employers. He took a shortcut, setting course between Seven Stones rocks and the Scilly Isles, and he finished up on Pollard Rock, in an area where no ship of that size should ever have been.

Her ruptured tanks began to vomit oil and great slicks spread over the sea in the direction of the Cornish holiday beaches. A Dutch tug made a dash for the stranded ship, gambling on the salvage money. (Where the salvaged ship could have been taken one cannot imagine, since no place would offer harborage to a leaking tanker). After delays and a death in the futile salvage effort, the British Government moved in with the navy, the air force and, on the beaches, the army. They tried to set fire to the floating oil which, of course, would not volatilize. They covered the slicks with detergents (supplied at a price by the oil companies), and then the bombers moved in to try to cut open the deck and, with incendiaries, to set fire to the remaining oil in the tanks. Finally the ship foundered and divers confirmed that the oil had been effectively consumed.

Nevertheless the result was havoc. All measures had had to be improvised. Twelve thousand tons of detergent went into the sea. Later marine biologists found that the cure had been worse than the complaint. The oil was disastrous for seabirds, but marine organic life was destroyed by the detergents. By arduous physical efforts, with bulldozers and flame-throwers and, again, more detergents, the beaches were cleaned up for the holiday-makers. Northerly winds swept the oil slicks down Channel to the French coast with even more serious consequences, particularly to the valuable shellfish industry. With even bigger tankers being launched, this affair is a portentous warning.

Two years after *Torrey Canyon* an offshore oil rig erupted in the Santa Barbara Channel. The disaster to wildlife in this area, which has island nature reserves and is on the migratory route of whales, seals and seabirds, was a repetition of the *Torrey Canyon* oil-spill. And the operator of the lethal oil rig was Union Oil.

III

Another piece of stupidity shows how much we are at the mercy of ignorant men pretending to be knowledgeable. During the International Geophysical Year, 1957–58, the Van Allen Belt was discovered. This is an area of magnetic phenomena. Immediately it was decided to explode a nuclear bomb in the Belt to see whether an artificial aurora could be produced. The colorful draperies and luminous skirts of the aurora borealis are caused by the drawing in of cosmic particles through the rare bases of the upper atmosphere—ionization it is called; it is like passing electrons through the vacuum tubes of our familiar florescent lighting. The name Rainbow Bomb was given it in anticipation of the display it was expected to produce. Every eminent scientist in the field of cosmology, radio-astronomy or physics of the atmosphere protested at this irresponsible tampering with a system which we did not understand. And typical of the casual attitude toward this kind of thing, the Prime Minister of the day, answering protests in the House of Commons that called on him to intervene with the Americans, asked what all the fuss was about. After all, they hadn't known that the Van Allen Belt even existed a year before. This was the cosmic equivalent of Chamberlain's remark about Czechoslovakia, at the time of Munich, about that distant country of which we knew so little. They exploded the bomb. They got their pyrotechnics and we still do not know the cost we may have to pay for this artificial magnetic disturbance.

In the same way we can look with misgivings on those tracks —the white tails of the jets, which are introducing into our climatic system new factors, the effects of which are immensurable. Formation of rain clouds depends upon water vapor having a nucleus on which to form. That is how artificial precipitation is introduced—the so-called rain-making. So the jets, criss-crossing the weather system, playing noughts and crosses with it, can produce a man-made change.

In the longer term we can foresee even more drastic effects from Man's unthinking operations. At the United Nations' Science and Technology Conference in Geneva in 1963 we took stock of the effects of industrialization on our total environment thus far. The atmosphere is not only the air which humans, animals and plants breathe; it is also the envelope which protects living things from harmful radiation from the sun and outer space. It is also the medium of climate, the winds and the rain. Those are inseparable from the hydrosphere—the oceans, covering seven-tenths of the globe, with their currents and extraordinary rates of evaporation; the biosphere, with its trees and their transpiration; and, in terms of human activities, the minerals mined from the lithosphere, the rock crust. Millions of years ago the sun encouraged the growth of the primeval forests, which became our coal, and the plant growth of the seas, which became our oil. Those fossil fuels, locked away for æons of time, are extracted by man and put back into the atmosphere from the chimney stacks and the exhaust pipes of modern engineering. About 6 billion tons of carbon are mixed with the atmosphere annually. During the past century, in the process of industrialization, with its release of carbon by the burning of fossil fuels, more than 400 billion tons of carbon have been artificially introduced into the atmosphere. The concentration in the air we breathe has been increased by approximately 10 percent, and if all the the known reserves of coal and oil were burnt at once, the concentration would be ten times greater.

This is something more than a public health problem, more than a question of what goes into the lungs of an individual, more than a question of smog. The carbon cycle in nature is a self-adjusting mechanism. Carbon dioxide is, of course, indispensable for plants and is, therefore, a source of life, but there is a balance which is maintained by excess carbon being absorbed by the seas. The excess is now taxing this absorption and it can seriously disturb the heat balance of the earth because of what is known as the "greenhouse effect." A greenhouse lets in the sun's rays but retains the heat. Carbon dioxide, as a transparent diffusion, does likewise. It keeps the heat at the surface of the earth and in excess modifies the climate.

It has been estimated that, at the present rate of increase, the mean annual temperature all over the world might increase by 3.6 degrees centigrade in the next forty to fifty years. The experts may argue about the time factor and even about the effects, but certain things are apparent, not only in the industrialized Northern Hemisphere but in the Southern Hemisphere also. The North-polar icecap is thinning and shrinking. The seas, with their blanket of carbon dioxide, are changing their temperature, with the result that marine plant life is increasing and is transpiring more carbon dioxide. As a result of the combination, fish are migrating, changing even their latitudes. On land the snow line is retreating and glaciers are melting. In Scandinavia, land which was perennially under snow and ice is thawing, and arrowheads of over 1,000 years ago, when the black soils were last exposed, have been found. The melting of sea ice will not affect the sea level, because the volume of floating ice is the same as the water it displaces, but the melting of icecaps or glaciers, in which the water is locked up, will introduce additional water to the sea and raise the level. Rivers originating in glaciers and permanent snow fields will increase their flow; and if ice dams, such as those in the Himalayas, break, the results in flooding may be catastrophic. In this process the patterns of rainfall will change, with increased precipitation in some areas and the possibility of aridity in now fertile regions. One would be well advised not to take ninety-nine year leases on properties at present sea level.

IV

At that same conference, there was a sobering reminder of mistakes which can be writ large, from the very best intentions. In the Indus Valley in West Pakistan, the population is increasing at the rate of ten more mouths to be fed every five minutes.

In that same five minutes in that same place, an acre of land is being lost through water-logging and salinity. This is the largest irrigated region in the world. Twenty-three million acres are artificially watered by canals. The Indus and its tributaries, the Jhelum, the Chenab, the Ravi, the Beas and the Sutlej, created the alluvial plains of the Punjab and the Sind. In the nineteenth century, the British began a big program of farm development in lands which were fertile but had low rainfall. Barrages and distribution canals were constructed. One thing which, for economy's sake, was not done was to line the canals. In the early days, this genuinely did not matter. The water was being spread from the Indus into a thirsty plain and if it soaked in so much the better. The system also depended on what is called "inland delta drainage," that is to say, the water spreads out like a delta and then drains itself back into the river. After independence, Pakistan, with external aid, started vigorously to extend the Indus irrigation. The experts all said the soil was good and would produce abundantly once it got the distributed water. There were plenty of experts, but they all overlooked one thing—the hydrological imperatives. The incline from Lahore to the Rann of Kutch—700 miles—is a foot a mile, a quite inadequate drainage gradient. So as more and more barrages and more and more lateral canals were built, the water was not draining back into the Indus. Some 40 percent of the water in the unlined canals seeped underground, and in a network of 40,000 miles of canals that is a lot of water. The result was that the watertable rose. Low-lying areas became waterlogged, drowning the roots of the crops. In other areas the water crept upwards, leaching salts which accumulated in the surface layers, poisoning the crops. At the same time the irrigation régime, which used just $1\frac{1}{2}$ inches of water a year in the fields, did not sluice out those salts but added, through evaporation, its own salts. The result was tragically spectacular. In flying over large tracts of this area one would imagine that it was an Arctic landscape because the white crust of salt glistens like snow.

The situation was deteriorating so rapidly that President Ayub appealed in person to President Kennedy, who sent out a high-powered mission which encompassed twenty disciplines. This was backed by the computers at Harvard. The answers were pretty grim. It would take twenty years and $2 billion to repair the damage—more than it cost to create the installations that did the damage. It would mean using vertical drainage to bring up the water and use it for irrigation, and also to sluice out the salt in the surface soil. If those twenty scientific disciplines had been brought together in the first instance it would not have happened.

One more instance of the far-flung consequences of men's localized mistakes: No insecticides or pesticides have ever been allowed into the continent of Antarctica. Yet they have been found in the fauna along the northern coasts. They have come almost certainly from the Northern Hemisphere, carried from the rivers of the farm-states into the currents sweeping south. In November 1969, the U.S. Government decided to "phase out" the use of DDT.

Pollution is a crime compounded of ignorance and avarice. The great achievements of *Homo sapiens* become the disaster-ridden blunders of Unthinking Man—poisoned rivers and dead lakes, polluted with the effluents of industries which give something called "prosperity" at the expense of posterity. Rivers are treated like sewers and lakes like cesspools. These natural systems—and they are living systems—have struggled hard. The benevolent microorganisms which cope with reasonable amounts of organic matter have been destroyed by mineral detergents. Witness our foaming streams. Lake Erie did its best to provide the oxygen to neutralize the pickling acids of the great steel works. But it could not contend. It lost its oxygen in the battle. Its once rich commercial fishing industry died and its revitalizing microorganic life gave place to anaerobic organisms which do not need oxygen but give off foul smells, the mortuary smells of dead water. As one Erie industrialist retorted, "It's not our effluent; it's those damned dead fish."

We have had the Freedom from Hunger Campaign; presently we shall need a Freedom from Thirst Campaign. If the International Hydrological Decade does not bring us to our senses we will face a desperate situation. Of course it is bound up with the increasing population but also with the extravagances of the technologies which claim that they are serving that population. There is a competition between the water needs of the land which has to feed the increasing population and the domestic and industrial needs of that population. The theoretical minimum to sustain living standards is about 300 gallons a day per person. This is the approximate amount of water needed to produce grain for 2½ pounds of bread, but a diet of 2 pounds of bread and 1 pound of beef would require about 2,500 gallons. And that is nothing compared with the gluttonous requirements of steel-making, paper-making and the chemical industry.

Water—just H₂O—is as indispensable as food. To die of hunger one needs more than fifteen days. To die of thirst one needs only three. Yet we are squandering, polluting and destroying water. In Los Angeles and neighboring Southern California, a thousand times more water is being consumed than is being precipitated in the locality. They have preëmpted the water of neighboring states. They are piping it from Northern California and there is a plan to pipe it all the way from Canada's North-West Territories, from the Mackenzie and the Liard which flow northwards to the Arctic Ocean, to turn them back into deserts.

V

Always and everywhere we come back to the problem of population—more people to make more mistakes, more people to be the victims of the mistakes of others, more people to suffer Hell upon Earth. It is appalling to hear people complacently talking about the population explosion as though it belonged to the future, or world hunger as though it were threatening, when hundreds of millions can testify that it is already here—swear it with panting breath.

We know to the exact countdown second when the nuclear explosion took place—5:30 a.m., July 16, 1945, when the first device went off in the desert of Alamogordo, New Mexico. The fuse of the population explosion had been lit ten years earlier —February 1935. On that day a girl called Hildegarde was dying of generalized septicaemia. She had pricked her finger with a sewing needle and the infection had run amok. The doctors could not save her. Her desperate father injected a red dye into her body. Her father was Gerhard Domagk. The red dye was prontosil which he, a pharmaceutical chemist, had produced and had successfully used on mice lethally infected with streptococci, but never before on a human. Prontosil was the first of the sulfa drugs—chemotherapeutics, which could attack the germ within the living body. Thus was prepared the way for the rediscovery of penicillin—rediscovery because although Fleming had discovered it in 1928, it had been ignored because neither he nor anybody else had seen its supreme virtue of attacking germs within the living body. That is the operative phrase, for while medical science and the medical profession had used antiseptics for surface wounds and sores, they were always labeled "Poison, not to be taken internally." The sulfa drugs had shown that it was possible to attack specific germs within the living body and had changed this attitude. So when Chain and Florey looked again at Fleming's penicillin in 1938, they were seeing it in the light of the experience of the sulphas.

A new era of disease-fighting had begun—the sulfas, the antibiotics, DDT insecticides. Doctors could now attack a whole range of invisible enemies. They could master the old killer diseases. They proved it during the war, and when the war ended there were not only stockpiles of the drugs, there were tooled up factories to produce them. So to prevent the spread of the deadly epidemics which follow wars, the supplies were made available to the war-ravaged countries with their displaced persons, and then to the developing countries. Their indigenous infections and contagions and insect-borne diseases were checked.

Almost symbolically, the first great clinical use of prontosil had been in dealing with puerperal sepsis, childbed fever. It had spectacularly saved mothers' lives in Queen Charlotte's Hospital, London. Now its successors took up the story. Fewer mothers died in childbirth, to live and have more babies. Fewer infants died, fewer toddlers, fewer adolescents. They lived to marry and have children. Older people were not killed off by, for instance, malaria. The average life-span increased.

Professor Kingsley Davis of the University of California at Berkeley, the authority on urban development, has presented a hair-raising picture from his survey of the world's cities. He has shown that 38 percent of the world's population is already living in what are defined as urban places. Over one-fifth of the world's population is living in cities of 100,000 or more. And over one-tenth of the world's population is now living in cities of a million or more inhabitants. In 1968, 375 million people were living in million-and-over cities. The proportions are changing so quickly that on present trends it would take only 16 years for half the world's population to be living in cities and only 55 years for it to reach 100 percent.

Within the lifetime of a child born today, Kingsley Davis foresees, on present trends of population-increase, 15 billion people to be fed and housed—nearly five times as many as now. The whole human species would be living in cities of a million-and-over inhabitants, and—wait for it!—the biggest city would have 1.3 billion inhabitants. That means 186 times as many as there are in Greater London.

For years the Greek architect Doxiadis has been warning us about such prospects. In his Ecumenopolis—World City—one urban area like confluent ulcers would ooze into the next. The East Side of World City would have as its High Street the Eurasian Highway stretching from Glasgow to Bangkok, with the Channel Tunnel as its subway and a built-up area all the way. On the West Side of World City, divided not by the tracks but by the Atlantic, the pattern is already emerging, or rather, merging. Americans already talk about Boswash, the urban development of a built-up area stretching from Boston to Washington; and on the West Coast, apart from Los Angeles, sprawling into the desert, the realtors are already slurring one city into another all along the Pacific Coast from the Mexican Border to San Francisco. We don't need a crystal ball to foresee what Davis and Doxiadis are predicting; we can already see it through smog-covered spectacles; a blind man can smell what is coming.

The danger of prediction is that experts and men of affairs are likely to plan for the predicted trends and confirm these trends. "Prognosis" is something different from "prediction." An intelligent doctor having diagnosed your symptoms and examined your condition does not say (except in novelettes), "You have six months to live." An intelligent doctor says, "Frankly, your condition is serious. Unless you do so-and-so, and I do so-and-so, it is bound to deteriorate." The operative phrase is "do so-and-so." We don't have to plan for trends; if they are socially undesirable our duty is to plan away from them; to treat the symptoms before they become malignant.

We have to do this on the local, the national and the international scale, through intergovernmental action, because there are no frontiers in present-day pollution and destruction of the biosphere. Mankind shares a common habitat. We have mortgaged the old homestead and nature is liable to foreclose.

¶ THE NIXON DOCTRINE AND OUR ASIAN COMMITMENTS
by Earl C. Ravenal   (January, 1971)

President Nixon entered office at a time of widespread public disillusionment with American overseas commitments and with the use of military power to support such commitments. The Nixon Doctrine, which received its first full exposition in the President's foreign-policy message to Congress in February, 1971, was less a doctrine than a general response to the public mood, promising a "lower profile" for American foreign policy. Earl Ravenal's article was among the first challenges to the Nixon Doctrine, pointing out its ambiguity, especially in relation to our Asian commitments.

The author was a member of the iconoclastic Institute for Policy Studies in Washington, and earlier had been director of the Asian division of the systems-analysis office of the Secretary of Defense. In this article, he questions whether the Nixon Doctrine would really lead to a fundamental reappraisal of America's overseas commitments and its active military role. He also raises the disturbing possibility of a return to dependence upon use of tactical nuclear weapons if conventional U.S. forces are reduced without a corresponding reduction in alliance commitments.

Ravenal argues that the old policy of forward containment of mainland China has not really been altered by the Nixon Doctrine. He proposes a more radical policy, which would present an alternative to containment through the removal of the U.S. military presence from the Asian mainland, without substituting a naval cordon or island bases, and he calls for the dissolution of America's security alliances with Thailand, Taiwan, and Korea. As Ravenal suggests, such a major diplomatic revolution may take a quarter of a century to implement, but, in view of the President's trip to Peking and the Communist Chinese acquisition of China's permanent seat in the U.N. Security Council, such a policy appears to conform with international trends.

THE NIXON DOCTRINE AND OUR ASIAN COMMITMENTS

By *Earl C. Ravenal*

EIGHTEEN months after its enunciation at Guam the Nixon Doctrine remains obscure and contradictory in its intent and application. It is not simply that the wider pattern of war in Indochina challenges the Doctrine's promise of a lower posture in Asia. More than that, close analysis and the unfolding of events expose some basic flaws in the logic of the Administration's evolving security policy for the new decade. The Nixon Doctrine properly includes more than the declaratory policy orientation. It comprises also the revised worldwide security strategy of "1½ wars" and the new defense decision-making processes such as "fiscal guidance budgeting." These elements have received little comment, especially in their integral relation to our commitments in Asia. But the effects of this Administration's moves in these areas will shape and constrain the choices of the United States for a long time to come.

The President's foreign policy declaration of February 1970 promised that "our interests, our foreign policy objectives, our strategies and our defense budgets are being brought into balance—with each other and with our overall national priorities."[1] After a decade of burgeoning military spending and entanglement in foreign conflict, the nation has welcomed the vision of lower defense budgets balanced by a reduction in American involvement overseas, particularly in Asia. Actually, however, the Administration's new policies and decision processes do not bring about the proposed balance; in fact, they create a more serious imbalance. Essentially we are to support the same level of potential involvement with smaller conventional forces. The specter of intervention will remain, but the risk of defeat or stalemate will be greater; or the nuclear threshold will be lower. The fundamental issues of interests, commitments and alliances are not resolved.

II

The objectives of close-in military containment and the for-

[1] Richard Nixon, "U. S. Foreign Policy for the 1970's, A New Strategy for Peace" (Washington, D. C., U. S. Government Printing Office, February 18, 1970).

ward defense of our Asian allies present us with a series of bleak choices:

With regard to deterrence: (1) perpetuation of a high level of active conventional forces, conspicuously deployed or deployable; (2) fundamental and obvious reliance on nuclear weapons; or (3) acknowledgment of the higher probability of an enemy initiative.

With regard to initial defense: (1) maintenance or rapid deployment of large armies in Asia; (2) early recourse to tactical nuclear weapons; or (3) acceptance of the greater risk of losing allied territory.

With regard to terminating a war: (1) large commitments of troops and heavy casualties; (2) use of nuclear weapons, either tactical or strategic; or (3) resignation to an indefinite and wasting stalemate, tantamount to defeat.

The only solution that transcends the triangle of unsatisfactory choices is to reëvaluate our interests in Asia; restate those objectives that implicate us in the possibility of war on the Asian mainland and diminish our control over our actions; resist the grand and vapid formulas of our role in Asia—such as the existential platitude that "we are a Pacific power"—that perpetuate the illusion of paramountcy; retreat from the policy of military containment of China; and revise the alliances that have come to represent our commitment to containment.

But this course the President has consistently rejected: ". . . we will maintain our interests in Asia and the commitments that flow from them. . . . The United States will keep all its treaty commitments." Thus the root problem of the Nixon Doctrine is its abiding commitment to the containment of China. In the furtherance of this policy our government hopes to maintain all our present Asian alliances and de facto commitments, profiting from their deterrent value but avoiding their implications. Yet it also intends to scale down our conventional military capability. The result is that the Nixon Doctrine neither reduces our potential involvement in Asian conflicts nor resolves the resulting dilemma by providing convincingly for a defense that will obviate reliance on nuclear weapons.

Let us examine the prospect of the Nixon Doctrine as a relief from involvement in Asian contingencies. The trauma that has resulted from our inability to win decisively in Vietnam has caused our policy-makers to suggest a limitation of future involvement on the basis of a distinction between external or overt aggression on the one hand, and insurgency, political subversion and civil war on the other. The President attempts in this way to avoid the strategy dilemma by altering the criteria for intervention and thus understating the probability of involvement:

> . . . we cannot expect U. S. military forces to cope with the entire spectrum of threats facing allies or potential allies throughout the world. This is particularly true of subversion and guerrilla warfare, or "wars of national liberation." Experience has shown that the best means of dealing with insurgencies is to preempt them through economic development and social reform and to control them with police, paramilitary and military action by the threatened government.

But this is nothing more than a postulation that the unwished contingency will not arise. The hard question remains: What if these "best means" are not successful? Under *those* conditions what kind of solutions does the Nixon Doctrine envisage? Might the United States be impelled to intervene with combat forces? The President states:

> . . . a direct combat role for U. S. general purpose forces arises primarily when insurgency has shaded into external aggression or when there is an overt conventional attack. In such cases, we shall weigh our interests and our commitments, and we shall consider the efforts of our allies, in determining our response.

But this formula for discrimination and discretion seems both unclear and unrealistic. At what point does an insurgency become "external aggression"? A definition sometimes proposed is the introduction of enemy main-force units, rather than mere individual fillers. But, even apart from the difficult question of verification, this event might be well beyond the point where our intervention became critical to the situation. The paradox is that in critical cases we might not wish to define the situation to preclude intervention; in less than critical cases we would not need to invoke nice distinctions to justify it. In any case, relying on formulas and distinctions misses the point: it is simply not credible that we would sacrifice our still-held objectives to the vagaries of circumstance.

Indeed, as long as our policy remains the containment of China and the repression of Asian communism, we are inclined to view even largely indigenous revolutions as objective instances of the purposes of Peking or Hanoi or Pyongyang. Consequently, if an insurgency in an allied or even a neutral country began to succeed, we would probably first increase logistical aid, then extend the role of advisers and provide air support. Since such moves might bring a countervailing response from the Asian communist sponsors of the insurgency, we might have to choose between sending ground forces and allowing an ally to lose by our default. In certain extremities we might be forced to the final choice among unlimited conventional escalation, defeat of our own forces, or "technological escalation" to the use of nuclear weapons.

Thus, with our formal or implied commitments and the President's open-ended prescription, the United States might yet be drawn into a land war on the Asian mainland or have to confront equally dire alternatives. In this respect the Nixon Doctrine does not improve on the policy that led to Vietnam. And, of course, our exposure to involvement in the case of more overt aggression, such as a Chinese-supported invasion in Korea or Southeast Asia, remains undiminished.

The only proposition that has become clear about the Nixon Doctrine is that its most advertised hope of resolving the strategy problem—both reducing the forces we maintain for Asian defense and avoiding involvement in conflict—is Asianization, *i.e.* the substitution of indigenous forces, equipped through enlarged U.S. military assistance, for American troops. The case for expanded military assistance has been stated with unprecedented urgency by Secretary Laird in preparation for vastly increased Military Assistance Program (MAP) budget requests for 1972 and succeeding fiscal years. Secretary Laird has characterized MAP as "the essential ingredient of our policy if we are to honor our obligations, support our allies, and yet reduce the likelihood of having to commit American ground combat units."[2]

But the Secretary recognizes the declining level of popular and Congressional support for military assistance. His solution, considered perennially within the Defense and State Departments but proposed for the first time in a Secretarial posture statement to the Congress, is that "military assistance should be integrated into the Defense Budget so that we can plan more rationally and present to the Congress more fully an integrated program." Military aid for certain "forward defense countries," including South Vietnam, Thailand and Laos, and consisting of

[2] Melvin R. Laird, "Fiscal Year 1971 Defense Program and Budget" (Washington, D. C., U. S. Government Printing Office, March 2, 1970).

about 80 percent of the total category "Support for Other Nations,"[3] is already meshed into the Defense Budget. This legislative ploy has not yet been applied to Korea or Taiwan, though the reduction of our troops in Korea and the insurance of Taiwan against communist pressure depend, in the judgment of this Administration, on the freedom to substitute U.S. matériel for manpower.

To merge military assistance entirely into the regular functional appropriation categories of the Defense Budget would be to institutionalize the dual rationale for military assistance that has become traditional in debate within the Department of Defense. The first element in this rationale is the argument from "trade-off"—a calculus that compares the costs of equal units of effectiveness of U. S. and foreign troops. This is essentially an assertion of "absolute advantage" and is the basic and obvious sense of Secretary Laird's statement: "A MAP dollar is of far greater value than a dollar spent directly on U.S. forces."

The second element is the argument from "comparative advantage," borrowed from the economic theory of international trade: "Each nation must do its share and contribute what it can appropriately provide—manpower from many of our allies; technology, material, and specialized skills from the United States." The proponents of military comparative advantage assert, by analogy, that the coöperating and specializing defense community can "consume" security at a higher level. It may be, however, that they can only consume more of the tangible intermediate trappings of security, i.e. the forces and arms. The essence of security, especially for the United States as the senior partner, might depend more on certain qualitative factors. In fact, there are several difficulties in the Administration's ostensibly neutral and technical arguments for military assistance.

First, both trade-off and comparative advantage assume and confirm the inevitability and relevance of the shared mission— that is, the forward defense of the ally's territory. But only if we cannot avoid this mission is it proper to confine the debate to the optimal distribution of roles and costs.

Second, the argument from comparative advantage, like the economic theory at its origin, stresses specialization. But the concomitant of specialization is interdependence. Thus a policy of selective reliance on allies, in order to be effective, implies auto-

---

[3] $2.443 billion out of $3.127 billion in the President's budget for fiscal year 1971.

matic involvement from the earliest moments of a conflict.[4]

Third, early experience indicates that U.S. ground forces cannot simply be traded off with precisely calculated increments of military assistance. They must be politically ransomed by disproportionate grants, more conspicuous deployments and more fervent and explicit confirmations of our commitment.[5]

Fourth, from the diplomatic standpoint the substitution of massive infusions of modern arms for U.S. troops is anything but neutral. To the North Koreans and their sponsors, for example, the one and one-half billion dollars of support and new equipment we now intend to give South Korea might look very provocative and destabilizing. A new phase of the peninsular arms race could be the result, with a net loss to regional and U.S. security.

Finally, the legislative tactic of integrating the Military Assistance Program into the Defense Budget would remove military assistance as an object of the broader concerns of foreign policy and assign it to the jurisdiction of more narrowly defense-oriented Congressional committees. The debate would be less political and more technical. The focus would shift from the question of involvement to the question of relative costs. Thus Asianization, which is the keystone of the Nixon Doctrine, would substitute some Asian forces and resources, but along the same perimeter of interest. It affords a pretext for reducing expense, but it does not enhance our security or relieve us from involvement.

III

The basic question is whether the Nixon Doctrine is an honest policy that will fully fund the worldwide and Asian commitments it proposes to maintain, or whether it conceals a drift toward nuclear defense or an acceptance of greater risk of local

---

[4] After the decision to reduce the ceiling on U.S. troops in Korea from 63,000 to 43,000, our government moved to base permanently there a wing of F-4 fighter-bombers. An American official explained: "Our aim is to reassure the Koreans during this difficult period. Despite budgetary cuts, it shows we intend to maintain our relative air strength here. They know that the minute an air attack starts, we're involved." (*The New York Times*, August 17, 1970.)

[5] The Administration proposes special budget requests of $1 billion over a five-year period for Korean force modernization, in addition to about $700 million likely to be provided in the regular military assistance budget. Even then, the Republic of Korea is demanding $2-3 billion, plus public assurances of no further troop withdrawals until after five years and the actual completion of the promised modernization program.

defeat. The most obvious change in our military posture is that the new formula provides conventional forces to counter a major communist thrust in Asia or Europe, but not simultaneously. As the President has explained:

> The stated basis of our conventional posture in the 1960's was the so-called "2½ war" principle. According to it, U.S. forces would be maintained for a three-month conventional forward defense of NATO, a defense of Korea or Southeast Asia against a full-scale Chinese attack, and a minor contingency —all simultaneously. These force levels were never reached.
>
> In the effort to harmonize doctrine and capability, we chose what is best described as the "1½ war" strategy. Under it we will maintain in peacetime general purpose forces adequate for simultaneously meeting a major Communist attack in either Europe or Asia, assisting allies against non-Chinese threats in Asia, and contending with a contingency elsewhere.

What will be the ultimate force levels associated with the new 1½-war strategy, and how can we assess their implications for Asian defense? Peacetime forces are obviously entailed by the extent of our commitments, but in no precisely determined way. A most important intermediate term—which could account for wide differences in strategy and forces—is the probable simultaneity of contingencies.[6] The Nixon strategy of 1½ wars is explicitly founded on the improbability of two simultaneous major contingencies. Thus demands on the planned general purpose forces are to be considered alternative rather than additive.

Can we then expect a force reduction equivalent to the requirement for defending against the lesser of the major contingencies? To support the previous strategy of 2½ wars, the Baseline (or peacetime) Force Structure was thought to provide seven active divisions for Southeast Asia, two for Korea, eight for NATO, and two and one-third for a minor contingency and a strategic reserve—a total of 19-1/3. Since the present 1½-war doctrine includes only one major contingency, in NATO or Asia, one might derive an active ground force as low as 10-1/3 divisions.

Such a literal expectation, however, is confused by the President's desire to insure "against greater than expected threats by maintaining more than the forces required to meet conventional threats in one theater—such as NATO Europe;" the fact that certain types of divisions are inherently specialized for certain geographical contingencies, so that all eight of our armored and

---

[6] Other sources of uncertainty and wide variation are: the readiness of our reserve divisions, the amount of available airlift and sealift, and the effectiveness of allied forces.

mechanized divisions will probably remain oriented to NATO
and inapplicable to Asian defense; and finally, the judgments of
both the President and Secretary Laird that the force levels
necessary to implement the previous 2½-war policy "were
never reached."

But it seems clear that the ultimate Baseline Force Structure
under the Nixon Doctrine will contain even fewer divisions for
the Asian requirement than the minimal proposals for a conventional defense.[7] The reduced conventional force is most significant as a reflection of the altered concept of Asian defense
embodied in the Nixon Doctrine. The constituent propositions
of this concept are: (1) the most likely threats to our Asian
allies do not involve Chinese invasion, and (2) with greatly
expanded military assistance our allies can largely provide the
ground forces to counter such threats.

There is a third proposition, strongly implied by the logic of
the problem and markedly signaled in the President's foreign
policy statement: in a future Asian conflict, particularly if it does
involve China, United States intervention is likely to carry with
it the use of tactical nuclear weapons.

—the nuclear capability of our strategic and theater nuclear forces serves as a
deterrent to full-scale Soviet attack on NATO Europe or Chinese attack on
our Asian allies;
—the prospects for a coordinated two-front attack on our allies by Russia
and China are low both because of the risks of nuclear war and the improbability of Sino-Soviet cooperation. In any event, we do not believe that such
a coordinated attack should be met primarily by U.S. conventional forces.

Though the "coördinated" attack described by the President is
improbable, it should be noted that "theater nuclear forces" are
prescribed as deterrents against the *single* contingency of a "Chinese attack on our Asian allies." Also, there are more plausible
scenarios that would, in terms of their potential to immobilize
U.S. forces, be the functional equivalent of a major attack: a
Soviet military build-up and political pressure in central or
southern Europe; or China's rendering massive logistical support to one of her Asian allies to the point where that ally could
release overwhelming forces against a neighboring country; or

---

[7] About five to seven divisions have been considered the minimum to blunt and delay an
attack along the main access routes in Southeast Asia, then fall back to a defensible perimeter. Against a communist invasion of Korea it was thought that the South Korean army
alone could hold initially north of Seoul until reinforced by Korean reserves or U.S. units
to be mobilized or diverted from other requirements.

the imminent entry of China into a war where we or one of our allies might have provided the provocation. It is conceivable that two such lesser contingencies could arise, in Europe and Asia, and that one of them could develop to the point of a conflict. In that event we would be reluctant to consider our conventional forces for either theater available for the other. Motivated by illusions of decisive action and immunity from retaliation, we might be tempted to dispose of the Asian conflict by technological escalation.

Therefore, if we remain committed to the defense of interests in both theaters, but maintain conventional forces for only one large contingency, our strategy is biased toward the earlier use of nuclear weapons. Of course, there is no necessary continuum of escalation from conventional war to tactical nuclear war. But the 1½-war strategy provides the President with fewer alternatives and renders the resort to nuclear weapons a more compelling choice, as well as making nuclear threat a more obvious residual feature of our diplomacy.

And so the "balance" promised in the new security policy is achieved—but not by adjusting our commitments, restricting our objectives or modifying our conception of the interests of the United States. Rather, budgetary stringencies inspire a reduction in force levels; a "1½-war strategy" is tailored to fit the intractable realities; and a series of rationalizations is constructed to validate the new strategy—rationalizations that simply stipulate a reduced threat, count heavily on subsidized and coerced allied efforts at self-defense, and suggest an early nuclear reaction if our calculations prove insufficiently conservative.

Thus the Nixon Doctrine reveals an apparent contradiction between objectives and strategy. Are we seeing the beginning of a return to the defense posture of the 1950s, with unabated commitments to a collection of front-line client-states, but with limited options and a renewed flirtation with the fantasy of tactical nuclear warfare?

IV

The new security policy not only shifts substantively down to a 1½-war strategy but also changes the model for determining defense requirements. Instead of the classic progression from the definition of foreign policy interests to the formulation of objectives, to the prescription of strategies, to the calculation of forces and their costs, we now see a constrained calculus that proceeds in reverse from limited budgets to trimmed forces to arbitrary strategies. The implications are not transmitted through the system to include a revision of objectives and interests. At best the system is balanced back from resources through strategies; the imbalance is shifted to a point between strategies and objectives.

But even the strategies and the forces may be out of balance. For the budget-constrained strategy revision is complemented by a fundamental change in the defense planning process. The previous system was requirements-oriented: there was, in theory, no prior budgetary restriction. Rather, planning began with the stated worldwide defense objective and resulted in forces and a budget which were recommended to the President and the Congress as systematically entailed by our defense objectives. Of course, the ideal system foundered on the institutional realities of weapons-systems and force creation. Indeed, the philosophy of unconstrained implementation of security objectives—"buy what you need"—encouraged inflated requirements within the framework of 2½ wars. And the attempts of the Secretary to limit forces only led the military to attempts to goldplate those prescribed forces, while keeping a ledger on the "shortfall" between the imposed strategy and the imposed force structure. But at least the direction and scope of the planning process compelled attention to the relevance and adequacy of the forces, and allowed the possibility of reasoning back from the rejection of excessive requirements to the questioning of overambitious strategies, extensive commitments and artificial interests.

By contrast, the new defense planning process begins simultaneously with "strategic guidance" and "fiscal guidance," established by the President and the National Security Council. The new procedure has attained certain efficiencies in managing the Pentagon budget cycle. But from the policy standpoint it is another matter: within the fiscal ceilings we will get the forces and weapons systems that the organization tends to produce— not the ones we might need. Of the two kinds of guidance, the fiscal is quantitative and unarguable; the strategic is verbal and elastic. If there is a coincidence of those forces and systems tailored to the fiscal guidance and those derived from the strategic guidance, it will be either accidental or contrived.

More likely, the Services will interpret the new guidance as a set of parameters within which they can promote self-serving programs. Under conditions of budgetary stringency they will skimp on manpower, supplies, war reserve stocks, maintenance and transport, while preserving headquarters, cadres of units, research and development of large new systems, and sophisticated technological overhead. In effect they will tend, as in the 1950s, to sacrifice those items that maintain balance, readiness and sustainability of effort, and to insist on those items that insure morale, careers and the competitive position of each Service.

Thus the Administration's defense planning procedure allows a second contradiction: between strategy and forces. This country may well end the 1970s with the worst of both worlds: on the one hand, a full panoply of commitments and a strategy that continues to serve an ambitious policy of containment; on the other, a worldwide sprinkling of token deployments and a force structure that is still expensive, but unbalanced, unready and irrelevant to our security.

V

The disabilities of the Nixon Doctrine follow from its insistence on the containment of China in face of budgetary pressures that arise not out of absolute scarcity of resources, but out of the nation's unwillingness to make large sacrifices for objectives that cannot be credibly invoked by its leadership. If the Administration is to be consistent in revising our defense posture and limiting defense budgets, it must consider a commensurate curtailment of our foreign policy objectives in Asia. Adjusting the intermediate-term strategies will not effect the reconciliation and will permit an honest implementation of the force and budget cuts.

But the Nixon Doctrine does not resolve the Asian defense problem in this fundamental way: rather, it appears as another formula for permanent confrontation with China. What are the issues that elude the perennial expressions of interest, by several administrations, in accommodating China? During the Johnson Administration the policy of containment ceded to a variant characterized as "containment without isolation." The shift, however, was accompanied by no tangible initiatives and induced no reciprocity from China. President Nixon entered office with a mandate—which he had created largely himself through his campaign emphasis—to bring about a reconciliation with China. His Administration has relaxed certain restrictions on trade and travel and revived the Warsaw ambassadorial talks. But such moves, though impressive as indications of enlightenment, do not touch on the essential concerns of China. However we ultimately conceive our interests, we might as well be realistic about the eventual price of a real accommodation with China.

This price would include three kinds of consideration: (1) diplomatic recognition and admission without qualification to the United Nations and the permanent Security Council seat; (2) affirmation of a one-China policy, even allowing the eventual accession of Taiwan to the mainland; (3) removal of the U.S. military presence on the mainland of Asia, without substituting a naval cordon, a ring of nearby island bases, a host of Asian mercenary armies, or a nuclear tripwire. The components of such a withdrawal would be: liquidation of the Vietnam war and removal of all U.S. forces there; retraction of all U.S. troops from other mainland Asian countries and Taiwan and closure of all bases; termination of military assistance to mainland states and cessation of efforts to create proxy forces to continue our mission; and dissolution of our security alliances with the "forward-defense" countries of Thailand, Taiwan and Korea.

Such a program would amount to a major diplomatic revolution. It might take a quarter of a century to implement, even with the most sophisticated public and political support within the United States. It would alienate client régimes, unsettle for long intervals our relations with the Soviets, and tax the understanding of major allies such as Japan and Australia. It would signify the renunciation of our efforts to control events in Asia; henceforth we would control only our responses to events.

But it is fair to ask whether we will not arrive at this disposition of affairs in Asia at some point, whether we will it or not. Should this occur after a quarter of a century of tension and devastation, or political manœuvre and diplomatic search? It is also fair to speculate that a more neutral, or even positive, relationship with China might give us a new scope of advantages. We might benefit eventually from a commercial relationship with China, rather than conceding the economic penetration of the mainland by Japan and Western Europe while we remain frozen in our historic impasse. We might also, simply through the dissolution of predictable enmity with China, make it more difficult for the Soviets to challenge us in other areas of the world.

And we might find it useful to have a counterpoise to Japan, which is still our principal Pacific competitor, economic and potentially military, and a possible future partner of the U.S.S.R. in such common interests as counterbalancing China and developing eastern Siberia.

The tangible expression of containment is our security alliances and the other strong, though less formal, military commitments around the periphery of China. These commitments, it can be argued, create the threat to us by transforming otherwise neutral events into situations of relevance to our interests; perpetuate the confrontation with China that gives substance to the threat, by frustrating the essential motives of China; lock us into a posture of forward defense on the mainland of Asia; and dictate the requirement for large general purpose forces or equivalent means of deterrence and defense.

Our alliances in Asia do not form a coherent and comprehensive system such as NATO. Rather they are a collection of bilateral agreements, plus the multilateral SEATO pact, contracted separately from 1951 through 1962. Even the purposes served by these alliances, as seen at the time of their negotiation, were diverse. Containment of China might have been a concurrent motive, but it did not uniformly inspire the creation of the pacts. Quite apart from containing our enemies, several of the treaties exhibit motives of containing our allies as well.

The ANZUS and Philippine treaties of 1951, though signed against the backdrop of the Korean War, related more to the fear of Japan which these allies derived from World War II. The 1953 agreement with the Republic of Korea was, among other things, a price for Syngman Rhee's restraint from attempting to reunify the peninsula by force. Similarly the treaty with the Republic of China in 1955 was in part a quid pro quo for Chiang's acceptance of "re-leashing" during the Straits crisis of that year. The SEATO alliance of 1954, which extended protection to South Vietnam, Laos and Cambodia, arose less from the vision of true collective defense than the desire of the United States to have a legal basis for discretionary intervention under the nominal coloration of "united action." The bilateral U.S.-Thai adjunct to SEATO, negotiated by Rusk and Thanat in 1962, reassured the Thais, during the events that led to the Laos neutralization accords, that the U.S. would respond to a threat to Thai security, regardless of the reaction of other SEATO signatories; this agreement, too, was a price to secure the acquiescence of an ally in an arrangement that suited the interest of the United States. The 1960 Security Treaty with Japan, revising the original treaty of 1951, reaffirmed U.S. administration of Okinawa and perpetuated our use of bases in the Japanese home islands, subject to prior consultation for nuclear or direct combat deployments. (The Nixon-Sato communiqué of October 1969 pledged reversion of Okinawa to Japan by 1972, a status that implies removal of nuclear weapons and submission to the "homeland formula" for consultation on the use of bases.)

Though deterrence has always been the primary function of our alliances, their military content has changed profoundly from the time they were contracted. The Dulles policy, in the pacts of 1953–55, did not emphasize the actual defense of allied territory or contemplate the dispatch of U.S. ground forces to any point where the communist powers chose to apply military force. Rather, it aimed at nuclear deterrence of overt aggression. In this concept the alliances served to establish a territorial definition. The implied countermeasure was the discretionary application of American nuclear force against communist airfields, supply centers, ports and perhaps industries and cities. The concept was not clearly resolved: it was semi-strategic and semitactical, partially punitive and partially for direct military effect. Also, cases short of obvious aggression, such as subversion and support for internal revolutionary struggles, were acknowledged to be imprecise and difficult. In Indochina in 1954 the Eisenhower Administration could not identify an appropriate enemy or target to fit the massive nuclear response and narrowly declined to intervene. Of course, it also sensed the lack of formal alliance protection over Southeast Asia as an impediment to intervention and moved to create SEATO within two months of the partition of Vietnam.

The refinement of tactical battlefield nuclear weapons in the middle and later 1950s made conceivable the notion of actual nuclear defense confined to the theater of conflict. The Kennedy-McNamara policy of flexible response, including counter-insurgency techniques and large balanced conventional forces, provided the practical means of containing a wider spectrum of Chinese or Chinese-supported initiatives. Thus the policy of close-in containment of China—involving the actual forward defense of allied territory—acquired its content.

There is a set of propositions that qualifies military deterrence: the more explicit and obvious our commitment, the more effective in preventing war, but the less effective in preventing our involvement in war; conversely, the more attenuated our commitment, the less certain our involvement, but the more probable a hostile initiative.

An administration with a more relaxed view of Asia might take the risk of the second proposition and look more neutrally on a communist probe. But this Administration appears likely to maintain its deterrent stance and take its chances on involvement in conflict. This would mean that it will not overtly diminish any commitment; indeed it is likely to reaffirm and reinforce any commitment that is beset by doubt. But to maintain the deterrent effect of our commitments in the face of reductions in budgets, forces and deployments, the Administration must replace deleted capabilities with some equivalent, such as increased rapid deployment ability or nuclear threat. This Administration could not count entirely on the mobility of our forces, which can be evidenced only by massive exercises and adequate lift resources, which are far from certain to be appropriated. Residually, it is forced to rely on nuclear deterrence, which need only be hinted. The point is that our mode of deterrence and our provisions for defense will now progressively diverge from the preferences of our treaty partners. Our proposed substitution of technology and threat for our manpower and presence might be equivalent from our point of view, but not from that of our allies.

None of our Asian defense arrangements is specific about the tangible support that might be evoked by an act of aggression. No joint defense force with agreed war plans and command structures exists. Our military concept could become, rather than the forward defense of all territory, a mobile defense, an enclave strategy, or even a nuclear tripwire. In another dimension, our commitment might be satisfied by various types of support, such as logistical, tactical air or nuclear fire. U.S. contingency plans are essentially unilateral and subject to uncommunicated change. And implementation of all treaties refers to our constitutional procedures, which are themselves in a phase of more stringent interpretation.

Because of this scope for manœuvre or evasion, our Asian allies will be correspondingly more sensitive to interpretive commentary by U.S. officials and to shifts in our military posture. Already they sense that the substantive content of our alliances is affected by the President's choice of worldwide strategy. The selected strategy is described as defending both Europe and Asia —though alternatively. But it is clear that Europe holds priority and claims virtually as many resources as previously; the major war case associated with the reduction in active forces is Asia. Although no alliances are formally disturbed, our Asian allies, as they count our divisions and analyze our posture statements and policy declarations, have cause for concern that behind the façade of ritualistic reiteration we might have altered our capability and specific intent to fulfill our treaty commitments.

Thus we can devalue the diplomatic and deterrent effect of our alliances without even gaining immunity from involvement, simply by shifting strategies, debating criteria for intervention and making arbitrary adjustments in force levels. In view of the liabilities of this course—which is the course of the present Administration—we might as well face the problem more directly and begin to consider the broader alternatives to containment, with their full implications for our alliances in Asia.

VII

As long as we assert interests in Asia that (1) entail defending territory, (2) could plausibly be threatened by hostile actions and (3) are evidenced by alliances that dispose us to a military response, we are exposed to the contingency of involvement. If we maintain this exposure through insistence on our present Asian commitments, while adopting budget-constrained strategies, we risk a future defeat or stalemate, or we allow ourselves to be moved toward reliance on nuclear weapons.

To avoid these alternatives, two courses are available. One is heavy dependence on allied forces to fulfill defense requirements. This is the hope of Asianization, offered prominently by the Nixon Doctrine. But this policy binds us closely to the fate of our Asian clients and diminishes our control over our involvement; and there is still the liability that U.S. forces might be required to rescue the efforts of our allies.

The other course is a process of military readjustment and political accommodation that would make it far less likely that we would become involved every time there is some slippage in the extensive diplomatic "fault" that runs along the rim of Asia.

This course is arduous and complex, and as little under our unilateral and absolute control as a course of military deterrence. But the consequences of not budging from our present set of ambitions and illusions—or of trifling with the unalterable purposes of China by limiting ourselves to insubstantial diplomatic initiatives—are far bleaker.

The situation calls not for a symbolic shift in strategy—such as the $1\frac{1}{2}$-war doctrine—which is founded on the hope that the contingencies that would test it, to which we are still liable, might not occur. The situation is not amenable to purely instrumental solutions, such as the calculated equippage of allied armies or the reliance on technological escalation. The situation requires a fundamental questioning and revision of the containment of China.

The confusion that surrounds the Nixon Doctrine is appropriate to its conflicting message and incomplete intent. While pledging to honor all of our existing commitments, the President has placed them all in considerable doubt. While offering promise of avoiding involvement in future Asian conflicts, he has biased the nature of our participation. Thus, in the attempt to perpetuate our control of the destiny of Asia, the Nixon Doctrine may forfeit control of our own destiny in Asia.

¶ ISOLATED AMERICA
by Hamilton Fish Armstrong   (October, 1972)

The author of "Isolated America" was Managing Editor of Foreign Affairs *from the time it was founded, in 1922, until 1928, when he became Editor. His article is an epilogue to those fifty years. Armstrong believes that foreign policy reflects a nation's character and that the United States will not regain the prestige that he believes it has lost until the American people recognize the ills of their society and vigorously set about repairing them.*

ISOLATED AMERICA

By Hamilton Fish Armstrong

SEVENTY-FIVE years ago, Archibald Cary Coolidge, who later became the first Editor of *Foreign Affairs,* wrote a book with a theme and title entirely novel at that time, "The United States as a World Power." In it he made the first attempt to define the new role in the world then rapidly being assumed by the United States. He remarked that all nations divide mankind into two categories—themselves and everybody else. And he said that Americans would be just as prone as others to cherish the pleasing belief that they had grown great by their own virtues and the favor of a kindly Providence, whereas the progress of other states was marked by unscrupulous rapacity; hence, they would demand that American statesmen keep sharp watch lest nefarious foreigners take advantage of their good nature and honest simplicity. The accuracy of Mr. Coolidge's analysis was corroborated before long by the alacrity with which the American people accepted the idea that they had come into World War I altruistically, in order to make the world safe for democracy ("American" democracy); and again by their readiness to suppose that President Wilson and his advisers at Paris had been bamboozled by wily European statesmen. The latter conception was promoted by American isolationists who depicted the League of Nations as a naïve and useless affair and a trap to involve us in Old World power politics.

The war in Vietnam has been the longest and in some respects the most calamitous war in our history. It has rent the American people apart, spiritually and politically. It is a war which has not been and could not be won, a war which was pushed from small beginnings to an appalling multitude of horrors, many of which we have become conscious of only by degrees. The methods we have used in fighting the war have scandalized and disgusted public opinion in almost all foreign countries.

Not since we withdrew into comfortable isolation in 1920 has the prestige of the United States stood so low. Following Harding's sweeping victory and his announcement that Wilson's League was "now deceased," the League of Nations passed out of the minds of most Americans. Having won the war for their allies, as they put it, Americans considered that they were entitled to attend to their own affairs exclusively. The world was stunned. The United States had won glory by turning the tide of battle in Europe and moral stature by sponsoring, through President Wilson, a program for organizing the peace that the world craved. In their disillusionment, Europeans did not forget America's achievements in the war or minimize what the American Relief Administration and other organizations continued to do in feeding the starving and restoring the wreckage in devastated regions. But something was gone from the picture that the world had formed in wartime of Americans; their adventurousness, their willingness to take risks had disappeared. There were Americans, too, who felt that the American dream had paled and who had twinges of conscience that their country was taking no part in the endeavor to make a new war less likely.

Efforts were made before long to demonstrate that the United States was on the side of peace even though it would not share the alleged risks of becoming a member of the League of Nations. One effort was made in Coolidge's administration, the second in Hoover's. In the summer of 1928 Secretary of State Kellogg took part in negotiating what became the Pact of Paris, the purpose of which was, in the popular phrase, to "outlaw war." It aimed to establish peace by fiat and was acceptable to the U.S. Senate because its signatories were not committed to take any concrete action to prevent aggression. It was harmless except to the extent that it led the American public to suppose that something effective had been done to compensate for the refusal to participate in the League. A second effort to show that the United States was on the side of peace was made by Secretary of State Stimson in January 1932. The League had been struggling vainly to find means to curb the Japanese invasion of Manchuria. Stimson sought to back up the effort by committing the United States to a policy of not recognizing the fruits of aggression. The plan was well intentioned, but its effect in slowing the Japanese invasion was nil.

This was not a period in which the United States was influential in world affairs. Materially, it was a Great Power in capital letters; morally, its greatness did not shine. When the Great Depression overwhelmed the United States, as all nations, Roosevelt's spectacular measures of reform gave the American people hope and trust again, but there was little energy left to think about the troubles and dangers of others. The European landscape was black. A new arms race set in. Hitler's advent was a portent of what was to come. Roosevelt made an effort to have the Neutrality Act amended so that the United States need not, by insisting on its rights as a neutral, break a blockade set up by members of the League against an aggressor; the possibility that it would recognize a blockade would be a powerful deterrent to aggression. The Senate refused.

Through the interwar years the picture of the United States in the eyes of the world remained much as it had been after the Senate killed the proposal to join the League, refused to ratify the Treaty of Versailles and rejected the Tripartite Pact which promised France protection against fresh German attack and which she had accepted as a substitute for seizing territorial guarantees of her own on the Rhine. Nor did it ratify the Protocol of the World Court. American policy was looked upon as quirky and unpredictable.

II

In the first issue of *Foreign Affairs* Elihu Root expressed a fairly obvious fact in picturesque language: "When foreign affairs were ruled by autocracies or oligarchies the danger of war was in sinister purpose. When foreign affairs are ruled by democracies the danger of war will be in mistaken beliefs." It is notable that Mr. Root, having in mind the collapse of four great autocracies following the First World War, referred to autocracies in the past tense, an error of which we soon became aware.

Since the United States is not an autocracy nor is it an oligarchy in the formal meaning of that term, the Vietnam War did not originate in what Mr. Root called sinister purpose. Did it, then, originate in mistaken beliefs? If we did indeed start down the road to war unwittingly and in ignorance, and if we failed to notice the points at which our leaders went wrong in time to curb or deflect them from a doomed failure, what are the characteristics of our society which account for our having been left in such a pitiable situation?

Discussions of the issues raised by these questions, indeed the discussion of all the problems of American foreign relations, are being carried on today in a denatured terminology. The rhetoric of good words and high ideals is everywhere heard; but the opponents of selfish or provincial attitudes are at a disadvantage which they did not face formerly and do not altogether recognize now. The words used to express the highest aspirations have become shopworn. Calls to duty or endeavor like those uttered 50 years ago by Woodrow Wilson today sound hollow and meretricious. The phrases have been used and abused too long.

It was in that period of American public euphoria, misleadingly called "normalcy," that *Foreign Affairs* was founded. Its purpose was not to promote specific policies, however laudable, but to increase the interest of the American public in foreign policy as such and stimulate their consciousness that they were an integral part of a world society and had a concern for its welfare as a whole. To anyone who had a share in that enterprise there seems to be a similarity in the situation then and now. Actually, however, the forces at work are very different. The risk today is not that the American people may become isolationist; the reality is that the United States is being isolated.

In these conditions, an attempt to write other than cynically about the present situation of the United States seems bound to be an exercise in futility. Yet the attempt must be made. Unless we evaluate and not merely enumerate the elements in our society as they condition the quality of our foreign policy we shall not make progress in changing what we feel is wrong with it. And wrong it must have been. Not, in the experience of the present writer, since the Harding era when we denied our enlightened self-interest and retreated from responsibility in our foreign relationships, while confessing to scandal and tawdry commercialism at home, has the world had such a poor opinion of us. American principles, which sometimes were characterized as naïve but in general were respected as sincere and humane, now are freely called hypocritical and self-serving; the weight of American material and military power, looked to in the past as a mainstay of world stability, is now mistrusted and feared.

III

Once again in the Second World War the United States saved Western civilization. The victory won, it took the lead in forming the United Nations and the Senate voted membership in it almost unanimously. It is now one of the two superpowers, unassailable in nuclear strength. Nevertheless its political power is less than its material power and its prestige is tarnished.

Our methods of fighting the Vietnam War are what have chiefly fanned world opinion against us. But there are other causes of resentment too. Radical changes in the structure of our foreign policy undertaken recently without notice to friends and allies have strengthened a feeling that American policies are conceived for American purposes only. Gratitude for the immense sums given for foreign aid since the war, and especially for the help given Europe in the Marshall Plan, has largely evaporated. Just as the war has sharpened all our internal conflicts, so it has accentuated foreign criticism of American civilization and intensified the resentment of foreign governments that the United States seems more and more to ignore their political interests and economic needs.

In the summer of 1971 President Nixon announced without warning that his National Security Adviser, Henry Kissinger, had been secretly consulting with Premier Chou En-lai in Peking and that he himself was planning a visit there shortly. A month later, he announced that he had unpegged the dollar from gold and ordered a ten percent surcharge on imports; this our allies considered contrary to international agreement. These actions, and to a lesser degree the later announcement that the President also planned to visit Moscow, confirmed the feeling in many foreign offices that American policy was erratic and egocentric.

The President's goal was to come to live-and-let-live terms with two great nations that had long sought to undermine our position in the world and that were hostile to our social and political system. His grand hope was to end the remnants of the cold war with Soviet Russia and make progress toward curtailing the arms race; and to open contacts with the People's Republic of China, with which we had no diplomatic relations and with which we had once come close to war on behalf of our protégé Taiwan. The objectives were admirable, provided the endeavor did not involve sacrificing friendships and alliances with peoples with whom we had had close ties, some of them traditional and in a sense sentimental, some economic and commercial, some rooted in similar concepts of constitutional government, democracy and freedom. In his preoccupation with methods of attaining the goal, and in his excitement as he seemed to near it, the President lost sight of the proviso. The result was a chaotic situation. The stability of the monetary system was further undermined, with our NATO allies among those most adversely affected. Canada, an essential friend and neighbor,

Japan, the rising power in East Asia, and India, the largest Asian democracy, were alienated.

The approach to Peking was not precipitate; it had been carefully prepared. But the announcement that the President would go there in person was made in a way that caused maximum embarrassment to the Japanese government. We had been pressing Tokyo to have as little as possible to do with "Red" China, "our mutual enemy." In so doing, we had opened Premier Eisaku Sato to domestic attack for sacrificing Japan's interests to those of the United States. Suddenly he found himself bereft of his excuse for having taken a position opposed in many influential circles. He felt betrayed.

Japan deserves consideration in the forefront of American foreign policy in its own right. Japan is now the world's third industrial power. Japan provides the second largest market, after Canada, for American goods, and a third of its foreign trade is with the United States. "Japan is our most important ally," said President Nixon on February 25, 1971. Our recent policies do not reflect a full awareness of these facts.

The end of our long-time friendship with India came about as a by-product of our efforts to please the People's Republic of China by averting our faces while the army of China's protégé, Pakistan, bloodily repressed a revolt in the eastern half of the country. India was overwhelmed by an influx of refugees from East Pakistan and took the occasion to help weaken her traditional enemy Pakistan and establish the independence of East Pakistan as Bangladesh, meanwhile accepting the support of the Soviet Union in exchange for the peevish "neutrality" of the United States. Our maneuvering included the futile naval demonstration—plainly directed more against the Soviet Union than India—of sending the *Enterprise* sailing up the Bay of Bengal (and down again). The gainer was the Soviet Union, which signed a treaty of mutual support with India and secured new facilities on the Indian Ocean, where the Soviet fleet will now face the American on better terms.

Canada is our neighbor and, we have always assumed, our staunch friend. The British used to take us for granted, a fact that irked us considerably; the Canadians have been similarly irked that in our eyes Canada is a natural extension of our culture and a part of our economic domain. This has been particularly exasperating because it is based largely on fact. Our periodicals sell in Canada almost to the exclusion of the local product. We have provided the greater part of the capital for developing Canadian raw materials and have acquired majority control of Canadian industries.

The increasingly uncomfortable character of the Canadian-American relationship remained unrecognized by the American public and apparently was given scant consideration in Washington, as shown when President Nixon made his economic and financial announcements, and Secretary of the Treasury Connally at once began negotiations with Canada (as with many nations) in an effort to see that the United States derived maximum benefits from its new economic policy. In the talks with Canada he stressed the need to "rectify" Canada's favorable balance of trade with the United States, and demanded changes in the 1965 pact which allowed Canadian-manufactured automobiles to be shipped across the border duty-free.

Canada pointed out that not only had she suffered annual deficits in overall trade with the United States in the 20 years before 1970 but that for the five years before 1971 she had suffered deficits in the automobile trade up to $625 million. Was Canada to understand that the United States was prepared to trade with her only when she incurred a deficit, and required concessions from her when (for a change) the United States incurred a deficit? And how was Canada, with a trading deficit, to pay the immense sums of interest, dividends and transportation costs arising out of American investments in her industries?

The effort to improve the overall American trade balance and balance of payments, even if this meant resorting to protectionist measures, was of course connected with the financial drain of the war in Vietnam. Canadian public opinion was strongly critical of the war and this increased the opposition to American efforts to secure Canadian concessions to help pay for it. Canadian official resentment was exacerbated by Secretary Connally's seeming lack of understanding for Prime Minister Trudeau's difficulties in submitting to American demands when Canadian elections were in the offing. (American officials are not the only ones that must take account of elections.) In general, Canada simply put down the controversy as an example of the usual self-centered approach of Americans toward their northern neighbor.

Our isolation from other peoples is the reverse of 50 years ago; today we are the object, not the subject.

IV

Our age finds it convenient to simplify everything. "Know thyself," a difficult proposition, is supplanted by "Know everybody," not "everybody" as diverse types but as a single prototype—glands, psyches, behavioral reactions and all. That we take refuge in generality is not surprising. Our society has become so complex that the multiplicity of its individual problems overwhelms us. To save our self-respect we turn from the un-understandable particular to the perhaps understandable general.

What is called for is a resolute attempt at complication, as the events detailed above indicate. Interactions must be understood as well as facts. Science and technology are adding to the world's problems, not solving them. Something better than a hit-or-miss relationship must be established between the knowledge amassed by scientists in a multitude of fields and the decision-making processes of those who guide political action. How are discoveries in physics to be related to population trends, urban blight, television addiction, substitutes for standard nutritional resources? The answers will not come out of a computer because judgment as to utility and aesthetic choice cannot be fed in along with the facts. Robert Oppenheimer once said to me that physics had become so recondite that the formulae that demonstrate one scientist's conclusions often remain intelligible only to himself. How, then, is a statesman knowing nothing of science to choose between alternative recommendations regarding, say, the development of ballistic missiles, presented to him by scientific advisers who may not know possible variations in fundamental factors involved?

Those who watched the negotiators at the Paris Peace Conference of 1919 struggle to find a realistic and usable pattern of the events that were transforming the world around them, and so to act to forestall new tragedy, redeem promises and justify hopes, were conscious that the leaders assembled there, men on the whole of unusual caliber and in some cases unusual idealism, were unable to come to grips individually with more than a single fraction of the problems they faced. Single minds could not encompass such complexities. Since then the condensation of time and space has magnified the complexities and made each component problem more immediate.

This ought to temper our criticism of our leaders as we look back at the remnants of half-understood policies and stumbling actions that strew the path of our involvement in Vietnam. It does not make us feel a need, however, to be lenient in our judgment where they disguised disasters in clichés or cloaked the miseries of millions of refugees, harried hither and yon under a rain of bombs, under comfortable terms like "resettlement" and "reëducation."

It must be made less likely—for it can never be made impossible—for American leaders again to take the country into war unawares. Proposed legislation to limit executive power to conduct an undeclared war by requiring the President to obtain congressional approval of his action within 30 days is misleading; in 30 days a war will have achieved a momentum of its own and will have introduced complications in relations with third powers that neither the public nor Congress will know how to limit or terminate. And of course no domestic legislation can prevent foreign attack, nuclear or otherwise. The prescription for reform is not written in specific terms. If we assume that mistaken beliefs, in Mr. Root's terms, have been responsible for the failure of the American democracy to curb actions of its leaders that are leading to war, the prescription is stunningly large and recovery can come only slowly as a result of a multitude of actions that could give our country a sense of direction again.

The direction is not backward, in nostalgia, to the virtues of our forefathers, except that we will draw from them an adventurous spirit and in that spirit will answer the question "What is wrong?" with the answer they gave, "Let's do something about it." The direction is forward, to recognize and accept the present ills of our society and to set about curing them—by rehumanizing ourselves, by readopting civility as a part of good behavior, by recognizing that history can inform the future, by encouraging the growth of élites in many fields, not in order to copy them snobbishly but to set intellectual standards to which everyone may in some degree aspire, by asserting that aesthetics is an essential element in art, by reëstablishing learning as opening doors to choice, by leavening the mediocrity of our culture with snatches of unorthodoxy, by welcoming diversity of opinion as an essential element of strength in a democracy.

Is this a dream? The crudeness brought by the mechanization of modern life says, yes it is. But science need not be against us, nor need we be against science. Almost 40 years ago Newton D.

Baker wrote in *Foreign Affairs:* "The triumph of science in the material world encourages us to do some laboratory work with the human spirit. A peaceful world would have been less amazing to George Washington than wireless telegraphy. We must not think too well of atoms at the expense of thinking too ill of men." If we accept that adjuration we may recover our self-confidence and self-respect and regain for our nation the standing in the world's estimation it once possessed.

COUNCIL ON FOREIGN RELATIONS

Recent Publications

FOREIGN AFFAIRS (quarterly), edited by Hamilton Fish Armstrong.

THE UNITED STATES IN WORLD AFFAIRS (annual), by Richard P. Stebbins and William P. Lineberry.

DOCUMENTS ON AMERICAN FOREIGN RELATIONS (annual), by Richard P. Stebbins with the assistance of Elaine P. Adam.

FIFTY YEARS OF FOREIGN AFFAIRS, edited by Hamilton Fish Armstrong (1972).

THE FOREIGN AFFAIRS 50-YEAR BIBLIOGRAPHY: New Evaluations of Significant Books on International Relations, 1920–1970, edited by Byron Dexter (1972).

THE WEST AND THE MIDDLE EAST, by John C. Campbell and Helen Caruso (1972).

THE UNITED STATES AND THE INDUSTRIAL WORLD: American Foreign Economic Policy in the 1970s, by William Diebold, Jr. (1972).

THE WORLD THIS YEAR: 1972 Supplement to the Political Handbook, edited by Richard P. Stebbins and Alba Amoia (1972).

AMERICAN AID FOR DEVELOPMENT, by Paul C. Clark (1972).

THE CARIBBEAN COMMUNITY: Changing Societies and U.S. Policy, by Robert D. Crassweller (1972).

INDIA, PAKISTAN, AND THE GREAT POWERS, by William J. Barnds (1972).

CONGRESS, THE EXECUTIVE, AND FOREIGN POLICY, by Francis O. Wilcox (1971).

THE REALITY OF FOREIGN AID, by Willard L. Thorp (1971).

POLITICAL HANDBOOK AND ATLAS OF THE WORLD, 1970, edited by Richard P. Stebbins and Alba Amoia (1970).

JAPAN IN POSTWAR ASIA, by Lawrence Olson (1970).

THE CRISIS OF DEVELOPMENT, by Lester B. Pearson (1970).

THE GREAT POWERS AND AFRICA, by Waldemar A. Nielsen (1969).

A NEW FOREIGN POLICY FOR THE UNITED STATES, by Hans J. Morgenthau (1969).

MIDDLE EAST POLITICS: THE MILITARY DIMENSION, by J. C. Hurewitz (1969).

THE ECONOMICS OF INTERDEPENDENCE: Economic Policy in the Atlantic Community, by Richard N. Cooper (1968).

HOW NATIONS BEHAVE: Law and Foreign Policy, by Louis Henkin (1968).

THE INSECURITY OF NATIONS, by Charles W. Yost (1968).

PROSPECTS FOR SOVIET SOCIETY, edited by Allen Kassof (1968).

THE AMERICAN APPROACH TO THE ARAB WORLD, by John S. Badeau (1968).

U.S. POLICY AND THE SECURITY OF ASIA, by Fred Greene (1968).

NEGOTIATING WITH THE CHINESE COMMUNISTS: The U.S. Experience, by Kenneth T. Young (1968).

FROM ATLANTIC TO PACIFIC: A New Interocean Canal, by Immanuel J. Klette (1967).

TITO'S SEPARATE ROAD: America and Yugoslavia in World Politics, by John C. Campbell (1967).

U.S. TRADE POLICY: New Legislation for the Next Round, by John W. Evans (1967).

TRADE LIBERALIZATION AMONG INDUSTRIAL COUNTRIES: Objectives and Alternatives, by Bela Balassa (1967).

THE CHINESE PEOPLE'S LIBERATION ARMY, by Brig. Gen. Samuel B. Griffith II U.S.M.C. (ret.) (1967).

THE ARTILLERY OF THE PRESS: Its Influence on American Foreign Policy, by James Reston (1967).

TRADE, AID AND DEVELOPMENT: The Rich and Poor Nations, by John Pincus (1967).

BETWEEN TWO WORLDS: Policy, Press and Public Opinion on Asian-American Relations, by John Hohenberg (1967).

THE CONFLICTED RELATIONSHIP: The West and the Transformation of Asia, Africa and Latin America, by Theodor Geiger (1966).

THE ATLANTIC IDEA AND ITS EUROPEAN RIVALS, by H. van B. Cleveland (1966).

EUROPEAN UNIFICATION IN THE SIXTIES: From the Veto to the Crisis, by Miriam Camps (1966).

THE UNITED STATES AND CHINA IN WORLD AFFAIRS, by Robert Blum, edited by A. Doak Barnett (1966).

THE FUTURE OF THE OVERSEAS CHINESE IN SOUTHEAST ASIA, by Lea A. Williams (1966).

ATLANTIC AGRICULTURAL UNITY: Is It Possible? by John O. Coppock (1966).

TEST BAN AND DISARMAMENT: The Path of Negotiation, by Arthur H. Dean (1966).

COMMUNIST CHINA'S ECONOMIC GROWTH AND FOREIGN TRADE, by Alexander Eckstein (1966).

POLICIES TOWARD CHINA: Views from Six Continents, edited by A. M. Halpern (1966).

THE AMERICAN PEOPLE AND CHINA, by A. T. Steele (1966).

INTERNATIONAL POLITICAL COMMUNICATION, by W. Phillips Davison (1965).

ALTERNATIVE TO PARTITION: For a Broader Conception of America's Role in Europe, by Zbigniew Brzezinski (1965).

THE TROUBLED PARTNERSHIP: A Re-appraisal of the Atlantic Alliance, by Henry A. Kissinger (1965).

FIFTY YEARS OF
FOREIGN AFFAIRS

Edited by Hamilton Fish Armstrong

On the occasion of the fortieth anniversary of *Foreign Affairs,* President John F. Kennedy wrote to the quarterly's editor, Hamilton Fish Armstrong, "By its 'broad hospitality to divergent ideas,' its high standards of editorial integrity, and its responsible devotion to the best interests of the United States, *Foreign Affairs* has created an unrivaled forum for those who should be heard, and it has served our country well."

Now, on the magazine's fiftieth anniversary, here is an extraordinary collection of articles that presents a panorama of the last half-century in international relations. If there is a common theme, it is the implicit acknowledgment of Elihu Root's thesis put forth in *Foreign Affairs'* first issue, in 1922 (in the essay that leads off this volume): that, in a democracy, the people are responsible for the conduct of foreign policy and must, therefore, be well informed. In articles of policy, biography, prediction, and reflection, the outstanding contributors—statesmen, men of letters, men of affairs—write on a wide range of fascinating subjects:

• In 1925, W. E. B. DuBois categorically (and prophetically) stated, "The problem of the twentieth century is the problem of the color line."

• Benedetto Croce was still in Mussolini's Italy in 1932 when he courageously explored the meaning "Of Liberty" in the face of Fascist ideology.

• The anonymous "X" (George F.